With One Fool Left in the World, No One is Stranded

Old City Khulm, May 1973

Also by Frances Garrett Connell

The Authoring of Selves: Literacy and its Indigenous
Forms in a Traditional Afghan Village (nonfiction)
Children Kept from the Sun (memoir and photos)
Down Rivers of Windfall Night (novel)
The Rest is Silence (poems)

With One Fool Left in the World, No One is Stranded

Scenes from an Older Afghanistan

Frances Garrett Connell

authorHOUSE®

AuthorHouse™ LLC
1663 Liberty Drive
Bloomington, IN 47403
www.authorhouse.com
Phone: 1-800-839-8640

While the journal which follow are based on real places, people and events, the names have been changed out of respect.

Published by AuthorHouse 01/17/2014

ISBN: 978-1-4918-3756-6 (sc)
ISBN: 978-1-4918-3757-3 (hc)
ISBN: 978-1-4918-3755-9 (e)

Library of Congress Control Number: 2013921885

This book is printed on acid-free paper.

Contents

YEAR TWO
KABUL AND TASHKURGHAN, AFGHANISTAN

YEAR THREE
AUGUST 1975-JULY 1976 KABUL, AFGHANISTAN

Dedication

To the children of Afghanistan, my own grown-up sons,
and grandson Gabriel and a new generation.

Note: The title comes from a Dari proverb:
"As long as there is a fool in the world, no one will ever be stranded."

Introduction

The past 40 years have taken us a long way from the world I knew as a Peace Corps volunteer in a small, ancient Afghan village in the mid-1970's. Not the least of the changes is the manner in which this once distant country now impacts the lives of every American, commentator, and schoolboy, as its name resonates with overtones of sorrow, contentiousness, and notoriety to the entire world.

When my husband and I returned to the U.S. in late summer 1976, we entered through Boston, where my in-laws lived. A white-haired Irish Catholic customs' official flipped through the visas and entry stamps on our passports for Austria, France, Germany, Italy, Greece, Turkey, Iran, Pakistan, India, Burma, Thailand, Malaysia, Singapore, and Hong Kong, places which we had visited over the past three years or on our way home. Then, he settled on the pages of vibrant green and orange insignia, three years' worth of Republic of Afghanistan work permits. Congratulatory, his large mitt-like hands warm and directed, he reached out to pat us on the back, then waved through our persons, along with three years' worth of trunks and articles nonchalantly never opened. "Welcome home!" he trumpeted. "I am sure you must be glad to back from that crazy African world and with your own kind again here."

When we continued on to Philadelphia, where Tom was starting law school, we found ourselves offered free cake as part of the Bicentennial Celebration down at Penn's Landing and in the shadow of Independence Hall and the new pavilion housing the Liberty Bell. As we moved into the paper-thin walled graduate housing at University of Pennsylvania, then into our own small apartment off campus, as I hustled to find work that fall, and Tom disappeared into law school, the career-training and career which would all but dominate his every waking day for the next 35 years, I volunteered for Jimmy Carter's campaign, and went through three teaching and two research jobs. Two years later, I started my doctorate classes at Columbia, commuting by train from Phillie where I continued to coordinate instruction and teach in University of Pennsylvania's English Program for Foreign Students three mornings a week.

By 1979, as we daily heard of the Iranian Hostages in the U.S. Embassy, and by December when the Russians invaded Afghanistan, Tom had graduated and taken a clerkship with a federal judge in New York City, I was finishing up my classes at Columbia and preparing for my comps, and our first child was only two months away from being born.

In the life of the world, our country, Afghanistan, and our own days, the thirty-three years which have followed, obviously, make a whole other story. In this turn back to the memories coded and buried in those years in Afghanistan from 1973-1976, and in the flashes to more recent events and reflections, this work tries to portray better what was lost, in the minute particulars and in the large, political and cultural strokes which made up that complex country of hospitable people who shaped my life in unpredictable ways ever since, and which—as a country, a region, an endless war—now impact a new millennium.

YEAR ONE
JULY 1973–JUNE 1974

Tashkurghan covered bazaar scene

Tashkurghan bridge with chadried woman

1

ARRIVAL

"If you see a blind person walking around a well, and remain quiet, it is a sin."

—Dari proverb

June 29, 1973

The brittle lion teeth of the desert rages, until we swoop down on a green strip in a salt desert, and see the New Mexico type adobe arches of an airport. We are at Kandahar, where natives are greeted like royalty as they descend from this miracle bird which has effortlessly soared over the hot sand hills. Dark, bearded, sun-wrinkled men push a staircase up against the plane, we glimpse camels and straw in one wing of the solo structure, then as quickly the stairs are pushed away, and we are airborne again, for Kabul.

It is Thursday, almost noon, when we land in Kabul, nine and a half hours from the ESDT. We had watched Kabul develop from the air, rugged, uneven patches of green and gray linked and edged by arteries of streets and roads, bowled by gray hills on two sides, and the ice laced Hindu Kush on the other—dusty hot, full of mirages in its large plain position in the middle. After deplaning, feet down on the cracked cement, we are dazed from the long trip and the falling heat like an out of season coat. Someone huddles us unprofessionally together for a group picture, collects our passports stuffed with visas like dealt out poker cards, as turbaned men and women squatting under thick scarfs, and children with dark round eyes watch us from the observation patio above, like so many strange intruders. We move into a bursting stuffed room of people to gather our baggage, fill out a form, then rattle through a sort of customs, to pause in a a waiting room/receptacle hall of *chadris*-ed women and modern-heeled, mothers-to-be, and skinny pairs of boys and girls clutching welcoming bouquets to greet their liberated brothers or fathers who have traveled beyond them.

Like limp laundry, we are scooped up, dropped in Peace Corps hands, cradled together volunteers, but not before the pajama-billowing, drab gray-dressed porters, one-half my weight, have carried away the baggage and shuffled disappointedly when we pay with the only funds we have, a German mark. Piled into an old Toyota truck, our luggage in another, we are swept into the city down one long straight street.

Now we know we have come to another side of the world: the baked faces of turbaned men walk stoically along the treeless avenues; donkey-burros and men carry stone-heavy long burlap bags, curved over their narrow backs like some outrageous sculpture of a hunchback; they sit on their heels along the *jewie,* the open ditches sewers loud with their filth and collection, as other vehicles swerve and scream by, driven without apparent rules. A bus swerves between us and another bus, loosely clothed men clinging out the windows like stickers on a bush, inanimate this moment. Women, ghostlike beneath their veils, or blatantly westernized in too high hairdos or raised shoes, appear as infrequently as ice in this broiled culture. Bazaars with their nut-brown owners settle among the rich colors of fruits or small packaged items, and colored soda water. But watching out of dry nervous eyes, we have not yet seen the fullness of this place.

At the Peace Corps complex, a repossessed hotel, full of wooden chairs with fine-rope supports, whitewashed walls, and a roomful of well-wishing Peace Corps volunteers (PCVs), we are greeted, warned, briefed and then as suddenly in line to be vaccinated for polio, tine-tested, shot to ban rabies, doused with malaria prophylactic pills (Aralen), and injected with gamma globulin by a sprite, white-goateed and teasing Dr. Jenkins.

Our group is arbitrarily divided; Tom and I are sent to the Ashraf Hotel, where a bulbous manager-guest with an idiotic fawning smile and a young thin boy with the posture of a coveted dreamer, proudly nod and point as they show us our rooms for the next two nights. We weave down a dark, narrow corridor and push open a door. Before us, resting on a linoleum checkered floor are two straw mattresses beds; their side boards and bottom rest alternatively on cinder blocks and akimbo wooden legs, as the beds lean wryly from the four corners. The mattress in its lumpy shape suggests an upright chaise-lounge; each is covered with two coarse sheets and a rough felt blanket. Against one white-washed wall (abundant with unidentifiable holes the size of potholes and loose cracked plaster, electric wires to engage the straggling bald bulbs in the ceiling to shine on call) stands a yellow-spun wooden dresser with drawers at the bottom, strangely heavy like the air in this room, a plastic table and two metal chairs with black vinyl covers for seats, a limp dusty pair of everyone's universal draperies over a design of glass and punctured screens, and a short door going out to a one and half-foot balcony ledge.

There is not yet time to absorb the senses of this places; we are whisked back to lunch at the PC training quarters, a lunch of iodine-basked tomatoes and cucumbers, *nan*, tea and boiled water, a *pilau* of rice, raisins and nuts and some mystery variety of meat; then we wander back to the bleak hotel room, test the water in the lightless bathroom which spits out of the spigot after long gurgling, nod at the spongy dampness around a tub and the putrid smell from the clogged waste just below the flush toilet, then sling our backs over sleeping bags, for a brief rest. We push ourselves awake again. It is 5:00, and seeking company, and wanting to sate our curiosity, rather than feed any appetite, we return to the PC office, where dinner comes large and plentiful, with mellow apricots and the national dish of ground beef and sauce (*awshak*), rice, carrots and raisins and yogurt, more nan, more tea. We drink unquenchably, our throats tight from the heat and dust, our noses full, even as we easedrop on the TEFL coordinator, our boss-to-be, who gives out details of our training and language instruction to begin the next day, as if dispensing rare, overly-culled mysteries.

It is 7:30 p.m. as we move along the streets of shadows, the darkness unnatural, past bent or staring men motionless along the bazaars, silent, suspended now like garish pus on a broken bone, before tailor shops and the guarded Iranian embassy with its Persepolis noble lion insignia, past night fruit stands piled high with grapes and round melons, beyond closed compounds, entrances and walls, where we are inaugurated into the the procedures of prayer time, families of women moving out toward some uncensored destination, single children floating in grinning lightness, a boy reciting the Koran in a lush-throated song, but mostly men, old and slow, bent and stretched prostrate on their prayer mat, turned facing Mecca's profound illusion in the west. Overheard, from open windows, come the shrill raucous sounds of modern music, an announcement rattles in succession from a station with brief English, then it is quiet, and we see a veiled figure leaning over the *jewie*. She coughs, begins wailing without explanation or identify, the sound plaintive, whirling up into the night as if smoke, and we wonder if she is tubercular, or in mourning for something else. But we can only pass on, more stiffly, up to our hotel rooms, where the heat shoots us like buckshot. Like retired puppets, our stings and handlers suddenly cut, we flounder, limp. There is energy only to settle in a *rigor mortis* abandon, and try to sleep.

Beyond our window in the courtyard, resonant with flowers and shade tress, cornered by straw roofed houses, or an undulated western fire escape, stretch the city houses of the ghosts who had passed us on the street. Suddenly out of them come the sounds, lonely as gathered time, of the final evening prayer, the strains assailing the mercifully cooling air of penetrated night, obliterating all other sounds during its solo flight, the deposited daily coverlet of faith, as a soul glides from the garden. Intermittently we sleep; the room like any other room where one struggles to settle on a hot night, in the dark forceless, strange, offering no rungs to let the weary climb a ladder of references or rest.

I wake at 3:30 Friday morning even before the birds and lay long before boarding the balcony to feel a maiden breeze, to see for the first time the baked gray-beiges of the compounds around us, their forms sharp in the not yet risen dust, mountains arrogant, unchanged, classic beauties marking the edges of sight.

On a rooftop in the distance, a small capped boy sweeps sand from his roof of straw; the square outlines of white-washed walls fall below, weedy.

We have read our list of recommended books, the humorous tales of Americans in Afghanistan in 1972, *Spies Behind the Pillars, Bandits At the Pass: the Misadventures of an American Foreign Service Family Assigned to a Hardship Post, The CIA and Other Disasters; Through the Khyber Pass; Following Bengal Lancers on Holiday; The Ganges & the Gurus* by Kathleen Trautman; as well as the definitive study by the American anthropologist team of Louis and Nancy Dupree, *Afghanistan,* so we knew about the country and this city, theoretically, like someone who has read all the books on sex education and human anatomy but never actually engaged in an intimate relationship.

What can we know?

We know about following any ridge of hills that crisscross Kabul down to the river, descending like a rock in quicksand to the warren of straw-thatched, leaning stalls, dun-colored, walled compounds, open, pungent sewage ditches, and men bent in half, donkey and camels stalking, burlap bags, boxes, heaved high on human or animal's dragging flanks and broad backs, as children collect their dung as it falls, a family's fuel to dry for winter warmth, or cooking fires.

And, we know, have been told, how difficult it is to stop before one of a thousand indistinguishable walls, knock on the wide wooden door, and enter.

We know something of how this city had been two decades earlier, how Kabul in the 1950's, like the captain of an otherwise sinking ship, flourished with authority and new status, at the heart of the Cold War's manic race to cultivate strategic alliances and invest Western money. The land, its leaders had learned from their still recent past, century-old tussles with British and Czarist would-be expansion, the secret to power and influence: Play one power against another.

Then, as now, as perhaps it would always be, the country was dirt poor.

Step by step in the 50's and 60's, the Soviet Union had built an international airport, provided cheap black-market flights north to insure markets for its goods, offered obligation-laden loans, equipped and trained the Afghan military with tanks, uniforms, MIG fighters and artillery. A network of rock and dirt roads sported man-pulled carts, camels, donkeys, taxi, and jeep travel. There were no railroads and no rivers deep enough for ships in this country.

Yet people came there, over and over, from all corners of the globe—in those years most recently from Saudi Arabia, India, Germany, Japan, Iran, the Netherlands, Turkey, Russia and the U.S. They descended regularly into this land-locked and slightly xenophobic country, where the price of basic food, lodgings and labor ranked among the cheapest in the world. At that time, the population of Afghanistan was 12 million, more than two-thirds of whom were farmers growing wheat and vegetables or nurturing orchards and livestock on the three percent of the land which was arable, in the snow-fed river valley's on the northern side of the 20,000 foot Hindu Kush.

People lived as they had for thousands of years without benefit of sanitation or medicine or literacy or government-services. Merchants exported dried fruit, found sellers in India and Pakistan—when Pakistan didn't close its borders—while lamb skins, karakul, was traded to the U.S. The per capita income was about $20.

A strong, rigid and conservative Sunni Islam ruled intrinsically every aspect of life. Pushtoons, Uzbeks, Tajiks, Arabs, Kutchis and Turkomen practiced the Pillars like drinking their tea or eating daily *nan*, while resident in the bleakest mountainous areas, relegated to low-paying menial jobs, the Mongol-originating Hazaras made up the small minority of Shi'ite followers, a group actively discriminated against, especially by the ruling Pushtu families.

But in that insular, isolated country, the culture of Islam, not necessarily the known "laws," ruled in those years. People looked to *mullahs* for authority on daily social issues, as well as advice on religion, medicine, and law. Anyone serving in the Cabinet had to be a Moslem. Foreigners were welcomed but carefully monitored in a capital full of spies and informers. And, technically, foreign marriages were not legal.

In the late 1960's, Kabul had bustled, lively with sprawling classical eastern bazaars and shops, broad avenues, a scattering of sparkling new offices, hotels, banks, government offices; and madly illogical foot, motorized and animal traffic. It was, also, the required stopping place for the WT's, "world travelers," the international youth traveling cross-country from the States or Europe to the fabled riches of India and beyond. Here were easy drugs and the cheapest accommodations and food in the world from a people legendary for their hospitality to everyone.

The Kabul we arrived in still pulses.

People moved in swirls of color: Traditionally garbed men in their striped silk *chapans*, intricately wound flowing turbans and woven ethnic caps, billowing *peron* and *tanbon,* blended with sandaled or high-heeled and veiled women in *chadris (burqa)*, or long, flowery shawls. School girls in black uniforms and demure white scarves, boys in monotoned shirts and loose draw pants stuffed into oversize trousers to attend classes, walked beside modern Kabul women in Jacqueline Kennedy-esque coiffures, high heels, and miniskirts.

For those with any money, the city opened like Ali Baba's cave. Here was a paradise for creative shoppers, treasure hunters who savored rolling up their sleeves, navigating taxis and buses between sprawling destinations, and bargaining over green tea and sweets in the back rooms of thousands of hospitable but canny shopkeepers, or off the donkey-borne inventory or rolling wooden cart of more itinerant salesmen.

The bazaars were everywhere. In addition to those on "Chicken Street," the nerve center for the WT's, there were those for locals and expatriates—at Jade Maiwand, Charahi Saadaat, and Bagh-I-Umumi, where one can garnish household goods, wild ducks and partridge, electrical supplies, silver jewelry, *chapans* (traditional long-sleeved coats), *gilims* (woven rugs), or hunt for knitted goods off the Nadir Pushtun Wat. The interested bargained for hours for *pusteen* (fur-lined embroidered coats) at Jade Wilayat; pawed through rows and rows of second-hand clothes imported by the ton from the States and Northern Europe near the grain bazaar at the Mandawi; searched for books and magazines and canceled stamps; or re-supplied lost photograph equipment or found a new camera on some corner, somewhere.

Besides ubiquitous food stalls, *kebab* stands, and the handful of "formal" Afghan restaurants (in the Afghan Department Store, the Metropole and Spinzar Hotels, and in Sitara), one could find Chinese, German, and Italian food, and even—although legally forbidden—beer and wine.

The standard "footprint" of the city, in 1973, as we learned quickly, began at the center of Kabul in Zarnegar Park, with its mausoleum of Amir Abdur Rahman, Queen Halima's ornately decorated nineteenth century home. To the northeast sat the Ministry of Education and the beginning of the Salang Highway going to the north provinces, to the south the Afghanistan Tourist Organization and the National Archives. Further on was the Arg or Citadel, a complex housing Afghanistan's monarchy, the site for coronations, audiences, and occasional *loya jirga* from the 1880's on. The Citaldel's main gates opened on to Jade Istiqlal (Independence Avenue), which ran past the Ministry of Defense and onto the Kabul River; to Pushtoonistan Square, the heart of modern Kabul into the 70's, with the Khyber Restaurant on one side sharing the Ministry of Finance building and the Kabul Hotel with its bustling restaurant just down the block.

The Pul-i-Khushti Mosque, on Nadir Pushtun Wat, beside the Pul-i-Khusti Bridge, sat like a crown in the oldest part of Kabul, where stalls, drying carpets and food stands crowded the river bank, while webs of unpaved streets, the entrance to the Char Chatta Bazaar, moved out from the wide avenue between the bridge and the Jade Maiwand. Four centuries before, a covered bazaar with four arcades, open squares, fountains and colorfully-painted walls, it flourished, a warren of open air commerce, cobblestone streets, livestock lots and stalls, housing the Sikh moneychangers, along with sellers of silk, embroidered caps, silver, used clothes and a myriad of other things.

From there the river wound through the city, shadowed by the mountains, dominant in any neighborhoods, with the plain, octagonal Mausoleum of Timur Shah on one side and the Shan-Do-Shamshira Mosque across the river. Continuing on, one entered the residential section of Share-Nau (New City), its sentinel fort, Kolola Pushta, watching from the hills, the adjacent Sherpur section boasting an azure-tiled "new' (1957) mosque, Masjid-I-Yaqub. Grassy, treed, or dusty brown, Share-Nau Park housed a cinema, a green house, a woman's condolence center, tennis courts, a book kiosk, and refreshment stands, although none ever knew what those spaces were or if and when anything was in reality open or used by the time we arrived there.

To the west, in the slopes called Sheri-Darwaza, the *chinar* trees (plane), summer pavilion, terraced gardens, and tomb of Babur, founder of the Moghul dynasty in India, offered a cool retreat. Here, regular as clockwork in this country where time seemed frozen, in the high promontory above the Babur's Gardens, two cannons fired at noon every day, permanent, untouchable, from the century before.

On the opposite side of the mountain, sprawled Jangalak, where textiles, furniture, pottery, vehicle bodies, farm equipment, and machinery had been manufactured since 1961. Further south from Babur's Gardens lay the spacious Chilsitoon Gardens and royal guest houses, shelter to generations of nobles and officials. If one traveled west, out another direction, past the Kabul Zoo and Deh Mazang, one reached Kabul University, at the foot of Koh-I-Asmasi, off Jade Mir Wais. On a hillside above the then central campus of new dorms, gymnasium, administrative building, library, and Faculties (Science, Engineering, Law, Education, Agriculture, and others), stood Aliabad Hospital.

Karte-char, a middle class neighborhood nestled against the foothills of Kabul's mountains in the flat valley in the west of the city, lay close to the university, a cleanly-chiseled place of family compounds with tall white-washed walls, modest two-story homes with gardens and garages, housing the university professors, government officers and professionals who valued its short distance, a reliable bus ride or cab away, from the hustle and bustle of center Kabul, land more spacious and less pricey than Share-Nau's embassies, foreign entrepreneurs, and international clubs. Other technical schools, some factories, and the usual cluster of shops and produce wagons flourished in the streets near by, while wide swatches of open fields and meadow still prevailed.

From there the city continued, until some six miles from its center stood Darulman, King Amanullah's "new" but shunned capital city from 1923. On the right side of the wide-avenued Jade Darulman, rested the Ministry of Commerce and the Parliament Building, ending in lush gardens and the never-used palace, the Ministry of Justice and the National Museum.

And, in this country where eyes pull upward, to capture the sky's dip starting a mile above the sea a thousand miles away, the many-domed Bagh-i-Bala, once a royal palace, briefly an elegant restaurant, straddled a hill to the north of the city, with a breathtaking view of the Kabul Valley.

In those years, as it had been from the Fifties on, the government, Kabul's educated and wealthy, its most enterprising shopkeepers, drivers, craftsman, and businessmen, embraced every new influence of "the Great Game," the historical battle by the "world powers" to influence and control Afghanistan. To those who could afford them, both Western styles and the idea of a democratic government, beckoned, embodied in the Hotel Intercontinental, panoramically situated to the far northwest,

Stretching up from the neighborhoods into the mud and stone hills, winding up to the Old City Walls and Noon Gun high above, lay crowded dirt lanes and tiny mud homes and shops, largely without electricity or plumbing, tenuous home to the armies of child laborers and day laborers, the vulnerable lowest classes of that city, then and now.

But those who lived below tended to see little of their detail, their drab, brown, miniature hovels unremarkable, blending in with the eternal beiges and powdery tans which defined the hills most seasons, their homes, their faces blurred like the soil, their voices seemingly silent, as the mountains—history, soon to break open again—pulled us up, and off the map.

We come to this country to learn about another way of life, to talk to the poorest of the poor and the most hopeful of the educated and powerful, to live among villagers and teach their children, because we believe this is the only way there can be a future, for any of us, in one world.

July 1, 1973

We have a delicate breakfast of egg toast and fruit, and then become the group for two experienced PCVs (Peace Corps Volunteers) who proceed to educate us a little to the ways and places of Kabul. Head drawn in forced modesty, I follow with T and the others into a world of men, flocks and mobs of men, in a Saturday-in-the-park array of bargainers, khaki bland in their layers of clothes, second-hand coats over tunics and tanbon, turbans looped over shortly cropped hair. From the empty almost shaded avenues of Shar-e-nau (New City) with their well-built bazaars, we move toward the densely crowded older bazaars—the used clothes bazaars, the electric bazaars, one for each commodity, it seems, more than can be labeled, among vendors of water and ice, the liquid fresh from the *jewie* in strange mixtures and colors that ape Koolaid or fruit punch, with others selling ice cream which resembles curdled cream. As it moves towards lunch, others conjure charcoal stoves on squat legs along the sidewalks to cook and sell *nan* and rice. We take a bus, snarling and segregated, back to the new area, and lunch on an all-American (Afghan version) of French fries, salad and hamburgers. In the afternoon, as a group, we take a cab to our volunteer leader's house, and from there walk to the USAID swimming pool. This is another culture shock, as, judgmental with our PC vows of poverty and cultural sensitivity, we see the array of other American expatriates around us as flagrantly snobby and arrogant, blithely using Afghan staff like cheap servants to fetch their tennis balls. But the pool water, and the safe ice tea we imbibe like ambrosia, rejuvenate.

Back again to summer, we are introduced to the couple who will be our hosts for the next five days, "real" people, more weathered volunteers from the provinces, Chad and Wanda Nelson, whom we follow as they shop for fruit in the bazaar. Retired early for the night, we are fit only for sleep but it is too hot, our bodies like overstimulated children's, too tired to relax. First we must repair T's bed whose leg has slipped off. No irony lost, we donate our thick pile of James Joyce books from our backpacks.

Waking in time to pack a change of clothes, and what we imagine to be the bare essentials for a few days, we hastily consume fresh *nan* and black tea, then move out of the hotel. What we had anticipated would be a brief pause at the PC office, stretches into more activities: we get more shots and a briefing on the two pills we must take daily so long as we are here to lessen but not really prevent the onslaught of bacterial and amoebic dysentery, write aerograms home, our words perfunctory and evasive for we are yet too flat to persevere and try to record the detail of complexity around us, have lunch in a modern snack place called The Red Lantern, and pick out books from the library. Soon we are joined by the Nelson's and their parrot, and all move by taxi to the edge of Kabul. At a dusty, open field, a bus "terminal" where taxi, rag tag bus and van drivers collect paying passengers for destinations south, we are surrounded by hard-core Afghanistan—unveiled Kutchi women, crippled beggars on sliding boards arrayed in clouds of dust, children sly and persistent who shout "Mister Ketchaloo" and stare, and dozens of black-bearded, milling men, as we board a Toyota van, our "bus." Heads turn around like bobble dolls to catch us and pin us with their eyes, as we sit waiting for an hour, until all the seats on our vehicle are full. The van lurches forward and moves out of the city.

Minutes beyond the ragged city edges, the world changes again, but already that trip eludes me: I remember the thin-haired man in front who offers us apples and feeds the parrot; the red-eyed driver's boy who mulls sourly over our worn bills presented for fare; the rustling *chadrised* woman beside her husband behind me, speaking in a quick shrill, almost commanding voice, yet powerless to our eyes; the young first seater in his shoulder shirt and round winglike cave of a turban, setting his eyes on us for the whole trip, blinking long; the sun-glassed, semi-Western dressed man with his dark, gypsy-colorful scarved daughter or wife of eleven, being hugged and rested from the sun; and the general in his military greens, hatted like a timeless warrior with his two twin sons in matching short suit coats splitting a seat like Siamese kittens. I recall the bumping across green shaded areas and the classic lines of walled villages, water running in a thin green-gray ribbon across the fields, the erotically rich aroma of clover fields, like some deliberately lost secret of perfume; the long labored move upland, toward the 11,000-foot pass between sharp barren mountains, a thin mulch of green coating the endless risings of rock to dust storms billowing around us, some unconsecrated falling of hot snow, the nomads' tents like large pilings of wound rope and skin, shaped like an overturned pot, clustering in the wasteland of dust and rock in the most desolate area; the pausing in the middle of this nowhere to let the engine cool down, then stopping in a teahouse while a leaking tire is repaired. In the teahouse dark men squat on wide shelves around the walls and drink from small pots and glasses, swaying away from flies, while a long looping water pipe for tobacco is passed to those who ask. The men are intrigued by the N's' parrot, discuss him, ask to exchange their fat, plain bird, a kind of bald falcon called *"cawk,"* for the tropical beauty. Then we arrive in the provincial streets of Gardez, and go to their compound, where we meet their cook, Jahandar, 75-years old and slightly lame, praised far and wide for his skills at conjuring up delicious dishes. He presses us to sit before a table quickly spread with dinner.

Talk follows, night falls, there is the whir of the generator and three hours of electricity. We look out from walled compound at a dazzling sky with every constellation visible, the cloudy sweep of the Milky Way thick as a felt blanket, then sleep.

July 2, 1973

We wake to the crescendo of sounds just after dawn, a radio whining a song's repetition, roosters vying with each other for the longest crow, chickens squawking, a parade of single men calling to each other as their feet scrape stones and they move along streets and across fields, horses clopping over a rutted road, and finally Jahandar creaking the well lever, winding and unwinding down the cool, deep shaft, filling a rubber bucket, its contents poured into the metal water can (*owdon*) to be boiled.

Yesterday in the hot dusty streets, we invited little children's stares as we went to the bazaar with Wanda to purchase *cat-ton* (linen) for *tanbon and peron*, and as the only *haragees* (foreigners) in Gardez, and soon we had gathered a crowd of all ages to see these strange people buy from a shopkeeper. But, yet, there are too many strange things to be able to capture them all and build a complete picture.

We went to Wanda's school for two hours of classes, and she officiated for us in the circle of twelve teachers in their blue vests and pants and white scarves, complexions often pock-marked, but of rich brown coloring. They spoke rapidly in barking lyrical Farsi, slipping into the more gutteral Pushtu of this Pathan region for more subtle comments, we assumed. As Wanda's guests, we are gawked at and questioned as to age and marriage, whether we are *dek* (sad) at their school or at Wanda's house, what we do back in *Am-ri-ka*, what state we come from (disappointed that we are, none of us, Californians), why we do not wear make-up or jewelry. After class we all sit under lean shade trees and look back at each other, the morning's chorus of "hello, how are you," behind for a while.

The school smells of dampness and caked mud, undecorated, its room indistinguishable, small square blocks with a double row of benches, short, warped desks, a scarcely balanced blackboard, a screen-less window, and the children's eyes. Dark, large, damp with their brownness. Today was "hospital day" and little girls smile shyly in their bright green scarves and red and black skirts, their hair looped over their shoulders in thick braids, decorated with ribbons. The boys wear tight formed western slacks and blousy shirts or the *tanbon*, their thin legs stick-like in the dusty clothes. The regular uniform for the girls is a black sack-like dress and black tights, but a few girls and boys, members of a service club, wear khaki green uniforms with neck scarves.

I first sit in on an Afghan teacher's class in geography, her Farsi rolling, as the children recite after her, or read from the shared textbooks, stiff and almost frighted as they answer a formula on the board or mumble to the cement floor. The teacher is young, fair-skinned beside her sisters, a long smooth braid like ebony rope scrapes her shoulder and her teacher uniform makes her eyes shine cleanly. She showed me pictures in a book—full, as far as I can tell—of depictions of soldiers and military operations, then picks out for me one English words as she points to a soldier's arms: "gun." Urchin-tagged, I go to Wanda's class where chain drills make me dizzy with their regularity, the students quick and then foggy, intent and distracted in turn. The eyes like burnt brick follow me and the girls giggle nervously at this silent visiting *haragee* (foreigner).

In the afternoon we are visited by a PCV from Kabul, not an English teacher but a botanist, here to collect a rare turtle and some cave moths and lizards for the Smithsonian, and also working as copy-reader for the *Kabul Times*, the English language newspaper where, he interjects in the middle of introducing himself matter-of-factly—he "laces up stories" at each opportunity.

But we are not the only foreigners in town after all. Summoned guests, we all go off to the German compound's garden, a place rented as a pasture for their leisure horses, for a picnic. On route we are observed closely as we snatch a few apricots from a road side tree, and as a man shouts fiercely, questioning our intents, we get out money to satisfy him. But he only tells us that we must shake the trees and get only the ripe fruits, and not the hard green ones. Behind us the stable keepers, in turban and calico robe, laugh at it all, this idea of trying to communicate with the foreigners. We tread a way back along the dry ruts, scattering children from their doors. Three goat herders encircling their lean flocks stand and see us pass, and a quartet of young bachelors, arm in arm, study us closely as our paths cross along the road.

Back in the compound, Jake, the single volunteer who shares the house with the N's, supervises the irrigating of the garden, a private drama enacted weekly on "water day "in Gardez as each homeowner is allowed five minutes of water from the field *jewies*, released, flooded from the river or *karez*. But there is an argument, for everyone wants more water, no one wants to lose this dam, earthwork masterpieces erected quickly to allow their owners to steal their share from the flowing ditches. Within the garden everyone works to channel the flow and soon the planted furrows and rows are full.

July 4, 1973

Again, we spend the morning at the school, but the teachers are much quieter, with only a few cornering me. Then in mid-morning Wanda gets sick and after battling with the public *tashknob* (squat toilet) briefly, beckons us to join her and go home. After rest and lunch, there is time to cut out and stitch T's wide *tanbans,* the type Afghan men wear, before a Tajik servant comes to claim us for tea at the house of one of the teachers—Spogmia ("Moonbeam").

Like an Alice in Wonderland entrance, we must come into our compound through a cupboard-sized door of dusty wood. We bend, following the cook who turns slanted eyes on us as if on a pursuing animal, anxiously. At the interior door, our hostess greets us. We enter a room with bright red felt-velvet pillows along each wall, an iron frame bed hosting two bulging suitcases underneath, walls sparsely covered with torn-off leaves of a calendar, and a full-sized calendar with a picture of a woman standing before a television set, and a short round table which holds a large radio, and is covered by beautifully embroidered scarves. As the flies buzz in the dusty cool room, Spogmia shows us her picture collection, snapshots of her wedding. Carefully, in patient English, she points out, one by one, all the relatives, then entertains us with "Afghan "sing-song" on the staticky radio. She finally summons tea and sweets for us, ceremoniously filling our glasses with half a cup of sugar, before pouring tea, but using no sugar herself. She shows us her handicrafts, the delicate embroidery on her husband's shirts and *tanbon,* as well as on the linen napkins which she brings with a mound of soft yellow apples.

A uniformed soldier passes in the courtyard, then enters a few minutes later, meekly, almost shyly in his home clothes, also made by Spogmia. Her husband has come home. He calls her a name meaning "little tulip". Minutes later, Wanda, having finished typing her tests at the teacher's school across town, joins us and she too is served tea and apples, and the conversation picks up. This young teacher and Wanda are fond of each other, and I study her youth; now that there is a Pushtoon speaker on our side we do not have to try to communicate in our nascent Farsi and sparse English respectively. We learn that our liquid-eyed hostess is only eighteen and has been married a year already to this thin, quiet man who teases her like a brother. He is, himself aged 24, and is likely in 20 years to become a general. Soon we leave, having stayed over two hours.

Dinner, falling light, reading in the dim room as Jake, drawling elegantly in his rich Tennessee style, sorts out the gift books he has gotten for his schools from Peace Corps's storeroom and the Asia Foundation. We pause, thinking this could be a winter evening in any home, a quiet family time, but in fact we are in a remote village of Afghanistan. Then sleep comes as we bundle in a corner under sleeping bags.

July 5. 1973

Back in Kabul again, we've been relocated to the Bost Hotel across from our training center in Shari-nau. Behind us the assemblies of Gardez, already memories, arise in the heavy air and the silence: I picture again Jahandar with his history of heroism during a war 40-years ago, when—as the king's elephant trainer—he had three elephants shot out from underneath him, and his present baked, sad face and arthritic knees and wide bow-legged walk, as he labors off to the druggist for painkillers. I finger my gift, *baksheesh,* from Wanda's student, of a beaded necklace. We study a Polaroid picture of Jake's presentation of the books to his school, and of our own group when we visited a *nan* shop to watch *nan* being made. We had been awed by the expert assembly of turned hands, a family of bakers on their heels rolling the grainy dough into small balls as perfect as tennis shots, stretched by two persons separately, kneaded to make the scalloped design, flattened mysteriously, by the head baker, then whirled against the walls of the underground stove, baked to a hundred year formula, spun out and laid flat, a warm, fragrant round of bread, piled in the window beneath flies.

At "home" the last night we were visited by Gulmamadudi, otherwise known as "the dude," the Pushtu tutor, a stiff, slight, whale-eyed young man in his crisp western pants and white shirt; and by Mr. Van Hollen, a UN expert from the Netherlands, thin-waisted and soft-spoken like his country, now in charge of coordinating instruction at the DMA teacher's school. While the younger native watches nervously—there will be no lesson today, as he's too late,—Mr. H. describes travel to Ceylon (Sri Lanka), its jungle tropics and lively culture, full of fat Buddhist holidays, the elements of color and beach life, in a world grown warm. But he tells us his favorite place is Nepal, where one hires personal guides to take you up into the mountains, and you stop—as the hills make you tired as you march upward—to frequent teahouses and rest stops, and just look out on breathtaking eternity.

As we mount the dessicated road the next day. I remember the line we made, five Americans, marching to buy bread on our 4th of July, as the all-male, tough warriors of the town stared out at us with lethal eyes. Was it just the *ghairat,* those core values in Pushtoon culture which dictate rigidly and unforgivingly a combination of zeal, courage, honor, pride, autonomy, and self-definition? And would we ever be allowed to understand, to benefit from, the Pushtunwali, that tribal code of honor which cloisters women and elevates men, which makes blood-ties the only basis for living, which offers hospitality to strangers but insists they stay at a frosty distance?

I picture how our return trip to Kabul began after breakfast, after the hostile stares: Jahandar receives his *baksheesh,* and has a picture taken. In the market we find a small, sturdy bus, and in a reverse of the trip down, wait again for the bus to fill. A few minutes out of the town, the man in front of us hails his friend from the road. The van stops and the man quickly joins the bus, shouldering a broad rifle which seems to spit at me, like a stiff snake over the seat. They press close to each other and one stares cautiously at us as we gurgle over some cliffhanging scenario, over the river bed and up into the pass, behind us the armies of goats in proud black file, a solitary camel statuary in the dusty sunshine of the horizon, thin groups of children weaving along the road to school or watching the animals, past the mud-wall villages, a study in rough lines, stunning green avenues along miracle streams, fed by the elaborate *karez* system, the land like that of New Mexico but with more sand, less red clay, the color all in the faces of the people.

Arriving into Kabul was like bursting the ice bubble in a pond, put to floating, struggling again. Carted to a hotel, hot and sleeping bagless, then going out—mistakenly, misguidedly, to a shock of Americana, hot dogs and cake at a Fourth of July celebration at the U.S. Embassy, complete with braless teeny-boppers, too loud beer drinking, a salutatory speech by the American *charge d'affaires,* all which stimulates a bout of the Kabul quickstep, and the need to hastily slip away.

In our hotel room, we find a scorpion large and liquid against the far wall, his tail curled like a poisonous wand above legs and a body so putty-like we initially mistake him for a joke. T. swats him, lamely, with his shoe, and the legendary creature scurries down the wall. As Tom comes down again, blood splatters, two footsteps remain on the wall, the creature is dead. Sleep is not easy: all the noises of the street, a party playing records across the hall, people shouting hoarsely in odd directions, truck doors squealing, a mammoth volition of awfulness and no wind enters our room, so we swelter, saved only by daybreak and a weary relapse into a day.

July 6, 1973

We walk down a Shar-e-nau street past world travelers and heat, to a park with shade and open waste heaps, to a bakery, back to a restaurant where we meet a girl from Macon, Georgia who has been traveling since January, including a long stay in the "South Seas." She effuses, telling us how she really likes Kabul. We ease-dropped on another girl who ordered the three forbidden things (water, yogurt, and strawberries), mute, unintrusive to her ignorance. Back at the PC offices, we sit, waiting for our time, along with the other returned new volunteers, to report on the provincial trips.

July 7, 1973

We are taken by hired bus around Kabul, shown it mostly from its hills, the old palace of King Amanuallah, who ruled fifty years ago, now a restaurant almost adjacent to the Intercontinental Hotel, than around Kabul University, Je-ma-mi-nat, the river, the noon gun, the Babur gardens, the tomb of Nadir Shah, the father of the present king, then around the ministries, back to the training center for the start of language classes.

July 8, 1973

We were moved in last night to a house in Puli-Suk-ta, a house without either water or separate kitchen, with dirt floors and un-white-washed walls, with flies and no screens. It is in an area where you can hear at night a continuous drum of horses along the cobblestones and dirt streets, the buggies (*gaudis*) carrying visitors and residents between bazaars and sleep, and replete with a lush garden fragrant in the night with close breezes cooling, coming up from the under stalks as you walk, and rope beds padded with newly tucked sheets and feather bedding where you can lay in the bedroom of the second floor and look up to a yellow squash moon. Moving out of the more commercial city proper with all our gear, earlier we scanned the place we left briefly behind—the pale mud houses moving up the hills, lights beginning in the corners, and the cars and taxes and lumbering buses sharing lanes with the man-drawn wood carts who trot out of centuries, between shadows, catching glimpses of the shrouded forms of women.

We have an evening tea of sorts on our slanting concrete mezzanine, listening for a moment as a *mullah* calls to prayer on a loud speaker, his religious cadence and Arabic song, crackling like an old-fashioned radio, and a guard and a gardener-cook, whose names we exchange, an Isaac and a Rahsul, have their own tea beyond us, move their beds out under the trees for the night, while we talk on, listening largely to Stephen an Abe Lincoln tall, gaunt volunteer, in his white *tanban and peron* a spectacle and cynic He describes his flight back from India to the States the previous year, how the flight went via Lebanon and then Munich. As it was just after the Olympic horror show in 1973, anyone coming from an Arab country was searched and only cleared for onward passage after being meticulously interrogated On his plane, Stephen explained, when they landed in Germany, a passenger disappeared, but his baggage remained, abandoned. What further plan was thwarted, this giant of a storyteller and world-traveler, a resident of Brooklyn, and former PCV in Toga, asks? Then, turning to less threatening subjects, he talks briefly of the courting scandals in India, where a single man is urged to take on a landlord's cousin's daughter, as any available Western male warm body would be appreciated. There were, he insisted, endless temptations there for a single, even a married, man.

Our gardener is a beanstalk-thin person with a lean, bald-by-shaving head, which seems to be at its peak as narrow as his chin on the opposite pole. Flapping his pajama-like clothes, he busies himself with a pail of water, to settle the dust, and a bristly straw broom like something out of an imagined German fairytale. The other worker, short with a fez and western shirt and pants, has one stunted hand, and speaks grimly, brows knit, about all subjects.

The first week of cross-cultural training and language study has begun. T and I and Stephen make up one "learning group," but I sense that none of us is the star of the class and I myself am feeling darkly less competent, shawled in my own thoughts, too often silent, as if all I had only wanted was peace and muteness. Yet Dari is principally just vocabulary, as the grammar is simple and logical, and while we are not introduced to written Dari, we have only to absorb and repeat, like toddlers learning to play violin by ear in a Suzuki workshop, the words and meanings. Before the move, the Bost Hotel had continued to be a challenge to sleep, with its music-loving drained travelers moving barely in between our doors, the *dhukandars* working late to close up shop, unrolling, resettling again at dawn. We expect to sleep better in this new neighborhood and separate dwelling, and to be immersed in the language, as this area resembles more of a village, than does Sha-re-nau Kabul.

Still, each day demands a senseless abandon to the questions of meeting people, not knowing any of our own, wrangling in our lost manner for a means of expression. We have lessons Sunday through Wednesday. As a woman among the male instructors I feel always supplementary, cautious that what they say to me is in its place strange, that coaching me strains a certain grace. Our teacher, in the dim room at the end of one PC office hall, has fine black hair, his every feature deeply and precisely chiseled, his chin and nose and eyes finely shaped. He wears colorful shirts, and speaks of clubs and restaurants, but underneath one senses his conservatism, as in a chance remark about how angry he was when a good friend of his once had the lack of decorum to inquire after his sister. Thin as young boys, these are our teachers.

To them, what are our ideas?

One evening we attend a restful party at the good Doc Jenkins' home, where we eat heartily and take in the air, quiet and fragrant from his porch lined with flowers, as music and a moist breeze drift around a circle, allowing us to imbibe a mellowness temporarily.

As a part of our language immersion, to insure we begin navigating this world completely, we now take lunches in hotel cafes or kebab shops. Yesterday we all set out on a typical outing. Once in a kebab shop, we join twenty-eight Afghans, seated on hard long benches, while little boys with men's jobs dart around swatting flies. The men duck their *nan i*n swollen salad oil and no women enters to be seated. The walls stare back, incongruous with poor prints of garish eighteenth century Greek revival goddesses in strutting loose poses, and calendar girls, likely imports from Bollywood, while the mugshot of the king, Zaher Shah, is wedged patriotically between the floozies and a picture of Mecca's Kaaba, the embedded black stone tantalizing to the pilgrims during the *haj.* Another evening we go out to a western shop, Salim's, with its pizza-ice cream specialties, where seven men with fly swatters struggle to keep out the street's flying vermin, and we seat ourselves in a clean flat room with booths and lights. We flash our tickets, which you in turn surrender for your food. Here, we meet some year-veteran TEFL (Teachers of English as a Foreign Language) teachers from small towns in Colorado who have taught and studied in Buffalo, N.Y. They talk of their own debut as teachers here, first there, and of their relationship with Lackawanna landlords, Polish hardy, and of the defense provided them by a neighbor once, a union leader from the Bethlehem Steel Company . . . .

Another afternoon over lunch, a beautiful Costa Rican women, a teacher's wife, talks of her own brand of loneliness, of her separation in this work from her homeland . . . .

July 11, 1973

Both of us are struck down with the Kabul quickstep, and pass a wearying day, in the pains of weak sleep and watchfulness . . . . The culprit is possibly the food at the AID compound where everyone had gone swimming the night before. Or just the flies.

We begin to feel a vast absence in it all of a place for us somehow, for Tom and me, as if we are the weak-willed, loud-stomached odd couple who have nothing but complaints to make, as if we are dragging out the details of our dearth like some sour toffee clenched in our teeth, sweet and enamel each ready to crack. We listen wearily to the stories of the "unrewarding life" our counterparts have found here, the "cultureless vacuum" of a too-often sacked land, which wears its age heavily, which has not yet recovered from the bout with a rampaging Genghis Khan. They paint a grueling picture of a land without its own art or music, with no philosophy or literature, with only a low stubborn pride in what it has always done and will continue to do, its slow manner to death, its bastardized religion, its guttural incomplete Persian, its bald puritan attitude toward women, its shadelessness. Particularly criticized were the Pushtoons, haughty and ignorant, who rule the country by the steel of their looks and their corrupt and hoarded money, essentially clans of retired bandits. Most praised were the Hazaras and the gentler, more honest life with them in the heartlands, the Hazarajat. Yet as much as these latter are gentle, they are also the most cursed workers.

We hear slander of the TEFL program, of directors in general, in all the raw particulars. Also we meet another volunteer who has experienced disillusionment. Susan entertains, and taunts, with her grim tales of life as a public health nurse in a town to the north, of its open hostility and unteachableness. The night moves on, ourselves sick and tired, as we watch some of our instructors retreat into forbidden drink. Yet the gossip envelopes us like a protection against all we can not understand and touch. So much for that.

. . . In truth, we were not given steady housing, and were more sick than others, in the first weeks, so PC staff begin trying to rally us and keep us alive and committed to staying. Consequently . . . .

The TEFL PC staff coordinator, M. informs us we are to move to his house for some "R and R," and by 11:30 that night we are mentally and physically "recouping" in the palace-like space of his home, sipping ice tea quietly on his Persian rug. Sleep comes on beds with real mattresses with a garden breeze, and morning includes fresh cornbread. While they go off with their toddler son Joshua to swim, and to handle their business at the office and elsewhere, we are left to mind house. But Tom wanes all day, I grow shy and distant, spend hours writing letters, and in the evening Tom revives enough to eat a bowl of rice. I locate some oatmeal and peanut butter and we sit on the porch watching the leaves move. When the M's come home, we speak briefly of grammar and pronunciation, and thank them for the quiet and comfort of their house that day. Then we all go to bed.

July 14, 1973

This morning, too early, we politely leave the fine residence, bid *ba mona xoda* to cook and *nana*, the latter a small grinning women with the shawl of all old women, walk to Sharinau's training center where we wait, and wait and witness a great confusion, then go out to the battlefront house on the edge of "town," then return to the training center for language lessons. Later in the morning, we share a reprieve with tea in a hotel window, lunch in the same neighborhood place with two teachers, then go back to finish the day, and tour some of the other volunteers' houses, Returning to our own home, we find ourselves shouted at, insulted by our night guard, for reasons we can not fathom. Still, we finally resign ourselves to stay right there, to have a dinner made by the cook, to sleep and rise early, and try this all again.

July 17, 1973

Tuesday. We are guests to a military coup which took place in the middle of the night, abolishing the monarchy (the former king Nadir Shah is in London with eye trouble), and placing under arrest all of his family (except those of the Uncle Daud, who is taking over). Today the soldiers and tanks stand jubilant along the streets of the capital, and people in the more western and educated levels of society speak readily of how their country has now become free, how the yoke of its forty years of stagnation under the present monarchy is now ended. The lean lone figure of our turbaned guard-gardener presents our teacher with a poem he has written in perfect, proud diction, his words speaking to the end of discord, the beginning of brotherhood, the existing of Afghanistan now as a garden. Our teacher reads it aloud: it is melodious, fragrant, harmonious. Like children given Christmas, among those we see everywhere, there is the element of wonder in the air.

In the morning we wake to the low sweeping flights of military planes demonstrating, half-exerting their own practiced power, half saluting the victory of their freedom, ten years in the hatching, now obtained. Rumors spread quickly; our instructors beam and congratulate each other, wonder some at the events of the night, and official word comes in the paternal words of Tim Macdonald and wife, our TEFL director: A republic has been declared. Those of the military who had not agreed with the Uncle Daud of the family have had to be done away with, particularly the son-in-law of the king, who has been in charge of certain of the military ruckuses in the past years when students at the universities were harassed and harnessed, and many of the girls speared by soldiers under their skirts. Apparently the new man—in truth the king's uncle, Daud—is fiercely socialistic and nationalistic, a leftist who vows to put a constitution back into force. The ministers are all under arrest, safe no more in their bloated, padded privileges, but their deputy ministers will keep all the offices open. The soldiers smile.

There is some fear that in the provinces the people who regard the king as the shadows of Allah will now join in their tribal alliances and fight each other, but our teacher, Wasim. explains that "when the sky is cloudy there are no shadows."

We listen, study, review Afghanistan's history, as we wonder how long we will be allowed to stay under this new government. The politics of the country bear more scrutiny:

This last king of Afghanistan, Zahir Shah, had sat on the throne since 1933. During the first twenty years of his reign, his uncles functioned as prime ministers in turn and dictated most political decisions. Their thrust was to strengthen both the army and the economy, and the eldest uncle, Muhammad Hashim, continued to develop Afghan transportation and communication, building on contracts for factories and hydroelectric projects first secured from Germany in the 1930s and also aided by Italy and Japan. Despite Allied pressure, Afghanistan had maintained absolute neutrality in World War II, and it found ready markets for its agricultural produce in India and other countries.

In the 1950's the famous Helmand Valley Project in Helmand and Farah Provinces, funded principally by the U.S., marked a new, closer relationship with the U.S. It was instituted under the prime ministry of the second brother, Shah Mahmud, along with recognition of the new state of Pakistan, whose contingency of Pushtoons arbitrarily separated by the British drawn borders, desired independence. Shah Mahmud's attempts to reform and liberalize the Afghan government failed, and in 1953, a public rift between the king and younger members of the royal family resulted in Mohamed Daud, the king's cousin and brother-in-law and a Western-educated man, becoming prime minister. While continuing to support the Helmand Valley project, and its potential for opening up irrigated land and creating electricity, Daud warily tried to reverse any previous pro-Western leanings.

During this time, liberalization efforts in Afghanistan—always more evident and practiced in the cosmopolitan Kabul, than in the provinces or in other cities—were small and positive, and they were instituted with cultural sensitivity. For example, in 1959, the government announced that women no longer **had** to appear in public veiled, but only that they must appear in a manner acceptable to "their society." There was no cataclysmic reaction or resistance. The government did not force the full abandonment of the *chadris* or the practice of veiling women. People were left to make their own decisions within the context of their personal lives, neighborhoods, villages, and believes, and to do so at the pace they wanted. Thus, during the Independence Day celebrations that year, then Prime Minister Daud asked his Cabinet's wives to appear in public unveiled. Likewise, the queen and the princesses, and the daughters and the wife of Daud, appeared at this Afghan National Day dressed in Afghan national costumes and without *chadris*. So this reform, or opening up of new freedoms for Afghan women, started at the top and was modeled there without threatening anyone else. The government never actively promoted the law allowing women to go without *chadris,* but a change had taken place.

At this time, Daud's foreign policy rested on a balancing act—the desire to improve relations with the Soviet Union without losing U.S. economic aid; and the desire to resolve the Pushtoonistan issue to the advantage of Afghanistan. The major trade agreements Afghanistan had developed with the Soviet Union during the 1950's, including exchanges of Soviet oil, textiles and manufactured goods for Afghan wool and cotton; the Soviet building of petroleum storage plants and oil and gas exploration in the north, and free access to ship goods across Soviet lands, remained in place. Further, Daud maintained a policy of non-alignment with respect to not joining the U.S.-sponsored Baghdad Pact (made of Iran, Iraq, Pakistan and Turkey); and in 1955 when the U.S. refused to provide Afghanistan military assistance, Daud turned deliberately to the Soviet Union for $25 million of military aid to construct military airfields in Bagram, Mazar-i-Sharif and Shindand.

When Pakistan closed the border for five months in 1955, Daud snapped up Russia's renewed transit agreement and some 100 million dollars of Soviet aid. Meanwhile, by 1960, he was so obsessed with the always volatile Pakistani-Afghan border and what he considered Afghan domain, that he utilized bribes to tribesmen on both sides of the border to challenge the Pakistani government, launch an aggressive negative propaganda war, and eventually deploy troops into the frontier area. In September 1961, Afghan-Pakistani relations were severed and the border again officially closed. Quick to find and secure its niche, the Soviet Union purchased and airlifted that year's Afghan grape and pomegranate crop, and the remaining goods were flown to India, all carefully engineered to avoid the now-rifted Pakistan. However, with the necessary supplies for building and other endeavors detained in Pakistan, many of the foreign aid materials and development projects were held up, events which cascaded into lost customs revenue, lost trade, and foreign exchange, all of which sent the fragile Afghan economy floundering.

Finally, in March 1963, King Zahir secured Daud's resignation, despite Daud's control of the armed forces, and a German-educated Mohammed Yousef became prime minister.

Not surprisingly, many believe that the turn toward the Soviet Union under Daud was less based on ideological reasons than on the most basic economic needs. In a pattern which would be repeated over and over in the following decades, the United States largely turned its back on any real significant long-term development of the country. The U.S. did build a Kabul-Kandahar Road, continue with the Helmand project (which would ironically provide irrigation for the first bumper crops of opium in the 1960's), provide assistance with developing highly nationalistic elementary school textbooks, and—successfully—start up Kabul University's School of Engineering. Meanwhile, the always pragmatic and neighboring giant to the north, the Soviet Union, was more than willing and able to fill the void in other areas. Then, at the height of the Cold War, both powers maintained spy networks to check on each other, and they maintained such espionage easily from Afghanistan's strategic South Asia location.

Once Daud was removed from power in 1963, the Afghan government acted quickly to make changes, initiating a review of the prison conditions, establishing a diplomatic and trade agreement with Pakistan, and drafting and adopting the 1964 constitution. In the spring of 1964, Zahir Shah ordered the convening of a *loya jirga,* composed of members of the Senate, National Assembly, Supreme Court, and the constitutional commission, with 166 members elected by the provinces and 34 appointed by the king. The September 1964 assemblage of 452 representatives, including six women, convened and signed the new Constitution. The representatives were heavily aligned with supporters of the king, but also included members drawn widely from the entire country. Significantly, this 1964 Constitution excluded members of the royal family, except for the king, from participation in politics and government. It also used the word "Afghan" for the first time to define all citizens of the country, and gave priority to the individual rights of provincial delegates over tribal ones. At the same time, balancing the role of religious leaders and deferring to the strong cultural basis of this country, the Constitution clearly identified Islam as "the sacred religion of Afghanistan." The language of the Constitution said no law could be enacted which was "repugnant" to the basic principles of Islam. At the same time, it provided for an independent judiciary, and the dominance of secular law, although religious leaders were included in the system and the interpretation of the sharia was to "prevail in all domains over which the parliament and the king had not passed a law."

At the same time, although a constitutional monarch and a bicameral legislation were to exist, the king retained most power. The 1965 elections, considered unusually fair, resulted in the election of many anti-royalists from both sides of the political spectrum, in fact, with the new Wolesi Jirgah (lower parliament) composed of "supporters of the king, Pushtoon nationalists, entrepreneurs and industrialists, political liberals, a small group of leftists, and conservative Moslem leaders still opposed to secularization." The new prime minister nominated by Zahir Shah was Mohammed Hashim Maiwandwal.

But at this time, at the height of the Cold War, nonaligned countries were seeking their own identify and nation-building, and their intelligentsia and sometimes more general populations were exploring the potentials of socialism and communism.

The People's Democratic Party of Afghanistan (PDPA) was founded in January 1965. It wanted to gain parliamentary seats in the coming election (they secured four) and it was led by Nur Mohammed Taraki and Babrak Karmal, both pro-Moscow Marxist-Leninists who had "cut their political teeth" over a decade earlier during Shah Mahmud's brief experiment with political tolerance and liberalization. Between 1949 and 1951, a strong student movement had been prominent among opposition political groups. Shah Mahmud, seeing his government threatened, had cracked down, dissolved the student union, jailed opposition leaders, closed down newspapers, and made sure that the 1952 Parliament had none of the liberalization of the 1949 one. Taraki and Babrak resented the demise of this experiment in political openness.

At the same time, despite his nomenclature of "New Democracy," from 1965 on, the king was largely wary of the aggressive street riots and parliamentary speeches instigated by the Communists, and thus never signed legislation allowing for the creation of new political parties. By 1967, the People's Democratic Party of Afghanistan (PDPA) had split into factions. The largest was Taraki's Khalq Party, made up mostly of rural Pushtoon followers; Karmalí's Parchami, with members generally from more urban areas, were of better socio-economic backgrounds, and predominantly Dari speakers.

Still, the legislative assembly that was voted in, in 1969, represented the national population, with a predominance of conservative business men and landowners and non-Pushtoons from city and province. Compared to 1964, however, most women delegates, leftists, and so-called "urban liberals," including Prime Minister Maiwandwal, lost their seats.

This is the government we have arrived to witness, one for whom the parliament has sat in gridlock for most of 1969-1973, a government which appears unstable, with political polarization drawing people to either extreme left or right parties.

Yet in the 1960's and this far in the 1970's, it has seemed relatively quiet in Afghanistan.

But, we have heard, it was inevitable that something would happened, sooner or later. There were always signs. The people, especially the Leftists, were strong and getting organized, and the ten years of democracy was a prelude to all of this because the Soviet Union took advantage of that time to strengthen its own alliances in Afghanistan. Unfortunately, they could do so partially because the West largely forgot about Afghanistan. This desperately poor country can remain stable only if they get substantial outside support, but the U.S. ignores that fact in a substantial way. When Eisenhower stopped over in Kabul in 1955, the story goes, the King's government had approached him to request desperately needed development aid—to build roads, schools, hospitals, and water systems to serve the people. The king was brushed off, in favor of alliances with Pakistan.

Re-enter Daud, then, with this bloodless coup while Zahir Shah is out of the country for medical treatment this July 1973. Initially he is to be welcomed, especially by those looking for strong rule, and especially by his most conservative Pushtoon military officers. The coup was carried out by junior officers trained in the Soviet Union, and although Daud has maintained relations with their leaders for years, it is believed to be Daud's alone, not something concocted by the Communists.

So university students are exuberant, marching in support of the new "republic," and celebrating the Shah's fall, glad to be rid of the old monarchy and confident that Afghanistan will now move into a new time, a more modern era, that Afghan society is ready for this change.

But this country is not ready. Society outside of the enclave of Kabul sees Daud as another King and assumes things will go on as always. They see no way to differentiate between a kingdom and a presidency or a republic. Most people, illiterate people, just desire peace, a semblance of stability, and readily available bread, tea and work.

In the evening, in our borrowed garden, we study the plants, sit lazily in the winds and feel coolness. There is still no mail, because the airports are closed. (Will they instantly take the picture of the king off the postage stamp? I wonder.) Hills around us stand like magnified samples of rocks, each of some unfathomable god's giant geology set. Worn down to their bones, the mountains watch . . . For tomorrow, we do not know if we'll be allowed to stay here: Our feelings are as wry as a bird's song, tinny in the mud houses. What do you do in a country where nothing is built with the intent to last? Night falls . . . the fourth prayer of the day, sallow, reverberates.

July 18, 1973

Yesterday a religious scholar with eyes as wild as melon seeds . . . lectured us in Farsi on the tenets of Islam, while our soft-spoken English-honed director of culture, Dr. Sahar, translated meticulously his every phrase. We took in long chains of phrases surrounding the truth, yawned and listened politely, perhaps finding nothing quite as strange as we would have liked it to be, posing as the curious and polite foreigners in our demureness.

Back at our house, our "courting" is heeded; the gardener begins to talk to us, tells us how nine people in his family have to live on the 2,000 *afghanis* that he makes working for PC, how he has a house with two rooms, how he works hard here every day, yet sleeps outside, without walls. He shows us blistered hands, then puts powder under his tongue (*naswar*) and offers us his beads, as *baksheesh.* Unaccustomed to bribes or such entreaties, perhaps, weary, we refuse. They are like olive trees, these people, each face twisted like a root, a smile, a child's terror from too many slaps on a sunburned face . . . .

> *[And sometime in the afternoon, as we gathered with other Volunteers, we heard about bigotry in Buffalo as experienced by other PCVs]*

. . . Yesterday in class, we discussed families, each of us naming the lines of our family, and our instructor making up or extending his own circumstances, how his father had three wives, how his father and mother are now dead, how his three younger sisters are apparently under his jurisdiction . . . . After supper we walked up to a house a mile away and in the crowded streets felt the stares like wet rain falling on us, curious and broaching, a tally of children and crusty men, floating women, a scattering of military, until we reached the living room of some other trainees. We chatted, sitting into darkness, then started back again in a subtle fear, uncertain as to what we look like then, coming back to our own row of chairs, a fan and light to write letters home, to read and be bedded . . .

[The next day the PC office is closed so we go to the USIS Library] a clean, air-cooled oasis of books and periodicals in a most unnatural order, to sit and read a while (There is a three-month-old *Atlantic* with Susan Sontag's description of a trip to China, a story by Jay Alan McPherson, preening); then we are off for a long walk through the new city to question and indulge and be overcharged at "the Khyber," a restaurant with big portions of meat and potatoes . . . Finished, we head over again to PC; it is still not open. So we take a trip by two buses home, to dust, to be presented a huge dinner of soup vegetables, watermelon, and tea, and then take in a lazy evening.

Rain comes mysteriously at sunset and our roof leaks. We scurry after pails, and bid the cook farewell. T gives a small lesson to our poet gardener in English, his primer well-turned, and we share the smell of mud, of dust settling, as the mullah calls, an epistle of another day rooted through us, our happenings like idle flies around its dry crust. We seem undiscerning, uncertain that we even placed the pans to collect the water right, or if we can. The leaks dry up quickly in this country. Only tonight there is the smell of scattered earth, of night coming in a like a desert wind, thick with the sense of miracles, of a grove of miracle trees sprouting at a waterhole. T tells the gardener he must sleep in tonight, rather than lie on his bamboo rope bed under the damp trees, and snare the damp. We don't know if its proper to just be. Tomorrow . . . .

July 23, 1973

. . . Our gardener explains that he is from Arabia, then proceeds to tell us a smattering of Arabic words . . .

We set out on the public bus for the Kabul Zoo; I am the only woman on a smelly stuffed vehicle weaving over the dust-trusted streets to stop in a puddle at the front of a walled estate, corralled by sleepy soldiers on their armadillo shells of tanks, for state hire. The zoo is a dry, fruitless place, a scattering of flowers suggesting a season to come, lining the walks with readiness, but the fields for the animals are bare or festering in turn. We note the black swan, the speckled coats of the long-legged flamingos, and the large, gaping mouths, nursing double chins of the herons. Before the dry pit of the lean gorillas, we watch a little boy steal water, and his lank posture in wrinkled brown pajama uniform, his opaque eyes, follow us from cell to cell, unchanging as we pause before the rupture-winged plumage of caged eagles, hawks, mirroring owl eyes. The child comes up finally with a request for money before the vulture poses, snarling giant creatures with dusty feathers crawling with cawing pain. We refuse him baksheesh, and like kicked dust he is beyond us, out of sight. A soldier with gun akimbo smiles into the sun, a chadrised lady lifts her veil before a maybe lover over in a receding corner of the yard. The lame lion and his matronly lioness rub against the weeds and blink, a stunted elephant from India defecates beside old piles of droppings and stares, and we go on to a scolded monkey, a gila monster with a smashed head, a long-horned deer from the mountains, an ibex, and the bird cage where we are startled by a cluster of grinning soldiery, young boys carrying metal sticks. We are harried as the bat is pointed out to us. Behind the cages of a shade tree, a young soldier watches his face in a stiff compact mirror, his black raisin eyes gleaning the surface, and the invisible boundaries of the zoo land end at a slim river where small boys tease and splash in the mud water, in this squeezed juice of their parched land. Behind them, old men with braying burros load and unload straw to flood an outlet of the river.

Departing before the crowd at the tapir's pelt, we are again on the street and hike up for respite to the oasis of American-style drink, four glasses of ice tea for me at the off-bounds USAID houses, a place flooded with PC Volunteers and trainers who speak thoroughly, willingly, of their disillusionment . . . .

Monday we go on a royal *haragee* tour to Pagman, to the Hill, and the King's Garden, remnants of a palatial lushness in this land of so little green, edging mountains that may still harbor snow, a long gushing babble of water moving beside our bus. Shade, flowers, and space. We take a small lesson as our instructor interrogates a young boy who sells cigarettes, and we hear, in slow translation, how the child is one of ten of a father in a house of four mothers, who has been cheated of all sympathy and family help by the step-relatives. His father, a mullah, earns 200 afs a year and the child works after school and on breaks to make a little extra, to make their bread, but the father lets them go to school, and he prays for a future for him. The boy, M''mood, is fourteen . . . .

Sometimes our Afghan teachers erupt in a too loud, coarse laughter which makes one cringe, and we see below them their near childhoods, blessed with the allowances of an adult . . . .

Perhaps as they take us to visit, they take in again the beauty of this oasis, a place where spring brings flowering orchards, their pink and white and purple blossoms showering down from almond and apricot trees, the *gul-e-maryams* sprinkled like colored sugar across the glens edging the village and moving up into the hills, the yellow and red roses, tall, slender gladioli, and bright marigolds stretching across fields. Like us, they value the cool green nestled between the river and the hills, from which you can look down over the grounds of Baghi-Oumami and Bala-bagh, the old formal gardens from 60 years before, the time of the reformer king Amanullah. Three marble columns, old gazebos, summer houses, landscaped lakes and fountains, stand out like strong bones.

Surely, we all marvel at how this place is green and flowering, how the hills and mountains explode with flowers each spring, and how the sound of water in the small streams lulls the visitor and resident to sleep at night, the thick fields, the spring wheat and corn waving in shades of green. Certainly, they remember their father's talk of the royal palaces here, and the way the king and his ministers brought all his relatives here in the summer, how they would stroll in the best European dress through he gardens and around the lakes and fountains, down the landscaped paths and terraces, between the kiosks. There was running water, channels and ponds everywhere, the broad avenues leading into and through the city were lined with walnut and pine trees, and the shopkeepers welcomed visitors, while the gardens and shades and water ensured it was always a cool and quiet place to come and rest and picnic.

And remember.

Kabul 1994, time of Mujahadeen Civil War

They did it,
squeezed all the color, light, and air from the city,
reduced it to gray-brown dust, its lush green hills and broad avenues
trampled into aridity.
The Id Gah mosque planted in debris.
shafts, minarets, loping balconies in the city center
resembling sandcastles washed away by the tide.

Then, among shattered windows, chipped stones,
the random wholeness of the Kabul Mosque and its minaret
glares, an over-decorated wedding cake at a pauper's party.

Row after row of gutted building, evaporated steel and mud,
gaping walls, paneless windows,
stretch as far as the eye can see.

The Darulaman Palace gutted,
roof and turrets collapsed, grounds striped.
In Amanuallah's western suburbs,
the Victory Arch bends inward, pitted by bullet and mortar shells,
its copse of trees obliterated.
Everywhere sprawl burnt out tanks, cars, trucks, and carriers,
collapsed walls and floors,
heaved up and over.

People huddle among bombed out buildings,
unnamed thousands buried under the demolition.
In the roofless buildings,
behind walls jagged like ancient weathered ruins,
families camp,
raggedy, barefoot children—
amputee victims of shrapnel and landmines—
scour for food among trash heaps and garbage bins.

Armies of widows in blue-tented chadris cradle infant or toddlers.
Their dry, weathered hands outstretch,

their voices rise like a Greek chorus
along the avenues
in the dusty back lanes:
"Nan, pisa. Nan, pisa, xonum. Xoda marabahn bashan"
(Bread, money? Bread, money, Mrs? Allah be kind.)

But others, fighters, attack women, mothers, sisters, school girls
fleeing their bombed compound walls,
women, girls gang-raped on the streets,
before their husbands

There are suicides.

Bloated, ideologues, empowered, armed
from the Russian Wars,
the splintered mujahadeen factors squabble
like spoiled and arrogant children
tossing out mortar, touting aerial bombings and rocket shellings,
planting antipersonnel landmines, torturing and murdering
soldiers and civilians in detention, using extortion, arbitrary arrest,
sexual violations to get their bounty

and people die; already 30,000 civilians killed,
a third of the city totally leveled,
half a million driven from the city by June 1993.

The fighters in a shabby potpourri of uniforms,
Russian, pre-Soviet Afghan, mujahadeen,
in small groups spill from the hulks of collapsed houses
and begin to shoot.

Between gun fights you see them:
survivors of the now demolished house creep out, tentative,
to take away the bodies of their relatives for burial.
Savagely, the fighters pick them off
like gamesmen downing ducks.

One or two corpses before each house in the area.
Some, the soldiers pile up and burn,
others they dump into family wells.

So bodies linger, festering piles of corpses,
strewn through the streets,
fill open fields and warrens
of once-thriving shops and offices,

left for packs of dogs
to scavenge and eat.

II

TRAINING AND TRAVEL

July 25, 1973

[News, via letters which finally reach us. I learn that my Grandmother Ashorn had died on July 4).

This morning the former royal family of Afghanistan was exiled. At 8:30 a.m., the king, his wife, the prince and princesses were escorted by military lines to the airport, and sent away.

July 27, 1974

. . . We set off on our always memorable bus trip down to town, settling this time for the crowds of early morning work and shopping; well-brushed teenage girls who will never see *chadris* grinning at me as they stand and sit in the composite women's section. Our second bus, caught at the corner by the zoo, is stocky and grows empty as we move closer to the Supreme Court-to-be building, then on to a past king's gigantic palace, around the corner from, our destination, the Kabul Museum. But first we can witness a stoic child's grasping a sandy hand over her injured eye, an old stumbling women weeping into her veil while her thin son or husband hovers a moment at her feet, a trio of mute suffering.

The museum is a gem, wise retained history, outstanding in its ethnographic trophy room: the bizarre wooden effigies from the people of

Nuristan, blond Caucasian people capable of intensive arts and dreams, muffled by the tyrannies of forced conversion to practical Islam within this century, still whispering in their wooded mountain valleys; the tinseled proud dress of Uzbeks and Pushtoons, silver and gold bracelets, beautifully carved and decorated muskets lining the walls, overblown pictures of the outstanding ruins around the country—at Jam, Golgotha, the old Lashkargar Bazaar, Bamiyan, old Kandahar, old mosques and castles and offerings to the sun. We enter the world of the 1st century A.D., a period of remarkably rich trade out of a key city here of Begram, when caravans from Greece, India, and China crisscrossed the river routes and mountain valleys of this land with silk and delicate pottery and statuary. Up until the third century this equilibrium among people prospered here, the area was wealthy with acquired skills, arts and literature, architects and philosophers, craftsmen, Kushans, Hellenists with royal Indian regalia, a touch of oriental balm.

Then it all varnished, in Islamic ups and down, conquests and empires, to be replaced by other empires and craftsmen, but alongside it the complete loss of earlier centers of Greco-Buddhist culture around Balkh and Bamiyan and near Kandahar where only the cells of priests like chiseled-out beehives settle, now empty of substance, huge statuary, the outline of villages, chips from painted ceilings and the motifs of the Buddha as Indian god. There remain a few earlier faces from 2000 BC, a grim man emerging from a stone, this artifact found in a town just outside of Balkh, a bounty of 2000 years worth, buried coins from near Gardez, and a few geometric Islamic pots and delicately brushed Persian miniatures, tokens for our anticipation. Yet we leave awed, thinking of all that might have been, hadn't the destruction without replanting been so thorough here. We reflect on the ivory goddess, the humanistic jugs and statues, the graceful arm of a blessing Buddha, dissolved.

And all that had been.

July 31, 1973

Now it comes. A miserable set of circumstances. We had been moved from the training house to a "new house," the move and the house itself quite public, without curtains, supplied with an untrained (later revised un-trainable) cook . . . . At noon, someone broke into our house. Everything we brought to this country has been taken, except our papers. All guilt is denied, its source as raggedy as our minds which try to digest it.

One night we go to a Hindi movie, circles or coincidences which carried a tearful girl into marriage, widowhood, motherhood, teacherhood, martyrdom, and back to a reunion with the people she had begun with, a self-metamorphosis. In the audience of the fancy cinema, we are the only foreigners. Both *chadris*ed and mini-skirted women, attendant men and families, don't follow our lead as we laugh at what hits us as apparent absurdity.

Meanwhile our ranks are thinning. One TEFL couple has packed to leave, and six TB staff also plan to go. What of the bureaucracy of an unhatched country? I want to describe only those things which leave me with some sense of continuance, something which I watched and then could no longer grasp, so had to write it down, to save it . . . .

That evening, I finish a lengthy teaching lesson before the hawk eyes of Fareiba, and a Kunduz "brownie," (an experienced PC teachers who is beloved by our TEFL director) and we then listen to what is missing, the nemesis after "the visitors."

And we note hostility like sour milk on the faces of the neighborhood. As for the robbery, there is a sense of inevitability as we begin the inventory, but maybe it is only our own weary frustration. Gone are everything of value, sentimental or otherwise we had manged to bring—the cameras, the typewriter(postponement again), as well as Tom's two overcoats, four pairs of pants, the long dress made by mother, all our sweaters, toiletries, the wallet with 8,000 afs, all my IDs, plus pictures of my family and friends, addresses, etc., the laundry bag and so on. Why? Why did this happen? Was it some poor conniving Afghan poacher off to render us poor, powerless? Or was it just too much temptation to someone so poor he knew no better? And still, in the aftermath, a boiling and simmering (picture that low pot on a fire fed with salty wood, snapping).

[We garnish sympathy, a meeting with Country Director G., where we voice lots of complaints. Later we go off to someone's going-away party on the roof of a house in Shar-e-nau]

. . . As night falls heat lighting frames the silhouette of dust mountains seemingly on one level as we look out. Amid a rustling breeze, there is the noise of people moving below us in their centuries of work, of arrivals and departures. Among empty streets, all of Kabul seems our closed secret. After bargaining for a taxi and a twenty-minute ride, we arrive, end short of our mark as the red car rattles away, and we stalk out, looking for a bald light bulb to mark our alley "home."

. . . . Morning does not befriend us. We shuffle out of the stifling *kenerab* alley with its smothering odor of decaying feces and garbage into the dust of street and people; children—the dung collectors—mingling over cans full of dung, shout "Mr. Ketchaloo," throw us stern faces and aping return looks as we try to shrink and pass by.

> [*The day is consumed with meetings with PC staff, disagreement and hurt pride with Macdonald. There is apparently not enough to keep us busy and we are wasting too much time waiting to learn what is going on and what we are going to do. Personally, we find the constant moving, when others seem long settled during this training period, troublesome. Still we move on as everyone gathers for lectures at PC on the role of women in Afghan society (formulaic), and a briefing by Ambassador Newton on the political situation.*]

. . . . Later we speak briefly with our cook for the first time. He tells of his previous work, and invites us to come for tea at his house some day. We find comfort somehow in the night, riding in this strange world, gray again, back to our ill-deemed house, among children and an old unveiled lady who smiles at us. T and I risk cultural insensitivity to share a chair, unheard of, this atypical integration within the ladies' section of the bus. At our house, the old guard presses his hand to his heart for us as he does at every meeting, then kneels to prayer when the house is right. We hear him cough loosely beyond our window, in pain like a baby's cry from a nearby compound. Heat has settled selfishly into all our corners and we've lost, except for early morning, our favored breezes . . .

August 6-8, 1973

. . . The dust chokes you, blinds you, expires you in this country, and you feel your head as empty as a dried gourd . . . I follow my feet up the road, breathing the noise, the stray stares, until I find our alley, our temporary wall in this land . . . I leave finally to teach the girls' class, performed and joked to schedule. Returning, a school girl of eight who speaks rapid Farsi accompanies me until a few blocks of the announced stop, her name and grade and sisterhood established . . . We are willed into supper, and a pleasant breeze, the long scared ache of our day temporarily dissolved . . . Old *baba* brings in Hussain Ali, after one knock, and the man's good heart applauds us, for lasting through the problems. He blesses us with a key, translates a compliment to *baba* for us, and is on his way. He is a Hazara, PC's director of transportation, but so kind, so decent, so encouraging each time we meet him that we want to stay on with him just to talk and be comforted. Directly we engage in a battle with flies who ravish our bedroom, until the lights are out, and we try to forget all wounds.

As simple as having a shady room, and a breeze guaranteed now becomes our concept of "ease," of "the good life." When a letter comes from the States, it pinpoints how among those we especially follow, time vainly stands still, but gathers his forces way behind you, well past, ungraspable . . .

Today a lecture from the quick-eyed 28-year old beauty, our teacher, Leila Doorani. on elements of dress. Under her untutored emphasis we're reminded again of the gulf between our worlds, among the best of each, and yet we can not converse equally on ideas . . .

Baba coughs like an old rattle, a child's family cries, and evening has put the sand to sleep.

August 10, 1973

[The days] gallop by again, a lesson taught, a sprightly . . . lecture by Ambassador Newton received. His rotundity joined with the mellowed conceit of his articulation weaves around us in and out of forced laughter and indulgent ignorance, a cross between German precision and logic and a nymphet's coarseness. Causality aside, we learn something.

. . . Then, we join in an afternoon with Senator Percy, chunky libations, to the scorching facts, his details more solid than politics (the brother-in-law of the Gainers), and we learn that Spiro Agnew is in his own little Watergate, and of the depths of that corruption. Earlier (seated at the Embassy and a kind of eternal California green back lawn, we heard the man's picture words, one image in particular of Kennedy falling instantly at the sound of a volley of shots). In our practice teaching classes, we teach avid children some letters of the alphabet, are invited to tea after a test, and then are initiated into the circle of concerns, and find our own less than those of some others in the listing of self.

It's decided pretty definitely we'll be in the "sorts unknown" site of Sherberghan, a good 12 hours from Kabul, west of Mazar, at the literal and figurative end of the northern paved road, blessed apparently with a bouquet of trees in its center, a small bazaar, and a contingency of Russians to the west in the number of 600 or so. These men work in refineries. Details are scant, nothing either precise or subtle. Now, to survive, albeit prosper, we have to correlate our own details and find a home. In a week then we'll head for Khanabad, to be housed for our student teaching duration at the Government Hotel, to work and to be observed.

Summer leaves abruptly every evening now, and the day lapses into cool, breezy night, a dampness and chill . . . an offshoot of the season. I think of a cat, one eye of blue, the other green, and of a baby starving, multiplied like unfolded paperdolls in long endless lines.

Our ceilings are made of bunches of thin sticks and rushes and straw piled, wedged closely together over irregular wooden beams, with a moss-like hanging falling like dry bats from the matted stalks, archaic cobwebs. Above this insulation is the patted, white-washed mud, a pageant before rain.

. . . The boys in the neighborhood, most children at least, seem won to our side now. They greet us traditionally, no longer scream "mister ketchaloo." In our four way walk to and from the school, the dust collides with our own thoughts, layering them through a thin filter with an unconscious sense of people, place, and time—but our feet just walk. Today we had six hours of lessons, Leila Doorani drilling us to the tee, leaving us to humor on some questions, like why (as the expected formula goes) do we have no children, or why is Stephen, our looney but beloved partner in the class, not married. Dry as four o'clock, we trudge home, the former blue sky and relics of mountains blurred by the dust around us, manifested as grit on our teeth . . . .

Last night a neighbor's house howled with musicians preening and crooning songs. It was a wedding. Baba grumbled, but tonight as he tells us what it was, he is no longer angry. Hopefully, he found a bed to sleep in sometime today, to make up for the lost rest.

August 14, 1973

Today we are treated to a lecture on folk medicine by Mark Havel. This is timely, as my own bout with an atypically strong cold made health and medicine the crux of all our thoughts. The lecture itself bursts with particulars, the beliefs about amulets and medicine men, theories for lessening pain: the use of the burning belly button, of shaving off a square of head to let out the bad air (bawd), of jinns both good and bad . . . .

I would later look up the reportage of these believes in two old British Raj editions, the first, "Afghanistan for the Afghan," by Sirdar Ikbal Ali Shan (Bharana Books and Prints, New Delhi. It taught about witchcraft, necromancy, charms, spells and divinations, and the supernatural, all with lots of caveats about what was considered evil, unclean, or the Devil's work. In his chapter on "Witchcraft, Necromancy," (Chapter IV), Mr. Shan explains (and I paraphrase and quote here directly):

> "To subdue a husband or a brother in law, it is considered most efficacious to cause them to eat the flesh of an owl."
>
> To be hailed as "an owl" in Afghanistan . . . is equivalent to being called an ass.
>
> If a theft occurred in the house, if you have a *saher,* he chants an incantation over some water, which is then used as a gargle by everyone in the house . . . and the gums of the guilty one will bleed.
>
> If the houseowner handles it herself, she is told to take an old slipper, drive a nail through the center, hold the shoe by the head of the nail and have two women balance it on their index fingers. Draw a circle on the ground and the Devil is invoked.
>
> The lady takes the mate of the shoe held by the nail and states the evil saying, "Oh Nani, I take the name of our husband, and ask you who is the thief. Is it . . . ?" She goes through all the names. If the shoe moves, as she mentions a name, that is proof of the thief.

> Again, using a necromancer or a witch, a pot full of grass, nails, rotten eggs, lentil, etc. is left to rise on a crossroads, and then charms are read to make it go to an enemy's house like "a bale of fire in flight." Some men may try to harm a client's enemy if paid—they go to the woods, incant, produce *"Kalla Pandee"* (swelling cheeks) which fill with puss and make the man (the victim) die.
>
> Or, one of the witches or necromancers can take a male and female frog, paint a black ox on the back of the male and a cow's face on the female. They are tied back to back, put in a pot and buried "amongst a heap of burning fagots." The result is a powder which can be used like this: "Throw it on someone and the effect will be to turn away his or her affection from whomsoever of the opposite sex had been deeply loved. The same can be done with the heart of a sheep and the horns of a bull."
>
> So, all of these mentioned evil spells use *kalamatil kaffir*, words of infidelity contrary to Islam. But another "form of enchantment is *"ufsoon"*, which may or many not be Kaffir. The legend goes back to "Samaree," who fooled the followers of Moses by making them think he could "put life into matter." Moses prayed for him to be turned into a stone figure.

The same author explains how witches *(kuftaras)* dwell in lonely roads or under ground, where acacias grow. They haunt people to eat their hearts and livers. They try to hide their faces, which look ancient, like an 80-year old person, with fierce eyes and huge teeth, and they have a paunch.

In Chapter V, "Charms, Spells, and Divinations," the writer describes the use of special charms and Koranic scripture:

> These are the results of religious and old regional believes written by mullahs or *faqueers*, called *taweez*, and are passages from the Koran. They are the work of a mullah or a village doctor, whose training is strict and who is called *wazaefa*. The man must prove able to handle this kind of work, so he fasts, or has a restricted diet, and sees apparitions which tempt him.

> But if he sits on the prayer carpet within a circle called the *diara* he is safe. But when a *djinn* is subjugated the mullah can use it to serve his client. There are levels of serenity (*jamalice and jalalee*).
>
> The charm is fastened to a person for protection. And people may pay the room and board, sacrifice goats, and fruit, etc. to a mullah believed to have the power to provide a protective charm, or a child. He does *amal,* special prayers to protect children from the evil eye. A charm or two is placed on a pedant worn around the neck. For a man on a journey, the charm is on the arm. To bring about domestic quiet, a charm is put under a stone.

Going on in his litany of cookbook superstitious practices, the writer explains the way "to soften a judge's heart, in a case or to heal someone." The supplicant will pray everyday by the river with dough made of milk and flower, which he makes into a small ball and throws into the river.

Spells are of two kinds; *noree* (light) and *naree* (fire), which come from the belief that Allah ousted angels from light, Adam from earth, and Satan from fire.

Usually the spells are taken from passages of the Koran and they do everything from protect the eater of white pudding from the evil eye potential of a servant who looked at the food to make a disease, to a woman alone in the dark, to a child going outside, to a box of hidden jewels, to a garden plant.

> To cure a headache, tie a charm into the hair, say a *sura qulhowulla* over the head and pinch the forehead above the nose.
>
> Entreat the grave of a *fakeer,* a holy man, and the trees which overshadow him also have curative powers. Women tie little bits of rags on the trees to wish for something. They make promises to cover the grave with a new blue covering called a *chader.*
>
> Among Hazaras, many tombs have no roofs, because they claim the saint's soul flows up during the night and returns during the day.

> There is a ceremony for women concerning a white pudding. It is made during the day of *shabbaaint.* It uses a special white flour. A curtain is set up and a maiden lady makes a three sided stage. She places a big pot with a wide mouth and the pudding of rice is prepared there. When it is ready, the lid of the pot is coated with a thick dough and the rice is allowed to cool. Then it is presented as an "offering to the Virgin Mary, Mother of Christ," as the women pray for their requests to be granted. If *punja* (the impression of five fingers) appears on the pudding, it means Mary granted the wish. All of the women are called to share the pudding and be favored.

Finally, in the chapter on "The Supernatural" (Chapter VI, 101) the writer explains that supernatural creatures come in three or four classes: *djinns*; ghosts (*urwah*) who are souls of the dead; fairies (*paries*); and giants (*dayoos*). *Djinns* are mentioned in the Koran and all Afghans believe in them. But the Hazaras especially believe *djinns* exist to afflict beautiful children, so they feed the *djinn* to make it happy and to leave the child alone. But the *djinn* can "throw its shadow" over a person and do it at a certain hour each day or every other day or on Thursday nights, and the victim, who is always a woman, is "seized with spasmodic fits and, throwing her veil, she roams about distressed and to all external appearance insane." The mullah is called.

Only s*ayeds,* who are the descendants of Mohammed, are immune from *djinns*. The ghosts can come in the form of cats, rabbits, or lambs, and frequent a tree, a plain or a ruin. They can frighten a person "as to bring about his physical dissolution." *Parie*s and *dayoos* live in the hills of Kahay Quaff or the mountains of the Caucasus. The *dayoos* protect the beautiful women (*paries*) and will tear apart any intruder. A beautiful daughter can be stolen by a *parie (peri)*, so a mother will not let her sleep outside or wear remarkably colored clothes, so she does not stand out. Also, *sayeds,* spirits of holy men, come in the form of deer and pigeons.

In fact, pigeons are held in high veneration because "they are continually at prayer; for the sound they make is similar to the Arabic word—ya ho—"for God," or at least one of God's attributes. Meanwhile, these *sayeds* and souls of the pure and pious take the form of a white-robed and white-bearded cortege of skeletons on Thursday nights.

Or so says the ancient, early folklorist writer from Pakistan.

We have lunch today with Leila Doorani. and her sister-in-law. The food is a fine spread, and we enjoy viewing all her pictures, family pictures, a cupboard full of the past, as well as ease-dropping on her father-in-law . . . The Alum's living room is full of old armchairs out of a cozy middle class 1950's home, rugs and curtains and an old Victrola. Her shy, blue-eyed daughter sets off for school.

. . . Old Baba took my treatment under his own last night. He had me sipping hot tea, with a bandanna over my head and a jacket on at the end of the evening. Just in case, I was set to nibbling at his offered Russian aspirin.

. . . Energy lacking, I would steal a view of the dead mountains, mount them myself, and draw suns to sign for travelers to these parts. What's in an old women's head, who has no need to be covered by *chadris* now, as she gathers her skins like yarn beside me on the bus?

August 18. 1973

. . . Friday morning begins at dawn. Baba brings us bread, and we unwind slowly. He gets us a *gaudi*, pumping on the first lap of a long trip to Khanabad. A taxi takes us to the insanely inept little blue and white school bus, and we wait for our colleague, Stephen. Soon we are all seated, then eloquently greeted by a Khanabad pharmacist and a teacher from the school there. The agony begins then—scenery green and lush, then absent, desert, desolate. The bus, stuffed, explodes with the tattered folks and bundles they transport. After a pit stop in Puli-Khumri, we roll on to Baglan and Kunduz, and the last stretch of non-road into Khanabad. No one meets us, greetings absent, like a chilly fortune. We are on our own. In a hotel room open to the world, we choke down despair with a quick dinner, and then sleep . . . .

August 19, 1973

Yesterday I sat through five rather languid classes while Miriam Hilcher taught, and my presence created a commotion that bored me.

My Farsi is still less than good. I sense how the girls in classes 8-12 seem to grow plainer with age, barrel-chested with stooped shoulders, padded bottoms, poxed skin by the 10th or 11th year, in this group. Many sleep as the teachers talks. What do they think about, these Afghan women? Is it of the man they haven't known yet, of the family they must have, the secrets they must keep.

I share a bench with a staring child who already has the snarled mouth of a female bargainer, a blend of shrew and urchin, ready to let loose her giggle of conquest. Engagements are announced. At 16 a girl has been selected to marry someone's cousin. Another girl was asked for just the night before. The school itself is segregated by ages. Each class has its own room, with the younger kids on chairs outside. They shout answers keyed in by the first students. Its all some stunted child's riddle for no one checks their answers now. They recite, they do not think. The school has its compound walls, guarded by a baba who eyes me quaintly, as if half expecting I may salute him and not offer a hand. Inside the narrow rooms open to a courtyard, in two rows, divided in the middle by trees. The men (there are only three women teachers, including Miriam) sit in larger chairs like a tardy class, headed by the principal who adds columns and rings a large bell in time to the motion of the clock. Inside in another dark cool room one disconsolate Pushtu teacher—a man reported to beat his wife and be insane—pouts darkly in a corner. He is alone and sleeps, unconnected to his questions. A smiling matron offers us grapes, but it is not time for them.

Crossing like an emperor with invisible cloak, I gather stares like loose teeth, and we follow the market corner into a residential tree-shaded street, to the teachers' house [the H's]. On route we exchange stories with a Food for Work volunteer, and a French traveler on his way to Faizabad and who had been a volunteer with the French Corporation in West Africa. Across town, dogs like lame wolves prance on every compound wall . . . .

Partial to our ardor, or lack there of, the local mullah, his loud-speakered mosque half an acre from our morning window, rouses us too early with his diatribe for almost an hour every sunrise . . . . How angrily the prophet flattens his song. A man with a crooked turban, a Pakistani, asks me what we are doing here. I am sitting like a lampshade in the upstairs window, squatting turban heads below. There is always this layer effect, parallel to their thought and life, in the people's clothes: over the traditional *tanbans* and lack of underwear, a suit coat, a vest.

August 21, 1973

[Visit from the coordinator and director of the TEFL program, after teaching, and more meals. We all play Monopoly one night.]

. . . We all sit on the mezzanine and count over two hundred swallows who moved as quickly as blinks out from the wooden roof of the hotel, endlessly darting, with a quick clip of small black wings, and more and more come, until it is dark . . . Stiff, dignified Dr. Sahar thinks me typical of Barnard beauties, those young women he had glimpsed as he studied at Columbia the decade before, and he finds in me also a semblance to native Tajik and Uzbek women in the area around Sheberghan . . . .

We learn that those much discussed 'swallows' we have been watching are a local variety of bats, called in Farsi, "a bird with a leather wing." They are blind in light, preying, moving only in the dark. Another instance of . . . deception—that what you observe you see is not always what you see.

August 24, 1973

. . . We leave the small town for a half hour taxi ride over ruts and dust (four school boys in front, one more in the back with the three of us) to Kunduz, a big city, reeking of horse droppings and bad plumbing, but vertiginous with shady trees and paved streets. We discover others of our group . . . . at the best hotel in town, a sprawling company monopoly, the Spinzar with parkland gardens around it, wooden furniture with maple finishes, German well water and fans.

[In the rendezvous with other volunteers, there is lots of gossip about how badly everyone feels they have been treated by the M's, etc., and some of the language teachers . . . A few intake beer off the bazaar, share pound cake, among the complaints.]

We find our way back to the hotel lobby's vinyl chairs, conducive to laziness and chatter . . . . and hear of the degrading snobbery of the Pushtoon students at their Sugar Club residence in Baglan . . . For a while we talk about Gulnar's knowledge; and she defends circumstances and asks questions, a bold, intelligent person in our midst, like a rose bud, in this country where women are viewed as walking covers without minds. She leads us to believe she has a story, that there was a wild love affair which ended only four months ago, when her boyfriend, a PCV who went crazy, finally left the country. The young man had been here for three years (back from a stay at the age of six in this land of memories), was very much into Moslem culture it seemed, and in love with Gulnar. But he was denied her hand, which set off a series of "honorable" suicide attempts by Gulnar's brother, Gulnar, and the boy, and a motorcycle wreck and more quarrels. It makes another incredulous tales, of a limited repertoire, of unrequited, denied, or shattered love.

We go by *gaudi*, after a stroll on the bazaar, to look for materials for our classes, and encounter not so nice sneers (the hecklers mistake Gulnar for a foreigner so bring out their best repertoire of swear words, which she of course understands), and a boy of 12 or 13 with a knotty growth on his face like a diseased tree gawks at us all . . . . All together again, we bounce and bound at the back of the *gaudi* which takes us to a knoll of trees and gardens, the Spinzar Club at the end of a cool pine-strewn path, where we can look out over a darkening plain, a ledge and Pushtoon village to one side, and fields of rice beneath us. Above a whining bit of a river, we look up to mountains which swallow the sun, a dusty red ball. We eat sun-soaked melon and walk further down the road and across a fertile stretch of green cotton fields, the plants bursting white now, with a UN worker, a native, who offers us tea at dusk in the yard of the experimental WHO farm station, a lonely vigilant crew of white buildings and a miniature barking dog. At dusk, a sing-song, and the mysterious noise of *gaudis* and taxis race out in the mist which is sprung dust, and we are ourselves soon among them after an Afghan instructor hails a car and becomes its driver. The rest of us huddle into a gaudy for a romantic scuttle into town, off the dust roads to the city of lights and stooping trees.

We finally escort ourselves into an uproariously crowded restaurant, sidling up to one table, all eight then, while the proprietor, a bald, wiry man who resembles an old pirate, takes our orders and speeds up the course. The air is electric. Then it explodes, and a fight is in progress—, men shout and push . . . The police come in and begin slapping two young boys crowded against one wall out of range. Cornered, the two youth are both thrown out; then a mullah is slapped, as men shout around him. Apparently two elderly men had both wanted the same "boy," this pink turban special. The whole crew is now ousted, the police taking them in tow.

. . . [Afterwards, we] wander uptown to a movie, but first we stop at a crowded corner to listen in one part of President Daud's speech . . . .

August 25, 1973

We came back from Kunduz in a memorable old Kutchi truck, one of the raggedly-painted tin contraptions that wanders from north to south, snorting dust and overcoming hills, its drivers as peaked as a hot day. The three of us sit in the cabin and periodically during the hour and a half sojourn in heat and dust, the driver shouts some question, his assumption age old that if we don't know what he is saying (being *kafirs*) he has only to raise his voice and it will become clear. In the back a whole repertoire of men and supplies are loaded and unloaded, people disappearing into waist-high rice plants in the middle of no where, a house with sand walls holding up the whole of a clear sky. Even behind the broken glass of the front visors, we are obvious and foreign, as long-legged boys pass and wink under turbans, shawled girls with eyes bright as their clothes, look intensely, and the eternal baked men from the dark caves of a coffee house or a straw pallet covered by branches and straw sat on a ridge over the fields like a pastoral hut before the sun, watch us pass. Everywhere is the motion of men with pitch forks in golden strewn piles of grain, tossing to separate the grain from the chaff, tossing up the glittery shafts which blow and fall according to their weights.

Khanabad is eerie with trees, and we soon join our instructors for a slow afternoon . . . . We . . . hear on the radio that the King has graciously relinquished all to the Republic (though he still holds its money), then set off to the movies, suddenly anxious in the darkness of the streets, wary of dogs and *jewies* to be dodged. To me, the only woman in the barn-like structure, a gray and brown tale with cracked words unwinds on the screen, men speak disrespectfully, and the laughter is not enough to look at . . . .

August 26, 1973

[School stuff, frustrations rein.]

. . . We walk to the bazaar to price carpetbags and long robes (*chablanks*), but the exchange is unproductive except to give us estimates. It has been a loud night of the wild hotel proprietors shifting and scooting things up, moving up an army of beds and knocking the walls down at midnight . . . .

Tuesday morning, school begins for the 12th class, our students sit docile under their social guises until cheering starts from the street and it becomes a strange day: This is, we quickly learn, Solidarity Day: even the girls must troop to the bazaar street and recite poetry and shout, and raise their flower bedecked picture of old Daud. The cheering and marching continue most of the day, and my classes are abandoned . . .

The governmental provincial officials, the heads of education and of the army and other such dignitaries congregate on the hotel mezzanine, a whole study of furniture brought up for their service, including a telephone which is spliced to the electric wire. It is all a scene from a forced comedy of German war plans, a scene of fat bellies and empty eyes reminiscent of any ignorant exchanges of power. This is stage 2 of the coup, of the Republic.

August 26, 1973

Last night, as guests, we attended a rich man's feast. Embraced as special and honored guests, we found ourselves sitting in his garden just as three satellites went overhead, eating a twentieth of the food set before us, nudging a new baby calf, ease-dropping as the host spoke to a girlfriend in America, watching his shy sisters, following the radio, courting a breeze, then going home to sleep. Ages clash, but less than we had expected. Pictures of this man's ancestors, which he eagerly shows us, resemble American Indians, and with his long straight black hair, the rich man looks a cross between Cochise and Joe Namath.

August 31, 1973

Ahman, the PC staff driver and cook, knocked on our door at a quarter to six yesterday. Behind us was the dawn sermon of the *mullah*, a night of mosquitoes, an enigmatic pocket of dreams, requests for water or motion. We gruffly got up, dressed and began to stuff our bags, mobile campers without a compass or a swim, until the room was empty again, the way we had found it except for a pile of papers knotted in one corner and the ashes of T's cigarettes laid in an old metal bowl. Scraping for dignity, as a concession (the first) to his first paying customers, the hotel manager, of that tribe of not so meekly inane, provided us with tea and nan. Before seven the truck was loaded and our Wasim and Ghulam, the teachers, Ahman and the unnamed driver, were leaving. We drifted away another hour, then went to our classes. My own was energetic and full of questions, the lessons I had pushed doggedly on verb tenses and vocabulary largely unlearned, except by a very few, for all my weeks' efforts. Then suddenly the students were excusing themselves, sending me off, when the cowbell rang and the class was over. By 9:30, T's class also finished, we were off toward Kunduz, searching for a set of double wheels to whisk us over dust and rills to the awaited cab to Kabul. We settled in instead to a Waz, the bench-lined jeep truck, and watched it fill up with men, as the driver and his helper argued over the precise number of bodies allowed in.

Faster than we'd hoped for the magic monster was easing into the sun, stopping a few more times to argue with new riders, none of whom ever got on because of the price, pausing at the advent of Afghan ingenuity as a lumbering dump truck threw out a new pile of dirt over the dust road, mysteries of engineering completely insane to us. Across from me was a white-haired Khanite, a small Marco Polo, his folds of eyes enigmatic. Somehow we walked through Kunduz and found one taxi (the beginning), a thin, bent man with child eyes who said we three could have the taxi for 1200 Afghani, the normal fee being 200 per head, with six people. Fanta-seized and nan-gripping, we decided to take it (my promised textile purse forgotten temporarily) and we entered the cab, only to be whisked to a back alley of town where the driver left us to a family's stares while he ran to his house and changed clothes, purchased a melon, and grinned. It was the open road, then, the hour almost 11:00, and we in a cab that ground at low speed and seemed to wobble, a driver who stopped too long at the toll gates, none of this settling us with much confidence.

Ten kilometers out of Kunduz, we enter desert, high, stark land scattered with nomad tents and strutting camels, the backdrop of Saharas, small indentures in the rills marking a path back toward other hills, back as they did when this country which was never young had less bends. Baglan comes out at the end of a river, rich-looking with its knolls of trees and village green squares, and there we see "Rooster David," a Norwegian named Norm, and later the student language teacher Nourshin. They ask for a ride to Fabrika, where they expect a PC truck. But this vehicle is never realized, so they come in with us for the trip (our assumption being to save money, our 1200 fee now divisible by six). On to Puli Khumri we shoot, with a story in my ear about a Russian compound near by with a swimming pool, as the land sweeps us, hot and dusty and frail. Until we enter an unnamed town at the edge of the Salang Road, and are again held up as the driver without ceremony finds himself food. We grumble, annoyed, have Fantas and bide our tongue as the soda vendor discovers a rusty bottle cap at his feet and decides we have purchased yet another drink and neither paid for it nor returned the bottle. Everyone is an entrepreneur. The obscenity abates; we feel trapped in a no-man's land of stale imagination, until a plump dwarf with a long white beard, raisin eyes, and shoes which turn up at the end comes whistling (to our minds) down the street—("Now if he had six brothers."). But it can't be; we are not in an Afghan fairytale.

We embarked on the long, stuttered ride up the Salang, with pauses for watering down the car, washing away the dust, taking pictures, clearing ourselves, before coming finally to the worm-like tunnels, and the view of the baldest rock conceivable. Our Norwegian doctor who had joined the cab tells us at 11,000 feet this is the highest tunnel in the world that traffic goes through. On the other side things grow markedly greener, the river bubbles and slides all along the road, and villages of brown and gray and green seem artistically carved out of the hills overlooking the road. Restlessly the afternoon moves up, we are two hours, one hour from Kabul and we sing. We hear about a cave beneath a bridge we've just crossed which requires you to go on hands and knees, crawling for an hour or more through the earth, before you come to a beautiful mountain lake, a kind of holy place, and how this site has been secret for centuries.

Kabul then, behind us the grape city, Istalif, and since everything about fares had never been resolved, a quarrel begins as we learn the driver expects another 300 afs, and wants to charge us three who began with him 1,000 each, plus for each of the others 180. Irate, we stop at Noushin's compound; she excuses herself as a crowd gathers, Nourshin ducks on to a bus, and poor lame Rooster minds the baggage. I think to shout angrily back, then leave, and the situation wobbles. Finally, Arnaud of Norway and Tom stalk away, another cab driver having asserted the justice of our claim that the fare can't exceed 1200 afs. In minutes the unpleasant misunderstanding is completely behind us.

Somehow yesterday I saw the country in its dazzling beauty, its ends of the earth loneliness, its miracles of green and running water . . .

September 2, 1973

(We gorged ourselves at the Hotel Intercontinental on Sunday.)

. . . Wandering into the hotel with our wits scattered and our stomachs distended, we can not imagine the feast before us, which (when it comes) is a table a hundred feet long laden with every good and delicacy imaginable, served on fine china with crystal glasses of water and solid silverware. We sit like jet-set models at the very top of Kabul, looking down over the rattle of clay compounds and the sporadic green, and then around us to the room where a subcontinent was dining. Overcome by it all, I manage to eat myself into discomfort, all the time listening to stories of how donkeys will bloat themselves on alfalfa and have to be deflated with a hypodermic needle . . . It is all as far from Afghanistan as the bedroom communities of New Rochelle, N.Y.

About 9:00 the Pushtoon language students return from Baglan . . . and . . . we collectively exchange experiences: we hear of a tour of a cement factory, of the executive's lavish riverfront home, of their food, and of the fate of mullahs who can't afford wives and so take boys, then in terror kill them. And, so on . . . .

Saturday we learn we are finished with training . . . .

In coming back to our Kabul north neighborhood house on the bus I find myself assaulted, pinched on arms and breast and waist by two heavily made-up Afghan women-girls. My Farsi curses dilute. Shocked at my capacity for anger, I think I want to scratch their faces in revenge. But I can't be like that. Instead, I mumble, turn away, and feel sick . . .

September 4, 1973

(Upon receiving letters from a ton of people, especially our parents:]

. . . Corruption is mounting, out in the open now, and the size of purgatory. *Time* magazine reports on Nixon and company and like scouring an over-sized score board, we watch for the details of their defeats . . . .

September 5, 1973

Daily we become more amazed at ourselves and our ability to take the peculiarities of this place for granted. Last night was our swearing in and "Afghan night" celebration, and for four hours we were suspended in a fragrant terraced garden, setting high in our pavilion in Babar Gardens (not the French elephant-king, a man dead some 400 years ago now, a grandson of Tamerlane, an odd fellow to be honored, scion of executors and destruction). We were invited only to think about lads and damsels, healthy helpings of stews and fruit and rice and some honeyed desert called "*seek kabob,*" and then to watch the sensual gyrations which pass for dancing of some of our Afghan counterparts. It was a place you wished might have been for you and your love and a scattering of poetic lonesome couples, open as the sky and a timid fall breeze, bounding like blown seeds over the ground.

We sat for tea with Fariad and his Swiss wife, enthralled as they spoke to each other in German, pointed out to us a shimmering hill across the city as the site of their house, and then the wise young Pushtoon told some of what he knows about languages (Czech was the mother, Latin had been like a Rosetta stone to his medical studies, and so on). His wife was quiet, somewhat nervous; they were acknowledged by the Gainers, who left early, gone when the meal started. This cross-cultural supervisor, a serious sort, delicate as a Chekhovian doctor's son, sat at our table and we listened as he spoke forthrightly of the shortcomings of Peace Corps, the graver errors of USAID, until his frank words and our queries were interrupted, postponed, so we might just take in the sky, although little had been resolved. This man is to be our coordinator/supervisor for the next phase of our lives here: we are Volunteers about to begin living and teaching in our distant and traditional village . . . .

September 8. 1973

[Lots of preparations, repair shop for typewriter, bank, coordination with our coordinator, then a trip to Fariad's house.]

. . . We met Fariad . . . and sped out in his muffling truck to his house outside the city, running first into his brother who was out of gas, and almost running out ourselves. The home is beautiful and spacious, well-conceived and executed to the arches between two room, the stage-like oriental raised portion of the living room, the delicate Japanese prints, a massive enamel inset sitar, a Maimana chest like a Russian puzzle, the stereo. His wife is quiet and gracious, a young girl with three beautiful children who mirror her, something fresh from a Swiss meadow, and yet speaking Farsi and some Pushtu (along with her German). The afternoon moves languidly, with a huge lunch and tea, and a tour of the grounds, where we meet a pet gazelle and 100 beehives in boxes, ooh at lush fruit trees, and take in the coolness of a mountain damp with water in the air.

[Later that evening going to someone's house, an AID showing of a movie, all the PCV's together, T and I feeling the emptiness, missing some real conversation . . .]

. . . An Afghan Jamal night, and we're invited for someone's mysterious party, but we know only one house in Jema-mi-nat with foreign residents, and have to find and ask the cook there where to find another. He offers to take us there. On a dark hill, lights lit inside dwellings sparse and flickering as fireflies, we stop to see if that is the place. It isn't, so we continue walking, surrounded suddenly by an open graveyard, and wander back into a lane. By some quirk of luck, we run into the kind Hussain. Ali, who has both a driver and a truck. They take us to the what they call, "The Big House," where we are met at the door by other volunteers, people on route to a movie down in Karte-char. We follow, briefly climb up the legendary housed hills of the part of the city where Mr. Ali. resides, a heavily Hazara neighborhood, and then are off down a hill and on the street level below again . . . .

September 9, 1973

> *[We were supposed to leave for Samagan, our posting site, this day, but Tom woke up sick. Then we set off anyway, and the others we were to meet went another route. I chased around between the Northern Garage, Sharee-Nau, and Kalow Shadalm, trying to determine where we were to leave from, then finally discussed it with T. and we were reconciled to leave tomorrow . . .]*

. . . Someone has put a pincher on all our dreams and now they've grown so little . . . . There is the feeling that you might make it through anything if you just have a book to read.

The languidness saps us. Yet there is beauty. Even the way the trees blow here, little rivulets of wind, illusion in a waterless land, leaves like gypsy spangles.

Chadris, Burqas and Veils, Pakistani Refuge Camps, 1995

You live in a world where you look out of meshing.
It filters colors and divides faces into sections.
The *burqa's* stiff, dusty silk and polyester cloth
pulled snugly over your head like a skullcap
pinches your forehead,
tunnels your eyes,
envelops your body in pleats that fall from your shoulders
like over-sized curtains on narrow rods.

Trapped in the heavy cloth folds,
the heat crushes your chest,
dampens your clothing
humid in the hot August sun,
drafty and clinging in the icy January winds.

To make your voice audible,
you must breathe out with all your strength.

From the moment you cease to be a girl,
your family, your religion, your government tells you:
this is your fate and worth.
The veil is yours to wear.
Your world reels with danger.

Perhaps, over time, within the harsh discord:
the artificial, tradition-broken domain,
homeless in refugee camps on hostile soil,
trapped on a dusty lane in the warren of camps
you even grow to desire the *burqa,*
a place of retreat and temporary safety,
of protective anonymity.

You welcome it as a portable shelter
days when you venture outside

from the filthy tent corner, your only home.
Or, it guards you, a surrogate companion,
when your son or husband or father is dead or distant,
fighting for your homeland
laboring legions away as cheap labor
for the begrudging host's menial tasks—
Pakistani cities' urban development,
whole sections of Peshawar and Islamabad,
cities in Iran, built by cheap Afghan refugee labor.

Perhaps you adapt to its narrow window on the world.
You look dully through the web
to see a blurred framing of faces and people,
the bleakness that stretches:
dusty plains bereft of trees or rivers,
row after row of tents or lean-to shelters
roofed with plastic or blankets,
endless lines of people
waiting for monthly rations,
a rare medical exam.

When you have no clean or decent clothes,
only the frayed, the faded ones you fled with
or collected from the NGO donations—
someone else's rejected and worn clothing
from a continent away—
perhaps you welcome the covering.
embrace this protection from the eyes of others,
the judgments on fashion or feminine beauty.

If you are forced to beg for money,
allocated to the notorious "widow's camp"
edging the refugee camps,
made to sell your body to pleasure soldiers
and feed your children,
this wretched burqa grants a shred
of dignity, of security.

In the crowded refugee camp, in the makeshift tents,
shoulder to shoulder against a neighbor,
privacy does not exist.
Each voice, a movement, some neighbor's quarrel,
broadcasts, known by the circle of fellow refugees.
The covering provides a preteen daughter
some modicum of self,
an abandoned wife a brief retreat from harsh pity,
a frightened child, a hungry baby
huddled under its fold against a silent mother,
sustaining warmth.

Or, as a family camps behind the skeleton walls
of a long-departed neighbor's compound,
or in the bombed out-carcass of someone's old store,
without electricity or water or sanitation,
a woman or a young girl might accept the extra cover.

Stumbling half-blind in the shadow
of a male relative,
in the climate of civil war and marauding armed militias factors;
or under the paranoid eyes
of the Taliban's fanatical Islamic Minatory of Vice and Virtue,
you know your vulnerability.
When you are out pillaging for food or trying to buy bread
from the local, understocked *dhukan,*
you know you could be raped, stoned, beaten, or imprisoned.

So you welcome life
under this ancient and restrictive gown,
rather than show your face or foot
and risk attack or death.
And somewhere in all that fear and defensiveness,
you catch at the blanket of dogma and tradition
and began to think,
perhaps I am more pure, a more faithful daughter of Islam,
a treasure of Afghanistan,
because I must be so protected.

Who will tell the story
about Afghan women and children,
orphans and soldiers,
about hiding reality for decades,
about different blindnesses,

about removing veils that hide the truth
and demean people?

III

HOME IN KHULM/ TASHKURGHAN: SETTLING IN

September 11, 1976

Like so much of Afghanistan, where the armies of Alexander (329 BC), Genghis Khan (1222 AD) and empire-builders in between and after, crossed, cultivated, razed, conquered and ultimately fell, and whose caravan routes and caravansaries hosted travelers, Buddhist pilgrims, and traders on the Silk Route between China, Central Asia, Greece and the Near East and North Africa, the province of Samagan hides numerous tottering and sandblasted remnants of ancient cultures and history.

Besides the Buddhist stupas recalling thriving communities from the third and fourth centuries and Takht-I-Rustam, honoring the heroic Rustam from Firdausi's *Shahnama* and his legendary marriage with the beautiful daughter of the king of Samagan, this province of fertile valleys and rivers, high plateaus and gorges, broad rice and wheat fields, almond and apricot orchards and domed mud houses on the edge of the Turkestan plains claims the village of Khulm at the edge of the Tangi-I-Tashkurghan gorge.

Nearby, on the banks of the Tashkurgan River, lies the Cheshma Hayat, "Spring of Life."

It was allegedly the only place where "the oceans of heaven meet the oceans of earth," according to the legend of Khwaja Khizr, told in Sura

18:59-81, and echoing a story in "the Gilgamesh epic, the Alexander romance and the legend of Elijah and Rabbi Joshua in rabbinical lore." Legend claimed that the true spring had been discovered only once by the Khwaja Khirz.

Invisible, Khwaja Khirz goes about the world, and occasionally makes an appearance as a very old man with a long white beard and dressed in green robes. He can only be seen by people who are lost or needy. People traditionally came to this site in the hope of meeting the green man, who was reputed to make his home here.

I have yet to see Khwaja, nor his perfect resolution of heaven and earth's rivers, although I have already seen my share of long, raggedy white bearded men and old *babas* in green robes. So I suspect that means we are not lost, nor as needy as others.

September 12, 1973

. . . We are in the hotel in Khulm, behind us several fast days stretched and taunted with circumstances: To begin, we raised ourselves a full hour late on Monday and still managed to be at the right motor stand and in a cab full of four other Mazar-venturing travelers by 7:30. (It took Baba's catching us a *gaudi* behind us, and borrowing some of his tea and heading to Kalow Shadan) . . . . Our taxi fellow passengers were largely of a loud, "*batch-bauzi*" variety, the two in the front cuddling up together at any excuse, their third friend in the back demanding full space for his middle body and posing sullenly as an excellent villain for an Indian movie with his flabby face wedged in tufting black hair and dull sly eyes; and finally the man-and-a-half taking up two seats, the fat man who exports karakul hats to America who fluffs up in his corner and looks progressively sadder and then just hungry. There is a tea and grape stop one half hour on the road, a gas stop at the capital of Parwan Province, then no significant stop until we are to the edge of Samagan city, and our companions have lunch.

The bleak deserts have stolen us, like the banishment of some unforgiving edict. At the traffic center in Samagan a police director hurries us into a lorry who takes us to the Girl's Lycee and with the location of the PC teachers house in mind, takes us to the volunteers' door (at a scalping price of 20 afs) . . . .

A weasily son of the Director of Education for the province has set out the details for some of our afternoon. He asks the men questions about all the women present (myself, other PC teachers) eagerly denying any female a chance to explain her own presence.

It is to always be like this, a light switches on: Pale and passive and prideful we are always going to have to hold back, to not be greeted or acknowledged or observed, to stand mute as a stone pillar in a scrawny forest of male trees.

At night, we move into the sleeping bags that will serve as our potable bed until we are settled. I think of the security of some womb . . . .

About 10:00 a.m. the next morning, we find ourselves in the office of the Modir-e-Mareft, a large, sturdy man who speaks definitely though wordily of the problems facing teachers and the chronic shortage and excess of vacancies they have here. This stretched to over an hour, during which Fariad called and announced he would be in by 12, to handle the reminders and then take us to Tashkurghan, our assigned village. Aloft, grimy and stone-eyed, some ten or twelve men have passed in and out of the room, I have accepted one apple I did not want, and the local volunteer, Jerry, forgetting his briefcase, finally secures us an exit with the excuse that he will take me over to see the girls' school. Back in the compound, we plot lunch . . . . There is another long session with the Modir-e-Mareft, before we go back to the house to gather our things, and find ourselves bundled into a truck and being introduced to Tom's acting principal. This latter seems to be a timid, non-authoritative fellow, capable of rather mild bursts of giggles, whenever he finds himself at odds with, or not understanding, the conversation.

The landscape is beautiful for the next 57 kilometers, sweeping and alien with the mountains squeezing the road at dramatic turnoffs, hordes of camels like scenarios of ancient trains stiff in their old postures, and bright bubbly narrow snakes of streams coming in and out of the hills. Through a winding gorge and out into the plains, a long mirage of green before us, round roofed huts marking each compound (an exchange of figs for *piesas* in between) and we are in Tashkurghan-Khulm—this, our new home, for the next 22 months.

Again, what have we read of this small village in its idyllic river valley setting, with its crumbling old castle/fort on the hill, with its orchards and fields, and round, nippled, Uzbe-style roofs like fecund women's breasts? According to *Afghanistan for the Afghan,* Sirdar Ikbal Ali Shah's study, this region had housed much, earlier in the century, not many decades before. Names changed but the site remained, he explained:

> The province of Afghan Turkestan is, perhaps, one of the most important in the country and is, indeed, equal to Herat or Kandahar. It has a number of flourishing industrial centers, among them Tashkurgan and Mazar-i-Sharif, a place to which the Russians have always attached much importance. From Tashkurgan caravans go to India and Bokhara. It is surrounded by a wall three miles in circumference and has about twenty thousand houses, each of which is surrounded by a mud wall of its own. The whole town is thickly planted with fruit trees, and through the middle of the streets run irrigating channels. There is a crowded bazaar, in which cattle, sheep, mules, goats, and horses are sold, along with cotton goods and silk from India, and fruit and nuts from the countryside. The Hindus act as moneylenders and bankers and exact exorbitant interest . . . .
>
> The population is a mixture of divers races—Tajiks Uzbeks, Persian, and Turkomen who are only united in their faith, which is, however, divided in this district between the Sunni and the Shiah sect (15-17).

Years later, from yet another text, in the chapter "*Mazar-i-Sharif and North-Central Afghanistan*" edited by Ludwig W. Adamec. (Akademische Druck Kahay U. Verlaggsanstratt, Graz-Austria 1979) as part of the *Historical and Political Gazetteer of Afghanistan Vol. 4*, and drawing from a 1914 Gazetteer of Afghanistan, we learned further about our new home, its origin and its current state and location:

> Khulm (332) consists of 139 villages which make up a *woleswali*, and cover an area of 4,234 sq. kilometers, with a population of 25, 264 to 74, 996. It is bounded to the west by

> Charkint and Nahr-i-Sha, to the north by Kaldaer, to the east by Kala Zal, to the south by Hazarat-i-Sultan Samagan, and Dara-i-Suf, and to the northeast by the Soviet Union. Khulm is the ancient name of the town of Tashkurghan which was adopted in 1946 during the reign of King Mohmed Zahar. It is 65 kilometers from Arbah, 58 kilometers from Mazar and 563 kilometers from Kabul. The historical ruins (334) include: the Shar-i-Banu, 13 kilometers to the north, where precious stones, ancient coins, and sculptures were found. According to legend, Shar-i-Banu was the woman who built the fort and ruled over the area. In Chiterabad, there are ruins of another ancient fortress.

According to Pierre and Micheline Centlivres, whose comprehensive study of the town remains the best resource on Khulm, the population is 45,000. In 1972 there were only Tajiks and Uzbeks living here. The 30 families of Hindis who sold fabric and medicine left in 1929 and the Jews, who had been dyers and merchants, and lived in 10-12 houses, left before WWII. The bazaar has 1,155 shops and workshop and there are 24 *caravanserois.* Bazaar days are Monday and Thursday.

The Teem is the covered bazaar where the road from Kunduz traditionally ends, and which dates back several hundred years, largely unchanged. The avenue Rostekalan was widened and lost its enclosures. To the southwest is a tarred road built in 1971 to go from Aybak to Mazar, at which time a new bridge was built over the Khulm River.

Tashkurghan was the last of the traditional towns, according to C.J. Charpenter's ethnography in 1963-64. He described it as "a city of low mud brick houses and orchards." The bazaar consists of nine specialized bazaar streets and open bazaars. The economy was based on grain, fruit, almond, karakul, and handicrafts made in the bazaar (leather, iron implements, turned wooden utensils, copper ware, rope, embroidered caps.) By 1971-72 a few houses had running water and some electricity.

But before 1914 (569), perhaps around 1906 according to the *Gazette,* Tashkurghan was "the largest and richest town in the province and the principle trade center between Central Asia and Kabul."

> It was unwalled, but had the *arg* (citadel) and was a mass of inhabited orchards, with the picturesque bazaar of covered shops. The streets are 10-12 feet wide, but fairly straight, intersecting each other at right angles. The houses are mostly domed, though wood for rafters is fairly plentiful, there being many *chinars* and poplars, as well as fruit trees. There were no wells; rather water came from the river through covered conduits, which take water from above the town.
>
> The . . . . Bala Hissar, the old fort, is of large extent, and stretches down the west side of the hill on which it is built. It contains barracks for 600 infantry, 400 cavalry, and a battery of 6 guns and 200 men. It is of no value as a defense against a modern army.

Someone, a "*maitian,*" describes:

> an inner fort on the highest point of the hill, which is on the south side; it is in good repair. From there, a wall runs north, along the crest of the hill dividing the Bala Hissar into two parts and terminating at a big bastion with a tall watch tower—the Burj-i-op-Jalewi (field gun tower) and commanding the town very well . . . . (but there was only one gun in the Bala Hissar) . . . . Between the foot of the citadel and Chahil Situn the houses are . . . pretty thickly clustered together. In this part is the large bazaar . . . . The town's population is 40,000. There is a wide band of sandy desert between the cultivated area and the Oxus. There you can see the old remnants of Khulm. On the edge of town rises the Tak Aazar, to 6700 feet, 5500 feet above the plain. Battles here occurred in 1845-49 with Mir Wali. The trees that grow here are the apricot, walnut, and *chinar* (574).

Kabul, of course, also has its Bala Hissar, the ancient fortress crumbling in the south of the Old City. But the day we arrive in Tashkurgan . . . . the road divides into a kind of back arch here. You see the white walls of some old manor house jutting up in the otherwise flat valley, and along a dirt road, which becomes the town. We drive close to the girls' school and weave on intriguing paths to its back gardens, along a murmuring brook crossed by thin rail bridges. Greeted by ten men teachers and the *modir*, we come into the office and begin to work out a schedule. I nod silently and gradually begin to understand (Fariad communicates: I mostly shake my head).

A call is made and we are off to the hotel garden to meet the sub-governor, a thin, tanned man in skinny striped pants and a Florida short sleeve shirts, and to meet others who shake our hands and vanish in our memory, except the police commandant for the town, himself only come here recently. He explains in precise official English his desire to be of help to us, and his determination to first make us entirely safe. He proposes that we take a house in the rest of the bank compound, "*sage*," because some ten armed solider are there at all times(!). A relic of a German count, thin, major-hatted, with a broom mustache and a quick step, he comes out of a school of national officers who value his broadest responsibilities as well as his job. In strolls a pale, blond man with blue eyes and every appearances of a Russian, his role still a mystery to us, and someone's daughter. We have tea, are excused perfunctorily to secure a room in the hotel, then, hours later, see Fariad off and tuck ourselves into our room for the night.

In the hotel, a gathering weakness finally claims me and I have a fitful weeping spell and cling to Tom's limp shoulder like salvation. Afterwards I begin to think it may all be possible to survive, that is, but sleep is mostly all we both require. We've finished off a double serving of *pilau* and some tea, and learned that electricity is on in the hotel until 11:00, been ceremoniously welcomed by the *baba* (all over Afghanistan it seems we are to have such friends, old silent men full of ceremony), Yeat's Chinese stone observers.

Days of sitting, or of being directed, or of being lost will follow, but we will persevere, and perhaps one day do someone some good.

Our hotel room has a circular front, with windows all along the wall. The floor is cement, the walls thinly white-washed plaster and mud. Besides two *chapoti* beds, the rope specials, we are blessed with two gross matching chairs, their legs a half foot from the ground, arms that come to your shoulder when you settle into them, some stunted relic of an old Nurustani or Turkistani design, perhaps coming out here in its lowest common denominator, and two round tables painted green. We have salt and pepper curtains, of a heavy weave, and one clothes stand with four prongs, two lumpish rugs, and our views. One large bare textured mountain stands strongest off to the southeast, the brooding paternal stones for this valley, and we remember my old landlady in Charlottesville and how she had studied her green Virginia views, looked out to those bowls of plush landed hills cradling her existence, claiming they were her strength.

September 13, 1973

. . . When I arrive at the idyllic Lycee Dagtars (Lycee Mahasty) at 10:00, a congregation of teachers are present and one begins immediately to give me my schedule, which includes 24 hours a week, four hours three days and six hours on two days, and no lunch. Briefly, the *modir* introduces me to each class, I begin efficiently to gather their names, stretch out the hour in trying to be understood, their English sparse and my Farsi stunted by shyness or dullness, abysmal. I have a long way to go.

The sun violates me: this sun is a sterling mirror, all its reflections make us boil, aging the dew skin into wrinkles of too much weathering.

Later, we are trapped in the hotel garden for a little while taking tea and pondering, and soon find ourselves invited to dinner at the sub-governor's house. After another exchange with Mr. Efficiency, the commandant, who less than reassures us about a house, we move into the gentleman's house, and learn that the leering Russian sailor from yesterday is none other than the brother-in-law of the governor. We talk and are talked to, the sister-in-law and a nephew and some nieces from Kabul stare widely, but kindly. To us a classic shifty-eyed exploiter, epitomizing the worst of "westernization," the blond man is a manager of a wild international club in Kabul. He speaks frankly, non-consolingly. The commandant comes to join us, for he has just captured an escaped criminal (100 men surrounded him as he slept in a garden!) and we all are made to eat . . . .

September 15, 1973

. . . The *baba* took us at 8:00 to a small apartment in a compound near the school, where a German nurse had lived a year before. It consists of one tidy clean room, and one den-like area, perhaps the kitchen, and is upstairs. We saddened the family by not snatching it. Leaving the place, we are halted by the frisky commandant, who entrusts us to the keep of a *saroykeeper.* This second man's idea of a place for us is an open, corral-like cluster at the end of a short bazaar lane, with cave-like structures hallowed out of the wall. We (it seems) were to get two or three of these rooms and have a *tashknob* and an open field behind a broken wall.

After a cordial cup of tea with the offerer of this prime but inappropriate real estate, we head out of town. Like sardines in a Waz truck, we witness an old scab of a man pull the ears off a little boy he fancies is bothering him (after calling Tom "Mr. Kalonast" ((Mr. Squash)). My feet fall asleep and I imagine in some wild flight that I'm going to have them die on me, as in frost bite, so before the whole congregation of pilgrims to Mazar I stand up and proceed to pound my feet viciously, sitting down only after the blood comes back and a pimply faced short-eyed boy, who periodically climbs across the truck to simulate the keeping of order, has stared a hole through me.

Mazar is big and flat and hot. We see the mosque and its whiter pigeons and its spiritual tiles and set off like lost buccaneers ejected by a sea wave, to narrow down the location of our compatriots . . . .

At 7:00 this morning, Tom and I go with them to Tashkurghan, arriving just in time for a pep lecture from our commandant, and as Tom scurries to school, I sink into reading. The closeness, the dimensions of the hotel room, give me an excuse to not really laugh or think or cry, to just be like one of those bleak scenarios stretching sporadically in the spaces of Afghanistan, until the time for my first class . . . .

The day's classes have snaggles. I meet with T. in the afternoon and we are shown one house which is fully a possibility, and hear of another one (with trees!) by my *modir-sibe* and the commandant. We were also visited by the sub-governor's nephew who out of some fame or sort of loneliness keeps wiggling in on our conversations, telling something we do not know. We steal a brief stroll out into the cool night to contemplate the lopsided hazy moon and a smattering of stars, until a wayward soldier in whose domain our bodies apparently reside, comes and stands, staring suspiciously across at us, and we realize the thin bounds of our freedom.

September 20, 1973

Last night we hosted the French couple, photographers Roland and Sabrina Michaud, and heard more of Pierre Centlivres, anthropologist of a seven-year tenure here, a world-renowned expert on Afghan antiquity, author of a book on Khulm. They spellbind us with specifics of the place, the old ruins, the Uzbek villages and tribes to the north, the valley and sites above the mountains, the places off the road. They speak glowingly of the old lame Esmaria who is the medicine man of the area, and one of the best in the country, cite him specifically as a unique raconteur, gifted and full of secrets and stories. They bewail the inflated prices of everything now, the gaming over *cawk* (pigeons) on Thursday market days, and how quickly modernity will overtake all cultures, once someone decides the area is worth "developing."

The house we have found has its own yard, with its own room, a whisper of a past dream, one fertile garden flower patch, and the prospect of cold and wind. But it could be.

Another bout of dysentery and its close cousin swamps me, and I am sick, stuck in the hotel. Finally we orally agree to a contract with a landlord, knowing full well we are hearing false promises as to when the house will actually be ready . . . . Visitors, on route to Mazar, stop by with welcome fresh baked goods . . . .

October 1, 1973

Like a long overdue symbol, Ramadan, the Moslem month for fasting, began yesterday after a night of cold dark, and a windstorm, dust-teethed and piercing, that kept out light and heat for some 18 hours. It was the end of a long week . . . .

The move comes in the afternoon. We tote our backpacks, bags and books, plan to have *toshaks* make for the living room/only room, and for the tiny space with a door where we will sleep on the floor. We must order *burrio*, straw mats, for the floors and have been told to have a canopy of fabric measured and stretched tightly over our heads to keep spiders and scorpions from crawling out of the straw and mud ceiling and falling on us below . . . .

In the house, sitting by lantern in the one securely fastened room, the poor windows on the other end rattling like acoustics for some nightmare, we sup briefly on boiled potatoes and eggs.

Then our landlord comes. He occupies, protrudes, settles in beside us, but we think him kind, [to change, to change].

He asks of Tom, "How much did you pay for her in America?" And so, at this point, the ailments of his own country staring down at us, his thin, clean features in little boy laundered blue *tanban,* he shouts out his life like a statement for innocent age (he left school to run the shop after sixth grade, as is the way here.) Morning into night, he leaves, and we finish the cold rudiments, board up the windows and sleep.

Morning is icy, but by 7:30 we have tea brought by the large-eyed neighbor boy, frail and silent, and I set out to buy some household items in Mazar . . . There are to be complications . . . .

Back to the insecurities of Khulm, where we enjoy an evening of pancake dinner; then I must sit it out like a dull statue as my husband is "visited" and I am left to sit silent.

October 6, 1973

A week now we've sat here, floor-less, our windows flapping, cut off from two of none-too-spacious three rooms by the owner's warped concept of propriety, but that's mostly all bitter grapes. I taught another week, find my words as much in Dari as in English in order to be understood, and am always wary as to whether or not anyone has learned. My students are frisky and curious; I represent so much more to them than a teacher of a language which is removed from their practical and expected lives . . . .

Sitting in the teachers' room, I am surrounded by: elements of maleness. The young he-men grin, in them, a rapid garble sets off the first looks. They further murmur of what can only move, mount: they lean expectantly as if to swallow each other's expressions. Recalling, rattling our papers, we vie to communicate. Today someone thrusts at me a bottle of Vaseline-hair pomade from Kandahar with labels in English. They play with this and that, and the small, aged face of the gentle first grade teacher, Esfandyar, who is lame, then bows and scowls at me, asking politely but persistently for the English meaning of some abstruse words: "litigation," "manuscript," "sponge."

(Behind us daily still, we are camping out with faulty equipment on the sand dust floors, moving our bed sack back and forth like some kind of corpse. Yet all is forgotten when the lights go out and we have only to sleep, wrapped in our sacks). Morning comes too early for our taste, the first rustle, scavenger size birds with the plumage of jaybirds and the voices of crows which settle on the roof and walls, punishing us. The first smell is the dust, chilly as lame dew.

Three of them, officials and soldiers, full of themselves like sails in a storm, came into my classroom yesterday. This class is the worst group, class eight . . . given to chattering over my voice, to teasing me in a language just beyond my full comprehension, to eying every morsel of me for critique. I stood for thirty minutes while they preceded to have the students tear out and scratch out pages of their books. (You think it must be materials pertaining to the government, you think of Nazi Germany or some Stalinist purge of the Fifties, of the Red Guards, of the indispensability, expendable nature of propaganda). The bell jangles, they again pass out and I want to tramp to the modir's room and gloat at him, and all his inarticulate rudeness in my rush of English articulateness, but I only pass to another class,. It is not the time to tell them that I hate their maskings at education, their pretentious games, that I didn't come here with two years of my life to rally with them as at a football game, that I have one of the best educations of anyone in my country, that I have written books and am qualified to teach at university, that I can do so much more than babysit for some hopelessly staffed and spoiled crew of students in the first form of life . . .

But it passes. I can not quite place the source of my anger.

I read into those school guard's eyes, the old *baba's*, little elves of contention, twinkle blue, white-haired, and red-checked.

And then there is the landlord, present now, who feels compelled to visit us for all our free hours every night, a lean hungry-eyed fellow with a matching child-son (the only survivor of four) who watches us cook and looks lonely, motherless the whole lot of them. We're to give them our ear, our hours. One of his sisters is in my class, another went crazy a year ago and now lies seeing spirits. They are all old souls: They come, these men, and move their worry beads about before us.

October 6, 1973

[Frustration with no progress in getting the house we are to rent ready, with the lack of privacy, and language skills appearing to "rot" rather than improve, plus an active dislike for the coarse and intrusive landlord's family, and the lack of a cook despite the pushy modir's insistence on our taking one of his friends . . . .]

With so many complaints, now, why can we be staying on . . . . Perhaps it is for those watchmen who call quarterly from the marketplace in the sterile nights when the stars stare blankly in their frozen seas, a mirror too big for us, and the voices like lonely thoughts float up and over the village asleep, flickering like lantern light, and an ass or a camel bellows with the sneeze of terror in his standing sleep, recanting an older dirge, and in our bare feet we squat close to the house to tend ourselves, all from this waking in the middle of the night and imagining the boarded up shops of the bazaar, their inanimate properties impersonally cloistered, and each man in his own home.

Or perhaps, it is for the one small wink, or intense wrinkle in one student's head in one hour in one day on one lesson, when something you say seems to have reached her and she excitedly tries to grasp your English, and you know most likely some decadent old man with half her brains will buy her for his wife, in a few years and she'll be filled up with children and never allowed out into the world except for petty things, marketing or kibitzing, and she'll never read a book nor have reason to want to, and the years you've taught her will soon be folded away like some little girl's dress into her box of the past—but maybe you forget all in that moment, and she is as strong as a tree in her carriage and you think her mind's future hopeful.

Maybe it is for the motherless thin child Iotila who comes to watch us cook in our kitchen hut or sell eggs or make potato stew, and the way he draws himself up, all bones, and thwarts his eyes and declares some commonplace, but precocious thinking in someone of his age; we see him then and wonder, and stop here.

Maybe all that sustains us is the night and the regularity with which it relieves us, letting us sleep, however simply, wrapped warmly in sleeping bag cocoons, and the prospect that no matter what tests us in daylight, in the dark we are again our own souls. (In the eaves of our memories, twenty years hence, will we think we built a rare home for ourselves in this, our adopted society, or will it all look like youth-struck wonders, distant and unabsorbed?)

October 13, 1973

We waited the whole week to record it, everyday bracing ourselves against the new insults, the grating promises that soon now, "we" will begin work, but it never came and finally it became clear we must give the landlord seven months rent before he would even start the work. Lies, lies, lies, and sly dealings until each night we'd go to bed sick with the thought of the eminent tomorrow, a clean slate for more teasing aggressions. School also has its deferred . . . promises and contending sessions, equally initiated by both teachers and . . . sadly indifferent students

One day Iotallah, the father, teased us about having children, but the worst of many gesticulating affronts came when his cackling sisters-mothers stuck in their scarf-protected faces this morning to question me in the same vein, but womanly scatologically, insulting my husband and our private life. And, of course, the long awaited day when the cementing was to begin, came like all the others, and left, leaving us limp, and without the work begun.

One day I was *maman* (guest) for a family of bread-makers and though they were all fasting, I was put upon to sample from some 15 pieces of freshly-ovened fare, and the family's son, who is as graceful as a dancer, skims the *toshak,* on visits to us four nights running, bringing us once a full course dinner and another time nan and almonds. And what are we to say to them all?

Yesterday we went to Mazar . . . . and then because it was almost dusk and no one would drive to Tashkurghan, we paid dangerously highly for private seats in a lightless taxi which swept across the dessert recklessly leaving us fatal tallies in the backseat, wondering if it could only make it a little further, and not break down here, in the middle of all the murderous lone leanness. It did make it, and all our prices were paid . . . .

. . . Today we had moved everything to the *balloi,* thinking the work was to begin, for had we not been assured of as much, but for tonight will move down again, another futile motion . . . . A gift of broad lace and stones . . . .

We remember other houses we had viewed, barns piled high with straw and dry manure—"Oh, this will be cleaned for you"—, places cringing in the middle of soldier's lots or camel corrals, or closet-size enclosures in a fringe village. Yet we can't even get this single place converted to a home. Everyone has an opinion, I find, the *modir* asininely framing thoughts himself, although he means well. Puckering a little, a prayer might lighten the nerves before this nursing hate does, but still we must balk at it, because we don't want to be sick—we came here to learn friendship and are only learning impatience . . .

But good news. Pomegranates are here. These, a great burst of tart red seeds, the ceremony of eating it unrushable, as one slowly strips away the skin, then sucks the seeds, a few at a time, like so many delicate rain drops, fresh flavors, ruby surprises.

October 14, 1973

On the way to school I see a snake charmer performing in the bazaar—pajama baggy pants, holding a drum cup and whittling a flute. A sleek, writhing body oozes along the sandy ground and raises its head; while the men loiter by on an ordinary morning and the school boys crouch and giggle or stare, as I pass by.

And all day the men carry cement and stone and sand in a small sling carrier from the alley to our yard, slowly, slowly, in the way of 4,000 years.

Our compound is behind Nagar Street, carpenters and metal workers' row, and until late at dusk, beginning again in dawn, there is the metallic beat of men roasting and pounding malleable ores, hot tin and damaged eyes in the scowling glint of blaring fire-shots. It is a war in waves of pounding, a dry sea.

October 16, 1973

They did, after the surface of the moon, some manner of cementing yesterday, and continue at it today, and in the unexpected release of a holiday (someone's Independence) we watch the workers and make cinnamon rolls (after a labyrinthine search through the market place for this tree bark spice, taken like gold out of a round stoic man's hemp bag, and passed to me for a high price), and finish off yesterday's cake, and for supper dine on potatoes. In the afternoon I go to Armoe Mohammed's house to sew the seams on our white sheets, and be stared at quietly by his womanly household, a mother and a daughter who has the uncannily northern features and paleness of some Turkomen blood, born princesses in their soft faces, I think, and a quiet younger daughter who speaks in a whisper, drawing in her breath and gesturing the way her father does, and a busy little sixth grader who is soon to be married, the gist of the conversation seems to tell me.

And we sit in the "kitchen" reading and working and listening to the radio until the dark sky has given rise to the cloudy moon, then move upstairs to the dust bins of our "*balloi.*"

October 21, 1973

(We hire the frail and elderly Armoe M'med, the *modir's* friend, to be our cook).

The much belated workmen finally have done enough work so that we can move our entire household within the three rooms. We did so two nights ago, and curtains and rugs and clothes were disposed of. There was a period when we despaired of our cook along with all the other fools, the mudmakers and stone takers, because it was seemingly impossible to communicate with him and he seemed always to be bossing us around. How flat. But he is an honest man before all the others. So it goes.

One day we open our bank account in Mazar, a staid gesture. The next day we inherit two delicious watermelons from our cook who had located them in Mazar, and along with eggs and lemons to boot, had brought to us to patch up "*jung mekonem.*" So no one will apparently get the carpenter to fix the ceiling, and the landlord's workmen will not fix the gaping hole in the *aushpas khona (*kitchen*)* and the whole Iotallah family is a pack of filthy despicable fools, but maybe we can barricade ourselves in here well enough so we don't have to have much to do with them.

But then the final sacrilege: they cut down our one little "beetree" in the yard to sell the wood, and no one even asks us if we want the only bouquet of green in our yard thus slaughtered.

I could go over all their boorishness, but where would it take us—the way the landlord has his dinner parties in our yard, the way his father comes and begins eating our melon, the way his sisters and little relatives squat and dribble all over our yard like some foul creatures out of a stagnant age.

Fresh nights though, and a million stars, and heavenward looking you forget there is any such land at your feet.

And then there is the way our northern director happened in one night and had some dinner and breakfast and filled us with eerie tales of a counter-coup in Kabul, and complicity with Pakistan and the royal patriots ending up being hanged or put in prison, about a fire in the Springar factory and random slurs against the royalist family, and so on, on travel and house arrests and investigation procedures, and a German volunteer recently ousted from the country for political fervor. (He handed out brochures in Kabul.)

I have three girls thrown out of the seventh class by the principal today and we actually have a full lesson, but whether or not the peace will keep up is frighteningly unlikely.

October 23, 1973

I am gathering a collection of witticisms from an in-class writing assignment: "The children's ears are yellow and pretty." "Their hands are clean and pretty." "This girl has many hairs." "Wali has no hair." "The girl's nose is very tall." "This picture is many pretty." "The nose is flat." "The head is big."

The new mood apparent in the *modir's* joke: "Hello, how are you?" "I'm foolish. How are you?" Then he is jesting with the plain newlywed, who is the clerk of the school, about her wedding and her not bringing me any *pilau*. "Now she must bring some for both of us."

October 29, 1973

We come to Kabul, 12 hours long on the bus, for meetings, and enter mythology—a cross wind of rumors about the end of Peace Corps here, strange plans for evacuations (it is only half in jest that they tell us PCVs leave just before the Marines holding down the Embassy), stronger notions and the consideration by which we could and should stay . . . .

It is a good trip but a lengthy one, as the bus lumbers through touches of autumn, in the valleys leaves turned a deep yellow, the hillside grass browner, milder, and a chilliness sweeping down on everything . . . . Upon arrival in Kabul we visit the police station because the driver claims we owe him more money (and he is right, it turns out later, though the police dismiss us all, with an indifferent shrug.), an awkward form of our asserting ourselves, it seems, disagreeing over less than a dollar . . . . All medical workers, TB-ers, etc. of foreign aid projects are now recalled to Kabul by the new regime, where they can only wait, inactive, until the government invites them to do other work, or the U.S. Government decides to bring them home . . . . Some see it as the forecast for us all.

November 1, 1973

It was back to school yesterday to a clamorous appeal for order and a few constituent teaching skills, the students genuinely glad to see me again, it seems. I present the Asia Foundation gifts and watch, bemused, as the *modir* and his bandy-boyed teachers stretch and tap them, then turn each one by one, upside down and backwards, suggesting Christmas children scrutinizing the presents of some eccentric now dead (but to their young minds a fact unfathomable) aunt. Within minutes, the *modir* has taken out a sheet of paper and is writing something down, telling me as he does so that he is requesting Farsi books and a typewriter.

This seems a certain kind of Afghan gratitude (sardonically), not to be confused with "give me-give-me." In fact, he has a few other slighting comments, but the success of my having procured these English science and math textbooks for the school is clearly questioned. Rather, by giving them to the school I seem to have violated some code which is kept sternly in place to prevent the "officials" from loosing face. A gift, then, can be an insult?

Later, much later that day it comes to me. In the politically fragile atmosphere of the country, the special surveillance of foreigners, these poorly paid teachers and *modir* and staff, are also being caution, lest they be accused of treason in some fabricated form, perhaps.

The chill of a panting winter begins here now. Our first night back a dust storm pelted mud, the air frigid. Mornings and evening are as hollow as an ancient dead tree.

We arrange for the purchase of winter wood, through a hunchbacked man who parleys with stones and dry timber, juggling the weights to count out each *seir,* one *seir* perhaps the equivalent of a branch of a small tree. We endure the afternoon squatting of Tom's student who stays, ordering *bookeries* for two room and having our future foretold by the pudgy and very attentive tenth grader: "If the *malim* would have a baby she'd be happy, "meaning I would be less prone in his eyes to argue with him about the audaciously high price. And I smolder . . . .

November 4, 1973

> *[There's been no mail in two months from my mother, in five weeks from the Connells. We have a continued discontent with the landlord, Iotallah, who is gossiping to the cook and to my modir. It is clearly a question of our Western sense of borders, of space and privacy, that makes us impatient with and also desirous of the company which townspeople feel obliged to give us.]*

Yesterday the *bookerie* man came and put in two, using mud to solder the joints—but in the evening when we go to light the living room's stubby one, we are engulfed in smoke, and only after Tom tried doggedly for an hour or more to get the pipes to vent, did we realize the *bookerie* outlet on the roof was non-existent: someone had simply muddied it over. Meanwhile we discover the intricacies of purchasing lime for our *hakendos-kenerab* (outhouse), and begin to put up the winter plastic on each of our windows to keep out the cold.

Two of my eleventh grade students, absent more than they've been present since they came to Khulm, are to return to Kabul. A favorite shy girl in the 10th class, an excellent student, left yesterday for Kunduz. So the ranks thin.

November 7, 1973

Winter came this morning, gray as a duck's down, with the mountains cloaked in clouds of cold mist, and a sunless sky all morning and afternoon. A wind scurries about the windows and tosses sand around the yard, and our *bookerie,* going for three warm night now, glows homey for me in the morning. The local *nan* boys and *kosmak* (boiled, sour cream, a specialty of Khulm) vendors stand in long lines holding their dishes like scales, the boys covered in stocking caps and too large old jackets, nothing visible of their bodies, and the *dhukandars* huddle behind burlap hangings trying to have business as usual and still avoid the bursting chill of the newly-come winter winds racing against light . . .

At school the girls have sweaters now. My classes are in rooms with windows and panes and when the door is closed we have the prospects of a warm hour, but Tom tells me that at his school, his large barn-like rooms in particular are like getting invitations to be windblown, and as he paces the class to keep warm himself, the boys in their thin *tanbons* and old summer jackets turn red and rusty. We realize the winter will be a long one. Old men, the school guards, carrier pigeon boys, vendors and sitters, squat chilled along the mud road I take from school. More pairs of huddled shoulders, obedient to the cynical wind, I have never seen.

. . . We are wrestling with a brand of Afghan absentmindedness.(Or is it the lack of literacy so they can not write down a list, or old age, or our own imprecise version of Dari, that keeps them from understanding or remembering something we said?) . . .

Our cook Armoe M'med was carefully instructed last night as to what he should buy as he sets off today for Mazar . . . Seemingly having understood he wandered out our gate last night . . . his gruff old voice reciting, "*arte de safed, dae powie, sub—*" (flour, salt,) a long silence, emerging gasp, his rheumatic old feet bending back: "Malim-sibe, malim-sibe, chan powie seib?' (How many pounds of apples?)

Then, entrusted with picking up a saw to be reputedly finished by Armoe's carpenter friend today, Tom set off. He inquired at several shops about his business and was getting no where, when a man came running up, listened to his tale, and then offered to help him find the person, this individual who was a friend of Armoe M'med and to whom Amore had given ten *afghanis* in down payment on an ax yesterday. After visiting about five or six *dhukandar* shops, the man turned suddenly to Tom, a light dawning, and exclaimed, "Oh, Armoe's my friend and I'm the one who got 10 *afghanis* yesterday to make the ax, but I haven't finished it yet, and was just now going home."

The darkness of frozen winter mornings round off the hours of our day now. At six, it is still starlight; by four it is as dim as down again.

. . . My students never leave off observing me. Yesterday it was a new sore on one finger; today a new barrette in my hair. With this much surveillance, how can I ever be self-conscious again?

November 10, 1973

[Walks and talks with guests, other PCVs from Samagan and Mazar . . . .]

We walk all over the town and go up on the domed marketplace where all the merchants were spreading new layers against the winter, and in a sharp angular wind climb up the hill of the old fort and look out on the valley, green and mud-dabbered, the mud brown round houses like so many beehives, the green stopping abruptly at the town's edges where the salty white desolation of the desert raises up again.

Mr. Kissinger, our colleague from Samagan, jokes crudely about Mullah Nasruddin stories: A man who had headaches, finally had himself castrated. Afterward he bought new underwear, and discovered—as the shopkeeper explained—the previous underwear was too small, had always been too small, and so had caused the headaches. Now, is that a parable?

. . . Looking out to the mountains we see fine salt snow in some of the crevices, and a full moon hugs the sky throughout dusk . . . .

Little school girls in their widow weeds salute me, berry brown liquid eyes and a chilly palm. Today is the second for giving lessons this week to the teachers, and to the others, of whom half of yesterday's fourteen appeared to discuss occupations, and the naming of government. We rehearse the subjects, and then I flee . . .

Armoe M'med asks for another month's advance in salary and in the morning his wife and daughter (or granddaughter) come limply to ask for medicine for a fever and a cold. I give generously of cough syrup and in the evening send on an orange, but being neither doctor nor a pharmacy, I can recognize the half absurdity of such small actions.

In the evening Armoe tells us of his three years working in a hotel in Sheberghan. He tells us the province is large. Remembering his workplace, he remarks how the foreigners—Italians, French, Russians—would each sleep in a separate room, and the way they would unroll a featherbed on the chapa (bed) every night, and just sleep through the death of winter. He spoke of 50,000 *afghanis*—surely not his salary for that time—but our language didn't let us know for sure . . . . Did he really once earn $200 a month, like a provincial governor?

November 11-12, 1973

. . . In the cold nights the soldiers hoot at each other from the roofs of the closed bazaar, keeping each other awake. Their echoes buckle you, lonely and alien, like no voice of man but of some caught desert animal or a tamed mountain lion: our desert coyotes.

We are strange, strained twentieth century misfits stumbling, planted in this 12th century sand heap, among sad stories. Nights like this one we feel every mile of the 8,000 that lay between us and the crazy old place we out of habit and breeding called our home.

Crazy we must be—we've lost our perspective so much we argue with our poor tubercular cook about using too much *roghan* (oil), who responds only with stubbornness against senility—And will we like every foreigner since time began, regress to curses against a whole race and their habits?. Is this being a model, someone peaceful? Is this how we are ambassadors, open to learn, or arrogant and impatient at losing our creature comforts and our control?

November 14, 1973

. . . Collections of the week. Looking up from the wall behind my school (river beside me crossed by four middle bridges) the old town fort a rumbling of collapsed mud walls, majestic in the league of homely ruins, and behind it the gorge, the winding split between the mountains where the road enters our valley. Our nights have been clear and jeweled, or overpoweringly light with the first etches of a full moon, like a magic potion to be ingested, and inside our chilly house we hug the *bookerie*, and sleep on our featherbeds . . . . The *modir*'s uncle (*caw-caw*) died and the *modir* was absent for three days. (In his house the people come and pause, offering the attendant mullah the symbols for a prayer). The teachers let down their hair (I am their "sister") without the *modir's* rather short-sighted barking. One day a team of doctors come and inoculate all of the student body against tuberculosis. The shy and frightened cling together, try hard to back away, and I recall the polio clinics of the summer of 1954 and 1955, when we were likewise rounded up and given injections with little ceremony . . . .

For three nights our never lengthy electricity comes on and then flickers out, so we strain our eyes by candlelight-kerosene lantern as the voltage weakens to nothing, then comes on again, only to go out. One evening a scintillating (though in its facts shocking) "Letter from America" session with Alistair Cooke, who spoke of Nixon and the oil shortage, and an indignation and fear on the part of the population . . . in the wake of a long, cold winter. How can Nixon stay there—all of his gang had been proven crooks? How can he still stand? . . . .

I am given a verbal litany of Afghan cures for my laryngitis, after badly negotiating a week of voicelessness—Drink no tea, drink fresh milk, eat nothing sweet, have no walnuts (almonds are cool but walnuts are warm, and since I have a "warm body" I must take in my opposite in times of illness, as with the medieval humors tale). A final word comes from the modern Pushtoon from Jalalabad who has me set up to secure penicillin lozenges from a local pharmacy. I wait out the lingering muteness.

November 20, 1973

. . . In our mud lane the hunchback each morning pops barrels and barrels of popcorn, puts it in plastic bags and lets little boys scatter and sell it for a few *afghanis*. And the town crier, a man with a deep, resounding voice, paid by whomever desires his means of publicity, walks up and down the lanes, in between shops and tradesmen, announcing what is lost or found or desired. For each man there is a price to the labors, each part of the body a commodity; for this man it is his voice.

. . . . Children rise here with the first sun and go out on their houses to fly thin paper kites. All morning the frail birds tumble and soar in the sky above us and the little boys pull them in to let them out again.

(How much we value our short-wave radio. One is ready to spell out a peon to BBC and Radio Deutscheville for the talks, news, and music wafted from a world remote from the mud lanes of tumble-down Khulm/Tashkurghan.)

November 22, 1973

(We join a Thanksgiving celebration with other volunteers in Mazar, to take in lots of food and mail which we had not been getting for a while).

There are 20 of us, for guests, plus the German volunteers and their adopted Indian baby, one rescued *jewie* puppy who resembles a chubby armadillo and a rat-shy kitten who defies doors. We all sink into a lazy comma of eating, and a little bit of thought—as if guests of some old grandmother in a Nebraska woods, the spell broken only when we glance out the window and see the hungry eyes of the Afghan neighbor children staring from a perch on the compound wall . . . .

The road between here and Mazar lies in its bleakest posture now, gray and horizonless, clusters of brown sheep clumping like scorched grass among the hard soil or bristly tumbleweed, a cold wind coming up from its secret cracks, as our clattering truck putters by, leaving us like strangers at the side of the road.

November 24-26

(Sickness, cook problems, Tom with a barking cough, too. As always discussion of our letters from home.

Odd to discover Mrs. Thaddeus had referred me for a position at SUNY-Buffalo)

November 29, 1973

I'm sick, feverish, the works, and over 24 hours take: five bottles of Fanta, two vitamin pills, two Diodiquin, four tetracycline, eighteen tabs of paregoric, six Lomitils, ten aspirins, the regular birth control pills, and as much (boiled) water as it takes to wash them all down. Alas, I am the daughter of a healthy stocked farm daughter who raised us without ever using medicine, except a bit of vapor rub when we had a cold or a baby aspirin if we ran a rare fever. And to think I am putting all this in my system now, routinely.

I dribble notes for future fantasizing (my authority here a Charles Heyward commentary on World Folksongs): Sentiments of Afghan songs are the highly praised honor (*nangi pakhtana*), revenge against evil and injustice (*badal*), and hospitality (*mailmastae*). The instruments (in person we've encountered only three so far, but perhaps we haven't frequented the right places), and the solo and ensemble: strings are: *sarinda (*three-sting fiddle, short neck, without frets), *rabab* (six-string lute), *ritchak* (two-stringed fiddle, played with a bow and often made of kerosene cans now). Vocal accompaniments include: *zourna* (oboe); percussion—*sir-i-baghali* (large circular drum with long cylinder resonator), *dhoi* (two headed drum) and *davow* (cymbals).

December 2, 1973

I feel that I've just returned from taking pictures of a whole crew of Afghan beggars. No, I am being flippant, for they are the family of our old, sad, ne'er-do-well cook who decided to have five pictures of his clan snapped—of the wife and two daughters, the latest nephew and orphan niece—all in their best dress. Whatever will it take to get the pictures back to them, for they must be first shipped to the States for development, then shipped back, and distributed?

Time, again here, is not measured by our breathless western exactitude.

In fact, our confidence and skills sharpened by the request of dear old Armoe M'med, on Friday afternoon we wander around the town and take some pictures, feeling finally "at home" enough to not be taken for preying tourists, perhaps . . .

Scenes from the first roll of pictures include:

> The Cook in his natural clothes—rubbers, apron, and turban;
>
> Tom carrying in wood for the *bookerie;*
>
> Our Home, our plastic windowed house, our timber white-washed pillars;
>
> The Mountain Pass, the Tangi, the mountain pass, the last mountains to the north, the road winding between them, the artery river, father of the green valley;
>
> An Old Man with his dull-winged *minah* bird in a cage;

The Craft Shop at the edge of the bazaar, tended by two boys this day—wall hangings, rugs, metal cups, jewelry of long ago found stones;

The Old Man at the Pottery Shop, a whole wing of a shady corner where men sit eating beside stony pots in sizes from simple bowl to trough, lined up against the wall and used for storing and cooling water and grain, and a few blue-glazed pots, and one so large it must be the earth's own womb (or is that tomb?);

A Local Butcher, on his haunches as he sharpened his knives for us first, hanging on the right of him the hind legs of lamb or goat, on the left the leg of cow which really might be fillet of camel masquerading as cow, beside him a pile of freshly cut skins set out to dry, lamb and goat with a cow skin or two at the bottom which will be used for hats, coats, boots, etc, the single fluffy brown one lying in a lump, and in the foreground an actual, freshly skinned camel, still with the blood on the underside, the worn patches where the fur was worn off, since when camels rest they always lie down, tucking their legs under, so they become mangy looking like worn bluejeans or old spare inner-tubes needing patches;

A Carpenter Shop with a young boy at work on the lathe, making part of an ornamental crib which Khulm is famous for, whereby the craftsmen use colored wood dowels, between an inch and two inches thick, for all kinds of things (coat racks, sides of cribs and dressers, legs for small stools, handles for hammers), and like everything the lathe is hand-powered. (The wood box which he has in his his right hand has a string attached to the lathe and he pulls it back and forth, turning the lathe quite rapidly, and in his left hand he has a chisel which he guides with his bare feet to cut the wood.) The paint, some visible on the left portion of the wood, is made separately. They burn colored clay until its soft and sticky, then form in into little sticks, like pieces of chalk, then apply it on the wood by turning the lathe and pressing the sticks against it. The process is actually quite delicate and the result is quite attractive.

Scenes to catch with the next roll of film:

A Kebob vendor, knees crossed behind his smoky grill, turning the skewers of meat and fat, waving the palm fan musically;

A Nan Seller with his basket on his head;

The Brightly Colored Cloth and Fruit *dhukans*;

Some Camels at rest in the camel lot;

Some of My *Chadried* Students;

The Old Water Wheel Granary;

The *Choi-xona* over the River at the entrance to the bazaar; the Hotel and Post Office;

One of Our Schools;

Us in the Republican Garden

December 3-4, 1973

. . . . There are so many things I like irrevocably about this place, this life. Goodness only knows there's always time to stop and recollect them, but usually you're not feeling well enough (could I have worms in my stomach to make it hurt so much—rejecting most any food through the grunting bowels minutes after consumption—vile subject but—comically—a much discussed one . . .)

The school girls who, midgets before you, yet only a few years from being "*chadris*-ed," chatter their morning "Salaam aleichems" as you pass by; students from the eleventh class who seek you out in the morning and daily without fail inquire after your health and your appetite ("Are you going home to have your tea?"); the *komak* (yogurt) salesmen at their morning pep talk, twenty or more boys tilting their scales of baked, scalded *kisem* and looking lost as some giant of a man among them divvies out the proper share; the train of camels lopping in slow motion up the dirt bazaar, a traffic jam at the corner before they pass,; the constant incongruence of talking with a ghost (the women in *chadris* who never show their faces).

Throughout, however, we encounter complaints, complain ourselves. There are always discussions of the *modir* at the boy's school and his attitude toward Tom. "I want money, money, money. Give us money." Then, there is the landlord who keeps coming to our house and just sitting there, often during dinner or our evenings when we really are tired and want no company. Further, he's removed a lock we'd put on the gate between his yard and "ours" as he clearly has no understanding of why we as renters have the right to privacy. There is a visit by my own (first) *modir* who comes and drinks tea and eats our cake and wants to know if we eat Afghan food and if we have science and math books to share. And, oddly, there are some rare village vendors who will not let us take their pictures.

Yesterday the legendary Afghan temper gave me an exhibition. If I were to be caddy, I would say the rather noisy personage of my *modir* graduated to rathood.

Tajenisa has the reputation of being one of the school's 'bad girls.' She is sharp as a tack, far from unintelligent, but she is blunt, often crude and disrespectful. She is in the current tenth class, although she should probably be in the twelfth. In any case, she had gone out of the room; it is her usual style to do so usually four times an hour. She dabbled in the hall with some other students within the modir's range and was run back into my classroom in a heat. For perhaps four minutes we all stood there transfigured, shocked and with that uneasy secret humor, while he screamed at her. She answered back, the screams grew louder, a sorry parley, ending when he finally took up another student's pen box and bolted it to the floor, turned to some call from the hall, and disappeared. Tajenisa, the student, just sat there, and the entire class held its breath. For a few moments I almost respected her spirit of dissent, yet it is so crude. She will yet be broken, everything around claims.

Mysteriously, I am handed the transcript for someone's semester in University of Arizona, delivered to me by a colleague. How did it get there? Did someone from Khulm make it to a university in the States?

Another story: Tom is out in the byways and bazaar more than I. He was standing in the street talking with a shopkeeper acquaintance yesterday, when a young man came running up to him, raced through the greetings, and began to tell him how good it was to see him. Tom was mystified, certain he had never seen this man before. It turns out he mistook Tom for the Mr. Tom who had once taught him in Kunduz, and having heard there was a "Mr. Tom," a teacher here, and that he was an American . . . . Afghan irrationality insists they be one and the same quantity, at least that time.

Boarding People on the Craters of the Moon (1995)

Hesar Shahee Camp,
100,000 people on a hot, treeless, waterless plain,
seeking refuge from
warring *mujahadeen* commanders in and around Kabul.

A scattering off the the pock-marked old Jalalabad road,
rows of tents stretch side by side for acres:
beige, sun-colored, a rare blue UNDP structures
anchored in ground bare even of weeds;
the ropes pulled taut, tarp over canvas,
a few hasty knee-high stone walls separating "the blocks."
The slightest breeze sets the ropes humming,
the canvas billowing,
like downed kites struggling to rise.

But there are few breezes,

People wear everything they carried,
women covered in layered dresses and pants,
long, flowered scarves cradling their heads and faces
fall behind them past their waist.
The children, heads wrapped in woolens,
girls in long dresses with loose cotton pants underneath,
boys in loose pants,
all topped with faded hand-me-down sweaters or jackets.

IDPs*, on the plain and war-sapped roads
above the orchard city of Jalalabad,
masses of people who have nowhere to go,
past, future decimated, everything taken.

In camp after camp, they cluster,
at Sharhabad 80,000 people crowd in,
new arrivals daily hunger
for tents to break the heat

wheat or rice or oil,
some kind of shelter.

But never enough.

In the middle of no where.
Delegated to a place
without water, shade, or trees,
this barren plain,
a land inhospitable to human life,
miles from a few remaining adobe villages,
among hulks of shattered Russian tanks,
the ruins of ancient forts.

Down the plane sits Nangarhar
famous for magnificent gardens and lush fruit trees.
In Jalalabad City, a very green city,
they could have stayed in one of the gardens
had water beneath the lit up oranges
as small streams weave through cooling groves.

By early 1997, according to UNHCR reports,
the total number of IDPs in Afghanistan would reach 1.2 million.

Behind a precious tent flap,
a women tries to sponge her feverish child,
an old women struggles to prepare hot rice
squinting out at the plain,
shielding their faces, hugging a child,
their eyes blank, stunned,
the prospect of no change making each day timeless.

Early summer, the temperatures soar
even Jalalabad dries and cracks under deathly heat,
temperatures topping 100 degrees at sunrise.

Near the front of the camp fields.

a huge, makeshift cemetery of shallow graves
sprawls to the horizon beyond the rows of tents:

children dead from snake and scorpion venom,
from landmines and untreated injuries,
from dehydration when their bowels ran.
Measles, mumps, tuberculosis
spread like wild fire at such close quarters.

So hunger and malnutrition took others,
their shattered systems especially vulnerable.

And water so rare.

Along the road up from the Khyber Pass,
hundreds of burned-out Russian tanks squat,
inside them children play hide-and-seek.
Around the outskirts of Jalalabad, below
stark images of burned-out buildings,
remains of trucks, artillery, tanks, and downed planes.
10 million Soviet landmines.
Just a mile from the camps,
prosperous, well-irrigated fields shine:
warlord's opium plantations
red flowered, large-bulbed
fecund with health and nourishment.

The stark Afghan-Pakistani hills
grow into tall sheer walls above canyons and gorges,
and the holes and caves in the porous borderlands—
now every journalist's fresh discovery—
still shelter traffickers, armed militia, religious jihadists.

But beyond this realm is the world of daily living,
where children are born and fail to thrive
and a women dies in childbirth every 30 minutes.

It is a life
where ancestral fields, compounds, basic shelters
in familiar quarters
were shattered overnight by rocket-propelled fighters
who only yesterday defended the neighborhood
but now shoot at the same people as an enemy,
veer far off to gain their own power,
a realm where men used to teaching, running shops,
crafting shoes or driving taxis find themselves
without means to support a family,
where they watch their sons abducted
to fight for a threatening warlord's forces.

In such a world people seek escape,
protection, sheltering, food.
Such a world offers little room for ideologies
on rights or feminism or even freedom.
There is only the language of bare survival
the pursuit of any means
to stay alive.

IV

FINISHING THE FIRST SEMESTER

December 5, 1973

. . . . To begin, pushing hard to run this English class for teachers, in addition to my Afghan student classes, I find myself at school at half paste eight with no students. The *modir* is there, waiting to receive wood for school for the winter. I come into the teachers' room and he writes up the books he wants from Asia Foundation. Finally, one of the teachers arrives and together we read the story we've been on for a week now in Book 3 . . . .

When I come back for my fourth hour class, I am escorted into the teachers' room again—It is a party for the new *saer-malim* Fakir Abdul. Prayers are said by the religion teacher who frequents the marketplace in black glasses. I imagine him in a leather jacket, his jaunty airs announcing hooliganism, and we begin to consume pots of tea and dishes of candy set down before us. Fakir does not eat, just watches, bashfully it seemed (and I think of birthday parties where some pampered little boy had sulked before all the guests, and who missed when he tried to blow out all the candles). Finally, Mr. Pomposity, our Pushtoon friend from Jalalabad, Ali-Jan (M'mood Ali) better educated and above all the others—and considerably so in wealth and ego—rose to toast the new honorable. His speech was so inflated even I could catch the gist of it: 'a salute among fond brothers, to this man who today has taken the high chair, and from this high chair will be a leader, a teacher, and a brother to the students and teachers of the school,' and so on.

Meanwhile, less animatedly, the others put up their congratulations, the *saer-malim* answers something about how the principal is like a father to him, and they are all his brothers. Somehow (in this all male gathering, its metaphors are all masculine) though I was very much in evidence, I can, as usual, only smile, until suddenly I hear the *modir* speaking of the greatness of the school, and slipping in these references to me and the books I was able to get for them, and the lessons I come to give at seven or seven thirty every morning "faithfully." He goes on about "my capable sisterhood."

Suddenly, with a quaint air the Pushtoon king is toasting me: "We drink to your health!" he calls out in English. A silence answers, for no one else understands his words, and in utter decency, I blush. The moment passes. There is another prayer, my hand goes to the right place then (over heart), and we are excused, as someone throws parting words to the effect that I could now go back to my 8th class.

The girls had been alone all this time: the walls giggle and roar and silence descends like darkness when staff again resume teaching in their classrooms.

December 6-7, 1973

Yesterday we stroll in the marketplace, a havoc-rendered place on market day when the strange farmers bring in their cows and sheep and goats and camels to be sold, and goods are sprawled out like a child's game of giant marbles.

In the riverbed, we see a group of men, all shapes and sizes, in robes and turbans, watching a magician, with a snake charmer's pipe and some skin of a tiny animal. He claims to be able to turn whatever is given him into a bowl of *pilau*—The miracle worker's ultimate gift in this society, ripe spectacle as all are who can transform nothing into matter. Yet the scene speaks of the Sea of Galilee in 95 AD, tents of fish vendors, hosting old men squatting behind the earthen stones, testing the wares, while the *nan* men, their wide, warm baskets full of loaves floating on their heads, pass back and forth. All that is needed further is a man to make a sermon.

And one is in the air, always is here, the silent ground up words of a murdered race, their ghosts moving witlessly to the chains of their old habits.

A catastrophe. We need to fire our cook. As to this inhumane and insensitive plight, we regret that he is slow and unteachable, admire his work bringing us water and chopping wood, but we need other food, and a guarantee that everything is prepared properly so we are not always sick. He asks for the cakes we make ourselves—like Marie Antoinette, we're the grumbling rich folk here.

I turn down invitations to sit in some young girls' house. T and I stay in and read and write and make deserts and play Scrabble and Monopoly. Perhaps from being rundown and ill so often, we indulge in self-pity: we recall how for us, the scholarship graduates of Ivy League schools, every friend we had ever had, had had more money than we. (Can we be sane in this thought in this land of such deprivation?)

Tom is so thin now, tooth-picked and scarecrow-limbed. In his Robert Hall, 1930's overcoat—procured from the Used Clothes Bazaar in Kabul—wrapped and bundled around him and two sizes off, he moves down the narrow streets, looking like nothing so much as an Irish emigrant set down by someone's cruel mistake in this gray land of camels and turbans and *chadrised* women, looking lamely among the mud for a single clover leaf . . .

I tutored my *modir* on a propaganda sheet in English he produced this morning about the merits of socialism and Soviet progress; then listened as the teachers stumbled through a chapter in our reader, passed on some words in my week-delayed story, and taught my own classes of beautiful, inquisitive, and mostly restless girls. The *bookeries* were in today, rusty and overfed for the season, and when I took off my coat, my students giggled and said, *"Tabreek"*, for they thought I had donned new clothes before them.

December 10, 1973

Our German educated PC Coordinator, Fariad, in the village to observe us at our classes, joins us for lunch back at our compound and is full of stories.

The former king and his nephew conversed one day at the former king's farm outside of Kabul. The king had forbidden the servants to feed the turkeys, so when the men strolled past the birds, they all came running to follow the king. Another day, he had them fed well, and when he walked past, they only nodded sleepily in the sun.

'Let this be be a lesson to you. Do the same with the people, keep them hungry and they will always be running after you,' he told the nephew. Both men followed this idea, and the people starved.

(We think always about the poverty of the people, who subsist on bread and thin tea, daily have only this as their regular food. We are, unhappily, discontented gluttons in their faces.)

Then he tells another story, this of a man who rode off to get a degree, earned one and began the journey back to his village where he would be called "Doctor-sibe."

But he soon turned back to his school, having decided a title was also needed for his horse. He presented his request to the leaders and notables of the university where he had studied, and they conferred for a day and finally told him that after checking all their books, they had found no precedence to allow such a conference.

'To date, the degree has been given only up to the level of donkey,' they explained.

And, of course, Fariad shares the old tale of one of Kennedy's gala dinners, when all the geniuses of art, music, literature, dance, etc. were invited to the White House. Turning to them, Kennedy said, 'This was surely the greatest gathering of wits and talents under the roof of the White House since Thomas Jefferson dined here alone.'

The weather always consumes us: The mountains hunker, sulky today, dark tempered with heavy clouds. In the passes snow lays like fresh cotton. Fariad told us of the storms which daily block the Salang now.

December 11, 1973

The weather: Now "Mudsville," is the world, the inferno of cow pasture. Today we wake up to find what the snow in the mountains, rain in the valley, had brought—mud to make every step laden with itself, the thick, adhering earth, out of its puddles burdening us. And the whole town, in the gray wintry blast with the winds from the mountains, lay sleeping, the bundled old men in their *dhukans* watching worriedly as thin human traffic passes, mostly children, light as dry wood, moving like sure-footed goats in the muddy trenches.

The mountains are mirage-like now with their dense white coats, eluding us in our squalor of puddles, gray and brown, down here. They are proud old men to our infancy, it would seem.

Our classes huddle around the *bookerie;* students come from their houses without anything but thin sweaters and plastic shoes. They all huddle as close as possible to the *bookerie,* until we all sweat, as if their small bones can store up heat.

Our modir tells me that Kabul Radio reported how Nixon's personal capital if equal to more than three times that of the entire country of Afghanistan, at present.

As I trod heavily through the marketplace, down the splotchy hill past the grist mill along the wall, going to my school, tiptoeing cautiously to keep my balance, a small boy in front of me starts clicking cautiously: "Bazaar finished, bazaar finished." Caught from my concentration then, I question him, until like thunder it dawns on me why he is saying this. He'd taken me for some poor lost tourist, waywardly taking in local culture and lost. So I tell him the truth of my residence and employment. He kowtows apologetically, and we each move on in different directions.

A little further on, the chorus of children on the wall of the family compound where the German Volunteer nurse had lived briefly some years before, shouts after me with a mimic's exactitude: *"Auf wedersehn, danke schoen, guten tag . . ."* As I laboriously pick my way through the mud, looking absently at the rich expanse of snowy mountains, for a moment it has all been transformed to a European Alpine village. Gone are the mud compounds and the strangely clad men, and the ghostlike women. Then my eyes fall down. It is Khulm, Afghanistan, spirited with one person's shadow across the muddy lane.

December 14, 1973

We bought 250 bricks to make raised foot steps all over our muddy yard. By night the white bricks shine, like the markers in a graveyard.

No sun today . . . the local word on weather conditions forebodes snow (or at least more precipitation). The thick clouds have eaten up the mountain.

It is a good day to sit in the gray room (like a charcoal bin, the air that rancid, but a charmed odor of potential heat, feeding our potbelly stove in one motion, and squandering words in the interior.

. . . Back to the five-day ritual tomorrow, biding time that, sparsely, makes the teaching enjoyable, the rare hours when they understand something I've said. Four of the girls are to go to the nursing school in Jalalabad, in three months; it will be a miracle of sorts, they say. I want to see.

. . . The sun's never going to come out. We wanted to find the meteor racing before the sun but our skies and timing have been too far off. The last few nights I've seen the hazy brilliant Venus and imagined it must be the sought after comet Kohoutek.

"No, it's Venus, and that's Jupiter, and over there is Mars," Tom shows me. We must rise one sordidly early morning and catch it before its down, if it is to be seen at all. And what of all those hot, clear nights and days? Summer is now long removed . . . .

Our bellicose chicken is gurgling up on the tree limb, seemingly inured against the sharp cold. Now he crooks, anamorphic, back to fowl.

December 15, 1973

I go early each morning to sit among the old men, the school's *babas,* as they mix lime for whitewashing or start the *bookerie* fires, or just sit in the building nursing cold limbs trying to keep warm, and I stay among them, waiting for my English class for the teachers to materialize. But somehow it never does; one or two bookless souls appear around 8:10. We recite together the sentences in the text like stale formulas, pass back and forth a few vocabulary words, and then surrender.

Yesterday as class began with only one student at 8:20, and a troop of others with the morning bell, the *modir* teased me, "Take their apologies for one day." But they are late everyday.

Some hours in the younger classes, the 8th and 9th, I imagine myself a tired, hungry old bat. I flare up at my students' slowness. They are not trained to listen, to reason, to respond, but only to jump on what I give them, to try to build back some non sequitur from the book they do not understand, all of it. It tries one's patience. And faith.

In one week it will be Christmas and in my better moments I picture myself presenting the teachers' lounge with a huge basket of fruits, nuts, and candy—with a slow explanation that this is what we do on our biggest, most important holiday of the year: we grow happy by exchanging gifts.

Nights now I people the wind with burglars, napping against the plastic and glass windows, prowling after our absence of goods. For 40 afs we pay a man one day to chop wood. Like the concrete layers of two months ago, who took weeks to materialize, I expect him to come back one day and chop down the scrawny, already diseased tree in our compound, stealthily as night. I am not hopeful of procuring the wood in small log sizes, as we need it for our *bookerie.*

We've lost the comet, having all the time, nightly, been thinking we had only to find it during one of the cold, clear night approaching Christmas, along with the sun, the way the wise men found the star, a thousand years ago.

> *[What follows is a taste of interaction with other volunteers, because of its comments on some other events earlier described. Note that although the journals are full of recordings of the endless stream of visitors—volunteers and tourists—passing through, the intent here is to focus only on Afghanistan as we knew it then. Of course, the two are interconnected.]*

. . . Three Volunteers came up on Friday, stopped in to deliver a little mail, ramble through the *teem* and nest in the *choie-xonas,* eat divinity candy and inquire after a *buz kashi* match that never materialized on a muddy, overcast day when half of the local team had apparently been sent to Kunduz for a match. We were still abed, debating the alternatives to remaining there when the pounding came on the gate. Well-versed in the need to offer western sweets and our warm bodies, I baked a cake. Off of the bazaar we bought some greasy fatty *korma* (stew), and a lot of warm, Uzbek *nan,* and we lunched, at noon. One visitor is a TEFLer in Kabul, a few weeks or days from termination (completion of service), the other had been with Food for Work or an engineering project. The Food Workers have been unemployed for most of the past year, so they travel and draw a salary, and this bearded, sullen fellow, is a former resident of a village between Maimona and Herat in the groins of the desert, a place apparently famous for its deep wells and pure water. They were staying in Mazar at the Balkh Nights, the town's only tourists this season, and came bearing gossip and truth on the facts of other people's lives now:

The N's and Jake of Gardez, with whom we had spent our first week and sampled life in a Pushtoon village, have been robbed and are leaving that den of secrecy and high piracy, the couple to go to Herat, and Jake to Ghazni (with his friend, the ghoul/ghazil).

The Leeks of Samagan have left.

Stephen and Ava Mansard. (our fearless language partner ended up marrying one of the TB nurses) are on a business trip to India, searching out the secrets of good egg layers in the beginnings of a poultry project for a farm outside Kabul which they are planning to start.

The TB program is hours away from being terminated, although rampaging TB is not, but PC must give all the nurses and technicians Completion of Service, Job Collapse and Other Country Transfers. A sad mess it would seem . . . .

Also, we are weary with the continuing misunderstandings with our dear old cook it seems, Armoe M'med. T's up for one of us to step aside. For days he does nothing, won't even boil water or stay around the house to guard it, and when he does do something it's only with the slowness of an old, weary man, made to stoop when he can scarcely bow. Small *afghanis* worth of goods keep vanishing; he eats three times the bread we do, and when we struggle all morning Thursday making our own *pilau* a la rice pudding, in the interim he sits sunning like a royal raj at the end of the yard, then cleans up perhaps half of the whole pot. He is content, still beaming as Tom boils water all day, kettles upon kettles to set our *oudon* up for once with a proper amount. We find ourselves cast as imperialists in that relationships—he must be scolded and coaxed to do our work for us and still doesn't do it. We are grown royally and racially irate and set upon him again. At this point we want to pay him to just leave, it seems. He assumes these are the limits of his job, that he need do no more, so he collects his bounty and goes home (probably his sixth or seventh or fifteenth trip that day already). It is better to work hard and to do it all ourselves. At least this week though we must keep him—and his limited repertoire of not exactly amoeba-free *pilau, kofta, korma,* and tea. Just playing the odds, when at least half the time we're not at the house, he is, and perhaps he actually keeps one eye out for stragglers as he chomps on raw carrots and walnuts and bread. Alas, we can never begrudge this dear old man food for himself and his family, but we do wish to have a reliable person to shop and prepare food and clean water for us . . . .

Teaching: Last week was a deadly waste, a complete and total drain, a ferocious drying up of resources. Every hour was something to be weighed and eliminated as quickly as possible—but the time was a slug and I was a swallow. We began the process of review, a dull, little appreciated method of re-hashing and re-teaching, as resonant and inspiring as its Farsi name—*"takiak"*—ing, like a crow's hoarse call. Having reached a halfway point in the books of at least three classes, I can almost say I've done what is required of me for the first half of the year. In theory. Now reality intersects: to measure its paltriness in the final exams will be disappointing. The morning teachers' class is dead already in my mind: a lean one or two struggled out for part of last week, there were none yesterday and this morning by eight o'clock no one had come either. The *modir* cautions me that now they will start coming again, because the days are longer, and it will get bright earlier. The *saermalim* apologizes profusely and then doesn't appear either, or (as once last week)wanders in at five of eight and reads indiscreetly for less than half an hour, making constant references to the time as he goes, then pops up at precisely 8:23 and moves to the business of the day—stirring up the whitewash for the day's painting.

One morning I find the younger Pushtoon there (the one who insists on greeting me as "sir," even today). He sits alone, as if waiting for something, but he never suggests it might be the English class. Still, we talk brokenly and it becomes clear that he's been unhappy here, that neither Khulm nor teaching suits him.

"It's not good for my head, my mind," he seems to say, gesturing. In three months he will return to the University in Kabul, hopefully to study something besides what led to being a teacher. The Ministry sent him up here; but he longs for Jalalabad. He winces, speaking of how the students won't and haven't learned Pushtu here (I could ditto him on English.

The young, married, "European model," who has a relative studying in Arizona (I long ago connected the mysterious transcript with him and his family), came in a few minutes later. Now it is his time to explain, and he launches into a description of why he is teaching first grade and physics both, how the regional director of education, that stout man in Samagan, had moved him from the school at the other end of the village where he had been teaching, to this lycee. He raises both hands, palms up, shrugs, and tosses out, as if asking the air, "And what could I do?"

Now enters the small elementary school teacher, with the pronounced limp and the sister Syfora in the ninth class. His face is swollen up: "This tooth, it is gone." he explains stiffly, unwinding a long shawl he had thrown heavily over his neck and mouth (for fear that *bad* would get into that pained mouth?) "I do not eat, talk, read, today," he explains again, in pain from the dentist's antics. (Only the day before we had noticed, in a strange coincidence, that the infamous fortress on the edge of the road, with the "Dentist Sign" in fact has a dentist whose hole in the wall, and chairless office, was open).

I rise to leave, a little English exchanged, and bump into the *modir*, who eyes us resignedly, inquires as to how the class is, accepts my "No one comes," without breaking stride, and tells me again that more will come because the days are getting better now. I tell him we will see.

Today it is clear and cold, the mountains as elaborate as coiffured old men, and as distant. There is always this visual image you can not catch. You focus like a sprung finger on the mountain, they recede across the desert and then return to you, and for all your hours of pacing them they are unchanged, exactly in their posture of one thousand years. But we know nothing of time. A generation, a millennium is only a pruned word we flaunt about us. Our bodies are bound to the cycle of days, the lean motion forward like the water wheel, whose pockets full of water push the old machine forward. Each pocket is dumped out, but others behind them have already filled up, then again they are dumped in turn, while further up is their source, in streams, so the water falls back into the same river from which it started. Like a mute wooden wheel we seem scarcely more conscious.

The women in the school *dhukan* smiles her toothless way and greets me, from underneath a pile of blanketing she shares with the small *sandalees*, a wooden table holding a clay pot full of burning coals, a small measure between the cold and its output. I find she has a daughter in the eleventh class, a quiet, heavy-eyed girl, always looking down at her paper to find some correction blurred, clear-skinned like most of the students, with a pristine glow. No one will touch her until a hundred people have said it is all right and then she'll have no choice. No girl will.

What has happened to all my words.? I mistreat them, use the dry flat vessels like iron cars; something is gone.

December 28, 1973

Christmas came and went in the land that would declaim it, signs of the nativity, the camels of proud traveling wise men, the low lean burros and sheep, the mothers and children beneath layers of clothes like swaddled timeless victims of their design, the deserts and mountains drenched in starlight and a partial moon, and the expectant meteor, racing beyond the sun now to come out as a blazing cone of light, the year's miracle or harbinger in a few more days.

[We share Christmas in Mazar with 18 PCVs and good food and music, then bring back with us new volunteers who come for a home visit (Darien and Lena.) The same week we set out again to Mazar to see other volunteers]

. . . With the help of the young gatekeeper, we find places in someone's car and are moving across the cold desert. A young Communist in the front seat, a former student of Trent Hatfield at the Teacher's College, engages us in a lengthy, sterling debate on the virtues of Russia and socialism versus the decadence and insular insults of America—mostly I listen while T explains and the car moves across the land oblivious to ideas and ages.

[Then, at the Hatfield's house, I make a person by person description of the new set of volunteers and some old ones, notably one Troy M., who is different and more engaged with this country than others . . . There a sharing of life stories and goodies and food, a constancy that gives us energy.]

We purchase a wall hanging rich as fine wine . . . . The sun stares back, a cleared window over the town, making a chilly day, but inside our house we nurture the fire and look across at each other . . . .

Tom, deeper in those words than I, says it better again: how the arctic cycle comes as the planets revolve, and threshes the land and the people, so in spring a stronger, leaner, hungrier breed is with us. We will see it here, when we couldn't in our own clans . . .

January 1, 1974

The week frizzles away in the slow agony of reviewing, pulling students' teeth to get them to remember what they should have already learned, and making up exams. We pass an odd New Year's Eve as we sit up past 1:00 a.m. by smoky kerosene lantern, slowly, painfully copying by hand (like two stodgy medieval monks, minus their illustrations and inspiration) exams for our students.

This week, too, Armoe M'mad had a tooth pulled. Poor fellow, he almost collapsed with the pain and fever surrounding it, and could barely even pretend to do his work. Once more we feel the natural empathy versus the real need to have food. We vowed he was finished with us, but it's never that simple. The morning I brought in the cold tea left from breakfast and he grabbed it and downed a glass, saying he hadn't had bread since the previous lunch, then asking for some kindly. What do we know of hunger? Why are we made to judge him then?

Gray skies, the accompanying heaviness (in the mountains, a storm, we receive its residue down in this valley as the thick obscuring clouds). Tomorrow night begins the Eid-e Qorban, the Festival of the Sacrifice, biblically wedded with the story of Esau and Isaac, of Abraham, and the end of human sacrifice before Yahweh,

Isn't there a certain irony in the notion? What is all of their life here except a constant sacrificing, a timbering of their lean days into a notion of religion? In theory, then, the people are to slaughter camels and goats and sheep and cows and eat heartily of the meat. The bazaars should be full of peddlers, the *buz kashi* players will have their hours of speculative glory, and friends will be visiting and feeding friends and family.

For two nights wedding parties trooped up the street beyond our compound, the musicians with a kind of fife and drum corps, bright lanterns dotting the darkness, girls with henna-ed hands clad in festive dresses, and the inevitable feast of *pilau* at the end of the march. My students knew both brides. Yesterday the eleventh class hooted Hamira, saying her father has given her away in a marriage to some one she does not want, and now she is angry with him.

I despair at the tradition, the unveiled senselessness and cruelty of making one's daughter a vassal, putting them in a role where they are forced to spend their lives with a stranger—what kind of love do they pass on to their children? Does something blossom out of the habit? I wonder, naively, not sure.

January 4, 1974

The third day of Eid of the Sacrifice. The afternoon on a bleak plane outside town where Afghans from all over the north had gathered to watch the proud mounted *buz kashi* players cut the ground in pursuit of the *buz,* over a hundred strong, fierce as the steppe winds blowing over us all. We gathered like some biblical crowd on the desert hillsides, behind us the bleak backdrop of frozen mountains, in front of us the deserted high plains leading to Russia, Siberia, the dead cold.

Children and vendors, sweets for sale from tents, open air *choi-xonas,* bus loads of people passing and going from town, chadried women like a pile of round ribbons coloring the top of one hill, underneath their anonymity bevies of girlish children fantasizing on the horse's mouth, a moment of running like a run-away stallion out into the world. We meet others "of our kind"—Trent Hatfield from Mazar, two single teachers from Jalalabad, the Pushtu-speaking genius of Logman, Jerry Kissinger and his wife Sara, the Samangan teachers, and other faces we've seen. We are solicited by the commandant, courteous to a fault, and then move out again to the edges of the field, to watch.

To go back to all that in a moment: but first the rest of the week:

> *[Janice Brown and Prissy from Mazar had come with goodies, chocolate chip cookies, etc. And our cook was off to the mosque "to pray for us.]*

. . . Back into the rims of the town, to the Republican Garden now closed, across the sparse earth of the expansive cemetery fields, in the distance an unknown man's shrine, before us the mounds of the dead, brass hands and poles crossed in signs unknown to us, and a decaying tomb, mud falling back to bud. We lose our way and come out in someone's cotton fields, go back to town and out past the old fort, heading to the washed out sand castle on the hill, the old city. In the cave-like shadows we imagine inhabitants, find all the turrets to be, brick ovens, peer over the edge of the cracked walls to the river below us, the whole mud village spreading around us, beyond to the white frozen desert as—a shepherd boy teases us, galloping gallant among his huge black sheep, posing a moment with crock to call us and stare, when Brenda and I move down the hill alone. From nowhere appears a band of ragamuffin musicians to wind a kite in one hand, a fife and a tin-based *ditar* in the other, We climb back into the past of the old town, its ghosts nowhere now except in a certain chilling wind that makes us suddenly vulnerable.

Far off across the crevice of the town's thin valley set round like an amphitheater for the houses along the hills, Prissy and Tom re-appear.

We set back for town briskly and while our guests start a fire we move like industry itself out into the kitchen, to pressure cook our meat and potato dinner . . . .

[The next morning] . . . at one o'clock they leave us, engaged for the two coming days as "mamans" (guests) for students and teachers in their own town (Mazar). They had entertained some 250 people off and on from Christmas on, largely Janice Brown's students, and Prissy's teachers. In our own town we have not the reputation yet, are not sought out for Eid visits . . . . And Thursday night, I was making copies of an exam by hand . . . . We keep looking for the comet, but the mountains are too high, the skies barely clear. In a few more days it should be high enough to clear the bowl of mountains, if we can match its rise and our viewing and find the correct time for that confluence . . . .

And we wake into morning, waiting for noon, and the long festive ride out to the picnic and game fields, troops of men and sons walking the five kilometers to the field.

Troops of horsemen storm across the plain, reins in the captive's mouth, each wed to his horse, the fur hats like wielded animal ears, the others in typically bound turbans. Horses large as Arabian royalty, majestic massive flanks, tall and muscular, roar. You thought of deserted Pegasus, a land removed from ideas and stripped to its concrete boulders, bleached and ravaged by the armies of earth and heaven. Before us then the racers, the men in their skins and floating silk or cotton *chapans* (flash-up to the tent city of female floating veils, back again to the thundering plains).

In the corners, along the roads, child's play: a hand-built carousel in triplicate, hand-pushed horses for little players, and the wooden wheelbarrows and windmills and rolling horses, made of cheap wood, hastily painted. In the field again beneath the wind, a player has battled the whole field. One hundred horses unwind behind him; he's dropped the bloody lumpy carcass in the circle. There has been a victory. But which team is which?

The ranks disband. Tom's students "salaam" us. We "tabrik" them; and the "misters" pass.

I am haunted by the picture—this game in which some one hundred fiercely riding horsemen, mounted on some of the strongest and most massive horses I've ever seen, attempt to carry a freshly killed "goat's carcass" (the *buz*) around a huge field and finally drop him for a moneyed point, in a designated goal circle. The players negotiate with whips, the horses charge and rear at each other, the spectators scramble from the nebulous sidelines as some vanguard player on a seemingly run-away horse gallops toward them—all and all it is incredibly brutal and exciting, new and fierce and illogical as is so much is in this country. The field where we watched it is a vast, barren plain outside the village where the land bends briefly in a series of bleak, grassless hills, forming a natural amphitheater of Olympic scope—while behind the snow-capped mountains brood over everything, and in the distance lay the stark flatlands that run straight to the Russian border (about 10 miles away), and then go unbroken into Siberia.

January 7, 1974

We have the coldest days yet; water and people begin to freeze, and there is a turn of events at the school. Yesterday morning we presented the Eid gifts. My modir wittily came up with a proverb but the gist of all the gratitude was thrown back to Tom; I was, it seemed, his lady. None of the teachers mentioned the gift the rest of the day. A conversation swam around me, about me, some absurd rendering of the difficulties involved if I were to grade my 50 question exam on a 1-10 basis. Were the disputers thinking me incapable of arithmetic perhaps, or maybe wanting to spare me so much effort, as in the grade matrix? So it went . . .

Kenning: the cook sits at my feet literally to ask for a piece of our cake. The *dhukandar* teacher and the youngest teacher—ask me for pieces of white paper. My clod-hopper shoes lose their heel in the middle of my graceless falling down the school steps. (The aged, old stale Brownie mix we had carried here from the States and finally, frittered over in the kitchen, turns out to have gone bad.) I further sit in a restive, dull stupor to copy out the examinations by hand.

There is snow again in the mountains, but we hear there is no meteor brightness above them, even if we have the time to wait for it . . .

January 10, 1974

Tom's exploits entertain.

On Monday he froze in a Waz to and from Aybak, and watched two *babas* arguing over the price of a fare. An old prophet figure came strolling in with a staff and began to pray loudly at the people in the Waz. sitting there like lumpy potato sacks, hunched over to stay warm. No ordinary beggar, he was a "religious." The Waz driver finally let him on, though he claimed he had no money. The truck started up and as the wind whistled another *baba* began testing the other.

"I've paid 15 afs for this seat and you can do the same. You've got money there. I can see you've got some in your pocket," against the old man's protestations of his poverty, yelping out a prayer provokingly as the old man stung at him more. Soon they were pulling each other's beards, while the captive spectators made a kind of rolling r-r-r-r sound of disgusted humor. One episode.

And the *kutchi* women, their hard brown faces burnt into an ageless wrinkled wonder, like American Indians, the old and young together, descend in the middle of the cold plain.

Tuesday, Tom went to Mazar for paper and tickets and to withdraw money from the bank, and yesterday he set of again for Aybak, to run off the detailed test and lunch on *cawk* with Jerry Kissinger. From the cab of the Waz, he brought back tidbits of a conversation with a fellow passenger, a very well-preserved man who claimed he'd been married for fourteen years, had a twenty-six year old wife who had borne him nine children, two of whom had died, and was himself a forty-year old land contractor. He spoke of the people in Tajikistan, Uzbekistan, Turkmenistan, USSR.

"They are good people, just like Afghans. They chew *naswar* and go to the mosque . . . In Moscow, they don't know God, but in these places, the people still can practice their faith."

Contending with the braggadocios at the back of the truck coming back, T. remembered one old local quizzer who'd been monitoring a nationalistic session on the virtues of Afghanistan, particularly its great fruits, and had finally asked T. if there were figs in America. T explained that some grew there but that most were imported.

"And where do they come from?" the know-it-all ventured. T told him.

"Oh, Arabesquestan." He thought a moment. "Is that close to America?"

[We hear of a near fatality, of a fellow volunteer staying with another volunteer, who had inadvertently swallowed poison instead of cough medicine He's been med-evacuated to Germany.]

. . . Yesterday was the first exam, and I was staggered by the massive confusion of the eleventh (my clever) class. In the long drafty classroom where the *modir* spelled out an algebra exam for his twelfth class, the *saer-malim*, and the young teacher watched me run from student to student to answer questions—for three hours. Worst, at the end, the governor and an assistant came in to inspect things. I was ready to begin my oral exams, was amazed when the whole quartet of *modir*, governor, and assistant, Pushtu teacher and other English teachers, seated themselves around me expectantly. The first student came in—Zahra. I breezed through her quickly; she was terrified and I was annoyed. The second girl entered, the clamps went down, a whole panel ventured to test her: the two outsiders launched into an inflated English grammatical command, and pulled at the girl to answer. Failing, she was sent out. I had no function there, it seemed; they wanted only to project themselves, their ideas of how it should be. There was something militaristic and—as always in such settings—male in the air—and what could best be called an inquisition dragged on. What should have been an hour ordeal perhaps, was strained into over three. Limp, disgusted, unseated, at their conclusion I stormed home.

> *[In fact, I was, am, foolish. What is it? Here comes my own mea culpa for not being able to tolerate authority or someone going over my head to do my work . . .]*

Other note-worthies: Amore M'med now eats more in a day than we do—rather he takes home for his family more than he leaves with us. He averages five loaves of bread a day, we less than two most days—and he lies openly, disputing anything said, and (worse, for it puts me in a role I can not retract myself from), he begs daily—for a salary advance, a gift of a new coat, some fruit or cake, and so on.

A duo of girls hang sheepishly around our gate one afternoon. Gathering courage they finally tiptoe to the kitchen door, where I am making orange bread, introduce themselves as sisters of one of my worst students, beg me to pass her, and stare. I give them tangerines, and they leave, wisely, having tasted more than the fruit it seemed. But, again, I go against wisdom by being so exacting, i.e. honest. But I wish to be fair.

January 12, 1975

. . . Yesterday T. discovered that his exam schedule had been changed and that he must be here Sunday morning. We were to leave that day for semester break, and there is a near showdown—the pompous incompetence—or is it more deliberate and a mild sabotage—of his *modir* almost triggers us to throw up arms and just get away from here. But we stay.

Morning, cold, the bleakest yet . . . . The Salang is closed, the buses won't go until later and no one is interested in traveling on a day like this anyway, unless with an emergency . . . .

The sun finally peaks out today, but the bitter cold persists. The *jewies* are frozen.

From the roof looking out to the road yesterday, waiting for Tom to come home from Aybak, I think about our days, our grumbles. Then all this strangeness doesn't seem so strange, because I embrace the distance, swallow hungrily the entire experience as some abstraction, and enter entirely within, easily occupied.

On Saturday the *baba* from the hotel comes in briefly, his kindly bright face, peaking around the gate, to tell us that his son has his exam "tomorrow." Seriously, Tom says, he would be fine, and as quickly the old man/friend is gone again. (On the exam, the boy, head's above others, scores a 96, unassisted.).

January 19, 1974

I am again in for my own share of balancing "reminders." The day of the 8th class exam Azarullah visits to remind us his sister Rokia would like to pass my exam. The exam itself has been a fiasco: it was set in the same hall as where a wordy group of seventh graders were having their Farsi or history exam. The snuff-taking old teacher was there, ostensibly to sleep by the *bookerie*, while I attempted to keep order. Lo and behold, when he left the room, all havoc reigned. The chaos enveloped only a minute, and then the girls stopped. I refused to answer questions for this class, my difficult tribe, and thereby managed a modicum of sanity. For the oral section: I was skirted by two English speakers, who wanted, as my proctors, to see the girls rushed through, and themselves relieved of duty. Obviously no grade is to be taken all that seriously.

The next noon brought me before my 10th class (again in an echoing large hall), girls with their white scarfs up and tight around heir heads and shoulders before their men teachers, spending time drawing straight lines on their exam papers, the vestiges of education. As the lackadaisical Farsi teacher nods a few calm, "Be quiet, students," I stalk and twitter around the room, barely keeping to my pledge to not answer questions, and the Farsi exam passes. Its examiners return to orally quiz the rambunctious students right in front of mine (still whining into their sheets).

Then a whole stream of men, proctors, enter: the head teacher, the governor, a chemistry teacher, the first grade teacher, Esfandyar. They parade, in and out, to glare or gaze, the governor to command me to speak English to my students, his assistant to conceitedly ponder one section of my exam and then leave, soliciting me indifferently for having created such a hard time-consuming exam.

Finally only my proctor is there, the all-American boy faces the newly married sir, who takes it all as a kind of elaborate joke, runs to my students with his versions of the correct answers, and in the *takiere* (oral section) goes out of his way to make me rush my questions and reduce this part of the testing, too, to a general farce.

. . . I spent a morning at school recording grade sheets and reading the correct pronunciation for a much-bored teacher, from his lexicon of irrelevant words.

[We get and read news of Watergate, Dean, Nixon's tapes from old Kabul Times, which arrive with our mail.]

January 25, 1974

. . . We wake up this morning in the twentieth century again, in someone's living room in Kabul, and while the snow piles up outside with the softness of tiptoeing angels, we sit inside on real couches . . .

We finished our exams on Tuesday and spent Wednesday as squeezed sardines on an old Haji-Aqub bus which chugged up the 250 miles of ice and snow and mountains between Kabul and Tashkurgan in a record nine hours, from 12,000 to 6,000 feet.

. . . I feel, self-consciously, a balminess that morning (the valley's judgment on me for coming to Tom's school early the day before to pick up his exams, not yet completed, to rush them home and correct them and return them so all his grades would be finished that same day?) The dissipated, scruffy flippant cowboy-looking modir had led me right into the middle of everything, so boys like Mexican jumping beans, leaped away. But today we rose before the sun, had tea, briefed Armoe M'med, and set off on a *gaudi*. Halfway to the Bande, we were joined by one of my teachers, who was carrying a bag of goods to be sold at the road. The village slipped behind us, and together the teachers told us the details of a kind of Tuesday night massacre (not quite American-style) that had just occurred here. Our Germanesque commandant and his arrogant *hakim-sibe*, the sub-governor, had both been "removed," apparently for stealing public funds.

Down and up as slow as sludge turtles, up the mountain on two slippery axles, we stop for lunch from a tuna can while little boys swallow our sight. We reach Kabul then, at 6:30 on a wintry night . . . .

> *[For an hour we had been trying to find someone in to stay with, having found the rates of the Spinzar Hotel too high, Then at PC office we heard stories of PC-Philippines from one volunteer (the Tanettas) who had been there in the first year of Peace Corps.*

Saturday's child, we feel the bitter cold with wonder, gawk at the transformed city mountains, get shots, share in colleague talk, and collect more books for the school . . .

Our village, because of the beauty of its setting, the traditional houses and bazaar, the old Teem (covered bazaar), aways invites comments and some envy. One of the PC staff tells us more about its history, the names involved, the history of our town: The Mausoleum on its edge, to the right of the road, was built during the reign of King Amandullah (1919-29) by Hakim Siksander Khan for his wife. The old town of Khulm, seven miles to the north, was destroyed by Ahmad Shah Durrani, (1747-1773) and he in turn founded Tashkurghan. What we see now (nothing remains of the old Khulm) is the citadel where Mir Wali lived about 1845, what is formally known as Bajr Johan Arie—Amir Adurmah's Palace.

Stealing the Past, Badakshan Province, Afghanistan 1996

In the mountains shadowing the high Central Asian steppes,
history has hosted every kind of conquest
and just as many kinds of destruction.

When earth rumbles across hard-packed rock,
splitting open its entrails,
it lays bare third century Greco-Bactrian graves
caches of unearthed antiquity
priceless, 2100-year old artifacts,
ready for "harvest".

With no government to control them,
opportunists and scavengers dig and hoard
as they've done for centuries.

From Alexander's march through Afghanistan in 330-329 BCE
near the confluence of the Oxus and Kokcha Rivers,
Ai Khonum sat, surrounded by Greek settlements,
military and colonial garrisons.

Then cultured Bactria was a center in the Seleucid Empire,
its rulers and artisans melded and syncretized
Greek, India, Chinese, Central Asian, and Persian cultures.
Here Alexander and Selucius's soldiers bivouacked,
in the shadow of Ai Khanoun's grandiose structures:
manor houses, villas, avenues, a theater and gymnasium,
temples, palaces, irrigation networks, baths,
indoor plumbing and heating systems.

Amid wars, conquests, defeats,
each new earthquake split open wider the past,
unearthed mass graveyards
which had housed the dead for thousands of years,
spewed hundreds of skeletons, spit out skulls
from tombs from the time of the Persians,

still intact jewels and period riches—
elegant robes and jewelry,
huge pitchers made of high quality china and gold,
delicate bracelets, necklaces and earrings;
gold and silver coins, seals, statues,
precious ornaments:

left bare for the picking
bleeding to death a world heritage:
Afghanistan's millenniums-buried inventory.

V

SEMESTER TWO IN KHULM

February 2, 1974

Kabul is behind us, maybe for four months. We leave it with its restaurants and people on the verge of modernity and decadence, its old mingle of austerely benign snowy mountains, its 6,000 feet, its *taxiwans* who race over ruts and new pavement in cars priced at 1000 times their values, its water-carriers, Hazaras, lugging *karachis* full of wood, its vendors with their asymmetrical booths or bags hung over a mule, its robber baron grocery stores where anything can be purchased, given the price, its movie theaters with American westerns, its over-priced, deluded foreign community. And our friends . . . .

We fired Armoe M'med today; he took it with dignity. We gave him an advance salary, all of all supplies of *roghan* (oil) and rice, and listened gently, guiltily, to his bravado, for he went on and on about his own efforts on our behalf and what good people we were, and how our friendship must continue as long as the earth. Then, he left, just like any day. We remain in this gray overcoat of a stormy day, worrying that he'll now have no more bread. (There is no justice. Inevitably, while in Kabul we were spending over 500 afs a day to eat out and buy crafts. This poor man's salary has been 800 a month).

It is so hard to explain, how in the stripped down life we have here, in a house without running water, and outdoor squat toilets, with the only heat the layers of clothes and blankets and the fickle, hungry *bookerie* with only a few hours daily of—on again-off-again electricity—with the limits in diet based on available produce on the market, with the hours daily needed to shop and boil clean water, and wash up ourselves and dishes and pots in mud-basins or by the *jewie*, with the requirement that the food we serve our Moslem guests be prepared by a Moslem so it is always *halal,* and—most important—with the great and logical need that food and water be served clean—iodine-soaked vegetables and all pealable fruit, etc., how important having a cook becomes. We inevitably put great store in having a reliable and creative cook. As much as we wish to help this sad old man, one on one, with our modest Peace Corps salary (yet equal, on paper, to what a provincial head makes), we can not just give him everything and get none of the services we—modestly—I still hope—require to function and stay healthy here.

It bothers us both. The worst part of this new life is requiring a servant, and that we can't play our role very well, are torn by the need to have a Moslem cook to prepare *halal* food for guests, clean food and water for us, so that we can be freed to do other things . . . . But always, someone is mistreated, it seems.

The new cook, Shah, is to come on Tuesday. He worked for the married couples whom we had met in Jema-minat last summer, and we are to pay him 2,000 afs per months. We expect miracles.

In the midst of the snow and roads that are never cleared, the trip back was cold and fear-inducing from the inception, starting with the battle with the taxi drivers at the Shohona lot. Hardened veterans, or desperadoes, they merely laughed indignantly as we inquired after chains and tires. Finally we boarded a Toyota, paid for an extra seat and a half, before setting out, and continued visibly wretched most of the way because of snow and ice. At some point the driver paused insanely first to remove and only later to put on again, the chains, and dodged some skids. We all sat through the ride in Allah's hands, wondering if we would ever get out of this vehicle alive.

There is something vulnerable in the very terrain of this land, the hard shattered rock piles of mountains. You could pick and pull at it, as if dismantling bookends, and a whole side would come down . . .

February 3, 1974

[I leave out, unrecorded here, my long dissertation on the volunteers we have met and their life stories; of Doc and his wife

Lila, and their life and travels in India, Nepal, Philippines; of rules for PCVs; of emergencies among old clients of the doctor back in Arizona, etc.]

February 8, 1974

We survive another bitter, hungry disappointment, because the alleged cook we'd so sanctimoniously enlisted the services of in Kabul, has still not appeared . . . and like a worried spirit, a ghost outside his body, Armoe M'med has come back twice to stare at us and ask if he can't help. We are bristly as he is there, regretful and ashamed of ourselves as he goes away; Tom tells him quietly there is no work for him here any longer. But he'll come back again, in his raggedy worn over shawl to tell us how cold it is, and ask again. He stares, shaking his head at the garbage pail full of bones and orange skins and thrown out tea. "I'll use your bones from your meat," he tells us. "I'll aways come back and get the bones for you . . ."

Now that there's no one here to guard the yard, we lock it up tight each morning, and go in and out through the woodshed. And now we can't just walk off together, as a day like this beckons us to, for fear someone will come visiting, pillaging, in our absence.

I am still struggling with the wearying and grinding ordeal of teaching daily, when so much of our energy is consumed with having to yell at these young charges, here more for social than academic reasons, urging them to be quiet, every few seconds . . . .

There's a man who speaks in Special English and comes over our short-wave radio every night at 9:00. He belches out each flat nonrhythmic monosyllable emphasizing all the numbers, telling us the world moves on in its petty rehearsals. This is our BBC god of sorts, I think, letting us hear of the world we left or never really knew, a lifeline to the current age as we move with glacial speed through this ancient one . . .

Feb. 13, 1974

[Before Class 11, I make a huge linguistic faux pas calling the mountains in Brazil in Dari, Big Vagina, instead of Big Mountains. I must not laugh with them, and try hard to mediate after their hysteria.]

These school children are like products of a nun school where everything natural is taboo. Their minds wander like river tributaries through all the flat unexplored land damned to them, lingering largely on what is private in a better scheme. But they love to talk of the forbidden, so perhaps I superimpose a puritanism on them that is not even there, aside from the obvious segregation of the sexes and repression of women's equality.

Then the other classes ask minutely after my husband, my sleeping habits, the kinds of food I eat here and in *Amerika* (calling it by that energetic form) not for the first time: the States represent that diminishing land of dreams, a figure of speech.

. . . . About the business of teaching, we move a little heavily now, for we've forgotten that excuse we had originally to pull us through, the illusory tension before the first exams; those half-gauged ideas about being able to transmit some knowledge, seem entirely gone now. Yet we are doing things differently by our approach. We entertain questions, have them write or speak stories. We like to use pictures and photos and re-written fairy tails. We let each student speak, not just the captain, and pull in lessons from geography, history, literature, or art, every chance. We ask them to think and not just parrot . . .

Yesterday the cook, Shah, appeared, his bedroll piled outside our gate so we hardly had seen it before we realized it must be him. He began immediately to wash dishes and rearrange the woodshed; he was going to move the kitchen to the woodshed. In the evening (he is to stay in the . . . *balloi* a few days, he says, until he can find his own place) he sat timidly (cat-like, the short, round body and the watery eyes, and the casual mustache like trained whiskers) in our room and T explained the most obvious to him; then he went off to the dark and chill of that sub-reptilian room and its dusty air. This morning he was up early, a little confused as to how we manage our *nan a*nd tea, but finally bringing it in, all things gathered there. By day's end he'd cleaned and ordered supplies and dishes and pots and *owdons*, each object in sight, and had shown himself to be a professional . . .

Feb. 15, 1974

. . . We read of a news reel which makes us think they may yet get Nixon to blanch.

Well-fed, protected now, we have a chance to wander, and so yesterday we took the road out to the Jemoriat Gardens, past the hotel and the post office, coming to our own secret pine-lined entrance to be wooed by the whispers of wind through the green, unweathered stoics. One lone gardener stooped over a corner plot as if waiting for the sown ground to cough up life, an existential figure in the presence of acres of over-run dried bushes, pods like gnarled gourds, tangled vines and vessels in browned, grassless veins. The old summer pleasure house has been almost entirely re-roofed now, the garish cement slabs edging the mezzanine like a roof hat, the white wash yet to come, the bald white skull cap of a dome staring out in the presence of mud walls, too precious for the time . . . .

Feb. 17, 1974

. . . . Last night the old father (*sibe-xona*) landlord took his lantern like a loaded gun, barged into the compound and began shouting at Shah in the kitchen, demanding that the room he was in must be let to someone else, that it couldn't be the kitchen, and asking after Armoe M'med. Tom followed the furius shouting man out to his stream, where he seemed, witch-like, contorted in postures of drinking and washing.

So now we wonder if we shouldn't move again. Shah tells us the "great Haji Aziz Khan" is crazy, that furthermore the people of this town are like donkeys, unlike the people of Kabul who know many things . . . .

[Lest we think we've grown too opulent and vulgar with good meals now being prepared for us, candidates for Gatsby's garden parties, in truth we have one bald light bulb to garnish up our yard now, and a plot full of dried up tomato plants.]

[And on school], where else can you walk into the principal's office and after being shown the best chair, be turned to by one of the teachers in a karakul hat, and get asked . . . "Technology for us please? Can you arrange it?"

Feb. 18, 1974

So the *modir* who earnestly, often to our insensitive notions, outrageously, tried to help us find a house, who patrolled my fits of nervousness and frustration, my incomprehensible stony moodiness, who received the books from Asia Foundation undauntedly, who in short had been a generous, though after his nature, a stiff fatherly friend, is being relieved of his responsibilities as a *modir*. He is supposed to be made a teacher in Mazar, and one of the Farsi teachers is also being sent to an obscure northern village this week, while their replacements come up from Kabul . . .

I learn all this like falling down a well as I enter the office before classes. Is it a political exile? Are his politics suspect? Which side is the relevant education director on? He is likely a communist, or is it the other way around? Is it exile for potential rabble-rousers who are communists, so Daud's men can control different factions of the communists, the Parcham or the Khalq? Or is it the other side he is on, and thus is he manipulated to lose status and position?

I think it somehow follows with the story of the brand new, stainless steel equipped kitchen at the private dormitory school for telecommunication in Kabul where two of our colleagues, the Leighs, teach. The cabinets, sink, stove and other equipment stand untouched, while the Afghan cooks build a fire in the middle of the room, squat on the floor and do all their work there.

Yesterday the assembled teachers and principals sat watching me in the office. Flustered, I could only look down, pretend that I did not understand.

"We are all very angry, "the *saer-malim* started.

"Angry?" I asked.

"Sad," the *modir* corrects him.

They all remained sitting there motionless, gazing into the fire or their watches, or out a window across the yard where the black-suited girls play, into our down-threshing eyes. In the afternoon, before, angry and trenchant, the *saer-malim* had stormed at me his bitterness, how in this country a man's not supposed to work, because no matter if he works or not, someone above can just pull him up and make him do something else. He was grasping in a spilled out English to tell me how continuity, devotion, and belief in one's work were not considered virtues here, it seems. Now we wait to see where else the scythe will fall.

Feb. 19, 1974

. . . There is a false spring now, the day before the month of Hoot, but though we still build a fire and feel a chill without it, the harshness, the darkened days of severe winter, seem past. But we know of the rains, and how winter finally goes out in mud-clobbered boots, an old man in a muddy wool coat.

> *[I reflect on being about to turn 25, on seeking warm corners to read, on studying Chinese again, and always, the mail from home we crave, want, seek as sustenance.*]

Feb. 21, 1974

. . . And winter, of course, comes back with a vengeance . . . then a wild day. We eat greedily (turnips and carrots, potato pancakes and toast, chocolate pudding) . . . take a walk through the mud luscious town, the snow in layers around us. At night we recall all the hours we used to spend, staring into the lantern after the electricity went out, the half-finished game of Scrabble, the dictionary and assortment of books spread out in a ring on the scorched rug of our floor, thinking about the future, and what we must do then . . .)

February 23, 1974

It is just after six; we've finished our nuts and fruit meal and emptied out the evidence in the kitchen, moved into our room out of the cold, muddy night, when we hear the gate open, and a figure moves quickly toward our house. It is Faroodullah, our old principal, who ceremoniously enters and immediately begins to explain how he was leaving now and would like to tell us good bye and that we have been appreciated.

Quietly we sit there, and the six and more months we have worked and lived here, the initial and often distrustful thoughts between us, pass behind us, like dross in a breeze, leaving only the thrashed and good wheat. I rise to go make tea, but he insists that there is no time. We thank him stiffly, speaking in English to show him that we feel he understands, then repeat our words in formal Farsi. In a few more minutes he stands up, shaking my hands, moving out the door without any ceremony, a duty executed to its end. So we wonder.

In a few more minutes our cook Shah comes across the yard; he had been out all day looking at houses, had found two possible ones some 45 minutes walk from here. He has begun to consider the difficulties of his wife coming here, from "modern" Kabul where she doesn't wear a *chadris.*

"There's nothing in this town but mud and cold," he tells us, sitting stiffly against the *bookerie,* looking out at the wall.

. . . Ghulam Azer the Peace Corps cook who had fed us in the first days we arrived in Kabul last summer came to visit us one afternoon last week (he has been working for the petrol station upon the highway, employed exclusively it seems to carry the 30-40,000 *afghanis* from the station to the bank every day). A small, active man he salaamed us and our future, explained a little about his five children, wife and home in Kabul, other Westerners he's worked for, returning always to ask after our health. He scolds the present government for selling all the country's goods to Russia as the the people are very poor again, and he seems to praise the old king who at least had kept up a strong friendship with the Americans instead. All this comes between business-like bites of Shah's peanut butter cookies and perhaps six rapidly swallowed cups of tea. Then he too is out.

Feb. 25, 1974

I live somewhat vicariously, stealing stories from T., who with a certain degree of mobility, can outdistance me at "experiences." Saturday I came home from school to find fourteen pairs of muddy, boot-shoes lined up outside the door. Inside, Tom was teaching his "special" English help class. They had been given a room at the school, but that day it was taken away from them (the science room, ruled over by the science teacher who feels responsible for the never-used equipment and imagines students lingering all around it to steal, is out). On the 15th of Hoot, the *modir* tells him, the weather will be warm, and then he can hold the class outside.

Then yesterday, when I came home no one was there. A note explained that Tom had gone to Mazar to look for mail, apparently grown disgusted with the whole thing. He explained to me later that the *modir* had told him the class couldn't meet at our house, because of "the Republic." The ministry in Kabul had explained to him that any assemblies of Afghans and foreigners was not a good idea (this reality was only implied to us, of course, but perhaps it is a fact these people are oblivious to—except the *modir*—because the government is so put-upon to keep its paranoid self going . . . .) So now, nonchalantly, our actions become suspicious . . . just when, for once, T. had found a group who really wished to learn English and might have profited from his instruction. In effect, though, the *modir*, the blessed representative of "the Republic," is acting as if his wanting to teach is just something he does to entertain himself. It's a debasing idea.

On his trip to Mazar, however, Tom found no mail and brought back a lot of non-necessities. Standing on a bus coming from Kunduz, that had paused to let him on, someone asked if he was Russian. Going back from Mazar, in a half-filled taxi, he shared a seat with a coarse, sprawling old men who expectorated spume onto the floor, angering the driver who threw a spittoon back at him, and then proceeded to talk to himself, about rising at 2 a.m., pausing only to whelp up another clod of spume, and to bless himself widely (spreading his arms out across the car like a scarecrow, pulling them in across his chest, making that gesture of pulling a mask over your face, every time the car passed a burial field or a monument) . . . .

Earlier, during his regular class, Tom had asked one of his students about his family, and the boy said he had two older brothers, who worked in the bazaar. Later, when he was collecting some papers, the same boy stopped him and explained that he didn't really have any brothers; he had just made that up so there would be something to talk about.

"I did have a brother," he said softly.

"Had or have?" Tom started automatically, expecting a verb tense error.

"No, I had a brother, but he died last week." The child had been five.

. . . . [We are inundated as we talk now, with other stories about students, gleaned from the essays, paragraphs they must write:] The boy who lost both parents, lives with his uncle, attends school in the morning, buys things in the bazaar, sleeps and eats; another who talks of his 80-year old grandfather who runs a store on Fridays in the covered bazaar, an essay full of dates, times and ages, atypical . . .

Yesterday morning the new girl from Aybak, Shahzadah, whose father holds a high position in the town, came over for some special tutoring. The teaching goes quickly; she learns, at least superficially, everything I ask of her. Then we move into the other conversation, when she explains how she is Pushtoon, that Pushtu is her native language, that she has lived in Lashkagar for 12 years, that she wants to become a nurse, as someone in her family—an aunt perhaps—already was, but that although the work was needed, "it is not good for women."

She looks through our Sears catalog, an artifact we had been encouraged to pack way back in our pre-departure days, almost a year ago, from a PC-provided list, and comments on the attractiveness of the women models. She stumbles before one black model, then refocuses and asks quizzically what the models' ages each might be. She doesn't wear chadris and never has, her father being of the enlightened variety at least that far. She nibbles dainty on a cookie, pulling the *toshak* up as she sits on it, looking up at our bookshelves. Then a servant is back at the gate; it is 11:00 and she must go home and I must go to school until 4:00.

A conversation, during the day, with Esfandyar, the gentle primary grade 1 teacher with a limp. He asks quietly "about things . . ." The large Pushtu Ali-jan heard of our dilemma in finding our Kabul cook a house and offers to find one. Finally, the *saer-malim* makes his loud, curt questions to me (from day to day he forgets how much Farsi I know, so covers up his confusion by speaking loudly to me as if to a simple-minded, deaf mute). I function fine in his language now, so feel slighted. But I know my problem, as it has been all my life, is my timidness.

February 28, 1974

> *[We are treated to an extensive, very detailed conversation with two backpackers, class of '73 from Harvard, who came through, experienced in many parts of the world from Turkey to Arabia and its history. They are disdainful of tours and people who will not try to be among and understand the culture they pass through, of people who view others' poverty like museum pieces established for their particular viewing pleasure. We adore them, share our own love for and frustrations with "our town," and the educational system, and then bid them safe travels . . . .]*

My new principal is officially welcomed into the town with a tea party at the girls' school, a mercifully brief ceremony to which I was invited, and where, in my asexual role, I sit at one of the two long tables before a dish of candies and a cup of tea and watch the new rulers of the region—governor, education director, etc., harsh-faced, sun-glassed in sinisterness, coarse and sour-tempered, I think, insular and arrogant perhaps, take a few toasts, rise general style, and leave. And the regular teachers, holding hands, troop out to see them out the front gate.

Earlier, before the assembled school, the girls, ridiculously blighted with their haggish *chadris* pulled over the back of their heads, I stand on the steps with the other teachers, while the principal, the big Pushtoon, and then the *saer-malim* say something fitting to the "dagtars" (daughters) about their lives and scholarship, their future and that of the "Republic." I feel myself shuttering, am grateful when I can find my way home.

March 1, 1974

> *[Shah does accounts, announces he must leave for Kabul, and likely will not return but will send Ghulam, another cook we had known. He just does not like this sad town and the hard work every meal represents. We inventory our discontent, but we understand his reasoning.]*

March 3, 1974

. . . A tragic day in this world, in every world. Tom's school is recoiling with the news that their recently transferred *saer-malim* (head-teacher), for that school also saw rapid transfers and changes of leadership, has lost his face. The poor man was severely burned when a kerosene stove exploded in his room in that northern village where he'd been transferred. In unknowable pain, he was trucked to the hospital in Mazar, and now it's not known whether he will survive

. . . . This word comes from one of the *babas* at the boys' school, but the teacher are all talking about something else, a headless body found by the old city palace, the remnants of some family feud, perhaps, but as yet the corpse has not been identified. And then in the evening (rain briefly stopped, our fingers are crossed but only the wall of the old kitchen has collapsed so far) comes news of the worst aviation crash in history: 354 persons, mostly British, with some French, Japanese, and Turkish, died when a huge Turkish Airlines plane apparently exploded soon after take off from Paris. "Sabotage can not be ruled out," some spokesman says, and one wonders, after the whole tone of violence and terrorism in the world, at the information that seven bodies were found as far as 10 miles from the huge crater the plane rendered in the forest north of Paris.

March 4 (13 Hoot), 1974

Marzia, the student, hasn't come . . . My new modir, Rashidullah, a fleshless tall person with a great beak of a nose, who wears three-piece suits and asks me probing but sincere questions, has now entered this school and our lives. Will we ever know why the other was dismissed or transferred, and why this Kabuli-academic was sent here instead? Who is being rewarded and who punished?

> *[The town is a miasmal swamp, ourselves ducks, everything dark and sloppy and heavy. Weekly we struggle with the feeling our students will learn nothing from us, that we are not needed here. Yet, like the sucking mud which pervades everything, we stay in place and navigate as best we can.]*

March 10

> *[Off to Samangan for a birthday for Jerry and Sara Kissinger, with the gang from Mazar.]*

Until, Friday night, limp with it all, returning to the unguarded house, we find the landscape muted, its grave austerity transformed in dusk and chilly late winter shadows, the beginnings of a new belly-growth green and purposeful on the foothills, off in the distance. The men of a village we pass cavort in a communal dance in their fields . . . Is spring then coming?

March 12, 1974

Yesterday Tom's student Azarullah came over just as we were sitting down for dinner. He enters with the usual frantic pounding on the locked gate. He joins us, the potions re-distributed, and then sets out to talk, almost non-stop, until 6:45. It has been a day of retribution for the town's and country's mistakes. He is first set off at the idea of *chadris* and a rumor that the principal at my school must soon announce an end to the wearing of *chadris* for the students.

Then he explains about Aminullah Khan in the early 20's and his attempts to rapidly modernize this country and how the mullahs had challenged him in their narrow and erroneous interpretation of the Koran. Although some roads and factories were started, and girls were allowed to go to school, the bigger, more needed changes in the minds of the people and government never came about. Now, like then, he thinks Daud and the Republic will begin to improve things, to modernize a backward society, that all the products of Afghanistan which are now being shipped out wholesale to Russian and the likes will be more judiciously obtainable by the people, either at face value or in an appropriate redistribution of wealth. He speaks of all the now legendary corruption, a young man strangely wise, all this coming from a lightly pockmarked face shadowed by a wound turban, of the age of perhaps 17)—how Afghanistan was like France before the Revolution when people had no work nor food nor education, and to get an education or job required an elaborate bribing and patronizing of the ones in power, or a banishment to poverty or serfdom.

The immediate realm of this city (Khulm) comes up then, and he explains (rumors again, I set it down against my own, perhaps myopic observations) that my old modir had been transferred because he, for three years, had been taking the rugs the weaving classes at the girls' school made and putting them in his own house to sell and then pocketing the value—rather than using them as an income for the school. Similarly other principals had been appropriated considerable means to paint the school building and keep up repairs, and only a small fraction ever went for repairs and the rest went into the official's pocket. He would "*put*" or "*doz makena*" (steal) all else.

Will honesty now prevail? Have the cheats in government been chased out and their methods scoured of corruption? I must doubt it.

Then, he gives us an ironical rendition on the incompetence of his teachers, past and present, who were/are teaching subjects they didn't understand. He cites one particular person, the current (or was it more feasibly, the past) *saer-malim* at the girls' school, who had been his 6th grade math teacher and didn't even know enough math to explain arithmetics, but who was now teaching 11th grade trigonometry and physics. Then he mentioned the curly-headed watch-maker who apparently doesn't understand his subject either and leans heavily on the members of his class for help. This whole assessment is certainly, undeniably true, but the part about my old *modir* is yet to be sorted out. Or not.

In his second afternoon of trying, Tom sits in the mud hut, the chilly chambers of the post office, for several hours while a cross-legged turbaned creature plays with the misshapen toy of the early 20th century, a battery-operated telephone, attempting to get a call through to Kabul . . . We hear that the TB specialists have all been promised "a transfer," but as it has been delayed . . . they're basically bored and unemployed. But TB spreads. It is just that the government does not want foreigners (Americans) wandering the country, so they deny there is a problem with this deadly illness, although it is at epidemic proportions.

I know a bit about this. Change must begin with the outsider gaining the trust of his host, and the people, listening to them, learning about their lives, then helping them articulate what their priorities are, and then, only then, attempting to help them change positively, in ways that make the basis of health, education, employment, more accessible, more equally distributed. But the change must come from the society itself, not from foreigners who would think to impose it. And does PC encourage, allow, that approach? And, more important, if it is not a priority of a government, can any progress in these areas be made?

Saturday and Sunday T. had gone to the local bank, trying to start a checking account, and after signing and transcribing an endless set of papers, he apparently had ended his business there (and I had come one afternoon to sign papers, too). Then yesterday an illiterate, limping *bab*a lugged a huge roll book over to the school and told him he must sign yet another statement—there were apparently pages and pages of names of people who had yet to sign and neither the *baba* nor T. could discern his space. Finally, a student found the line. We are thinking that if it has been this difficult to put money into the bank, we'll have to requisition about three months in advance if we ever want to take any out.

. . . Another fresh tidbit: Mr. King Pushtu himself, Ali-jan (also, always sadly misplaced in this village) got word that he will be transferred to Kabul by the end of the week. He is ecstatic, and clearly which ever evil bureaucrat put him on the list to exile here, has been displaced or bribed into removing him, almost unheard of, after just one semester.

March 15, 1974

We set off this morning, a spring dawn, (with Brenda and a volunteer from Baglan named Bob) into a blindingly bright sun. We move, off past the foundations of the mud-tottering ancient fort, to a winding sand-rutted country lane that winds between the impossibly stiff foothills of purple twisted clay, and pocket valleys of greening fields, families squatting in the long, lean rows in bright children's skirts and bare legs, through two villages beneath the road where brown-baked workers handled drying camel and goat hides, the ghostly shapes of the skinned animals laying over mud wall and in the narrow road. We pause before an old men, toothless as a pirate, who sits by the road with a just-born goat, the tiny creature's umbilical coil still hanging between his wobbly legs. The old man scolds him in Farsi to stay near his basket. On we go, in the shadows of the hills, along the narrow path, between the small fields and brown-walled compounds to the river, pouring out below in muddy glory, the salvation of the valley (the children scattering as we round the bends, an early warning system which sends the women like haunted shadows clustering in their doorways to stare at us, too) the lean craning bodies of the families pausing with their shovels and wooden plows in their tiny fields and orchards.

Then we come upon three bow-legged cows dragging their half-yoke plows while their proud owner straddled his black stallion and spurred them on from the rear. And then we emerge, five centuries later, on the modern paved highway, the Russian-built northern road, and for a moment are deceived by it. Suddenly, a motley dressed, full-figured old merchant emerges from one of the beehive like mud huts beside the road and after greeting us lengthily in Persian, gestures wisely towards the bleak mountains and slowly greening fields, lord of all he surveys, it seems. He begins to explain, like two options for life—the destinations we might take. There is the city that lays in one direction up the road, or the Tangi (or Gorge) in the other. He offers us fistfuls of popcorn, then we move on.

March 17, 1974

> *[News from home, Dan is in school and needing maintenance to eat, David has returned home, the first time in 13 years, and is needing help. I worry at my inability to help either brother, yet the pressure remains, and mother is left to deal with it all . . .]*

It is in that, then, the lack of initiatives in changing century-bred nations of life and land and Allah, that we find most frustrating. The government, the programs, would have us sit down and listen to them, rather than grant us the freedom to sit down and present our version. Radicals, Christians, what would we say . . . . But in the best principal, of course, that is exactly where all "development" should start. With the people themselves who want change.

Volunteers from Iran, full of stories of outrageous prices, the challenge of having no support for their endeavors there and very limited food in the villages, stop in to buy Uzbek silk wall hangings (designs like candle drippings, old and running, faded maroon and rose colors) in our Teem (the covered bazaar) . . .

Today I help the *modir* translate the titles of the books we had brought from the Asia Foundation last November, and we speak with two Afghan boys, sons of a member of the Ministry of Foreign Affairs, who had lived in Washington a while and now live in Kabul, nephews of one of the teachers at the school. And will such children want to stay in Afghanistan? It is doubtful.

March 23, 1974

It is good to be anchored somewhere temporarily above it all, looking down and praising the immediate, the mellifluous subtle majesty of almond blossoms and green returning like a shy bride's train to the earth. Spring. It comes upon us with the suddenness of all the seasons here. By noon of its first day it is hot enough to be summer . . . .

Fariad appeared . . . this regional director has sour words for a new development in Kabul: the Ministry decided last week that 35 of the 40 recently-trained volunteers must stay and work in Kabul, rather than be sent to the many and far-flung places to the north, as originally planned.

Their alibi is that it is now new government policy to make all those (Afghan) teachers who had previously brushed off an assignment to the "sticks" in the past in order to stay in Kabul, to now go out to the places, as natives. Foreigners, likewise, should stay in their own "terrain"(Kabul). The implication for ourselves seem obvious: Are no other volunteers coming to the northern sites? Will we be the first and last English-speaking *haragees* to teach here? What of the much disregarded word, continuity?

Later in the week we are to hear a more precise, damning reasoning for this, voiced by a German-trained Afghan doctor visiting Mazar with some of the recent cycle volunteers. The intention of such government mandates, he claims is to gently phase out the too-balanced cold war tactic situation of American and Russian aid, while encouraging more neutral aid from Japan and Germany. Without straight-forwardly abolishing any project, the government wants to slowly cut back the impact of U.S. projects so that they will pretty much retreat of their own initiative for the immediate future.

. . . So there are now two incredibly remote sites in western Bamiyan to which someone may/must be sent, plus the agricultural school in Baglan, and Herat which is almost its own county, so full of solid schools it is. These are the only provincial sites officially "open."

[School: the saer-malim having to quiet some classes, the 9th class trying to convert "this kaffir" the day before Na-Roz . . . .]

Finally we set off on a crowded road in a tight taxi of sons and one *chadrie*d woman, for Mazar, to take in the excitement of Naroz eve, giving everything a mischievous tinge of delight . . . .

Eagerly, we move into the festival streets, where people parade around the mosque square or gather in the temporary tea shops and restaurants beside the carnival grounds (and children swing on wooden merry-go-rounds and ferris wheels—like those of our own childhood only in more basic form). Somehow we find ourself in one of the carnival tents, seated in a VIP section with a few other foreigners and a flock of richly-dressed, over-made up wives, sisters, and daughters of the carnival's promoter; all in front of us cut from one mold. When the program begins, a motley quartet sings the song of the Jemoriat (Republic), their funny man clown accompanying them in seeming fervor, just as he had when the same group had carried out the flag. There is singing of a popular song ("Black Eyes are Gone") and a series of slapstick conversations, and then appears a jungle gym playground of acrobats, whose rudimentary gymnastics barely keeps us awake, until at last we can leave entirely.

Thursday morning, Tom runs out to watch the raising of the *jantala* (flag). We walk again and watch in the crowded square, and . . . I meet one of the 13th class students at the Higher Teachers' College, one of three girls there from that class. She launches into a description of the hardships there, how women are highly persecuted, and the staff remain prejudiced against their presence. I am none too surprised to hear. Last year she had actually gone to see the Modir-i-Mareft to protest the mistreatment of women, and in particular the need for some facilities reserved for them. The men get dormitory, food, all priority; but the girls get nothing, not even rooms to share . . . A round-faced girl with soft eyes and black hair, she gives the immediate impression that she can not be very bright, that she must be a tad foolish, because one eye is crossed. But that passes as soon as she begins to speak, as she does with us in an excellent English. She is alert, polite, and intelligent, and dreams like all of them of perhaps some day going to study in the States . . . .

> *[I remark on the gathered people, multi-national, multi-agency, in Mazar for this holiday, and on the new and old volunteers, with whom we share a meal.]*

. . . . From Mazar, T and I go to Balkh, highlighting it all with one mistaken trip to a shrine outside of town. We were first picked up by some students in a *gaudi* who saw us walking; then brought by a wily old driver of 50 years with only half of a left foot, to the Haji-Piadaw shrine outside and to the south of the town. We saw a former masterpiece, the ruined halls, bone-ladden of the once majestic city, the old mosque from the Timurid times, now a pile of felled tiles and unfinished arches. The old shrine of the walking pilgrim is beautiful—the legendarily giant's throne, a mound of man-made caves. Its perfect skeleton of arches is carved in beautiful vine-like relief, shamrocks or wings and a thumbnail indenture—and obscuring the dates for these things, over time, it has been allowed to disintegrate, with most of the mud and plaster fallen.

I recall the words of a traveler in these parts at the turn of the century, who said of this site, after visiting Khulm:

"Balkh, a city of ancient fame, lies some 50 miles to the westward. The place, which once covered a circuit of nearly 20 miles, is now in a state of almost complete ruin. The whole of the northern half of the old city is one immense waste; the walls have been torn down into the most fantastic shapes by wind and weather, and the citadel is nothing but a mound . . . ."

March 24, 1974

> *(School opens again, with some logistical changes, The starting time of school is changed to 8 instead of 8:30. We are visited by the Provincial Inspector who demonstrates the elements of a good lesson. We now have other women teachers. This is a major change, of course. Ahmed, the PC cook from the previous summer, who has been out of work for six months, returns and tries to help us find a new cook, in a discussion which includes such options as the Nelsons' old cook from Gardez. We get news of a volunteer couple off to Ecuador because their program has failed . . . . and I get to host a visit by my favorite class . . .]*

Today the 11th class comes, full of gigglers bearing a box of candy for me. I bring out banana and orange cake I'd made yesterday; they try pieces without much comment, eat some nuts and candy and tea, tidy up behind themselves most graciously, look at the infamous Sears catalog, and listen to the radio and to some simple songs by me. The day before amid general hysteria, I had "taught" a song to the 9th class, and some sing it now by themselves. They watch me and my walls. Shogul dances an Indian maiden's soliloquy, Gulsom hums, Soliha sings a proud, sad Arabic melody, amid a lot of popular songs from Hindi movies. There is a short round with apples and oranges, another clean-up session, this latter also out of my hands as they insist I must do nothing, only sit, for all my trouble. They singularly make the inevitable expeditions to the *juab-e-choie* (outhouse), and soon it is 5:00 and they move homeward to chores . . .

. . . Tom volleys a ball all afternoon at the boys' school; he'd been afraid my students would be afraid of him, but he still got a peak of the small round of raised *chadris*, students at the gate, before he could safely flee . . . .

March 30-31, 1974

Yesterday we walk up the highway, then back through the Gardens where a shiny headed batch of freshly shaved draftees are having a picnic in the grass, and some brave duet is playing badminton, without a net.

Imagine those girls here then, coming with their *chadris* raised as Tom fled at the invasion, to sit and stare and sing, and nibble exactly three hours, and then to flee again into their 12th century streets, to go back to their houses to cook dinner in a mud oven and wash their hair (in a Saturday night ritual) with a concoction of fresh yogurt and river silt.

And on the days I am happy . . . my students smile up at me like dreamy princesses from some Arabian Night, the mountains are stoic and tranquil shoulders around us, the spring moss green on their bellies, a growth of substanceless magic; and every shopkeeper and farmer carries the proud, nobly molded head of the greatest sculptors, every arrangement of lines, eyes, countenance more elaborate and intriguing than the last . . .

Reading Jawaharlal Nehru's *The Discovery of India,* I am pulled in by his description of the crushing burden of the past in India, and most of Asia. I understand. It is the same strangling, tubercular burden that haunts Faulkner's individuals. Here one can see it on an epic scale. The pruned submission from being slapped so many times, the conqueror's highway; and the ultimate reduction of one's life to the barest motions so there is seldom the time or inclination to begin to change the quality, to up-raise it, to improve.

It's a morning as gray and damply drizzly as English spring. Wind and rain, after a dust storm, strip all the trees of their blossoms. Are we back to winter again? No, the valley is green.

April 1, 1974

. . . We see three generations of frogs in trio jumping out by the outhouse every night.

April 4, 1974

. . . And we discover a supposed phantom mountain, rising like dense shadows over the flat steppe lands to our north, what is in fact a mountain, but one we had not seen clearly before, or not at that angle . . .

Two or so days ago, I found myself alone with the principal, his gaunt, stooping figure, his plain, scalding mien, his actual shyness. I had come to school early, determined to finally present my respects and queries to him and his wife (about whom rumor in the form of the 11th class said she had had a miscarriage and been hospitalized in Kabul). I asked him how he was and if his household was well, and he explained, yes, but there had been a little problem, and he explained that his wife had had a baby but the child died; they had had (to another question, awkwardly named by me) no children, although he had taken the woman four years ago, and since she had lost three babies. Lamely then I said my Farsi resignations of pity, and the conversation ended.

Then the next day his wife, large and talkative as a patron of old wives' tales, is in the office with her sister (a mistaken guest in our class some days before, about whom Tajenisa had lied, "This is my cousin.") And again yesterday I speak briefly with them. The girl, sulky and bored, has taken the university entrance exam and is waiting to hear the results.

The sun is dripping in and out like a head of washed hair; cold weather chills in the air as long as the sun is absent . . .

Early this morning (spring-spangled), when I went out to buy some fresh breakfast bread (Amore M'med is in Kunduz for a few days—for yes, he is again helping us) the old *saroykeeper*, a fast-talking individual who rents stables like rooms in the middle of the bazaar to the unwary for the equivalent of $2 a month per cavern, and entrepreneur-like has both thumbs in most all village functions as well, came up to me with a large almond tree branch full of perhaps a hundred tiny silkworms. The clusters hang in the first webs of their raw spun silk threads, and he asks me in his growling sweet Farsi if any creatures like these lived in the almond trees in my yard (we've only got one). I tell him, "No," and he moves away, further down the mud-rutted lane, stopping to ask other people, waving his precious bough like some royal scepter, motioning at the sun to suggest the brightness of the magic threads . . .

Later, when I mention the man with the silkworms, one of the teachers at the school tells me the legend:

The most famous silkweavers have always lived on the border of Afghanistan and Turkestan, not far from this village, perhaps. They claim they learned their trade from "Tales of the Prophets." The story goes that once Job had been severely tested by God, he was reinstated and healed. Specifically, a stream was made by the Angel Gabriel and Job was put in it and all of his sores closed up and new and healthy skin replaced the boils and other ailments. Then, the worms that had been in him were recycled, so to speak. Some, after leaving his body, crawled up the trees. These were then "fashioned into silkworms." Later Imam Jaffery Sedique, the first silk weaver, was given the directions of how to use the worms and the threads they spin directly from Saint Daud. So, his worms began to make silk threads. Because of its origins among the most saintly, there are still special rules for those who can handle silk worms.

April 7, 1974

. . . Going back to school . . . I learn that one of the teachers has died, as of last Thursday. He was an old thin string of a man who spoke slowly, but who always tried to greet me, to give "salaam" and an encouraging nod. Today everyone asks me why I haven't gone to his house. But I had not known and now the three days for visiting are past. I quickly tell them I offered prayers for his peace. One day, then, he sat in his morbid firmness, austere but good, and the next he was just gone.

For an hour I sit in the half-light of a thunderstorm; it passes, the wind stops rustling, the air is cool again.

April 9, 1974

Yesterday the *saer-malim* stopped me to ask why I don't stay at the school after I finish my classes, and talk with him, why I am always so quickly running off home. A whole flock of students gather around us, and I am too embarrassed to answer in either English or Farsi, for fear of one or the other understanding and laughing. So I bow, nod my head and smile to avoid his question, and leave, after asking him to please forgive me (*bubakshane*). I am staggered by my lack of professionalism. But I can not overcome my shyness. And there is no way to explain that silliness, pervasive as it is, to anyone. I fear that I will, as an old lady of 60 or 70 one day, yet be afraid to sit and talk or test myself around others, because this shyness will dominate me my entire life, cut short careers, limit friends and social interactions. Who can say, and is it not a silly western thing in the midst of these people who try to survive life itself, so often futilely? . . . .

T and I wander through the bazaar for an hour, price some snuff boxes with bone miniature painted lids, listen to the price of *gilims* (woven rugs) and watch some jewelers shaping bangles and pearls out of copper and silver-colored wire.

A knocking at our gate this morning materializes as the *namsad* (fiance) of Zahra's cousin, come with an invitation to her wedding tomorrow. We wander to Tom's students house to ask after the etiquette of a local wedding, to find out when we are actually expected to come, and if we must bring a gift.

Afterwards, he leads us, at beginning and end, to a *cosah* (water jug) factory, a young man's potter's wheel and the heat of Hades for the kiln, and to a flour grist mill where wheat is shattered into powder. In between we sit in his house over tea and nuts and hard candy, meet his father, sit and then are blessed with *bakshesh* (a silk scarf with a small girl's Kandahar stitching).

We finish a dinner too large for either our eyes or our stomach, are near its end, when Armoe M'med appears at the gate, surveys the "new" kitchen a moment and then comes inside. He has scarcely exchanged his wealth of greetings and told us about how he sells goods in the field in Mazar and then sleeps in a a teahouse, when he asks if he might finish our bowl of rice. We give it to him, with some tea. He eats like the starved. He requests we send more wash for his wife, who has been doing our laundry, and since his work in Mazar is finished, he wants more work from us if there's ever the occasion. His hands shake. He tells us that he has seen my old *modir* almost every day; and the man now wears a white turban. He stares after our Kabul cook. And what do we say to a dying man's questions? Is it nerves, then, his mind, that are slipping away?

April 12-13, 1974

There is so much tradition in an Afghan wedding. We've sampled bits and pieces of several in our months here, but, reflecting, try to recall its elements, its preparation, its protocol. From "Afghanistan for the Afghan," Sirdar Ikbal Ali Shan's writings, comes the following, roughly paraphrased and excerpted (Note: I use his transliteration, which does not match my own):

> Betrothal and marriage:
>
> A woman acts as a social spy, the families negotiate, always mindful of class, sect, or friendship between the families. A proposal is made two or three years later by a "party of ladies" who visit the girl's house. The mother listens quietly, then asks for time since the girl is still young and does not yet understand the *nashaib* and *faraz* of the world (the ups and downs). The visitors eat "*duktar talab*" (daughter seeking). A back and forth exchange is expected. An expression explains: "consent is not given until the young man's people wear out their shoes by paying calls, until the soles are as thin as the thin layer of an onion."
>
> . . . When an agreement is reached, a date is set for the *qand shikini*, the "sugar breaking" which designates a betrothal. The family holds a *mahfil,* a scene of mirth and singing. Everyone calls "*khush amad*i," "*mada nabashi.*" In warm weather they will serve "*sharbat;*" in winter green tea. Then the people retire and formally re-enter the hall, with the women veiled and the men now present. The grandfather stands and takes from the tray the gifts for the family and says who they are from and what they are. The father of the groom brings a tray with four sugar cones, each 1.8 inches tall and covered with red silk embroidered with gold threads. They break the cones and say a prayer. If the cones break into many fragments, it is a good sign . . .
>
> The daughter is meanwhile in a room alone, and no one can see her.
>
> There are more visits and a wedding date is set. The girl begins apprenticing in the kitchen and also makes gold-threaded hats for her father and brother. She is sad. The announcement of the date reads like this:

"We shall give our boy your daughter's slavery on such and such a day."

. . . Six to eight months ahead of the marriage ceremony, all the women in the household sew, and embroider a trousseau. Specific gifts are given by the mother to the daughter for her wedding.

The bridegroom sends out the invitations, and writes a poem.

A *shadi-khan*a, or marriage house is built.

The bride is made up, including pulling out her hairs, powdering her for the "buying green grass" (*sabza kadan*) ceremony.

At the wedding, dishes are served, usually eight or nine courses are served. These include: *nan, shorba* (curry, meat, potatoes, meat), *korma* (meat fried in butter with curry onions and other flavors); *kofta* (round balls of minced meat fried in butter); *shami kebab* (flat, minced meat fried in butter with ginger or mint); *biryani* of pilau (rice, meat, salt steamed); *zarda* (rice sweetened, boiled, steamed with currants, almonds, saffron); *firini* (rice-thin pudding); and s*hir mal* (round flat cakes, slightly sweetened).

The breakfast dishes are fried chicken, *samoso, shir mil.* No food is served at afternoon tea . . . Then there is a procession to see the gifts, after lunch, during which people call: "*khanaysh abad,*" meaning "May this house be full and prosperous." There are breaks for the call to prayer, the *zuhr* at midday.

The bride continues getting beautified. Her hair is perfumed, her face powdered, her eyes brightened. Stars will be put on her face.

There is another call to prayer (*asr*), after which the gifts are given out.

The next day is the *nikah naman*—the marriage certificate and the *mahr nam*a—the legal document which states what the wife's legal position will be during the marriage.

> The ceremony goes on all night. The *qazi* reads the documents and signs them, with the father of the bride, the father of the bridegroom, and four witnesses, the *shahids*. Then the bride and groom put their thumbprints on the documents.
>
> Then the bride shows her face to her husband, first through a mini "unveiling. They sample from a silver bowl full of sherbet and white rice pudding. Then there is a concert.

So now we've seen, from the seat of the honored guests, an Afghan wedding of someone we actually know. In the morning three boys came at 9:30 to accompany us to the house, Tom to go to one, me to another. We weren't quite ready, so had one of the boys, a cousin of those to be married, come back a little later while Tom dashed out to find some candy, since our still-muddled thinking was that it would never do to approach the house empty-handed, and that we might at the least offer a hostess gift.

Down the village lane, around a corner or two or three, and I am entered into a large yard where a hundred brightly dressed women stand like butterflies flitting on a broad veranda porch. In the figures, I find some of my own students, the favored cousins of this family affair, Zeagul of the eight class, Zahra, Falora and several others of the eleventh, Ruhna of the ninth, gaily, almost gaudily decorated with broad thick spangles, necklaces and earrings and broaches, hand bags and high heels, wide mascaraed eyes and tinted nails and lips, and a flutter of bright shining dresses and pants. I am salaamed and welcomed, discreetly set down the courtesy gift as I shed my old spring coat, and scarf, and am moved toward the honored corner of the first room of women. Stared at not unkindly, there I sit awhile, with the radio tape deck blaring Afghan-Indian dances, as first some of the tiny girls, lithe as spring weeds on a river bank, dance traditional movements, and then outbid each other to have the older daughters of the household dance.

In a bit the *modir's* wife and his sister, Kabul standard bearers, appear and are seated beside me. They invite new conversation. In the long hall the women sit taciturn against the walls, under the windows, and look out without talking. The faces shift, two young princesses in long-skirted gowns and stiffly crowned hair sit silently opposite me for a while, old grandmothers are lined up, in their matron caps and white scarves, directly along the wall beside me, and children made up like favorite dolls move in between these relatives' arms.

I next go into the bride's room, Tiara, a slim swanlike girl in her white *tanban* and simple top now, who is standing behind a curtain in a deepset medieval window seat, her hair in curlers. She holds two burning candles in each hand, in what must be a Moslem rite of prayer and purity, I imagine. Then I move back to the veranda, to sit on (obviously the family's pride) a large, overstuffed fake leather coach, and am served with my students' conversation and a tray of tea. The first is whisked from me and replaced with another when I unwittingly indicate a preference for black tea. I meet Zahra's mother, a rather cloudy-minded, withered creature, but with her daughter's large, soft eyes, and I soon learn that this woman had born no other children. She gives me her wrong hand to shake, consternating her child, but she soon brings a chubby boy to smile at me, who is also her son but—Zahra explains in a strange English—"she had him from another place."

Back into the room of maids and matrons, I go, joined now by the semi-suave *modir*'s wife's sister. The *modir's* wife's stockinged legs covered by a blanket in her corner, her large body in a dark black and blue velvet dress, she looks the part of another place and age. The dancing contests begin again, from the gyrations of the Kabul student to the young girls' graceful songs, and then the harsh, jarring movements of a professional performer take over, a woman who with her band of two small boys, one on a harmonium, the other on a drum and tanbor, regulate the feeling of the room and collect money in between her brawling song and gyrating dances.

Then it grows almost quiet for a while, and the big clay painted water pipe, the *choki,* is brought around for the true matrons of the gathering, who roll the tobacco leaves into a thinner powder in their hands, then stuff it into the pipe and draw greedily, old cronies missing only a beard and dagger eyes.

I hear from the Kabulis that this is all different from such affairs in Kabul, where men and women are together, where a wedding and reception now are all catered in a hotel. And the maidens talk about staying maidens and the matrons with their gathering wrinkles tease them. I am led back again to the bride's room (here are all my students, the *tanboned* ones in simple summer silks, their long hair down where other decorations hadn't been afforded, and with them the whole 12th

grade class, the bride's friends.) There is more dancing, and a little singing from the dancer's sons. I meet a second year student from the Mazar Teacher's college, who speaks excellent English, all made up now like a daughter of Jezebel, but beneath her mien obviously warm and with a quick mind. She speaks to me politely, as in the corner the bride's mother tucks a few more stitches into her daughter's green gown, and claims that next year she will teach here, at Lycee Mahasty.

By now it is almost 2:00 and dinner is laid out the whole length of the veranda. We (the *modir's* wife, sister and I) are the first seated, at the top of the assembly, and we are pushed to begin to eat the *pilau* and *korma* and peppers and bread, that make up the feast. A spoon is brought for me, and the others, my partners at imitating the Afghan dexterity of fingers, are quickly sighted. Then the feast is all cleaned up and while old hooded women, like weathered nuns, move up and down the table clothes dismembering it, our own "service" comes from a dark, jolly deaf women with the square hands and nose of Van Gogh's "Potato Eaters," who grins and politely inquires after the "foreign" guests. There is more talk, this time with the 12th class, one of whom looks strangely like my niece Leslie . . . .

But the marriage throne is being set up, the couch is covered with an ornate rug and in front of it is set a green basket of flowers, plates of powdered sweet bread and the sweet syrup juice {*shabat*) the newly weds are to feed each other, bowls of oranges and apples and candies, and a cracked, thickly iced cake—brought heavily from Mazar—and which is now rather pathetically balanced in the center of the table. I am made, with the other two women—the *modir's* wife and her sister—to sit directly beside the bridal throne, to better see it all, and be seen. Now children and cronies and all assembled crowd around, the dancer and musicians play again, and the bride and husband and mother (clutching her child's thin arm as if to hold up a broken limb) move slowly along the length of the porch. They solemnly inch in like bearers of the dead to the honored seat. The song is now the traditional wedding march. The Koran, wrapped in green silk, is held like a canopy over the couple. They stand weakly, the girl's chin buried in her chest with modesty. She now has the green gown on, is stockinged, wears a green, tented veil, and both she and her husband have a stiff harness of green paper flowers around their necks.

Finally, they sit, mutely, both shaking. Candles are lighted on their tray, one by the groom and with the same match the other by the bride. The box of rings is opened; the rings are put on, two for the bride, one for her husband. Meanwhile wrapped in its green silks, the Koran like a baby pillow has been held over the couple's head from the moment they entered. Spoonfuls of the sweet juice are fed each to the other, then spoonfuls of the traditional crumbs, than a morsel of the cake.

Then chaos begins. Like hungry animals after a kill, children and old ladies and the fair maidens close in upon the richness on the table, each more afraid than the other that they might miss some of it. The newly-joined couple sit meekly, crumbs get scattered in the *modir's* wife's lap, the tray of candies is tottering to the floor, and someone has begun to cry and another has pushed. The scene is coarsely comical. The engineer (the groom) is to go to Russia for five years now and get his doctorate, then return and teach at the Polytechnic (his alma mater) in Kabul; his bride will follow and be able to study at the university as well. Of this country jousting—if he even notices it—what must he think?

But now we must leave, the roles set. Tom is fetched to take me home, given eye none of the other men are availed of, sees the bride and groom and is much seen by everyone there. We walk to the road with the Kabuli duo, wait with them until a *gaudi* is fetched, watch the army of ghosts, all the *chadried* young girls, leave soon after ourselves, and quickly find ourselves on the road home.

Tom tells me that his side of the house was much more sombre than ours, that the men sat largely without talking, ate two full meals, then went off to the mosque. He had observed the legal part of the ceremony, at which the bride's procreative powers are purchased (this one for 20,000 *afs*) in the presence of a mullah and the so-called Koran wedding, with the groom and the bride's representative, in this case the uncle, Zahra's father. There was one joke, played leanly by an old man who claimed his wife was near a hundred now, had no more teeth, and so he reckoned he was entitled to a new mate. And Tom was taken to the top of the house from which he fathomed where the house was in relation to the rest of the village and countryside, and heard the groom's story also. Honored as well with the chief guest's seat, he had been well-tended.

. . . Home, feeling warm, we nod together, thinking again of the kindness and generosity, if riddled often times with strangeness, that these people are so capable of, and of the never-ending deference to and respect for the stranger, the guest. We know we will go to many such social functions now, that the stubborn shyness and sense of boundaries with which we had arrived, can be abandoned gracefully.

. . . And the night is like a boat on a stormy sea, the wind a heinously large bellows, the windows rattling . . . and a cold wind dances around the valley.

April 17, 1974

As I finish off that pulsating version of destruction's tale by I.B. Singer ("The Family Moskat"), feeling ill with it all, I feel too cloistered by the non-abating pessimism of life, everyone's life, the Jew's burden of the past, the Moslems who have no future. Reading a new shipment of the *Kabul Times,* heavy (among the naïve political salutation), my mood plummets further with its predictions of more drought and famine in every continent, except Europe and North America, it would seem, where the energy used to route television reception would be sufficient to purchase the fertilizer needed for underdeveloped countries to grow food . . .

We are debating . . . some quotation, that (to the effect) beauty exists before and after humans perceive it, and (a second) that nothing is beautiful but that it is marked by a certain strangeness, even a grotesqueness. The first I interpret as existing within a chain of natural beings, the separate life of natural phenomenon apart from man. How can we condone the kind of anthropocentric thinking that has made man, taking free reign of at least the externals of this world, bully and pervert and ultimately destroy himself, his own kind, the land and air and water that maintain him? Yet not all men have, nor can they ever have equal power to so shape their environments, so are they then not men? Words could veil anything. So the people in the Sahel lands, whose lives have never been more than subsistence, in the face of the galloping Sahara's spread, have now eaten all the seeds they should have planted. Two-thirds of the children born in the Middle Eastern countries don't reach adulthood, or see childhood, the rest reach it deeply scarred, mentally and physically defective and ailing . . . and in the States people still play their games in the name of causes, vacuous and jarring as atomic holocaust, and we, too, have our ignored poor, and our ingrained racism.

What do two people who can see it . . . as from a gradual distance, do about it? What right or power or sustaining wish have they to intervene—even if they and a million others like them choose to?

April 19, 1974

[Guests arrive . . . . I decided to take off the afternoon and peruse the market with them]

A haggling, rather subdued, or alternately too loud session of purchasing, seems to be the style of this chain of foreigners. Then along come the largest crowd of Russian visitors on an Afghan Tour bus, I have witnessed here—substantially-built, gesturing people, old ladies with bulging upper arms, bare, heavy bosoms and buttocks, garbed in stretch tops and pants, and followed by two barrel-chested men. They could not be more culturally jarring, or insensitive. But we do not talk with them, so how can we know anything about them?

[Books from the Asia Foundation are delivered by Fariad]

I set off to take the books to the school, then encounter a student who explains that the principal has left and set off to Mazar . . . . We go up to the road in a taxi, are soon the center of a ring of questioners who only half know us us after the winter's reclusiveness, but have spotted us for new blood . . .

[Some elderly couple with fine principals, speak with us in the bazaar, people careful of, caring of, the culture, the residents . . .]

Thursday morning in Mazar, on a shopping spree we mingle our sweating bodies and red-burnt eyes among the crowds of brightly dressed Turkomen families and Kutchi jewelry sellers along the booths and sidewalk, dropping—like a penny—1900 *afs* . . .

April 21, 1974, 1st of Saur

Yesterday, I set off to the school to present the 75 books which we had gotten from Asia Foundation last January, and which had only now gotten up here. The first step should have warned me of the indelicacies of those that would follow. After all, I had been through this ceremony of reserved concern (only much later articulated as gratitude). Aman, our new cook from Kabul, loaded the two spilling boxes on a *gaudi*, and bracing myself alternatively between the seat and the boxes, I managed to stay intact as the *gaudiwan* steered his horse and buggy across the bazaar and down the bumpy road beside the river. He stopped the horses and carried the boxes to the gate of the school where the dwarfish *baba* preceded to carry them about ten feet, before delegating half of them to the tiny fretful half-blind janitoress. In this slaving arrangement, we arrived at the modir's desk.

*I explained briefly about the books and gift and program, gave him a copy of the Farsi edition of the Asia Foundation program, and watche*d as the secretary began writing a list. A few other teachers wandered in, but none greeted me as such, as they fingered the books cautiously, and one or two asked where they came from. Hearing the secretary nod quietly in my direction, I was frightened and disappointed, as both the *modir* and the *saer-malim* seemed genuinely annoyed by it all. Perhaps my sensing was wrong, but half sad and angry I finally set off for class. The Farsi teacher stopped to thank me; I can never quite know if he laughs at me or with me

After lunch I checked again in the office, and spoke to the secretary-clerk. Again, after class, I came for the list to be sent to Asia Foundation, waiting quietly as the secretary made another copy of the list and as the *modir* scribbled some unknowable message on the face of the paper. (This all in contrast to Faroodullah's timid note in English, six months ago, after his initial restraint, when he was a little awed, seemingly thankful for these beginnings of a library). And I left, more or less dismissed, sensing again the *modir* was less than pleased with it all, sensing I had somehow offended him, discredited him. I don't know. I can not understand what is the source. Politics? Or responsibility no one wants to take, for caring for these gifts?

Then walking home, it hit me, just as it had back in the fall. With the new restrictions of what and where foreigners can do, and obvious censorship of materials, all post-coup (if not before), and the tenuousness of positions here as judged by one's political appearance, perhaps they were all frightened of getting in trouble for housing a collection from westerners . . . . But a library?

> *[T. has written a letter to the Peace Corps PRIST people, about how to prepare future volunteers better. We talk of how we are eternally the outsiders here because of stark differences in our societies; how no one talks about literature or poetry or other cultural things despite the history; and, in fact, how one is struck by an absence of any sense of real history or place despite this having been a cross roads for the world and civilizations for millenniums.]*

Note: Twenty years later, in 1993, I will read William Dalrymple's book, City of Djinns: A Year in Delhi,*and find a net within which to lure, catch and see the reality of Kabul and Afghanistan, the city and land where I had lived the decades before.*

There lingered, unarticulated, unknowable, from the centuries before in the Afghanistan of our day some of the same elements which defined Delhi, and its Moslem intelligentsia discontentedly exiled to Karachi following the Partition in 1949. I recall the words of Ahmed Ali, who had written Twilight in Delhi, claiming angrily: "I never opted for Pakistan . . . the civilization I belonged in . . . the civilization of Delhi came into being through the mingling of too different cultures, Hindi and Moslem. That civilization flourished for one thousand years undisturbed until certain people came along and denied that great mingling had taken place." (Dalyrimple 63).

It makes sense to go back to the common stock of what also ruled part of Afghanistan in those days, or atleast what marked both the end of one kind of glory and the beginning of its empirical days, the Mughal Empire. For it was Genghis Khan who demolished much of Afghanistan's treasures and inheritance, and the Moghul emperors, were all Moslems and direct descendants of Genghis Khan, through Chagatai Khan and Timur. The "classic period" of the empire started in 1556 with the accession of Akbar the Great.

Just as the period before, under his father Shah Jahan, was the golden age for Mughal architecture and arts, with the construction of the dazzling Taj Mahal, Red Fort, Jama Masjid of Delhi, and the Lahore Fort, it had been during Aurangzeb's reign that the Moghul Empire reached the height of its territorial expansion. The Empire stretched to more than 1.25 million square miles, ruled over more than 150 million subjects, nearly a quarter of the world's population, with a combined GDP estimated at over $90 billion.

Persian influence across the swath of lands and peoples was paramount, and Afghanistan was periodically at its epicenter. Babur, the first Mogul emperor, was descended on his mother's side from Genghis Khan who had conquered Asia from the Black Sea to Beijing, and Timur-i-lang (Tamburlaine), whose empire had stretched from the the Caucus to Delhi on his father's, began his sovereignty and intense state-building by conquering Kabul and surrounding areas. He cultivated literature, science, and music, struggled against the insubordination of the Afghan tribes, and eventually conquered Pakistan. By 1523 he controlled Lahore, then he moved on to India, a land whose gold and silver he admired but little else, and from which he pined for the cool crisp mountains and gardens of Kabul. The fifth Mogul emperor, Babur's great-great grandson, Shah Jahan, redesigned the Imperial apartments in Kabul to impress his father Emperor Jehangar, eldest son of Akbar. During much of the supremacy of the Moghuls, classical Persian was the language of the educated at the court

As with the lands to its west, the kingdoms which eventually became parts of Nepal, Afghanistan, Russia, Iran and Pakistan, visitors came to Delhi and the city thrived. In the end of the 1600's and early 1700's when Sogfsrjung, a Persian nobleman from Nishapur in Iranian Khorasan arrived, and when Aurungzeb was still emperor, Dalyrimple describers the Delhi which he saw as "still the most magnificent and most populous city between Istanbul and Eno (Tokyo)." Larger than Paris or London, it had over two million inhabitants and sparkled with its gold-topped domes and mosques.

But by the last emperor's death, Nadir Shah had come and gone, had taken eight generations of accumulated riches, seen the murder of three emperors, and Delhi was "a city of gutted ruins."

History speaks of "the Twilight," the period between the Persian massacre of 1739 by Nadir Shah, which hastened the decline of the Mughal Empire which had begun with the death of Auranzeb, the last great Moghul, in 1707; and the vicious hangings and killings following the British recapture of Delhi after the 1857 Indian Mutiny. This latter, in September, included the British capture and razing of the Red Fort, the trying, execution, hanging or shooting out of cannons of 3,000 Delhi-wallis, the exile of the last emperor to Rangoon and the shooting of his children, the banning of all Moslem residents from the city for two years, the locating out of the gates of the city of all its inhabitants, to starve, the selling of the mosques to Hindu bankers to be used as bakeries and stables, and the explosion of what Dalrymple called "the worst of British qualities: philistinism, narrow-mindedness, bigotry, and vengefulness," even as the Brits looked at their route of Delhi as "a proud victory."

Blue Babies and Drought, 1998-2001

Nature itself conspired
on the heels of Soviet war,
the five year civil war,
an already rainless half decade
turned into a major three year drought.
It swept through Afghanistan's northeast and southeast areas,
combined with the steady deforestation of fragile valleys and slopes
as people struggled to find fuel for cooking and heat,
and factions competing for power,
burned and razed fields and villages.

Unabated, poverty, destitution riddled,
ravaged Afghanistan,
removing would-be breadwinners
leaving women and children destitute.

Driven from their homes and villages
people flooded internally displaced persons centers,
young children in Kabul or other cities,
landed in children's shelters, orphanages
left over from the Soviet era
or opened by the few humanitarian groups
still working in the country.

The cycle moved around and around,
repeating itself as Afghan villagers and city dwellers fled,
then with each possibility of order, returned.

They came back,
hungry to be back in their *waton*, their homeland,
a pull so fundamental it belied political reality:
charred earth and waterless plains,
a million home shortage of shelter,
land-mined or poisoned fields,
the treacherous Taliban.

Sometimes, though, a scale of sorrow all its own:
hundred of thousands of starving people,
several days walk from Herat
followed the rumor:
The UN has sent food, fuel, water, shelter.

Thousands from other provinces pulled up roots,
set off to what they thought would be survival,
only to end in "Kumpa Masa," or "Butchery Camp."

Young mothers looked for days for their blue babies,
infants starved, dead from the cold, exposure
but mothers still kept cradling
the small corpses.

It never had to be that way.
People struggled to be resilient,
determined to survive.
They needed so little:
warm clothes, clean water,
heat and food and simple shelter.
But it did not come to Kumpa Masa.

For winter's survivors,
the next season's heat festered and clawed,
the sun piercing dark clouds
hanging above once purple hills and circles of mountains.
Amber high plateaus receded on the horizon,
as a brown haze enveloped everything.

A rancid fire, the dust moved,
distributed from some ancient plain
and forever restless.
In dry motion, like human ash exhumed from quiet graves,
it drifted indefinitely.
It sifted and ground, stung eyes,
stiffened hair, choked lungs and nostrils.
An abrasive cover, it permeated clothing and flesh,

melding human effort and form to the dirty fog,
relentlessly dismissing geography and history.

On such a stage
grown men and women gathered like old rags,
desperate to absorb the largess of humanitarian aid,
waited with dented pot and outstretched hands
for flour, oil, blankets, tents, and water to keep them alive.
Small children looked out of scabby faces and bold brown eyes
made old beyond their years with violence witnessed
and families shattered.
In Mazar. In Sare-pul. In Maimana. In Kabul.

VI

APPROACHING ONE YEAR

April 22, 1974

We attended another wedding last night, at a house with a spacious garden out of Eden, and a hundred courtyards and rooms where real carpets spread, and 1200 people (counting those for lunch). Another session of divine stares, in the eyes of students and their relatives, as we sat (again I was beside the *modir's* wife and her sister Zudrah—who has just heard she was not accepted to the university) from 6 until 10, rising only to give the three kiss greeting expected of all women, each time with an introduction. How strange to sit so long among so many people who barely talk, and to have them tell you you are beautiful, to have them ask what kind of cream you use, and why and how you don't have babies, and to turn to watch them yourselves—the raven-headed young girls here on their best behaviors, perhaps to be sighted by a future mother-in-law, the elephant-bosomed mother letting down one corner of a dress and feeding a tiny sleeping infant with her weight of richness, the tribe of shawled matrons lining the walls in postures of repose, and the 16-year old married child, powdered white, in spangles, grinning back at you like a large porcelain doll.

Outside the musicians are ringed by the younger girls, and the light fades one moment and comes on again while a hundred large lamps dot the gardens like giant fireflies. By 10 we still haven't eaten, but Tom sends a messenger to say we must leave. I explain to the hostess, call on the excuse that "my husband needs to return home for some important work and I should go with him." One of the new women teachers at the school (her sister-in-law is the bride) nods, then insists I eat first. This is done after a quick fashion, and I finally excuse myself, after stealing one baffled vision of the bride. Her hair is in curlers, her eyes swollen from crying, and she sits in a room apart, seemingly engaged in rocking a baby's cradle. It is mysterious. A lantern bearer walks us home, the village now a dark shadow of the unknowable, a land of barking dogs and specters who cry out from the side of the road upon seeing us. A hot breezeless night and we stand pounding on the first gate, approached in one moment by a *dhukandar* who stays every night in his shop. Then Aman has opened the gate and we move into our un-curtained box of yellow lights

Today . . . playing the Emperor of Ice Cream as we squatted in a cloud of cotton in the afternoon, beating it and then stuffing it into our should-be mattress, we ended up with a lumpy, considerably diminished mound of air and cottonseed.

There is a splattering of rain and a breath . . .

April 26, 1974

•

The sounds of the town: the harbinger of everything, birds, crows, wrens, pigeons, scattering and starting in great choruses of cacophony. In the background a diesel tractor is eating up the stone hills between the road and marketplace where trees are to be planted. The metal workers in their alley are only a dull background now, as if their motions, distorted by heat, are of the realm of night crickets.

We watch a horse ant carry the carcass of a cricket or waterbug up the wall and into one of their cities.

In the early dusk Tom's student cames to sip tea and talk. He explains how all day people have been praying at the mosque, and how those who have much are giving away rice soup to the poor, all in the name of Allah, to elicit the much-needed rain.

"If there is no rain (for there was little snow this year), there will be no wheat."

He explains how people starved three years ago, when there was no wheat crop, when camels and cows and sheep were sold for a tenth of their value, rather than be starved to death in the grassless field. How slim the border between drought and subsistence and plenty always hovers here, where people's survival is so closely dependent on the seasons, the gift of rain and water.

The blind man comes a third time to our gate. We give him coins, then send him away, not wanting to have beggars haunt our gate. But should we? . . .

Hamia and the teacher Jamila and Rozia . . . from the 9th class and a bevy of girls, along with old wilted women who must be their aunts or mothers, greet me as we walked toward the Gardens before supper. They give me all their roses, and ask if I feel unhappy in this country, at home . . . .

Old men clutching them like handkerchiefs, moaning adolescents in spring love, the town's full of rose-sniffers. It seems a public cult whose members emulate the great friendly bull Ferdinand who spent his life inhaling buttercups in a Spanish meadow, for all his build and breeding, unsuitable to fight . . . . There was a tractor in the town lot, down by the river bridge, surrounded all afternoon by onlookers, who watched five men's weeks worth of work being done perfectly by one small turbaned operator in the great gyrating cab, his pair of scurrying claws chewing and smoothing the ground. Tom's student says the loud, drawn-out noise is making his head hurt. "With this work's noise, none of my people can sleep . . ."

And the air is full of bursting spots of black, flocks of migrating birds, "the mulberry eaters," who come here for a month each year from India; and then disappear. These are patterns of life that go on so much more evenly than man's, creatures who move by the scent of the wind, their time ripe, while we stand expecting a startling message, deaf to the subtleties.

And if no more rains come, and if the encircling droughts of Africa and central India spread, and if no one can halt it, and if a million people die in a week, and another the next, and so on, . . . and if we can't even imagine what the record of these happenings can mean—are we any more alive? What right is ours as privileged westeners to remain fed and standing, while they are swallowed by hell's sands? . . . .

Last night we heard wedding drums and a flute pass through the bazaar: a 13-year old girl and a 16-year old boy were married.

We learned the name of the silky black and white winged birds with the long tail, who glide with wings outspread and perch with possessiveness: it is a magpie, the creature common to the whole world, but perhaps not at this size, the bird famous for its loud chatter and its ability to collect potentially useful odds and ends for its purposes.

A thunderstorm comes, the ground is allowed a quick, thin downfall of rain for a few seconds, then puckers dry again. We crush the crippling life out of a small scorpion in the *tashknob.* Within 20 minutes an unbroken file of ants had entered to carry away its body.

The night huddles, as warm as a mother's lap, but broad, so broad it makes you feel empty to stand in it; yet I stand under the moon-less sky in my night gown, fancying myself a wanderer in thought, wanting like some pain to reach up in a dance and draw those stars closer, always watching for the corner of light from the end of the wall where Tom stands on the shed, wanting him to ponder me like a night's poetry, to see me as he comes out, and to understand, by all the ways I was there, how very alone this creature has grown . . . .

April 29

[We punctuate the days with philosophical talks, the latest long discussion with T. about world religions, and which of the Christ, Buddha or Mohamed had had the better philosophy and life; and later we worry,] concerned about how conservative we will have to become in the States, how difficult it will be to have sympathy with a particular cause—laborers looking for a second car in the garage, college students' spring freedom with long hair and organic greens, when the people of this world, what we'd experienced here, lack even the dignity of daily bread. I suggest it is perhaps a matter of levels of existence, that here there was little above that basic, bare animal purpose of survival; whereas in the States there was a security and abundance that gave man's mind free reign to pursue other goals.

"Yes, but . . ." we both agree. How much more perverse it still all is that people who are themselves out of danger, think only of their material comforts,—not knowledge or thought as something particularly divine. And they refuse, will not even begin to consider the problems of the rest of the world . . . But none of this thought is even vaguely new, and we who criticize what our cook brings us evenings, are as much hypocrites as the rest.

How little time I give to thought in these pages, to re-creating, invoking ideas or images from those million pages and voices I've read. this past year, in the long silences and weary rests . . . .

I was . . . saddened today at the way the 8th graders made fun of the new Persian teacher at the school: he is quite heavy, with one scarred eye, and they jeered at him. I had thought this was one thing startling good about Afghans, that they had too much humility and hurt to make fun of a physical handicap in another. But, thoughtless cruelty as this appears must be learned, or is it an instinctive response, to reject what is different and strange as beneath you? Or, is it only these girls, cowering on the first step of what they fancy to be the trappings of modernity, trying like barnyard cocks to exert their own superiority against all odds . . .

Or, is there perhaps some story about this man which they know and I can not imagine?

In a country where the poetry comes from stones, where there is everywhere the response of two elements, man of the dust, returned to the dust, man and dirt (only water a gurgling reprieve, lost to the relationship) why can't I find the words of a Tolstoy, or the vision of a St. John, why haven't I the discipline of a blind child learning to read, seeking to unlock the secrets of a dark world?

And the night comes up again, a poetic refrain, the suspension and yet the support of all reason. We are Shakespeare's substance, for dreams, yet ourselves the dreamers, moving across the shrouds of night with heads like empty chalices seeking wine.

Sometimes I see the mountain shadows of Thomas Wolfe's childhood with its effigy of a home, sifted to the naked motions of family life, and wonder where the incubus child has gone to. Better a Nashville afternoon with Agee's father's sudden death than the hostility lingering image of our own forgetfulness. You see that so entirely what I write is a stripping back of my malformed present to resuscitate those images more carefully bred into me . . . but I picture them leaner than they could have ever been and have neither Daedalus's sea, Faulkner's dark histories, nor Chekhov' s sad humor, to doctor them into life . . .

April 30, 1974

Have we already plunged into the past tense of Fitzgerald's gilded people, who reach that day in their lives when the three o'clock of the soul has so frightened them, time has so decreased them, they're lost forever from their delicate early dancings in a callow sun . . . .

> *[It comes back to me, an anxiety, a regret for all I had not done for the Peter Taylors during my time there, two years ago, when I house-sat their Rugby Lane house and they traveled in England . . .]*

. . . This feeling now, that if everyone who had seemed to support you has forgotten you, you've ceased to be worth remembering . . . .

Grotesquely, at 6:00 a.m., tuned into BBC World Service, we heard the mouthings of Nixon, saying he was turning over transcripts of the long-requested tapes to the Judicial Committee, and granting the right to the Committee chairman to verify their accuracy . . . How sick that man makes me. I can think of no one more despicable . . .

Alas, so much is explained. There is a second (all hearsay) scandal at the school. The Persian teacher whom they brought in two days ago has a reputation among these Victorian maidens of mine, who all eagerly explain to me today that they don't like him because he only came to this school so he could be with girls. They insist that he had flirted shamefully with all his students, so that the *modir* and *saer-modir* have both finally asked him to leave.

"He is like a woman, but he is a man; his body is fat like a woman's with child. When he was at the boy's school he was always hugging and kissing the boy students, and from there too they told him to go."

My students giggle frantically, one grabbing a *chadris* and stuffing it into her dress, another demonstrating how to nuzzle the ears of her neighbor, the others winking lewdly at each other. They act cruelly, but what else can one expect of them. Perhaps this is really a sick man, a pervert. But what of the young ladies?

[T had "cast an atmosphere to take your breath away," peeved because I had written a letter to Joan Bennett and Mary Gordon . . . and sealed it without letting him read it, "holding on to, hiding [my] secrets again from him—"] And living in this cocoon, so close, is there no right to my own voice, apart?

May 3, 1974

The day, like unfed puppies, turns into squabbling imbalances, but largely, wholly, we spend it in writing eight exams (each). They must yet be copied into the ditto sheets and run off, and—more difficult—their principles must be drilled for another three weeks, until they themselves are administered. But now we can truthfully begin to breath (a little) in anticipation of successfully finishing off this year . . .

It is a day as clear as birdsong is cluttered: we stood on our roof stairs yesterday watching the rain come in, the town bending and bursting to get out of the downpour, a carnival of birds of the same feather (a thousand cut from one mold) clustering in the big mulberry tree behind our wall, the dust laid to rest for a few hours like a contrary child at nap time . . .

May 5, 1974

. . . After school today I walk with Tom to the post office. Again we imbibe the startling scenario before us which we've so long been able to take for granted: An old white-haired man in cotton wound turban, and faded hanging clothes, edges step by step down the road, his legs steadied by two stalks of wood. In the time we take to go up to the P.O. from the corner, he has only managed to cross the street from the hotel to the hospital side. One bandy-legged child throws stones at another, then sets off, bare feet slapping the pavement, to catch him. An old work horse minces by as slowly as an old spinster, behind him a wooden *karachi* piled high with chopped wood, and two cross-legged men. A *gaudi* full of brightly-capped men in their karakul capes, the baggy *peron* and *tanbon* hanging down over their plastic sandals, bumps by. And the ghosts, my sisters, move in their stooped pairs, *chadris* as thick and worn as old sheets. The mountains, in their spring undergrowth, a dense green moss across the shoulders, look more like hills this season, with the sun's glare diminishing everything.

And in the evening we wait for the lights to shout "dark," sitting on our mud white porch watching the effortless flights of the swallows, and then the spastic bats . . . .

We hear everywhere of cowards—The Arab terrorists who murdered over 40 people in Athens last autumn, have been released, expelled by the Greek government, which had originally convicted them of murder . . . .

May 6, 1975

In a bow to mores and modes and customs of Afghanistan, Tom has his *modir* and one teacher and the visiting inspector of education here tonight for dinner—and I am put in a most Afghan position. For to save them from any awkwardness and undue embarrassment which might arise at their having to share their presences with women (i.e. me), Tom and I have hid me, in best purdah fashion, away from the men folk. The only difficulty is that our house, consisting as it does of only two inhabitable room, doesn't lend itself to the intrigue of a normal Afghan house which has separate courts and entrances for the females of the household, and a separate room apart, the *mamon xona* or guest house for the purpose of entertaining (i.e., feeding abundantly) all male visitors to the family environs. So my "hiding away" consists largely of my being in the only other inhabitable room, directly next to the first room, and separated by a door full of cracks. Here I sit then, feeling like nothing so much as a naughty girl who's been sent to bed early for punishment, while a gay party at which I can't be welcome goes on next door. Alas, I am one thin door, but centuries and societies away, from the old European notion of a hostess in one's own home. And, to finish the scene, I am required to make my entrances and exit out the window.

Today under the mulberry trees, the 5 to 8th grade students take a ton of elementary exams, mostly consisting of translating a few sentences or answering some questions on a most unprofessional corner of paper. A bit like a left foot when only right footers were allowed, I proctor for an hour, then exit in relief to the wild familiarity of my own classes . . .

May 10, 1975

. . . Another of my classes, the 9th, has regional exams, so the teaching day ends early for me . . . By 3:30, Tom and I, dittos and papers and yogurt pie in hand, are sitting in the cabin of a Waz speeding through spring greens and brown edging river to Aybak. The *malim-e-sports* from Aybak, who had been up here on some business, a tall thin man with high hallow cheekbones and thick jet black hair, shares the cabin with us and generously passes the time, asking Tom all the particulars of our lives here, listening carefully to hear of the differences in America. His questions, arch or sincere, include: what kinds of meat did they eat (and here he pulls a faux pas, surely taunting us, explaining that at the dormitory school in Kabul they were served meat from a tin once, and he's always wondered what kind it was, the intention obviously being we should admit it must be pig—*guste-hukh*—((since everyone knows those *kafirs* in America feast night and day on this dirty meat)). And did we think he should buy another wife, or just be content with the one he has now; and what about friends of his who had gone to study in Russia on scholarships and met women there and now had to come back to Afghanistan with these non-Moslems? What did we think of Russia? Hadn't they done a lot of good things for Afghanistan?

He speaks of his brother who had died only five weeks before and how since then he's had little desire for food or anything else, and that was why his coloring is now so bad; and he describes how he failed a class with a Russian boxing coach one year. This leads to an admission that "those people" hadn't read any of "the books," and the question as to how many of the four had we read. Or, do Americans read them (referring of course to the omission of the Koran among our "masterplots")? But in fact, we remind him, we are all "people of the book," since the Koran shares the Old Testament and recognizes the New Testament.

> *[One of the sustaining joys of PC life is connecting not just with local folks, and their culture and perhaps daily useful work, but also sharing time and stories with other volunteers. One of our favorites are the Kissingers in Aybak.]*

So during our visit, we get a sketch of the people next door to the Kissingers in Aybak. There is a husband who is a lab technician, a wife,

Parween, who was trained by Americans in Herat six years ago and is now a practicing midwife, and three children, Parweena, Darius and Diana. The children had been there when we arrive. The youngest is nine months old now, and was delivered by the mother herself. She is a black-eyed mischievous infant, ready almost to walk. The oldest, a beautiful four-year old girl, is shy, just woken from a nap, a plump, universal child. We hear how the wife, proudly, at seventeen, had chosen "this man" herself, after her cousin had rejected him for his one eye (when he was five he hurt it somehow and his "treaters" poured Mercurochrome on it, obviously burning up the cornea). But Parween thought he would make a good husband.

She has a job at the hospital, but with no examining room takes all her patients at her home. In five years she claims to have never lost a child, and yet the people talk of her, claim that she takes too much money from them. In the middle of the night people will come and pound for hours on her gate, expecting her to go alone with some strange man to the old city; while in the day women wait around her gates like stone pigeons, clustering and waiting. She delivers more than one baby a day many times.

She is 25 perhaps . . . .

But, we hear about the way she delivered her last child, a real ordeal. Sara ran over at a grandmother's insistence after lunch one early afternoon, and she already had the placenta delivered, had bathed and knotted the baby, and our colleague found herself holding a child only a few minutes old. Then suddenly Parween became quite delirious and couldn't stop bleeding. A doctor came over and gave her some "bad" thing in a shot which Parween pulled out of her arm as he was giving it, saying it was like fire or electricity in her arm. Ointments and tonics were prescribed, but the Kissingers called our PC doctor, Dr. Jenkins, who said to get Pitocin (emphycidan), and in 24 hours the brave mother was perfect again.

Then there was the story of the old mullah, who used to be paramount in the mosque beside the house, but who was recently replaced by a more strict, fundamentalist Moslem character. The old fellow, short as an ogre and always wearing sunglasses with one lens cracked, accepted their *kafirness* without comment, and their money. They had seen him only a few days before in the bazaar . . . stopped in front of a pharmacy where he was attempting to buy a large bottle of lean-blood topic for sixty afs without his sixty afs. Sara lent him the money though there was reason for real skepticism about how much this tonic was really needed for the little man, or if she would ever see the 60 *afs* again.

Another day they speak of Maury M., a PCV nurse who had worked both in Aybak and in Mazar, among the Kutchis, vaccinating for TB eradication, etc. But she has been in Kabul since the Health program collapsed, with everyone being recalled to the capital at government edict. This strange girl came from the second family of her father, who had come to the States from Pakistan at the age of 45 or 50 and left behind another family (there were three daughters, and allegedly three sons had died in infancy). He made a fortune in sheep and cattle grazing in Texas and California, and raised both families, the first via mail, Maury claimed, by sending them $6,000 every half year or so by way of his family's village, with the intention that this should support his brothers as well as his wife and children there. But the brothers claimed to have never seen any of it, thanks to the wife, legend goes.

And now Maury insists that the family has a contract out, to kill her, as the most immediate kin in the immediate vicinity, and therefore responsible for the 30 year slight. This old man, her father, Mary told the Kissingers, had a heart attack last year, had an operation for cataracts, had hysterical blindness for three months, broke his leg, had another heart attack, and is 81 years old. Maury is to leave and go home to see him as soon as possible, but by last report she was still waiting (visas and vendetta to boot), in Herat . . . .

Thursday morning is the celebration of the unveiling of the new republic's flag. We go with Jerry Kissinger to try to run off our exams, but fail to find a single machine that will do them, so finally give up after a brief view of the marching field, and go home where—like naughty little boys, Sara's husband and mine decide to fight the tiny white scorpion (captured from the living room the night before) with some aggressive ants around the yard. In a jar with ten ants, the stinger-wielding critter is quickly defeated. Alas, Buddhists or Jains, we are not.

. . . Sara who made it to the Republic celebration, tells us what we had missed: after the red flag banners had made the round of town streets, everyone gathered in the adjacent field. She sat in one of the tented areas, politely acknowledged as the "malim-Amrika." There was first the flag raising, and everyone clapping as the banner refused to unfurl, but just lay limply at the top of the pole, tangled. Finally someone manipulated it to show its stripes, but they were now horizontal instead of vertical, and its wheat and mosque emblem had been changed to an eagle (a "morc" or chicken by one man's description), while the rest of the flag was red and green and black. This wondrous act completed, three soldiers came out with loaded guns, apparently intending to set off a salute, but instead two of them fought over who was to shoot. At one point, at least in their movements, each pointed his gun straight into the crowd. Then there was the "aton," the national (men's) dance, in which the town's "da wa-nah" (crazy man) joined in; and finally there were the Pushtu speeches no one could understand which signaled time for everyone there to leave.

. . . In the afternoon [we] set off for the Buddhist stupa, Tahkte Rostum. We move along the rich green fields, a forest of small flowering trees giving way to a spacious valley of wheat golden in the sun, the dark liquid river plowing beside us. The stupas themselves are like the cool echoing crypts of an old church, all of its patterns and statuary moved, destroyed, blackened by the non-pious fires of generations of travelers who had camped inside the old monk's chambers since the 8th century. The cells are carved out cleanly as one continuous series of chambers, scooped out of the unruffled hillside 15 centuries ago. Up at the top of a hill is the large egg-like rock, perfectly circular, with a round belt of a path around its bottom, and more hallow chambers within the natural cliffs. From here one almost sees the images of a sleepy Buddhist valley. (How had it been? How strange that Afghans would find this place beautiful now. Their forefather's blood had destroyed it and all the ideas it had nurtured.)

. . . We start back, trying to gather into ourselves the peace of these plains and hills, the bent backs of workers in the late afternoon fields, children guiding the family flock of sheep back toward the town or village, old men resting in the shadows of the walls; then again the main street shops, business in its small scale, and finally the allusion of a western home, their home again.

This morning's taxi driver, a dark, sharp-featured southerner, announced at the edge of Tashkurghan, that his people, the good people, are the Pustoons, and that "these Dari-speakers are not good . . . ."

May 14, 1974

Our friendly creatures of the lower realm: the speedy quick-tongued lizards roll a lidded eye at us and vanish; the black, rolly-polly beetles the size of turtles waddle across the porch.

Yesterday I was cooking dinner when an old grandmother and six children from nearby came to the kitchen door to study me. Mostly I was transferring boiled water to the *owdon,* but later when I was making a fritter batter, the barefooted children's eyes bulged. I invited them in, offered a sample, but—as if my Persian words were exploding lightbulbs—life goes on denying them sense rather than illumination—they just nodded, giggled, and fled.

The first fruit of the season, home-grown Tashkurghan apricots (*zardoloo*—yellow plums) come on the bazaar yesterday and Tom was out before seven, old basket and 10 afs hot in hand to have the grinning, cross-legged young fruit merchant measure him out a pound.

Hallowed and colorless as silt in a riverbed, the *modir* has returned from Kabul again. Yesterday we exchanged greetings . . . . There is such a sadness in him. Is it just the childlessness? Or is it a political exile, for him to have been transferred here

May 17, 1974

Tuesday night like a choking arm the full, unmitigated heat came upon us . . . *[Exams were delivered, classes restless, reports mediocre. We had visitors, including a photographer from the Afghan Tour company with lots of gossip—of travelers arrested for drugs, of a Swedish girl who died of rabies, of PCV's who are terminating early, of the death of a AISK student, of his hatred of Texas and its punk cowboys—He'd lived there in high school and gone to U Texas-Austin. He speaks of his brother who was a helicopter pilot in Vietnam, of his work for the Duprees, of Fariad telling him that he had close ties to M Daud who wanted to make the Afghan Tour a successful company, of having his passport and everything else stolen just before he left Washington, of his shared 6,000 afs a month Kabul house . . . .]*

This morning at 6:30 a.m. we go with the visiting volunteer Dan and Ismael the Lame (the knowledgeable antique seller), and a rambling storytelling Pushtoon driver, and Ismael's *cawk*-shooting son, and the pudgy, smooth managing Afghan Tour official photographer with his Russian camera and the Baktar News agency reporter (slim, sallow, sunglassed and in embroidered hat) in a Landrover, out 15 kilometers to the cities of the old Khulm, the site last occupied 1200 years ago, they claim, and Tashkurghan, lived in until about 170 years ago when everyone moved to what is the current town. Great scattered piles of broken pottery, gopher hills and lizards and snakes, and the flat, unburdening desert, are all there is left now. To the north the green blur of trees mark the Oxus (Amu Darya) River and the beginnings of the Soviet Union. We pass a small herd of camels and one young camel is chased for a kilometer or more by our driver, apparently the fellow too dull or frightened to realize he has only to move to the side of the road. And in the villages at the edge of the desert children stare at our mechanized movements, but no one talks . . .

May 21, 1974

> *[Foolishly, I wrote a note in Dari excusing myself from school because I had work at home, although it was actually food to prepare for guests. Then the landlord, haji-sibe, arrives, snoops around and then leaves; he is followed by Armoe M'med. Finally, we say we can not help him, but then we go out to the bazaar and bring him back in. He offers to keep our house for free, make us a garden, etc. Quietly we nod our heads, listen, and then feed him.]*

. . . The night outside is wondrous: a dust storm, lightning, thunder, and a brittle rain. Our lights flicker on and off like old childhood memories, but the air, once the dust had been laid down again, surrenders with coolness and light.

Monday's school, well-known to be the last day for formal instruction, brings out the teasing questioning side of students who clamor and claw and hug at me to confirm that I am loved and (for a good many it would seem to have followed) that I must certainly give them all passing grades. I sit first with the *modir's* wife, as I had the afternoon before. This time she stays in the 4th classroom with two other teachers, who are grading the embroidery work of the students. They all make much over me, I smile vacantly and respond specifically to their questions:

Do you wash everyday?

What do you think of these clothes? Won't you take them?

And I was the inheritor of the captain's best work. They marveled again in their whispering kind of excitement about how pretty they thought me . . . .

The letter of excuse for Sunday has so impressed my dear and hollow sallow *modir* that—thinking to honor me, could it have been—he had posted it on the wall behind his desk, where everyone can know of it. Some eighth graders tell me it isn't good writing . . . and the *modir's* wife quickly teaches me how to correctly write "Mahasti."

Tajenisa is lolling in her apparent dismissal from my brother's affections—or so she had created this betrothal for herself—on the basis of my telling them I had an unmarried brother, and now, half-joking and half-frightened, I tell the class they must forget this idea. Meanwhile, someone has a stack of post cards, mostly of red flowers, which Tajenisa quickly points out I like (I'm naughty and full of life, that's why I like red), but one postcard shows a seemingly nude girl clasping her body so that nothing shows but her nakedness and Zeagul (Tajenisa's half sister) quickly explains that this was the note Tajenisa will send to my brother.

Hailed by the 5th and 6th graders, in the hall of their *takerie* awaiting the cruel mullah's Koran Sharif questions, I am again the center of sighs. The girls claim they must look at me carefully because before I came they had never seen a foreigner like this before. So I do not chase them away, this last day until the fall.

Today was to have been the Teachers' Geshwen or Roz-e-Malimeen, but taking cues from Tom (and a conversation last afternoon with my *modir* and the Pushtu teacher, both of whom confirmed that no celebration, only a holiday, was planned for the next day), I left with T. to go to Mazar . . . But—awkward, inexcusable, a most unfortunate and unintended cultural slip—upon return I learn that I shouldn't have missed the party in honor of my likes. Further, . . . Tom's arrogant *modir* taunts him about his request to leave town early when his "convention" isn't in fact until the 15th of June.

May 25, 1974

. . . Then it is Thursday, my first exam. The young "black widows" sit stiffly under the broad shade of the mulberry trees in front of the school, chewing their pens and ruling the thick official exam papers set before them by the inspector from the Ministry. With the first grade teacher as my proctor, we begin the exam, or the reign of coquettish discord, to name it better. The Pushtu teacher and the second grade teacher alternately confuse my directions, but largely the exam just goes on, and I lose all reservations or desires except to see it ended. After two and a half hours the proctors have become so conspicuous in giving out answers, I decide to call it quits and collect the papers. Furiously, I began the orals, with the young teachers prompting the entire class through the windows after I temporarily succeed in diplomatically banishing these teacher outside, and they scream, giggle and tease. The students being examined stumble self-consciously, and I work faster. Then it is also over. Taking the teachers' final words to me, "Don't fail any of these girls," I set off, after first looking at Esfandyar's boiling cauldron of soup in the rear of the school, food for all the teachers.

. . . In the afternoon I finish grading exams and turn in the grades. As the *modir* and *saer-malim* read off the brazenly high grades for the other class, I stumble over the wavering results of my own. Meanwhile, Tom is kidnapped at his school, made to sip tea and sign exam papers . . . .

. . . Yesterday we walked out to the old fort town, the sun scorching us like a reprimanding parent. Below the river flows coolly and the valley shimmers, a rich green . . . We doze in the incomprehensible heat . . . then set off to the bazaar . . . And we find a circus: a busload of Afghan Tour's skin-exposed Germans, the men strangely fat or tall, the women in cut-off pants and bare legs and arms, uncovered heads, and—presumptively—money tumbling. Their hot sweaty words invite insult and chatter from the shopkeepers, as they occupy the shade of the covered bazaar like a crazy corridor . . . insensitive . . . as if the world owes them an explanation and they can tread heavily on their pleasure through everyone's private gardens . . . But, again, I apply standards of my own. The shopkeepers, of course, invite and welcome the business.

Evening upon us . . . Armoe M'med's wife and a sister from Mazar appear before our half-spread dinner table to survey the house with a dozen little girls and ask of my ideas and plans, and quiz me about some medicine. The sister is perhaps 13 or 20, had been married after the sixth grade. She has two children, the youngest about four, but has had no more children, so everyone assumed she had become sick and rushed her to a doctor for some kind of medicine. The prescription was unreadable, like all doctor's prescriptions, but there was something about a cervical infection. The women looked on gently but I really couldn't help them, except to say she had a sickness "where babies grew," and that she needed to get the medicine to make "that place" healthy again . . . .

My 10th class exam goes well, the grades fairly good, obviously some learning took place, but in the middle of the test under the trees, the *modir's* wife and other teachers appear to hover around two poor students at the front. When I give them some gruff answers they quickly pass on, and I have to pretend to be occupied elsewhere, as they return and deliver the answers . . . .

May 31, 1974

. . . Then I spend the afternoon going through the motions of the exams and finding, to my stock amazement and pleasure, that more than a handful of students had actually learned something . . .

Wednesday we made a last efforts to finish Tom's exams, then pack up and exchange directions with Aman, our cook, who is being paid to stay in our house during our absence. Going to bed, our heads spinning at 9:00, we wake at 4:00 a.m. and take a bus for 9 ½ hours to Kabul. Entering the city, we feel like country bumpkins . . .

Yesterday. We carry a request from my principal, Rashidi, written in his painful English, to see if Peace Corps would hire him to teach Farsi, or if they could help him find a job in an American school. And the landlord, lone, moody Iotillah, has asked for medicine for his mother who has been constipated for ten days, as he himself slumps against our pillows and sticks his hands into a pocket of my knapsack to fetch out a jar of deodorant and ask what it is. Then grinning mutely and lecturing us on how we should come back from Kabul in a month and be with our students (and him), he edges out of the house.

The young Pushtoon teacher appears in the afternoon of T's last exam, embarrassed, to plead help for his good friend, who is slated to be failed. These are our neighbors' ways. Our own are foreign.

Again, we look at the growing wonder of the country, crossing it, climbing the Salang, its goldenness and blunted deserts, and the life-giving rivers, and the faces of the strangers. The bus is full of children and *chadried* women, sitting in their thick envelopes against the window, mute as the dead, their husbands scowling elderly beside them.

Entering Kabul, there is the obligatory fight, in fact two fights within a few minutes, between the *motorwan* and policeman, and then between two *taxiwans*, the obvious heat of deprecation, this readiness to quarrel . . . Or is it a way of life?

At dawn we see a Dutch or German traveler stretched in the street, on a bad drug trip. A crowd hovers around. We plead with the police for him to be taken to the hospital but—while he is gone when we return from buying *nan* at the corner— it is frightening to think of someone alone in that situation. Will he survive?

Background on the Civil War and the Arrival of the Taliban

During the decades of armed conflict in Afghanistan, no force has consistently respected human rights or parameters or principles which supposedly dictate international armed conflicts and are intended—as the human rights documents state—to "protect civilian lives to the maximum extent possible." Rather, over and over civilians have been targeted and killed, in "deliberate and indiscriminate attacks"(Amnesty International). These attacks involved mass killings of civilians from specific ethic groups, after a particular city, town, village or locality was captured, and employed bombing or shelling of homes, schools, and other civilian buildings, The statistics are sobering: During the ten year Soviet invasion and occupation from 1979 to 1989, Afghan communist military and civilian collaborators clashed with *mujahadeen* fighters in a dirty war which brought torture, uncounted disappearances, mass killings, indiscriminately blanketing landmines, and the world's largest number of refugees. More than a fifth of Afghanistan's population, over six million people, fled the country, a number which peaked in 1990 when the UNHCR registered 3,272,000 Afghans in Pakistan and 2,940,000 in Iran.

As early as June 1982, Pakistan and Afghanistan began proximity talks through the U.N., and the U.S. and the Soviet Union later joined them. The talks resulted in the Geneva Accords, an agreement in April 14, 1988 between Afghanistan and Pakistan. By the terms of that initial accord all Soviet troops were to withdraw from Afghanistan within nine months, a neutral Afghan state was to be created, and millions of Afghan refugees were to be repatriated. Meanwhile, in 1986 Karmal had resigned as secretary general of the PDPA (Parchami). He retained the presidency briefly, then saw power shift to the former head of KHAD, the Afghan secret service, Najibullah, whose reputation and alliances proceeded him and who—not surprising—saw Karmal's every move uniformly resisted by the *mujahadeen.* Once all Soviet "uniformed troops" had left the country in February 1989, the communist government held on to power until 1992 as the U.N. struggled, unsuccessfully, to cobble together a transitional government acceptable to all sides.

At this time, however, the U.S. and its allies abandoned the field entirely, severely undercutting the potential for international engagement which might have secured peace in the country. While a trickle of humanitarian aid came in sporadically through the decade, it was always way under what was actually needed, and most Afghans were left desperate and destitute. As Soviet leadership moved from Brezhnev to Andropov to Chernenko to Gorbachev, and the Soviet Union collapsed and its Central Asian republics became independent, the U.S. and the world's attention shifted to places other than Afghanistan. The thinking was that Afghanistan was no longer needed as a Cold War bargaining chip or rehearsal hall, since the Cold War was "over."

The Northern Alliance, made up of the Tajik forces of Ahmed Shah Masoud, the Uzbek forces of Abdul Rashid Dostum which had been allied with Najibullah, and the Hazara faction called Hizb-I-Wahdat, was formed in early 1992. At that time, Najibullah attempted to leave the country, but was stopped at Kabul Airport by non-Pushtoon militia forces who had previously been his allies. For the next four years, he was forced to take refuge in the U.N. compound.

On April 25, 1992, Masoud entered Kabul. A coalition government excluding Hekmatyar's Hizb-I-Islami faction was agreed upon the next day. Undaunted, Hekmatyar began a strategy of random, major rocket attacks on Kabul, which continued until he was forced to withdraw in 1995. Meanwhile, Burhanuddin Rabbani became acting president, and the Hazara faction (Hezm-I-Wahdat) and Sayyafís factor (Ittihad-I-Islami) began to fight. By the hundreds, civilians faced death and abduction. Rabbani cleverly packed the *shura,* the traditional governing body, with his own supporters, and the council granted him re-election in December 1992. However, he was ousted in January 1994 when Hekmatyar joined with Dostum against him and Masood, who was then the defense minister.

Full civil war erupted, as well-equipped factions supported by other countries struggled for supremacy. This period (1992-1995) was marked by new atrocities and abuse, and the almost total leveling of over a third of Kabul with aerial bombings, mortar shell exchanges, and rocket shelling. At the same time all factions planted antipersonnel landmines, engaged in torturing and murdering soldiers and civilians in detention, and used extortion, arbitrary arrest, and gang rape to get their bounty. Anarchy reigned.

By summer 1993, according to the British paper, *The Guardian*, some 30,000 people had been killed, 100,000 wounded, and more than half a million civilians driven from Kabul. The number continued to soar, during 1994, with many claiming a toll of more than 25,000 civilians killed by deliberate and indiscriminate attacks by *mujahadeen* factions, between 1992 and 1997. At the height of the fighting, over 3,000 rockets were hitting Kabul per day. No one knew who was friend or foe at that point, as civilians left and right, and families by the dozen, were killed on the streets. In addition, rapes, kidnappings, torture, and burning of houses continued, and rocket bombardments singed the skies. In the areas near the university, in Karte-char, and the northwestern suburbs one report claimed over 10,000 people were killed in two days. They were all civilians, brutally killed by different factions.

So before the Taliban swept to power, people had long since tired of the atrocities committed around them by the warring forces—both those in power and those struggling to get power. This was Afghanistan's darkest era, so people initially would welcome the Taliban, as they successfully occupied each area and managed to restore peace there. They promised the prospect of ending the looting, the attacks on women, the rapes, and the stealing of children.

Chronologically, the advance of the Taliban was swift. As the Taliban, the movement of armed religious students, systematically defeated local commandants, they moved to take over Kandahar and other southern area in November, 2002. In their sweep, along with opened roads and the disbanding of exploitative road blocks, came their strict religious law, banned videotapes, public music and dancing; and harsh restrictions on beards, burqa, hats, and turbans.

Throughout, Pakistan strongly supported the Taliban, as its Pakistani traders sought the guarantee of a friendly government in Kabul to replace the banditry and violence blocking their trade routes to Central Asia. By September 1995, the Taliban had taken Herat and the trade route to Iran. A year later they took Kabul. At this point, Masoud retreated to the north, got aid from Iran and Russia and became the major, if not only, opposition group to the Taliban. Into this murky picture came Bin Laden, who returned to Jalalabad in 1996 and went on to Kandahar in 1997, where his fighters joined the Taliban fighters. Meanwhile, from 1997 and 1998, Dostum ran his own 'mini-state' made up of five northern provinces, headquartered in Sheberghan. Allied with Hizb-I-Wahdat, he controlled Mazar and its large Hazara population.

The details of the tenuous alliances, purges, and resulting abuses and their results read like a date book for genocide and internecine affairs. Different factions were armed by different groups, with each group getting arms from the neighboring countries—Russian, Pakistan, Iran, China, despite the "on-paper" arms embargo. In truth, little else except weapons was imported into the country at that time, including cheap Italian-made landmines.

In August 1996, there was a three-day summit in Washington, called so that the U.S, could determine how to end conflict in Afghanistan, including establishing some kind of relationship with the Taliban. Afghans from all walks of life were invited to participate. At that time the *mujahadeen* were still in Kabul, and although they had taken over 90 percent of the country, the Taliban had not yet occupied Kabul. They did so in September. It appeared that the *mujahadeen* had made some kind of negotiations behind the scenes with the Taliban leaders, because as soon as the Taliban reached the outskirts of Kabul, these factional leaders left within 24 hours. Amazingly, the whole establishment of the *mujahadeen* just disappeared, including the full extent of their weaponry, machine guns, artillery, tanks, and vehicles,

At first there was an eerie calm. Then within 24 to 36 hours after the Taliban had taken over, things radically changed as these Wahadi religioius zealots spread out over the city and immediately, relentlessly, began to implement severe *sharia* law. The new rulers had come less to liberate than to control and punish Kabul, a city they detested for its worldliness and a citizenry they viewed as having committed every conceivable sin, especially during the previous 35 years and in the Communist times.

As explained by Suraya Sadeed, Director of the NGO, Help the Afghan Children, who was in Kabul when it fell to the Taliban:

"Of course in part, the Taliban acted to destroy the legacy of earlier decades, the reality which had always given women more freedoms and participation there. Many Kabuli women and girls were educated, still attended schools, and taught, practiced medicine or worked in offices. What applied to Kabul had nothing to do with the more conservative practices in most of the rest of the country. Although beginning under the mujahadeen, there had been strong repression of their rights and their role as members of society had been minimized, many women still moved and worked outside of the house. Often because they were the only breadwinners for a family, they still had some relative independence.

"By the third day after the Taliban had come, the tribunals had mandated that all schools for girls be closed and that women not be allowed to work outside their compound walls. They had started to go around the streets and to impose the *sharia* law with their long sticks, as ubiquitous a part of their uniform as the long beards and black turbans. They beat everyone and anybody who would come along, because they dictated the use of corporal punishment for certain "crimes," including any violation of the strict dress code, or the failure of a man to have a beard of a certain length. Under the many-footed, fierce domain of the Ministry of Promotion of Virtue and Prevention of Vice (al-Amr bi al-M'ruf al-Munkr), they started slowly but surely to impose an inhumanly harsh sharia law on people.

"Kabulis, like city dwellers anywhere, had witnessed many things in their lives . . . but no one there had experienced this kind of fanatical rule . . . especially women. At the very beginning, along with closing all the girls' schools and closing the university to women, they even shut down all the hospitals for women. They forbade women not only to work outside the house, but also to even go outside on the street without a male relative. So within days, out of fear, no one went out, not even those who had initially celebrated the Taliban's entrance and the end of the civil war. People literally disappeared from the streets, and overnight the city went from a noisy, lively city to a graveyard.

"I was an eyewitness to the effect of the Taliban imposing *sharia* law on average people. Imagine these individuals who had had such high hopes and then found themselves suddenly confronted with tyrants. Further these religious tyrants had nothing to do with the culture, had nothing to do with generations-bred ideas of hospitality and respect for women and the elderly. These new boys in town had nothing to do with what had always been—if flawed—Afghan customs, believes and practices. It was almost as if the Taliban came from another planet and thus had no knowledge of, or commitment to, the 5,000 years of Afghan traditions and culture."

As she explains further:

"They were just entirely different, a combination of all types of things. Most of them were born and raised in Pakistan where they had more or less studied in the religious madrassas. In those institutions, part of what they were taught was—if not literally hatred—than a great resentment of and intolerance toward women. They had lived in a male-dominated world, quite often completely separated from family life. They had been born and raised to believe that women were second class citizens and the narrow Qoranic interpretations of their Wahabi roots taught them something like, 'Women are here to serve us, the men. They have no other worth.'"

With that kind of mentality, and the particular Saudi Wahabi agenda, the Taliban, these new rulers, had no restrictions on extremism. The specific political and religious basis of fundamentalism for the supporters of the Taliban was the Deobands school. All these Wahabi-funded madrassas were enmeshed in the principals of the Deobandi's very strict interpretation of Islamic law. In fact, historically, the Deobandi school originated in India a long time ago during the British occupation of India. At that time the political issues which the British government had regarding the creation of Pakistan had a lot to do with its structure and its popularity, and the issues it raised and rebelled against.

Geographically and ethnically, in 1996, the Taliban was a combination of Afghans from the southern part of the country, some foreigners, especially Saudis, and a mix of different Pakistanis who were from this area called "no man's land," or Pushtoonistan. This area properly belongs to neither Pakistan nor Afghanistan, but remains a tribal land created at some point by the British as a buffer zone between Afghanistan and Pakistan. Further, most of the Taliban spoke only Urdu and Pushto, while the vast majority of Kabulis had been and continued to be Farsi speakers. Like further fat on the fire, the Taliban carried a huge resentment toward people who spoke Farsi. In fact, the Taliban actively recruited the young Pushtoons from particular tribes, especially those in the South, knowing they would be more accepting of all the religious indoctrination and "jihad-building" which was going on within the religious madrassa. At that time, then, the control of the Taliban was very much about Pushto and non-Pushto, as well as about rigid Islamic laws.

While the initial development of the Taliban, as students in the madrassas, is well-known, the process by which the ranks of the Taliban swelled from region to region within Afghanistan is less discussed but also somewhat typical. In fact, most followers were not the fanatical religious fundamentalists we associate with this group. Pragmatically, most were local farmers, shopkeepers or wealthy warlords who simply followed what they saw as the winners. The movement was highly localized initially, with local village leaders installing their personal followers on the side of the Taliban, as the movement grew. As more influential commanders soon combined the local village groups, the numbers quadrupled, until a patchwork of militias was commandeered under one strong leader who could draw on as many as 2,000 men. Any of these same leaders worked just as quickly and treacherously to change sides at will, depending on who was winning, and who was paying him. Unabashedly, he might take money from both sides at once. The Taliban came into the country with funding from outside (principally Saudi Arabia) and they managed to buy off many local commanders and their men, and in this way, to take whole areas without ever firing a shot.

As soon as the Taliban began to "collapse" eight years later, the U.S. effectively used the identical technique of buying off these same warlords and commanders. They did so in the end with horrific results.

VII

SUMMER 1974

June 1, 1974

[Denise Blake, a volunteer in Kapisa, has drown. Her husband of a year was unable to rescue her. They'd been married a year, after serving together in Brazil. We realize again how tentative all our lives are . . .]. In the afternoon there is a memorial service in the chapel of the Italian Embassy, and, a congregation strong, all of Peace Corps sits there mute and grieving, as a small priest speaks St. Francis's words, about Sister Death and Sister Water and Brother Sun—how it is all equally near and part of the human experience, how there must be eternal life because there must be a purpose to all this, how when John had reached his hand out to hold back his wife, she was taken out of his hands, because of God's purpose, a mystery that none of us can understand . . .

A year ago in this same chapel the priest had married them . . . . Outside on the long embassy driveway the pine and willow trees whistle mournfully in the afternoon breeze, dust returning, in mock battle, to its own, while the life-giving (and taking) rivers in this country, continue to rumble in cool righteousness and enigmatic violence across the hills beyond this city, into the valley of Kapisa . . . .

Historically, the site of Kapisa, called Begram when it was a Graeco-Bactrian city 2,000 years ago, was always above the Panjsher River. Capital of a far-flung Kushan Empire during the early centuries A.D., it was once a city of sumptuous palaces and bustling bazaars full of international goods. In the 20th century, Kapisa has been the site of one of the most spectacular archaeological finds of the entire regions. In the 1960's, a cache of treasures were excavated here. The finds included Chinese lacquers, Graeco-Roman bronzes and plaster matrices, Alexandrian vessels of porphyry, alabaster and glass, and exquisite Indian ivories. By this era, however, the only thing again visible is a mound rising above a bleak plain surrounded by low hills, and marking the spot from which a citadel and a fort in the ancient city had extended. Buddhists stupas with reliquaries also dot the areas near Begram, many alleged to be full of unearthed gold, and silver cases full of pearls and aquamarines, and other precious items. Like much remembered but not legitimately pursued or preserved here, the stupas and their treasures have all been long since been plundered.

June 3, 1974

[We fill out forms for vacation leave, change money, dine with other volunteers, by candlelight noting their Nuristani shawls as brilliant as ecclesiastical robes, and get our summer job assignment at the university.]

And we've come again to count our days like cheap trinkets, which we must sell to make our living. One day we observed our potential jobs at the university, a sphere in which English is more than functionary, a pure tongue; and another day we were swallowed by a conference, . . . and by forms. In the afternoon the Ambassador spoke, optimistically, of what he has seen and can expect from the new regime, and later a former PC turned accountant for the Embassy spoke of the origins and rituals of the money bazaar. It began with seven Jews in the late 1800's and by the 1930's was still a non-Afghan market; now it is a Pushtoon market and most of the exchangers have accounts in banks all over the world, although to have a foreign bank account is illegal.

[The small details of bodily maintenance: Dentist check-up, discussion of Living Wage, party at Doc Jenkin's, and my own restlessness and sweet talk with one apparently genuine volunteer.]

. . . In the house of James and Lena, the primitive stone carvings of animals, stallholders, gawk from the imperial embroidery clothes. The walls hold with dignity the carefully folded hangings, some women's monthly work, molded to string and flowers. In the roof beams families of scattering mice find their footholds and a wind tousles the ancient trees around their yard, travelers in the inner sanctum.

June 14, 1974

We will not begin teaching immediately. We have leave to go explore another part of this land for a few days.

We have heard from others about the magic of the Hazarajat, of the peaceful ancient village of Bamiyan and its two Giant Buddhas from the seventh century. People have told us how standing in this town among its Hazara residents the sun pours over you like honey, the air so clear light engulfs everything, sunrise pinks and maroons, the rim of azure sky, green weeping willows hug the riverbanks, as purple, brown mountain layers, stretch beyond. Then at the end of the valley, we know, stand the Buddhas, majestic, peaceful guardians silently ruling the north side of the valley. From the dusty, ground they rise above: chiseled heads on giant forms, a posture echoing the slightly quizzical and calm faces, the wide checks, and folded eyes, of the local Hazarajat farmers and small shopkeepers.

The folds of the stoles, noble and precise like a Roman senator's toga, float as lively as real cloth, suddenly frozen. Inside the bee-hived caves, cells and staircases unwind on either side of the largest statue, secreting paintings, details of the chipped frescoes in ceiling vaults, as fresh and vibrant as their initial painting more than a millennium and a half ago, when monasteries, training schools, markets and craftsmen congregated here from all over the world, at the height of civilization. Each statue, monks' cell, stairwell, and meeting room was meticulously constructed, bedecked with simplicity, and lavished with gold and jewels.

Mounting the Big Buddha, one can find the remnants, the warrens of intricately interconnected rooms, these cells of a beehive, which lead upstairs to other rooms and vistas, either side of the statue in stone. One must hover in open archways to view some rooms, to sample a few chambers' mysteries

Nancy Dupree had recalled "the scene as it was during the moment of greatest splendor:"

> each surface painted with roof beams, carved doorways, windows, in deep hues and shades, the statues dressed in cloaks, blue and red silks, gold-covered faces and hands luminous, jewels hanging from each raised arm, each ear. And in those ancient beginnings, outside the yellow-robed monks chanted, their monasteries sailing under wind-borne tall flags as pilgrims journeying over centuries from the conquerors and civilization-builders, armies and tolerators, rulers changed a hundred times: the Achaemenids to Alexander the Great, the Selucids, Maurnsya, Ceylanese, Scythians, Kushans, Sassanids, Hephthalids, Hans, Turksw, Tibetans, Umayyads, Abbasids, Tahirids, Safavids, Ghaznavids, Seljuks, Qaraqitans, Ghorids, Mongols, Timurids, Chagatals, Buddhists and Moslems and Central Asian nomads, monks and writers, scholars and scoffers—Fa Hsien, Hsuan-tsang, all wandered through the mountains.

And from atop the smaller Buddha, its ornate faded paintings and niches, alight with fragments of seated Buddhas in each seemingly undiscovered corner, one looks down to the thin stretch of tree-lined river bends, far down this strangely perfect basin between harsh, mud-colored mountains and the long stretch of cliffs, the world in which it had been created, ensemble of monasteries, chapels and sanctuaries nestled in the valley's foothills, chanting and prayer, shimmering candles and incense in 12,000 caves housing monks and visitors, caravans laden with Silk Route goods, kingly entourages seeking solace in the otherworldly light of sandstone hills, farmers and herders tending fields and herds for thousands of years.

We've been told, as well, of how inhabitants of Bamiyan and the nearby village of Korghan "speak of a cave in the hills from which cold blasts of air issue during the day, and at night a phosphorous light emerges out of it and blazes in wild and bright flames."

At 5:15 a.m. on our first officially-sanctioned vacation day, we are in front of the Peace Corps Training Center waiting for the Toyota to take us away. In the early streets we seek out some snack food, and by six are tucked away on the hard seats of a blue truck, full of three Afghan drivers (only one essential), a strange girl named Mary who clings to an Afghan boyfriend and seems immune to all knowledge of cultural sensitivity and who simply appeared, like a parcel on the inventory; the E's—Doc the Vet, and his wife Leila, and their three daughters and one son, and one son-in-law; and a Mrs. O., mother of Lorna H., grandmother of one of the PCV babies who arrived last February; and Dale, the Michigan dairy farmer's son whose work in Lashkargar has collapsed, and who is the only one among us without a camera because he doesn't believe in having to pose pictures.

Outside Kabul, then, we move up out of the city's valley through the small pottered villages and grape valleys on the road to Charikar. Finally after 70 odd kilometers, we turn off on an unpaved road, the surface of our dreams for the next four days. Immediately the road hooks between the mountains, the impervious white caps receding but prominent. In the foreground the green thin rills are full of wheat or potato fields, and the river, clear and icy, winds its way like life blood along the hills. Suddenly, the people are the flat-faced, Oriental-eyed Hazaras, waving to us from their low houses beside the roads, or in their fields. Their women in bright red and green dresses hide their faces, but they look as baked as Navajoes, behind their shawls.

Behind us lie the roads to Begram, the ancient Kushan capital of 2000 years ago, and the steep roads leading to Panjsher's torrential rivers. About nine we stop in Baughi-Afghani. In a teahouse above a bridge full of old men we had tea, and scattered to the fields and a mountains stream in search of nature's relief, after a style. Caught in our female acts, (six females strong beneath a mulberry tree) we are screamed at by a Kutchi woman from behind the wall, not sure who is more embarrassed by our imposition.

The terrain shatters out of the green valley: the carved houses nestled into the hills become scanter, the river leaner and more hidden. We pass through another one-street town, and then another, and then are caught by the grim claws of the barren landscape, in a road winding up into the Shibar Pass. To either side of us the Kutchis and their battered tents and yawning herds scramble for the scatterings of green, and the invisible river. Six hours pass as we crawl; later we see camel caravans and carrying trucks, dust-coated as if dunked in a river. Then we enter the green miracle of Bamiyan's valley. The raging river, the gentle people, a thousand strong, wave to us shyly from their weeding in the green plots, or from their cliff-cave houses against the hills, or as little identical marching school boys winding along the road, or as a toothless grin in an old warrior's face, a peaceful farmer for all his descendants.

And the Red City (Shari-zahar), where the carved facts still hide the notions of war and fortifications, where one of Genghis Khan's favorite nephews was defeated and killed and Genghis Khan for revenge moved into the Bamiyan valley, past the playful rich streams and green, elaborately irrigated fields, and the mudhouses, and groves of popular trees, to Shari-Golgathe, the City of Screams, where his men murdered everything alive and ravaged the land so that today the former Islamic gem of construction stands like a harsh brutal scar, a bleak white shrine of collapsed and broken walls, an archway here, the curve of a walk there, speaking of a time when its inhabitants had lived here. Built in the 7th century, it was destroyed in the 12th, and has remained arid and lifeless since the blood bath.

The town of Bamiyan is a narrow street wide, with small shabby shops up one end of the road, and a restaurant and teahouses up the other. Like an overcooked bakers' dozen, a tin-roofed two-story hotel and two dozen white imitation yurts crown a steep plateau to one side of town, reached only by climbing a thickly tree-lined road that winds up to its level head. Lining the whole valley are the old grottoes, a red hillside-chiseled and riddled by a thousand caves, most of them dating from the Buddhist monasteries built initially 2500 years ago when the first Buddhist monks entered Afghanistan, added to again in the 3rd to 5th century A.D. when the giant Buddhas were constructed, and finally abandoned in the 8th century, and others with a rough outer shell added on, the homes for poor farmers or wandering sheepherders. Then we see them, silent gods of a lost age, the great carved Buddhas standing against the face of the mountain, their faces and limbs chiseled away by Islamic conquerors 1200 years ago, but the stately folds of their robes, the awesome breadth of their stature relatively untouched in a millennium. They are present somehow in each resident of the valley, Shi'a Moslems, these Hazara who are strangers in their own land, the gentle, mellow people, the unrecognizable, descendants of the mad Mongols. One finds the same tranquil dignity in their humblest work, as in their stark mute rulers of the valley.

Our first night we climb both Buddhas, revering in the other worldly quiet of the place, thanks to our Farsi and established position as teachers, allowed to view the upper chambers, and to climb almost to the very top of the Large Buddha's mountain. Sitting on each god's head, the valley wings below, the patterns of rich green and yellow, molded in the fields, raising up to the brown gray mountains, and above them to the snowy peaks, we speak with the monuments' guides about this place they are rightly proud of, and study the faded remains of once elaborate frescoes in the archways around the statues, and in some of the grottoes. Dizzy from the settled time, the notion of so many years between ourselves and those small pious worshippers, we move, stooping, through the dark passageways, up the circular stairs, around chilly vaulting rooms.

For dinner we all settle in Pascal's Teahouse, sit on carpets in the dim lanterns' light, watching our reflections against the gaudy calendar-slick pictures on the wall, and listen to another volunteer, Mike P. play songs with the regular *rebab* players and drummers. Toward bed we move finally, carrying a lantern like a fire bug across the deep cool dark of fields, wet with watering, the sky arching above us with the million constellations. At the PC volunteer's house we wrap ourselves in sleeping bags and forget everything in a sound sleep.

By morning we follow up the dew, eat heartily of our host's soft spread of bread, fruit and tea, and set out to find Golgotha, the City of Tears. Two friendly soldiers escort us to the base of the hill road, then entrust us to a small pale boy carrying a bag of rocks or ground grain (we are never to learn which), who speaks at us animatedly all the way to the ruins. From the fields, brightly-clothed women and children smile shyly toward us. A young student stops to speak about his plans. After a few miles, we take the child's picture and give him some money to buy a pen, thanks for his guiding us, then move into the realms of another guard-guide, who leads the way across the frozen destruction up the steep winding path, to the roof of the world. From atop, we can see the whole magic valley stretching green and temporal in all directions, to the hills behind riddled with more caves and the now empty niche of another former Buddha, and the larger compounds of generations of families growing out of the land.

For lunch we are piled in the truck again and driven several miles outside of town to a place where two mountain streams seem to converge, called Six Bridges, Puli u-Shash. With the wind and rapids we lunch, and then, to the delight and consternation of some 20 tiny school boys who gather in the road above us to stare and talk a little, the E's, gymnasts, put on a brief acrobatics demonstration. Later we climb up to Golgotha again and that night—from the walking, the mountain air—we sleep soundly.

Our second day, we set off to Bande-Amir in the morning. The fertile valley is quickly abandoned into stone, stone sprouting camps of sheepherders and yellow thistle flowers, and three hours of rocking in an old truck puts us above the blue creation of the lakes, all five of them stretching with a rich color that made even the clear sky look dull. We wander around them, climbing the natural dam edges, studying a storybook scene of a hundred little shaven-headed boys spilling out of the windows of the mosque shrine at the edges of the largest lake. The woman we are with, Mrs. O., wants to learn more about the poor people who tend cattle or crops in the narrow rugged valley and live in caves in the mountainside.

We visit two of the gristmills powered by an overflow from the large lake, and she takes pictures of the structures and of the local children, and we wonder what dignity such people could have left, and if we don't diminish it by staring at their poorness. Most children that we see have white, leathery skin, worn by hard work and the elements or malnutrition . . . We find a man who keeps and rents out horses for "visitors," and horseback ride for two hours, picking our way on rather dull but careful horses through the rugged valley, past more tiny houses and sheepherders fields, up again and around the high cliffs above two other lakes, feeling free, observers of the miraculous, letting the land talk to us in a mute whisper, as the wind moves across the heads of wheat 75 kilometers back. Here we sense the silence of mystery and bleakness, shared by miracles which somehow let life survive.

It is time then to go back to Bamiyan . . . and the small boys with hoops racing up and down the Bamiyan street, as dark falls . . . .

In Bamiyan, in this time enclave, then, Hazara women are equal, farm, and work as doctors, nurses, or teachers. And schools for boys and girls, few and inadequate, still run. The women are everywhere in long skirts and blouses, their black or gray-streaked shocks of braided hair pulled back, dusty under brightly patterned green, blue and red scarves. As they carry water from the river, a child inevitably straddles their shoulders, or they wave from the pocket-size fields off from the narrow road. No one has on *chadris*. In the small Bamiyan bazaar, elfin-faced men, Asian steppe-featured, dark narrow eyes, flat noses, and broad cheekbones, grin and offer us tea. Capped boys and their stooping fathers squat beside nearly empty shops, gesturing at small piles of onions or nuts. Typically, rural and mountainous houses seem hunkering nearby, low, walled, mud-made, the shops basic straw stalls.

One reaches other villages by foot, or jeep, on roads no wider than a hiking trail, with bone-jolting boulders and deep rutted potholes pacing every movement, past hamlet after tiny village, each bound to the sheer bluffs and cliffs above the valley, crossed by tiny icy streams, the mud wall houses grasping the edges of each other, the red mountain walls behind them. Bereft of trees or even weeds, the land still thrives: local herders and farmers have carved out small vegetable plots in the rare, narrow ravines between cliffs. Most hamlets stare back, bleak and tiny, one row of a street with a few limping store booths, perhaps a few dozen families and their livestock. But the hamlets build on each other. Further up the valley cluster more houses and sheds, with the lower one central to several nearby villages. There, flat-roofed houses are built against the boulders, only a few feet down from several attached to the ancient caves which riddle the porous mountain terrain.

It is a long ride back to Kabul . . . and we rest, quiet, musing on route, remembering only the edges of that enchanted picture . . . .

June 18, 1974

Teaching at Kabul University is a bit sterile and tedious, at least the eight hours with a Freshman section thrice a week, largely repeating and re-repeating basic grammatical structures before a sleepy bunch of would-be teasers, the bright engineers of the future (their minds don't move like mine—could I ever introduce a poem?) In our office there is a bullet-like but gentle Afghan instructor, Mr. Shokor, who stutters in his impatience to voice a thought and brags lightly that his son, 13 and in the 11th grade, is able to do all the same work he gives his college freshman and sophomores. A trim crisp-speaking women, Mrs. Azur, whose husband has a doctorate in geology from a German university, teaches from the dull green book of grammar, asking the Americans questions with the eagerness of a learner. She and her husband came back from Germany, where they had been for two and a half years, just ten months ago. Our other colleagues include a burly-haired PC volunteer who resembles a squinting Austrian spy, tongue lashes his lazy students, and poses as an Arab at official parties; a thin balding effeminate slight man of 23 who has settled in here for two years already, moves with a pursing indifference but some exertion, a bachelor born and bred; and then the new recruit, jet-settled, sun-glassed, mumbling over his slowest sections (the B3 and B4s who should—theoretically—not even be in this faculty), and who is to be married soon.

June 22, 1974

> *(We teach and we taste the expatriate and volunteer life of Kabul, with a second anniversary, birthday for Billy, introduction to the game of MONOPOLY with Kabul places, and to Gayle Pinder, a Black PCV whose sister plays cello at Julliard)*

. . . The wind of Kabul nights, feline-like, rushing through and rubbing against the trees, and the windows rattle like intimidated ogres, crashing across the panes. Outside a slinky, frisky tongue yodels at the moon and the motions of strangers behind our wall.

June 25, 1974

> *[Mail comes and includes pictures of my brother John and Katherine's wedding in Iowa . . . We entertain memories of Mr. Shetab of studying in Carbondale at University of Southern Illinois in 1967—He recalls he flame in the gasfields near Alton, an early Easter egg hunt in a park, a sunrise service by a lake, the Anheuser-Busch demonstration team and the brewery, and in my sort-of home town, the Gateway Arch and the zoo]*

Living at the edge of an Afghan middle class (or above) neighborhood, we hardly seem to be in this country (except—there are wheat fields and manure piles and *chadried* women doing their wash and livestock roaming behind the university; and a mosque sounds off ritually at regular intervals despite its neon lights, and a *nan* shop and a meat and vegetable vendor indicate the unchangeable, and school girls in their black dresses and white scarves gawk at us passing, and we can never cease to be unaware of the stigma we have as foreigners.).

The cook at this house where we are staying is a priceless gem of wit. Hossain was a shepherd until three years ago, in Ghazni. He had never been to school. Somehow he took a secretarial course at a place called the Wanton English School in Kabul upon arriving here with his mother, once upon a time back then, and he learned to type fifty English words a minute. But being unschooled and a Hazara, he had no possibilities for employment. So he began taking English classes at the Peace Corps Secretarial training school and his vacuous mind began to fill up with every name and phrase conceivable. He recites stiffly the chronology of world leadership, the changes in name and power, his aspirations for life and those of others, standing there now in his eighteen years, (can it be?) in his pants that are patched behind the knees and with a zipper suitable to an arctic lumber jacket holding them together for the full course of their front. And his English phrases startle: "Would 6:00 be suitable for you for your evening meal tonight?" came out one afternoon like a Victorian butler. A few weeks ago he was married, to a child of sixteen, and now the three of them (with his mother) live in some tiny room near Jema-minat . . . What a mind, such precocity. Why can we not enrich his life?

July 7

> *(As with all small communities, we find the Kabul PCV community full of tension. We hear criticism of some volunteers and hangers-on and are "cornered" by the Faculty of Engineering Dean who wants to tell us of the incurable arrogance and indifference to work he's encountered in "some person," current volunteers working at the university. T and I were brought in to insure that PC looks good again, but in the process will earn no points among the current volunteer staff. With so many stuck here but no longer gainfully employed, this behavior seems inevitable. And with the advent of a new country director expectant soon, one who might sweep the Augean stables in a Herculean task, we can only hope for positive change.]*

Even with all this unwinding, the Afghan government itself has systematically starved out every worthwhile project here, specifically those in agriculture and health care, because they view foreign workers here as suspicious, and leave only the rather innocuous PR job of teaching English intact. This work, sadly, may at best affect and even help less than 1% of the people in this country . . . We hear we are also losing 30 dollars per 350 dollars of cash, because the government has a monopoly and people are having to plot ways to smuggle cash out since the xenophobia here is over a distrust of foreign currencies against the *afghani*, as much as of people.

> *[One night we enjoy a long talk with the quiet and conscientious volunteer Jason McCabe, about literature, Nabokov and Marquez, Faulkner and Welty, all this in his Kabul backyard under moonlight and the real or imagined scent of jasmine. How hungry we have been to discuss our old favorites.*]

The dog, a sleek black misfit here who prefers chewing the bark of trees or captured birds to any more civilized fare, barks at the shadows of tomcats on the wall; the moon is full and a thick wind hustles the branches of the trees above us. Someone tells how he met a professor from Columbia here, a twenty-eight year old language specialist who is an expert on the pre-Islamic Middle East and is fluent in Pushtu, Dari, Turkmeni Uzbek . . . (Is it Bernard Lewis?) Wondering what could possess someone to bury his life in such a narrow study, the speaker asked him. This scholar's answer was immediate: he had become interested in this area, and could only afford to support his interest by becoming an expert in it, mastering a rare field and developing as a genuine scholar, knowledgeable in all its languages and area studies and history.

> *[We learn more of the wonder boy Hossain, his letters to Joe's younger sisters, his way to practice his English, and his desire to tell his story]*

. . . My musing, most often boring, time is going most recently to correcting and grading sophomore compositions written on such stimulating topics as "The Future Role of Women in Afghan Society,"

"Living in a Kabul University Dormitory" (12 boys live in room designed for four, but they have hot and cold water and modern equipment), "The Best Movie I Ever Saw" and "Advantages and Disadvantaged of a Large Family." In the latter, I find a certain pathos in their praises for a recent heart-breaking moralistic India movie . . . .

July 14, 1975

Eerily, one day this week we take a taxi back from Shari Nau and the driver, noticing our Farsi, asks if we are teachers. We nod, and then he begins to explain how he had been the one in Gulilibakar (Panjsher) who finally went into the water to retrieve Denise Blake's body. Over and over he relates the details, how wild the river is and how he managed it briefly because he is a strong swimmer, but how it is a place of death for almost anyone else; and how his family lives just down the stream from where she fell in and how they all rushed to the bank to see what to do. He goes on, his face pale but animated, to tell how finally the husband had offered a lot of money to him for doing what he did, but how all his people and he himself told him he could not take it, how sad it was for a person to come to die in another land, far away from family and friends, and how sad the husband of only a year must be. This driver must tell that story now to everyone who can understand it . . . .

. . . Rumors to choke your life off abound here: for Jeshewn all of Kabul is being blocked off so no one will be allowed either in or out. We are wondering if we can get to the airports . . . .

I finish the university job with feelings of having accomplished a minimum, but of also having seen a slim, if real, potential for education in this country in the Faculty of Engineering. The physical plant of the university is good and the school has an excellent faculty for the most part (educated and devoted and Afghan) to train future engineers and scientists—It is clearly an insult that the volunteers sent to work there have not always been of the highest motivation or caliber. As for the other departments, there may be reason for real doubt . . . .

Part of my issue, and Tom's, of course, is that we were there such a short time, like substitutes perhaps, just following someone's syllabus without the chance to define it or the students as our own.

July 18, 1974

Kabul is then behind us like an ancient dream turned rueful. We leave in a calm flutter from the airport which had swallowed us thirteen months before with such a dry appetite . . . .

[We took vacation, flying to Istanbul, taking a train in Greece to Athens, then going to the islands of Rhodes, Patmos, and, then up to the Peloponnese and to Delphi, then back across Turkey to Iran and Afghanistan, the first part by train, the second by bus and foot, to return five weeks later.]

September 8, 1974

[From Meshed, Iran]

. . . Unholy to the end, we see nothing, only rush for a bus to the border town of Taybad . . . sit warmly through desert dryness for another three hours and a half, until we are at the fronter, with a Doctorate of Agriculture from Afghanistan, one thin singular traveler, a Japanese youth, and two Americans, a loud 38-year old and his dainty wife, bound for Herat. Customs passed, we bargain in no man's land with a driver to take us to the Afghan side and from there to Herat, finally strike reason and are off, in moments in Afghanistan. We wind our way through that labyrinthine custom check, and as dark falls heavily are in a rattling Toyota heading for Herat, a truck which stops on the bleak, unpeopled road to pick up other passengers, is stopped and searched once by a hoarse-voiced young soldier—who seizes some former smuggler from the seat in front of us and waves us on—and then we suffer one be-wailed stop for dinner. Behind us stretch the acres and miles of unnamed Iranian cities, as we move into, within this country we had chosen to return to, until Herat is around us. But when we seek buses to Kabul, we find the good ones are all sold out. Still, we finally choose the 5:00 a.m. bus, one of the oldest fleets, eat cold *pilau* and drink Fanta at a hotel, crawl into a flea bed for 20 *afs* a piece in a building of grim would-be travelers and seven loin-clothed Pakistanis . . . Awaking we find this bus is not going after all, so venture into the city to visit and end up leaving at 2:30 on a more reliable bus line. We are prisoners to this tin contraption and moveable feast for a 24 hour trip, survive one flat tire outside of Ghazni, free our bodies bond in weariness from the hard bench-like chairs, and arrive in Kabul at 3:00 p.m. It is the following day and we seek much needed sleep.

But in the quick visit to Afghanistan's famous western gate, we came quickly to understand this most literary and Persian of Afghan cities, the beautiful Herat:

This city shows off its elegant Friday Mosque, the ancient minarets edging the town like sentinels, full as the giant bronze cauldron before the mosques and mausoleums from the Ghorid Empire, with unscathed treasures. Beyond its medieval citadel, the Arg with 18 towers, bazaars radiate from the Chahar Su, the heart of the Old City. We gawk at the minarets, mausoleum, and small *madrassa* of the blue-tiled Musalla Complex, all of which date from the time of Timurid (1417), and at an enhanced garden of irrigation ditches and *chinar* (mulberry) trees. Aways, we sense, here is a strong and somewhat autonomous entity, coyly capitalized for millennium on its location between the Iranian Plateau and the Central Asian steppes. It never ceased to be a center of Persian culture, lovingly attended, fought over by Central Asian, Persian, Afghan and Middle Eastern rulers—Ghorids, Timurids, Seljuks, Safavids—but firmly independent and classy.

On rising ground north of the city, the elegant eleventh century shrine of Gazar Gah honors the Sufi poet Khwajah ʿAbd Allāh al-Anṣārī, its blue marble calligraphied panels of poetry, exclaiming:

"From the unmanifest I came,
And pitched my tent, in the Forest of Material existence.
I passed through mineral and vegetable kingdoms,
Then my mental equipment carried me
into the animal kingdom;
Having reached there I crossed beyond it;
Then in the crystal clear shell of human heart
I nursed the drop of self in a Pearl,

And in association with good men
Wandered round the Prayer House,
And having experienced that, crossed beyond it;
Then I took the road that leads to Him,
And became a slave at His gate;
Then the duality disappeared
And I became absorbed in Him."

We have heard of, but never find here, the grave of a famous and saintly old woodcutter. Said to have lived for thousands of years, he was called, the "shah mullah"

So, we tour fleetingly, then board a bus, to travel all night and day to reach Kabul. Then, quickly, we go on to Tashkurghan to arrive in time for the first day of school.

Hazara and Hazarjat, 1999-2004

Thirty harsh years later, when the Taliban came, the villagers in the Hazarajats and in other enclaves of Hazara, were the first to die, in targeted and punishing destruction. Taliban forces burned their clinics, killed their teachers and medical staff, and gutted and torched the villages, 4,000 homes, shops, and fields. Then, in March 2001, on orders from leader Mullah Mohammed Omar, the Taliban turned to the Buddhas and destroyed these gentle giants from the 6th century A.D.

As Rory Steward (*The Places in Between*, 2006) described the area a year later:

> *No where in Afghanistan did the cruelty of the Taliban seem so comprehensive or have such an ethnic focus. In a three-day walk from Yakawlang, where the Taliban had executed four hundred, to Shidan, where eighty shops had been reduced to blackened shells, every Hazara village I saw had been burned. In each settlement people had been murdered, the flocks driven off and the orchards razed. Most of the villages were still abandoned.*

But the fate of the Hazaras throughout Afghanistan, not just in Bamiyan, remained brutal. Because of their Shi'a religion, their Mongolian, Central Asian features, their alliances, and their century-old casting as the lowest classes in Afghan culture, they were targeted over and over again by the Pushtoon Taliban. In Mazar-i-Shariff, historically a site of conflict and a place of many ethnic groups, including large numbers of Hazaras, there was major retaliation. After some 5,000 Taliban were killed following their failed attempt to capture the city in 1999, the following year the vanquished Taliban returned with revenge. They hunted down thousands of Hazaras, trapping them in the streets, then hacked off their arms, and massacred them.

Year Two
Kabul and Tashkurghan, Afghanistan

Frances, at Old Fort, Tashkurghan, 1975.

Tom tutoring Mirad

Tashkurghan bazaar 1975

Cart and hauler in town, 1975.

Eid carnival outside Tashkurghan, 1975.

VIII
BACK TO TASHKURGHAN

September 11, 1974 (20 Sunbullah)

. . . . We find a taxi, a quiet fellow who carries us across the freshly green valleys in their last dresses of summer, into the unchanging deserts and to this town again, in less than six hours . . . . We half-doze, and . . . glance up only to catch the aqua tumbling streams of mountains waters, to wince at a catapulting Kutchi truck outside Puli-Khumri, to settle for tea beside a Salang valley, to study the first view of Tashkurghan again.

Under the blinderless afternoon sun we unload our bundles beside the road, are stopped by two previous teachers from school, and a new Pushtoon one, apparently a language teacher from this summer's cycle who had worked earlier at Samagan Lycee and was now transferred, quite against his will, to teach here. Disregarding our obvious disarray, our newly-arrived state, he immediately plunges into an explanation of himself and an appeal for help with his "problems". He proudly waves a note from the new couple in Samagan which implores us "to help their good friend." A bevy of baggy cotton-panted boys offer to carry our abundance, and finally we set off down the mud lane to our compound, a shuffling Amore M'med following, mutely. We are "home," again.

That afternoon we report to our respective schools, me to meet a roomful of newly-sent teachers. The young, soft-featured karakul-hatted teachers from last year help me figure out my schedule. I exchange words with my closest friend among the teachers, the tiny 1st class teacher,

Esfandyar, and am interrogated about starting a help class by the young Pushtoon, and then go home.

We had hired this cook (alas, our third) Aman back in April, and left him in charge of the house while we were in Kabul and then on vacation. Alas, upon our return, we find ourselves in the middle of a necessary drama. He must be dismissed.

He snivels and begs even after we give him a large, extra baksheesh, claiming he should have a bed, a watch, clothes. It makes for an ugly, distasteful time, calmed by night when we sit without electricity and finally leave off wondering and go to bed. In the morning this cook leaves us at 5:00 a.m. We have an unexpected holiday from school, so we spend the day cleaning the house, collecting a little food, having our clothes washed, and learning the truth about this sad-sack thief of a cook we had just fired. First we hear from Amore M'med's wife, then from Iotillah's son:

They tell us that ten days after we left, Aman himself left, after locking up the house and announcing his intentions to all the town, and bragging that he had been paid "thousands of *afghanis*." And, we are told, he had only returned a few days before we were due back. Having become 8,000 afs richer for doing nothing, and universally acclaimed as lazier than any in town, he had ridiculed our trust.

I hesitate after Aman has left, for a day or two, wondering if he had in fact done this heinous act and betrayed our trust. Or, was it *drough* (lies) which these two very wounded people with their own self-interest had been intent on telling us? It is possible, but somehow this time Tom and I do not distrust them and their motivation, so much as we believe in and mourn the unreliability of the lost cook.

Traditionally, Afghans believe that 13 creatures were once men and were turned into animals—*muskh*—for specific faults. Thus, as a sampling, they were as follows: elephant (cruelty), bear (theft), rabbit (false oaths), scorpion (change of faith), fox (pride), tortoise (embezzlement), crow (drunkeness), and mouse (a woman who used to weep aloud). Other creatures who once were men, are dove, sparrow, owl, and porcupine.

And among us, who is the bear, who the rabbit, who the tortoise?

At night, Tom kills two scorpions, unwanted guests who had kept their own vigilance and grown a family, perhaps, in our absence, and we sample a homegrown melon, then try to burn out some bees in our outhouses. Yesterday, in the cool first hours of morning, we discover the bees are still intact in the walls of the *kenerab*. A neighbor comes to dig out our dirty ditch to give himself a channel for water from the landlord's land, and three neighbor boys, twins to a quartet of puppies who haunt our dry fields before the ditch digging blocks their entry, run away with our toilet paper, taking it for a kite . . . .

My first day of school dawns and passes, with me basically teaching the same grades as last year. I welcome my student's beautiful faces, even those who I know will learn little and be disruptive. There are new faces for the 8th class, but the new 12th class is someone else's charge now. I tell about my summer's adventures boldly in Dari and English, greet the *modir's* wife and Najiba, the new teacher from Mazar whom I'd met before, then apologize profusely and try to sincerely explain to the *modir* who had beguiled my failure to contact him in the summer, how the summer had passed. It was my shyness that kept us from looking him up and sharing a meal while we were in Kabul, but it comes across as yet another unprofessional mistake, and a culturally insensitive one. Why can I not do this right?

We are also greeted with an incident with one of Tom's students, who had failed English. All the Pushtoons in town demand that Tom pass him. Zeagul and Tajenisa (10th class) come over with dried fruit and an embroidered handkerchief to plead his case (since he is their half-brother), so though the boy knows nothing, he is promoted to the 12th class and the family shame is mitigated. For it seems he is to be married, but can not do so until he gets into his right grade and has the promise of completing the *lycee*.

So, we can compromise, know our own limits, bend when asked . . . .

Today, I have six hours of teaching . . . and find, not surprisingly, that even my best former students have forgotten a lot. The *modir's* wife pops in during a break to tease and scold me. First she tells me I am to teach her English three afternoons a week, and then she reminds me that I must now remember to present myself in the office before going to class each day (the old "protocol"). And, there is an invitation to a wedding tomorrow night . . . .

Out in the world, beyond the quietly corrupted social modes of this village, under the diamond splattered sky, the cool night breezes, and I wonder at all the still unanswerable, unchangeable family secrets—beyond all this—back in the States. Ford has granted a full pardon to Nixon and the world weeps again at this distortion of justice, the separate standards for rich and poor. And rumor has it that a pardon for each and every rascal involved in the insulting destructive charade of Watergate is not to be long in coming. Our stomachs sink at yet another instance of betrayal. How small it makes all these little lies look (passing students who have learned nothing, paying a cook who lies to us), for these people are powerless by comparison while the others are semi-gods, "leaders of the western world." . . .

September 15, 1974

The town seems to be having a taste of every ritual before Ramadan begins. As was the case in the spring, there have been weddings almost every night, as well as a funeral for the father of Folora (a 12th grade student and uncle of a clan here that includes our new teachers Najiba, Zahara, and others.) Thursday night I go to the wedding of a student from last year's 12th class, Fazuddah (or Fouzia, for short). Tom goes to the men's quarters for lunch earlier in the day, so I am *"tona,"*(alone) for the evening. At six, gathering in my unwomanized dignity as the night falls, garbed in my Greek dress (the "maxi" tomorrow's gossips will knight me with wearing), I walk as far as the first group of women with Tom, who has dashed home for something, then am escorted by two richly *chadried* mothers and their three children, to the gates of the party, into the yard past relatives who carefully inspect me, and to the consternating circle of discerning females, all the way to the side of the thin hair-curled, chain-smoking and green-brocaded bride.

And so begins another famous night of sitting, of moving decorously from the honored guest parlor with its rugs and real chairs, accompanied by a train of students to prevent me from going through an open window instead of the proper door, to the bristling outdoor cool with its massive wedding canopy decorated with colored paper flowers and lanterns, to the porch of sleeping children and brightly dressed neighbor women, to the courtyard musicians, *tambars* and drummers. Here in the lantern light each favored family beauty spins a few graceful steps, and the hovering cousin boys perform giddily, the night heavy with the held breath of festivity, bursting out like a breathy soprano with each dance. Lithe ageless girls wind their hands and legs into soft undulating circles, small movers of the audience, hand-keeper of children' precious secrets.

Sometime in the evening three old haggish women with stretched tambourine drums come into the guest room to perform. Toothless, rustled, and comically old they sing a folk tune like a metronome, while their pudgy, potato sack-sequined fellow crone dances heavily across the rugs to gather money. I eat pilau, the only spooned participant, and lightly as befits a stranger. But I am in good company; there were no hardy eaters; and I also have tea, well-welcomed in its time.

I talk with some students from last year's graduating glass, Mogul and others, two who promise they are going to enter the university in the spring, another who is married and already the mother of an infant. Then I am introduced to another young woman, the sister of one of the new teachers at school who is from Samagan and knows the whole history of Peace Corps staff teachers there. This young woman speaks politely and simply to me about my life here, and my 'medicines' and work, and tells herself what she knows, claiming to be one of Sara's former students. At first she mistakes me for someone else, someone who had visited her house last year and taken pictures. But as we move outside to watch the procession, long eminent, she squeezes and leads. It makes me uncomfortable and involuntarily I instantly pull away, none too discreetly.

Then the long awaited union of man and wife follows, the ceremony ends, and it is the stroke of midnight. As always, it seems, a Cinderella escaping fearfully at 12, I made a rather insensitive scene in my haste to leave the house, bowing out with neither grace nor greatness, accompanied in the pitch dark by three boys, who are kindly but startled I think, as they lead me by lantern over rutted, unseeable road, to my house. On route, we are stopped once by two policemen who insult (this is a first) me with some question suggesting I might not be all I should be to be thus about, a woman largely alone at this hour. Finally we reach the old door of the outer compound; I bang heartlessly, bid my accomplices a sleepy, grouchy adieu, and enter the safe hole of our home . . . .

More invitations come quickly, some taken, others delicately refused for now as I immerse myself in the rituals of teaching class. The classes so often seem scarcely aware that they should have to learn, but always within each group there are a few stars.

Armoe M'med, forever part of our life, has began a systematic fluffing of our bedding and *towshaks*, and one day manages fulfillment. He advises paternally about what good grapes must be bought, how cheap melons are in Puli Khumri, and how wicked the landlord's family is, and had been. We learn more of Aman's treachery. He apparently paid the landlord 500 *afs* to lie and say he'd preserved the house for us. Then Amore M'med coaches me on how best to receive invitations aplenty from my students: "Let them know you are at home. Visit each one. Invite them here, of course, kind teacher." . . .

All Friday Iotila (old Iotallah's grandson) plays with some puzzles, observes a game of checkers, introduces some games ("Frisbee, he cowers) to his cousins, and then advises us after his own fashion about things. I think of the paucity of toys, of time to be children here, and the wonder of childhood's simple games we'd so often taken for granted, those constant supplies of picture books, puzzles and balls. A taste of these things suggests a new realm, a new reason to him, to them all . . . .

The bees *(zambaris)* seem hushed now. We see only one a day sluggishly hugging the *tashknob* door. Perhaps our one night's stand, that comedian's farcical purge of burning tea cans and kerosene lanterns, has brought a slim success. And the dumpiest of the four orphaned puppies from next door has befriended our feeding hand. And the stars here are again nightly wonders.

So the days have passed.

We are going to live here for another 40 weeks . . .

September 19, 1974

It is 6 a.m,. morning cool, the day as yet unprovoked. There is the hush of undisturbed earthlings, a few braying donkeys, the wind in the branches. The third day of Ramadan begins in our host country, in sleep. It is, by contrast, an easy week for us, barring my infected tooth and our waiting for Mirad, our new cook . . . . The tinsmiths and carpenters, the sleepy *dhukandars* and fruit vendors, the alley of tailors in their bent knee stances beside their machines, the ragamuffin unveiled girls relaying bowls of honeyed fruit and *mass* (yogurt), the mule drivers and the setters on, the hallow-stomached teachers and the accusing-eyed students—all of these have found the week a little harder, I dare say.

One night Azarullah, Tom's always visiting and assisting student from last year's 11th class, comes over again, and we sit out on the dusk-cooled mud porch, sipping the bond of tea. He spilled out the atrocities of the school system, and the particular evils of one teacher—the little watch maker who teaches physics and knows nothing, who failed most of his class because he didn't know the answers himself, who deliberately erased Azarullah's exam paper because this student had audaciously confronted him, who quarreled with his wife and took out his hatred on the classes, until his wife went to her commandant because he refused her foods, and then left him for good three months ago . . .

Azarullah speaks also of how little the other teachers know, because they are products of the same crippling system that requires them to do a new book for each subject each year, so it is ignorance heaped on more ignorance, students and teachers constantly pushed through for the sake of the system.

. . . . The fruits of Fouzia's wedding last week are still flowing over: a timid boy brought us a huge platter full of Afghan cookie meat pie-grease bread last night. Our table was already laden with Mirad's first meal, rice and raisin and onion and potato stew and melon and salads; then our neighbor's son joined us for a plateful, and then left, eyes daunted, and we sent some of the food to Armoe's family.

We examine the fate of one adopted puppy: we fed him minimally, scraps, and now he seems to hang on to us for affection. In the night he yelps in the *jewie* like a banshee's yell, terrified by plopping frogs ostensibly, or by the narrowness of his hole through the wall, or some unforeseen puddle of water, or one of his nibbling brothers . . . But we cannot keep him.

And my students, my sisters, how can one not love these girls . . . .?

September 21

> *[Another set of distasteful relays from Kabul . . . . It seems that the new PC Director has fired Koshan, Wahidullah, and Mary, the changes all to do with Volunteer support services, and moved the PC office to a small house near his own home. The*

implications of all this? It seems that mail delivery will now be though the Afghan system and not by way of PC. Volunteers will need to handle all their own paperwork; and there will no longer be a PC switchboard . . . A newly-come doctor is already preparing to leave, we are told. All these cutbacks will impact the Volunteers, although people like the Country Director will continue to make 20 times their/our salaries, etc. [But likely he is 20 times more effective than the median level of accomplishment of the Volunteers.]

. . . Strolling through the bazaar, I face the usually laconic shopkeepers, possessed today, with a mad zeal in their eyes to sell: An Afghan Tour bus had just pulled in and spilled out its moneyed explorers.

September 23, 1974

Classes waver, but are largely tame: the 11th class can always surprise me with their picture descriptions. There was one today of Tajenisa's parents, another of an Iranian man who dresses as a women, and another by Magfirat full of characters and genealogy, about a widow and seven sons (three of whom were twins, the others separated only by a month in age!) For the 10th and 8th classes, I am always having to strain the reins . . . they remain abnormally antsy-pantsy, always fluttering to run out of class . . .

[Tom's shared, so rare with him, some childhood recollections] . . .

This morning was a forewarning of winter, chilly and dark, but by eight it was again warm, with autumn not yet bending to more Nordic commands . . . . How will it be, another winter in this tiny village, with the inevitable cold nights and the long, often unpredictable trips down to Kabul on swerving icy roads?

September 25, 1974

Tonight it is raining, a soft tumble of irregular drops, and we sit, full-bellied and lopsidedly weary, in the house we've befriended a year now. But last night we had a thunderbolt, as the father of the father of the son, the Haji-sibe, (another Iotallah) himself permeated our lightless room with his full sense of nonsense, and told us we have to pay 300 *afs* a month more to live in his house; we boiled with injured pride and justifiable annoyance—for the old batty leech has done nothing to make this place livable. We have ourselves painted the walls, put in new doors, patched up walls, put in electricity, laid bricks—and now our investments are presumably to become his assets, and he wants to squeeze us for more. We smolder today, but not because of the money (a $ 5 to 6 raise) but because he will never see us as anything but *haragees* to be taken advantage of, almost as a point of pride.

But we did one good thing. One of Mirad's nephews came from Sare-pul to see him last night and asked if we knew of any jobs for him. We decorously wrote out a map and letter for him, to the people in Mazar and this evening his uncle heard that he had gotten employment with Allison Kennedy, the new PCV there . . . .

About the family who resides behind and around us . . . they are rude, dull people, ignorant and without grace, their children as dense and unruly as their elders, never once taught anything in love or interest and pitiable now for their having been reared in a nasty vacuum.

We will have to look long and hard for another house . . . .

On Saturday we are to begin lessons with Ziadeen, an old PC teacher, Persian reading and writing for three hours a week, at PC's reimbursements . . . It is a grand idea which I look forward to, one allowing us to move up in basic Persian literacy

As I enter the school office today, a man, in full-fledged navy blue band uniform, with gold-braid and harp insignia, is talking unabashedly to the *modir.* I am reminded how, with the clerk at T's school, there was the argument about whether or not to sign and acknowledge the receipt of permission for the conference we attended five months ago, and the rapid reversal of the *modir*'s reasoning to not change Tom's schedule because it would make too much work for the *modir* himself. And we also wrestle with the petty quarrels between otherwise reasonable school boys who have refused to come and sit inside together at the same house (ours). It makes for a strange vision.

I have tea at Fouzia's (the newly wedded) house which we are considering renting. As always the honored guest, I am seated in the gilded wedding cushions with three plates of sweets and hot tea pots in front of me, while all of the family (Zahra, her sister, and the other cousin, Tiara, now five months pregnant, another aunt, and a neighbor) fast this Ramadan day. This is an impossible situation. I do not wish to break the fast in front of them, am not desirous of food at all, and yet can not deny them their obligation to treat me as an honored and well-fed guest.

September 28, 1974

I'm tickled by, adoring of, the little girls going home from school, uniform in their drab black dresses and short bobbed hair, clutching their slate boards. A hoard of them crosses the bridge beside the mill, when one of them drops her slate by accident into the water. She sits down on the bridge and howls. Her classmates look flustered around her. A man comes out from the mill, silently pulls the slate out of the water, and gives it to the girl. She goes from tears to a smile to tears again when she discovers all her "alefba's "have been washed away.

In the office, a new student, a tottering four-year old, barely beyond babyhood, is asked to say her name and alphabet. Shyly, she mumbles; the *modir, saer-malim*, and teacher nod heads, and she is sent to class. How many days, years, will this young girl be allowed to study?

Sept. 30, 1974

Our new lessons have started with Ziadeen, hugely self-confident, albeit, rather arrogant, yet also undirected. He is seemingly incapable of gauging where we are at in language and yesterday came up with a most simplistic presentation of the "five important verb tenses," some point of Persian we actually know. With his tutoring he is making as much salary as we are; yet he bums cigarettes, questions our salaries and our life here, seems to enjoy deliberately taunting us, and—in general—is frequently less than likable. We dread his staying for dinner or beyond his appointed four hours a week, but are helpless to just tell him to shoo! Again, sad to say, it is the Pushtu attitude, the machismo, the proud warrior, behaviors complicated by his being out of his own territory and driven to master this one. Alas, we must learn from him.

Tom's gotten worm medicine via a long route—We made a call to the Country Director Howard himself on Friday afternoon, got a return call from Fariad, and a relay from the Afghan Post directing a bus en route to Mazar to leave the package at the *bande* . . . .

Yesterday I lingered in the office after class a few minutes, as the modir, his long knotted face sallow as always, took out a brochure about some company in England which finds work for other nationals wishing to work abroad. The jobs are primarily for laborers and, as I immediately suspected, the inquiry came out of his own desire to leave this country, to find a way to serve his own interests. I blunder, too quickly telling him these placements are not jobs for teachers or educators, and doing so in front of two other teachers . . . .

In the same day, I discover that his wife, Muzdah, with several other teachers at large, no longer fasts. I am sitting in the second grader's class room with her and the tiny teacher Parwin, and the returned 12th grader from last year, while they squeeze and tear apart a pomegranate and suck out the rich red juice. It happens all behind closed doors, but before an open window looking out on the school yard crowded with the students in recess. She bewilders me, this women, unhealthily flabby, dark-skinned, harsh-fingered. Yet I know she once studied both French and English. Coyly once in front of me, she wrote a tiny excuse in the notebook of Shirngul (2nd year, 8th class). In French she had crafted: "Le professor est dans le salle de bain . . ."

We walk out into the afternoon, through the town along the road, past the dark crazy man who patrols the silent and remote streets as a half spirit, shoeless, shirtless, in winter and summer alike. Further and before us sway the wizard wand and cape of an old sorcerer, his long gray white hair tucked untidily beneath a high crown-like turban with the Arabian's canopy. We go as far as the Garden. After a summer's work it is still little changed. Some of its mud walls are freshly whitewashed, pointedly. We gather some fresh-secreted resin from the pine trees, the sap clinging to the ends of newly-trimmed limbs like subtle teardrops, and then move back across the bony desolate outer ring of the town, into the anonymous mud lanes, grasping for their secrets in the overhanging branches of green fruit trees behind the plain brown walls.

Each morning we wake to the pounding ocean of the tin and iron workers' day. Then, like a closed-in tunnel in reverse, we hear it stop in evening. We catch the mad "hee-haw-ing" of donkeys and the chatter of birds overhead, lifting all from one tree or wall like an expiring breath.

Always, we are surrounded by antiquated people, their motions as well worn as the stitches in some old magic robe.

The pomegranates are in harvest now. Most of them are shipped out of town, heavily boxed and bundled, on trucks, camels, and cars, but the bazaar stalls are still full of the pink, thick-skinned fruit bursting with their red jewel-like seeds. At recess at school the tiny first graders pour outside to sit mischievously under the thin ring of trees in the school yard and nibble at their personal pomegranate, their red juice-tinted faces seeming to testify to a new discovery of "happiness." Is it any surprise, the women teachers crave them, in defiance of the fast? But then recalling the time and place and gender, it is likely they are all pregnant and do not have to fast, or that more educated Afghans tend to disobey this pillar, seeing it as unimportant, as irrelevant as a sundial in a modern hour glass.

October 6, 1974

We had a full day yesterday, a solid six classes in a row, and today I do an interview with some of the teachers, who want me to teach an English class again before school. The first grade teacher Esfandyar shows me the list of words whose pronunciation he wants (as he had started by presenting me with last year, too, dear soul.) I startle, worried, realizing how the repetition of all his recorded words had proved to be a past time last year that stretched beyond both of our attention spans. A small, youngish teacher who had scarcely said two words to me in the last year, pops up with an explanation for formal versus informal speech—in perfect English—and the *modir's* wife tries to entice me to substitute for the second grade teachers. I confess an inability, claiming I'm only in the first grade (Farsi-wise) myself. Baffled, as by everything about me, she looks away. In the afternoon language class, our own instruction, we learn the words for a religious discussion and hear Zia's own misgivings about the tyranny of organized religion. It is exhilarating.

The cold grows daily now, and each day the light recedes. We have yet to find another house, though our month runs out in ten days or so. We remind ourselves we are leaving the on-going feud with the Haji's family, and seeking a better place big enough to also house our fine new cook—Mirad's—family.

Last night Tom's student Azarullah was our guest for dinner.

He explains in great detail the state of poor people in this town, people who support a family and work all day only for the price of four loaves of bread and water for dinner. A few years before when there was a drought linked with a long cold spell, poor people in the mountains had to sell their sons and daughters. He continues, explaining how for a population of 30,000 there is only one doctor in this town, and how the clinic has insufficient medicine and the doctor's services are expensive, 20 *afs* for one prescription, or 100 or more for a visit. We discuss births, and differences between Afghan naming ceremonies and Christian christenings. Following that we talk of how a birthday is a large celebration, especially for children in the States, and in cities here like Kabul or Herat, among the Western-style adopters, it is celebrated in about the same way. Yet most people may not well know the exact date of their births.

Moslems contend that their third book, i.e, our New Testament Bible, once had references in it to the coming of Mohamed, the last of God's messengers, but that Christians changed the reference, altered the original book of *Eassawur* (Christ) to erase any sense of this. Where are we left then, with Revelations or the Moslem Holy Wars?

. . . As is always the case with this delightful man who is not only a cook but a trusted and delightful new friend, we see a small child's joy and pleasure in Mirad as we show him how we can make copies of something with a carbon, and tell him how a ditto works. He gives us a firm explanation to our own in return, when we tell him why separate papers are needed for a test or something, to keep the students from cheating. He seems pleased and surprised to hear learning so balanced, with enforced standards and rules. He had told us how his own father was "maybe a little crazy" since "the man had thought I should not go to school . . ." and then, perhaps to reinforce for us his having learned something of the world, in any case, he tells us how to say father and mother in Uzbeki: "Ota" and "Ona" or "Oyim," respectively.

October 7, 1974

Errors, mistakes. After all, I am only a second year teacher for all my Masters and Ivy League education. In fact, I thought I had all but written out our ticket home today.

We entertained a visit by all the big wigs of government and education, a heavy bulk-some lot in several senses, who stopped in my 9th grade class for a few minutes, when the hour was already exhausted, their objective clearly to intimidate me soundly. Instinctively I found myself fighting back, I guess, when a student wrote the wrong conjugation on the board and they all applauded her. Rather than sit mute and facilitating, I stepped in and told her, that that was wrong, and corrected the work. I insulted these supposed panel of experts with a modicum of truth I suppose . . . . They barely looked back.

October 12

> *[. . . Grumbles . . . admiration for the modir's wife's gutsiness and discomfort with her overly large presence in all I am supposed to be doing . . . another change of staff with the sulky and women-avoiding saer-malim from the boys' school replacing the more gentle saer-malim at Mahasty. A visit from the volunteer from Lashkagar, a kindly soul, and negotiations for the new house, even as there is work on the old one and more intrusions by that landlord.]*

. . . Pat Gruner, the sweet Nebraska agriculture specialist PCV, tells us that his cook in Lashkagar who has never let his wife out of the compound, and whose daughters, of course, don't go to school, and who is trying to convert him to Islam, had a rather shocking introduction to the men and women of his town, (once called "Little America" and built by American engineers hired to design and implement the Kaji Kai and Helmand river dams). At last summer's Jeshen celebrations the uprising (foreign imported) youngsters and elders of the town came out to celebrate in their best finery. There were no *chadried* women; rather, with so many American families, it was like the streets of Peoria, with men and women both in shorts, sandals, and—as often as not—blond hair.

October 16, 1974.

The first day of Eid. Last night the lights came on at midnight, drummers batted the pavements and the whole town woke up in the absence of the moon to find their daily month of fasting was finished for another year.

[Anticipating visitors, Mirad cooked lots of food, but only a few visitors came by. Meanwhile, we proceed with our planned move.]

Armoe M'med brings over his explanations of prayers for us today and in exchange for a tiny amount of cake and some candies, he gifts us with a walloping tomato and an elongated sweet melon—and his blessings. How strange, pathetic often, to listen to him talk, as he tries or seems to try to explain things to us, for he seems to think we yet understand no Farsi, and his own head, grown soft with hard age, can only formulate this style of repetitious words. But it is in fact his growing poverty that is drummed hollowly out to us.

One night a windstorm unfurls itself against our windows, moaning like a man's voice and we rise frightened and put on the lantern, and see only blowing dust, and the crack of teased window panes.

It has come to this: A general state of war between ourselves and the Haji family, our planned exodus well-known to all by now, I guess. Others in the town comfort us with the news that this family has always had a bad reputation, that though rich they never give to the poor or offer tea to guests (and it is true that they have never once brought us anything or offered us the basic social exchange of tea.) But then Afghans always seem to try to say what they think you want to hear. Still, we have evidence that the family stole from us, things however small in value. They complain because we never put the cloth on the ceiling, but then they never thanked us for the plastering, the paint, the extra electricity money—all the food and snacks they took with us, even the cups of tea. The women over there are dull and ignorant; the men crooked or demented with self-pity; the little children too tough and imitative. We are sad we are not leaving as friends, and are eager to see what our new neighborhood will be like.

Snapping pictures of this place that's housed us for a year, I feel a certain pride in having found comfort in the bare exteriors, and having made almost something attractive of the interior. The dome-ceilinged tiny middle rooms of the new house are dark by comparison to this one; the two end bread loaf vaults have bad windows; the whole house has mud, tick-infested floors. But it is more Afghan, built in the Uzbek "*gimha'er*" style, and making of it a place of clean solitude, if not always quiet comforts, should be a worthwhile challenge. It is on a busy residential alley, so we are moving into the warm breast of a neighborhood, and yet being totally walled and separate from the net compounds, we will have great privacy. It is adjacent to an orchard of almond and apricots, and there are huge mulberry trees in the large-walled compound. Adding to its virtues, there is an adjacent yard with a house for Mirad and his family. But best, the family who owns it is among the most revered in the village.

We catch, beyond this world, the bad news on the radio, race riots in Boston over the busing of Black and White students from South Boston and Roxbury . . .

October 18

. . . . We are in the new house with its spacious, rather eerie yard, and its white-washed rooms freshly made over in the last 24 hours to resemble those we had made in the "last" year's house. Yesterday morning we dissembled everything and slowly, via a *gaudi* and Armoe M'med, Tom, Tom's student Azarullah and my own shoulders, took everything in bits and pieces across the street, down the mud lanes, to this new residence of "the *malims.*" Largely my job was to sit in the old yard, guarding our paltry gear, while *hazardan* loads were disjointedly relocated. After four hours, it was dark, the day over, that episode behind us. Weary and dusty we sat down to a timely dinner brought by Azarullah, who, like an always hovering angel, appeared at the moment we needed him most.

Sleep was disconnected. Too many new noises roused us and our ears were attuned to suspicious sounds, our minds racing, while our bodies lay limp, just too tired to relax.

Morning, the light a guardian seer, we like the day. It becomes another day of ordering the household, with one room to paint and some wiring left to redo. *Eid* visitors knock on the big gate off and on all day but because we never realize how hard it is to hear the knocking from inside the house, for hours we do not let anyone in. How strangely alone we are these two days as the town dressed to its best, bright new dresses, turbans and shoes, hennaed hands and mascaraed eyelashes, parade, walk, stroll and watch celebrations on the desert at the edge of town, pass from family to friend's house with food and gifts, and take in the brighter fuller days after the theoretical (or real) month of daily fasting.

. . . A few *chadried* students and one unveiled girl, greet me in the falling afternoon with invitations to visit their houses, and I hurry to the bazaar to find some fruit and candy in case another *"mamon"* or two wanders in.

October 22nd

[Tom turns 25; we have no cake, just a buz kashi hat as a gift.]

. . . My 11th class class students come over for a very brief stay—only long enough to look over most of our household goods and books, and some pictures, and to wolf down cookies, tea and fruits, and then to have their own pictures taken. Tom sits on the roof reading the *Hounds of the Baskervilles.*

In the night we wake to the rattle of windows and roof, a slight earthquake . . .

Yesterday Mirad returned.

As scheduled, I begin the teacher's class this morning. The *modir* and I sit in silent embarrassment for half an hour. No one else appears.

Tom's favorite student surprises us. He borrows our little camera to take "a few pictures" and uses up the whole roll of 20. Now we must send it to some kind soul in America, on credit, to have it processed and returned. It is okay; this young man gives us so much.

October 26, 1974

. . . *We indulged in a folio of happenings this past week with visitors from Baglan, Mazar, and Sheberghan, each with his experiences to share . . .]*

Then Friday morning we go for lunch at my *modir*'s house, where Rashidullah and Muzdah have made a spread equal in quantity and flavor to nothing we've ever had here. We are served elegant and flavorful, *awshak* and fried eggplant and potatoes, *kebab* and salads and fruits, and candy and nuts . . . all the while speaking hesitantly of the weather and history of Khulm, of the provincial approach to education, of the country's needs for literacy and sustainable employment. We look at all the wedding pictures, and those from their families, especially his wife's, and his classmates and fellow teachers from various cities, his gaunt

Lincolnesque plainness and beak nose evident in each gathering, her fullness from middle school on a prestigious mark of how prosperous her family was and how well she was cared for, I had been told.

I spend an hour, just after our luncheon, at the house of Shiringul next door, one of my students, where a household of women are sorting and embroidering items under the stern if myopic stare of an elderly relative, a Van Gogh peasant-nosed woman, to be sold in the bazaar. Another old grandmother "*behee*" lectures me on the bad manners of the foreigners she sees in the bazaar who have bare arms and legs and faces, but have better clothes than any Afghan. And they all discuss my Farsi, my posture, my apparent effrontery at not drinking all their tea. I take *nan*, smile, chatter about anything to win their approval.

In this house there is a design—the 65 teapots on a shelf around the room, a single tattered photograph, the *toshak*s and open window doors, unpainted or preened mud walls, the oven in the yard for baking bread, and the cows and chickens in special barnyards, the water running like a clear voice from compound to compound. I recall how plain, unadorned the walls and guest room of the *modir's* house were: one solitary chess set and a book of photographs . . .

There had been nothing to suggest permanence.

In our Farsi class today we have a lesson on religion. We discuss similarities between Moslem and Christian believes about the beginning of man, of his spirit given by God, of how those who have not lived by God's laws on earth will never see His face and will be sent to hell, how God has promised the poor, his special friends, ten times the blessings of others when they reach heaven, how all work that men perform is done only with the help and permission of God. So on we go, discussing these "heavenly topics" disinterestedly like the plot of some new story, me the liberal Methodist among a doubting renegade, one lapsed Catholic and an intolerant, non-practicing Pushtoon Moslem.

The classes are going well. Also, I made up a book for the teacher's class, which officially got off the ground this morning, with conversations and sentence patterns . . . I can use part of it with the 10th and 11th classes, too.

October 29, 1974

On Sunday night we have a long discussion with Mirad about the government in this country; he has a few theories about what makes it up, and speaks quite candidly about kinds of thieves, about how if Daud left quickly there would be war between the tribes, but how if he doesn't go quickly there will be a bad, ill-prepared for, war between Afghanistan and Pakistan, in the name of Daud's bad judgment. He reiterates what we know already, how in all the places of the north, Pushtoons rule the roost although they have no citizenry in the towns per se. They are the governors, *modirs,* police and army captains.

"What do the people think of them?" we ask.

Mirad replied, *"Gaep zadanametainane."* They aren't able to talk about these things.

. . . . [Mail, things to be taken by Fariad back to Kabul. A confirmation that some of the film from Greece had been lost.]

. . . I sit waiting for Zahra (11th class) and Najiba, one of the new teachers while Tom tutors two unexpected male guests in the bedroom/ lounge . . . It has taken us a good year and then some, but we are finally genuinely part of Tashkurghan now, our selves, our stories, our house to be sought out, approachable and respected. Was the fact that we were housed by the dishonorable Haji-sibe the earlier deterrent to more visitors? At the same time, now we comfortably welcome all the visitors, the back and forth, although for me—a shy and withdrawn person—perhaps each day of socializing is a challenge.

October 31, 1974

All Hallow's Eve. We carve out an elongated, chubby thick-squash and make a sinister Jack O' Lantern, its candled glow unhealthily fierce but reminiscent of all those lost nights of fall's frolics when we were little kids and beguiling beggars.

Tonight we lamely tell Mirad the history of Halloween, how years ago people feared that on this night the spirits of the dead rose and came back, so they prayed, and how vigils, and eventually the use of lighted shell-like pumpkins had evolved as a means of scaring away the dark folks, and this was gradually changed into a way of mocking the past fears, until now it's a child's fantasy night, when all his mischief is rewarded with more candy.

Then Mirad tells us, when we use the example of *dijnns* to try to point out what these spirtis of the dead might have been like, his good humor abruptly dropped, how *djinns* are real, how many, many people in Afghanistan are plagued by *djinns* for six months sometimes, once or twice a week. "Why?" he asked, incredulously, clearly angry.

Then we hear the sad tale of his wife, who, four years ago was beset by *djinns* who visited and haunted her for six months, once or twice a week; she would scream and run around and could not be held down, claiming she was being hit. There would be loud noises all in the house. In childbirth she was particularly difficult, and they lost their first two daughters. After forty days both infants had turned blue; and the mother had convulsions, tongue-swallowing, at their births, so they were never real children. Rather, he signed, the *djinns* had snatched them away at birth and left the changelings to die.

This same wife is clairvoyant, too, it seems, being able to foresee what her neighbors do sometimes. But her craziness was more than apparent in the years Mirad had been married, especially with births. But they had had two more children since the time of her attack by the *djinns.* One son has now almost reached two, and another was born within this month. Eventually Mirad had gone to the local mullah who demanded a lot of money and then told him to kill a goat kid when the last son was born. He did so, desperately, and so far things have been better.

How strange, this primitive fear, the last resort, because there is nothing else to help. In his town there is one doctor who "looks" at everything, but poorly, and no hospital. Once Mirad had asked at the hospital in Kabul for some medicine for his wife's fits, but "no one" had time to help him.

There have also been a barrage of robberies in Sare-pul of late and on the road to Sheberghan. Families put all their goods in one room and lock the others, and take turns guarding each night. Before, this was never a problem, but now—as both Mirad and Fariad have mentioned—people are fearful from this newest pest. The thieves are never caught, but remain at large to go and steal more, because the police are in their confidence and are paid off quite as often as not—then ask the supplicants to pay them again so they can "pursue" the thief. The cheek! Always it is the most vulnerable people who suffer.

November 3, 1974

> *[Inherent in the script of being a teacher, surely, is inevitable frustration with one class. Last year's 9th, this year's 10th, taunt and challenge, inevitably stealing even a "modicum" of my dignity. And the teachers' class, likewise, is full of stragglers, and has inconsistent attendance in too short a time. By contrast, there are some good stories, if all of a mold, from the 11th class]*

On our roof three squash are drying, and a last kite is anchored under a rock . . . With three classes worth of notebooks (*ketab chos*) to read spilling between my arms, I weave a hurried trail to the house, as a study line of raggedy school boys beg for one "ketab" each, and are denied with a quick head nodding; and a solider . . . at the crossroads stares a hole through me.

. . . On Friday afternoon Azarullah's mother, aunt and a bevy of cousins (12 strong) come over for tea and a very brief session of looking me over and studying my few photographs, and the state of the house. I am inundated with all of the regular questions (Where does my salary from where? Why do I have no child? Am I sad? What's the rent of this house?) Someone of them asks me to sell our things to them when we leave. Then they offer me an invitation to go to the great large women's house in Mazar. Be-chadried, they leave as quickly as they had come, leaving only nibbles on the huge platter of bread, almonds, and pears behind them . . .

November 6, 1974

What can you expect of a day which begins with an old huddled woman and a small child greeting you at 7:00 with an invitation to come to their house for a wedding at 10:00? The woman kisses my forehead and I answer that I must be at school, and therefore can not attend, a but I thank her.

Then yesterday Tom's *modir,* three supervisors (*emirs*), the inspector (*mafetish*) and a *saer-malim* came over for lunch. They plow through the food we had intended for four and converse jokingly on *kaffirs*. I eat in the kitchen with Mirad, remembering the uneasiness with which these men had shared our rooms with both of us present last time.

As always Tom is peeved with the Pushtoon arrogance of the group. They are all top brass, i.e., all Pushtoons. They don't take off their shoes, send our cook out for (free) cigarettes and fall to eating uninvited the moment things begin to be put on the table. Again, is this something cultural, some rule we simply are not grasping? How can we find so much deference, respect and gentility when we are guests of (or guesting) the local families, and yet be confronted over and over again by these behaviors which would be rude anywhere in the world?

Our complaints later elicit a story from Mirad, about how different the Afghan tribes are. He shares how according to one rarely publicized story, four years ago, some rich Pushtoon land owner in the west of Afghanistan quarreled with his Uzbek tenants and one night quietly gathered them all in one room and set fire to them. Although evidence was well-documented, when the Pushtoon officials from Kabul came to investigate, they were bribed by the Pushtoons involved, despite an Uzbeki attempt to gather enough money to try to purchase their integrity, and nothing was done at all to the man. If they had been Hazaras, they would have killed an equal number of Pushtoon, as has apparently happened before, but since they were Uzbeki and Uzbeks do not like to fight, the incident rode, was dropped.

Last night he told us other stories, about the perpetually sad shape of medicine in this country now. He explains that since foreign medical teams have been thrown out, particularly in Jalalabad where western doctors used to teach at the medical college, cheating is again rampant at that school, and people think two years of bad studying is enough to make them doctors entrusted with life and death decisions. We tell him how American doctors study for 22 or more years to become qualified, and then must take national exams set by a medical board, and then practice another four tears as residents, under an experienced doctor's authority. He shares how he has had an appendix taken out last year by a Dr. Shawn in Jalalabad. He survived.

[Back in the States, we hear of Primary Elections in the states—with wins by Democrats, Hart in Colorado, McGovern in South Dakota. The loser is Ramsey Clark.]

A student asked me on Wednesday, pointing to a picture from an old *National Geographic* which I had given her as a writing prompt: "What color is snow in America?"

And looking at a picture of an Oman village, all mud-earthen walled like their own here, with men on donkeys riding through the rocky dusty streets, and dressed in long white and brown robes, turbaned or beanied, and with few, no, women in sight, and with two-story mud buildings instead of one, my well-enlightened eleventh class decided excitedly that this must be America . . . .

I had a series of misadventures yesterday as I attempted to invite the *modir* and his wife to lunch for today. My modir claims he might be going to Kabul but if he doesn't, he will come, the ambiguity leaving me in a fine state of indecision. Then he kindly tells me that we shouldn't wait for them.

"Fine," I explain truthfully. "We'll find another day that is good for you." But then it hit his wife and him that I had come all the way to school this day just to deliver my invitation, so they started thinking again, and I finally protested that it simply didn't matter, and left, half in fear that they perhaps still hadn't figured out that they weren't in fact to come and half relieved that they weren't.

[Meanwhile, other PCVs, annoyed by directives from Kabul, grumble.]

November 12, 1974

I'm swallowing this week like a bitter pill, because I started quite ill on Saturday, but taught the full seven classes anyway . . . and worked scandalously long on Sunday and Monday, trying to make up a book of student (corrected) essays, and a whole lot of picture stories for use in all my classes—Meanwhile the weather has tuned cold and wet. Last Friday a student, Shahzadah and her slick-dressed brother brought us *awshak* and sweets, after we had pleaded an inability to go to their house, because we had guests who were about to leave (and the next day's dizzying extent of classes capsized my intentions to be good.)

Fed to my gill with notions, romantic and visceral, of being whisked off to Kabul with an appendicitis or some equally deadly attack, I manage to heave my way though that morning, only to fall away asleep once safely back home . . . .

Sunday is more guilelessly passable by merit of there only being the three classes and because the students who question my health clearly do so with genuine interest. They call out and smile, telling me how glad they are that I have recovered. And Monday afternoon, I meet two Australian girls in the bazaar . . . . who share some of their around-the-world stories. Mirad is quite surprised and baffled by them, it seems.

Unmarried girls traveling the world alone for two years? And how do they do it? *"Dawah?"* (crazy) he asks, without identifying exactly who he means.

So they set off for tea with one of the antique sellers and we review our first class Farsi reader in preparation for a lesson with Ziadeen.

Then Tuesday, unnerved and un-nerving, I go in to six classes (the teachers' was first, and I encountered dull stone stares, a general lack of understanding, my colleagues floating in it all, as if I had staggered in on them at the oddest possible time). Hourly I seem to grow angrier and less patient as other classes go on, worrying, eating at me, until sad and broken and furious at once, I let the eighth class blow up and—inexcusably, like a crazy lady—I run from the school hysterically, fending against the burst skies, running in hurt and anger, just going home to cry . . . .

Our old house has occupants again, at 500 *afs* a month. It seems that we were never wanted there, and thus—the way the Haji did it—were eased out. Now Shahzadah's family lives inside. Must they also keep the gates open?

And Mirad seems sort of clouded with the weather, though he has bought himself a noisy white chicken.

Today my 10th class, devilment's damp delight, challenges me again: I had taught them the word "menstruation" one day and now every girl hops up at least once an hour to demand to be excused because she's "got the menstruation." I simply am not witty enough for their quick (and devious?) minds. We are observed by an inspector from the Ministry in Kabul, who watches quite stoically as we look at pictures of exotic animals and talk about how many legs and teeth they have and where they live.

. . . Tom, among a cackling gaggle of giggling girls, meets me by the schoolyard gate, after my classes today. Alas, for all the love in God's world, he'll be reticent to face that mob again.

By lantern light we crowd over our squat table while my head buzzes without thoughts and Tom tries for the fourth time to pen a letter to our venerable leader Dr. Howard. Each day is so short; we are busy.

Alas, now a bounty is out on the ladies at my school, as they grumble about the lesson plan the *mafeesh* (inspector) claims they all need, and claim they have too much else to do to handle this. Then comes their inevitable teasings about the machination of sex, with the small Sherafad claiming she has great trouble at night because her husband is too tall for her, and the *modir's* wife Muzdah chiming in. "How is sex with Mr. Tom?" they ask, wide-eyed.

I say, distractedly, a seventh grader's shyness and resentment in it all. "Fine." Then I ask them why they tease so much. Alas, I am better on the wing or reading words alone . . .

To a one, their faces look surprised at my query.

November 17, 1974

We are host this past week to the squire of our new "manor house," our landlord, a lovely, resonant old man, who comes in wearing his ceremonious striped *chapan* (a kind of lordly stole wealthier Afghans hang around their shoulders) and his karakul hat, to sit cross-legged on our pillows and write the receipts for our rent in a painfully slow Farsi. He excuses himself from eating any of the nuts and candy we offer him with his afternoon tea, because he is "without teeth." Business completed amid much mumbling of his head about how high all prices have become, especially how high the price of the workers we had used to fix the walls here were, he then begins to tell us about his family (he has two of them, by two wives), his teacher sons, his various grandnieces and nephews who had been "grift" (taken in marriage by a number of good young men.) And he talks about other things, the Persian sounds always slightly humorous in their setting of a toothless mouth and kindly bobbing head. He praises the help of our "country fellows," ourselves, claiming the misfortune of how Afghanistan is slow, but promising how some of its people are getting faster. Not wanting to slight his own village or that of Mirad, who is present, he proudly announces that Tashkurghan and Sare-pul, after Kabul of course, are now getting to be two of the progressive, i.e. "fast places." Soon he bows out politely, as venerable as his age, leaving us with a humorous sense of things, and not a little wonderment at the courteousness at his old heart.

The day passed, evening brought some stories. First Mirad told us it had been an interesting day in the bazaar because one of his friends had told him how our landlord Mirzad M. Daud had been a big man at the time of the Batcha-e-Sakow rule and the restoration of Nadir Shah (though he spoke of another, Amir Abdul Rahman Khan, who had died in 1901 and built the garden here). Mirad explained how Mirzad Daud had owned most of the land in present day Tashkurgahn. He had apparently gathered some men and gone by horseback to Kabul through the Salang Pass to confer with the new king. And he was told to redistribute his land back in town, and so he did, giving away most of it to the townspeople. The king, who often visited the town, would stay up on the old city hill. All these legends of history perhaps confusedly put the present Mirzad M. Daud and his father as the same person, unless he is over a 100 years old. And now everything this venerable mans says is considered law.

(And all the time he gave his land away, we speculate, the Haji of our last home was gathering it up to use just for himself).

The landlord's wife and two other women, and their small boys come peeping in the windows about 4:30, but they will not come and sit down. "Sorry, it is too late. We do not want to disturb you. We'll all be back for *Eid e Coran.*" And with at least one turning at the gate to inquire about my childlessness, they are off.

Meanwhile Tom and Mirad have been off at a match at the boys' school and its story comes out when Tom gets home about 6:45. Carefully he relates the absurd details, how the Mazar team had not arrived until 3:00, having only begun to look for transportation at 1:30 and having fought over this for an hour. Then once on the field, how everyone had to shake everyone else's hands, since all the *modir* and mayor and police chiefs were there, and finally everyone was settled down around the field and the teams were, they thought, ready to begin. Then the *modir* suddenly called everyone back to participate in his "jemoriat" ceremony: Boy Scouts carried out a blackboard-painted flag of Afghanistan and sang a (hilariously bad) version of the new republic's song, and a few long-winded students declaimed original poetry, which they had learned from classical *diwans*, the collections of Persian poems. Then, finally, everyone was allowed to move back to the soccer field, only for a fight to break out over whether or not three teachers from the DMA should be allowed to play on that school's teams. They were thrown out of the game and made to switch their multicolored "uniforms" with three eligible players—and the game started. The referee was a bit of a fool apparently. He made unbelievably bad calls, two calls were recalled entirely. But Khulm won.

With night drawing on (sham) it was now time for the basketball team to perform, but as soon as all the audience was gathered in too tightly around the "court," it became painfully obvious that the DMA didn't even have a real team. A few students were drafted, among them two miniature boys whom Tom thought must be the janitor's ten-year old sons, the school's sports teacher and two other unknowns. Barely able to trace the basket (which has no net and consequently must be watched constantly to determine if a ball goes through it or not—the players fouled and Tom mis-called for fifteen minutes, until the *modir* finally acknowledged himself that it was too late to continue. Contented, dignitaries, teams, and teachers all dissembled to go inside for a *pilau* dinner.

At this point Tom tried to explain to the DMA's sports teacher that he had been playing American Basketball rules (hee-haw) and that fine man was employing International rules, and consequently there had been this added confusion.

At some point the Badakshan *mafatish* (inspector) came over and summed it all up: "*Ujah komoon baine e mullalle, inja Khulm!*" (A bit after the tailor's speech in *Endgame:* "But look at the world and look at my pair of pants.")—"There is the world outside and then there is Khulm."

Meanwhile my 11th class continues to send daily greetings to Tom—whose handsomeness they gossip about. Nonstop. As well, they comment now on his "kindly behavior," how he has helped me carry my books home one day and even met me at the school. And why shouldn't they be surprised?

. . . And Ziadeen informs us that last week when he went to Aybak to tutor the PCV couple, the Rawls, he heard "*gaep-e-ajeb*" (strange talk, gossip). The *modirs* at both the boys' and girls' schools claim the PC couple has not been to school for a week. Meanwhile, the neighbor boy said that one night there had been a lot of noise next door and he and his father had run to see, thinking someone, a thief, was in their house, but it had been Marguerite, claiming Rob had gone crazy and was banging his head against the wall and also hitting her. The next day Fariad came and took them to Kabul . . .

[Mail arrives, some lost, some found, others months old and newly found. And, as always, a string of visitors whose surprising and contrasting trips to see us we both crave and enjoy,.]

November 23, 1974

Today at school, I discover that my schedule has once again been changed, so that I am unnaturally in the wrong place at the right time, unfortunately in opposition to the bearded mullah malevolent. So I sit in the sun for one free hour answering all the usual questions from one of the new teachers from last year's 12th class, who informs me that her father is the *modir* of the Bande of Iretank, the border town to the north of here, on the Amu Darya, only a long spit across to the Soviet Union.

Yesterday the *modir* and his wife came over for a much-rehearsed luncheon—we had asked them before and never quite gotten all the details straight. But this time they come and we serve them the fruits of all Mirad's toil, meatloaf and pilau and potato chips and onion rings and vegetables, and so on. We show them our scanty collection of pictures, explain the fate of others stolen, and to their great disinterest offer them a few views of two slides of historic Greece. They eat well, but politely, fondest of the chips and Fanta it seems. We talk, inevitably, briefly, of the troubles of education in Afghanistan, all good words being hosted by the *modir*, while his wife grumbles and makes amusing but rather inappropriate questions and turns in conversation, quite after her fashion. Properly, again, we confuse each other.

Today Mirad is off to Sare-pul to fetch his family for half a year, perhaps, if his patriarch allows it.

[We hear now from other volunteers what Ziadeen had hinted at: The volunteers in Aybak-Samagan had a domestic fight, and the wife was beaten. They were taken to Kabul, and this probably means the end of their service, and perhaps their marriage . . . .]

And once again we must deal with more tricky workers, who claim to work and then never appear. Mirad, in turn, agrees heartily with us that there are only a tiny percentage of people in this town capable of telling the truth, it seems.

Tonight's lesson from Ziadeen ends with his rendering a sociological discourse on prostitution and homosexuality, and unwed mothers, (of which there are a fair number in this town, he claims). But I know nothing of this side of the village life, or might he—as the Pushtoon conqueror—just be speaking disparagingly of the mostly Uzbek-based people here?

I earned praises last week in the official book, for my teaching . . . .

. . . And now we have regular Friday dog fights (*jangi-sag*) in the valley between the river and the old town fort, and the last of the summer fruits is almost finished—the grapes at least are gone, but now there are succulent pears and the first oranges are coming up from the south, and a few melons haven't become scarce enough to be expensive.

Alas, in these in between days, there is great comfort in a *bookerie* fire.

November 24, 1994

Common conversationalist now, I again have a discussion of sorts with one of the new teachers, a student from last year's 12th class, tall and quiet and stately somehow. I am reading, admittedly poorly, a book of mystical poetry by a Persian of the 13th century (born in Balkh), Jalaluddin Rumi, during one free hours. When she comes to sit beside me and sees my book, she decides that she wants to read it. So we go painstakingly slowly over one paragraph, translating it all quite literally. It is full of the usual Song of Songs mystical images of God as the beloved and the writer as his Bridegroom—until she stops and asks what it means, apparently having caught nothing from it.

I explain lamely and she nods, and says, "Sufi."

Then I decide to see what she would think of some pictures I have in a *National Geographic* on the Arab world. All goes fine until she notices an illustrated page from the Koran showing the angel Gabriel before Mohamed.

"Do you know Mohamed?", she asks.

So it goes, her face falling and white as she realizes I am not a Moslem. Hastily rendered, all my fine theoretical gesture to effect that Christ and Mohamed had both been prophets of God and that to know of God alone is all that really matters, gets us no where. There is simply no room in her head to conceive of another way of life or belief, even with another "adom-e-ketab" (person of the book).

November 27, 1974

We get a call from Kabul. Mirad is still in Sare-pul. A dinner is planned in Mazar for Thanksgiving. In a response from Dr. Sahar to a letter we sent in September, we learn—sadly—that, Fariad has been let go. And there is confusion as to how and if Tom will be sitting for the LSAT, which he is booked to do in Kabul in a month or two.

Classes seem undisciplined, as always . . . unless they are reading or copying the book. How can you tell a child you only want to open up her eyes a little . . . help her be freer, wiser, show her that education also requires thinking, analyzing, getting tools to solve problems? It is not just rote memorization . . . . The teacher's class continues rather slow. The *modir*, a fine man, comes and the others are quiet, so he winds up giving a literary translation for everything I say, much to my own confusion. A new approach is needed . . . . I must find one.

Teddy Roberts, the banking specialist from Kabul, is discovered eating dinner with the supervisor of the bazaar, Shahzadah's father. We hear of many misbehaviors by volunteers, real scandals in the PC office, along with justification for Howard not coming in November because he is afraid to get stuck in the Salang . . . I am enthralled with quotes on painting from "The Spirit of Man in Asian Art" by Lawrence Binya (1933-34 at Harvard), as if a thirsty man seeking an oasis.

November 30-December 1, 1974

As our guest, PCV Teddy R. tells us more about dinner with the *modir-e-maleyah* (taxkeeper), and shares his perspective on grievances and processes at the PC office. Some volunteer, unidentified, serves spiked brownies and shows blue movies and parties nonstop. Teddy's background is in Mongolian, oceanography, geography, Russian, and

California. He is exceedingly diversified and a bright young man, our contemporary.

Today I am waiting at home to pay the water carriers, while Tom and Teddy go off to a kimah-tardi—a breakfast party of sorts at the house where Teddy had been a guest the evening before. At 8:30 Tom comes dashing back for his books, and as he rushes off to school I am hailed by the postman with a bundle of mail.

I went on to the highway to sit out a ride to Mazar, and shared my letters and pictures with a few passengers as the car slowly filled up and I read all my mail. Then I sat stiffly and tight between the driver, whose door kept flying open, and a chadried ghostly quiet woman, while behind me the nine other occupants of the station wagon sat silent. One parakeet in a large cage sang fitfully, as we passed bleak desert.

In Mazar I set off for the Hatfields, kind hosts for the Thanksgiving get-together. My *gaudi* driver is stopped at one point by an apparent creditor, who seems intent on taking his horse and *gaudi* on the spot. The creditor shouts; the driver gestures and whines, and the transaction is deferred, at least temporarily.

> *[At the house I met new volunteers and heard their stories, and then Tom appeared.]*

The best of the evening that followed is talking with the wives of Hossain (Alyson's cook) and Maurice's cook, both little girl fresh, with tiny babies like play dolls . . .

Friday . . . we all set off to the bazaar to gather a few unnecessary things, but as the brilliant fall morning weather and the market day crowds of robed men and turbaned ancients, modern girls and anonymous shopkeepers, move around us (or vice versa), my shoe sole falls apart. We stop at a tiny shoe repair booth, whose proprietor takes Tom for an Afghan and who proceeds to tell his story as he bangs nails into my unworthy shoe bottom. He used to make shoes and things from leather, until the price of his materials got too high, and then he took up the easily learned-trade of repairing shoes. He compliments us on our conversation and such. Re-soled, we move on to collect fresh vegetables, and one new stove wick, to do some bookstore business, and gather some sweets (from a gold-toothed Haji at the "Different Sweetness Shop.") In town we meet one of the old Afghan workers, whom we recognize as formerly on the AID staff house staff, now freshly drafted into the army, shaved and scruffy.

We got a ride back in the front of the Waz. The driver is well-traveled and speaks of the paradise of social progress in Kuwait, the roads of Germany, a smuggling ring between Afghanistan, Pakistan, Iran, and Germany (hashish sealed into cement blocks) and so on. Between us a small boy, batcha awal (1st student) in the 5th class, listens.

Back in Tashkurghan, I hurry over to meet Mirad's quiet wife and doll-like two-and-a-half-month old baby, Mohammed Ali, and ghostly thin shy brother. They had come the day before and finding the room above too drafty, moved into the cave-like room below. I sit with them a little while, growing chilly in the late afternoon shade, while the brother hovers beyond the door, and the wife, Zeebee, finally nurses the baby. She speaks of the warm days in Jalalabad, of having lost their first two children, of the death of Mirad's aunt, and of all the people in Sare-pul she has just left—and then her face grows sad and she smiles, but her eyes tear, as she describes her 2-year old son who is there still with her mother and father-in-law.

I tell Mirad and Tom to buy a *bookerie*. The family plans to move back upstairs, then.

That night, we have a lunar eclipse, the moon blood-colored, which launches the town in a flurry of fear, shooting off guns and banging drums and pots. Mirad tells us that this eclipse will be taken as a sign that bad health or war or a change in the king is imminent. The cold wind gallops and on our mountain, tilted stiffly to the sky, some poor shepherds hover beside a flickering campfire for the night's terror.

And in the morning, there is a discussion, the explanation at school about the "moon eating." The mullah-versed response is that this geographical disruption of the events was only the talk of "kaffirs," that God and nothing else was behind it all. And that, I am not really rebutting. But of course I need to respect the faithful on this one, not stir up my students and make them choose between the harsh mullah's dictates and my own persuasions. I keep my tongue silent. For now.

Today one of the workers from (our former landlord) the old Haji's estate comes over to talk—He is one of the few who took up Tom's casual invitation to come and visit some day. I have to tutor Shahzadah, who is back, and don't hear all of their story, but from a few words eavesdropped and Tom's recollection later, the man had spun a tale of his family and how he came to be here now.

He had a very wealthy brother, a mullah, whom he greatly feared. This man had one son to whom he had left all his money when he died. (This is the famous Pendarullah, now a government official of small sorts here. This Pendarullah is also the father of Bashir, one of Tom's best students, and—as far as we could surmise—one of the few good apples in that whole family compound.) So the Haji had six children, by two wives perhaps and his oldest daughter married Pendarullah and is the mother of Bashir, as well as of one of the small girls who used to haunt our yard last year most sweetly, more thoughtful than the others. The Haji's other children are—and we are cruel to have ever labeled them, I know, but—Assadullah (the mooney), the dull brother whose inarticulate stares last year earned him the name of "the turkey," another little boy, Rowkia, and her middle sister, and Iotillah (and Iotila?). Assadullah has already married away one of Pendarullah's daughters. So, the family has a mix and a match of uncles who are also grandfathers . . . .

The workman, eager to gossip, spills out the scandal. Recently the Haji was taken off to the local jail because he owes the government 100,00 *afs* for salt he has bought over the years. His nephew bailed him out somehow, and he now has six days to raise his full fee or begin to lose all his land. As compensation, meanwhile, he has moved the *modir-e-muliyah* into the old house of ours, certainly with the intention to bribe him? Will justice be done?

But the world is smaller. People deal darkly with issues of life and death. Mirad's wife will not use the cradle left here by Mirzad Daud's family because she thinks a baby might have died in it, and that's why it's been left behind . . . .

December 5, 1974

[Tom had left for Kabul to take the LSAT. There are lots of letters and things to take care of.]

Tonight, tomorrow, Saturday and Sunday nights then, he will be gone. The wind whips beyond the windows, the *bookerie* smoke wafting into the dog-barking chilled still night. I am to be alone here.

This week at school, the first biting cold of winter will ravage the students in their thin dresses, uncoated, small-sweater-ed. The classrooms are an assortment of warm cave-like refugees or halls for entertaining the howling wind through broken windows.

My long wool scarf became a popular piece of shelter, however temporary. Students took turns wrapping it around themselves, their only bit of wool and warmth. At such times the absurdity of vaulted ideals of English teaching feel so tawdry I could throw them all out, and instead find a way—regardless—to give these people, my neighbors, my students, shelter, food, clean water, work, health, education and peace. I write out a greeting in Persian . . . to a bevy of people from "the other world," send out on the back of post cards a few dry words. I have to go make duplicates of tests typed over and over again, address envelopes, and read instructions.

And after this arctic week, whose start we had "honored" with full-time use of our own *bookerie*, and a gift of one to Mirad's family, tonight, a chance conversation turns up the fact that Mirad hasn't been using any of our wood for his stove. Thus he is scarcely using the stove. While I sat here toasting for seven days, he and his family, the infant, the toddler, the quiet brother, the quick girl-woman mother, had likely not had even one night of warmth . . . .

> *[T's Dad seems exuberant that his son will pursue law studies; we had told him, pondered ourselves, all the logistics of making that happen. Among the letters is one from my sister Evelyn whose family sounds wonderful . . .]*

The radio tells jarring news, of plane crashes in Washington, DC, in upper New York, in Sri Lanka. This latter was a planeload of 191 Moslem pilgrims on route from Indonesia to Mecca. And lives aside, every country is seeping itself in depression, economies festering without any chance for a quick healing. Will it all turn around? . . .

And I, I am in an unnamed retreat, a room with a few shelves of books, a loudly clicking clock, a typewriter and a now a silent stove. It could be Virginia and the Zukowski's basement, where I lived during my Masters work at University of Virginia, or some strangely sterile apartment house in New York where I was to babysit for the night during my undergraduate days. But it is Khulm, Afghanistan, and I am somehow duller and yet more alive than I was in either place, either time. Only for a few nights alone, I remember what it is to speak out of myself . . . .

December 6, 1974

I finish some typing and reading, on a dark day when I am totally alone—Tom remains in the chilly streets of Kabul, and Mirad is off to the orchards beneath the mountains to find another 100 seir of wood. There has been neither visitor nor counter-self to alleviate the day or plot an outing

Mirad's brother brings me bread, tapping me awake at 8:00 this morning, five hours later than I had risen with Tom on Thursday, and at the end of the day Tom's student Azarullah comes by to sit in the dark room and ask me if there isn't something his family can do for me. Don't I need him to buy something or to stay himself for the night, or to notify Amore M'med to come over? I feel more awkward than I can remember being before, unable to speak Farsi in anything but mumbles, and searching my head for a real subject to discuss the whole time. As he leaves, he tells me how sad and afraid I must be here alone; I begin to feel exactly that, and even catch myself on the verge of tears whenever either of us makes a reference to Tom. The young man leaves me rather shaken I think, good-heartedly worried, having wanted the assurance that he could help me. He tells me, brotherly, to sleep soundly and not be afraid, and that he will check again tomorrow, to see if I have changed my mind and want some help.

All of which reminds me of how ill at ease I am with men these days, how awkward I have grown to be alone in a room with one. *[Diverted, I remember my "crush" on sweet Pat Gruner in Lashkagar . . . . then veer back to admonish myself that T is the only one, the "fire," even if I sometimes look at "sparks." . . . .]*

December 7, 1974

> *[Tom is still in Kabul to take the LSAT, the logistics of that happening having been harrowing. I wish Tom could find a career he likes—Strangely, I hope he really will go into law,*

though that's a rather a far step from the romantic poet/ stage actor that I first met, or the humanities professor stock, I foresaw for him somewhere else, some other time back there. Mostly, were he to return to his high school teaching or become a lawyer or go back and read English in some university, it wouldn't really matter whatever he was doing, just so he somehow felt he wasn't wasting his time, and—just so I were also doing something besides being "Miss Isolation," as during the our first married year in Bel Air when nothing and nobody could find a place for me, my MA in English floundering.]

. . . His student, Azarullah stops by twice today, in the best tradition of ancient chivalry concerned for my well-being. The first time, dog-wet from the cold rain, he merely questions; the second, as dusk had invaded further the all day dark room, he repeats his invitation to find me a guardian or a new home during T's absence. Briefly, our awkwardness dissolves a little as he tells me his version of the scandal associated with the "Haji's" family. He explains that the present "deal" of no rent for the *modir-e-maleyah* is little different from how debts and such are always handled. Then in a lighter vein, he talks about the problems of boys meeting girls here (couldn't it be anywhere in the world, not a chilly dark day in this minute village?). He repeats how few manage to defy their parents and choose someone, to have a few talks with him (or her) in the street, and how most girls, and boys too, are beaten by their fathers until they concede to the marriage match proposed for them, no matter how distasteful it may be to them.

Further, I learn that Ziagul of Class 11, has an "understanding" with one of the students in his class. But when the boy broached the subject with his parents, he was beaten and exiled to Kabul for six months. Now he is back (and what will happen?) I breath in sharply, hoping this lovely girl will not be snatched up and married so young. I want her to go to university, to rise with her clear intelligence and natural beauty to be in a place where she can change the world. And yet if she loves her cousin, if he seeks her hand, is not a good marriage something also to be sought after in this stubborn medieval society?

Then he gives out one anecdote about the Turkomen wedding custom—how everyone plays war in flour! He leaves, good-humoredly.

December 13, 1974

Tom came home Monday afternoon like a favorite uncle, bearing gifts.

He has a hundred anecdotes about the bizarre ways of Kabul, where he had entered and left a conquering hero thanks to the elegant articulation of the letter he had dispatched last month to Dr. Howard about changes needed in PC/Kabul. The man was quite impressed with all he had to say and even had a three-hour conference with him and two other staff members to give Tom a chance to fully flesh out his ideas and Howard and the other the full benefit of his expression. Excellent.

> *[He had gone to take the LSAT at the Embassy, had been admitted to the test center with a cable from Henry Kissinger, Secretary of State, and had found the exam difficult . . . . Then there is the always prevalent Kabul gossip—]*

Our literary and decent friend, Jason McCabe, left a week or more before Tom came, keeping the promise he had made with himself that if his work was meaningless, he would not stay. Lena and James Auchincloss are still in Kabul teaching Engineers, have yet to be sent to Kajikai Dam and are now by mutual consent sated with learning Dari. Someone's father has died; Patrick and Shelly West are unexpectedly off to Beirut, med-evacuated after Patrick suffered through a blocked urinary tract scare, dispatched back to his village for several days, until—virtually paralyzed—he was airlifted from Kandahar in the ambassador's plane, after a slight duel between the AID driver who had picked him up in Grishk and the soldier guarding the gates of the new military exclusive Kandahar landing field. And there is word from Mel and Heidi of the old health team, and now in Korea. They have been inoculating against TB in the demilitarized zone near the northern border, while "the rooster" of our group, Devon something, is about to marry "a prostitute," ("slut?") a woman who has been known to have slept—none too discreetly—with all the singles in Peace Corps Korea . . . . Human nature? Men? A bad process for screening volunteers?

Back here, then, Ziadeen seems to mind yet another vein of arrogance. He spends one afternoon outlining for us all the impossible ailments of Afghanistan and how his own head aches from thinking about them—but what he bewails to us is painfully obvious—poverty, inept government, illiteracy. But he casts so much of it in terms of "inferior" tribes and ethnicities. Bad. Meanwhile we learn that a friend of Zia's from Jalalabad was dismissed from the boy's school under a heavy veil of complains and accusations of "*batcha-buzee*", of behaving improperly with students. Finally, the boy's school *modir* is moving his family back to Kabul, at great expense, because he plans to save money. (Or, for this staunch communist, is it his way to insure he has an entry back there, when the government changes, as it doubtless will, again?)

In our own household, Mirad's baby has had earaches. The little boy shakes his head back and forth, and Zeebee believes he is here only as a kind of gift anyway, and thus almost nothing she does can help him. Still, she talks about herbal remedies she does not entirely believe in—the old egg broken on the head, some mountain herbs dropped into the ear, all this to get out "bad bawd."

Tonight, Mirad explains to us how things are affected by the moon, how on a night of the empty moon, at the end of a month or beginning of a new one there is great danger. Accordingly, many people (such as his father who follow the stars,) sleep in a different part of a room every night so as not to be under certain ill ominous stars. Further, if the third day of the lunar month falls on a *shambay* (Monday) bad luck is due. He explains how when he had meant to take his family to Sare-pul just before Christmas his father wouldn't let him because the stars were wrong for their traveling, and how when the star of Aqrab is in the sky and you want to take a journey, you have to turn your back to it and take seven steps and only then will you be safe and ready for a journey.

Always, there are more wild stories from Tom's student, Azarullah, about more scandals at school. We hear of the insane old science teacher who by night lives in a rich man's house as his private mullah. He had the whole "faculty" over for lunch one day, all under the pretense of producing the goods himself, when in fact it was his "bey's" (rich man's) estate. Not surprisingly, he took bribes last exam and most everyone considers him incurably crazy about religion in his vigilance to the key of the "science" laboratory and its equipment. Who, what, is he protecting? It is all for himself, the boy explains.

Meanwhile, the long-bearded mullah at my school who always quarrels with me, or rather does not hide his distaste, started a kind of civil war in his neighborhood by calling all the other families "kaffirs" because their children went to school or to the university, or wore western clothes, and so on. He tells them they are not Moslems, that only he is a proper Moslem.

And then there are the abstruse readings in the Class One Persian reader, the first text the "national" song chant, that little children memorize, which claims that if any enemies come to Afghan soil, the people will pull out their eyes, while other songs claim that Afghanistan is famous over the world for its pure "Moslemness," and its fighters, and its love of its king (this old hat now, of course)—The line has been replaced by "republic," the word "king" crossed out. All this sort of nonsense is commanded for a five-year old's mind, in a society where literacy is barely 6 per cent.

. . . And one day I went to Mirad's bare room, where his wife Zeebee unbound the tiny-faced baby from his cocoon restrictive swaddling clothes, and I looked at his ears and throat. Shaken from sleep and howling quite healthily, he stole the show, but in nothing could I find infection or the cause of his constantly turning from side to side as if suffering a bad earache. His mother (at 21, already having buried two babies) told me again how babies were only gifts from Allah, who could take them back any time he wants. Again, she explained some of the "home remedies" she has tried—amulets and blessing from the mullah, various herbal ointments, and so on.

And what can they know, or not know, children themselves, and yet have survived . . . .

[I continue working on revising the old novel from college, but am embarrassed at its bad places. In this country I read constantly, always two or three books a week.]

The Orphanage, Kabul 1999

Dickens would have found himself at home
breaching the tall iron gates
separating Tahee-e-Masquin from the outside world,
as decorous as any Victorian workhouse,
but only full of children.

Crossing the frozen gray, late winter's hard-packed,
discolored snow and ice,
fields bereft of trees or other life,
one enters the bowels of the partly ruined
bleak house.

In stark filthy rooms,
drafty, black-ceilinged,
their walls dripping spiderwebs,
splintered and broken plaster and mud,
the bareness startles:

no books, balls, toys,
a single pitted blackboard, blurry in the smoky air,
pushing against one wall,
one dented potbelly stove, sputtering,
casting the smallest circle of warmth.

Urine-stained and torn-sheeted beds
line up in rows in each room below for the youngest.
But on the third floor,
in crowded, windowless rooms,
the girls are contained, secreted like prisoners,
not allowed to go anywhere else.

Only the children.

The children, thin, sharp bones
buried under layers of sweaters and scarves,
some with parkas,

a cacophony of colored cloth in the dun-hued room,
scattered in hallways and cell-like rooms,
tiny arms wrapped around themselves,

eyes glazed or hotly beseeching,
small, sooty-faces leaning into each other
as they sit mute on the bare dirt floor,
barely moving,
others coughing painfully,
others hiding.

Sockless,
they shuffle in cheap plastic shoes,
despite the piercing cold,
the round brown eyes weary and hollow.
At night they wake with nightmares and cry.

Down a dark hall,
Bibi Xonum, a sparse elder, squats in the kitchen,
a tiny closet with only a stone slab for drainage,
a place to make a wood fire, and wash a few pots.

In another space wilted Bibi Jamila,
red hands frigid,
leans into a puddle on the floor,
wringing out clothes
washing old sweaters, skirts, pants
in cold, soapless water.

A bathroom boasts shower stalls
but no hot or running water.
Instead, someone has set out
a bowl of water in each booth
to be used for washing,

the way one might put out pet dishes
in a Western home.

IX

HOLIDAYS AND STORIES, YEAR TWO

December 17, 1974

. . . Today Mirad was looking at the *National Geographics* on Mecca, thrilled to see the holy city's pilgrims, and he begins to explain all the business and ritual involved in a haj.

Glowing, he talks about the house of the devil (*shyton*) and the black Kababa and the stone-throwing pilgrims before the former, garbed in their white, simple robes. He speaks of the holy city itself, open only for the length of Eid-e-Qorbon when pilgrims from all over the world came there, and how the buildings for prayer and sacrifice are filled up with crowds of the faithful—"the whole world"—and how the door to the shrines are open only this short time.

"And anytime that the place is not full, angels take up the remaining places," he explains. He had seen in all in a movie shown in Jalalabad several years ago.

People are allowed to go (once they have the money) only if their name is drawn in a lottery, which takes place once a year. And he speaks incredulously of the huge airplanes that carry 150-350 people at one time. Worried at their heaviness, he asks "And are they safe with so many people and all their boxes?" Then he reads us a page of the Koran in an earthy and stuttering Arabic . . . Yet the vowels soar.

The flip side of this reverence and sincerity, as if on cure, arrives also on our doorstep. One afternoon this week a young socialist-communist, a teacher at Hajie Boran out at the edge of town, comes by to discourse on dialectics and materialism. He tries hard to thrust his ideas down our throat, as he shares his feelings about various mullahs in Afghanistan who thwart the people and keep them ignorant, hawking the Koran's unwise, age-old prejudices and narrowness. In fact, he claims, all mullahs should be murdered so Afghanistan can grow. Continuing, he then names, as if an exorcism, all the culprit mullahs in town who hate foreigners and oppose any signs of progress. Fury-eyed, he continues, bragging about how he has read many book on philosophy and politics and history, all this with the incongruous sort of arrogance and flaunting that under-educated, literate Afghans seem to have. (Yes, I've also read many thousands of book in my life and . . . what of it?)

Is he, likely, another of the wild Parcham (communists) Daud's government exiled to the provinces, to prevent their assembling opposition in Kabul, or Jalalabad, or Kandahar? Or, is he, and others like him, here to stir up support?

Teaching, somehow, feels like pure drudgery this week again, with the teachers' class coming in first for most troublesome. They're so unevenly matched, and I want to do reading with them but what chance is there when the reading passages I have are either absurdly easy or philosophically, linguistically hard? Again I seem to show my own lack of skills or imagination, to project my own expectations callously on people trying to figure out many more important and immediate tasks and needs. But my own classes also grow lax, as they see now all that we are doing is review. So they fidget and talk and its like pulling teeth to make them understand they should listen. But more, there is something about the dark mornings, that makes rising from bed an impossible feat, wearying me for the end of time. So perhaps I just do not have the energy to squander in chasing a few overly-hatched ideas around school rooms . . .

I breath deeply, reflective, as I sit in the back of the stunted crop of first-graders in their smoky room, among their thin bodies and raggedy, assorted clothes. They chant out religiously the letters of a word; the word today, "*xalos,*" finished.

December 20, 1974

We are back to school tomorrow . . . but only for two days this week because Eid-e-Qorbon will begin Tuesday, and Monday is a public holiday.

We are wakened late (8:00) this morning by the disoriented pirate wrath of the one-eyed barefooted, raggedly-cloaked Turkoman trashmen-water carrier (*shoow*) as he spills our two goatskins full of river water into our tin can containers (*owdons*). And by the time we've gotten dressed and Mirad is bringing tea, and Tom has gotten fresh bread, half the town is noisily gathering on the old fort hill a few alleys (*cuchas*) down from us, to behold the Friday dogfights (*saag-e-jehad*). Tom and Mirad walk off to the milling crowd, where they behold a lot of likely competitors, but no fight, for with Tashkurghan's usual gift for giving everyone a sounding board and no follow-up, everyone with dogs to fight preferred to argue prices rather than spur their earless, blood-heaving hounds to action.

I indulge in a hot "bath" with boiling muddy water, and spend a poor afternoon typing up Tom's—likely—ill-fated applications to Harvard and Columbia (for none of the others have materialized yet, due largely to unknown forces, i.e., the Afghan postal service).There is always the unreliability of the mail, and no other way to "hasten" the process from this far afield. Yesterday, Peace Corps's lovely, literate, deputy country director Arthur Alpert and Rashid Parwani, the director of all programs . . . came by, paused for a brief shopping spree (they bought one *kebab* stick, a prod for a fireplace, and a beautiful cradle), and knighted us with the gist of more shop talk, rumors of people leaving, plans for more language teaching, the likely resolve that we could not be replaced, the substituting (good, good) of Afghan staff in lieu of Americans for some positions.

December 26, 1974

Behind us a strangely filled week.

There are two days of school, just Saturday and Sunday, then the sadly reminiscing, rampaging holidays. Monday Roz-e-Arafat, the day the gates of Mecca are opened, we spend gathering in the bazaar ranks. There's a midday chill day in which to observe a banner headline crowd collecting goods and selling them: turnips, potatoes, carrots, onion vendors everywhere with their piles of hard vegetables and fruits—oranges, dry grapes and a few treasured melons, apples and nuts. Others hawk rainbow-colored candy bits, and sweaters and hats and clothes new and used to be picked over and donned (we bought Mirad's baby a monster large sweater). There are the fish vendors at the river and the wooden horse man putting in his stakes for a children's merry-go-round.

Back in the kitchen I cook fudge and pumpkin pies, while Tom gives out bits of an English lesson . . . and we host and share, between guests *(PCVs Goodmans from Lashkagar, Fred Cozzens from Kabul, Teddy House from Mazar . . .)* . . . and go out again to wander in the bazaar . . . . It is a world gone wild with children's noise breakers, little painted rattles, wings and pushmepullyou's, rudely chiseled of a pattern from wood and painted in strokes of green and pink. Little girls in bright new outfits peek out as shy as spring flowers, while *chapaned* strollers pass beside us in the wet world . . . We end up taking an unplanned trip to Mazar via . . . a raucous route, getting our money's worth of *gaudi* and taxi . . .

The next morning, a shrouded, foggy day, T and I bicycle to Alyson's house to poke a head in on her and her guests and collect a debt from Hossain for Mirad. In a lazy afternoon we walk to the mosque as evening falls. Crossing the grounds of the mosque, we chase the sunset, a winter's eve of solemness, to snatch pictures and buy holy tiles . . . .

We head back to our town. Mirad has stood three hours on the highway seeking a ride, and finally catches one as we pass by . . .

We take a nap, then entertain a visit from Armoe M'mad who fills his pocket, little boy like, with candies, and then with Najibullah, Mirad's brother. We trek out to the *buz kashi* field, observe the murdered calf . . . take in the ethereal wonder of ancient plains, tent stalls and stands. We see bouquets of dressed children, the *chadried* women making up a whole hillside apart, the thundering ephemeral horsemen engulfed in tornadoes of dust clouds as they race, the huge snowy peaks above the dirt, the etched out lines of round roofed villages to one side. Then the scene springs alive, all eyes drawn to the horses galloping into the eras of past mischief and mystics. Turbaned men watch, run off the corners of the field, at a false turn by the swift-riding players, until dark begins to call itself and we take another ride back into town

I have a long sit with Zeebee and Najibullah and the baby, which turns out to be a dinner and tea (rice and potatoes and bread). She tells me in a wild desperate humor about the shame of debtors in Mirad's family (Hossain had only paid up half his fare), about Mirad's inconsistency in saying he wants to take another wife (I am shocked), about the wrong done her when her young son was not allowed to come from Sare-pul with her. Najibulah asks about traveling to America, and about electricity—What wonders run wild in his head that we will never hear him tell of? And then I go back to my house where Tom, bemused by the intricacies of making pancakes, stands hungrily waiting for some goods. We relax in a lazy night beside the fire, catching at the images past us now like the whiffs of smoke in our potbelly stove.

This land in all its simpleness, its tangled secrets and ungracious loving, teasing ways, endears itself to us. Now, as time grows shorter, we hunger, wanting to miss none of this life and its lessons, but hardly knowing well how to catch as much as we would also give . . . .

December 27, 1974

Visitors: Out at the *buz kashi* field, always lively for Eids, today the crowd of *chadried* women sit like colored toadstools on the bare hills in front of a tiny VW. We arrive in time to witness the throat-slashing of the calf, the game's 'buz,' as fog and morning surround the arches of the mosque seen from across the city, a visual gate we move toward in the uneven *gaudi*. Each person is a messenger: the Hazara baby in his pink and green hooded cap, bedecked with charms from unknown places, one claiming "Mr. Dapper" in plastic letters; the Turkomen women's bright flowered clothing and high headdress, moving ahead of us in the distance like some mobile vase of roses and greenery; the all-male crowd watching my mouth move, hearing what they recognize as Farsi, but awed and excited to see a "malim," a foreign woman and a Farsi-wan; Mirad's brother Najibullah, with his hobbling, half-dragged sprained foot (his brother had told him not to play soccer in the alley, so now he has gotten hurt, which Mirad felt should teach him a lesson for a while) moving up and down the frozen desert dunes around the *buz kashi* field; the student from the university, who is another relative of Mirzad Daud and asks us quietly to come to his house nearby for a feast of sacrificed beef and lamb . . .

December 28, 1974

It is a calm day as Mirad's brother, Najibullah, sits looking at our *National Geographics*, until the crazy radical of Hajie Biron barges in to collect his tests from us, to sit and say nonsensical time-consuming things. Tom escapes to the bazaar while 10-year old Najibullah continues looking at the magazines, and I point out a man under the ocean taking pictures of fish. Najibullah looks at the image, than claims, "This is a donkey," and I realize I have misjudged the picture and been quite unceremoniously put in my place.

I napped for half an hour, then wake to find our landlord at the door. He greets me with great seriousness, stiffly, but cordially, and then leaves. Then I visit Mirad's wife, Zeebee, who is just rocking the freshly-bound baby to sleep. She speaks of missing her oldest son and of the injustice guarnteed if her husband really does contract himself to another women. Najibullah's foot is well-healed now, the sprain apparently slight, and he watches us talk, hovering in the background, then runs to open the gate

It is Ziadeen, forlorn and pitiable, who comes to sit in the house and softly scold us for not inviting him to the Christmas party in Mazar (but the invitation had not been ours anyway). We have scarcely talked of anything, when Najibullah comes in again, this time leading Shahzadah's brother, who explains that an American doctor and a women on a truck have come to their house, thinking it was "the *haragee's*." I ask him clumsily to please direct them here, and go back through the gate into our own house, extensively to see Ziadeen excuse himself (all this time Tom is at the *buz kashi* field). But the guests are the new PC doctor, a tall articulate, intense man and Jan, the nurse from our cycle, and a gauntly quiet driver, at the gate (with Tom behind them soon after). Ziadeen half bows out the door, misplaced, and I head to the kitchen to make pilau, French fries and scrambled eggs, while Tom and the doctor bring in fresh nan. Then everyone else sits by the *bookerie*, talking causally until dinner, my quick creation, comes, and we all fill up.

Still we talk some more . . . Jan describe some of her tales of infant care and otherwise, the binding, the pulling of the ears for a headache, the twin killings; the WTs loose in the Kabul hospitals. The new PC physician, Dr. Stern, fresh from two years in Togo, tells us of volunteers there and the warmness of the people, of one chilling experience of anti-westernism when the President was almost killed, and about fetching water from muddy ooze and contracting meningitis . . .

There is much that can be learned about medicine and illness in this country. The old turn of the century South Asian writers (in this case Ali Shan, cited earlier) spoke in detail of child birth, of special ceremonies and taboos surrounding that event, and of the subsequent milestones in a child's early years, in this land where so few survive:

> Following delivery, the mother is fed *ajwani*—soup of *ajowan* seeds (carum copticum), caraway seeds, sliced ginger, cloves, meat, chick, and sugar) to help her regain her strength. This mixture is boiled until the fibers of meat dissolve and then it is given to the mother every three to four hours . . . Meanwhile, in the corner of a well-heated and dim-lit room, there is a pedestal on which sits a dish in which incense of benzene and joss sticks burn.
>
> The child is wrapped in a silken quilt, and over it is put a white cloth with sacred verses inscribed. A thick silk cotton cord is wound spirally from the neck to the toes, around the child. The child is placed in a hammock made of thick Persian carpet, and swung. If a wet nurse is hired, her character is checked. She must be of high character. For the first ceremony for the child . . . the imman or mullah reads into both ears of the child a prayer, which makes the child a Moslem:
>
> "God is great, God is great. I am witness there is no god but one God and that Mohammed is his prophet. God is great. God is great."(*Allaho akbar, allaho akbar, ash hado. Ullaelaha, illalla, ash hado, una, Mohamedar, vassul, allah, Allaho. Akbar, Allaho akba*r.)
>
> . . . There is a naming ceremony at five or six months, a ritual which is pronounced by a *mullah* or a *sufi*. Also, when the child is a few months old, there is a hair shaving using rose water in a silver cup. The child's hair is shaved regularly until he/she is four or five years old.
>
> . . . The people have a huge dread of the evil eye: so to protect the child, the child can not be taken out at night,

especially not on Thursday night when evil spirits are most malevolent. Similarly, on starry nights, the person nursing the baby can not have white cereal (rice). Also, one can not take the baby out at noon when the sun is bright because vultures or birds of prey "may at that hour drop eggs of corrosive liquid on the child."

Further, special protection is needed during a thunderstorm, and the child is not ever to be near the gaze of "beggars, criminals, or others of ill repute."

When the child cuts its first teeth, there is a celebration. When the baby teeth are all out, "they are thrown into a mousehole, so that the new teeth may be sharp and strong" like a mouse's.

The child receives a milk diet until he/she is three years old, then the diet is changed to grain and a hard diet. Parents recite the Koran and the child is given charms around its neck which may include luck stones, luck words, the carved claws of a lion or tiger, and a sacred pendant (a coin, a piece of metal, a jewel, silver or gold). At age 8 or 9 the boy is sent to the mosque school.

[The teaching is going well] . . . sparked by the dedication of my 11th class and a few of the 9th graders. One day the women teachers led by Muzdah, the *modir's* wife, and Najifa plotted to go to Mazar to see the drama/cinema "Bobby," but they lost permission from the *modir* . . . .

I race home to a quick and lazy lunch, and a moment's reprieve. Then Anifa, from last year's 8th class, hovers at the door with her mother. I invite them in, but they take nothing, sit mute for a minutes, then thank me and leave hastily. Moments later, Shahzadah pops in for a lesson, that program also cut short by Ziadeen's entrance.

The lesson has only just started, when Najibullah jumps in the window with the uncontainable news, "Mohammed has come, Mohammed has come," and before we quite figure out that Mirad's oldest son had arrived, our dignified landlord comes in for a quick cup of tea, and some formal talk. Of course, never to be outdone, Ziadeen informs me haughtily after the noble man left, that the landlord didn't eat my cake because it was cooked by a foreigner, that no one would eat any of my food here because they thought I killed it myself without saying the Moslem prayers. All of this may be true but it should not apply to desserts, and for another thing a Moslem cook prepares everything in this house (which is why we hired one) and further, M'Daud has only been kind and polite to us and has, in fact, sampled our "sweets" (brownies) and our cooking before, as has his family, so I doubt that Ziadeen's gruff observation has any relation to reality at all. (Rather, I remember the first time we met this man and how he had politely apologized for his semi-toothless state and how that limited his chewing.).

Then Mirad's father, fresh from Sare-pul, came in with Mirad's two-year old son (the "Mohammed" of Najibullah's calls), grandson and grandfather. Just behind them, entered Najibullah, holding the baby. I notice Ziadeen balk, his whole body visibly repulsed, it seems. We all feel ill at ease until the baby farts, the family giggles softly, and the little child is rushed out. The son, who is actually called Habibullah, whimpers then, so Mirad's family excuse themselves to go back next door, and our aborted lesson finishes itself. I start dinner, the fire sputtering . . . then duck next door to greet Zeebee and her reunited family quickly, while Ziadeen tells Tom about his "successful" relatives who have gone to America, then finally saunters out.

And night closes in on us a we eat bread and *pilau,* wash dishes and bake cookies for more expected guests tomorrow, then read and write a few letters . . . . This, then, our ritual for the year now. Still, there is an uncanniness with which Mirad seems to be gone, every time we have a deluge of guests . . . and we must fall back upon ourselves for the necessary basic motions. But so it goes.

Tonight, we do not have the full moon of yesterday, but a thoroughly bright one, and the mountains around it gleam white as phosphorescent waves coming in on a beach, these snow-binded, the other salt liquid bright . . . .

Beyond our immediate scenario, the mountains stretch, to higher and higher land leading to the Himalayas eventually. I lean back against our cool wall, flushed with *bookerie* glow, and imagine places others have told us of, where subcontinents merge:

The plains and narrow valleys of Taloqan, high loam-rounded mountains carpeting the horizon secreting pocket plots, wheat and rice seedlings in the lower meadows, interspersed among razor-sharp peaks.

The snake of a barely discernible trail skims fractured pinnacles, crevices falling down to bare hills, treks which summer will turn into moonscapes of dusty, boulder-riddled riverbeds.

Further north, following the rusty colored Monjan River, the rock-barren skeleton of the road to Faizabad weaves over millennium-old ruby and lapis lazuli mines. Stark glacial peaks tower far to the north and east. From the air, one could imagine how they rushed in front, some filmstrip in fast forward, while below, soft white shadows outlined the snow-blocked passes, patches of raw amber-colored earth marking where the ice has broken and mudslides cover the slopes. Here, where Badakshan and Takhar Provinces, edge each other, and beyond, the Hindu Kush and Pamir Mountains collide into long, narrow river-splayed winding valleys, high passes which lead, unbending, into Pakistan, Tajikistan and China, land once the heart of the Bactrian and then Selucid Empires. The Kokoram and Himalaya peaks, the valleys of Hunza, Kashmir and the North West Territories across the artificial British-drawn Durrand Line of the late 1800's, are cut of one cloth geographically. Valleys echo valleys, mountains rise into gargantuan peaks across unfettered frontiers, like the green, orange and brown hues of an old topographic map, hills giving way to mountains, sheer rocky cliffs perpendicular to cloudy river banks, from the Oxus to the Kokcha Rivers, from Central Asia's endless high flat plateaus mirroring the Afghan land below.

Time is lean and untouchable: an imaginary tight rope suspended across the sharp upraised peaks and their dizzying threads of valleys far below, where lives and villages hang in the balance, in tenuous perched land, between the raucous earth and the expected seasonal punches of ruthless winter snow and early spring downpours. From above, one could see the plunging valleys and harsh mountain cliffs, move past rugged terrain, over bleak rocky outcrops where copses of raggedy poplars, pieces of mud-brick adobe structures cling to the edges, until it seems one valley widens, the muddy river rushing and broad with the spring rains and melting snow. Amber and green-terraced fields mark a small inhabitable area like a child's stubby step stool mounting a few feet against some superhuman giant's ladder to the clouds. Then the fields and remnants of orchards thicken, a brown film of a high meadow spreads out below, and one reaches a homestead.

Up in this realm, of course, in Badakshan province, is also the mythical city of Faizabad.

In the 70's, Dupree described the mountainous Badakshan province, the approach to its provincial capital of Faizabad, as a timeless world still encased in the language of myth: a rugged place of spectacular scenery, hairpin serpentine paths, high winding passes, and tiny villages with green valley and orchards connected to each other by swinging bridges over deep river gorges, and mountains still holding the secrets of both legendary lapis lazuli and gold mines. Faizabad's narrow bazaar had stretched over a mile, vibrant with shops selling multi-colored knitted ski socks, cumin, walnuts, apricots, and a luxuriously soft wool gathered from wild goats. History had granted it, one century, to host the Cloak of the Prophet Mohammed, beckoned guests and conquerors who wrote about it, from the Chinese pilgrim Hsuan-tsung in 644 AD, the Mongols in 1220, Tamerlane in 1384, to Babur the Moghul, Humayun, and finally Abdur Rahman Khan, Afghanistan's "emir" from 1880 to 1901.

In the end, they all left, the isolated valleys, rugged terrain, indigenous people unconquerable, and the local chiefs maintained power.

In late spring, rushing water, the fierce brown-gray Kotchka River flooded as it wound between high mountains and down to green valleys, fractured donkey trails climbing to high villages, pencil marks above the huge brown slate river. In summer, emerald green meadows, fields wedged between jagged breaks in the mud banks or rough rocky outcrops, vibrated. Trucks, diesel clouds hanging, spun and sputtered on the pitted narrow overhanging road, less road than a wild goat's trek or rocky river bed. Vehicles shuttered to a halt, stuck in the mud or off-balanced by boulders, over and over.

All of Afghanistan, not just this broad northern patch, well beyond our central Asian steppes, was always a fierce terrain whose people hungered, held on against war, earthquakes, floods, but also where the cultivation of the poppy, scarlet, pregnant-bulbed lady, swelled.

Dec. 31 1974-Jan. 1 1975

. . . A New Year's Eve. Mirad . . . came back from Jalalabad on Sunday with frightening tales of being sick, and thus not being able to return earlier. Meanwhile an earthquake in northern Pakistan kills nearly

5,000 people, and its tremors can be felt from Nangahar to Badakshan. How uncanny that I had imagined that land the day before.

Yesterday I visited Mirad's household, the grandfather clutching the 2-year old son, Habibullah to his arthritic body, the child whimpering in best toddler style out of jealousy for the new baby, Nazar the 10-year old brother-uncle dunking the youngest in a pale of his mother's wash, the mother weary, aged, trying to gather back the last son who has been away from her for over a month and acts distant from her since the new baby came, even as she cradles and nurses Mohammed Ali into sleep . . . . Domestic life.

Today we are inundated by another stream of visitors, but there is a sort of nuance, a pattern about them: First is the crazy teacher from Hajie Biron, who sits for three hours, typing over a few whole exams, crumples our box of crayons, melts the type . . . then breaks two staplers, and offends everyone else in sight by saluting us as his "fellow Kaffirs," or "Comrade Communists" or some other such nonsensical salutation. Next, along came two boys with a list of English verbs requiring the second and third parts of their conjugation, the sons of the judge here, it turns out, and originally from Paghman. They are preparing to take a make-up test in English next term. Then sad and more subdued than ever, (after Armoe M'med announced him), perhaps because we have not come by his house for Eid (we visited no houses in fact, out of a lack of sensitivity, or just of preoccupation with our own visitors), is Tom's student Azarullah, who seems down about many things beside. He makes no pretense of his distaste for the Hajie Biron teacher.

Protectively, he tells us, "That man is a rogue and has not come for the right reasons. His being here is just not right. It is as if he is here as a spy, somehow in all this center . . . ."

January 2, 1975

New Year's Eve Mirad tells us stories about bribery in this country, past and present. He claims that a new commandant has come to his home town of Sare-pul who is cleaning out a lot of the *"riechwort"* (bribe-takers). He explains how any time you need official approval for something you first watch the motion of the official's pen posed in his hand, the fingers moving back and forth in the understood gesture of "Okay, give me the money you think my signature is worth."

He retells one of Mirzad Daud's stories, about how one of his sons studied well and seemed an ideal student, but then at the time of the exams got a *"na khum"* (failure.) When the son inquired in turn about that, he was told that the father was expected to bribe the teacher or principal or someone. So the next term the boy did a lot of work for this teacher, carrying his water and such, and also working hard, and he passed easily.

But Mirad also shared a tale of Zeebee's brother, her only living relative it seems, who has been in jail in Sare-pul for six months. When Mirad, or his father, or anyone tries to find out why, what the charges are, why his case hasn't been presented before the "judge," they only meet with requests for money for signatures, etc. So the boy sits there, virtually family-less, with no food except what someone may bring him a few times a month. And his case must be multiplied a million times, certainly, since there are still people in the States, too, with unclear cases, held without bond or bail or formal charges for long periods, and without the means to get themselves cleared of charges filed against them. So how many more years will it be for Afghanistan to even start to wake up to its lack of judicial order?

It is odd, turned as we are to our window on the world, the radio and BBC World News and VOA, to hear these of the voices of the past year—Nixon's resignation (one line repeated), the agreements made in Moscow or Arabia or the Golan Heights—for whatever these men's words are worth. *What happened this year? I think back, finger old Newsweeks we received. From the end of OPEC's oil embargo, to the nuclear disarmament meeting between Nixon and Breshnev, to the overthrow of the dictator in Portugal, to the successful testing of a nuclear bomb in India, to the collapse of Haile Selaisse's emperorship and a military monster's ascension, to the kidnapping of Patty Hearst, to Nixon's resignation and Ford's ascension to the Presidency, to his pardon of that man. And in the arts, we learned of some song called "Hey Joe," of the ballet virtuoso Mikail Baryshnikov defecting to the U.S during a tour, of the start of a magazine called "People," and movies coming out called "Chinatown," "The Godfather Part II," "Day for Night", "Blazing Saddles," and "The Towering Inferno." And there were thoughtful, deep books (and just poplar ones), Robert Creeley's poetry,* <u>Sitting Here;</u> *Annie Dillard's* <u>Pilgrim at Tinker Creek</u>*; Gail Godwin's,* <u>The Odd Woman;</u> *Stephen King's* <u>Carrie</u>*; Toni Morrison's* <u>Sula</u>*; Grace Paley's*

Enormous Changes at the Last Minute; *and Robert Pirsig's* Zen and the Art of Motorcycle Maintenance.

Mirad and his family go off to Mazar as a pilgrimage to the shrine there and to visit Hossain. Already my students are talking about my leaving, and how I'll be missed. Will any of them be able to write to me, or want to?

There was . . . something rich in a few moments walking across the mosque grounds on Christmas Eve in Mazar, and seeing the other people there, and ever so briefly feeling we were all about the same thing after all—until we were again, very quickly cordoned off and sent out to the street, the outsiders, the foreigners, to be teased, scorned, suspected . . . .

. . . Weather-wise, it's a sunny, balmy day, fit for escorting us in a timeless walk around the city. [Hours later, we haven't taken the walk, which leads to a rumination on how the differences between T and I stem from different activity levels—my needs to be in motion, his to sit.]

And our secrets are strong. Already we do a delicate dance around each other, I pull back least he come too close and know how haunted I am by the writing and the need to write and thus how he does not really know me unless he accepts this as a part of me. Or, bigger, how much I am troubled by the madness and dysfunction of my first family back home, the generation-stretching siblings.

He can know nothing of nor care much for my brother David who is clearly mentally not healthy, having battled depression and alcoholism and unsteady work despite his degrees for most of his adult life; or really much either (beyond my embarrassment) of my sister Louise whose madness so suddenly breached her own first life—as the scholar and wife of the rich oil company executive's spoiled son, and mother of two small girls—all—the life and the daughters—taken from her by the husband; and then a second life now as a birthing machine to a petty thief, an ongoing welfare case; or of dear, dear John, only 16 months my elder, so full of fire and poetry, yet also off the track, given to violent breakdowns and hospitalizations, then reduced to a zombie pill-taking simmer, and now in the throes of some security and an actual marriage to a beautiful and loving woman, and some success with his writing, but—will it all be temporary, again?

And what, for all his care for me, can he feel for my parents in their middle 60's and 70's respectively, struggling to understand what to do for these children who are so long gone from being children. And likewise, what does he and even I really know of the other sisters, Eloise and Evelyn, who are seemingly fine, and their children and husbands who now seem to be thriving. And then there is my youngest brother, the brightest of us all by far, Danny, off wandering the world . . . . in his own way forever unconnected, a dreamer.

And Tom can not understand all this, sees it as not my responsibility, coming from his New England Catholic family where each child claims his independence early and brings only good news back to the parents, where love and respect are a given, not something to be hacked out daily as a reason to stay alive, where no one shows signs of mental illness or hysteria or violence, or failure.

Of course, I then wonder if I likewise do not know his core, either.

And so my fear, the timidity, the hard-to-break habit of retreat from any testing or confrontation, even those which would nurture and make me grow. Here. Back there. Can I help anyone?

January 4, 1975

> *[We are expecting our homestay guests, the new volunteers who will live among us for a few days to sample life in the provinces and in our schools, and who have not gotten here yet, although we walked up to meet them at the bande and have had a huge meal prepared for their arrival.]*

. . . This morning I try to call Kabul, an experience Tom had been sheltering all to himself previously. I sit for perhaps three quarters of an hour in the mud room where a long-nosed man hovers cross-legged on a rope bed manipulating a small electric battery-ed switchboard. He screams and curses in his continuous tempo. At one point he actually "gets" Kabul on the line, only to have the connection abandon him as he keeps being interrupted to fight ferociously with some would-be line-snatchers from Mazar, Puli-Khumri or Samagan. To each he screams the necessity of my connection with Kabul, explaining he has the foreign English teacher here, all alone, and her house is in trouble and she must reach her directors in Kabul.

So he argues over and over to the brazen soul out there somewhere disregarding him—until it becomes clear that "Kabul" is lost, encased and downed in some wires stretched over the rugged Salang Pass and Hindu Kush, and has to be found again, but that will not happen, at least not this morning. The operator seems about to turn on me when I calmly get up to leave and learn that Tom is back in town.

"Oh, the *malim-sib*e could have called himself? Later?" the kindly telephone operator asks me.

It is a brief teaching morning, the last formal day for teaching this term . . . .

January 5, 1975

> [Our guests, PCV trainees—the Mahoneys.—arrive. I go to school to give exam to the 8th class, and Brenda, with her long curly red hair and tiny bones like a bird, is wooed. We read diligently through all the Christmas cards and all the mail they have brought us from "the sack" in Kabul.]

. . . We take an afternoon walk and sit for tea with Mirad's wife and kids, then return back to the house for an evening to correct papers.

. . . Today we receive a telegram, a Christmas salutation sent from my parents: I get it from a student in the 8th class whose brother brings the mail from Samagan. Standing in that bare, scattered classroom, I open it, thinking about everything else, caught off guard and near tears by the beauty of the action . . . ."Blessings in this season to our wandering pilgrims in an ancient land. Love, Mother and Father Garrett."

I am stunned, a whole life rushes over me, and I carefully pull back my feelings, secure my face and return to my classroom, where my sensitive young charges see immediately something is different.

"Later," I tell them, smiling. Later, I will sit down alone and think through all of this, the parents, the family, the vulnerability, the stages this communication has gone through to reach us, the message, the love. In fact, I am sure, I will think of these very things, never quite to be resolved, for the rest of my life . . . .

. . . The modir always shows me such kindness. He watches my exam for five minutes initially while I am handing out the papers and giving directions, but mostly he wants to be sure I understand where the students are or where they should be—My proctor, the lovely and lively Mr. Esfandyar, interested in everything except proctoring, guides Brenda around to his first grade classroom where a feisty, petite child captains the others (or a small number of them) in chanting the alphabet.

January 6, 1975

Yesterday seems a long way back there. We had a night of pouring rain and rustling wind. Morning comes to carry over yesterday's grades to the school, along the mud puddles, to chat cordially with some of the teachers, then to come home. We entertain a short visit by two neighbor girls, who measure out our room in lives, in the snapshots of the town and of my family.

In an afternoon walk to the old city with our guests, who inspire us with a modicum of faith at their curiosity and humor and knowledge, we enjoy ourselves. They point out to us with fresh eyes so many things we'd not taken time to remember looking at before, or thinking through: the anachronistic signs all along the northern highway with the men in business suits and hats silhouetted; the scrub forming along the bleaker slops of the regions where people already labor to break the hardy fields for winter wheat perhaps; a blind form lumbering suddenly before the bus, who turns out to be a chadried women with a child; and before whom the bus suddenly stops;the inevitable disconnect between our literary-saturated minds and this place which refuses to share with us its deepest written poetry; the new varieties of PC people who come over here now—a few shiny-cheeked optimists, and a lot of healthy skeptics. On the later, there are, we are, I surmise, totally out of the hashish-seeking stereotyped single male WT-style 1960's prototypes, are to see put in service now only professionals, preferably stable couples.

Tom shares a tale this morning about the roguish distempered old man who sat beside him on the bus, who griped and grumbled about everything in sight at the first chance, claiming he couldn't take it any more. So Tom stoically continued to sit with him, until the old man's bare-fanged senile spitting brought one solemn burst from Tom of "Christ!" at which input the old man turned to everyone on the bus to say, "Look what I've done. I made the foreigner go crazy (*Haragee dawah shudom*)."

The never tiring views fall around us when we climb to the old city hill, in every direction a different world somehow, one with the foreground of breast-topped houses, the garden and tin-roofed little boys' school, and the lonely lean wound of road stretching vast and silent to the desert of Mazar; the emerald green fields of winter wheat and cross-patched with the dry brown rustling of cotton plants being sheared, and the tidy terrace plots for irrigation; the bloodline river rambling on beside; and the town proper in its circle, its hundreds of roofs and its walled communities, the secret family households, and guarded gardens, the shops and eternities, impressions of a rustic land's unaltered patterns for "a city."

I think again about the way my parents' telegram arrived here for us: It was sent by my father on Christmas Day, with his sparse but deep words, to a telegram station somewhere, relayed on and on, to be printed out and delivered to me by hand as I stood outside my classroom two weeks after Christmas . . . .

What is to be made of Mirad's outburst about his visitor last night, a man whose family he had lived with last summer; he had borrowed 500 afs from him and early this year sent that sum down to him by means of a mutual friend, who is now a soldier. Well, the man apparently never got it; so the man had gambled 200 *afs* to come up here and try to get what he thought had been denied to him.

We lend money to Mirad for the sake of his honor and today he moves more freely in his ways . . . *[We had lovely talks with the Mahoneys.—about Oregon and religious Irishness and trips, people and believes . . . science and poetry. And I find I can talk with Brenda about my own family, and she nods and holds my shoulder, and says she understands how hard it all is.]*

January 8, 1975.

Today I proctor Fakir Khan's English test for 47 seventh graders and as we take turns walking around and corralling the excitement (actually they are very quiet and only a few at the end plead "*siphel*" ((0)) and refuse to write, gazing intently at a neighbor's paper all the time), Brenda, our guest, watches their faces. Her attention to their rows of exotic beauty calls them back to me—so I remember their rareness, their large, clear black and brown eyes, their regal rich dark hair, their alive complexions, the way each one of them is like a princess of some long lost generation. And the exam is just an exam.

But then time changes: in the afternoon Brenda and I go for a walk out to the garden and en route meet my old *saer malim*, a crew of taunting school girls (but none my students) who shatter my dreams, the kind young teacher with his garden and two guests, who wants us to come in for tea, and the Iyotollah of our last residence, the land-lord-grandson. Today he is as well-dressed and dignified as a little prep school boy . . .

January 10, 1975

> *[Rumors always proceed the arrival of would-be royalty. Just, so a PCV couple. We host a visit from the famous Gwen and Jack, brilliant and classy—Princeton and Harvard—(Tom and I, hailing from Princeton and Columbia, are less classy by nature, apparently, or just way less pretentious) fresh from Balkh and time with the volunteer there. There, we hear, Gwen had been "learning Farsi rapidly while sitting in the women's houses around the compound and being a cross-cultural Barbie doll," being dressed in everyone's best clothes, and pawed and exhibited, while her husband sat in the volunteer's humble, humble hut, surrounded by children who came to them like to a Pied Piper and hovered around him. Alas, is there more to being a Volunteer?]*

I sat with Zeebee a few minutes. Mirad's sister's husband was visiting and as he proceeded to spread his cloth for afternoon prayer, Habibullah, fully a mischievous free-hearted young boy now, threw pomegranate seeds at his uncle, 10-year old Najibullah, while Zeebee nursed the round-faced 5-month old.

> *[We have one more talk with our guests, then say our farewells]*

. . . . Tonight Mirad told us a story about where our new hat (a velvet and gold one, a gift from a PCV in Mazar, Janice Brown) . . . had come from. It's made by the people from Kazakistan, "*pahra-dahrya*"—people who fled across the Oxus from their ancestral homes in the 1930's under Stalin's mauling hands. He claims his own father's family is from this place, from the Lahiem Kazak people, who settled all over the north of Afghanistan. He has an uncle still in Tashkent.

So he describes how when he was a soldier in Badakshan, he was stationed right on the Amu Darya and could look across from his guardhouse at the Russian soldiers in their realm. Of course they could talk to each other. This wasn't allowed officially, but each marched on his side and raised a flag, and Mirad claimed some of them prayed like his people do. One day a Commissar came over, in a basket-pulleyed boat of four from his description, to check on the "boundary stones" to make sure they were accurate for each side of the river. Some of the accompanying soldiers spoke Farsi, but what they talked about on this notable afternoon Mirad doesn't share. And Mirad speaks of being drilled and taught by the army teachers, instructed in "border policy" and what to do should a war begin . . . A strange image that: the young Uzbek or Kazak across the river who could have been his lost cousin. He is not a Hazara, then, alone, but a blend. I pause, reflecting again on the arbitrariness of national borders, dividing families and heritage, setting up sibling rivalries for war.

Reading some of Reuben Levy's *[I did not know it then, but I would have this professor at Columbia several years later]* book called *The Social Structure of Islam,* and its general introduction to the spread of Islam, of people converting to save paying the tax to the conquerors, of others selling their children to raise money for the money bondage. It is amazing also to concede the sheer numbers of Moslems in the world . . . . engaged since that day, July 15, 622, when the Hegira began . . . .

January 12, 1975

. . . Today I am back in front of last year's 11th class, 12 strong, now 12th graders—Paregul, Sohliha, Zahra, Shegul, Gulsom, Monira, Katzah, Kamila, Foolaria, Rabia, Mumlekat, Suraya. They are taking a standardized English test . . . carefully administered by Fakir Khan. I see only one mistake, in the use of "how" on one question, but then he launches into an argument with me on how some "word-wide" grammar book had told him never to pronounce the "g" in "ing" endings and that it had to be correct because it was written there as a rule. I told him it was my native language and people simply did not speak that way, but although he smiled wistfully, he still was simply unconvinced. Meanwhile, the students who began English class just last year, Class 7, can't letter even a word in English. They are his students, but I can not blame him for their failure.

The Grinch has stolen winter here it seems, with more unseasonably pure blue weather. It looks as if the trees may start to bloom.

January 13, 1975

Mirad gives us a vivid description of the religious day coming up, the ten days that end with a day of mourning for the "Shi'a people." He speaks of the new month, begun with last night's full moon, and how everyone who knows about the significance of this time goes to the mosque and prays, and listens to the sermons that tell them not to steal or covet or do anything dishonest, but to give to the poor, to feed and cloth them, especially at this time. He is quite perturbed that Tashkurghan has no enlightened Shia population.

Then he explains how some people think all Shi'a are like the group living in Doshi and Shebar, who believe Ozret Ali had been God, and that he came once a year on this day (the death of Dazod) and put his hand print on the mound of the collective *pilau*, but that really a mullah had made that imprint, since Ali could never have been God, since he himself prayed to God (This is most interesting reasoning, which makes us wonder what he had heard of the Christ). He explains further how his people, the Shi'a, do not believe these words. Still, Zeebee wants him to take up two hand clothes to the shrine in Mazar and get them blessed, one for each of his sons.

It is Ashura, of which he speaks, the tenth day of Muharram, when the martyrdom of Hossain is commemorated, a day sacred to the Shi'a, who consider Hossain to be the 3rd Iman and the rightful heir and successor of Mohammed, the prophet. To show respect, Shi'a people wear mourning clothes and pray and recite poetry about the original deaths of Hossain and his family.

> *[I work on an old manuscript, finishing a draft of* Down Rivers, *excuse my lack of energy, as I am on medicine for dysentery and also sport a cold.]*

Today it is more wintry: the sun never come out, but I brazenly set out to shoot the last of the colored slides, wandering down a nearby lane to find a gracious veiled women beckoning me to come to her house. Then announcing me to her son up the road as "this women is my sister," she lets me move clumsily on. I dare intrude into the livestock sale below the old fort, am poised to take my shot, when the film clicks empty. I cannot record the moment, but smart at how I looked the foolish foreigner in the weathered faces of the old crowd.

January 14, 1975

> *[I cull through my pages of quotes from i.e. cummings, Italo Sveno, "Great Conversations," Willaim Penn Warren, Ignazio Silone, Joyce Carol Oates, Oscar Lewis, Nikos Kazantzakis . . . I've read decades of U.S., British, and foreign literature, and to what avail? Only, it seems, for my own pleasure, the passing of days, the easy detachment from all that is around me . . .]*

Winter comes with a vengeance this morning, and a blizzard wind brings snow that howls against our doors and windows, while the whiteness mounts outside.

This morning, Gahwar, an eight class student, and daughter of this household . . . comes over to visit. I give her tea and cookies and show her my pictures, and before she leaves take one of her. Although hers is a brief stay, we talk about several things—She is shocked that Americans don't knit or embroidery while all Afghan girls do. I tell that her many Americans actually do, but that I just am not one of them. She speaks of her various married relatives and their present and coming children, then looks me in the eye and asks softly why I have no children. Further, she tells me how all the students are afraid of me now, since that day I left class in a fury and the *modir* had scolded them for their rudeness and told them how I was a guest in their city and must be treated better than that. Then, inimitably, she smiles and tells me to come soon to her house to be a guest again.

Tonight, there is another story from Mirad inspired by T's question about Ouzret Ali, and how another Shi'ate he talked with (Joe's cook Hossain) had said that Ali's real burial site and shrine is in Iraq or

Iran, and that he had only come to Mazar and prayed once, not left his body there. Mirad claims that he doesn't really know himself, can only repeat the stories of mullahs and *"moie safeds"* (elders), However, he knows that there is another smaller shrine in Mazar dedicated to the old Baba who—legends tells—held Ali's horse for him when he was there.

Warming up to our curiosity, our raconteur-cook-friend tells the folk story of the origins of Bamiyan and Bande-Amir. For years the people living there hadn't been able to control the overflowing lakes, until one day Ali himself came there. Legend has it that all the men left and a few strong women stayed to pray with him and after that he made seven dams, and then told the women they were the strong ones now and should wear the turban (and so, to this day, some Kuhistan women wear a long wound turban). There's a shrine in that place where he left his hand and footprints. Further, Mirad goes on. He describes the *adjhar,* the gigantic dragon who used to haunt the valley near the Red City (Shari-zahra or Sorkh-ra), eating people, until Ouzret Ali came and slew him with a sword. The huge crevice by the city now (the stone turned dragon) remains to show how deep he cut the monster. From a spring in the rocks, supposedly where his head would be, a bitter turpentine-like liquid flows slowly out, making a gurgling, moaning noise.

And he mentions one more place, Yohawlang, in the Hazarajet, where a hospital for TB and leprosy was built, but which the government has now closed.Years and years and years before, at this place the dragon's child was killed. Mirad walked up from Bande-Amir to the village once, stopping to visit some of the houses. People live a strange life there, boarded up for the whole winter, with dry weeds to burn for warmth in one corner, all their animals in the other, themselves and their ovens in the middle. Somehow, he said, they survive the long months of cold . . . .

Mirad is so funny when he speaks of religion with us; he gets very animated and enthusiastically paces out the dimensions of the places he describes. It's as if he forgets we aren't his Moslem brothers and just accepts us into the whole mysterious ring of his religious conscience and imagination.

January 15, 1975

The exams are completed for the ninth class, and no one has failed, although there are some low numbers. A student needs only 25 out of 70 . . . to pass with a "three and a half." My proctor, good-hearted but rather distracted Esfandyar, caused more *"taklef"* (difficulty) than my students combined, carrying on a lively conversation for most of the morning with my students themselves, or dawdlers he had invited in from the hall to share the fireside *(bookerie)* with us. Alas, I fail miserably in trying to impress "justice" in these realms (!)

> *[I fill the pages here with quotes from Yeats, some later used in* Down Rivers . . . *.]*

January 16, 1975

A bitter cold has descended. This morning an old shawled woman and her two thinly-clad daughters meet me outside our gate on the way to school. They had walked three miles from the Tangi because the littlest girl insisted on being allowed to go to school (although she was sick and without transportation) because she said there was a warm stove and she could keep a good attendance record. The mother seems good-humored, although the small daughter has cried the whole way (she has "gotten too much cold") and the woman, who could not have been more than 40 or so, doesn't seem to begrudge me my warm clothing. It is as if she just accepts this inequality, although I offer to give her something of ours . . .

Why do any of us accept such inequality, when every religion, every faith, has begged us sternly in tome after prophet to the fictional Aloysha (in the *Brothers Karamzov,*) to treat all men as our brothers, to love our neighbors as ourselves, to do good?

Today the body of a student from last year's 12th class is brought back to town. He had been working in Lashkagar, but fell suddenly ill and died. A truckload of students go out to Hajie Biron to his funeral. We can't help but think of all the commotion that would be around a similar tragedy in the States, how memory plaques and scholarship funds and such would be up all over to bewail the passing of so young a person, cut down in his prime. But here people just chalk it up, another death, another dead son, Allah's indiscernible will.

January 17, 1975

I go again to Mirad's house to give the two-year old Habibullah something for his high fever. A quarter aspirin seems the best I can offer.

"How can I know what will become of a small child?" his mother asks me.

She says she is uncomfortable, that her nipples hurt.

I tell her she must keep feeding the baby, to squeeze the milk out, if the baby's sucking hard irritates her. I coach her not to give up, just because she is having trouble nursing, apart from the distraction of tending two boys. She says again that her breast hurts and so she had stopped nursing the child with it because she thought it "sick."

"No," I tell her gently. "You can put some balming lotion on the nipples, but do not stop feeding the child . . . ."

Mirad has another story, of finding an old man asleep one night beside the river, between the outhouse near the Haji's house and the water, in a tiny room too small for a man to stand up in. The man explained—after Mirad had seen him by lantern—that he was there to guard the wood beside the river and keep it from being taken during the night by some person, and thereby cutting off the gristmill's source.

Of water—this leads to a story about how some people had drowned last summer in the spring nearby. Ultimately he tells us why he has come to be terrified of water. When he went to the river in Jalalabad with some friends, several years ago, he got swept in the current and had already given himself up for dead, when the river leveled out and his feet again touched ground, and he was able to walk out . . .

January 19, 1975

With yesterday's last exam finished, today I sit in the office watching the mountains all morning long, trying to earn my holiday for tomorrow, except for a few minutes in the mad house of the 7th class, where students drew models vases from the blackboard and then displayed their embroidery for a grade. They are a loud but gifted needleworking group. I easedrop a few minutes on their geography test, given by Najiba, and on Esfandyar's diminutive Class 1, then am off to an Afghan party at Azarullah's house (Tom's faithful student).

With his little sister leading, I enter into the large high-ceilinged room where six women sit under the blankets of a broad *sandalee* (the table with burning coals in a pan underneath it and covered by a blanket). They are white-scarfed, under it their dark peasant faces, marked and large nosed, their layers of clothing stitched together with those dry aged hands. I become the honored guest next to Azarullah's mother and the conversation begins, with her the careful matriarch sifting out all my answers for the benefit of the others there. A few grinning children try to touch me; neighbors and relatives of the family watch me, one old toothless crony encourages me to speak or learn Uzbek. She is deaf but eager before my answer. Of course there are the initial everlasting inquiries, branching away from me as each asks about prices, a dowry set for one woman's daughter. More and more come in until there are perhaps 12 women and six children, one tiny doll-like baby nodding her miniature head, her eyes big with make-up, and with each the ritual of kissing, then sitting in the room under the big *sandalee* with its small pots of coals under the blankets, savoring the heat.

Dinner itself comes hours later, after the waterpipe has been passed to all the crones and the sugar water blessed and shared, and the parade of 170 men in the guest house and garden viewed, scrutinized, commented upon with true un-maidenly cynicism . . . The food itself is rich and expansive, with huge mounds of carrot-raisin *pilau,* spinach and *korma*, oranges and tea and candy, and with my plate made up for me by the large mountain of Azarullah's aunt, I am expected to eat well beyond my capacity.

When leaving finally, I watch each of their faces shyly in the doorway, taking in a picture of light and dark, some old dark faces, the light Turkomen blood, one pale hazel eyed thin beauty, Elizabethan stage right, in Afghanistan, without an age. All the children later comment upon my future, comment on the curse of childlessness as well (for in that household immune from their matron scarves, the religious smoking, the sugar water drink, I am like a child, grouped with the children to be tended to.) Thanking them all, I set out. Azarullah walks me home and gives Tom a "*bomona khodah*" for the journey we are to leave on tomorrow.

January 21, 1975

Yesterday we woke to a cold, gray morning, and snow falling around the skeptical steppes as we set out for the highway. Mirad carried all our gear (at his insistence), there to make sure we got off well. We stood a while, waiting for the razzle-dazzle bus line, Gulhana, and the front row seats. We stay warm during the trip behind the burly bearded Haji Pushtoon driver, *naswar* rolling between. varied lips, and en route see the victorious and newly sainted, bus and taxi loads of returning pilgrims from the Haj. The land clears as the altitude soars; we eat lunch beside the road part way up the Salang in a frail teahouse.

January 22; *10 of Maharrem.*

I is a morning of wandering the junk shops of Kabul looking for small items to take "home," to someday grace the households of America—Nuristani woodblocks and old leather gun powder pouches, water pitchers of Ghazni's handcrafting, and musical instruments of antiquity and modernity blended except in price.

> *[We visited with Brenda and Chris Mahoney and heard stories of the Yellow Man's Coyote Tales from Brenda's professor's time on an Indian reservation; the American International School of Kabul (AISK) where Sara and Jerry Kissinger. were now staying/working and its very American clientèle and postures; Jeb and Caitlin Leigh and a discussion on the implausibility of Hindi movie plots, the only thing any of us got to see in the boonies; the always shared and bountiful meals and other connections with former and departing PCVs.*]

Jan. 23, 1975

We set off with Patrick and Shelly West for Jalalabad . . . a hard ride through the rich Kabul Gorge, red-shawled shepherdesses like cardinals on the rocky hills, sharp mountains and winding snake bent road leading to square mud compounds, orange and fruit groves, winter wheat and narcissus bouquets. Entering we feel the hum, the bustle of Jalalabad where all the wealthy of Kabul have come for the three day holiday, to admire and warm up, among other things and places, in the Charka Garden and in shops and restaurants along wide avenues and tucked away in green parks. We exit from our squeezed back seat of the Toyota, along with the little boy who has been our drowsy scapegoat, tumble out to find a hotel and lunch, then settle down to the "high sights," and eat kebab in a packed masculine room. The streets seem overrun with stylish Afghan "dagtars," stylishly-garbed and chadris-free. Best is a ride out to Hedda, the Buddhist-Grecian archaeological site, the largest mound of the once-thriving 2nd to 6th century Buddhist monastery and reliquary and votive stupas, where Buddha's earliest reincarnation—legend claims—had taken place centuries before and where he had killed a viscous dragon and where his skull and teeth were supposedly preserved. Here were the beautiful stucco remains: animal gargoyles, cupidlike corners, fabled sea monsters, the austerely royal feet of the Buddha, the decorative shrines left behind by centuries of worshipers come to take the cast of the Buddha's holy part, along with the amazing Greek like followers admiring the Reincarnation, the teacher, the gods, the Nrioma—all in a mound now called Rostana Jethur Camel Hiri . . .

We walk through more streets, approach a peaceful garden hotel and eat a small delicious dinner. There is a story hour afterwards with Arnie and Kayla Bond . . . of Puli Khumri . . . .

January 24, 1975

We wake to a delicate fine day's view, up to the sun sounds of 7:00 in Jalalabad, what may be a million (it seemed) Kabulis setting out to return home after the holiday weekend. We have breakfast and negotiate for a taxi to Logman, a ride out past the blue reservoir into green valleys shouldered by the White Mountains (Kuh-e-Safed), groves of oranges, and barren stretches, all willed by the river and the high snows. We enter market day in the village and all the neighboring hillmen have come in to sell goods; little boys sell stripped cane, and oranges like bright jewels, the lean-lined Pushtu faces stare back at us. We wander beside a garden of old cypress and palm trees, note a few delicately ruined fort turrets, along with the massive manors like fortifications of family compounds scattered across the valley.

On we go by taxi to Charbaugh, a gem of a village perhaps 30 minutes from Logman by cab, built upon a hill, with its bazaar of old

Nuristani-style, wood-carved booths. A pied piper of children seeks our pictures and points out the dimensions of the bazaar, and everyone tells us welcome. We stop for tea and a chat with a local teacher, who is now working up the valley a ways, and all the venerable shopkeepers apologize for the children's discourteous behavior, and pour us tea, explaining it was fine, that the children were only curious and well-meaning. We study the dark winding covered bazaar, the carved balconies hanging out over the hillside, like something from a Swiss mountain village or an old English half-timber house in Shakespeare's day. The effect is a touch of pastoral peace, with streams braiding the valley, crossed by little wooden steps and miniature bridges.

We move back by camel-lined, unpaved rocky road to Jalalabad, and stop in at the compound of volunteers there, then go out to bargain for hats and a *shawlo-blanet* (the Afghan overcoat), before taking a long walk back and forth to the volunteer house for dinner [and hear of Shelly's family, like all it seems, with its sadness, its sibling(s) lost.]

What is the story of each Afghan we met today? Are we out of step, wondering about the lives behind the cardboard and our own *chadried* visions of reality in ourselves and others?

January 25-6, 1975

In this, our exalted semester break, from Jalalabad we get up from our room at the Ansari Hotel, to consume the greasy omelet special, then go out to the volunteers' house to leave off our stuff and seek a jeep to Shawa. Procured about 10:30, it is a wobbly strong vehicle driven by a native Pushtoon from the valley going toward Nuristan. He is clear-skinned, Western-featured, with dark curly hair, and speaks both Farsi and Pushtoon as a second tongue. We move across more green valleys to the town famous for its old craft of making wooden things and painting them with bright colored crayon wax (lacquer), all this using a hand and foot-run lathe (as in Tashkurghan), one of the last places where this craft prevails. We pass a garden where our driver insists that silkworms are commercially raised, and the turn off for the road—he claims—leads on and over the highest peaks into China. We see much praising and imaginings in the tiny half block town bazaar, chicken grease soul on the porch of a *choie-xona* . . . . Then, Sunday morning, we go by cab to Kabul, and use an afternoon to price things in the streets. In one surprising visit, we go up to the loft room of an old Turkoman carpet seller, who carries us off the street to show us his things. We buy two Lokaii pieces, and feel as if we plucked them from his dark collected arbor of aged and exiled skill . . .

January 27, 1975

We are up late today and I troop out to the USAID Gift shop, where contemporary American woman wearing tasteful make-up transact intimate business, imitating French tête-à-tête beside matronly young Germans. I am in the middle, spotting out embroidery and leaving with the most expensive thing there . . . .

> *[We lunch with the assistant country director, and dinner with the Mahoneys. and Benson and Susan Marek at the Aga-gul's. We learned that Trent Hatfield's wife, from our cycle, was pregnant.]*

Jan. 28, 1975

It is another day of shopping, and since our decisions have already been made this time (yesterday's rehearsal), we just collect objects and pay, while a dreamy white wet feather bed of snow falls mutely all morning and into the night.

> *[We have a delicious dinner at the Howards . . . recall a few insights from Trent and Candy Hatfield, who had seen a neighbor try to take medications for amputees when her knee was sore . . . and hear of a sadistic Class 1 teacher who made up a ridiculous situation to punish the students and humiliate them: the children were made to stand in the tashknob without their shoes . . . .]*

Hotel Continental, Kabul, 2000

In gray Kabul, the self-appointed "mullah-ocracy"
controlled and regulated all life,
a rope choking its citizens' normal breath and movement
cataloging and imprisoning its rare visitors.

Huge Toyota pick-up trucks with their black-turbaned,
armed Taliban, caroused the streets
dispatched by Kabul's "finest" from
the Ministry for the Prevention of Vice and Protection of Virtue
(Ministry of Amr bil Marouf).

They covered the city,
rounded up and jailed people
for not covering their heads,
not having long enough beards,
not going to the mosque,
not heeding their ban on listening to music;
not wearing a long enough burqa
or showing their ankles.

Their black turbans screaming off their dark-haired heads,
wound loosely and high like decaying mushrooms,
they shadowed, thick beards embracing chins,
pushing up to broad noses,
blurring the plane of stern faces or bold boyish faces.
Quickly their eyes bulleted their target
as they spilled out of the Toyota pickup trucks,
Karishnikovs pointed, wooden sticks dancing.

High in the northern hills,
from the stark, ghostly void of the Hotel Intercontinental
tottering, frozen in time, like everything that year,
the world beyond the bullet-holed windows and balconies,
lay empty, denied sounds of music, television or traffic,
the only noise the haunting wail of the call to prayer,
regularly puncturing the silence like bullets.

Besides the fleets of Toyata pickups,
only rusty bikes scuttled like dying insects
among squatting hulks of buildings, buckled streets,
burned out and bombed ruins,
a shattered city, its pitted streets, open sewers,
rubble heaps of neighborhoods:
a ghost town of squatters, beggars
and unmarked graves.

Only everywhere, springing up every few feet,
new mosques and shrines, gleamed coldly.

So the buzzards ruled.

X

CONTINUING

January 31, 1975

. . . We catch a slow starting Toyota out of Kabul . . . to be delivered to the fairytale white land of the Salang and its brown villages perched like homely birds . . . . and a morning, gray without sun . . . .

Our trusty second set of eyes on this world, Mirad gives us more stories, This is about killer camels and how some, angered with being burdened, grab their persecutor with the teeth, knock him down and then kneel on top of him and crush him to death. Mirad claims to have seen two instances of this. Also, he confirms the danger of these seemingly awkward animals who can also outrun a horse (I recall the time last year when the jeep raced the young camel; the wild motion of his running across the desert from the road beside the reservoir outside Jalalabad.)

There is a ring of clouds around our mountain as the afternoon clears, the white snow border like a fancy confections . . . .

Feb. 2, 1975

[Our mail arrives, along with an attorney who has traveled the world . . . .]

. . . School without our *modir* (principal) is rather lax. I've begun with a full bag of tricks and am liable to run down before too long. Today our *kouteb* (clerk) is talking about making the "*haj*" on his bicycle, only half joking it seems as he embellishes his story of how he would make a sail to catch the wind; and the cruel, deranged dark mullah is wearing his Jalalabad hat today, to the amusement of all, the donnish wool cap looking demented and out of this realm on his half-witted and haughty head.

Feb. 3, 1975

The weather is cold . . . . I begin "Aladdin" with the teachers' class and they have trouble envisioning a magic garden. But clearly, something is not being communicated, since all of Persian literature is full of such places.

> *[I am wanting to write about the committed versus the uncommitted—in any situation, thinking also of how effective Graham Greene is in describing people's affairs and actions bloodlessly . . . Oddly, a letter from Ms Thaddeus, my undergraduate advisor, extols me not to try to write as an Afghan but as an American . . . Will I ever know what she means by that, much less be able to act on it?]*

Feb. 4. 1975

This morning's snow has covered everything, the soft white frozen flakes has made a burst feather bed of the brown land. In the classes, the grades, like epistles from unreliable heavenly bearers, are passed out and a lot of children cry. Status had shifted; Zahra, who is always first, has slipped to second, Mazari is third and Shahzadah, our Lashkagar import, has moved to first.

I have only the first four hours of teaching, plus pre-school, this morning, so I return home about 11:30 and go over to visit Zeebee. Her two sons are asleep in their corners, a small fire of brush and kindling glows in the *bookerie.*

She sits washing a cup for me, a saucer and a teapot, carefully scalding everything with the boiling water, and then, perched under her layers of clothes, her shawled cap like a veil above her head, she leans back on her heels and tells me stories, first about the snow in Kabul, Mazar and Sare-pul, that never came to Jalalabad, then about how necessary the snow is for the crops, her people ("*ma modum*"), who had known years of drought and subsequent starvation.

Somehow this leads into a rich description of all the things the Lyttons (those previous Volunteers in Jalalabad for whom Mirad had worked, and with whom Zeebee had also lived) bought to take back to the States with them. Some, Zeebee explains, they bought for themselves, and some as gifts—silver bowls and embroidered caps, materials and rugs and braided cloth, wooden Shahwa boxes—on and on she itemizes the objects like a great scroll spread out across the floor behind us.

And, remembering the Lyttons and Jalalabad, she speaks also of Mirad's operation last year and how he'd been in the hospital a few weeks and had "the tiny red thing like a fat snake inside removed," and then (going back) she carefully detailed what had happened to make him go to the hospital and how while he wasn't there she'd been alone with Habibullah. Kindly, Theresa Lytton, had asked her what she needed and brought some things for her, including wood. This latter entailed another story, how they weren't using the Lytton's wood because Dan didn't want them to, and how actually God was good to them with the weather and they didn't need it, but once Habibullah was walking outside and the weather was chilly and Dan must have asked why he was outside and not in with Zeebee, and she told them because it was cold in there without a fire. So it circles back

And as she tells me, I am reminded of the matrix of some story where a young girl sits at an old woman's knees and the women slowly reminiscences over all her life, bringing each thing in its time, a little at a time—But Zeebee in years is a young girl, for all her experiences in sadness (the sickness, the deaths) and lack of experience in my other worlds. In this she is already old . . .

And she explains how the last time when we were in Mazar, Mirad and his sons and Zeebee and the brother had walked all around Tashkurghan to see "what there was" and she (they all) concluded it was really not much of a town, certainly not like Kabul, Mazar or Jalalabad are. She tells me that she had never really seen Mazar either, until the last time they were up there for Women's Day Prayer, and she got to walk all the way across town to Hossain's house.

Tashkurghan, she nods sagely, has hats and some nicely colored things, and an old city above, but little else, except now, the snow . . . .

. . . So I leave to come sit by my own fire . . . and listen then to Tom's stories about his school. He has just read "Hansel and Gretel" to the students in his class this wintry day and they had loved it. And (in another realm, or not) he shakes his head. Twice in this past week he's discovered pictures of naked women in his students' hands. Is it a coming revolution in this protocol of provincialism? To be humored? Or, more likely, are adolescent minds the same the world over?

Feb. 5, 1975

. . . Now that Tom and I have launched a storytelling program for our last semester here (having decided that we'll never succeed in embedding good pedagogical techniques so at least we'll make this last period be time with context that our students will likely remember) we come home each day and compare how his lanky, lean-suited farmer boys and my mischievous, soon-to-be tamed in marriage girls responded to the Candy House, the Witch and the wicked stepmother in "Hansel and Gretel," the long rope hair of Rapunzel, and the Sleeping Beauty's industrious dwarfs. All the stories we had read to us as wee children are like pieces of free candy to these gangling adolescents who've never had even a picture to set off their native imagination. We'll do nothing to make sure they always have shoes or food, justice or even a book, but perhaps we can give them a small blue patch of childhood they can tuck away and maybe one day use on their own children. Who knows. At the same time, it is absurd that we must bring them western stories, when their history embraces millenniums of literature and stories from multiple cultures.

Feb. 5, 1975

The snow that had cushioned our days and kept them immoderately cold, melts in a great mess of piss and puddles today, especially evident in every spot I have to walk in, the schoolyard with its all but disappeared hump of an *"adomee barfu"* (snowman), the *cuchas* (alleyways) between our house and the schoolyard . . . .

Mirad's world broadens daily. We smile at his excitement at learning some English phrases of greeting, in their perfect grammar set down in the first book to be read; or his going thoughtfully over the spellings of the colors whose true names he doesn't even use in Farsi. Then tonight he came in after supper to ask for a telephone number he had given us of a friend in Kabul, because he heard on the radio about a very bad series of bus accidents in the Kabul Gorge between Kabul and Jalalabad, a route his brother Qorbin goes over frequently, and so now he wants to call this man in Kabul and find out if he has any world of Qorbin ("the Sacrifice," ironically)

Feb. 6, 1975

[Days pull, demand. We prepare for a conference in Puli, and write letters appealing to Asia Foundation for a mimeograph machine for each of the schools here.]

After lunch, just as Tom is describing to me how his student had prepared tea and music for him at his shop yesterday when he went to buy a pen, we hear a call at our gate. It is the first grade teacher from my school, Esfandyar. He has come ostensibly to invite me to his sister's *takht-jami* ("housewarming"). This is a gathering of all the women, neighbors, relatives, and friends at the bride's husband's house to bring her dishes and furniture, look at all her wedding treasures, eat lunch and have tea, and share fruit and candy. But once he sits down and precedes to drop lavish hints about what a fine teacher he would be for us, and how he had an excellent rapport with all the students in the school, we pass a full hour with him, highlighted by a presentation of—always—our photograph collection. Each of them he surveys with a rather crazed laugh and a question.

He has barely left when Tom's student Azarullah comes out shyly from the kitchen, wherein he had been talking to Mirad and waiting for this teacher to leave.

After a lot of general greetings I leave him and Tom and set out to the bazaar to finish off our roll of colored slides, so that I can take pictures tomorrow of the *"zahni* gathering." Through casual eyes I catch a shot of the fort and mountains, a kindly carpenter, a ghostly gray *chadrised* woman floating across the river bridge, the bazaar behind it, the muddy *mandalee* commerce center in the late afternoon, a *karachi* driver pausing in the road with his old nag and cart . . .

Back to the room, I discover Tom and Azarullah performing a postmortem on this new *"rafted" modir*, a conversation that soon leads to the announcement that only five of this year's 12th class have passed the term. Then Azarullah describes his own traumas from the tests, the lower grades easily explainable by the fact that he had been a little sick that day, or because the teacher was notoriously unfair anyway.

Night falls; there is a lone dog's bark, and we sit in our clutched metaphor, figures out of time, most common beside a wood burning fire.

Feb. 7, 1975

A strange day, one of those for which you want to sum up all the details to tell to a grandchild, or to cronies grown old, one day

. . . . Tom sets off to Puli-Khumri . . . .

I eat breakfast and watch a bright morning come up over the mountains . . . . when suddenly I hear Mirad talking to someone and quickly realize that Esfandyar has already come to take me to his house. It is 8:40 a.m. He sits totally still in the chilly room where a fire has yet to be started, both of us awkward, myself feeling more neuter than ever in my present, unprotected state. Then I fumble and start to talk. We speak about small, irrelevant things, how the weather is warm today, how snow has been only slight, insufficient, in the town for four years now, and the crops have been smaller than usual, how corn, oats, and wheat are planted in the late fall and sprout in early winter, provided they have been well-nourished by the winter moisture, how (he said) people in town out of ignorance complain about the girls' school, not realizing how good and necessary it really is, how his sisters miss me and so on. Somehow I introduce the topic of Mecca and the Haj, which the perfect time for him to ask to see my magazine on Saudi Arabia.

He pours over the pictures taken by the narrator, a blue-eyed Minnesotan turned Moslem, asking me almost nothing about the pictures yet obviously not fully understanding them all either (the two pages of various Moslem women baffle him—the Nigerian with decorative scarred cheeks he takes for Buddha, an old Persian miniature of the Crusades in Jerusalem he thinks is about a war six years ago).

Then it is 9:30 and time to leave.

An easy foot shorter than I, limping, salaaming as we pass by a never-ending stream of *"malims,"* he starts us out down the narrow muddy ways, to the paved road. We are doubtless an odd couple. The mountains shimmer beyond the town, the thin white coating on the high fields beneath them glows like a grave painting, a timeless backdrop for the old town fort, its "modern" persons moving in the foreground. Neither of us talks in the road much; I think the little teacher may be embarrassed. Yet he begins with the best intentions to point out to me various houses and landmarks he felt I might not know about—the Gardens, the old fort, the graveyard, the home of his uncle.

In his own compound, which we reach in a long 15 minutes, we hail his brother, newly returned from the army, where he won a first for tent-pegging for his company. An excellent farmer, gardener and cook to boot (Esfandyar had carefully coached me), he is in the process of looking after the cow. I see the same generous smile and open eyes on him as always rest on Esfandyar.

I am taken to sit with their mother and little sister, Sabera, until the kindly-faced father, his oldest sister (the three girls all are "one face"), her adoring two-year old daughter, and the dark-haired, porcelain-faced girl-next-door, Esfandyar's wife-to-be, could all be gathered for some pictures. I did my best to catch them, but in typical Afghan style, they neither know where to stand nor how to look happy. I capture a largely unsmiling group.

Under the *sandalee* in their first room, I sit with Esfandyar's fiancée, his sister, and mother, while the niece crawls across me like a tenacious but lovable ant, and I rise and sit and rise again, kissed by a stream of aunts and cousins of the family, until in walks a dark-eyed, pure-skinned beauty, perhaps the most perfect looking child I have ever seen in this land of exceptionally beautiful young girls. Her dark long hair falls on her slim just-turned 15 shoulders, a green dress sets off her rosy clear colors softly. She was some aunt's child, unnamed, I am told.

When a respectable number of women and children have gathered there, each kissed and salaamed, we all set out for the house of the husband of Syfora (the newly married sister, my former 10th grade student). During the walk along the wall, for we are only going a bit up the lane, the talk is all of how much each person is bringing in her "*paket*," and who has brought bowls and glasses and pitchers and saucers for the new bride. I walk ahead of them after a while with Sahera, the young sister, and a few pre-chadris-aged girls.

So we arrive at the large estate of the new husband. By now we are almost to Hajie Biron, behind on the non-paved road farmers in fields turning in rows, the tilted earth of a plateau pushing up toward the mountains, a gothic stillness, and permanence about the scene, prevailing somehow.

The yard is full of a row of houses. We are led up to the second story of the largest house to the living quarters and greeted by Syfora, who looks splendid in brocaded white silk, although made up heavily like someone's version of a pretty doll. Here we would be until four o'clock.

The first hours pass as we just sit there among the women, complimenting each other, being softly watched, finally shyly touched by the old white-shawled women with their faces like ancient maps of a quick-blown life, and again and again rising and resettling around the warm fire as each new guest enters. I have never been ceremoniously kissed or kissed back so many times, although every social gathering is the same. This time I am completely embraced as one of all of them, a sister, and so—in effect—undergo a kind of initiation,

I take some pictures of the honored ones, the new wife and the expectant one, sister and aunts and mothers, outside with the couple on the roof, in the sun, before the courtyard. As a parting gesture I try to take all of the groom's family, but it proves a task beyond me; I managed to loose a few heads. Once I get scolded by a jet-black headed women, the mother of the beauty I had seen earlier, for trying to take a photo of her child, for which I apologize profusely. Her face is not to be among those documented; I must recall it only in my head. Silently, I wish on this child a life of such respect and protection.

Intermittently we all have tea and candy, and conversation, about the usual: childless versus child rich, language versus speechless, English versus Farsi, teacher versus wife-mother—as the coals steam and the cups are passed and children are nursed, and the looks move to each face and each new entry.

I have no sense of outside, where the food was cooked in a kitchen, and then finally carried in on steaming platers about 1:30. There are huge mounds of rice to be shared among us, set down on great plastic sheets stretched the length and width of the room, and again I am fitted out with a spoon, while everyone else uses her well-molding fingers.

Somehow the afternoon passes, women kindly asking me the questions and lapsing into their own descriptions of their daily life. I am struck again at how practical the conversation is, how much concerns the prices of things, quantities of stories, the amounts of rice, roghan and flour. To know how to bargain, to balance, is that not a way to survive?

The import of the day's program, the distributing of the household goods (which are mostly all dishes and some money) comes at last. The chubby family matron, a plain, loud-voiced girl, or woman, as the afternoon's joke about Syfora went ("she is now a *zahn*, no longer a *dagtar*"), announces who each piece is from, then holds it up to be seen as everyone looks on approvingly.

Out of it all, at last, with little sister Sabera and her 9-year old brother in tow, I set off on the long road back home in the shadowy afternoon. The town lays still, except for the neighborhood boys playing in the street on their holiday, until we reach Sabera's house. Again, I say goodbye and keep walking, only to have Esfandyar yell for me from the street. Numbly I pass back to greet his brother and father again, to look at their gardens, the cows and a new calf, to thank them for the invitation, to join them and provide the day and their family an afternoon guest for yet more tea. The little teacher then walks me home, back to where it had all started . . .

Alone now in the house, secure beside a warm fire, I let my mind soar and send up a kind of gauze net to catch all the small impressions of a very Afghan day, and keep them as I said before, until I have neither the leisure nor the peace of this village life to be setting them down in, and in that future time, I will to look at them again like little fall roses in an almost frozen garden . . . .

Feb. 8, 1975

. . . Classes here have their victories. They are our work, our principle purpose. Then, after them, a class for an hour and a half with Mirad, as we help him with basic literacy. He has barely finished when Shahzadah comes strolling in, intent on a few new words in a lesson, and for once she stays a full hour . . . She is ushered out and in comes Hossain, Mirad's cousin, with the news that he has just been fired by Alyson, over some, as he tells it, apparently far-fetched thing ("Her *modir* says that I smoke hashish"). He has left his things in Mazar at Maurice's and brought his family (Shiringul, Mina and Zmaria) here to stay while he goes to Kabul to secure other work. It all seems rather strange, particularly the timing which left Alyson's house with no one there, just when she has gone to Puli Khumri.

There are strong hints after that of something even crazy: Hossain claims Alyson has an Afghan boyfriend who stays with her a lot of times, and that she believes in having several "friends"(these exclusive of Tim, it would seem). Then more comes out. He claims that Alyson hasn't paid Hossain for the time he didn't cook, for the time when she was in Lashgakar for semester break, and then again for these last six days which made it a month he was short of pay.

I venture next door to the roomful of people, Hossain's pregnant wife and energetic children, Zeebee and the brother Najbullah (thinking already how it will be when he goes off to Sare-pul for the new school term just short of a month hence) and Mohammed Ali and Habibullah. The little boys are chopping, picking up chopped twigs, snapping them like whips, while Hossain is peeling carrots for soup. Against the wall, the wives are busy nursing and holding children, then squatting, washing dishes and passing comments on better ways to do things (You shouldn't let Habibullah eat raw carrots; you shouldn't let children play with sharp pieces of wood) like relatives the world over.

Sitting there I remember Saturday night dinners with my Uncle Herbert's family when I was a small child, before my older siblings married and moved away or went off to university, before my parents and myself and the three remaining brothers moved from Houston to St.Louis when my 56-year old father's job was transferred there. After that we were never all together as a family again, never near any of them for more than a few night's visit, and then there were decades when we did not see them at all. In those early weekly gatherings, there had always been slight tension, but also an easy-going familiarity, the crowded sense of everyone being in one place without the right to privacy, and yet an acceptance, a comfort in being so immersed . . . .

I envied the young cousins and their parents the gift of family shared, and I realized how much the seeming normalcy of Tom's well-settled family, had drawn—and still drew me—to feel safe and loved somehow.

So tomorrow Tom should be back with my news or terms of punishment, and Mirad will go off to Mazar to look up a sister and to get money for us from the bank. Tomorrow the teachers' class will again commence, and with it, likely, a beagle's ear of expected troubles . . . .

Feb. 10, 1975

. . . A rabble-rousing school day that sends me home pleading bedlam, but walking through the village, as always, I grow revived by the pure day, and blue spring mien. Just outside my gate, four *chadris* accost me and greet me formally, then one (the mother of the third grader who frequently visits) called out to ask why I hadn't ever visited her. Of course I reply jollily that they must visit me, which they do within seconds of my entering my yard, but only briefly, to ask the usual questions and acclaim my hard work and wish me well. There is lunch, soup, and no lesson for Mirad.

Then along come Shiringul and Zeebee and their foursome of beauties, their children, and lone Najibullah. I put on tea and bring cookies and candies and want to begin some conversation, but in walks Shahzadah primed for a lesson, which eventually gets off the ground, as the two cooks' wives eye it all with strange unknownable thoughts, I'm sure, as they nurse their youngest and quiz their eldest . . . They leave, and I fear I have slighted them, and yet I could not have failed to deliver a lesson for my tutee, for all her Pushtoon pride. . . . Then Tom appears . . . . and it is a bustle . . . to get dinner on, all this interrupted by Esfandyar who brings in yogurt fresh from his family cow, nibbles a few cookies with us, and gently corrects our Persian grammatical construction as we try to explain about some political issue in the States. Then, now so fast, it seems to be time for bed, which I seek like a soft lighthouse on a blind, stormy night.

I am off early to school the next morning, for a good reading of *Aladdin,* a strict order to my classes now, and then about 11:30 I am interrupted by a note delivered by Tom's student on his behalf and pleading that Yasir and Rashid from Peace Corps Kabul had arrived and would be with us for lunch, but that Mirad still has not returned. So, the note entreats, I should get some stuff for them as soon as I could from the bazaar . . .

The above named themselves are waiting to go to my house. They are making definite plans for two volunteers to practice teach at my school (and four at Tom's). Typically, anxious to help, half my 11th class volunteers their own houses to host the guests for lunch, when they hear that I don't have anything ready at my own house. Finally, dear, bright as a new penny Paregul (she wants to become a doctor and certainly has the intelligence) pops up philosophically with the information that these guests were "only Afghan" and "human," and therefore worthy of no particular worry.

So, classes done, I leave with the two men, who make quite a show of turning their truck-jeep around and then driving down a narrow rutted road and—worse—down our *cucha*. But Tom has already returned from his school and stepped in and fetched *pilau* from the bazaar. There is fruit and tea and cookies galore, so everyone eats well.

We are in a scurry as they leave . . . and then Mirad walks in. He had visited his sister way out in the hills of Balkh, where her husband had been paralyzed on one side for 15 days now (though a mullah and some shot cured him of his facial paralysis earlier). His was again a sad tale to put all this bustling vacuousness into perspective.

There is a claim that the son of Noah, who was named Shees or Seth, is buried at Mazar, and that a piece of the ark is in Samarkand (Turkmenistan), and that the land that appeared after the Flood was the Hindu Kush range and that the country where they arrived was Balkh. Could not any of this mystical and profound history and legend muster up the grace and magic to save one poor man in these wild and empty plateau, the swath of land stretching off to the horizon now in every direction?

Mirad also asked for Alyson's version of Hossain's downfall, which Tom gave, after much apologizing. There was a silence. Then Ziadeen and Kabir arrived to visit, to collect . . . money, and ponder his daughter's negatives, and to discover where they stood in our eyes: The main undertone was: Won't you help us find work for the summer in PC? So Ziadeen is not going to teach us anymore, it appears. Meanwhile, Kabir sat stiffly and unspeaking, in both English and Persian totally inarticulate. They are ushering themselves out (Ziadeen 900 afs richer, thanks to our paying the Rashed's debt—which we'll be reimbursed for later, I guess), when Esfandyar appears, small and a little shabby. They scarcely greet him, I note, which makes all the more reason to welcome him.

In minutes he is seated with a pot of tea and some fruit and nuts before him, spinning a tale of having just come from the home of an old friend, who had lost a hand, having broken a wrist in an accident some time ago. Yogurt pot returned, two oranges consumed, he too leaves, all the while dropping compliments to us like great sighs . . . .

Feb. 12, 1975

A great calamitous storm last night, with wind and rain and a howling cold, turned the season back to a convincing winter. This morning I wake to find our yard covered with water, and as we putter around getting on our "mud suits" to confront the mush and wet and cold, we joke about the need to build an ark to save the last examples of mankind

What a pathetic sight my students made in their billowing *chadris,* trying to weave their small weights through the deep mud and puddles, but behind the patched, screened holes, their eyes barely able to see their steps in front of them.

I find a moment of captive audience as the *modir* attempts to discern the meaning of "buffer" in the 12th class history book. I explain its significance with respect to wars and boundaries, and Ziadeen accepts my gist and then explains it again, paraphrasing it for the others, while the *modir* takes my spelling and looks up his own meanings. It seemed they agree, my explanation is accepted and understood, and the lesson moves on.

The six Peace Corps volunteer teachers due here on Friday have a challenge awaiting them: they are expected to watch and teach in our places, but my students have already decided that I'm to let them take my place only for a few days . . ."because you will be gone too soon and we now want everyday to just with you."

Inside our box of a house like a great animal's rib cage, we listen to the growling wind in the air beyond us, and think about floods of history and histories of floods.

Feb. 13, 1975

. . . The next day our eyes open to a sun-blessed day with all the mountains around town crystal white with the new fallen snow and the radio's announcement that the Salang Pass is closed again, and there have been 400 new avalanches . . . .

Mirad tells us a lot more substantial sort of stories than the fake trappings of forced plot give room to. Last night . . . he told of a trip he took a few years ago, the year of the great famine that started out with blizzard snow late in the season. He and his brother Najibullah were on a bus (going down to Kabul, was it). In any case, the weather was terribly cold and snowy and the bus put up in Jangaluhan in a storm at the edge of the Salang, where a pretty bit of Moslem brotherhood was soon exhibited. The teahouse keeper started by charging everyone 20 *afs* for just sitting room, and of course there were so many stranded passengers there, none could lie down. Likewise, the price for all food was rapidly doubled, despite the hoots and mumblings of the religious and the common who were appalled that a fellow Moslem could be so cruel and mercenary. The whole bus load was apparently near to rioting and tried to force the driver to go on into the Salang, to take them to their destinations. But it was too dangerous. They lost the argument and all stayed there.

There had been one man among them trying to get his sick wife to Kabul for treatment, and she died during the night. In the morning, a mullah (Mirad named him, but probably some others pitched in, too) gave the poor man about 500 afs and found a cheap taxi to carry him and his deceased in their sad poverty back to someplace in the North. A few cars eventually started coming over the pass, down the blood-wrenching white mountain, and a lot of them had damaged or crushed roofs from where the snow had fallen on them. There were others that had just vanished in the falling white death, so that that assembly of would-be travelers shied with genuine fear when their *motorwan* began to scold them for their protests the previous night to go on. "Don't you see the sin of all those good Moslems sent to their deaths, and if I had listened to you there would have been even more."

I suppose they eventually got to Kabul, and back, but the story was not really complete there. It seems that on the final way back to Sare-pul from Mazar the road was washed out by rain and snow, and Najibullah and Mirad had to start walking with the group of others when the Waz could go no further. Najibullah somehow hurt his leg and they fell behind the others, and Mirad was rather worried about wolves, the lean, hungry animals bred on the unproductive desert, a kind who Afghans swear attack men, because they are starving. Throughout this whole ordeal, the small boy Najibullah didn't cry, it seemed, but just clutched harder at the can of roghan Mirad remembers he was carrying. Eventually, they reached "the samovar", great Easter image of salvation in the form of warmth and fellow men, and—he said—one Moslem boy had been saved that day. The people were thrilled and told them how lucky they had been to survive . . .

This afternoon Azarullah comes over again . . . He shares his story about some wild magician who comes through town at times, and who may even live here now, who can cut off the students' heads and then put them back together again using a kind of magic salt-like powder to get instant reconnection.

We shake our heads politely, noncommittal.

Also, he explains how two mullahs, from Tom's school last year, one a kindly old prophet figure, an Uzbek who would salaam us graciously in their first weeks when we came here last year and had wandered the road rather forlornly looking for a suitable house, had been reported by some students one day as saying things against the government, the new Jemoriat. It was soon discovered that they were old time-born advocates of the Mullah Party, the most conservative and possibly feared "hez's" of them all, so they have been arrested and had been sitting in the jail in Samagan ever since.

Tom has a story about the old farmer (on the ride on the way to Puli-Khumri) who introduced him to the whole Toyota as "the *malim*" and then went on to tell all around how good and decent (always with covered head and legs) his "*honum*" was, and how all in all we were both such good people, it was a shame we didn't convert to Islam (for converts get all sorts of special benefits in the miracle department, it seems) and stay in Afghanistan for ever *more.* And then, as briskly as he'd expounded virtue and religious ways, the old man went into a graphic demonstration, to the delight of the attentive passengers, of how when Adam first rolled over to Eve and wanted to go at it (finger in and out of the thumb) Eve had looked at him and asked what purpose That Thing had. It must have been delightful.

[Mirad prepared a huge feast for the teacher trainees due today, but who do not make it because despite the clear sky and billions of stars here, the Salang is still closed.]

Feb. 15, 1975

. . . The *modir* is in Mazar with the students waiting to take the national exam, which entirely made it up from Kabul yet. All my own students are waiting and worrying why my own guests haven't arrived as it had been announced previously. Then, all is forgotten as I listen: here is a moment of sheer pleasure and pride as my 11th class begin to read the stories they have composed, based loosely on the cut out picture prompts I gave the . . . .

> *[Valentines quoting Shakespeare materialize from Tom, and dinner is held. We make eager trips up to the hotel and highway in search of the expected arrivals. But there are no guests . . .]*

I type up about half of the 11th class stories today. They are each given a cut out picture from a magazine and told to write about what they see. There is much that is amusing, but I am really amazed when I come to Paregul's opus. The plot must be something which she lifted from a Hindi movie—Cousins are promised in marriage from childhood, then find themselves separated on a trip back to Poland. The girl grows up with her father, but sets out one day to find her betrothed,. On route she gets held up by robbers and helped by a policemen, then goes back to her father's house to hear that the fiancée has returned,. Cautiously, she looks at him and discovers he is one of the thieves who had accosted her earlier, so she calls the police,. He escapes as she watches him, and is killed by a car. Then, she ends up marrying the kind policeman—All of this is encased in another story of three engineers reading it out of a book to each other. What these girls manage to find in a small picture?

We have more clear crisp weather; like a well-set poem the mountains keep their legend of snow upon them . . .

One of my student's cousins, a wealthy 8th grader from Kabul, slipped by me today in her chic elevator sandal shoes, her borrowed *chadris* flying . . . What a lot of secrets these people live within, without.

I remember the day Mirad came back from Mazar, where he had gone off to find his sister near Balkh. When he told of her husband, partially paralyzed now, miles and centuries off the road and helpless, he just kept saying it was very bad. Yet he didn't seem to particularize it at all, as if what was wrong wasn't even his brother-in-law's particular tragedy, but the fact that it had happened the way it had and that it could have been anyone. Another time he spoke of how there used to be Baktar flights to almost every town in Afghanistan (or at least close to them) including Puli Khumri, and they were cheap and really sick people, women in difficult labor, for example, could be taken by this means to hospitals and help . . . This was all abolished, it seems, with the Republic.

We took a walk yesterday to the hotel via the back road of the city. Before us were the great mud palace walls, the bleak stony graveyard, behind us the silent austere mountains, the secret gorge. We came out of the mud streets and daily life and emerged on eternity, things ancient and chthonic and impervious. Walking there we thought about what it would mean to try to stay here, knowing there are not other places where we could find such a blend. But . . .

The old *baba* at the hotel, our dear old friend, greeted us like his lost children, and then we turned back home.

Feb 18, 1975

[We broke down and later ate the prepared food, since no trainees arrived, although the Salang is apparently opened now.]

. . . That night Mirad sits after dinner with us telling us about when he was a soldier in Badakshan, and how other, poorer soldiers, hadn't been able to survive—on one *afghani* a day. They had to get money from their families just to keep their boots blackened. They were given so many *seirs* of wheat a month and from this had to make their own bread, and as far as the arts of soldiering go, they never had the equipment to really practice, considering that they were allowed only 12 bullets a year. Thus, when the great occasion came once a month to do target practice, they naturally didn't even know how to hold the gun, how to aim it, how to use it for its full destructive, precise powers. Of course, the guns themselves were all left over from the First or Second World War, with the kick of a dragon in them. Meanwhile, across the river from them in Russia, everyday they heard the guns pounding, their equipment plentiful, and each soldier, unlike his Afghan counterpart, had a horse to ride to do his border patrolling and a "*gorg*," (wolf) some kind of trained police dog.

Tom describes the bread man at the corner on cold days, how he takes his wooden crates apart slowly, breaks them in small pieces to feed his clay pot of a fire, and toasts his cold hands in the flames, turning them over and over, like cooking meat.

We read Aladdin's story in the office one day, and all of the teachers passing through—little Sherafad from her second class duties and the *kouteb* (clerk)—stop to go over a few pages, eager to better understand what has happened. They ask, incredulous, about the *djinns* and wizards and magic spells.

The entire orchard land perhaps will not be ruined, but it seems that the almonds have blossomed, and if the month of Hoot brings a frost, there will be another bad year for the farmers. As with everything, our neighbors speak of better times, of cheaper living, of years gone from them now.

I slip next door to see Mohammed (Mirzad) Daud's orchards; Mirad's brother, Najibullah, carefully hops up and escorts me through the rows of trees and points out the flowers in the pink buds on the long, dry limbs.

My student Shahzada informs me at our recent lesson that her father has had a great quarrel with the Haji, their present and our old landlord, and consequently they plan to find a new home, post haste. The quarrel was over the electricity, which was to have been included in the rent. Then, suddenly one night the Haji came seeking this extra expense, and the food tax collector with all the proverbial venom of his well-antiquated profession, told him where things must end.

Mirad, hearing the tale, says the Haji was merely getting what he deserves for ever chasing us out.

Last week's storm is a long way off again from today when there is a summery cleanness to the warm air, and a stillness, far from the wild panting of the wind in those cold days, when it struggled like a fitful, great winged bird against our window panes.

Yesterday our seven volunteer/trainees from Kabul arrived. They have tales galore to tell of their misadventures trying to get out of Kabul. They had chartered a whole Haji Aqub bus, the one and only luxury-liner in their stocks, but this delicate bit of machinery refused, sensibly, to take off until a definite all clear was given for the Salang. Fool-heartedly, the volunteers had taken their places at 7:00 on Sunday morning at the end of the great traffic jam winding out of Kabul toward the Salang. They moved tortoise-like but steadily until they entered the road going up to the tunnels, at which point the snow was only cleared from one and a half lanes; and as lorries like armadillos and snow plows like scurrying overgrown crabs and daredevil taxis and pudgy bolstered buses, and all manner of occupied vehicles, began to ascend, each had to take its time to take off chains for a clear spot and then to later put them on again; to shinny and shimmer in impossible passing positions, to wait their turn behind the slower but unmovable vehicles of age and neglect. After a number of adventures, including seeing their bus pulled unsuccessfully by a thin cable, which twice snapped, and watching a highway worker buried to his waist by a snowplow, and noticing how it was the snowplow itself that had really gotten them stuck in the beginning, they were on the road again, squashed further by the excesses of traffic. After a novel full of worries and observations they finally reached the Khulm hotel at 10:30 p.m., while the rest of their group went on for another full hour and a half before reaching Mazar . . . .

> *[Koshan, a Peace Corps language teacher . . . who has a kind and bright demeanor about him and seemed quite capable of finding his own place within most parties . . . was with them.]*

Feb. 21 1975

> *(My 26th year to heaven . . . a day without the gaiety of a youth's days or the reserve and dignity of celebrations when you are old, just another day to look around and find that myself and me are not the best of friends . . .]*

. . . A cool wind falls down from the steppes, although the sun is out splendorous. We rise, five of us in this house . . . and set out to climb the old city citadel, the ancient hill of history we've come to befriend with our walking thoughts so many times in our months here.

But back a few days to Wednesday and Shiringul telling us about the eggs that are due to hatch, and asking if I'd had mother's milk, and telling me about Maurice in Mazar who was born premature and had lived in a machine for a while. Then, she launches excitedly into her trip to the bazaar with Zeebee and buying hats for the little boys and nuts and raisins and embroidery thread. She's a beautiful young girl, my brother Dan's age (20), but a mother four times over already. That same afternoon, Mirad's brother Najibullah, Shiringul's son Zmaria and Mirad's Habibullah play ball and tag on our mud-walled terrace, while we watch them . . . .

> *[Again, these pages fill with PC talk, lists of who was there and what they "represent," and the ongoing and predictable, issues we daily face with teaching here.]*

. . . The next day we set off to Samagan (the boys had classes in an old rundown bus so full of people it seemed incapable of moving), and arrive there to find that their volunteers-in-training are occupying the top floor of the local teahouse . . .

. . . Then, we move out to Takhte Rostum . . . the ancient Buddhist site at the edge of town, to explore the vaults and grotto-like enclosures, the tunnels of carved columns and lotuses around several niches of misplaced statuary, up the hill to the great round carved stupa shrine itself, and the view of the valley, winter gray and brown now. An old woman and her sister and daughter send us some bread from their perch across from us on the hill. Walking down with me later, she asks about my home, my husband, and my childlessness . . . .

> [More, on the *PC supervisors, my students, food, the student teachers, etc. A former volunteer, Bruce Letts, resurfaces as the new TEFL coordinator. And, as in all small communities with too much time on their hands, there is gossip on who was with whom, and which exotic trips had taken people away.*]

. . . Our volunteer and friend, we enjoy meeting is Kirk. He speaks of the good quality education of the Afghan Technological school, but how it too had lowered his once sterling standards . . . He seems a modest but efficient and very conscientious teacher and student of Afghan life, watching it all from his Jema-minat house, and beyond.

But back to other realities here; Mirad's son Habibullah falls down the stairs and sprains his foot, which an old *moie-safed* plasters up the next morning with eggshells and spit and mud . . . much to our fear that somehow the break is real and hasn't set right, insuring that the child will be lame for the rest of his life—But it seems that this time the old solutions may have worked.

That afternoon while I am giving a lesson to Mirad, his wife and Habibullah and Shiringul and family come over to watch and the little cousin's succulent wife stays on after Zeebee has gone home. There is something incredibly ripe and coy and beautiful about her sad posture (for at this point Hossain has been gone for 12 days), and Mirad seems very conscious of her presence, as might be any man.

That night Mirad tells us of his old mother's belief in omens, how if you take a chicken or a sheep and rub its hair a certain way and ask a question, if he animal shakes you'll get your request; but if it doesn't, nothing will come of your wish. And, Mirad explains, he has done this himself; he consulted the shakings of a goat when Zeebee was pregnant with Daud. He had asked for a boy and the goat shook and then when the boy was born his mother laughed, saying he had had good thoughts. He told us also about a game with the wishbone which requires the participants to accept nothing from each other once the game has started on threat of having to invite the whole gathering over to dinner; or of a similar test of wits (or memory) using the kneecap of an animal, which is served up with a meal. One person challenges the others to break the tough old cartilage and if a person accepts the challenge but fails to break it, he has to carry the old kneecap around with him indefinitely until the other challenger asks him about it one time, and he is able to take it off quickly and give it to the original owner.

And, speaking of folk believes, one day Mirad also tells us about trouble he had with several soft spots in his teeth and asks if we know any good ways to have them treated. Then, marveling, he describes an old woman from Sare-pul, so old her back can never be straightened, and who walks almost on fours, at a sharp bent over angle—who had grown a third set of teeth, baby-like like his son Habibullah's . . .

[Hossain returns and has landed a job in a USAID household for 2600 afs a month plus free rent on a 300 afs house.]

Feb. 26, 1975

> *[We are fourteen strong at our house, eating meat loaf, baked potatoes, spinach, carrots, pomegranates, oranges, bread and butter, corn cake and orange bread. There are visitors from other places, working with one of the trainees doing student-teaching. Increasingly, I find so much in common with Brenda Mahoney—on marriage, feminism, Anais Nin, writing, etc.]*

. . . A brilliant, eerie full moon's night, the whole world illuminated, the old city haunted on the hill.

I gave the teachers their test early, first off for the day, and the whole school was ten minutes late starting because the *modir* needed that much extra time to finish! This morning when I pass back graded papers, there is a lot of confused good humor as the modir and Magfirat try to compare notes, and they all laugh at my grants of 10/10 when they had confused tenses and spellings.

"That's only for perfect and we are not." No one is fooled. But in fact, the numbes mean little. I am just pleased at how much some show they know.

. . . I remember vaguely, recollect hearing Anais Nin speak once . . . at Barnard, her face like a sad Italian clown's, her voice small. Or had I dreamed it after reading one of her diaries in my over-heated sophomore days? . . .

Mirad makes a thwarted reference tonight after dinner (the lights were out again, they have been every other night for over a week) to a Dr. Wilson who had lived near the Italian Embassy for many years and been liked by the monarchy—"He is a kind of Mullah," Mirad suggests. He was more likely a minister in a Christian church, I think first, then listen. Mirad felt this man had known "about everything" and had done a lot for prisoners and travelers and sick people in Kabul. We wonder how many people he must remember in his quiet head, what judgment he makes of all these foreigners he has met, how much he learned from each of them . . .

[Tom begins a discussion] about how people here discipline the students, how physical violence is accepted as a culturally reinforced thing. This leads to a discussion of how little right we have to intervene when we see something violent being done (beating a student, throwing

a stone at a dog) simply—though not simple at all—because our very presence here is a much more subtle but just as bad, a kind of violence. That is, that every time we have food in excess and clothes and a million opportunities, while these people have nothing, are daily worn down by the very tendons of their existence, then we, too, tender injustice. Yet, because Westerners are so eager to separate mental and physical violence and are not able to recognize them in more subtle forms, they are quite apt at criticizing these kinds of outward demonstrations of violence (physically visible) and be barely receptive at all to the slow murderous violence the whole wealthy greedy West renders upon the East, and within our own country, with the haves versus the have-nots, etc . . .

Feb. 28, 1975

Yesterday it rained all day and night, and the whole valley was swallowed by the interminable gray fog and clouds . . .

Last night Mirad talked about his old friend in the bazaar named Halifa, who now sells spices and knows a lot about the condiments of flavoring and is general consultant for the bazaar. He was once a cook for our landlord Mizad Mohammed Daud and endured rather grave treatment at the time of Habibullah, the Batcha Sagaw who reputedly once came up here to consult with or censor M. Daud. Halifa, fearing for his master's life, kept him out of the wealthy and powerful amir's lands, only to have himself beaten and dunked in the river by Habibullah's thugs. He had been kept in the river without being allowed to sit or stand for a whole night, until his mother came and apparently freed him and sent the bloody Habibullah away.

The man, Halifa, has never married, is "lame" of sorts as Mirad explains, and apparently this means he is impotent, and so could not marry. Mirad smiles and says how the man is his good friend, and always invites him to sit down with him when he's in the bazaar, and listen to his stories. He is apparently full of his memories of the days when "royalty" lived in the old city hill and a gatekeeper charged one *af* for every person who went in and out of the monopoly of a gate; of the time when land was only 5 *afs* a *jereb* (although it is now 100,000 a jereb), and flour and rice a fifth of the present price.

I begin to wonder if this is the famous traditional healer about whom Charpentier had written in his ethnography on Tashkurghan, and who was mentioned as well by the Michauds, when we met them soon after we arrived in town the first September.

Mirad took his own son, ironically another Habibullah, to the old spice seller when his foot was hurt and the old man cautioned him to take good care of the child, to make sure a reliable person looked at him and treated his foot, because—he told Mirad—little Habibullah was only a small Moslem boy-child and must be protected for the future.

This morning we wake to a bright gray sky and by 8:30 the sun has burned off the thick clouds around the top of the mountain so their rough, sharp spines tower into a growing blue sky and the clouds hover like modest robes around the midriffs of the hills. In the afternoon we take our favorite walk, up through the back of our neighborhood to the old road to the Gardens, passing on our way the fruit rich pastel clusters of blooming cherry and almond trees, their fragile pale blossoms like a small child's skin among the rusty old gray trunks and ravished ground of the wintry . . . trees. This week the whole valley should blossom and then surely spring will be, irreversibly, upon us . . . .

Kabul had its second most heavy snow fall this winter . . . the whole city is freezing and Arctic white.

"Oh man, make peace with your mortality, for this too is God" Who said that?

Supplies Come to An Internally Displaced Person's Camp, Herat Province, 2000.

Brown tents, brown earth, brown hills
dominate the edge of Herat
where sprawling tents and desiccated cold ground,
displaced peoples' camps
hover,
the settlement and forms
small aberrations
on the vast sweep of bleak mountain-rimmed plateau.

Men and boys in their ancient baggy pants and long shirts,
bony forms under layers of vest, jacket, shawl,
wound turbans or peaked caps,
spread out across the dry cold plain,
silent and staring.

Then people move,
a dry and weary pageantry coming to feeble life.
Like suddenly freed butterflies in some dun-colored room,
tiny girls in faded flowery dresses,
thin *tanbon*, and plastic shoes,
their dark hair powdered with dust,
began to peer out of tents.
They paddle across the hard ground,
toward the gathering crowds,
to wait.

The isolation haunts:
time frozen in this desolate, wind-blown place,
where the desert encroaches in piercing gasps of wind,
where the allusion of blue, a haze choked with dust,
hovers atop every circling hill.

Stunned, unsmiling, people come up and stare.
Spokesmen
indistinguishable in uniform turbans,

white skull hats, jackets, shawls, *tanbon and peron*, rubber shoes,
huddle near the trucks, ready to distribute.

Each family cups a bundle of supplies,
absently swats

the clouds of flies circling everywhere,
swarming, dotting the rich but washed out colors of
patterned dresses and skirts,
layered and gathered coverings,
contrasting with their surroundings,
the muted wintry wash.

Each child leans with swollen stomach,
sores on tiny faces,
bare feet and hard crusty skin
from walking through winter terrain
without socks or shoes.

The faces around consume
huge dark eyes, peaked, olive skin,
fine featured Tajik, Uzbek, Pushtoon heritage,
Hazaras and Turkman-rooted peoples' round eyes and chins.

Alone in their dark tents around sooty, open fires,
the girls and women seek light and warmth,
shelter and food, medicine, education,
peace.

The rest of the world looks elsewhere
calling for 20th century solutions
to 12th century inequalities,
content to let the Afghan people
who had led the final effort to end
Soviet hegemony and communism
as it had existed for decades,

bury their children and flee their homes,
again.

And again.

XI

ONLY FOUR MORE MONTHS IN THE VILLAGE

March 2, 1975

Morning begins with the three foreign women, the new PC volunteers doing onsite teaching, observing Class 1, where Esfandyar put on his usual spirited performance teaching, drilling, reviewing, and reinforcing his class of tiny timid girls. We sit like Gullivers among the Lilliputians, and brave Deborah even venturest to the front at the teacher's invitation to pick out which little girls (or boys, for now there are two special students, two tiny boys) should go to the blackboard the second hour to write pre-learned passages. There is a lot of cuteness and dignity among the students, writing crookedly as the small statures stretched below the blackboard, sharpened bamboo pens in hand creating good solid black strokes on their already cluttered notebook pages.

In the office between acts, the *modir* suggests we take up letter writing and singing in the morning teachers' class. In the afternoon, we have our lessons with Mirad and Shahzadah, and then the crazy radical teacher from Hajie Biron comes over to wheedle Tom into making the other foreign teachers play a tournament out at the school, something which can not be arranged, it is explained to him several times, though he acts tortoise slow and weasel quick to catch it.

All of us *mamons (guests)*, we set off to dinner at Azarullah's, a sumptuous, well-cooked meal served in the boy's room, introduced with conversation by his father.

The old man praises the teachers here and speaks of how the village people know nothing, about nothing and so have barely even profited from all they could have from (our) presence, and how the girls here are hid as children until their husbands take them and hide them; and then—how all the 10,000,00 of the 15,000,000 people of Afghanistan are thieves! In a folkloric role, he tells us how he is "*bey-car* "(without work) "mislay modumn" (like the people). When we protest that he should not be giving feasts for us if in fact he is without work, he demurs and corrects himself, saying that he only passes on gladly what little he may have. Our hosts continue, telling us of the need to sell land because crops are bad and how sons can no longer find work after high school, but so few of them can go on to college, and so on.

We stuff ourselves on the good food, then "the girls" want to see the women and we go to sit under the cozy *sandalee* as these matriarchs and girls praise us and ask all the usual questions which the majority of them could already answer for me. We compare ages and nursing methods and family allegiances, and then the Azarullah's young jellybean-energized brothers proceed to dance, while his dewy-eyed cousins sing, and the old women play the *dipola* (tambourine) and later a *dola* (drum). Then, it is time to leave them and pass into the starry night and its brisk spring breeze, and our own sleepy words again . . .

Classes and sitting, lessons and time past. We eat dinner at the river teahouse with the whole trainee crew plus Tim Macdonald . . . . then walk them to the hotel in the lightless streets into pockets of hot and cold air, and then back in the pitch dark because there is no electricity in all the town.

. . . And through it all we seem to have strong feelings that we should extend our contracts here, go hastily around the world and then return to teach in a good Kabul job one more year . . . .

In the teachers' class the favorite story today concerns the "Three Billy Goats Gruff" and a goat who fell into a well after a fox. They like the idea of a fable, a proverb, although these should perhaps be a little simplistic for them. Or, perhaps wisdom about human nature is just that simple.

I return in my mind to Azarullah's house: the Islamic blessing in strong glass-cased letters on the door. The mother's womb environment of the *sandalee;* all of us gathered under the warm lap blankets. The wide-eyed laughing daughter of the house, the widow cook with the four-year old twins and five other children. Azarullah's mother, dignified and adoring, the old one-toothed aunt or neighbor hiding the tambourine under the table, shy as a young girl so the men of the house wouldn't hear her playing foolish games when they go by, hugging me and calling me her dear child, her face bright with a long overblown beauty so she just sits quietly some moments, grows alive and ageless again as she plays the music for the dancing boys. The gossiping next door neighbor, Ahlia's mother, speaking of her daughter newly married (my 8th grade student last year) and living now in Samagan, and how her own husband is now sick. The shadowy bare room, the great door-wide windows being opened to the spring night, the simple, confused loveliness of people making themselves a full time, three foreign women novelties among them, but fully taken in in their wide warmness . . .

March 3, 1975

It is a day with every style of weather . . . I wake at 6:15 to a bright sunlit day and a certain distrust of the time, imagining that it must be well past seven and yet our informative knock has not yet come on the window. By the time breakfast is over and I set out for the teachers' class, a mountain of gray clouds has already begun to move threateningly across the valley, and as the morning moves on it grows darker and darker, and then pours rain and a frosty hail, setting every riverlet and road to puddle brown sogginess, deblossoming the early blooming almond tress as their spilled white petals across the wet ground look like pale shadows of tears . . . .

The lights are out all across the city; people who until four years ago had not had electricity at all complain mulishly now that they have been returned to "dark ways."

March 5, 1975

[Sitting in the school office, I recall the desserts and late night recitations and games with the visiting trainees, the poetry

read by Tom, and wonder what it means to each of our guests, including the Afghans.]

Last night the weather turned frigid, not quite cold enough to skin the trees and kill all the fruit yet, but certainty cold enough to spill snow on the foothills off to the south and west again. Mud-luscious below, we all seem more stuck to the ground than ever . . . .

. . . . Juggling the world in my head like stale pomegranates, invariably but wistfully hoping that they'll fall and burst and send the red jewels carpeting the ground around.

The old *nana* at our school, a poor, tired little creature with her single eye and wizened form and face, wrapped in her clean, worn rags and skirts, asks everyday after my health . . .

March 7, 1975

A full spring day with just a hint of coolness in the air and the sun saved from brashness by virtue of the clouds . . . . we take our historically traditional walk out to the old city, to gaze on the fuzzy-headed white and pink trees in blossom across the gaunt, ungreened valley. Boys with their appendages of shovels and giant spoons are everywhere digging among the old mounds, looking for sheep bones to sell, like toddlers on a sealess seashore creating castles in the sand. But there are other real treasures there, as well, as an old turbaned baggy-pants-ed elder informs us, as he pops out of a small window of a worn-down mud hut behind us and begins to speak like a contestant for the absurd staging of "Laugh-in."

"A young boy found a 4,000 *afs* wedding band here yesterday, and others have found gold coins. There are a lot of things to be found here, but I have never found anything." He *salaams* us in all properness, having told this much of the story, and saunters out of the dollhouse-sized building dwarfed by years of rain, to join his friend in the bowl of the rolling brown hill.

We take our own formal pictures among the ruins over the muddy river, interrupted by one of my students (Nacia, 10th class), her aunt and cousin and some gruff, bully-looking boy, who all come puffing up the hill to speak with me and coyly ask for a picture . . . . They explain they are out walking too, looking at the pretty scenery because that is all people can do in a place like Tashkurghan that has no cinemas. Graciously, they invite us to lunch and the Garden and an afternoon with them, then stay discreetly in their *chadried* corner hoping Tom (around the other side, away from them) might come into view and send them giggling. An old man, lean and sullen with dignity, his face the wrinkled map to these ruined hills he walks among, stands above, looking down on our posed picture-taking with great disapproval, then moves on within his own un-tellable story, like so many others. We watch the bent figures of farmers working in the turned fields around us, see the party of my student and her family winding down the hill toward the river and then up a narrow lane, out of sight. After following the curve of the watch towers, arch windows, cannon-like upright shapes, and round central roofings, we move down the hill ourselves, along the lip of the river and around a quiet neighborhood between flowering orchards, where another old man, gaunt and thin and straight in dark shirt and wool cap, looks like an old Norwegian fisherman set down in a barren land to scratch for lost water in the brown earth, wearing his moisture in the deep colors of his eyes and skin.

Yesterday I went out into the town myself to take pictures, webbing the soft streets and lanes in my Amore M'med boots and sloppy old corduroy jeans. First out to the edges, the back street between the town, the graveyard and the old palace gardens, I catch a few blossoms spilling over the harsh mud walls. Kneeling at the imagery of the solid wooden carved gate into the Baugh-e-Jemoriat, I catch the long pine tree-edged path leading from the entrance gates to the white-domed building at its end, and the thin clouded, snow-capped mountains behind and above it. In the little boys' school behind me, the children shout their alphabet and the old crumpled *babas* nod in the sun against the crooked stairs leading inside. Back across the orchard edging town, I am drawn to the old man's heyday, the bazaar day crowd of farmers and outlying villagers, old men backward and unsmiling, secreted in their simple faces, sunbaked splendor and poverty.

I linger awkwardly on the edge of the crowded field of camels, goats, cows, donkeys, and sheep for sale, then walk quietly, inappropriately but excused among them, to catch an old man kneeling on the ground with a newborn calf, as a trio of old timers watch two twin lambs be nursed by their tottering mother-. Everyone is gracious, finding me odd (which I am, being alone) but respecting my right and ability to do anything, most knowing me know as "*the malim-Anglasis.*".

From there, I move among the bazaar proper, potatoes and oranges and broken candy, almonds and *gor* rock, old *chadried* women like humped crows squatting on its edges and among the shop stands, buying, looking at goods. Then it is into the shadowy covered parts where these same women sit mutely against the wall holding greet sheens of spun cotton and thin wool thread that they have come hoping to sell.

In and out of my own back lanes around the school, following a little girl who had adopted me in the middle of the bazaar and is intent now on taking me home, I am awed, stopping again late to catch all the school girls stopping at a candy stand behind the schoolhouse, the first and second graders out at 11:30; and out on the road overrun with the little school boys, a sad chorus of their non-meaning, mischievous "mister." But I am now in the company of two tiny first class girls, one of whom tells the whole crew of boys that they are *"shack"* (naughty) and they should leave me alone. But, seeing her animated face and flushed color I know she is secretly quite thrilled by all the commotion on her usually uneventful walk home from school. I just walk on, waiting to be far enough out of the center of traffic to take one quick shot of the sweet child.

Then I move back to the bazaar to look at some *ghulims*, which later in the afternoon Tom and I walk back to buy among the usual exhausting and confusing rounds of bargaining.

The trainees left for Kabul yesterday morning, all their days here by now the fabric of gossipy stories to retell and to nostalgically wonder about . . .

Mirad is full of stories . . . and tells us about the fire-eaters who used to work the wedding route in Sar-e-pul—young boys and sometimes older men whose routine consisted of filling their mouths with kerosene, then blowing accurately and quickly out at a lighted match. But sometimes (and Mirad had witnessed the sometimes) they would breath in instead and the fire would consume their stomachs, and actually burn them to death before the too-soundly entertained audience.

Last night some entrepreneur from Jalalabad brought up about 25 boxes of honeybees, and perched them on the open lot next to the river. This morning he let them out on the flowery town to fertilize and feed, and eventually to produce their honey. The whole town buzzes with their activity and you imagine the drunken richness of their flight among the orchards, while their owner sits in his tent among the bee boxes, camped out for the production line. Bees (honeybees) are quite advanced social creatures, their elaborate system of class organization, the queen and drones, a grand story well-known but still mysterious in its precision.

But it takes Mirad's very literal description of how the bees work to make me really stop and think about the industrious little creatures again. He explains that each house has its own king (queen, surely) and that soldier/guard bees are stationed at the entrance to each beehive whose job is to sniff at and inspect all would-be entrants, and to kill them if they've "sat" in a bad place in the course of their flyings about, so that only the pure bees can get back into the hives and leave what they have to make pure honeycombs. Piles of dead insects lay quietly before the entrance door, mute messengers of the sinful lives which have made them be lost and killed by their pure, discreet guard brothers . . .

> *[It would take a book to write up just our visitors. Today, another typical adventurer spirit arrived. He was another WT, but Harvard Divinity School-bound, a reader of Pynchon, resident in Kenya by the seashore and sated with all the elephants and lions he saw in the northern wilderness, and briefly imprisoned in Kuwait for "insulting" a government official at the Iraqi Embassy there. He had been a traveler since 1972 . . .]*

. . . Mirad informed us last night that the Presidents of Italy and South Vietnam have both been visiting here, and in their honor the President of the Afghan Olympics Association (or maybe the President of the International Association) has organized an official *buz kash*i match. It will be played for thee days in Mazar (starting today). Mirad, sent to Mazar to take out cash from our bank there, gets all this news first hand from the taxi or Waz driver and then hears it confirmed (at least the part about the official visits) on the radio deep in the night.

March 8, 1975

[I record, for who knows what reason, a long description of how bees work . . .]

. . . We show Mirad some pictures in the biology book of various bees, and he listens to the observations of the famous naturalist quietly, then acknowledges that the man was right about bees talking to each other, something he had discovered in his own experience. When he set out to kill one bee, she saw the creatures go into a kind of dancing, waving of his antennae and legs, and in a few seconds found himself the protagonists before a multiple number of bees.

Another time he was carrying something on a donkey from the mountains to his house (the thistle, dry brush for stoves) and he decided to give the donkey a rest about halfway down the mountain. The donkey immediately began his "*hagmalee kadae*" (rolling in the dust in the road), but the poor creature managed to put himself on a beehive (wasp nest) in the process of his excited wallowing and the large angry creatures stung him by the hundreds. The animal attempted to run and disgorge them but the creature was not quick enough and within an hour he was dead.

When Mirad got home his father asked him where the donkey was. "He's dead," the boy had answered. "Can't you see I'm carrying the things myself?"

The father laughed until Mirad explained that the donkey had been "eaten" by the wasps, and then his father "pulled out the wood" to teach him never again to let a poor dumb creature get himself into a wasp nest and be killed.

. . . . This afternoon, after Mirad's lesson and Shahzadah's, Azarullah comes over. He sits with Tom for our usual evening conversation while I run back to our neighbor, the Turkomen "racketeer" shopkeeper, to give him the 500 *afs* remaining on the *ghulim* we had bought. Back in the warm room, he is telling Tom about a boy from last year's class, Abdul Sahdar, who had taken the Concorde and gone to the Polytechnic in Kabul, had an epileptic fit and been discharged from there for a year at "doctor's orders," even though he had earned the third highest grade of his class of several hundred on the placement test. The child comes from a very poor family and now eats perhaps one nan a day, while during his two weeks at the institute he had full, healthy meals and the pleasure of studying. He has always studied, although an epileptic for a long time, and does not mean to be stopped now. Yet it looks as if—without proper intervention by a powerful someone—that he'll never get to go to the university, will be encapsulated by his family's poverty and his disease that modern medicine has medicine to control, but which have not yet reached here or are not affordable here.

Then enters our gallant landlord Mirzad Daud and a long gracious silence until we initiate the idea of paying our rent and then he in turn directs all his energy and figuring power to discerning our debt. Grateful, he silently excuses himself . . .

After dinner Mirad recounts another bevy of stories, beginning with an explanation of our landlord's possessions and their loss. He used to own a booming *seroi* where the present bank is, and this used to be a busy, thriving road between Puli and Mazar where every bus stopped for lunch, and where people purchased the famous wood products of the town (stools and cradles). But five years ago when the Russian-built road came through, the whole old raw road dried up. All its commerce ceased, people no longer bought anything from these shops, and no one ate at the hotel and restaurant, except for the occasional Afghan Tour bus. This is the story for all the little towns off the main road (Samagan, in the past famous for kebab; and Aqcha, 30 minutes from the highway now, full of rugs and good people, very isolated now in this modern age of paved roads, whereas in the past it was a real center). So now Mirzad Daud rents out the big rambling *seroi a*nd its buildings to the bank and the army barracks, but makes little.

The story somehow leads on to a description of the *"motorwans"* and we hear how one of Mirad's friends was in a Toyota on route to Mazar showe-Eid, and his Toyota was somewhere in the Salang when the driver suddenly informed his passengers that unless they gave him 50 afs more than that agreed on he would run the truck in to the river, off the mountain, and kill them all. The passengers, disbelieving, stayed on, refusing to pay, and the crazy extortionist leaped into his truck full of people and headed for their death leap, until the people, terrified, told him to stop, saying they would pay. One meter from the edge, the vehicle stopped. Then, all the way to Mazar the crazy man played the radio loudly and laughed. At Mazar the customers tried to take the driver to the traffic police to get their money back, but the police only told them that the money was gone, that the man was crazy, and that they could do nothing but let him keep it.

Another driver, a young boy who lived near Mirad's house in Sare-pul and had a reputation for being a fast, rather reckless drier, is the subject of Mirad's next story. This driver had a good private bus and one day he was asked by some government overseers to take a batch of new army recruits to Kabul. He refused and the overseer insisted, telling him that if he didn't do what he was told, he would lose his vehicle entirely and himself be put in jail. The boy then pleaded (lying) that he couldn't take the soldier because his car was in bad shape, that he couldn't control the steering, and the route was dangerous.

"If I take the trip, I will end up killing all his passengers," he allegedly pleaded. Finally he made the governor of the province sign a paper saying that if anything happened to the bus on route to Kabul, the driver would not be responsible. The paper was duly signed.

The story goes then that the boy driver started out, his bus loaded with some 60 soldiers and when he had been going for a little while, he announced to the passengers that he was going to kill them all now by letting the bus go over the edge of the road (to a valley or a river) and jumping out himself.

The soldiers protested, "Why?" But the crazed man went on. He ended up killing 35 of the passengers; the governor came and found all the dead gathered, put the driver in jail for a few weeks and told him he should never drive again.

"So much for punishment," Mirad concludes cynically. "Now the driver has two buses and is prospering in his trade . . ."

March 9, 1975

. . . Last night the rain turned to snow and this morning a cold blast of retroactive winter seemed to have doomed all the trees. I rather wade, than walk, to school, my pants cuffs dragging so that I have picked up pounds of mud along the road. Like church mice in the pantry, Paregul and Magfirat and myself steal into Esfandyar's clean classroom and borrow an old feed sack to wipe off our feet, but I hurry and have scarcely improved my appearance (that of a mud rat) before it is time to start the teachers' class.

. . . I have to sign the class book for the 11th and 8th classes because both Debra and Brenda had forgotten, so busily sit in the office during my free hour constructing "had beens" to record. It is then I overheard a conversation between the *modir* and Esfandyar (class 1), . . . that the man has been transferred to parts unknown, effective tomorrow, and though it will be next to impossible to find another good first class teacher, he has to go where his work dictates . . . . The *modir* seems intent on getting a changed decree from Samagan, but the chances of this happening seem rather slim

Why can this be? This is Esfandyar's town, and everyone knows his passion and skill as a teacher at the school here.

Home then to eat lunch . . . and I overhear Najibullah telling his brother that as he brought water, there was a poor woman sitting by the river weeping, and her husband was also there, sad. She had lost a child and was begging for someone to lend her 50 *afs* so she could buy a shroud for the dead child and bury it. When I ask Mirad about this a little later, he tells me that he thinks it is better for people that poor to never have a life, if they must always suffer and go without everything other people have—houses, food, clothes, warmth—so it is perhaps better that the poor child has died. ("Ieen kesm zinda az na zinda kadae, na zinda xubtar'as.")—"To not live at all is better than to live a life like that."

The whole valley is like a messy sucking child, with the rain, the light all gone away, the lowlands muddy and dark and gray, and in the cloudy mountains beyond the bowl the pure white snow looks down on us like some proud clean god figure before a crowd of mud-besplattered mortals.

After supper tonight Mirad asks innocently about traveling from Afghanistan to the States, and if you can go the whole way by car, Tom explains a little about the oceans and planes and distances, and then begins to talk about time differences determined by the shape of the earth and the way the sunlight moves across the earth, lighting only one half at a time, so that you may start from Afghanistan at 7:00 a.m. Kabul time and fly west for 12 hours and arrive in Turkey just as the sun of day is beginning to show there.

Mirad looks baffled and a little hurt, as he often does when something seems so unlikely to him that he must think it is a fact contrary to the Koran, perhaps. And then a faux pas, we make a bad mistake, when we mention the prices involved in a transcontinental flight . . . how government workers like ourselves can save as much as 30,000 *afs* from our ticket money by going overland . . . 30,000 *afs* more than this man can ever expect to make in a full year of work for just such foreign employers here . . . .

March 10-11, 1975

The most human consuming mess of mud any creatures should ever be forced to negotiate a route through totally invaded the town today, as we move from worse to worst, and even more than before it becomes a mortal impossibility to just move one's feet from one puddle to another.

. . . Last night brought no drying to the land and today again we moved like muddy slugs trying to catch our balance between precarious steps.

In the 11th class we have a "casual" discussion the last hour about the U.S.'s lifting of the embargo on arms shipments to Pakistan and India and how Kabul radio had announced that if Pakistan and Afghanistan were to fight, Pakistan would be helped by the US and Afghanistan would be assisted by Russia.

I explain that when I heard of this policy, I was "sad," that I disliked all wars, that not the American people but some figurehead with power in the government was in support of such things and everyone else hated the idea. At this point Tajenisa gushed into quite a tirade about how both Pakistan and Afghanistan were Moslems and they should not fight, but that Pakistan had already fought so much with itself and India, through some method, that it would likely start a fight with Afghanistan.

It is also the day I give out birth control secrets after one timid articulate 12th grader from last year came to ask me the name of pills for her sister. Everyone else pops up to ask about this "custom" and to get down the name for future family references, although—certainly, each explained—not for themselves

Mirad's story, our eyes on the world, the alive and the dead: He tells us he had heard on the radio that M'Daud had left that morning to go to India. Tom responds by saying that he thinks Daud is not as frightened as he had been for the longest time, and so now is entering into foreign travel. This speculation elicits from Mirad a story about last Jeshen, the

17th of Saraton, when all of Kabul had gone out to the Jeshen grounds to view the various booths and exhibits amassed for that day in honor of the first anniversary of the coup d'etat.

Mirad was separated from his brother in the crowd and his brother ended up sitting on the edge of the field with a lot of university students. This was an area heavily saturated with government spies, it seemed, just cringing in anticipation to take in any would be revolutionaries on the weight of a few misplaced words. One huddled up to the end of Corban's group's conversation and demanded to know what they were talking about. When they refused (out of common sense, although they had actually said very little that could have incriminated them), he immediately gave a signal to some eight other spies loitering in the crowd and they grabbed two per person, Corban and his friends, and took them off to a makeshift "jail" made of several tents at the end of the Jeshen field.

Meanwhile Mirad saw the procession go by. He had been sitting in the field since midnight the night before to get good seats, and he claims his head had just gone *"xarob,"* as he tried to find out what had happened to his brother. But until 3 in the afternoon, he had to be content with seeing that a lot of people were being detained, rather indiscriminately. Later he learned that they had just been held and finally questioned and asked to produce witnesses and then released. The government spies followed them around for another day, Corban recognized the faces, perhaps, and then it was over. But it had certainly been more than enough to spoil the great holiday for Mirad and his brothers, the great celebration of newly granted "freedom," when for no reason his brother and others were detained, ironically.

Mirad articulates the general fear in Kabul, even now, that a man is not free to sit with his own family and intimate anything against Daud, or they will be (and in many instances, have been) carried off in the morning by groups of police.

"Spies are everywhere," our wise friend admonishes us. "Every word spoken in public is carried out like a radio announcement to the ears of some government official."

. . . Azarullah sits one afternoon discoursing in new, perfect, if slow English, as Tom prompts him with questions. He is again a shy turbanless graceful young student for the afternoon, dreaming perhaps of success in another world simply by the words he lets come out of his mouth in our presence. The next afternoon Fakir Khan's son, 20 and in the 11th grade (his second time, he can't learn math it seems) comes over to buy some film from us. Tom tries to discourage him from taking it until he is sure he has the right kind for his camera. They eventually begin to talk about taking pictures and what kinds of pictures that should be, and it comes out that the boy wants to make a film and then show it for the Afghan Film company, and get launched into a career as a movie producer. He looks with admiration at some of our colored slides from Greece, asking direct and relevant questions about how they were made, and how the slide viewer worked, and so on. He seems to have an excellent grasp of the mechanics of photography, if not quite the sure knowledge or—obviously—the facilities to do very much beyond exploring his interests right now.

In the afternoon, I take a trip to Zeebee and Daud, Najibullah and Habibullah and Mirad's household, up the slide-like mud staircase which Mirad has tried to anchor with wooden nails and bricks on each "step" and some regularly spaced nails along the face of the wall—to enter into the bare room which now houses ten 2-week old chickens and their irate, fussy mother. The creatures had been placed, in theory, behind the rope bed turned into its side in an alcove of the long room. But they pretty much wander at will, until Habibullah scoots up after them on his stomach or throws a stone at them, and the mother hen begins to peck angrily behind her screen, and the chicks scatter. Then Najibullah gathers one fluffy ball and pretends to drop it down Habibullah's shirt, which sets everyone rustling, until the actions are all repeated. A little later, Zeebee, her long black hair exposed today, asks me at one point how old the child must be, comments on the crazy weather here and the odd things that happened in Jalalabad with them having the coldest weather ever there . . . She shows me the pretty colored bead applique, and Habibullah's hat, and a pair of embroidery loops she had gotten in the bazaar the day she and Shiringul went there several weeks back.

When I leave, the boys, Najbullah and Habibullah, follow me through the archway into our yard and into the house. After some initial unfreezing, peekaboo and candy, . . . the little child looks at some pictures of animals . . . vehement that they are all *"gao"* (cows") and that there is *"lock"* (one) of everything.

Mirad . . . tells us of the chicken coop he had discovered in the shed near the *kenerab* where the bricks had fallen out. He maintains that it is used to protect the chickens at night from prowling animals who eat them along with grapes and melons, an animal—he describes—that is yellow and has sharp yellow eyes and has the ability to hypnotize a chicken from a tree above him until he falls to the ground. Then the dog-fox-wolf—like creature (a relative of the coyote) takes him away. Mirad demonstrates his elaborate howling patterns, a kind of 'woo-woo" with valleys, insinuating up and down, so convincingly that the little boys cover their ears.

In the teachers' class today the physic's teacher Abrahim Khan, Najiba, and the modir seem thrilled with the story behind the song of "Lemon Tree." Despite a few overly salacious phrases which prove too difficult to translate entirely ("love," "faith," lie" "lost in love") they seem to like the gist of it and though the *modir* hastens to tell me this is not the Afghan way (such a love affair) and I hasten to agree with him, they like the images and the simplicity of sounds enough to rate it as a real poem . . . .

March 13(ish), 1975

In a bit of a cross-over seasonally, one foot in spring (mud-ladden and blossom-blessed) and the other in winter—the blossoming pastel fruits and nut trees now stand in full glory in the town below, while above them the stern mountains still hoard their regal white coats. And a wind, still far from balmy, cuts through the strong sunlight of a day clear and blue.

. . . . Yesterday . . . we made the indiscretion of trying to snatch "a nap" in the middle of the afternoon, only to wake suddenly and find Habibullah, Najibullahi and Azarullah all nosily gathered a wall away in the kitchen. Getting out of our "*estawaht kadan*" (napping) we are soon in a long discussion with Azarullah who has come full of invitations to the home of the two young girls I often see being driven to school in a *gaudi*, unchadried and well-dressed sixth and seventh class students who live only an alley away from here. The boy launches into a praising description of how Americans are loved more than any other nationality in this town, because almost everyone knows or has known some American who visited here and left friends behind.

It is always hard with the invitation to be fair, to be sensitive. Were we to accept all, several each day, never short in and out affairs, we would be "*mamons*" full time and do no work.

We soon find ourselves in the middle of a story within a story, the tale of an old man who had been at Azarullah's house one night. The old man had described how he had been forced to flee from Bokhara when the Russians over ran that area after WWII. He had taken an old horse and his wife and come across the river into Afghanistan, thinking now all his problems would be solved. His first night in the country he came across a tent in the desert and was approached by a tall man with a huge mustache who introduced himself by saying he was a thief, but that the man should not worry because he only practiced his profession across the border in Russian (for in those days there had been no such thing as border controls and whole bands of wandering thieves would sweep into the steppes and plumage large landed estates and then ride back to Afghanistan with their bounty).

The mustached man, in a regular Robin Hood tradition, gave the old man (then young) a tent to stay in and a good supply of *roghan* and wheat and rice, surely from his stolen coffers. The man went on eventually with his wife and lived in Maimina, where he made a living selling things in a small *dukhan* in the bazaar. Later, he learned the barbering skills and worked in Mazar at this, until barbering no longer yielded enough income, and he took up baking.

In Azarullah's living room that night, the boy explains, this old man shared his story to illustrate how bad the Russians had been to take all the land from the people, how they had been much worst thieves than any of the infamous bandits. But another guest, a young man, had interrupted him to say that, no, the Soviet Union had done good things for Afghanistan and that the best future for his country would be to become a part of the Soviet block and share its industrialization and society. At the word "society," one of Asadullah's uncles who worked at a Russian factory or export business in Mazar explained how unfriendly the Russian people he had met there were, how when you went to their houses they would be laying on a couch sleeping and at your appearance instead of asking you in and offering tea and conversation, they would ask suspiciously why you had come and what kind of business you had with them.

In contrast, obviously to this tale, Azarullah begins to talk about his friend Abdul Salaam, the brother of my eighth class captain, Hamida, who is in his fourth year at the faculty of science in Kabul. Abdul Salaam had asked him once if he ever visited his English teacher's house (Tom) and Azarullah had answered him that yes, he was always a guest there and Tom went to a lot of trouble each visit, giving him tea and cookies and candy and walking him to the gate when he eventually left, so much so that he was ashamed of having accepted so much hospitality from someone who by all rights was his guest and not the other way around. To which Abdul Salaan answered that he shouldn't feel ashamed because this was just the American custom, to be kind and generous and that was why these people are loved all over the world first, and after them, the English . . . . Strange prospective.

Alas, it is correct. One-on-one we are good people, but out foreign policies have so often been for selfish gain, ignorantly, sinisterly, administered.

> *[We continue our powdering of 'next steps;', I continue musing on my lack of a professional goal, my desire to become "a veritable chronologist of other peoples' tales, as if to find my own disposition and place among them." We are still considering the extension for a year in Kabul, but are wary of the cold winters and our own ages and worry about our families back in the States . . .]*

How often I have had to sit and think about my position, the conditions within this society. Most of the first year here I was always politely but firmly distancing myself from every social experience, too much aware of how I didn't like always being out in a role where I was the petted darling, the clear-faced young woman to be squeezed and pawed curiously, the person to be given the biggest platter of greasy food or the tea and candy and nuts when everyone else was fasting, the freak at every female gathering because I had no children and was in no hurry to create them, and because I took walks with my husband, and could always be found in the corners of my compound with a book (not embroidery, weaving, or knitting) in hand. For I haven't learned a thing about these crafts though I am surrounded by them. But this year I've come to enjoy sitting among the mild gossip sessions of old ladies and children and teachers, the enthusiastic but often illogical questionings of my students, and hours can pass with me barely conscious of them, warm and so much loved in a role I shall surely never be allowed to play so fully anywhere else again in my life.

These people are beautifully gracious and everything new must fascinate them, and yet though they tend to scrutinize me quite throughly, they are always very admiring. I'm a little wary of my own shyness, the fact that I will never really talk to them as much as I should. But, in truth, that is me and how I am and would be "back home," too. Still, I think now I've begun to know them, and thus have a certain right to consider them my unforgettable friends . . .

March 14, 1975

Birds sputter out their versions of spring heralds, topping the mulberry tress as some newfound stage for courting. It's as warm as a spent season already today, although the sun's still shrouded with some clouds, and the thinnest coat of snow still rests this morning on the heads of the mountains around us.

Last night was the death of one moon month and the beginning of a new lunar month, Safar (Sawr?). Mirad explained the significance of this month, which is generally acknowledged by those who consider the heavenly bodies, as a month with four bad-luck days. During these periods people are not supposed to look at the moon, nor should they travel, or something bad will befall them. Punctuating his explanation with the comments, self-consciously, that his mother who is very old has always told him about these things, but that he doesn't really know if they are true (comparing their knowledge of this with how he imagines the scientist who wrote the article on bees came by his observations), he speaks of instances when people he had known had attempted to do something on the 1st, 2nd, 3rd and 18th of this month and met with misfortune.

Once his father had a fat mother cow whom he had taken to market. He had bound her with rope to exhibit her while prospective buyers gathered around, bargaining, arguing, trying to find a desirable and acceptable mutual price for her. The cow got impatient or angry. In any case, she had some super-animal fit and tried to burst the rope binding her legs. She succeeded in freeing herself, but the explosive force also managed to shatter her own leg. People standing beside her had imagined it a gunshot or a bomb. The cow was then killed and slaughtered on the spot and Mirad and his father went home richer only "by the price of one hat," to discover that it was one of those "unlucky" days in Safar.

Similarly a wealthy man in his town once had a strong beautiful horse whom he had kept in winter pasture until the day he thought spring had arrived. He mounted the fat creature, and the creature immediately began running wildly across the desert. It fell down suddenly and broke his neck, and ended the man's fortune. The date was the 18th of Safar.

It would be interesting to find the sources of these folk religious believes, but they seem to be so subtly rooted in the lower class culture that no one even thinks about how they must have first come to be believed. They are one with the land and the water, the rugged bare mountains, and the eternal call to prayer.

Mirad talks, as well, of the star-watcher who slept in several different places each night to avoid the bad light of some particularly cursed star when it is at a certain place in the heavens and moves its rays across a non-suspecting sleeping human with a power that can kill. He had spoken before of his father's habit of moving with the moon.

Outside with Mirad . . . Tom points out the bright planet Venus still low in the sky. He is about to ask Mirad how his people view this particular "star," to ask if they have a name for it, when Mirad begins to explain:

The past week this star and another brighter one (Venus and Jupiter) had been in one place and this was considered both a blessing and a vulnerable time, so the mullahs cautioned the people to read their Koran during this period to prevent anything bad from happening. However, for the five minutes or so when the two planets are actively touching, all the water everywhere in the world stands still, and if any person takes some water from the river, in the exactly right moment, the water will be turned to "*jahwar*" (jewels or grain—it could be either). Simultaneously, all things that you wish for (like the candles blown out on a birthday cake) at that time can come true. Many people sit up for nights and nights waiting for the magic moment.

Such hope.

Bees buzz dizzily on the horizon, flies crawl back for the succulent feasts of spring, and ants who have never really gone away all "winter" cluster in their military lines across the ground toting crumbs and dry shells of dead insects . . .

. . . One day when I was walking to school two *chadried* figures on horseback moved casually down the street in front of me. I think of the playful image of Syfora, a 10th grader now married, who always claimed she went bicycling in her *chadris.* It was a real spoof of the inane *Afghans Learn English* drills, which always centers on playing soccer, climbing mountains, riding bicycles and listening to the radio.

> *[I record the cycle of games we play kindly and childlike with each other]*

March 15, 1975

The mountains, always the stark mountains, seem gathered now around the pubescent spring of the valley like proud gods present at the creation of the world. We sit outside in the warm sun for most of the afternoon and explore the ground for ants and worms.

> *[We reminiscence on childhood springs and summers, activities and bugs . . . . and the end of the school year as it wound down in our little children's minds, the annual ritual of getting school photos taken, the advent of softball and Hide and Go Seek . . . and the contrast and similarities with this time and place and activities drawing from T's childhood and my own repeated here . . . .]*

Zeebee and her sons sit down beside me. The six-month old grins so widely his head seems shadowed in two, and Habibullah sets out extensively to get into the kitchen and beside his father who he remembers usually has food to nibble (or, as Mirad calls it, "to thieve") but after working the screen door for a few minutes he decides he'd rather try to squash big "*morcha aspekee*" (horse ants), which his mother catches and throws in his pathway. But for all his strong stomping he never manages to floor one, until he takes his piece of wood (from a game in which a player has to hit the end of a smaller piece of wood with another larger piece to make it jump), then, in true conqueror mode, he proceeds to wave the wood omnisciently all over the immediate area, at his mother, at me and at the scurrying ants. He still can't catch any insects, and when one crawls on his shoe he is irate and jumpy and demands to have the creature removed.

Peace reigns briefly when Najibullah comes in with his buckets of water, but that too leads to a two-year old's version of a quarrel when he is told to keep his hands out of the dirty water. Reconciled again later, he stomps off to the patches of what Zeebee calls *"qon-gush"* (weeds), ground cover which she claims make good feed for cows. After his uncle Najibullah has pucked him a healthy fist of greens, Habibullah comes back to us and takes turns distributing and recollecting the bounty (which Daud is anxious to stuff in one fist into his mouth).

About then, I notice a timid head pushing around the corner of the gate, and in a moment a whole stream of *chadried* women with their *chadris* pulled up, one student of mine (Ruhara, class 9) and a crying boy in arms and two small unidentified girls, are gathering in the yard in front of me. Taken off guard, I stare a minute, mute. But they are just curious, and the oldest, the bony-nosed one among them, proceeds to explain that she was the mother of the groom at the wedding I had gone to last spring, and that her son is now in Russia and has a three-month old *"bacha"* here, and that I should come and visit her household again.

Meanwhile, Ruhia introduces cousins, aunts, and a mother in the person of the others there, faces I recognized vaguely from parties or weddings I have been to, or a glimpse in the alley or a raised chadris coming out of a gateway before the veil was lowered. I think immediately to have them come in and have tea, but am at a loss for a moment as to how to get Tom and Mirad out of the living room without scaring away these visitors. Slow as always, I don't take the hint when one of them starts to push in the locked window to the bedroom.

I offer tea several times and Zeebee identifies herself and makes her invitations, too. But the visitors insist they can not stay, keep saying, no, thank you, that they are just coming home from the bazaar, and in passing my open gate, Ruhia had suggested they just come in and look a moment. Now they have done so, they must hurry home because there are unattended children back there who will be crying up a storm.

Still there is time for the inevitable questions, "Why have you no children?" Zeebee, to my surprise, rather tartly I thought, informs them that I don't like children and therefore take tablets every month to keep me from having them. It is quite the wrong tone, too quickly introduced into the conversation in front of all these women who have been conceiving since they were eighteen or younger. I try to correct Zeebee's outburst, invite them in again, but make little progress. They wander next door to look at the orchard from Zeebee's yard, to hear the story of the chickens, to be invited yet a third time for tea. Then they leave in a great blowsy replacement of *chadris* on heads and feet, spilling out into the alleyway, inviting me again to come visit their house.

I sit a little longer with Zeebee, who goes over line by line, like memorized script, all that had just been said . . .

[After dinner] we try to explain to Mirad what television is, as he has heard a report that President Daud had appeared on national Indian television in Delhi the day before and talked about Pushtoonistan. . . . He seems to grasp it quickly and speaks of some sets in Mazar and an antennae he had seen on a house here, all of which must receive programs from Russia. I remember the TEFL coordinator, Macdonald, and his story of going back to the Iranian village where he had once taught and finding—two or three years after the fact—television sets all over town and electric ice boxes, dairy cases in every restaurant, but unreliable electricity.

The Hand and Foot Tree, Kabul, 2001

At Masjed-I-Sham-shara
a massive poplar tree rises before the mosque
where people, often the poorest of the poor,
come to pray for miracles.

War widows, old or aged beyond their years,
their toothless mouths like old wounds,
shuffle and bow beneath their heavy *burqa*,
eyes, hands, sunk into their shrouds
from which, haunting a disconnected silence,
their wailing rises,
a sound gathered deep
under the pleats of the cumbersome veil
rising into the air.

Above them,
memorial to the Taliban justice,
the tree canopy
shimmers:

Severed hands hang.
like shriveled claws,
turning brown and splotchy as they rot.
Some strung up like pairs of fleshy gloves,
others pale and deathly white,
only the bones picked clean
beside single feet, unshod,
hooked to the wood,
stark as hooves.

XII

THIS IS HOME, YOU ARE OUR FAMILY NOW

March 16, 1975

. . . An amazing number of students are absent today for at least part of their classes because they have gone to the *hamum* (public bath) in preparation for the coming New Year. Women can use the *hamum* here only two days a week, thus the usual Saturday morning absenteeism, and then some. A new teacher, as yet unnamed to me, having been introduced at a meeting I had somehow missed, begins teaching today. He is a soft-faced, thin, nervous man with the broad forehead and receding curly gray hair of a poet or an intellectual. By a series of sleights of hand, he has been reallocated to teaching the lower classes (7,8,9) and Ziadeen has moved up in the world to teach senior and junior Pushtoon classes in place of Kabir's tyrannical reign on that subject.

I was teaching such impractical words to the 8th class today as "poet, famous, beautiful." and used the picture of an old women, claiming she is a famous Iranian poet who is old now, but had been beautiful as a young girl. And, everyone wants to know her name, and a few decide she must be Rabia Balki who—for the record—died about 600 years ago . . .

[Lunch, lessons with Mirad, Tom a little sick, Shahzadah appears]

Today Shahzadah opens up a discussion on, among other things, her father's old American engineer friend from Helmand several years ago, a Mr. Steele whose address she is eager to find.

He had apparently liked Shahzadah's family and the girl especially and had promised to send money to her when she was older so she could come and study in the States . . . When they were living with him, he used to give her American clothes, let them use his bathtub, and drive them around in his car . . . . Marzia informs me that all Americans are wealthy and have every opportunity to work and play in their country, while Russians, for example, have dull, unproductive lives, and a constant shortage of food, clothes, and extras. I also hear of one of her relatives who speaks six languages fluently . . .

Tom's student comes in later, to sit down, and talk. What follows in the next hour and forty-five minutes constitutes a grand and eloquent vein of gossip. First as a kind of introduction to the juicy parts to come, he explains how Afghanistan has several tribes and that the non-Farsiwan Pushtoons have traditionally exerted an upper hand in ruling, running Afghanistan, and keeping other tribes in low roles. Zahar Shah's branch of the (non)Farsi-wan Pushtoons, from some village area around Jalalabad, have for years been in particular control, given all the appointments and high positions all over the country, although the appointed representative themselves are typically ignorant, boorish, and totally undeserving people. Sometimes they are callous criminals and once given their positions take quick action and release other "clansmen" from jail, sometimes as quickly as in a week, even if those once incarcerated have killed ten people each. He notes that the Hazarajat especially has been denied all opportunities and that until recently the Hazaras were not even allowed to go to any of the higher schools.

We know, sadly, this is all true.

Then he coyly turns to me and asks if I have any news about the fight that took place at my school a few weeks before between a teacher and a student. I plead total bewilderment. I knew nothing of it. He begins to explain how it had been between Tajenisa and the teacher named Kabir and had started when Kabir refused the girl permission to leave the classroom although she pleaded sick. A strong-willed young woman, she took her leave anyway. Upon her return, he (verbally) jumped onto her with a lot of *"gaep-e-xorah zada"* (bad talk), to which she answered in imaginable spitting rebuttal with more "bad talk" about how he was just a dumb stupid Pushtoon from Jalalabad who was only a little man in his own area, but who came here and strutted and pretended to be big.

This talk, of course, fired the vain man on to new heights. He attempted to hit her, at which point, she exploded that she doesn't even let her father hit her.

Somehow they, by themselves or with the help of others, were separated. But—after that—everyone in town has begun to let out his or her real feelings about the egotistical little Pushtoon, who it seems is bound now to be transferred. The quarrel is particularly bad, because little Kabir has lived with eight different people since he came to this town last year, all of them his own native Pushtoons from Jalalabad, and all of whom he finally left in implied states of quarreling. But, he has been eating and staying regularly at Tajenisa's house, another sign of her family's fairness and bounty. Further, he has always been good friends with her brother—for the past couple of months—and so this was even more of an insult since he was turning on the very hand that had fed him. Such behavior, of course, is an absolute and much-remarked upon taboo in Afghan culture where the benign face and outgoing hand are social duties never questioned and where one will swallow the strongest aggravation or anger before turning it on someone who has had you as his guest.

Then out comes more venom from the 12th grader who maintains that Kabir's walk is renowned in town, as are his cigarettes trailing in the street, and that some "naughty" boys from the school regularly mock his smoking with pieces of wood in their mouth and his strut with their own version of his pigeon-toed stride.

Our little student holds back nothing. Next he moves on to the crazy watch repairman Jaglagar (who burned his wife's hair, drove her out of the house, and regularly flunked his students after one of his periodical rows with her). This man is teaching second-graders at my school. Next, then, we hear the infamous Lawalahan's unexpurgated story, how he's always insulted students with "bad talk," but resting on his Pushtoon laurels, he never expects to be reprimanded, until one morning one boy and a supportive native teacher led him to the office and what should have been his dismissal from teaching, period, but which he somehow managed to turn into a prize for himself. Unbounded, I next hear of how Azarullah had one day gone to a tailor in the bazaar to have his pants sewed up and witnessed an exchange of "*reshwot*" (bribe money) between Kabir, my *modir* and one of the shopkeepers that he would never have believed had he not seen it himself;.

And up then came the next tale, this of Shahzadah's brother, a ne'r do well, who had indelicately failed 11 subjects last year but—although rich—managed to stay failed so that if any attempts at a bribe were made they just weren't sufficient to the weight of the boy's renowned ignorance. Azarullah maintains that his head is "*putch*" (empty).

Then we get a sad, final update and refinement on the poor brilliant student who had been removed from the Polytechnic, supposedly because he is epileptic, although he had had the mildest of fits. He claims that when he first got back to the town his mind and thoughts were not very clear. He thought, in fact, it was his illness. But now he has figured out why the school really dismissed him. It was in order to admit a rich, dumb Pushtoon, in a fallback to the years in the crowded classrooms full of what he called dullards with the right tribal background, admitted for their money and political pull.

And, that is quite enough—justified or not— character destruction by our dear student, I am just deciding. But Azarullah goes back to his berating of Kabir, then tosses down like a gambit, the tidbit of "information" that people all over Afghanistan are afraid of people from Tashkurghan, because our townspeople used to take out contracts on people who insulted their families. All these hired murderers are all living elsewhere now, in the big, lucrative cities, but their origins in Tashkurghan continue to give the town a certain reputation. Was there an implication that Kabir had best get out of town quickly before justice was extracted on him in the old-fashioned ways of murder?

Then, setting me up with a social engagement of obligations for the next days, he praises us (Tom and me) as people he will never forget all his life, and then leaves, politely nodding and refusing T's rising to walk him to the gate.

So . . . all this time the young saint of the town who believes everything he hears and retells twice what he knows for sure, still manages to be a bright, diligent, and dignified 19-year old. Is it all true?

[When we showed pictures of an elephant who carries loads in Thailand, Mirad wrinkled his forehead in amazement and showered us with questions about the details of this creature.]

This led to a description of deer and fox hunts when trained *tauzis* (Afghan hounds) sniff down and chase the animals. The *tauzis* then corner an animal by catching its tail in their mouths. The deer who uses his strong antlers to pull himself up mountain sides and supposedly to charge antagonists, turns every which way to escape, but the speedy and strong *tauz*i can dodge him, and fence him in until the hunter arrives and kills the deer. The fox is wily and flaunts his tail in an opposite direction from the way he runs to get the hound off his real scent, so it always takes two *tauzis* to catch one fox. Mirad's mildly picturesque way of telling stories, and the wealth of his anecdotes, never fails to amaze . . . .

Yesterday the bill collector from the electric company came to announce that wires would be cut as of noon today if all accounts with them weren't paid off. True to our fears, Mirad went to the office this morning, a place so crowded there wasn't even standing room, and finally paid our share. But in typical Afghan confusion, and irony, he could only pay for three of the five months' worth of expenses, because "the company only sends someone out to read the meters every few months, and "he had been around for two months now, done those calculations, and won't be back for another month."

March 16, 1975

. . . The skies are blue, the weather warm and scintillating as a single bell's toll. I teach "Blowin in the Wind" to the teachers and discover they didn't understand it very well. Not to be defeated, I give them the words for "Row, row, row," and they like the idea of comparing life to a dream.

I am honored with an introduction to some of Muzdah's sisters (the modir's wife), a farewell ceremony for Kabir (the departing and much disliked Pushtoon!) in front of all the students, a long lesson with Shahzadah, and another chat with Tom's student . . .

Tom is out to play (coach) basketball and me "to eat the air" on the main street full of everyone and his uncle out in the spring sun. (Strangely, suddenly, a car full of well-dressed young women stop in front of the compound beside the boys' school and a woman jumps out to say, "Salaam, Frances," and then the vehicle drives into the gates). Mirad takes his son to see doctors and gets a prescription for penicillin shots and some sort of syrup. He has a respiratory ailment, something like bronchitis.

Word comes that the tax collector's family is moving out of the Haji's house tomorrow because he continuously tries to cheat them, His latest idea is to tell them they owe 500 *afs* a month for electricity in addition to their high 500 *afs* a month rent . . .

. . . Sitting in the sun with the principal and his sister-in-law during my free hour, I am showered with his opinions. He tells about the smallness of life in this town, and the tiny school population compared to a Kabul school with 45-50 girls in each class, and fifty classes. Here there are only as many girls as their class numbers from 10 to 12 it seems. The *modir* also selects this minute to tell me that he will also be leaving the school after exams, because he wants to find work with some government office in Kabul, or else just become a teacher there again. It seems—and this he divulged in English—he doesn't want to be a principal any longer because: "In all the world other people do what they have to by themselves; only in Afghanistan do you have to tell people to do something before they'll do it."

"I do not like this role or this reality," he repeats then in Dari.

I focus on a stream of people coming into school: old stooped *babas*, broken-shoed turbaned fathers, alone or usually in the company of a poorly-dressed and awkward soldier, his clothes hanging on his gaunt form like scattered clods of dirt, his shaven head giving him the dumb, stuttering expression of a scolded child (and most of them are only boys).

The students count as "business," because with the end of the fiscal and government year this week all records of attendance have to be closed up. If a student has been absent for a certain amount of time, more than a few days, the principal must send one of the *chaproses* (janitors) to her house to fetch her. If she is absent for more time than that, and the student doesn't come back with the old man, then her name is sent to the commandant and he in turn sends soldiers to the house to gather the fledging. If the child herself isn't there, then a father or brother has to go with the solider to school and explain that the child or family is no longer living in this town.

How effective is the system? Only a tiny percentage of the children in this town attend school, especially after the first few grades. Who is responsible for the child not going to school? And how does one change a culture that discourages girls from advancing in an education, and one which gives the poor, who constitute the huge majority of the population, few opportunities or encouragements to continue studying?

March 17, 1975

While sitting in the office for my free hours, I listen once to an old man explain that his granddaughter doesn't come to school because she and her mother had moved to Kunduz, "years ago," he claims. In the face of the blatant lying the *modir* holds firm, persists, to say that if she hasn't come to school to this day, if 20 times a *chaproses* has been sent to knock on their door, and no fit answer was given him, it doesn't matter now, but that if she is school age she should just report here and do as she is supposed to. Then both parties will be clear of any future trouble. All the tale is confirmed later in the day yesterday when Azarullah explains it to Tom over tea and candy, with respect to his school, and before he sets off for his house . . . .

[I read of Twain's life, of Gorky, of love]

. . . We watch the repercussions of a small incident involving Mirad's little brother. He was playing in the *cucha* (alley) with the boy from the house across the way and a piece of wood fell into the *jewie.* He waded in to get it and found a 50 *af* bill in the water. The little boy from next door immediately demanded some the money. When Najibullah refused, the boy went home and shortly thereafter, his father and other relatives came to the house to demand the money.

Mirad tells them, "This is children's work. If you need this money so badly I will lend it to you, but this is not something about which adults should be wasting time." They leave and Najibullah keeps his bill.

March 18, 1975

. . . Coming home in a gaudi, late wedged between two students, I see a camel rampaging in the street . . . Then I hear the two unchadried girls announce that they think they will be buying a *chadris* very soon, because they are often bothered by the Tashkurghan people, "whose eyes and mouths never close." This, a fine retroactive step.

There is lunch, and afterwards I go out to stroll in the garden, to absorb the flowering trees. There are new plum and cherry and apricot bushes laden heavily with darker petals and delicate whites . . . Zeebee . . . gives me a complete rundown on what each tree is, whether blossoming or still bare, . . . and how Mirad has always liked birds and that is why he likes raising his chicks, and how he had had a *cawk* in Jalalabad last year as a pet, but ended up giving it to his brother, and how the yard was so good for chicks and roosters (and Mirad's father would not have let him keep them) and how, here, the chicks have everything they need to be strong . . . .

[Azarullah came to take me to his aunt's house . . . "because the aunt and the cousins were always asking him to have me visit and this once he would take me over and after that I would be on my own."]

We come into the big compound through the empty hall, first where the *gaudi* roof lay without its frame for the afternoon and a dog napped under the roof, into a yard with several brown mud buildings, two bird cages hanging in a tree, three big wide door windows open. Behind them faces look out and then exclaim at seeing me, for I was not technically invited for that precise day or hour. Next, I am ushered by two of the five girls of the house into a large carpeted living room with old bridal wreaths of paper flowers all around it, a painted tapestry woven design of Mecca and the Black Stone, a sounding chime clock, several pictures of the family in flowered frames, and a Japanese calendar showing a small village scene in the mountains with tapir-faced Japanese matrons sitting on a braided wooden porch.

I don't see the father when I first come it, something he definitely took note of [although he did not speak to me the visit] . . . Instead, immediately I am seated and seven dishes of sweets left over from the great engagement party of a near relative in the house the day before, are set before me along with tea. Soon tea is brought for the others . . . The house pets wander in and out, Leelah (class 8) a cousin of the house's brother from Kabul, the son who has read up to the 13th class somewhere and has an English vocabulary book and Persian volume of biology diagrams. He plays the harmonium for his beautiful sixth class sisters singing in a live session of tambourine and harmonium. Eerie and sad, he goes on himself in a strained small girl voice after we have heard all of the family performers from the night before, recorded on the tape recorder.

I stay an hour and a half . . . a specimen and a gentle inquisitor, as people discuss me . . . the firmness of my nose, my brown sun-turned hands, my school coat, my smile— . . . Yet none ask me directly although I am expected to smile at the music, reveal my cook's salary and our own, tell whether we miss our parents, answer if cousins married cousins in my country, and explain if I had a radio or tape recorder. And then I have to defend myself as to why I have not come before to their house . . . .

> *[Punctually one day, as they have these past years, we entertain a visit from PC, Macdonald and Howard and some old PCVs from Thailand, etc. We accept an invitation to dinner at the hotel, give in reluctantly—anticipating "takleef" (difficulties) to this protocol of being "honored. We would rather create a feast right here. And, in truth, there are many delays and poor food and very little conversation in the interval, because our administrators who have taken charge to plan this do not really have the negotiating skills or local contacts required to pull it off; and the hotel is not equipped this month to prepare huge meals.*

So, unfortunately the meal is a fiasco.

In the larger picture, then, we hear of the usual silence of the Afghan government toward Peace Corps, which seems more mystifying than ever.

Macdonald makes us laugh as he recalls his mistake as an Iranian volunteer with his new wife, when he confused the word "pill "and "spoon." So people were bemused as to which of them swallowed "the spoon" every day to avoid getting pregnant . . .

We hear that a new census has put the population of Afghanistan at 10 million, not 17 million, a fac which will reduce the total of U.S aid, based as it is on a per capita estimate and allocation . . . .

So, eventually, we are irretrievably off then, a fair amount of misgivings correctly in tow, (for we would have gladly hosted everyone here) to the Tangi Restaurant, where we park the PC truck in the stone lot and walk across the wide arch like bridge across the river, the mountains dark and sheer around us, the new building a lot like a birthday cake in the damp palm of a great god's hand. I remember the ancient legend about Khoja Khiza, the pious old man who gives directions to those lost in forests and deserts, and how he is said to have lived some of his centuries in the adjacent Tangi, existing within the pure waters of the spring there.

A poor young man dressed in white has apparently just begun his cooking over a fire in the patio outside, but we still go blithely inside to wait, expecting miracles. The mayor of Khulm takes us for a tour of the hotel's three bathrooms and six sleeping rooms—clean, *kaleem*-covered, metal bedded—then back to sit in the Great Salon where a brief conversation with the mayor is temporarily cut short by a light failure. We are all introduced to his friend the mayor of Hezrat Sultan . . . and then the village mayor *(wahil)* tells Mullah Nazruddin stories and explains how everything is new here so there might be some problems—Subsequently, the meal limps forward. There is—no electricity as the generator has shut down—and some singular boy keeps cooking outside on a stove—ashamed. But finally a meal arrives; and we eat. And the bill comes to 540 *afs* (way out of range, although only $10.

The next day I led a class for the teachers about "nomads," which interests them not at all . . . and later we endured a duet of inspectors from Kabul for the entire morning . . . .

March 20, 1975

New Year, Naroz. We have come to Mazar.

Gray clouds hang all over the valley like bracelets around the arms and legs of the impervious mountains.

But before leaving Tashkurghan, I spend the morning typing up "Pandora's Box" and "Puss in Boots" for my teachers' classes . . . then set off to the crowded, vehicle-thriving main road where thousands of people are on their way to Mazar and where I join Najibullah (in his fresh clothes) and Mirad in the back of a Waz. After a lot of haggling by the driver the truck joins the stream of cars and trucks and buses. We endure a cold, dark ride, the mountains clouded and chilly with the lonely poised airs of an exhausted season. A little girl falls asleep on the floor against my legs while her *chadried* mother dozes, and an old man with a face of a million years, thin, with hollow checks, high-boned, asks Najibullah about me, then smiles to see me help the little girl. Beside him, so close in looks and age as to appear a twin, another baba clutches his striped three-legged stools and tens of lantern holders to be sold in Mazar, his thin and whittled face like an old oriental sage. The boys in their hooded corners laugh and rough-house, the miles pass and it grows colder and darker as we near the wind-throwing city. Sidewalks and streets bustle alive with huddled figures and free-striding visitors and well-dressed women and slow-moving cripples and Mirad and Najibullah get me into a *gaudi,* then set off with their *anor* tree (pomegranate) and bag of small things to find a place for some rest . . . I am welcomed into an always graceful dinner and sleep, a tour of fellow PCV's home, Trent and Candy Hatfield's.

Morning and we are off with the crowds to see the flag-raising: the *jedda.* We get in front of the mosque to see the ceremony, only to learn that he flag had already, 20 minutes before, gone up and that all the people on rooftops and around were beginning slowly to move away. We continue on, into the strange crowds of the mosque gardens and courtyards (though not the very central ones) to see the scarved Kutchi women begging, the crippled old men and children for whom this year had not brought a miracle either, the amulet sellers, the long-haired heaving *malangs* chanting their Allah-praising dance, the gatekeeper with his ceremonial sword cutting off an overflow crowd before the inner chamber, the few poor souls trying to get to the flagpole and pull down the streamers, but being beaten off by Boy Scouts lamely swinging belts at them, and finally the promenade of women coming out of the square, whose ranks we are allowed to join only for the last turn out of the gate . . . .

Back at the house . . . we find Mirad, who stood sleeping on his feet . . . . He had never found any of his friends, had paid 50 afs for his brother and himself to sit up for several hours in a noisy teahouse with Afghans screaming, until 2:00 when he went to stand in line outside the mosque so he could have a good view of the flag-raising. At dawn, the wall of cement which was overloaded with people had collapsed on his group, had just missed hurting Najibullah, and not so fortunately injured a lot of other people standing there. Then the rain had come, as he was trying to get the boy off to Sare-pul. Now he had come back to talk to us, and then would set out for Khulm.

We have lunch in a room behind the Mazar Restaurant with some bigwigs from Central Statistics in Kabul. They all speak perfect English and have traveled or studied in the States, and each claims he is going back to projects or more work within a half year. They share some candy and nuts; we share pistachios, as they lead a casual enough discussion, speculating on how bored Americans must be in this country, touting how Americans remain "the best people," but how America continues to have the worst politics in the world . . . .

March 23

. . . Back in Tashkurghan, we both bath in the boiled mud water of our *tashknob* and wash our heads with silt, so after it all we are wet and greaseless but hardly clean.

On his visit, Azarullah tells a gory story of a man who had come to his house the night before, and how this friend had lived in Russia years ago and been rich and had a wife and two children. But then soldiers had come to his house one day and raped his wife. Furious and in shock, the man killed both the captain who had violated his wife and the woman herself with a huge rock he threw on their heads. Then he took his two sons and drifted across the Oxus, and ended up down stream in Kunduz. Soon he took another wife there and one of the sons died of smallpox or some childhood disease; eventually the man went to Mazar to work, to make a living, to raise his son. Now his son is full grown, but he and his son continue to have bad feelings about the Russians . . .

Azarullah . . . storms on about how he knew that if anyone other than the Russians had lived there, they would have made Afghanistan into as rich a country as their own by now, and allowed Afghans free access to their cities and factories and universities. As it is, he claims, only a few students from Afghanistan are invited to study in the Soviet Union every year and nothing is done to significantly change the level of poverty of the Afghan people.

He mentions an incident of his own, a trip he and some family member took to the border town of Iraton. They saw some Russians out on a boat and asked them to come to shore and pick them up, but the Russians ignored them and moved away—[because] they were rude and their country could not be a good place to live if its people were always so unfriendly . . . .

Last night Mirad told us about the origin of various dairy products.

Animatedly, as always, he explains that yogurt (*maas*) is made by heating fresh milk and then causing it to curdle with sour milk or something acid, and that after this yogurt has collected in a bowl for several days, it is put into a bag and pulled tightly. It is churned in unique Afghan fashion: the two ends of the bag are jolted and pulled quickly back and forth for several hours, until the butter fat had all coagulated into "*maska*" (butter). The wheys of the yogurt left in the bag are called "*dal*" and many people drink this straight, while others take this watery solution and wrap it into several thin clothes and hang the cloth in a tree for several days, so that all of the moisture falls out. What is left is a very bitter stuff called "*chauka*." Other people take this "*chauk*a" and roll it up into hard, tight balls and this product is called something else. It is sold in the bazaar and when a person wants to eat it, he turns it back to a semi-liquid form by rubbing it hard against a porous clay ball. These two latter specialties are often used on *ashak* and other dishes, famous for their unrepeatable flavors . . . .

Most intriguing, however, is Mirad's version of how certain cheese is made: To begin properly, a baby sheep is killed and a substance taken from its belly, the residue of the milk it has taken from its mother. This "milk clod" is wrapped in goats' hair (*moie buz*) and then some of it is squeezed into a bowl of milk every time some cheese is needed. In twenty-five minutes, the milk turns to cheese. Mirad visited some shepherds once, a special friend of his, and watched this kind of cheese being made, but what especially intrigued him was the clever way the old shepherd had of churning his butter. He filled the bag with yogurt and then tied it on the donkey, and as the donkey traveled up and around the hills, in pursuit of the sheep, the "*maas*" was quickly changed to "*maska*."

March 24, 1975

. . . . *I experience a* real joy reading "Pandora's Box" with the teachers and with my others class, too. They all like its notions of beauty, curiosity, and disguise

. . . Mirad . . . asks if we know anything about why Daud's eyes should be red and swollen . . . Azarullah comes in just then and explains that there were some times in Khulm when all little children's eyes are swollen and sticky from trees and pollen, and he thought it might be now at the time of Amal . . . .

> *[We giggle watching and hearing about Habibullah's shoes and his* "gauz zodane, *"(passing gas), Zeebee's frantic shopping for Naroz . . . and another slapstick picture of Habibullah. This lively little boy tries to chase out the hen and her ten chicks with a broom four times his size, and they persist in coming right back in . . . .]*

. . . Mirad tells us again, in detail, of the people in his family: a brother older then him and a rich shopkeeper in Sare-pul who "keeps apart" and who has a son who has finished the fifth class; a sister with three girls, who is a little older than Mirad; and a brother and a sister who died after the next brother, Corban, and before the birth of nine-year old Najibullah. And, he tells us of a sister younger than him who lost her only child to a strange disease: The boy literally wasted away, until all of his bones and skeleton were exposed and his face was bruised and transparent. Although he ate tremendous amounts and was always hungry, this child—who was only a week older than Habibullah—had died about five months ago. Now this same sister suffers further. Her husband, "out of worrying," has become paralyzed on one side, can do no work, and wants to be taken to Sare-pul. Mirad's father and mother had eight children, and lost two of them, this a higher percentage of survival than others in this country. There is not a household which has not lost at least one infant, and usually each has lost several.

Standing over the sand house and scurrying armies of the Horse Ants . . . Mirad talks about people he has known who can carry up to 500 pounds at a time: One man in Sare-pul, a strong, wealthy fellow, mocked the hired movers in front of him once and told them to put the load on his own back. They did, but something "cracked," and when they took the things down and carried him into his house, within two hours he was dead. Another man fell down while carrying his 500 lb load and merely broke a leg. Somewhere in here, among the points Mirad sneaks in . . . is a description of a man who lived alone with his wife because he was "impotent. "("You know there are some men in this world who can not have children," Mirad explains matter-of-factly).

Tom speaks of an 11th grader, bright, lively, athletic, the brother of the post office clerk, who has TB. In his thin paleness, untreated, he seems doomed to stoop toward early death.

March 27, 1975

.... On the 25th we have a day off from school to honor the Prophet's birthday . . . Something called *"Youzdaorum,"* a unique gathering of all the town's women and children was scheduled to take place in a compound on the edge of town, but although I expected a messenger to come and get me . . . nothing ever came of it . . . .

We amble out to a warm, balmy morning, a little overcast, but otherwise clear, though not a scintillating blue day . . . . to the Jehmoriat Gardens, where the groundskeepers and his younger brother (together they were less than 20) invite us to inspect the work of the restored palace which, after two years of constructing and whitewashing, now has a strong porch, roof and basement set of rooms. Still a lot more repair is needed for all of its main buildings and its gardens. The original contract was for two years, the boys tell us. A minor miracle must be expected for the next 12 months.

We take in the mutely vibrating, lugubrious cooing of the white pigeons under the graceful eaves and porticoes of the building, the darkly echoing, still mud-floored entrance hall, the watchtower circular staircases that carry you to the rooftop, flat as some motif of desert falling out from beyond it on the road to Mazar. Before us is the spectrum of spring's earliest turns on the steppes coming out of Russia to the north and east, leading up in gentle rhythm to the big wave peak of the Tangi.

Two carloads of wealthy Afghans, sleeveless sleek women in halter pants and platform shoes, squint out, and bald-headed, suited men in canvas shoes, and a flurry of perfectly dressed little boys—descend with absent aplomb onto the rustic gardens. The turbaned gatekeeper and the young guards disappear briefly before the visitor's impervious and imposing style. The group climbs up to the roof and looks out test the water in the Egg Pool, and then collects themselves in the Mercedes and Volkswagen and speeds back on the road. If I may generalize, brazenly wealthy Afghans seem to be even less inspired and more perfunctory at a "monument" or "historical place" than even their American counterparts on speedy tours of Europe under some guidebook's "check off as you go" instructions. The group "encamped" exactly 4 ½ minutes.

As for ourselves, standing on the roof with the whole valley before us, it seems impossible that we have already been in this country almost two years: There is a certain lesson in the way the surface of the land has not changed in that time, how we can scarcely measure our own changes, although we must know there have been some, how a certain ageless tranquility blended with belittling drudgery shapes every house, every action, every appraisal in this town . . .

. . . Mirad brings in the news that King Faisal of Saudi Arabia has been assassinated . . . He was shot by an insane nephew while holding court in Riyadh in honor of the Prophet's Birthday . . . . Then he tells us, hesitantly, the story of the fox and the tree:

A fox was trying to get hens and ducks and saw in a garden a cock picking a worm. He jumped over the fence and was going to take the cock, but the wind moved the boughs of the tree and he heard the beating of a drum. Then he saw the drum and immediately desired it. He thought it was better than the cock. So, up he climbed to get it and—for his greed—he got only a dried skin.

Morning . . . . six hours of classes . . . . the modir's wife is crying most of the morning over the departure of her mother and sisters . . . and Sherafad, the tiny 2nd class teacher, finally escorts her to the gate so she can return to her home. Her gentle, stork-like husband, stands her up in the laboratory door and tells her all will be fine again soon.

> . . . [*I muse, thinking how well I am treated but how I am still in no one's inner circle, likely because I am someone "who has her whole life managed to quietly put people off with a strong but mute kind of distancing, a quiet concession to the fact I don't think or talk nor wish to think or talk, the way they do." Classes, between holidays, seem to be struggling. I am missing being*

surrounded by . . . "the mumblings and soliloquies, threads and melodies of old American English . . ."]

Lunch is bazaar pilau, great greasy mounds from the chubby cook behind our old house, and as we sit on the porch in the clear hot day, the old landlord comes by with a man to dig up the garden. The stately old fellow, Mirzad Daud, speaks in his great rolling Persian with obvious witticism and formal endings of "*bedenk*" and *geranke*," these rhymings a kind of graceful equivalent of "behooving" in Old English, it would seem.

About 2:45 Paregul (11th class star) and her sister and six-month married, five-month pregnant sister-in-law, and the sister's two-and-a—half year old daughter, and Jamila of the 8th class, come over with a silk embroidered handkerchief, oranges and several pounds of almonds. We sit in the shadowy house and and watch the nieces' antics, speak of school, America, nuts (the edible kind), and look at the same collection of pictures I have presented before. Once again the wedding shots of my brother John and Kathy prove head-over-heels better loved than anything else.

They make up a gentle and reserved group, and Paregul is one of my favorite people anywhere in the world. As she explains that she is a student, while the others are early pigeon-holed mothers and wives, I want so much to tell her that I am too, and that this is how it should be. How frustrating it is to know there is nothing I can do to help that young mind and gentle spirit. Or, is there?

Tom brings us tea (just to the edge of the room) and hides in the kitchen and after my guests eat and talk good-humoredly of me and of the goodness of this man for serving us women, and the crazy, expensive purchases of foreigners, we move outside to take a picture (though I explain they will probably never see it), and sit quietly a minute in the sun. Then they leave about 4:30, claiming that Tom is being held prisoner in his own kitchen and, besides, the time is late.

It was a pleasant visit, their softness and generosity made me feel sick at my own inadequacies before them, but perhaps they came not so much to judge, as to just see . . .

Tom goes out to play basketball with his new eager team of 8th and 9th graders; apparently the older boys had too irregular attendance records so the sport teacher dropped them all from the team and invited the younger boys.

Mirad returns from Mazar, where Zeebee has visited the mosque with a thousand other women and Mirad has walked and minded the children's shoes outside the soldier-cordoned off area of the women's courtyard. He hadn't found his friend's house, so the whole family had come back. He is tired and asks about the Israeli-Arab war, which he had thought involved Faisal's country. I show him in our world atlas the difference between Arabestan Saudi and Arabestan Mesh (Egypt) and he comments on how he has been afraid of more war now that Faisal, who had opposed war, has been killed.

Our wise Mirad.

[Reading old Time magazines in the evening, I find the world as war-crazy as ever . . . .]

There is still the pathetic sorrow of Southeast Asia with the neutralist Cambodia that American military stagings turned into a new pit of murder, corruption, and desolation five years ago when Nixon's 'incursion" had us all in chanting tears and indignation against that soulless government leader. There are the 500,000 dead and twice that many injured, and a whole population denied their village homes and life-giving farms, and the Buddhist stoical peace they had learned to carry over them like an umbrella in the tropical land. And there is still the Lon Nol government, on the verge of collapse daily it seems, and the Khymer Rouge and exiled Norodom Sihonouk in Peking. And there is Vietnam, blemished, self-murdering, whose putrid head of state we still laud with money to be swallowed up in hopelessly corrupt expenditures. There are those peasants dead and dying and the half-bred children left from 15 years of French and American involvement there.

And yet the U.S. has not yet even begun to learn its lesson. Now the magazines document for us in bold black print, columns of statistics and diagrams—how the States will sell weapons, sophisticated war equipment, everything short of the hydrogen bomb to the countries of the Middle East and to Pakistan and Iran—so that we can always insure for ourselves a new war, a new conflict, a constant source for the wealthy arms manufacturing companies in the States, and the mercenary Pentagon. France and other European countries sell their souls too for silver, so that the rich get richer and the poor just play a constant game of Russian Roulette, only none of the cartridges are empty; they're all totally full of ammunition, and trigger-ready soldiers (U.S.-trained) to set off the test.

And there is unemployment in the States, over 10% in New York City, the highest percentage among Blacks, and with this comes the loss among millions of people of the dignity of some work, of the ability to support themselves or their families—a more "sophisticated" torture than the bare hunger, death, and homelessness among the South Asians or the Africans. These people will never starve to death, so on the surface it seems less ferocious, but in so far as it cripples people's minds and bodies, their hopes and their vision, the future, it is as much a deadly specter as any other.

Then there are the rich playboys and playgirls who con the "personalities" columns everywhere and make some cute comment on water temperature in Malibu or a shocking cocktail and cocaine party with their dizzy see-through blouse—those superficially infested realms of existences too, where the people live like armadillos under the thick coats of their easy decadence and sporting associations, but are as empty, most of them, as some dead husband in a battle somewhere in the world whose heat and ignorance and cruelty these people will never allow themselves to know about . . . . [Some other writers editorialize on the merits of euthanasia, the definition of "right to life" and where, if ever, an abortion is okay . . . .]

March 28, 1975

> *[Letters come, always mother's so gracious and determined to give me no cause for worry. There is news of Dan's itinerary—he is on route to Dar es Salaam. My superficial first feelers for jobs bring other rejections, and notification of Tom's mostly incomplete law applications (forms, files did no arrive) insure him discouragement. As always there is Kabul news and gossip . . . . and little introspective discussions of individual PCVs.]*

We hear a bizarre tale of how the Shorts, PCVs of Kandahar, got arrested one night as they were coming out of their compound. They were put in jail for the evening by the local commandant, on the charge that they were spies for Pakistan. (In truth, instead of going out of the country through the Khyber Pass, they had gone through Quetta over winter break, to visit Pakistan, against Afghan and Peace Corps policy). Our Afghan coordinator for the southern and western provinces, Ghazni-jan, bailed them out but one can't help wonder exactly what kind of opinion the Afghan government, local and national, must have of us, if they are so quick to round up a pair of American teachers, to allow and expect such incidents to happen easily . . . .

The gentle breeze against me as I stand on our roof at the end of day is like the after breath of some giant bird's flight. High above a lone hawk turns and glides, beyond him the dancing sweep of a flock of pigeons play among the still blueness like silent music for a great audience of mute spirits . . . Summer is upon us already it seems, and by this week's end we must reach a decision on whether or not to stay in Afghanistan another year . . . .

. . . We have had a strange ride back from Mazar in a taxi. It is hot and crushing with people. Next to us sits a man and his *chadried* wife and their two-blond haired, blue-eyed children, their coloring fairer than mine, their hair like something out of a German nursery. Yet, they are Afghan, Uzbeki origin, and—the blue-eyed, gray-bearded turbaned father hastens to tell us—and they live in Tashkurghan.

I think of Alexander's campaigns here milleniums ago, of his love of Roxane, a local princess, of the intermarriage of ethnic Central Asians and Slavs, of the legendary pale-faced and blond-headed Nurastanis, of the whole blend of people in the cross-roads for centuries of East and West.

As we are waiting for the car to fill up a man is struck by a "hit and run" cab on the highway across from the *seroi*. The traffic policeman comes running, apparently records the man's license from sight or a crowd's contribution, and onlookers congregate spontaneously, appearing out of no where. An ambulance comes. (From where? It is the first I have ever seen?), and people speculate on the man's condition, as the limp body is carried away to the hospital. The crowd excitedly continues to tell itself the story of what each has seen. Meanwhile, the traffic policemen at all the toll gates around the city are alerted to look for this car. Later, as we pass through the traffic circles ourselves, our jocose gossipy driver contributes his opinion over and over.

The desert spreads out greener than I've ever seen it, the winter grain a lush green, flocks of sheep and goats with their young, shepherds dotting the horizon and in the flat fields near the road. In Mazar, the Turkomen women with their high, ornate head dresses and colorful long clothes and fair skins, shop in the holiday air of the teeming *dhukans*, and huge river fish from the Amu Darya are piled up on ice for sale, raw in the market or at the carnival grounds, fried. There are well-pressed, flashy Kabul families, high-heeled women and sun-glassed men and children, and the inevitable shiny car somewhere, along with a certain posture of walking as if to disdain all these surroundings and yet acknowledge it as their ancient heritage. And, of course, there are children of all the couples, rich or poor, of all the tribes, representing that union at some moment between a man and a woman, out of love or sheer animal instinct or desire, and how someone carried that creature inside of her for nine months, and nursed it, and saw it first walk. All these children now, little people, speak of this ritual of all living creatures.

March 29, 1975

The story from Mirad tonight is of the spring blizzard five years ago. He had been invited up to see Naroz with a friend of his from Kabul and they started out from Kabul in a cruelly cold bus, paying four times the usual price because of the crowds going to Mazar for the holidays. Prices were equally inflated in the city and three of them shared one bed in a tearoom for 180 afs. It snowed for several days and they couldn't see anything in Mazar, because of the bitter cold, so they set off to Sare-Pul, again in a truck at four times the usual price, only to have the trip take 13 hours, instead of the usual two and a half. At one point the truck fell into a groundhog hole where the unseeable road had collapsed under the riddled ground. The whole vehicle almost crashed over, and the passengers screamed and complained. That year all the sheep of the huge Kutchi flocks were killed; they froze to death and starved because they had already been taken out to spring pasture. Many of the newborn and the mothers, thin after birth, were especially vulnerable, and all of the winter stock of "*cou*" had been finished up. When the unexpected snow came the animals had no food and they died by the millions. Mirad spoke of "*cou*" as selling at 120 *afs* a *seir* (usually about 5 *afs* a *seir*) and livestock being fed on regular wheat and bread, because they were cheaper than the usual feed, and because of the late freeze and snow all of the spring grass was killed.

The Kutchi nomads, whose whole possession in the world is entailed in a thousand-sheep flock, were literally going crazy upon discovering the death of all their animals. One man whom Mirad met on the road to Sare-Pul had gotten the news and his mind had shattered, never to recover again. He died a few months later. Another man rode out to the shepherd camp to check on his flocks and found the shepherd there alone with two dogs. When the shepherd showed him what had happened, the man shot the shepherd, the dogs, his horse, and then himself.

The price of lamb has never recovered since then. Before it sold for 10 or 12 *afs* a pound; now it is 28-30 *afs* a pound. Beef, too, was a good 12 *afs* cheaper before this time, selling for 6 *afs* (it is now 18).

. . . Two "middling" girls from last year's 12th class have been accepted to the university, in the Faculty of Letters, and in Engineering, we are told. This is much to the surprise of everyone who had figured that other students, higher in the class standings, would have had a better chance. Four from T's school are also going, though rumors have it that another four are still waiting in Kabul to hear of their results . . . .

. . . Someone had initiated the idea of allowing the 11th and 12th classes to go to Samagan for the day, and the students were aglow with the notion, until our modir Rashidullah, called the modir-e-mareft, who promptly vetoed the whole possibility . . . .

Ziadeen comes over for a stilted hour with his shy, whining daughter who would look adorable and precious if she weren't always frowning and contrary. He sticks to his usual style and talks only to Tom, about the scale for teacher salaries in Afghanistan, about the uninspired townsmen here, exemplified in the students who won't come to sports now simply because no one is pressuring them, of the sickness his daughter had last week which required a trip to the doctor in Samagan and several shots, of the *rowshakt-xordi* system that still exists in the government jobs (bribes), so that medicine is not free, so that a doctor may not be in his job in the hours for free care that he is supposed to be because he prefers to stay at his home and collect house-call money.

He is a well-read and intelligent man; I regret he could not be our honest friend, for whatever reason. Perhaps, he will do well elsewhere.

. . . And Shahzadah reads her English exercises . . . and looks at the pictures of the coronation of the Nepalese royal family (which appear in my recent magazine). We talk (in Dari . . .) about the size of her family. She has four sisters I did not know about and one dead brother ("Do people cry in America, too, when a young person dies?" she asks), and about some *Time* magazine photographs, about the Kennedy assassination which she claims to have read a book about in Persian, in which the claim was made that the U.S. government had been responsible for his death (like a coup) and that she was very surprised to hear that his wife wasn't in jail now for her involvement in it, presumably. Where did this book, or this mis-told gossip, arise?

A caressing sort of night. The stars are clear enough to be seen but slightly blurred, as if being viewed through a think layer of gossamer, the wind is a brazen, fresh young man after all the green-foliaged virgin spring trees, and Tom and I are sleepy heads writing by candlelight . . . .

March 30, 1975

T. is off early to school, me to another discussion of "Pandora's Box," with the teachers' class. The scientist in the group firmly claims that actually all the troubles in the world didn't come out of that box. The 10th class is classically inattentive to a story about a lizard and a turtle, stimulated instead by Rozia's query on the word "vagina."

The 11th class reacts squeamishly to the picture of amphibians in the American second grade science book I show them, but Magfirat and Paregul tease the others gently, saying that it is good to look at the pictures because when you study medicine you have to learn all about animals. My voice again wanes; I have galloping laryngitis (*gulloo-dart*), so the students offer medical advice (a yogurt pastiche around my neck) . . . .

I trudge home past a busload and market full of Iranian university students, here on their way to Mazar for *waxt-e-gul-e sokht* (the first 40 days of the New Year) . . . I sleep and wake to hear Amore M'med's sister and the orphan niece at my window . . . The sister explains that her niece had seen me in the alley today and has come to my house now to get some medicine, because I had given her some last year that cured her of her cold-croup. So, realizing again how little long term good I do, I half-heartedly dispense aspirins . . .

In the next room Tom and Azarullah are reading "Aladdin," and the smell of garlic floats out from the kitchen . . . Today is the legendary 9 ½ day limit for the danger period after Naroz for the orchards and animals of the country, because in a half day once, Amal 10th of one year, all of Ghazni was destroyed by a sudden storm.

. . . Mirad tells us . . . his sick brother-in-law has died, and his sister has gone back to Sare-pul, while a daughter by a first marriage (her mother had died) has been sent to live with a family that had taken her as an adopted child. It seems a process, like buying her for a future marriage. Yet I know she will be treated as a stepchild, likely be used as a servant. But I say nothing to Mirad, just tell him I am sorry for his sister's loss.

April 1, 1975

Yesterday it started to rain, suddenly turned cool and continued to rain all afternoon and night, turning the hard ground again to mudscape.

In the teacher's class we finish off "Pandora," and discuss the plan to start the tale of "Puss in Boots," a cat in clothes, tomorrow. Relevance? Good sources of vocabulary and structure. And engagement.

I am invited to demonstrate a mimeo-hexogram machine and a silk screen that had been discovered in the bookkeeper's shed after years of disuse. With five people crowding around with at least as much ceremony as was given the first demonstration of movable type, I proceed to demonstrate how copies can be made of a master copy. Unfortunately I do not realize I am getting an upside down image until Ziadeen tries his own hand at this task, and then it becomes evident that we are missing a middle sheet of images to transfer to the gelatin surface to get the correct copy. The teachers . . . almost riot when I tell them we need paint and other equipment to demonstrate the silk screen, and only after I have applied some indelible purple ink . . . and finally walked out about ten minutes late to class, does my role in the exhibition end.

I think the stored and incomplete equipment will be squirreled away again.

[*Wie have another guest, an Iranian PCV volunteer named Brad, Princeton 1973]*—We venture to the bazaar to talk to the "one-eyed bandits," our friendly *dukhandar's* son who just finished his agricultural degree at Kabul and is about to go into the army(mandatory). In his excellent English, the graduate informs us that his brother has been accepted to the Polytechnic in Kabul. Along with three other boys, they represent the only ones to get into the university by passing the Concorde (along with the two girls at Mahasty Lycee). But, the four boys who had gone to take pre-engineering and pre-Polytechnic classes in Kabul have all failed the Concorde . . . .

Brad's conversation intrigues . . . He says that conversations during his first year in his village of Ghaf, near the Afghan border, a Shite village in a Shi'a country, had been circumspect and dull. No one would speak of anything except religion and prices . . . Eventually he was befriended by the university students and another Iranian teacher at his school. The uneducated there also wear turbans and *tanbon* and *peron* . . . there is only one paved road which washes out with flash floods, and the school is overcrowded. (He has 240 students). He lives about seven hours from Meshed, Iran's holiest city . . . .

The Shah saw that televisions were given to all junior high schools in an effort to utilize the new national television educational station, and make up for the teacher shortage. But many villages have no electricity. Although teachers in the high school are supposed to have a college degree in their subject, they still end up teaching subjects that are not their specialty and many lack the degree. There is also a lot of cheating among teachers who want to have extra hours so they can make more money and they cut-throat each other to get as many hours as possible. But they do not necessarily teach those hours. They just record them as "taught."

Much resonates with the way we find life and educaiton and values in this country, it seems, although Iran has a higher over all literacy rate.

We learn, now, the route our ill-fated bus had taken in the deep dark the previous summer from Tehran to Meshed. It had gone from Tehran up through the mountains and along the northern coast of the Caspian through the cities of Babel, Gorgan, Sahruyd, and Neshabin, the opposite route from that of the train which stays on the other side of the mountain range and passes rather monotonous desert. Subsequently, although the train has been going for forty years, most Iranians still prefer to take a bus through the green north . . . We also learn that PC Iran and its volunteers use local Iranian doctors, or in a dire situation, the U.S. Army

Hospital, so the policy for Afghanistan is different, or the level of medical care in Iran is comparable to that of "the West."

He describes Persepolis, the traditional royal city of rulers and kings of the Persian and other empires. It is located south of the official business center, and constructed on a selected site where the sun rises on the first day of the New Year (NaRoz by the solar calendar). Once a year, the sun sends certain arching shadows across the columns constructed on the historical site; this corresponds to the exact moment the New Year begins. Historically, every year the king and his court would travel in full regalia to the site for the festival. As part of the ritual to bring both good luck and fertility to the kingdom, the king was required to impregnate a few virgins. In his later years, if a king was unable to perform this necessary ritual, he was often aided by a slightly hallucinogenic drug called *"hama,"* which is found only in Siberia. Here, then, everyone ate plentifully of pomegranates, the symbolism of fertility and abundance obvious. When the rulers could no longer officiate properly at this initial procession of the year, it was a sign that his reign must be abdicated; he resigned or was killed.

> *[We recalled also the story of the "White Revolution," under the prime minister (Mohammad Mossadegh) who in 1953 had attempted to establish a more constitutional power in connection with a communist-socialist party. He nationalized the Iranian oil, and the Shah fled, but the CIA—this under Dulles and Eisenhower's watch—had Mossadegh killed and his party disbanded. The Shah was brought back and given almost total power . . . and—sad irony, sick American errors—the present Ambassador is the former CIA agent Helms, who had assisted in the Great Reinstatement of the Monarchy. Of course, none of the textbooks tell this story, and the anniversary of the monarchy's return is treated as a holiday each year.]*

Brad also tells us how politics are simply not discussed in Iran because of the all-reaching intrusion and supervision of the secret police. Even among good friends, no one will broach a possibly oppositional opinion, unless they are totally certain of everyone present. Students are arrested on as tiny a pretense as having a mimeographed carbon in their hand, which the secret police take as a sign that they are about to run off tons of critical leaflets against the government. The students are killed, imprisoned, forced to leave the country . . . . the mail is censored there. He was talking to his local Postmaster one night, whose son had just been sent to San Antonio for an Air Force training program, along with several thousand other Iranians. The letter back from the son stated, there are stores in San Antonio, Texas which have prices in Persian and which sell Iranian products. The father casually asked about censoring and just as casually had gotten an answer:

"Yes, things are, because the government is particularly concerned about what Iranians write to each other, in or out of the country."

This same country still has beautiful rustic villages, almost totally cut off for most of the winter, and in one such up in the north between two mountains is the old mountain fortress near Mashad of the great conquering, and vicious, Nadir Shah of Ashrafs in the 1700's, the man who pushed the Afghans out of Khorasan, reconquered Iran, overran Kandahar, and sacked Delhi, in the latter of which cities he and his Persian army massacred some 30,000 of its citizens in six hours.

[*I think back to the Delhi we heard about in the 1970's, and which Richard Dalrymple described ten years later as still a "low-rise colonial capital," dominated by long avenues of white plaster Lutyen's bungalows, "where "shady avenues of janun and ashupat trees" open to "hundreds of rambling white colonial houses with their broken pediments of old Ionic pillars (25). Connaught Circle had not yet been shrunk by mammoth high rises. People still wore the shalwar kameer or the dhoti, the main cars were the Hindustan Ambassador and the Mariti, and red betel juice (paan) speckled teeth and street. People sat on charpoys, rope beds, before tiny shops, while everywhere one was accosted by the fumes and desolation from Trilopypur, the major slum on the far side of Jumma and the ancient mohailas, the old city quarter, which had sunk into the stench and refuse of landless, starving shelterless famlies, and the jhuggis, the eternal shanties on the edge of the city full of penniless migrants. Even the poorest merchants had a chowkidor, a guard or a policeman in his keep, even as the cotton fluffers still wandered in a halo of feathers from courtyard to door sustaining themselves by puffing up old mattresses, itinerant musicians unleashed their harmonium and tabla and performed on the corners, and the damp, humid walls bristled with the quick motions of green geckos, and banyan trees as expansive as a forest stretched out their weblike roots in the last bare spots and parkland, and deodar trees sighed.) It was a scene which captured much of how Kabul looked then, too.}*

But here in the present . . . Iranians look down on Afghanistan as a backward little brother/urchin, not to be pitied but detested, it seems. Is it the Sunni-Shi'ite split? Or is it that they think of Afghanistan only as the stereotypical pushy and arrogant Pushtoons, whom few, I think, can "like."

> *[So after Peace Corps, Brad had gone on and done work in Sweden and language training with third world students, and attended a conference on the environment and innovations needed to preserve the earth . . .]*

. . . We're craving a *bookerie* fire, having gone without the sun for three days now. Life is: the luscious fundamental of unshod mud, the vulgar and comic reality of trying to navigate a route through it, between ditches of cow-pies and splatters of horse droppings and broken chunks of once high walls, and deteriorating slips of pathway edges, and the wooden bridges across the river with missing rungs and slates, and the ambitious puttering, splattering boys racing behind you, before you, to the bazaar, and with the stoic, mud-crusted hem of their *chadris*, drooping students and women braving the tiny peripheral vision through their mesh masks to walk between school, bazaar and household.

Mirad speaks of the *dhukandars* down by the Char-Darya grist mill where several men and the sheepherders were sitting during one of the rains, calmly drinking tea, when one of the walls began to tumble. They all jumped clear and saw their produce buried and broken in the tumbling mud and rock and wood—shattered teapots and pitchers and glasses, bottles and dry fruit, and paper goods, tins of grease—all brought low, and with it their earnings and livelihood.

April 2, 1975

Mud, more and more, so that the school is close to a 25 minute inch-by-inch walk through brown luscious water, all slipping and sliding and splattering . . .

Mirad's story is of how a *mullah* becomes a *mullah*. He explains that once a student studies under another mullah and learns the Koran and all, he must continue studying for many years before he is really capable of having a position that will support him and a family. But, each mullah is supported by his congregation, which depending on the number of families around his mosque and how much money they have to spare, will be minimal or very comfortable. Many mullahs make 20 *afs* a month for each child they teach in the mullah school, working all morning and half of the afternoon, a pitifully small amount by anyone's calculation. When a congregation needs a new mullah, or when it is time to pay one and to judge him, to decide if he has given the Friday prayers well and recited during the 10 days of Doe (Shi'ate) and at other important holidays, all of the mosque neighbors come together and the Khans of the village manage things. They requisition out how much each family must pay according to its resources, and select a permanent mullah. The best mullahs go each year to Kabul to be tested by the head mullah there, and these are then appointed to mosques where they can make 50,000 *afs* a month or more, from their congregations and adherents who seek them out.

We hear also of the man in Sare-pul who is childless, although he has two wives. He is a tiny round imp of a man who built a mosque first for himself on his lands as an act of goodness and who now supports the mullah himself on 30,000 *afs*. Each year he gives a feast for all of the town, buying and preparing 50 *seirs* of rice and 20 *seirs* of r*oghan*, and going to the houses of the townspeople and inviting them to his house. He has made his relative fortune from candy, has a huge "car-xona" (factory) with assistants and students, and a truckload of sugar delivered every month and twenties of donkeys carrying bags. He also gives clothes and shoes to the townspeople and is much beloved for his good works. But he has no heir.

As always that story ends with a Moslem turn, a nod to the obligation to help your neighbor, but also to pass on your religious seed. Is this not also the Jewish definition of immortality, or "life after death?"

Today in the 9th class . . . . as part of the conversation practice, I ask Suraya, as I probably have callously other times, if her father is a shopkeeper. She sits down crying, the question having set her *(yawd amad kadean)* remembering her father, who died three years ago. After that I can do no more with the class, feeling I have trampled on a child's soul without respect or caution . . . . Her classmates try to comfort her, tease her lightly for crying about something that had happened years ago, but secretly they love her for her hurt, so much like their own, and want only to make her remember as lightly as they have made themselves come to do, such tragedies, such losses . . .

I enter, nurse, a different vein, as I read the stories by the 11th class, all quite well-written and with the precociousness of little creators of mythology imagined from the small particulars of pictures I gave them, and their own memories and hearsay and imaginations.

. . . Mirad's father had prophesied that a king would die—so far that is fulfilled by King Faisal—and that the crops will be good this year, but that many women and children would still die . . . . We hear the story of how Corban's wife's brother, with a Pushtoon from Jalalabad, had made a lot of money carrying things across the Pakistani border to Jalalabad, and how the brother himself had done runs for a season, and made a healthy profit. But the work is illegal and spies are posted everywhere along the route to catch smugglers, but those who make it through, make a good living . . .

This no-man's land of the Afghan border is no where as daring and bustling, we had been told, than in the passages, the camel's way, between Peshawar, Pakistan, the Khyber Pass and the first major city in Afghanistan, Jalalabad.

I remember.

If you begin on the flat Peshawar plains, the road groans under scattered, limping mud-brick and straw stalls, drying fields of vegetables and wheat. The local Pushtoons haunt, *kohled* eyes starting, wild hennaed beards like cotton candy, turbans neon-lighted pastels twisted over raven black or gray hair, the air assaulted with burning tires, spit *naswaar* (snuff), hashish, dung, grilling meat, diesel oil, and gunpowder.

It is here you can find the brightly-painted trucks, flamboyant road ships, dinosaurs. Their taj, the overhead wooden prow, jut out over the truck's cab. They are brazenly, brightly painted in florescent greens, reds, yellows, ancient Bedford trucks, overladen with anything that can be carried—people, lumber, cattle, stoves, clothing, bedding, guns. Gaudy drawings depict flowing waterfalls, shrines, peacocks and fierce tigers, pithy sayings from epic poems, or prayers in ornate Urdu, Dari, Pushtu or English script. Other images straddle time and cultures, the sacred and the profane, carefully painted F-16 fighter jets, the Mona Lisa, Arnold Schwarzenegger, Mohammed's winged horse Buraq, Hindi movie stars, romanticized portraits of sports or military celebrities, a protective eye. Reflective strips resembling diamonds frame each, shaped in bright greens, yellows, oranges and red, signatured with more bouquets, the decorations cover every part, a movable visual feast—body, flaps, undercarriage and hubs. Inside, as well, the trucks ripple like overdressed women of pleasure. The exterior, ceiling and windshields are covered with lace-like diamonds, stars, gold tinsel or leaves, mirrors, fringed brocade cushions and pillows, glowing lights, draping bead chains, pompons, artificial roses and silk marigolds, pressing the carved wooden doors or plastic inlays. The trucks snort and ground, strain up curving roads, swallow distant miles, still young at 25, chassis and springs seemingly indestructible.

At the border, small children are often used as couriers, tiny creatures bent like hooks as they carry things on their backs, along with local people, who walk back and forth through the border gate seemingly uncontrolled. At the frontier, Pakistani border guards, tall, khaki-coated man with cloudy black eyes and hair under uniform hats that shimmer with grease or water, jeer, look officious, show off black beards, and let you through. Whether one advises you, or not, once you pay your *bakshesh*, you can always find a route across. You can travel for hours along a remote, mountainous route, through an area more porous than a sponge. Anything and everything gets absorbed and passed through as the mountains swallow everyone, making one as insignificant as flotsam.

It has always been this way. Then you see that you are actually part of a silent parade, all who have defied the human order of marked border stations, milling people, with their transport of contraband items, and counterfeit goods.

You watch then, in the bleak, cratered hills, and swerve with the hairpin turns carved into the rugged terrain as if by an army of knife-wielders who had set out to sculpt the most fantastical and irrational designs. Painstakingly, you move, slowly along the route, the dust coating hair and eyelids, and giving faces a powdery look even with windows up. The heat scissors its way into the feebly blowing AC like daggers, as you wipe away sweat. Soon, if you have persevered, you realize the extent to which you are an honest interlopers in this world of thieves, like the dry wings of cicadas buried in their holes for a decade and a half and then swarming everywhere. The judgment of those who ignore you but follow you, swell in those hours. The others there "on business" laugh long and hard at your foolishness, but they do not bother you.

So the old caravan trail runs alongside the regular road through the Khyber Pass, a single lane with sharp turns, an eroded macadam pavement, potholed and cratered from harsh weather and traffic.

Sheer granite walls and cliffs shoulder the pass through the mountains and rise between 600 and 1000 feet high. In the plateaus occasional fields and villages squat. Much of the year, except the early spring and summer, everything lays brown, the land dry, the terrain craggy and severe. Through the frontier, past Tokham, inside Afghanistan, the light slowly begins to change, to shrink, silhouetting sharp, jagged mountains, catching the glitter, the twisting Khyber River paralleling the road way below, until you reach the gardens of Jalalabad.

April 3, 1975

We listen again to Azarullah's stories about the crazy antics, sad, illogical and otherwise, of his school, students and teachers. One teacher in particular is the subject: Haagi-sibe, the university graduate who is reputedly brilliant in everything from books, science and English, but who is a prototype Mullah Nasruddin in his inability to conduct his own life. His son rides a donkey bare-backed and coat-less in the dead of winter. Every year he buys heavy boots in the spring, having worn rubber plastic shoes all winter; and the overcoat he finally puts on at the end of the winter he wears well into the beginning of Saraton. He calls all his students by their father's names, for he has taught so long he taught the fathers. When he speaks of "microbes," the students mock him, telling him that examples of all of them can be found on his own body, for he visits the *hamam* perhaps only once a winter, and when he shaves once a week or so he only takes part of his beard, leaving a mustache or part of a chin fuzz until the next round, so that he is never clean-shaven. He always complains about having no money, his miserliness is legendary; yet he has a huge garden and land, has just completed a several hundred thousand *afs* extension to his house, owns a meat grinder (but doesn't know how to make kebabs), a pressure cooker (but he never uses it because the price of kerosene went up and cooking by wood is cheaper), and an electric blender he has never used either.

Once, last year, it was announced on the radio that he had been awarded a medal by the government for his many years of service as a teacher, but when questioned about it he claimed he had never seen any such award, that it was something talked about on the radio only. At the funeral party of a fellow townsman, all of the teachers from the school and several students were sitting one chilly afternoon. He excused himself to go to the *tashknob*, borrowed a jacket (*chapan*) from the master of the house, soiled it and—half way back to the house—went back to the *tashknob* and made it even dirtier, then to save his own honor, claimed to the owner that the master had just given him a dirty chapan to make him look ridiculous . . . Yet he is much-loved and forgiven all for being a true eccentric.

. . . Azarullah also gives us a catalog of student methods for *"naquel kadan"* (cheating) . . . . Boys cover their *perons* and *tanbons* with answers, catalog answers in tiny folded up sheets of papers pressed into the palms of their writing hand, in their shoes and legs and—in a truly ingenious gesture, some boys write answers on a Trojan, tie one end to their undershirt and pull it down to their palm when they don't have the teacher's eye on them, then let it lose to disappear when the suspicious looks come around (but, of course, this name ((or its real use)) was never discussed by the student).

A swallow has lost his nest and, trying to find which beam in the dark supports his family, flaps himself almost to death on our porch. We open the door to give him some light and he rushes in to become another prisoner. Finally he leaves again to circle tirelessly in the dark shadows of the porch where he can not find his home. By morning, he will have fluttered himself to death.

> *[I read books, everywhere, one on painting by Maurice Giorsh.]*

April 2, 1975

A strange day all told. With my new schedule that leaves me free from second to fourth hour, I was sitting in the office writing a letter and with half an ear turned to the clerk's joking, and the *saer-malim* and bookkeeper, who were taking inventory and discussing consistencies of mud.

In sweeps the new history teacher from Samagan, coming in on the tail end of the *saer-malim's* comment on the planes that had crashed en route to the U.S. from Vietnam with 200 children aboard (of course, I learned latter, the numbers and destination was confused).

The teacher, Kamshad, proceeds to ask me what credentials I had needed to come to Afghanistan. "Do you have a high school diploma?"

Ziadeen interrupts to tell him that I have a Masters.

Then he asks if I will earn prestige when I return to the States, for having taught here.

I tell him, "No." I could explain more subtly, point out how the experience would be counted in my favor for future work or study, etc. But I sense he does not really care how I answer and he irks me with his overbearing arrogance.

"Then why," he demands, "why have you come here?"

To my answer that I want to teach and also to see the way of life of another people different from my own, he bursts out fiercely, sarcastically: "Oh, so Afghan life must be like seeing the cowboys for you? Surely you've come to my country just to look at it like a cowboy movie?"

Stung, even as I detest his tone, I sit silent, and by this time all of the other teachers have come into the office for the recess break. I choose that moment to ask him why he thinks it bad that I have come. "What makes you so angry that you would ask me such insinuating questions?"

All the other teachers immediately try to tell me that no, he has only meant that life in the States is easy, while here it is difficult.

Brushing this aside, he then asks me if I know the radio, and inquires whether I know what Lon Nol is doing and particularly what the U.S. is doing with respect to him. Before I can express my disdain for this despot, my hatred for such a policy and for any U. S.-alleged support, the radical plunges on with a demand to exact from me a statement of support for, or rejection of, the American policy.

I explain, too hastily, that I do not accept it, that I think it is horrible, that if I believed in such American policies as perpetuate war, I certainly would not be here now, when I could have been back in the States in my "easy" life.

They ask if Rockefeller/Ford (one entirety in their mind, for now some other teachers were ready to quiz me) was a good man and I tell them I consider him quite *"awmaak"* (stupid), that as far as I can see all of his interests stop and end with planning wars.

"Oh, no," the outspoken Kamshad interjects astutely. "His interests are toward making money." Kamshad then informs me that 15,000 Americans could not find food to eat. His statistic brings a hush to the room, and several query as to whether or not this is true.

I answer that there is food enough for everyone, but that right now with high unemployment many people were struggling to pay bills. I explain the there are government programs to provide emergency food and social assistance to the poor, but that the current administration might not be fully funding these programs.

Ziadeen then interrupts to say that 5% of the working people in the U.S. are now unemployed.

I switched into a direct acknowledgement then, that I know there had been no war in Cambodia five years ago and that the U.S. has brought it there, a terrible and unconscionable decision by a now ousted President, to which he declares in perfect English, "Yes, I know all about these things."

Then the discussion moves on. They want to remember to which party John Kennedy had belonged, and who his brother the Senator was, and what Johnson's policies (more domestic previously than international in focus) had been.

Finally, changing the subject abruptly, Ziadeen announces that a Dutch anthropologist would be working for the next three weeks here and all over the north, and how good his English was. Eight minutes late, I run off to class, chagrined.

I have no desire to defend anything the U.S. is doing or has done. Yet, the assumption that I, as an American, might share the worst of that country's policies and inhumane priorities frustrates me. I wonder how long these teachers have talked of these subjects among themselves, and only out of politeness not confronted me with questions before. Or, I think, perhaps the anti-U.S. coverage on the radio has increased under Daud, and that is why such questions burn so immediately. Or, perhaps, America and Americans just are worst than they have ever been and also more visible as they err on.

. . . Paregul and her sister Nefaz visit . . . Shahzadah's lesson includes a discussion of how—according to Shahzadah—people outside Kabul know nothing about fashion because they all wear the same thing all the time . . . Then I look at a huge embroidered flowery tablecloth someone had given her to show me, for the price of 1800 *afs* . . . but the girls are quite open telling us the price is good but they will ask again. Then a discussion rages about who can or can not embroider well, and why haven't I learned.

At this point they ask about birth control pills, and insist now it is time for me to get off them and to have a child. They find it odd that there is medicine to keep me childless but for childless women, like the sister-in-law, who has born no more after her ten-year old, there is nothing to make her fertile. They are interested in the typewriter and I give them a brief demonstration . . . and also show them my magic marker collection. Next I am quizzed as to why I don't wear makeup and am told how an Afghan man would hit his wives if they didn't make themselves up.

And the talk moves, as such always does, coming at last to a debate about husbands hitting wives. Someone claims that Russian men never hit their wives, and that in Afghanistan, also, really a man never hits a woman unless she is bad. They waiver on that point for a while, and hear that T. never hit me and that I would never allow him to.

"Good," echoes around the room.

Then they decide he is a good person, and pause a moment. "But why is he so *'payshanee torsh'* (close-foreheaded) and never talks to us?" So, I explain that he does this only because he thinks it is their custom that men and women shouldn't sit together, and he doesn't want to insult their custom . . . .

Somehow in the afternoon's conversation the subject of bread comes up, and I comment how the bread in the bazaar had become smaller, and they ask if one piece was enough to fill me. Then, I find myself explaining self-consciously that I never eat only bread . . . and they ask me what I had for dinner. Again, I am caught off guard and speak flippantly, dropping my usual reserve. I tell them I have only to request a dish and Mirad will create it. What can they think?

[In the evening, alone, T. and I are full of reminiscences about childhood, summers, old neighbors, the intense love we felt when we first met . . .]

April 4, 1975

Rain, rain and more rain and the mud mounts. The state of the weather inspires another Mirad story, this one about Noah's Ark: Hezrat Noa had gotten word a long time back that God was going to flood the earth. So he built an ark ("a big ship") and put families on it. Also on this ark were some animals, like the mouse, who ate a hole in he bottom of the ark, but God told Noa not to kill the creature because it too was a *askare-xod*a ("soldier of God") and must have some purpose in this world. So, it rained for 40 days and nights, and the land was covered and then God told the water to go down and what was left of the changed earth was now the mountains and the valleys and deserts (because before that all the land had been alike).

Also, we heard about why the common worker can never be satisfied but must always work everyday, never to be full. This anecdote goes back to the the time of Hezrat Daud (the Prophet King David), Mirad thought, when many men worked and make a lot of profit but gave nothing to the others, so they stopped working and had an easy life, while others worked and had nothing. One day a man came to Daud and asked him why this should be so and Daud then uttered a prayer and said that if the man accepted it, that from that "amen" on no man who was a laborer would ever be able to sit back on his laurels; he would always have to drive to work to try to fill himself, and he would never be filled. Merchants would be rich and prosperous but would have a sacred trust put on them that they might always be exacting and honest in their work and generous with their profits—and so to this day has it been, Mirad thinks . . . .

. . . When the subject of the tablecloth comes up the next day, I turn thye purchase down. And in the teachers' office we note the disparities in the male versus female teachers' workload . . .

April 7, 1975

As I am sitting in the office during another *bey-car* (free) hour. the male teachers talk about going hunting for *cawk* and other birds when the weather gets warmer and the mud dries. Islamadeen, the former English teacher at Hajie-Boran who teaches classes 1 and 2 now, and who is always reminding me to ask Tom to go to the mountains, describes some bird as tall as a man's thigh with a wing span of a long desk, which he has named after the yogurt-sour milk specialties of the town, *"maas-mast" and dall-dal.*" The religious Persian teacher, the soft-spoken white-turbaned man tells Islamadeen that if he doesn't plan to go too far, he would also like to go on this expedition. "But," he explains, "I get weak if I have to walk too far" (and how he had once walked to the village on the other side of the Tangi only to ask a farmer if there was any water, and when told there wasn't went no further.) Ziadeen then interrupts with a description of a man he had seen in Mazar during NaRoz who had a bird whose beak was four feet long, and which he was apparently planning to sell to a museum or a shop . . . .

I wonder at these novelties.

April 8, 1975

. . . Yesterday as we were moving through the second grade science book, we came to a picture of astronauts in their lumbering spacesuits going toward a rocket, and even the beautiful and brilliant Magfirat wanted to know why anyone should want to go to the moon. And, specifically what value could it possibly have.

Cloying, at the core of irresolution and such questions is another topic entirely, I quickly realize. The girls describe how the mullah had lectured them that morning and told them they must use their scarves more completely and have them always on their head, covering their hair and chins with them, and at night they must also wear a scarf wrapped around their heads while they sleep, so that they do not insult the angels and other Moslem spirits of the dark who overlook the Islamic world, even as they try to rest every night.

Of course, the students want to ask me if this is true . . . and I flippantly nod to someone's suggested "drought" (lie), only to catch Fazilat's eye and a shocked cry.

Catching myself, I withdrew any implied criticism of their mullah and concede that all people have a right to say or believe what they would, and that they must honor their customs.

Walking through the rivers of mud, splashed by *gaudis* and myself, I feel furious and grow stony as I reach the school, for once insensitive to the laws of the land, which place the men as first-class citizens. Thus, of course in their eyes, as I doggedly try to keep my balance on the seven-ten walk to school, as a woman I am no more than another child to be pushed aside as they move past. So, I am almost falling into the river as a soldier, a *chapaned*, thick-striding shopkeeper, and an old farmer with his donkey plod blindly over land and wet, bristled by me and my armful of books, and move on to their day's work. Of course, it is only the universal Afghan law that you would be insane to step aside for a woman.

. . . . All afternoon I type excerpts from a reading book for the teacher's class, 30 pages, and another page of questions . . . and into the evening, too . . . I am optimistic of their progress and interest . . . .

"Chekaks" (leaks) have sprung up in everything, and Mirad discovers that the old kitchen has lost part of its wall, and that soon all of it will fall. He also brings another chicken . . . .

This morning the teacher's class has only Magfirat, Abraham Khan, and the returned *modir* . . . I endure a cross-examination by the *modir's* wife about the "badness" of my *"cucha* (alley) for walking and whether or not my house leaks, since everyone else's does.

I stand a moment in the 9th class room looking out at the blood red river flushing past like some soiled vein split in a royal body, and behind me the black-uniformed girls copy my scribblings off the blackboard, my scribblings about how to make questions. It strikes me all as horribly absurd since they can not even learn in their own language how to question, how to draft a question about anything important beyond the curtailed movements of their lives . . . .

. . . Meanwhile, my radical (or perhaps rational) inquisitor, Kamshad, asked me if I have a historical atlas he can borrow . . . .

> *[We host a visitor, the notorious PCV who had opened his own export business and skipped protocol and laws while in Bamiyan, been thrown out of PC after the hotel owner there questioned his intentions—and now runs his company from California. The man had lots of complains about primitive living conditions as he and his wife travel in country now . . . .]*

Coming through the stile-like lanes of the neighborhood in my painstaking splashing, I am approached by a man who calls out, "Mister," and asks for help. I respond to something in his voice, and turn around demurely. He holds up a can of powdered milk and asks if it is okay to use. Then his child-wife comes out, beautiful dark-haired, soft-eyed, with a baby, and they ask if it would be okay for the child . . . Before I cam examine the can or answer, he runs across the narrow muddy lane to grab a pants-less boy from another compound and carry him to the *jewie* where the child can relieve himself. The young wife retreats back into a compound wall. This is surely a symbol of it all, the fear and need and distrust and question, and the always incomplete questions . . . . The option of nourishment for an infant, but also a possible poison, since it will be mixed with bacteria-rich water, as all *jewies* run into streams from which water for washing and drinking come . . . .

Afghan Refugee Camp, Pakistan Summer, 2001

To be refugee is to have lost everything.
To be an Afghan refugee in Jalozai Camp near Peshawar in 2001
was to be caught in a crowded, unsanitary "hellhole."
To be among the 20,000 Afghan refugees
who arrived in Pakistan late in 2000,
the so called "invisible refugees,"
was to struggle at the lowest level of subsistence.

You were a squatter,
outside the already squalid and sprawling official camps,
desperate to find an open area
in a city alley or ditch or waste-filled yard.
Nameless and unregistered,
you were officially not entitled to rations, food, tent, or space.

Even as fighting and drought intensified in Afghanistan,
the Pakistani government limited
the number of Afghans still in the country.
Hoping both to further isolate them
from their own population,
get them in position for repatriation,
end Pakistani responsibility,
the government shifted Afghan refugees
to camps in unsecured border areas.
At the same time, neighboring countries—
Iran, Turkmenistan, Uzbekistan and Tajikistan—
officially closed their borders.

At the edges of Jalozai,
the heat begins to claw at you,
the noise of thousands of people pulls you in,
you are staring at bedlam,
pain-filled and roasting as any Dantesque Hell.

The camp spreads out, row after row of frail structures,
shoulder to shoulder of torn plastic bags,

tattered cloth blankets draped over wooden frames,
held up with ropes and string.

Inside these frail shelters, people curl up
trying to escape the heat,
they squat at the entrance to seek air—
elderly women in frayed scarves,
mothers balancing nursing babies,
crippled and aging former soldiers,
children with imploring faces.

The temperature hovers at 119 degrees
chimeras of heat create halos
above the hot, paltry shelters.
Block after block
stretched, baked, entreating faces,
look back:
lined with sorrow, weariness, hunger,
hopelessness

XIII

BEGINNING THE END

April 10

Azarullah talks on and on . . . . We hear of the melancholy, politically-motivated bad luck of a certain family in town, and how my best teacher Ibrahim Sayyed is of that family. One brother who taught at T's school last year and had studied Arabic and Persian at a special school in Mazar, had been offered the job of "*kosi*" (judge) for his knowledge. But he was been put in jail this past summer and still sits there because some rascally (paid?) students had created a lie about him, accusing him of saying things in class against the Jemoriat. The same boys had been part of a gang in Tashkurghan who picked fights and carried guns and had robbed some homes.(One had drawn the gun in class last year on the tailor, when he refused to give him 2,000 *afs*). They are bandits, thieves, liars, destroyers of people and their fortunes, and yet they remain lose to continue doing as they want . . . .

We ask about Ibrahim's brother and what chance he has of being freed and his name cleared.

"Truth has nothing to do with in," says our astute young friend. "Which ever group politically decides to rule against him has all the power. And they can pay off the worst of the worst to ruin his life. His real integrity and truth count for nothing here."

Then changing the subject, he tells us proudly of the questions for a conference he has prepared for his class and which is to take place on Thursday. It's a sort of oratory or speech contest it turns out. As part of the program, students must recite tongue twisters and give correct answers quickly to long lists of names. Further, they must improvise a lecture on some subject for so many minutes without using two words (such as "but" or "then") and make sense of scrambled sentences, and palindromes (These latter are words you read one way as well as the other, and so on.) Is the event like the Lebanese Zajal?)

The "kid", as we lovingly nickname Azarullah among us, also informs us, shrugging his shoulders and wringing his hands to point out that one really can't expect much else from people who have no work, that Tashkurghan is famous throughout the land for its unemployed people. While every other place has factories that manufacture cloth, Tashkurghan has one factory that never stops manufacturing. That is the factory of *"bofton"*(talk). This a well-worn repetition of the old Franciscan adage that idle hands are the devil's workshop. Listening to Azarullah is always akin to being at an old-fashioned kaleidoscope show. He spins and drops a hundred images which can be shaken up to make one basic pattern, or a whole tawdry style, with black bursts of disconnected particles. There is nothing so mundane as a single truth in any of his stories. Yet he craves the truth and usually tells us facts, albeit they are sometimes surrounded by highly charged and emotional descriptions.

But he turns now back to the his first concern, He gets his cuts in against the "*kosi,*" (judges) and all the government officials who accept huge bribes, and routinely expect them. They will let you purchase your freedom (deserved, or otherwise) for 50,000 *afs.* In the past six years a whole stream of *sharwalis* and *commandants* have passed in and out of the offices here. Of our own initial stalwart friend of our first September and our arrival, the First Commandant, the kid confirms that he had done an excellent job of keeping thieves under control here; there had been no burglaries during his time. But he himself stole freely, most specifically from the *pista* groves (pistachios) in the valley outside the mountains, orchards which the poor people tended all winter, but then were denied access to.

Today brings the first sun in ten days and the mud which was so deep before has dried up like dead figs in mid-summer in most alleys. Brilliantly clear, the sky is a sea dream, with white doves, and the winking quick swallows with the velvet split tails, glide above us.

Yesterday, the son of one of the *chaproses* at my school died. It was his last child. The others have all died at birth. In a kind of memorial service, as the dark, squat man in his heavy gray turban and pock-marked, hallow face and downcast eyes sat in the office among all the teachers during the recess break today, Sherafad, the tiny 1st grade teacher, chanted a prayer in Arabic for the lost child. We sat quietly in the sun-drenched room as the tones rose around us, the vowels sweet profundity. But the man's face did not change. He seemed focused on something far across the floor, beyond us, the words only impressing themselves . . . falling, into that unusual terrain of harsh, rapacious earth.

I recall the process of burial among my neighbors, their tradition going back to all generations: the rules for grave-making are precise. Each grave must be at least six feet long, two feet deep so that the corpse can sit up on the Day of Judgment. The feet of the deceased must face toward Mecca, so the dead will wake to see the holy city first. But if the dead are improperly buried, the soul is damned and it can return, to kill and enslave other souls. Then people must use special magic potions to get free again. Further, nothing must be planted on the grave, because spirits could hide in shrubs or trees.

Afterwards, the "arguer" asks me if I have understood what has happened and then if we "kafirs" pray. I nod, but to myself note how Ziadeen did not pick up the blessing at the end of the prayer. We are all up again in a few minutes, after the modir's "Xoda Bubakshan" (God forgive him), referring to the All Mighty Himself or the snatched child, or the saddened earth dwellers, perhaps a little ambiguous purposely in the Persian phrase. We move again into our classrooms, to say our words to children who have survived this long already, who have the best chances to survive a little longer because they are now beyond the most vulnerable years (excepting, wrongly, childbirth)—but each of them, if not to die himself, perhaps, is bound to see more deaths, in the immediate family.

Today I receive a gift . . . a handkerchief embroidered, from Suriya of Class 9. Proudly, she shows me the birds she has embroidered from the picture in the book I had lent her—this creation of tiny creatures in yarn and colored string something that can set within her pretty head like a snug cat in a rag bed by the fire.

Mirad's story again opens our eyes. Once an old *paghmanhar*, unnamed, (a prophet) was being persecuted by his enemies and fled up into the hills to find shelter in a cave, for he was only one man and his enemies were many. In the cave were many spiders who, seeing quickly what problem the prophet had, wove a thick web across the face of the cave where he had taken shelter, so that when he enemies came up and searched the cave and came to this one, they passed on realizing that their man could not have hidden there because of the intact web. So, since then, people have had great respect for spiders and never kill them or destroy their webs carelessly.

Zeebee and sons come over to sit in the hot sun and chase fallen blossoms and tall pulled weeds around the yard. Zeebee, small and gentle, looks proudly at all the trees and tells me their names, and remarks on what fruit trees she has (or had) in Sare-pul in her *owlee* (yard). She thinks the fruit will be rich this year after all, although everyone has warned that the strange warm winter could kill the trees. Habibullah imitates the rooster's crow and wrestles his little brother, swats his mother with a long stick and giggles at peek-a-boo. Then, he runs, screaming from the anthills and prances on the wall like an emperor for a few minutes, demanding to touch the leaves high up on the newly green trees, and to peek into the windows in the house and storage shed. Daud grimaces and jumps in his mother's arms like some round stuffed bouncy doll on a string, as their mother looks to sky and ground enigmatically. Inside Tom and Mirad read their lessons.

. . . Later, Zeebee brings us a loaf of freshly baked bread . . . She reminds me again this afternoon that Daud's eye has entirely healed, thanks to the (expired?) medicine and advice we had given her.

> *[In this debate, back and forth as to stay or go, today we come down on the side of not extending, because there are no jobs that we want in Kabul . . .]*

Yet walking out alone to the bazaar to self-consciously price several *pardas* (embroidered wall hangings) again, and negotiating one small purchase of "*ghoraz-e-anger*" (brown butcher paper) in the easy-spirited atmosphere, we are awed by the clusters of old men basking in the teahouse porch like great Confucian soothsayers inspired by the sun; the barefoot boys with their trays of yogurt or bread or boiled spiced chickpeas, selling their snacks or dinner treats in the gentle whir of passing; people sitting, the school girls weaving a petulant route through the puddles of soft mud going home for the day, and the enigmatic *chadried* figures, billowing out across the old road, hovering like frightened, faceless birds before the dark shop booths. Waking to walk through those few minutes today, I know again how sad it will be to leave this tranquil prison, to break out again into harsh freedom.

. . . What do we see?

Grass growing out of the muddied patios around the yard, a swell of green mold across the stagnant corner of yard, the tiny green berries in the mulberry trees, a single bush of mentholateum (camphor?) smelling odors in one *jewie* side, two dandelions-pussy willows poised in a sea of weeds waiting to be blown and turned to wishes, and a single winking white butterfly crossing the forest of green, We watch it, sensing our time too has mellowed, toward an end.

April 12, 1975

We get up at 6:30, heads spinning with the notion of climbing our famous "wave mountain," the Tangi. Tom sets off for the long-awake bazaar, on this breezy morning with enough clouds to keep our heads cool, and brings oranges and eggs to boil, and bread for four. After breakfast I put on my old Swiss mountain climbing shoes and we sit on the porch to wait for Azarullah, who had invited us the night before to go with him this morning.

He comes weakly in, feverish and with laryngitis, at about 8:00, then explains that he cannot go this week after all, because he is ill. He grew quite flustered when he discovers that we will go anyway, insisting he must find a person to show us the way up, insisting all the way to the door that his feet are fine and that he could go with us after all, since we are all ready . . . . Tom dissuades him gently and sends him home to mend.

And we move down the road to meet several hundred Tashkurghan residents carrying bird cages, all coming back from a big *cawk* fight up in the old city, proudly holding their squawking birds out in front under their tie-dyed coves, grinning, some of them over the fights that had never become, the money put down or received, all enigmatically concealed in their likenesses, walking down the hills and into the city.

We wind around the direction they had come from, until at the base of the old city two little boys and a princess white dog come bounding from the wall toward us, as several *chadried* women behind them flutter in the gap in the wall as they stretch their forms up the hill. The boys come from Azarullah's family and insist that we join them on the hill for a day's picnic, but we tell them kindly that this time we will continue in our direction toward the Tangi. As we move up the road, the old citadel falls away. Soon we are on a deeply rutted twine of road moving among the hills, passing fields and several families in transit to the fields or marketplace, gaunt old patriarchs leading the family donkey, their dry faced women and sapling children carrying bundles, moving docile-like behind. Along the lane we move, thinking still to find the road up to that proud mountain, Then, just as we had been warned, we realize the route will not be so easy to discern, so we change our plansa and decide to walk out to the Tangi and the Chesma (springs).

After moving along the rich green fields, we cross into a small grove, then quickly through a graveyard and into the tiny village of the tanners. Its entrance lays as still as a ghost town, but then as we enter, we see it is alive with the dark-skinned men in their stained, rolled up *tanbons,* wielding the strong skins of cows, camels, and sheep, immune to the acid, pungent smell in the air of rotten carcasses everywhere. The men want us to take their pictures, so Tom sets off on a tour of their various houses to have the whole process explained. First, the skins are taken from animals and covered with a solution of salt and lime (lye) which eats away the fur and leaves the toughest hide. These hides are then dunked in water, a great dark pool out between the houses where the men with their bare legs and poles push the hides deeply into the water and thoroughly soak them. From there the hides are taken to be beaten and with a combination of stone particles are partially cured. Men with huge wooden hammers suggesting the props a giant at a circus might use in his act, pound the shattered stone bits into the hide, pounding and pounding in the shifting air full of broken dusty stone, their noses stuffed with cotton, until the hide is taken over to be dried in the sun for some time, and later beaten more to soften it. We never get a sense clearly of how long the whole process takes. Our guides tell us that perhaps 100-150 hides are done each month, and that these men all work full time for their special livelihood.

We take our appointed pictures and the young children ask about our basket and the old straw hat resting on the top. With thanks for their interesting demonstration (but it is their lives), we move on, out toward the nearby stream, which since last spring when we had walked this way, has "grown" a sturdy stone bridge, this latter built as part of last summer's water redistribution project. The cliffs of another mountain range tower above us on one side, and further down are the willow-like shade trees, orchards, mud houses with the waterway coursing through them like a constant secret.

We have reached the road then as we head toward the great gap in the earth, the gorge, Kholm's Tangi, its porous-looking stones cleft perfectly, cliffs building up from it into the mountains. We pass a sullen boy trudging beside a donkey loaded with "*boteil,*" the dry sagebrush the people gather from the mountain and use for fuel to bake bread in stone ovens. A man and his son scamper across the river and up into the thin path to the hills. We stop to catch the damp coolness of the Tangi. Looking up to the sheerness, we imagine its age, and how the whole valley had millions of years ago been carved out by a great river. The moss green across the crumbling red earth-loam hills is beautiful, a rich festive kind of coloring deepening and brightening in turn as rain clouds pass over, and the sky grows blue. Further on the clouds are again over us, further yet we emerge in the clear sky. A crusty, dizzy looking shepherd comes up the road, makes a motion at Tom for a cigarette, watches him shake his head, then slouches tiredly on. Beside him, his brother, dim-sighted and grinning from atop his slow donkey, offers me some roots from his saddlebag. It is "chicory," the famous spring fruit of the mountain streams.

We walk tranquilly, growing warm, then cool as clouds shield us, and a farmer hails us from his field where he moves painstakingly slow behind a cow and a wooden plow trying to guide the unwieldy team through the tough soil, to turn it up for planting. We pass a few solitary compounds, nestled at the valley-mountain edge, with patches of dazzling green groves, the now-turned earth, brown walls and green patches like pretty snatches of a rich song.

Then the *modir-e-mulliyah* (tax collector, Shahzadah's father) hails us from the river and we go down to pass the time with him, one kilometer from the springs. Under a bridge behind him are half a dozen men playing cards, surrounded by pots and pans, and fishing nets. He invites us to join them for fishing, but Tom refuses because I'm there and obviously would not fit into the all-male scene of cavorting, gossiping gambling men. Later, on our way back, we will see them again, the modir's pink pantolooned, red-suited son, peacock-like watching the highway.

Is it for spies? I wonder.

He gives us some odoriferous herbs he had fished up from the river, called *"shogfar,"* a handful of red poppies, and then we continue down the road to the springs and a dolorous old man perched on the concrete wall around the parking lot with a basket of bread.

The spring itself is a shallow pond, marsh green weeds on one side, white ducks on the other. We eat our lunch under a cement mushoom pavilion, then pause to take pictures of the rich red poppies crawling up the hills like a rich woman's jewelry, the elegant blood red flowers in the bright green grass, yellow and white stalks among them like court tenders to the royal train. We climb up the hill to the first ridge, and look down into the valley and up into the bare mountains beyond and out to the winding road and the small figures of people coming to sit in the hotel and out by the springs. A man takes off his shirt and rolls up his pants and swims a few minutes, goes back out again and Clark Kent-like redresses, complete with wound turban.

It's cool on the hillside, a young hawk circles in the sky, a moment blue, then gray, then somewhere half between. The craggy grays and red and green with their dots of yellow life, frail red flowers, reach out around us, stern statues to time, and always beyond them are the desert. After a while we climb boldly back down, following our jagged footsteps, making a new path deeper in the soft hill.

We are at the heart now, off to put our feet in the cool, clear water, and to see the source of the spring, to sit quietly a few moments. Our reveries dissolve; a crowd of loud and staring men (Pushtoon workers from somewhere across the highway) come over. They watch us, talking all the time. A gruff man with a son and a fishing rod, intent on watching the springs for signs of a rising fish, ignores them, continues casting,

Soon we are off on to the road again, refusing rides from cabs and jeeps and trucks who stop to offer us transportation. Each driver shakes his head, amazed at our craziness when we refuse them. I realize that like lost children in a fairytale, by venturing alone outside the civilized and very much controlled parameters of the town, we have entered a world of unpredictable and uncensored behaviors.

In a moment we are back again close to the Tangi, where a father and his two sons with chicory baskets and poppies, and other men, fish along the rushing rusty river.

The poppies: what we know of them is only their beauty.

The poppy flowers capture a rare beauty. With the deep red petals and a branded purple-black inside each center and the delicate pollen stalks golden within, uncannily they grow almost out of the rocks in some places, the land hard but near a source of water. In all the full-blown hedonism of some opiated dreams, one could imagine some half-crazed pilgrim wandering out of the stony winter desert to find one field of green alive with the millions of red blessings, and stretching himself down within, crushing the flowers with his body until the yellow powder is all in his clothes and the red petals cling to his skin, seeming to nurse his dry body. Then he would get up having seen his vision; he mirrors the blue sky above caught in its opposite in the red and green fields, caught again in the small tight moss spreading across the iron clay hills, going back up again to the sky.

Some students from Mazar greet us, and with a detailed listing, one by one, remind us of all the Americans they have known there. Later on some tall, high-heeled women in *chadris* pass us with a welcome word, exclaim over the good air and beautiful scenery. Some are also from Mazar, and one is the mother of Tajenisa I learn the next day, when my student tells me excitedly in class how her mother had seen me hot and flushed "on the road," and been worried that I had gone to so much trouble . . . (*taklef maekedan*). We pass one of my student's mansions, a huge compound with spreading orchards and except for my hot dusty state and Tom's determination not to stop, we would have gone in to honor the persistent invitations. A rich man and his *chadried* wife stop in a *gaudi* a little further on; he insists we get in. Quietly then, we are carried into town, and to the end of our street in a *gaudi*. At 3:30 we are back in the compound again, blistery-footed but at peace from our outing . . . .

> *[We learn there have been visits by Daud and 10 women while we were gone. Workmen come to repair the cracked kitchen wall; and Mirad admits that he will allow his roosters to fight.]*

So, not in the least to our taste, Mirad takes the Calico Cock to his yard to embroil his own White Wistful. The challenge set, he carries the Calico Cock around the yard while the younger cock races after them. When set down (we feel squeamish already), they spit at each other, then ruffle feathers bristly, begin to claw each other and duck away. The white creatures are soon streaked with blood, and I think of the Spanish mystic's images of the beauty and horror in the blood of cockfights, the sort of incredible sensuality in the struggle between such proud birds. But it is mostly just barbaric and cruel. We tell Mirad, "enough," and as Habibullah trails the birds, he catches one bird and takes the defeated white cock home to wash.

. . . There is now a regularity, albeit comfort, in teaching the morning classes, in having time and language to socialize with the teachers, to even play ping-pong with Najiba, to joke about taking everyone to America . . . and to watch the interactions during recess (*tafrie*) . . . The Kid appears in the afternoon . . . and invites us to go with him again, this time to the mountain . . . this time with him as the guide.

Mirad talks about the mountains in Badakshan and a city across the border called DuShambe, where the language is also Tajeki . . . .

We are taken off guard, but delighted by the appearance of Daud's women . . . Daud's tranquil smiling wife, his daughter, an English teacher in Mazar, 15th class student Fazia who is seven months pregnant and had been married seven months before, Mary from Class 9 and her two sisters with cropped, fuzzy curled hair. We have tea and look at my small collection of pictures, answer questions about teaching, invite each other over to the respective houses again, stroll in the garden, take pictures, and sit on the porch until Tom comes. After another look at the kitchen, they get ready to leave, perched on tiptoe as if ready to dart off. Then we separate, they back to their *chadris* and family, me to watch the sunset from Zeebee's roof while she holds diarrhea-sick, belly-aching Habibullah over the edge (he had eaten unripe almonds off the tree all day); and the baby giggles and cries too. And the sun sets . . .

> *[We hear how the U.S. Embassy has evacuated personnel in Cambodia . . . how a Vietnamese pilot tried to strafe the Presidential Palace, how Libya and Egypt exchanged unbrotherly words . . .]*

April 13, 1975

. . . . Mirzad Daud is still here today, patiently but firmly overseeing the reconstruction of the kitchen . . . Mirad explained how he and other *moie-safeds* had been invited to a marriageable girls' house recently, to study her father's opinion of her, and propose a match, and set terms and prices for various parts of the formal agreement . . . somewhere in the vicinity of Zahra's house. True to the custom, without ever expressing their purpose in coming one way or the other, all of the gathered party well knew that the preliminaries to an engagement were underway and the role of the old men in keeping everything just and proper was invaluable. If an agreement is actually reached, soon there will be an engagement party, the *sharee xorie,* at which time the girl's family gives handkerchiefs of candy to everyone who comes, breaks bread and lets a prayer be offered. Thus it is solemnized. (This process is more direct than earlier ones I've read in descriptions.)

The harsher side of it all (not just that a woman is sold here) is the fact that the prices are so high, never less than 30,000 afs, and that a man is a debtor often up to his fourth or fifth child because *the wife's* family wants only straight money. No goods, "in lieu," are accepted. What an obviously negative way to start a marriage, like killing all the young buds on a rose bush and then sitting back five years watching for them to sprout into full blown flowers again. So one understands why bearing a child, fast, is so vital.

Some stranger bird whose name we don't know has come to perform in our mulberry tree. Punctual as sunrise and the noon gun, he hoots out boldly, softer than a factory whistle but equally even, taut and flat.

We haven't caught sight of him but I half expect him to be as tiny as a hummingbird, with a great flexible gullet he blows in and out.

The raw almond rage has hit my school. Mischievous eight graders sneak out to the orchard behind the buildings, on the pretense of going to the t*ashknob,* and come back with greedy fistfuls of the tart green fruit. And later the bellyaches.

April 15, 1975

. . . I've been waking at 5:00 and unable to sleep, lay here empty headed expecting an alarm to go off any moment, until I go outside for the "john stop, "and find out the actual time and still can't get back to sleep. This morning I see an exotic bird, a tan color with black and white striped underwings and stomach and a crest like a blue jay, who seems to be scolding his look-alike brother in the tree, until they both flutter away. I think them the authors of the great *lub-lubbing* echo we hear every morning, but I'm not sure that song has two voices, and I distinctly heard the shrillness. Are they magpies?

> *[Among other chores, I remain the roaming photographer. Today I was asked to take pictures at school . . . in the muddy fields.]*

. . . Mirad claims that certain birds are hypnotized by the golden eyes of *bocums* (owls). Thus the birds dive down if they ever see one with his eyes open during the day and try to eat the creature's eyes out. This is why the owl does all his prowling at night and uses his sharp eyes to make a livelihood without getting himself in competition with the day birds . . . .

Tom just returned from a disillusioning match between Tashkurghan and Samagan, during which the fans and umpires and teams were all poor sports, or poor participants, and where he passed two hours trying to rid himself of the persistent odious comments and requests of the crazy English teacher Rahinee from Hajie-Boran. The Samagan team actually quit in the middle of the soccer game when the near-sighted Tashkurghan coach came up with an imaginary goal for the home team. They were finally induced to stay for *pilau* dinner, a gesture of reconciliation, although obviously their impressions of Tashkurghan were unpleasant ones.

Tom says the teachers from the opposite team were all dark, with the stark features of Pushtoons, and that the students, with their bald-headed sheared expression, and tight suspicious manners, looked old, like convicts in a work gang. Who knows?

April 17-18, 1975

Tom's *mamoonee* for his teachers, including the Rooster, goes forward, a feast, with a potpouri of dishes, and home-made potato chips, etc. I stay in the bedroom and only greet and retreat . . . In the end only four attend, although he had planned on a dozen or more, and had had Mirad prepare heaping platters of food.

. . . . The star of the lunch cast is the famous Hagie-sibe, whose tiny cracked voice, equally incomprehensible in Persian and English, ejects itself periodically with explanations, only to be answered by a rather brash history teacher from Samagan, who loudly paraphrasess or restates in its entirety each utterance. The other two teachers seem fairly indistinguishable; one reported to be a very meek recent graduate of the university, the other Talhan Khan (King Peacock) who teaches history and 12th grade English and seems to be the most decent of the strange Jalalabad crew sent up here last year. The men talk about the origin of the names Khulm and Tashkurghan, and who had founded the towns, and when and where. They concede that Afghans can never agree on a date in history because they have a rather foggy notion of things in time anyway, that 200 or 1000 years are really not much different from 50 years ago. The most interesting thing to come up is Hagie's contention that Khulm meant "sticky mud," referring obviously to the better grade of mud here, because it is wet from a steady water supply, something vital for building and living. They also rationalize why the Afghan has always built with mud and not stone . . . . saying that it has just always been the custom.

Hagie asks about dating and how Tom had met me in America, and I remain absent for that explanation, coming in again just as they begin a debate on why women are chadried and unequal in society, and what basis each "practice" has in the Koran. They justify the "one boy equals two girls" theory in inheritance because daughters leave the family, but sons bring in new family and must support them. The *chadris* is not in the Koran at all (as we already knew). The *suras* say a woman's head and arms and legs should be covered out of modesty . . . and the custom of covering the face only developed among the wealthiest—was it the Mughals?—and spread to everyone later. The Kutchis and those in the villages out in the farms, do not veil their women, though, they are careful to point out. These women must work the fields and to do so under a *chadris* would be impractical.

Hagie and his old *modir* have been good friends and we hear of the examination for the American University of Beirut which they had each taken, and failed.

Meanwhile Tom continually urges them all to eat . . . with the story of an Afghan student who got to the States and was offered food only once (instead of the customary three queries) and was afraid he had landed among the rudest people imaginable. They reassure Tom they will not hold back. Even so, tons of extra food remain.

. . . At school I learn that the father of a student in the 8th class, wealthy Nazifa, had been arrested and jailed the day before on charges of criticizing the Republic and Daud, or of having taken too many bribes, or of being too rich, or some equally nonsensical or illogical charge. There is a hesitancy to name the cause of the arrest, since its impossible to imagine . . . on the first score, that anyone would be foolish enough to speak against the government publicly, at this point, and on the second instance that it could even register with the authorities that one of their own is taking bribes, since the majority of officials at all levels do this as a matter of course. Why are some targeted?

Thursday . . . . Mirad and family go to Mazar . . . The ninth class, minus three students, followed by Tajenisa and her sisters who hastily explain how I must come in the morning to their house, appear for a visit. I had expected them at 2:00 for afternoon snacks . . . so I just proceed to feed them as if they had all already had lunch, with nuts and chips, candy and cookies, oranges and tea, and later bread. They are really such little girls; yet, there is a tremendous difference within each class, and between them.

After I get the teapot on, we begin the first stage of entertaining . . . examining the photographs, which they all but maul in their eagerness to touch and see each one, the best—always, always—being of my brother John's wedding, and of their own class, which brings on the cries of "Give me this one." They seem totally uninhibited in the house or in their roles as guests. Only the half-crazed Seeman persists and sulks when I, big-sister like, gently ignore her. Then we partake of the feast . . . they eat daintily of everything except the cookies and oranges and potato chips. Then we wander out to walk in the garden (after a rash of *"tashknob"* stops) and then back to see Tom, who in a rare abandonment of his normal retreat, entertains with the caterpillar-looking stalks of wheat which Suraya especially wiggles her hands to demonstrate to him; and to get pictures taken, myself among them.

We all go back inside to cool down, set the radio blaring, and as Tom exits, off to the bazaar to take what turns out to be untakable pictures in the covered parts, the girls sweep out of the room, set up the table as a drum, and take turns singing, drumming, and dancing. Lulah and Seeman show an amazing gracefulness and suppleness, their movements quite beautiful to the rather jangling music, They seem older than the other girls in their movement, totally self-possessed and wise to the very air around them, with each rhythm of their hands and feet and hips. Yet they are both young enough, the pubescence just beginning to turn to womanliness, to not appear repulsive, too sensual or coarse; they are just good dancers. About then Shazan begins begging the others to leave with her (from the beginning she has been the most nervous, worried, almost crying when I brought in the food or promised more). Finally Zegul (little miss quiet industry, gathering cups and sorting orange peals while the others played) and Leelah walk her to the corner, then come back to dance to more music from the radio and a menagerie of looks and comments as I give them my stocks of *National Geographic* to skim over for half an hour. Before long, they all leave, after I take a few more pictures, at least one of which captures the girls with the *chadris* down.

They were funny in their timing, in their insistence that they had all eaten at school before coming. They also showed an odd terror of a lizard on the garden gate (which they considered some sort of filthy *narakh* (Koran forbidden) creature, a kind of devil child I think. Consequently, they hadn't wanted to cross through the gate once they had seen it, and only did so with extreme fear and caution. Likewise, they showed their uniqueness, were curious, in their childish demonstration of the wiggly wheat stalk. Not a group or age notable for their capacity to ponder, after one-second looks at the millions of images in *National Geographic* they seemed content to just fly over everything they had glimpsed with a shriek or a nod, and no questions or comments.

. . . . A persistent pounding comes on the gate . . . . and when I finally open it, the old gardener comes rushing hotly in to divert the water to another direction; then out comes Zeebee with the bucket for carrying water, a pair of Mirad's shoes whose story I didn't catch at all, the baby and the rubber boots three sizes too big for her . . . She talks about how her sons had not originally been given their real names at birth, but only after a year or so were given them. She smiles proudly when she recalls how the visiting women had asked her baby's name, and then said, "Daud, that is our name, too."

Zeebee gives details then on Mirad's widowed sister. She can not remarry . . . is childless . . . must live as a kind of nonperson with her old parents or oldest brother now. She describes something else about nursing children and how long Habibullah had nursed compared to this one who seems ready to stop already, and how her people don't give food to the child for the first few days because the milk is sour—Is the essential colostrum considered unclean, or does the milk of someone else get given initially until the mother's milk is in? She laughs at how Mirad had been surprised to find a baby born when he came to Sare-pul after Ramazan, since her people—separated from their families by soldiering or work as it has happened now—have no way of knowing about such things. She recalls the advice she had gotten on Habibullah from some student at the other volunteers' house in Jalalabad and whom she had asked for birth control pills, before she found she was already pregnant . . .

And then she mimics how Habibullah pretends to leave with his father in the morning, calling out, "I'll come back soon," and then kissing her . . . .

> *[In the evening we follow a BBC coverage, a feature on Ezra Pound . . .]*

Up the next morning at 5:00, we scurry about as Tom gets ready to go off to fish with the teachers at his school . . . Someone, another teacher, comes just minutes afterwards to collect him. Graciously he invites me to come to visit with his family another weekend in the mountains, carefully reassuring me that he doesn't want me to be left out . . . Later, I am off myself to visit Tajenisa and her whole clan.

April 19, 1975

Yesterday, staggered and delighted, a full day in every sense.

I leave by gaudi at 10:30, riding as a kind of solitary princess in glory through the town, out to the fields and past the bazaar roofs like so many round buns in a baker's tin mold . . . Arriving at the great medieval manor house of Eqromboy's compound, I confront the labyrinthine passages going into court yards and upstairs to all the separate compartments. The Class 7 student, tall, lithe Nasreen, greets me and takes me to the women's guest room upstairs, the stage for about half of the afternoon's action. After a while all the other women and children come in, the mother in pale blue splendor, a mother of nine children, the older mother who sits toothless and mute in the corner, while the other children pass in and out, and the oldest sister who only studied to the sixth class and then was married, and now is twenty-one and has three children. The youngest nurses from her tired body.

About her, Zeagul tells me: The life of an Afghan women is very bad (she speaks in English, not wanting to hurt her sister, though usually they are very frank with each other). Because they must marry early and have many children and live in a stranger's houses (their husbands') and grow old quickly. I ask her if she worries about her own future and she tells me yes, because she has been "namzad" (engaged) for five years, since she was 12 years old and will probably be married after she finishes twelfth class. Her "intended" works in Kabul and she claims that she has never seen him, although his father's house is near her own. Later, as we walk from garden to garden of her various relatives, we pass the stout, pink-skinned father of her "fiancée, "who salaams us on the road.

My favorite for the day is the tiny sister, Hushi, who stays by my side most of the time, telling me *"tashekour"* in a parrot sweetened voice every time I turn around to catch her hands again. I ask about another girl, whom I've seen at school and who looks just like Tajenisa, and they explain that this girl, although a natural daughter, was given to a childless sister when she was two-years old, and that the girl is being raised in that family as a daughter, calling her real parents, aunt and uncle, although they know who birthed her. This is a common practice.

And, as they day moves on, I met three different women who can't have children, despite all sorts of of money they have spent consulting doctors about children and conception, all to no avail. One of them, who lives in the compound which is our last stop in the afternoon, is the oldest sister of the teacher Najiba, a petite quick women with huge deer eyes and long black braided hair, who speaks with a childish sadness and gentle way, She is an excellent tailor and keeps a magnificent flower garden, whose best blossoms she plucks for me and gives as a gift as we wander on through the compound. A large, bowlegged cow-faced women had just given birth to a child the week before and still moves as one heavy with child; and in another room a girl (a distant cousin, someone's new bride) lays on the floor covered with rugs and blankets, pounds of raw green mulberries spilled on the floor before us. They tell me she is very sick, with some sort of bleeding (dysentery) and they are trying to cure her with a broth of berries, along with other things.

We go then back to the main compound, where we sit and talk about the mother's operation for an eye aliment at the big foreign-staffed Noor Eye Clinic in Kabul and how she had been there a week and had recently come home to rest. Very thin and vulnerable, she caught something else, and so had to go back to Mazar for ten days, difficult days, in the cold winter until she was able to come home. She is still a delicate women but walks the whole long way with us in the afternoon, and supervises all the feast cooking.

Tajenisa tells me how the women of her family make the food for the 30 people of their compound and their cousins' next door, on alternative days. Consequently, they are always used to having a lot of mouths to feed, and in the process consuming as much as a *seir* of rice every day. Their father always hosts several men. Today the *saer-malim* from my school, and Kabirmullah who lives in their brother's apartment in the compound, and Esfandyar who is also a relative, are there to eat hungrily of the feast after I have finished, (in a rare reversal of the usual order of feeding the men before the women.).

After the mother tells of how many children she has had, and of those of the silent first wife in the corner (who has also given one daughter away at birth), I chronicle my own family and relationships. Then, we start talking about birth control pills. A frisky younger brother brings in a pen and paper for me to write down the magic "anti-baby" medicine, "the pill," which they all vow promptly to disperse to all their one-babied relatives. The girls and women were up and down the whole time, going out to check on the delicious food they are making (*mantu* dumplings full of meat, a sweet white pudding, fresh onions and parsley, yogurt and rice *pilau* and huge meatballs, and spinach); then come back again to sit. Finally, it is the hour for *nan.* It is brought in quickly and we all eat huge quatities. Plate after plate is pushed on me; I eat heartily because the flavor is excellent and I enjoy it, but with a considerable amount of discomfort because they expect and enforce that I eat three times what everyone else is consuming.

A cousin (from the family whose father had recently been arrested) joins the women's circle. She is a tiny first grader, and some food is put royally before her as well. Our dinner is over quickly, the dishes and floor covering cleared away, and new and refreshed dishes are taken into the bright front room, where the men are assembled for their lunch.

Halfway through their feast, I am taken in to "make a picture," I had previously tried one of the inside of the women's room, but this one is straight into the sun and obviously not going to work, Yet, one just doesn't argue with the *"sibe* of the *xona"* (men of the household) so I ceremoniously, if sceptically, take these pictures.

At some point I ask Zeagul about the Koran and if it speaks of women having to cover their faces and she tells me it says right there Moslem women must wear this kind of *chadris* (sic). Another time she and her sister Nasreen caution me anxiously about going to the witch's house with the 10th class on Monday.

"But I know nothing about it," I explain. So they tell me the woman there does spells against *djinns* and *kaffirs* and will beat me and say terrible curses against me since I am not a Moslem, and if I go I will have a lot of trouble. I assure them I will not go, that the mysteries of the smoke-filled room and magic spells will remain unknown to me, for all my curiosity, because I value my own faith and person more than the raw facts of experience in this case.

Lunch is finished then, myself well-stuffed. Nervous Tajenisa has had one eighth of my portion, I discover, and her other sisters have eaten even less, but I think I succeeded in convincing them that I both liked and appreciated their food. I stretch a few minutes as they all scurry about to serve the men, and then bring in tea (the second of these batches it will turn out).

We stand and everyone combs her hair before we set out to the first garden. I am carried away in the eager arms of Tajenisa and Zeagul and Nasreen, and the little Hushi. We are a crowd: The mother and first wife, and another brother's wife and the nursing sister-mother, another brother's wife who hasn't been able to conceive, and three frisky little brothers like stairsteps. Also with us are the three orphan children of another sister-in-law and the woman herself. The man—he must be a brother or an uncle—had been shot to death in some demonstration or riot five years before. The children have fair skin and gigantic eyes reflecting their mother's hazel tones, and the mother is thoroughly round and Irish-looking. In the garden we gather for pictures, and the whole crowd is excited, pointing proudly to the water irrigation ditches, the basin for washing clothes, the line for drying them, and the trees of pomegranates at the other end.

We leave, pass back through the house and move again into the street to a wide shady orchard, the estate of an older half-brother (these are all the children of the first, oldest wife it seems, darker-bodied than any of the other, younger children), who is there with several workers and a 10th class student, a real brother. Among the rows of trees and a small barnyard with the brother sitting with his cow, and in between flowers, more pictures get shot, myself among the others; this time Tajenisa snaps away and then Zeagul, in turn, as I stand with one or the other.

We parade back to the house, past Islamadeen Khan's garden (my teacher is their neighbor, and another relative), and we sit in the cool upstairs for a few minutes. Then the old squirely father asks me to take his picture with his whole clan; I do so in the bright sun of the first courtyard. Before lunch I had gone out to the back courtyard to the *tashknob*, quite a journey, with Zeagul leading in a regal procession, past the new calf, and the roaring oven fires where all the women were gathered to make the meal) carrying a roll of TP they had gifted me with, special for the occasion.

After another rest inside, during which the daughters all change into their best clothes—bright silken pajama tunics tops and wide flare pants—we set off to the desert beyond their compounds, down the mud wall lane to a small stream, past the old mosque and house where the daughters had gone as tiny children, on and on to the open meadow where one woman stops in disbelief to ask me who I am, refusing to accept that I could be a foreigner as foreigners have never been here before. The woman lags behind us and we move on to "a high spot," and sit and have more pictures. We meet another group of visiting girls out walking, and Zeagul moves in a special dramatic pose against the mountain. Then they all line up against the hill, with the backdrop the city below.

Finally Zeagul, tall, long black-haired elegant and graceful, takes my hand and we run barefooted through the fields, out among the thistles and grass and wild flowers. We meet two boy with a teapot and slingshot who have been in the mountains gathering flowers. The others catch up with us after a while, and it is on to another garden, flowing riverlets between shade trees and workers against the wall. At each field as yet gray and fallow, someone in the family points out to me which land belongs to them, and what grows there, while the little children frisk ahead to steal green fruit and almonds from the hundreds of trees.

Down one lane we meet some other students in the shadow of the family compound, and talk a while until we can again gather ourselves. They feel, at 5:30, that I must be starting to be tired, so we move again into another relative's compound, and gather flowers. I find the old white-haired patriarch is the very man whose guests I had been on our first night in Tashkurghan, 20 months back when the commandant took us off in the dark to the rich man's house, and I sat rigid and awkward with the men until I had semi-collapsed from some exhaustion, fear, and very real malady and they let me go sit in the garden with the women, at that point just secretive tending shadows in the dark.

From that house, then we go back to have tea and exchange farewells at the main house. Finally, the visit ends. I leave in their paid *gaudi,* my arms full of violets and roses, to arrive home at 6:30 p.m. In the cool air, I sit with Zeebee, over tea and and a tiny sliver of cake, as the neighbor boys vault over the fence with mud clobbers from a battle in the alley, the broken pieces almost showering us, and night comes in.

Tom appears about 7:30 and we share bread and cheese (from the 9th class). He presents one of his "caught" ducks to Zeebee and later gives her another, but keeps the fish for ourselves. So I hear the details of his day: visualize the place 30 kilometers down the road, and the goatherders in the hills who gave them fresh goat's milk, and the teacher's recreations of net fishing and card playing. He shows how the men took turns wearing Tom's straw hat. There, too, there had been a discussion of birth control pills, a concept and medicine which, his colleagues had told Tom, they only object to because their wife must to subjected to some sort of internal examination to get the pills. Once the picnic and hunting and fishing were over, the group struggled to find a way home: the road was empty, no transport evident, until someone sighted one Waz with binocular from far away. It ignored them, whizzing by (it held two women being rushed to the hospital in Mazar, they decided), until finally an empty Waz came and they climbed on . . . .

. . . The next day . . . Janice the nurse from Kabul appears . . . . In the evening we hear of the social life of Kabul, the small circle of people there, and the many cultural events through the embassies and USIS. The previous week the international school had put on a production of "The Mikado."

She describes the nursing assistant program at her school, which takes seventh graders and turns them out to "practice" in 18 months, students who have been exposed to a lot relevant to medicine and care, but who absorb very little of it. Then she treats us to the details of a recent trip she had taken to Russia and the "tourist-oriented bubble," whereby foreign visitors are separated from the Russian people, shops take only hard currency and the clerks perform their duties with major indifference. Yet the major cities are heavy with the huge monuments and memorabilia to Russian heroes and czars, from Lenin to Peter the Great, and the massive Orthodox cathedrals and onion-bubbled towers haunt the avenues, most open as museums or for other purposes now. And traditional worksmen still make the petite, intricately-painted lacquer boxes.

We hear of Woodbury (from the U.S. embassy) and his theories on Islam, and how it is a religion oriented entirely toward actions of unquestioning obedience to certain established laws and procedures that a good Moslem must be always aware of, while Christianity bases itself on an individual having a personal commitment of faith. Thus, this animated and thoughtful woman and fellow volunteer explains, we can sum up the whole unquestioning nature of this society in a few thoughts: first, students think it is foolish to ask questions, and, second, the concept of exploration in sciences, psychology, religion, everyday life, is largely nonexistent. There is never any logical or even mystical (as with faith) foundation established or encouraged (except the sufis . . . who are buried among the persecuted Shi'iate minority here.)

But I wonder about the other eons of Islam, its ability to create, absorb, syncretize art, literature, medicine, astronomy in the ninth to the 13th centuries and the richness of its kingdoms. And when, and if forever, that synthesis and creativity has been turned around.

> *[I am chagrined to have used a picture of an electric dishwasher torn from a recent magazine to—unthinkingly—spur conversation in one class . . . . The students move dully, automatons about them . . . . and my mind has become like my bowels, gaseous and sieve-like . . .]*

. . . There is rain and a little lightning; roses bloom bounteously over all the yard, the soft, huge pink ones now. There is the beginning of mulberries and other fruit on the small shrubs and bushes.

I learn today of a great mistake . . . Zeebee always hides a present for Mirad's birthday and she had brought over a pair of new shoes for him and told me to hide them last week, but I had not understood and had put them in the kitchen instead. Of course, he quickly saw them, and thus we ruined her special ritual and surprise. Worst, I earned her disappointment . . .

April 22, 1975

. . . At sunset, we are visited by Suraya (9th class) and her mother and an elusive third figure. The women claims she is 42 and has had 11 pregnancies, none of which has led to surviving children. She tells us once she had gotten birth control pills, but they had caused her trouble, and now she wanted to try again. She had heard there was a doctor at our house and has come looking for pills. She had not had a period for nine months, so perhaps did not need anything, but she claimed that her sister had produced up to age fifty. Convinced she has had enough, she demands to know what I use. Uselessly perhaps, she takes my empty Ortho-Novum box and sets out. I have dispersed so many, to help woman know a name.

Yesterday we saw the first scorpion of the season . . . actually the second, and we realized we have accepted living in a certain abandonment to the possibilities of scorpion stings as close as the floor under our heads when we sleep, or when we sit on our *toshaks* on the floor.

Now we must look to ourselves.

Like a tocsin, an old fashioned bell of warning, jangling at us, something has again entered our lives and requires attention. Tom begins by telling me, after Janice left today, that he thinks we are wasting each other's time. As the talk moves forward, he says, sadly to my agreement, that everything with meaning in our relationship has died and that now we are co-existing stale, living on dull mundane shared table manners and nothing else . . . What ensues, then, is a long discussion of how he finds my comments on him critical, like saying we have soup all the time for lunch, or that his feet stink, or that I already know something he is about to go off on and explain, such as writing Macdonald about a job in Kabul which I had already looked into. He is unhappy with my general failure to be sensitive to his needs.

None of this is too surprising.

When we were talking with Janet about the couples in the last cycle who broke up for all practical purposes, Tom kept saying that the pressures for or against a marriage working, were (a) the fact that there are no other women (or men) to interfere and create rivalries or affairs, as a pro; and the fact that the two people are thrown so entirely on each other, as a con. The fact he puts so much emphasis on that "a" makes me wonder if it is not some great trauma in each of us that threatens to make shards of our relationship, but just that he is grown tired of my presence, my sexlessness or my non-striking body, or my unexploring mind, and thinks that along with looking for some future, binding career, he should also look a little more closely at the great field of women he had always been too serious a youth to explore before. He says I am no longer sensitive to how he feels, that all I can see in him is an anger at or rejection of me, and that I am not capable of looking into him any further or caring about what his real state of mind is.

I can echo that thought, convinced that he no longer has the desire to really know what I think or feel, just that we have known each other for seven years and in all that time he has never really wanted to read my "stories,"(granted I have held back to him instinctively, realizing the truth long before I read the quote by J.C. Oates, that she doesn't want her husband to read her things because she would tend to put too much emphasis and value on his interpretation and reaction to them, and never write just as herself) . . .

I say then . . . if we can not keep a tenderness here, where we can sit on our roof and watch the birds fly above the great fruited green mulberry trees and the swallows dart in the rich groves of fruit trees beyond the wall, and take in the scented sweetness of fine rosebushes like beautiful girls in their rich greens in the yard around us, and watch the sun set and the stars come up, and hear the quiet of the ribboned hills, as ancient and peaceful as a perfectly preserved tale of life, and where we only really must teach half a day and have the other time somewhat "free," and where our food is mostly cooked for us and we have only to take care of our responsibilities to ourselves and our professional duties as teachers and social exchanges with students and neighbors—if in such a situation we can let that tenderness die, what chance could there before us when we're in some dumpy apartment in a big city and he is grueling over three years of dull law books and accumulating $15,000 of debt and I'm furthering my way at some job as yet unknown but one certainly without the rewards I would want from it, and our childlessness grows into an embarrassment—what chance then? . . .

So I let out my tears, in the face of his bizarre (to me) examples of my shortcomings, each of which makes me feel little and also makes me think one of us is totally wrong, or ill, or something . . . .

Is this a conversation we will have for 20 more days or 20 more years? What can I do to change? What about him? Something is wrong, for we are each always lonely, I think.

. . . It's time to work, so I go off to school where my 11th class asks me with great concern what is wrong with my eyes.

"Have you been crying? Do you miss your family? Have you quarreled with Tom? Are you sad because your guest has left?"

They persist, not believing my lie that I had had a bad dream . . . . The tenth class is equally inquisitive, and so on for the ninth, each of them telling me I must have cried a lot to get my eyes so swollen and red. (Still hovering, the thoughts too close to forget, so that I know I am yet on the verge of tears and must control myself in front of my students, is Tom's comment that he wonders if we would take very long to adjust to a separation, once we decided that that was what we needed, and that this would be a measure of how much feeling we actually shared.) I tell the girls, "It is nothing . . . ."

. . . I remember what our visitor Janet had said, about finding in one small garden in the middle of Moscow a memorial to Peter the Great, which meant more to her than all of Russia, because for a moment her mind could focus on something small and memorable (two old men, and their canes and babushka-ed wives on park benches in the shade, beside an old ivy-coated stone guard house); and where, briefly, she could walk in the cold air without being forced to concentrate or be trained. There is in me, then, that kind of sense.

Or the indignity she witnessed in the old Indian chief at the state hospital where she had worked in Nebraska, who spoke only Sioux. He had a massive operation for cancer and had to excrete out of a tube. She recalled another from Rapid City who was in for multiple knife wounds (his name was Wounded Head), and while he was there massive floods in Rapid City left him isolated; she had tried to track down his family through the Red Cross, but found no one.

In a world of such lost souls, such real grief, how can we create animosity, false traumas?

. . . I wind my way home . . . and sit outside among the rose bushes and under the mulberry tree, to read. But soon Habibullah and Zeebee and Daud appear at the garden gate and finally, when the gate is opened and I walk into the yard to find them, we begin a slow promenade through the green gardens full of some wounded trees and some rampant weeds. We let Habibullah blow away all the dandelion balls, *"puff kadane"*—ing at every pause. We find worms sunning on a stalk stripped of its leaves now (later Mirad comes out and kills them all), and Zeebee shows me where water had flooded yesterday and undermined the wall because the water gateman did not divert the stream in proper time. We look at a rosebush against the wall, until Habibullah leads us to the shed at the end of the yard where their chicken first hid her fertilized eggs. After the little boy is content that he has seen all there is to see, we exit back into our yard where he proceeds to entertain himself by wrapping and unwrapping a piece of wood in an old patched handkerchief, while Zeebee and I sit on the veranda and watch him and the roses.

He had told her he was going to school in the morning, then shook her hand, and trotted to the gate, then returned hastily, saying he was back . . . . When Mirad returns from his lesson with Tom he shooshes them all home . . . We avoid a visit by the Hajie Biron Dawanah (CrazyOne), as Tom sets off to a basketball game at his school.

Mirad tells me why lizards are considered very dirty animals: old people say that if they have a *jewob-e-choie* (defecate) on your head or any part of your body, the skin will become ugly and sore like the boils left by a blight; and others think the creatures can look at your teeth and make them fall out . . . .

Finally Tom returns, we eat too much dinner; and on the porch afterwards I tell him all the bad Mullah Nasruddeen stories I'm teaching my classes now. Earlier I describe the little old gardener men at our school and their constant battle with the students and teachers to keep the trees, bushes and flower gardens unmutilated . . .

We remember the folk story of the crow and the snake, one of many. The crow's young were always being eaten by a snake. So Crow asked jackal what he should do to protect his young. "Blind the snake when he is asleep," the Jackal said. But the snake was too far in his hole, and none could reach him. Then jackal's wife said to take a garment from a wall where it was drying in the village. They fetched one and the snake crawled out of his hole to sun on the cloth. Immediately, the village people killed him to regain their garment. And, so, the crow was always safe from the fatal fangs of his neighbor.

Mullah Nasruddin stories come up and over us like a tap left running in a basin, flooding the floor, soiling everything, bringing our attention to both the fragility and resilience of humanity and its foibles:

Once when Mullah Nasruddin and his son were on a journey, the Mullah let his son ride the donkey, while he walked. Passersby scorned him, asking why he spoiled the boy, so he switched with the child and rode himself, while the boy walked. Again, people criticized him, so he secured both himself and his son on the animal and went further along the way. Seeing this, people began to jeer at him, calling out that he was cruel to make the poor animal bear so much weight.

"Very well," thought the good Mullah, who proceeded to dismount and take his son with him. They continued with both of them walking, and the donkey bare.

Now, of course, people made fun of him for wasting the donkey, for having the creature carry nothing while both son and Mullah walked. At this point, the Mullah lifted up the poor creature and placed him on his shoulders.

"Come on," he called. "If we do not do this, it will be impossible to make people stop talking." And so they walked on.

In another story, Mullah Nasruddin was sitting under the shade of a walnut tree. As he looked out, he noticed a huge pumpkin that was growing on a skinny vine nearby. Studying the tree above him, he saw the small walnuts growing everywhere on the huge tree.

"Now, why is this?" he addressed Allah.

Just then, a walnut fell from the tree overhead and landed on his head.

"Oh, God, forgive my questioning. Where would I have beem now if pumpkins grew on trees?"

In yet another tale, the Mullah and his wife were at home one evening, when they heard a strange noise. When Mullah Nasruddin went outside, he saw something white moving. He reached for his rifle and shot it. Immediately, his wife ran outside.

"You unlucky man, "she shouted, "You just ruined your best shirt, which I washed and hug out this day."

"Oh, no," he insisted. "I am the luckiest of men. If I had worn that shirt today, I would have killed myself."

There are hundred of them:

When invited to a banquet at a very wealthy man's house, Mullah Nasruddin dressed in his everyday clothes, so as not to appear pretentious, and sought entry at the host's gate. No one would let him in. So off he ran to his house and dressed again, this time in his fanciest and finest robe. Upon approaching the host's gate, he was immediately ushered in and seated at the guests' table.

When the soup arrived, Mullah Nasruddin began to dunk the sleeve of his robe into the bowl and admonish the robe to eat up and enjoy.

"Why are you doing that?" The host asked him,

"Well," said the Mullah, "I can only assume that it was the coat and not I who was invited to your banquet, so I am making sure it feels welcome and is well-fed."

Again, once Mullah Nasruddin was riding his donkey backwards. People, noticing his odd position, called out to him. "Why are your riding your donkey backwards?"

"No, "he replied confidently. "I am not backwards. It is not that. Rather, the donkey is going the wrong direction."

Another time, the Mullah was sitting on a chair and eating an egg, when a man came by.

"Are you sitting on a chair and eating an egg?" the man asked?

Mullah replied quickly, "Why? Should I be sitting on an egg and eating a chair instead?"

Yet again, Mullah Nasruddin got a new donkey and showed it to a neighbor. "I will be glad to lend him out," he told the man, "whenever you need him."

So the neighbor came to borrow the animal one day and the Mullah told him he was already loaned out. Just then, however, they both heard the sound of a braying donkey.

"But Mullah, I heard your donkey now in there."

Mullah responded, indignant. "Do you believe me, or the donkey?"

Reflections of An Afghan-American

After the initial Soviet influx, from 1979-1982, everyone I heard from was losing family members, having them disappeared or killed or imprisoned or forced into exile. Every family came with stories of how their houses were burned or looted, or how they lost their babies. The horror stories were endless. Yet Afghans abroad remained silent for years because those who had managed to escape were in shock. Later, they would speak of what they had heard or experienced, the loss of everything they had—their family members, their livelihoods, their friends, their memories.

Those I met, in Germany or the U.S., overwhelmingly showed deep psychological wounds, not just from losing country and material goods, and children or other family members; but also their pride. They woke up to find themselves poor refugees, at the bottom of everyone in society, compelled to start all over among strangers in a strange land. Not only did they have to adjust to a new environment and culture, but also they were under the terrible weight and memory of this recent history and its hurtful effects. They knew they would never go back to their own country, that that life and all it involved was gone forever. They grieved, knowing all that remained of their past was some paper, a picture album, or some reflections

I learned about people's fates from the people themselves. As I met them, they shared bits of their own lives and what they had been through and lost, escapes through the Khyber Pass over a month by camel and by foot, being hidden for days, then moved on a little further, then traded off among different smugglers. These human traffickers sold off refugees to each other, and in desperation people paid huge amounts to get smuggled out. The trafficker would set a price for a family, based of whether or not it had been wealthy, and then the family had to pay the amount the different traffickers bid on as a price to get that family out of the country. By the time these families reached Pakistan, or the States, they had practically nothing left. Although, they had taken what they could when they left, they had had to give it all to the smugglers and the traffickers. They just managed to save their lives and that was all they did or had.

Beyond the devastating conditions in the country at that time, the murdering and torturing of people, there was also the whole Soviet indoctrination, the Soviet attempts to oppose traditional life and to impose new social rules on the people, an approach which sparked the resistance. A lot of people were terrified. People could not even listen to BBC, because that was considered anti-government. In the classic totalitarian style, sons were turned against fathers. The push in every institution from kindergartens to high schools, even in the gardens or teahouses, everywhere you went, was this talk to get rid of the old life and embrace the new life, to trust the future and to not obey your parents or respect traditions. A generation was being told that the new way of life which the Soviets were introducing was the one to follow.

Because of Communism, the talk was, Afghanistan would now move quickly to take its place among modern nations. People had to do as the government told them so this progress could happen, the indoctrination went. In this period, the government even took large numbers of high school and college students, more than 15,000, and sent them to study and stay in the Soviet Union and Eastern Europe, to indoctrinate and train them as the future cadre leaders. They were to serve in a future Afghan Politburo and were trained as traitors. The government interjected itself into everyone's daily lives, so that people could no longer trust each other, and feared to talk openly to each other. There was this teaching that children should turn in their parents, sons must betray their fathers. Rapidly, the very basic fabric of the society was destroyed. That was a major change.

So that began even before the initial Soviet invasion, this taunting and deprivation of Afghans and of their culture. Sadly, in a different way right now, Americans are doing the very same. We are following a policy that makes the Afghans angry and which calls up aspects of the Soviet era. Our language is about democracy, not communism, but still we preach that democracy is good for them, that democracy is the only way to go. In fact, they do not want our version of democracy and that is why they are resisting or failing to enact it. Such a democracy is unrelated to Afghan history, and most people do not like to be told either how to live or how to govern. While we want them to know a whole lot about this new civilization, "globalization," this new modern life, we do not know ourselves what should be the prelude to any change in society. Such changes can not be forced, but rather they must come from the people themselves.

People have to accept a new government first. No matter what we do or say or try to train, if people do not want this for themselves and it is not part of what they define as what they want, it will not happen. They will not accept what another government imposes on them. It is ironic that our initiatives since 2002 will all come back to haunt us because of the resentment. Seriously, if someone wants to eat with his hands then he will eat with my hands. And, likewise with government.

I can get up and talk about this issue for hours: I am sorry that in this respect of alienating people, there is nothing different between what the Americans are trying to do and what the Soviets did. We each just insist on prevailing in our way. The Soviets paved the roads so the tanks could go on them, but Afghan people did not want the roads paved nor the tanks on the roads.

Then the thinking is:

Take your pavement for your own purposes and shove it. We are satisfied with the way it is. However, if you do pave the roads, stay with us to use the roads. But, if you are telling us you are building these roads for us but they are really just for you, then that is not acceptable.

Unfortunately, as well, American soldiers in Afghanistan in the last six years, act even more arrogantly than the Soviet ones did, because there is a huge difference in the expectations and lifestyle of the present American soldiers and that of the Soviet ones. The Soviet soldiers came from a poor country and with low expectations; they were satisfied with a piece of bread, some cheese, and some vodka, so to speak. But our soldiers come from twenty-first century America. They are pampered all the way and what comes across too often, the way they look at ordinary people in Afghanistan is "You are cockroaches. Get out of my way." Obviously, no one likes that arrogance. Many of the Soviet soldiers sent to fight here came from Central Asia and were Tajiks and looked like Afghan Tajiks. They also were of their ethnicity and spoke the language. Yet they knew the culture, more or less, and they still quickly acknowledged the impossibility of winning the Afghan's "hearts and minds." They thought they were bringing "freedom" and "modernization" to a backward, neighboring country. But they were hated as invaders and enemies.

There is no way the U.S. can win this war, not in a million years, not with bombs. They can never transfer democracy in the shadow of B-52s or cluster bombs. It just can not be done.

At the same time, our servicemen are often angry, because they can't understand why the Afghans don't want their help. But the pervasive thinking in the country is that these are people who invaded Afghanistan, that they are no different than the Soviets in that respect. Further, the mistake of trying to impose a lifestyle, a political style, is just like the Soviets and the failure and humiliation will be the same.

I have no doubt in my mind that the U.S. can drop a few big bombs somewhere and then call it a "victory." But they will not conquer Afghanistan or the neighboring regions. Strategists can bomb these people to ***the stone age****, where they essentially are now, but no one is going to win. Now even a 7-year old whom you encounter on the street will show hostility toward the U.S. It is tragic.*

—Notes from interviews conducted in Fall, 2007

XIV
DEPARTURES

April 23, 1975

A huge English rose, a single one to each stalk, deep dawn-colored, dons our table this morning. It is Mirad's gift from the delicate bush outside, which we've been eying for several days. He is also working himself up to sheer joy over the imminent ripening of the white mulberries. For all his years in Jalalabad he never had this berry which he loves. Several times a day he runs outside to chase away birds from the huge bower of a tree and last night he explained how the ripe berries are gathered. A hug net of cloth is spread out by several people under the branches, and as one person climbs up and shakes the branches, one at a time, the bounty catches in the net. Then all can feast.

A student presented Tom with the gift of a hat today at school, one he had admired the day before, and which precipitated his getting his head measured. This is the student who last year tore up his own exam paper when Tom had persistently told him to turn around while he was writing, an action that set off a full investigation by the proctors and inspectors and a testimony by the class. As a result, the boy earned a zero on his written test, but the teachers let him pass with a 3 ½, thanks to his remarkable performance on the oral part of the exam. But this boy misses about 80% of all his classes, because he is the head boy scout of the school and consequently is forced to do all sort of work errands for the teachers and administrators. Alas, education or position?

Tom is a bit grim about the collapse of order at his school with the new *modir*. The fact is that students don't go to class anymore, that no one can keep order, that the new *modir* is a gentle jesting Yusef who is four and a half feet of good wits and unstinting allowances. It takes so little to make a good school from the point of view of discipline, Tom persists, and because this element has been undermined so badly no one can even call his place a school anymore. (It suffers from more than just the way it ignores always poor standards of scholarship). At least the old arrogant principal could manage things with his iron hand, and for appearance sake and undercurrents, the school ran smoothly with him, although he taunted Tom and others wretchedly, and the teachers and their methods were no more skilled or effective for the most part.

. . . On the radio news, we hear of a pre-conference in Nairobi, Kenya about "the habitat of man". The point will be to discuss environmental problems and man's discontent everywhere with the way he is ruling his surroundings and ruining them, especially in the First World, which consumes 80 per cent of the resources and creates that same amount of pollution, but contains a fraction of the world's population. A larger conference will convene in the future in Vancouver . . . . Will an international movement be able to halt greed and rapacity, to reverse capitalism's fine dance to acquire comfort and huge wealth for a few, at the price of the earth and all its people's future?

April 26, 1975

We were up at 5:30 yesterday . . . and at about 6:30 Tom and Mirad set off for the old city ruins for a much advertised *cawk* fight.

Tom later tells me of the hundreds of people gathered and the absurd, almost dull ritual of the fights, where two stumpy-footed plump birds are set down in a small ring with their cages (bottoms removed) still over them, Then the fight begins, and it consists of the birds pecking each other with their sharpened beaks until they get tired and dry. Then one begins to run in circles around the other. Their cages are clamped over them again and the two keepers squat down next to them and fan them with their *peron*, get water, drink it themselves, then squirt it into the bird's mouths to cool them down. The absurd bodied, now viscous nature of the birds make the fights odd and a little boring, but Tom and Mirad had stayed among the crowd there until 10 . . . .

Azarullah, the Kid, comes over then and we plan a walk to the mountains. Tom finds oranges and eggs and bread, and I make Koolaid and we eventually set out about 11:00 with the basket of simple fare. This time we hike out past Najiba's house, along the old road to Kabul, past the fertile gardens behind high walls, reaching the highway eventually, and then past the old men sleeping in the sun, stopping in a curve of the road to watch some bright-colored (pale blue, yellow and white) birds flutter across a thin mountain ridge. Later Azarullah tell us these birds are used for medicine, their meat having a tart, curative quality. An old *cawk*-fighter watches us from across the highway and when Azarullah runs up the hill to get two doves nesting in a crack of rock to fly up and show their colors (though they stay still) he exclaims indignantly that they are holy birds and it is forbidden, a sin, to bother or strike them. We move on then, and the old man lags behind, finally calling out from a kilometer back to some figures further up the road, asking them if they are dead or alive.

The villages are green beyond us, men working barefooted in their elaborately carved up fields to catch the water, planting rice and cotton now, while the fruit trees fall behind them and the richly covered town of roofs and walls, glows like a beautiful emerald curtain.

It begins to get cloudy; there is a moist shell in the air which we are going to have with us for the whole day. Outside the Tangi, Azarullah asks us to guess how many "seat" (volume of water? Resident villages?) there are along the gorge way. He tells us there are 200. The river is rushing full and violent below us now and as we enter the gorge we see the shattered concrete markers along the cliff where there had been a rock fall several weeks before. The debris falls from high up in the gorge hills, gathering, a whole army of pelting heaving particles as it pounds on to the highway and ultimately the river bed below. We plan to cross the river and go up to a meadow somewhere on the other side, but for a few minutes Azarullah seems overcome with the difficulty he imagines such a crossing will cause us. Finally Tom steps in cautiously, finds he can go all the way across, with the water only a little above his knees. He carries the camera and basket over, while I roll up my pants immodestly and Azarullah starts out ahead of me, insisting I grasp a long stick he holds out to me. The other side reached, we put on our shoes and begin up a sudden steep hill, which sets me huffing and puffing like an old hog. I am glad to reach the expansive meadow we are to sit in for the next few hours, a green soft stretch of grass and poppies, which is a little pungent with sheep dropping like shrunk grass.

Azarullah tell us that when he was here two years ago the whole field was covered, carpeted with the thick growth of flowers. We explore the meadows a while, then sit down for our lunch and speak of little in particular, just watching the curtain of folded hills beyond us, the velvety red and green colors manifestations of unknown things, grass and iron or copper. We wonder.

Speaking of the significance of the poppy flowers, Azarullah tells us there are more than 55 varieties of this red flower, each more beautiful than the other, but that in poetry, the red petals of the flower are said to represent the red lips of the loved one and the diamond white design in their center is representative of the clear teeth of the same beloved.

The boy is flustered today, trying to explain the word "awshook" to us. He says this flower is also always associated with this feeling, bearing the sense of lovesick or love starved or sad love or such. Tom tells him of the poppy fields over the dead soldiers in Europe, and the poem about it, and the notion of the blood of the dead growing out again on the earth, as a living memorial.

It grows dark and calm in turn. Far away we see the rain coming, but we play Frisbee a while, before setting out again up the mountain. Here we run into some old hill men who have been up collecting chicory and now give us some. Going on, we capture a formidable picture of the gorge and the flat, blinding bright plain beyond it. We go slowly up ridges, stopping under a pistachio tree as the cold chilling rain falls down indiscreetly and the whole land slides down below us, the pens built by the shepherds for the newborn lambs looking like gray designs of ancient Stonehenges from our visage point high above them. We gather wild flowers, then sit again as the clouds lift and blue sweeps over us for a few minutes. I go down the hill ahead of Tom and his student and watch bright red, green and yellow parakeet-like birds dive down the ravines, and have to marvel at the delicate rootless lichen growing on the bare stones in places where there is no soil. I wonder, thinking that there must be some plan for all of this.

We climb down then, to meet an expedition of chicory carvers and hunters coming down from the craggy mountains well beyond where we have hiked. Their scrubby donkeys ford the river and they carry great loads of thistle and chicory across. We ourselves cross and move back through the gorge as the rain starts up again in full fury. We meet two more of Tom's students, one a handsome 11th grader in a suede hunting vest and with dark, long black hair, the other the brother of Foolara (12th grade), who at his gate pauses and beckons for us to come in for tea. But we just go on after many and profuse apologies, for it is late and we are all wet and the way to our compound is another hour at least. We walk quickly, finally coming again to the old road to our house. Sighted by Najiba's family this time, I must be polite, so I duck in and see the garden briefly, and then beg my way out as they come running after me with fresh flowers.

[Mirad has gone off to a wedding this day, and before that walked to the old city and the gardens . . . with his family.]

. . . This morning Mirad tells us at breakfast what a fine wedding there had been last night, with two tons of *pilau* and tea and candy. There were two loudspeakers and a phonograph and loud and clear music everywhere, and a foreigner and his wife had been guests and they had been hennaed . . .

We are off to school . . . and a quick targeting in by the Samagan "spy" about Vietnam and how the U.S. Congress has now finished their term. He confronts me, speaking of the U.S. in general, claiming how rich "we" were to have paid so much money to such a small country so that there must have been something awfully important for "us" to have stayed there all those years, and how "we" should leave now.

All of these comments lap over me like flood water, painful, as if I were personally responsible for each act of degradation and folly rendered to that land, or the decade of destruction brought by foreign policies by the U.S. Government. I take a deep breath and tell him I'm hoping it is all finished now, that any American money spent there had been poorly spent, that innocent people have died, that people with needs in the U.S and in other countries have been denied the life they deserve—

But he persists until the *saer-malim* reminds him that it was a private business between governments and that I (Frances) have nothing to do with it. He leaves, and the *modir* and *saer-modir* together tell me that all governments make mistakes. They bring in the example of Pushtoonistan, which Afghanistan for years has had and led quarrels over, and how everyone knows this is not good or just. Yet "the bad bawd" (bad air) continues, and thus it was the same to them, the individual people, as the Vietnam question was to people like me, and to most all of the American people. So that conversation is laid to rest. Again.

April 27, 1975

Yesterday's full schedule involved school and tutoring of Shahzadah . . . We had a feisty discussion of what god and prophets we all believed in; and which people were rich and which poor, and who should marry and why, and why her "old school" teachers in Lashkagar had taught her better, and how Afghan girls have to endure the "ignorance" of the mullahs who tell them they shouldn't pick flowers because it is not good work for young girls. Or do anything. She speaks of a cousin who went to France seven years ago and has not come home since, although his mother in Taloqan cleans the room for his arrival everyday, and everyone except the mother suspects he has married a French girl. Since the mother told him he must marry a Moslem, Shahzadah believes that he is afraid to write otherwise . . .

This is a smart, successful family, one knowledgeable of the world beyond not just this small ancient village, but also this country. They've tasted, actually supped fully, on Western, i.e. American ways and lifestyles, and the kind of expectations they have can not help but clash with the reality of life here now. And yet, in the malcontent in this young girl, Shahzadah, I think, too of one of Mirad's stories, the folk tale of the blind man and the youthful carpenter. According to the story, there was a blind man who was a good musician, but had a "viciousness of mind," and there was also a youth who was skilled in the craft of carpentry and had "a frank disposition." They set off on horseback and after they had traveled together several days, the blind musician, who did not trust the carpenter youth, felt for his whip and found something smooth. The youth told him it was a snake, but the blind man would not believe him. Then suddenly, as they entered the sunlight, the creature came alive and when the blind man reached for what he thought was his whip, he touched the snake. The creature bit him, injecting his poisonous venom, and the man died.

> *[My 20-year old brother, Danny, traveled from Europe to Afghanistan. The letter announcing his plans would not arrive for another couple of weeks. As he appears in town, he stops to play soccer at the boy's school, before being led to our house.]*

April 28, 1975

. . . Yesterday I caught a lame *chim-chuck* (sparrow) under the mulberry tree and took it to Mirad's boys to show. In a great bursting of energy the creature fluttered off the porch several times, and Mirad showed his terror of it, when little Habibullah let him snuggle under his shirt. After a while the creature came back to my feet and chirruped up a mighty wave of sadness and protest, and lamely fluttered down to the ground where he must eventually have lost life . . . .

Mirad's sad sister, Zeebee tells me, does not want to live anymore, for she has no life, being a non-person without child or husband.

"Rahnee Dawanee" (the communist teacher from Hajie Boran village) was over at the house and has asked for the following: a typewriter, dictionaries, diamonds, a plastic watch, a job with Peace Corps, a hunk of *lapis* for him, and a fellowship to the States . . .

Five a.m. Monday morning. The birds are already gathering in the mulberry trees, they've lost their fear of the colored people clothes Mirad has wittily thrown up there. So Mirad has brought himself a slingshot and certainly should be keeping the creatures under a strong eye. A full moon is still out, about to go down, the day clear with a touch of cool. Far off a donkey brays. We are to have lunch today for several *haragees* in town, a Dutch anthropologist and an American doctoral student from Harvard, Margaret Mills, who reads Persian and has been researching Afghan folktales in Herat for six months . . . .

I read my note on Indries Shah, an Afghan-Indian and English translator of the Mullah Nasradeen tales. He sees them as basic to Sufi teachings, a medium for conveying much deeper ideas than the surface impression, and thus an acceptable means to convey the ideas, morals, and humor from century to generation.

April 29, 1975

It was quite a full days' happenings starting with my school day yesterday morning when I was given several hundred "*chesma-ton rashanees*" (your eyes are bright) by teachers and students upon the news that my brother had arrived . . . . And the lunch guests were exceptional, of course, too.

The folklorist has permission from the Ministry to go out to likely places with her tape recorder and record stories, etc. So, she has been collecting folk tales for months. Today she shared a sample.

She told us the tale of the bride at one wedding who climbed up a tree and refused to come down and be with her betrothed. The ox had been slain and the guests and family were all gathered around for the festivities, but she would not budge from her seat in the tree. In fact, she claimed that all of those gathered below were old meanies, not the sort she wanted to mingle with now, for forcing this on her. Though her father begged her, and the mother and sister and brothers each presented their pleas, she wouldn't descend. Finally the groom himself asked her, and then she asked him why didn't he come up to her. He did. Then they were both turned into white doves and flew away . . . eternal, independent lovers, the end moral might have been, or something entirely different.

The anthropologist and folklorist set off to try to rent a truck to Bamiyan, and then my student Shahzadah comes by to invite us to lunch for the next day, followed by Azarullah and his invitations. Dan and Azarullah talk, initially in response to Dan's question of, "Do you ever think about the meaning of life?"

Azarullah pauses, but graciously rises to the occasion, answering what he takes the question to be. So he rattles on coherently in English about the time of civil war here, forty or fifty years ago when there was blood and fire in every household and a lot of fighting between Pushtoons and other tribes. A lot of it was centered around hatred of the Hazaras, he said. These families would be mounted on horses or against a wall and just riddled with gunshots, and there was no follow-up to protect them, from the government. Since then, time has improved the country in those senses he claims, but now it must learn to utilize all its mineral resources, gold, oil, iron, sulfur, and others . . . .

Dan blinks and says he is glad life has new hope and meaning.

We finally leave to go to Mazar, but not before Dan has a conversation with a blue-eyed, silver-bearded man who welcomes him proudly and asks all about him, and then as he answers thank you in English to everything, the old man ends by saying to Danny, "thank you, thank you." We meet Amore M'med who greets us proudly on hearing this is my brother and so on, greetings and congratulations, until we go back to find Azarullah. He takes us up to the old city to view the rich green fields below us, and to recite a Persian poem.

The gist is this: friends were made to be close together like the blossoms on a tree to their limbs. They may be scattered over the whole field, yet they remain as of one tree.

We move on to a feast at Mirad's, to which we enter as the honored guests, to a mat on the floor with cut roses and his glistening dishes and full pots of warm food. His sons laugh or are shy on the porch or over a rice bowl, until they fall asleep. The lights are on us, and we begin a meal of great depth and magnitude—*pilau* with nuts and spices, thick rich *korma*, spinach and tiny fruit with stones like pebbles that Mirad bought from the bazaar (a fruit plentiful in Jalalabad, he tells us) and several kinds of candy and cake and tea and nuts and pistachios. All of this he puts before us, humbly presented, along with Fantas and cakes and his generous hand.

It is a beautiful evening, we speak in snatches, praising his ability to tell stories, hearing of his father's great knowledge of them, and how Najibullah, his little brother, has learned many more . . . We get a view of the newly pipped chickens, hear tales of catching *chim-chuk* and other tiny birds and preparing them for a special meal, and learn how Mirad had vowed to war against the birds in the mulberry tree . . . .

Tuesday, there is school and lunch at the tax collector's house. We find our old house (the tax collector had never moved after all) quite changed now with rich rugs and posters of Hindi movie stars on the walls. We enjoy a rich meal, talk of languages and visitors and the famous

Mr. Steele (Stele) from the States, who had been a friend and mentor in Lashkagar . . . .

Ziadeen and Rashed come over to tell us something, later when we get back home . . . and we are soon to begin a trip to Kabul . . . .

May 2, 1975

To go back a few days and pick up the pieces. We got up at 5:00 a.m. on Wednesday and set off in scattered glory to the *bande* to catch a bus at 5:30 or 6:00. As we exchanged our usual questions with others waiting on the road and the sun cleaned off the damp sheen on the encroaching hills, I again caught a hint of what it would be like to leave this place for good one day soon. There will be a veil of tears.

The first buses started coming about 6:30 and as their order established itself and no number four Haji Aqub appeared we began to panic, in what is my usual reaction to unrequited waiting, no matter how many times we confront it. The traffic policeman and several helpful passengers all gave their opinions on the lateness of the bus companies. When it finally came on we bull-headedly boarded, only to be told unconvincingly to get off again. We thought to get a Toyota with two wheeler-dealer type drivers, got in and agreed to a price, only to have the driver break out into a great row with a man on the street, at which point we bounded out.

Intrepidly we ran up to a non-official bus and boarded it. With entreaties from Tom and the traffic man and the cab drivers and all assembled, that Tom's money would be gotten back, and with me in tears spelling out the story to everyone around, and Dan looking stoically distracted, we set off on the "Friend of the Highway." Of course, this was a bus which was so intent on getting customers that it would stop whenever it saw anyone on the road—a child crossing, a man in the grass washing his hands, a shepherd with his staff—so that it was perhaps two hours to Samagan, another three to Doshee, and all the time I chattered at Danny every story I could recall about anything . . .

As they always do, the trip passed, the land everywhere more green and vivid with red fields of blood-red poppies, soft purple sprays of white lavender, yellow sprouts like clear, clean images after sunrise: people working with their simple plows in the ground, carving out their beds for more plants. In places, it was so green and patch-worked one thought of meadows in Switzerland or the tilled Irish countryside. At 4:30 we finally reached Kabul; once we had passed the "local" status from the other side of the Salang, the bus finally went over 20 kilometers an hour.

The soldier in the next chair asked Danny if he wanted a cigarette and then hashish, and I told him these were not good questions for a soldier. An old timer chimed in that "yes, in fact, one was not always a soldier," while the man in a waist-ankle brace cuffs, a prisoner in transit to Kabul it seemed, looking uncomfortably on. We finally left the old bus, grabbed a cab from Sho'ra (Northern Depot) to PC and sauntered in in time to be rebuffed . . . Danny to get his shots . . . me to collect the "Noxema" skin cleaner, which after eight months of traveling had finally reached us. Then we went to the Mahoneys for the night . . . .

Chris Mahoney had been asked to send back a package to the States for another couple, Volunteers who had left. It was mostly 57 kilos of old clothes, but the customs people thought they knew better. When the police at customs took one look at it they decided it must be full of all varieties of illegal drugs, which they most certainly had better find, since the very first thing they found was an (unused) hashish pipe on the top of the pack, and everyone knows even crazy foreigners have better sense than to spend several hundred dollars sending home old junk that is worth ten dollars on the Used Clothes Bazaar, so there had to be some other reason for the stuff.

So the search started, with every boot sole and heel and every wad of clothes, every collar and seam and sock being throughly shaken, poked and assessed. It seemed they had looked their fill when a husky-voiced official suddenly came in with a package of oil paints in tubes in which someone could (and he assumed someone had) put away a lot of cocaine. Then the Interpol began their search anew with more intensity, taking samples of each tube, poking them with pins in pursuit of false full ones, testing the paint with others, but that too eventually cleared and it was time to put everything away . . . . accomplished only by leaving behind two scruffy pairs of shoes and exiting, two hours after arriving . . . .

[So we met with volunteers and PC staff, and after getting shots for Dan, we hear of returned volunteers' funny experiences in Bamiyan . . .]

The best that night was hearing two musicians at the Springar Hotel, a wizard of a *zia-belogh* (drum jug) player and a a player of a *ghucha (ghuzah?)* of wood and mother of pearl, this latter an old man from Mazar who—like a loose board—moves his head and sings sensuous bawdy notes. The drummer is magical, his fingers nurse and pound the stretched skin, his fingers dance and dawdle and caress. I have never seen such masterful, violent. and exciting music. Likely the closest of this caliber is the master of masters, Ravi Shakar, and his rendering of the sitar, the long, broad-necked, three-string instrument which was traditionally an Afghan instrument. Some Afghan students sit a while, dance in their seats, and leave, and are shortly replaced by an old American couple who nod over barley juice, listen intently, then leave a good tip. Later a calypso dancer's mate, a black-clad and muscular, Afghan dances in and out to the *ghuzah* playing.

I think of the *daira*-players we had heard at weddings in Tashkurghan, the simple tambourine-style drum which is almost entirely played by women; and of the omnipresent *tabla*, another set of hand drums endemic to traditional Afghan music.

Our hosts ask the drummer for names of teachers *(usteds),* and he bewails the small circle of musicians in the country, and how music—although ancient, of the very rocks, has not been proudly preserved. He says sadly that no schools exist to keep it from dying. He mentions the Shawqi movement, music which started in the 1950's and was a mixture of local and European instruments, still with a strong traditional style.

But there are professional musicians here, among them Ustad Sarahang, the "Mountain of Music," "Baba Music," who co-hosted a radio show called "De Ahangoona Mahfil," "The Music Gathering." There is Nashinas (Sadiq Fitrat), and the main pop star of the 1970's, Qahmad Zahair, flamboyant in life, the son of Dr. Abdul Zahair, who had been Prime Minster during Zahar Shah's reign, and who is a performer famous for his renditions of poetry from Hafiz, Saadi, and Rumi.

And, of course, Sorban, whose "Ahesta Buro," "Walk Slow," has been a standard wedding song for Dari ceremonies.

We murder one scorpion . . . . I wake up hearing voices beyond me and the landlord puts on the light in his upstairs window. Before sleep—irony, irony—I break the bottle of Noxema accidentally, sweep up the pieces and collect the cream as best I can. In the morning Brenda tells me she had dreamed of an orgy with Noxema cream, all of which—in the dream—her landlord overlooks from his shadowy lighted upstairs window . . .

In the morning . . . a cab rushes us to the bus stop and we are 25 minutes late; they leave literally as we step on, but a certain justice has been validated. It is a fine, sunny day, and we reach Khulm at 1:30, the *bande* is alive with policemen and motor control and *gaudiwans* telling me how Tom had gotten the ticket money back, and how sorry they had been to see what "bad work" was being done to me and my brother.

Dan, Tom and Mirad gather mulberries in a sheet and both families eat from them. The landlord Daud arrives, and asks patiently about cutting back the roses and getting someone to clean up the yard. Then he ceremoniously gives us his address in Mazar . . . and an invitation.

Vietnam is finished, and finally the war is over. It has been years.

> *. . . [We have school and I tutor Shahzadah. We clean up a room just big enough for a sleeping bag and his pack off the kitchen for Dan.] An evil stormy wind rattles the air, though it is nothing after the previous night's thunder and lightening.*

May 7, 1975

. . . This week has been a delightful one, full of little moments suddenly of sheer beauty, like retracting back into our ancient soul.

Sunday had the chalk-stained local inspector at school writing up tests for the 6 to 9 classes, to be administered for most of the morning under the mulberry trees, with a dead-eye obliviousness to details of score accuracy or honesty. I missed my first two classes, given over to collaborating on simple algebraic problems, and a few other subjects, and when Magfirat, having finished her test, came running to our class with a simple problem in two unknowns to solve, I was really shocked to hear she couldn't do it because it had been at the end of a book the class never finished in the 9th class.

It was Mirad's birthday and we tried to contain the secret. In the afternoon, Tom and Mirad wander in the bazaar and see a magician who makes a card fly up out of various hidden places. Later, we give Mirad a party . . . he is 30 years old.

Back at home Dan, Tom, and I set off for a walk . . .

The terrain stares at us, so familiar and yet always full of surprises. We go out the old city road and then into a farmer's field until we just start climbing the stoical mounds. We follow, the lane leading on and on like some elusive road up to the foothills, the first ridges of the famous "wave" mountain. Dan moves far beyond us toward a small white tent between a patch of winter wheat growing horizontally on the face of the mountain and a snake zig-zag path moving up one face; I lag behind (I had worn my school sandals. Blisters and slipping footing are making my pace a slow one.) We reach a vista.

Up then and the whole world below us, shades of the colored hills, a brisk wind, turned into a howling chilly blast, and for a half hour I am alone on one small peak as Tom tries to catch up with Dan so we can start back. On a milder path back, we watch the green town emerge below us, pass through a shepherd's flock, come home to relive the notion of when we would actually go "up the mountain" next time. How many times we have come close, or perhaps we never have. What is his elusive mountain?.

Then Thursday at school comes the news that a second-grader has died, along with the father of Gulahad in the 12th class. Everyone is getting ready to go over to the wakes.

Life, death, journeys. In this land where one is ancient and wizened at 30, the death of a child at seven, or a father at 45 elicits only a small sadness publicly. The rituals unfold and the people declare, "This was Allah's will."

Today, for lunch we set off walking with Mirad down the road to the Tangi, ford the river, a swelling cool muddy current; go up to the meadow we had found a few weeks before with Azarullah; eat eggs and boiled potatoes, Koolaid and bread, cake and fudge and bananas; play Frisbee, soccer, football; climb a small hill and delight in the gorge clear as a graceful cleavage in a female land. Then we start back again, going through the tiny village and the tanner's silent rows, and through the rich orchards and barley fields of one of the town's wealthy families, Sulayman.

We stop to eat mulberries along the road, and Mirad tells us it has always been the custom for a man who can afford it to plant mulberries along a roadway so that anyone passing by can always have fresh fruit, like water, to help him on his trip. As we near town we sniff our picked licorice shrub, chicory, (to be dried for tea) and talk with some of Tom's students, the son of the orchard owner we had gotten our winter wood from, the potato seller in the bazaar. We see the pastel blue *"Khaghar"* bird, whose meat people with congenital lung and chest problems eat, because the bird has no song. Near the river, we try to find a nightingale's nest, a *"bilbour."* Mirad has told us how beautiful they are and how much he wants to have one some day.

He also tells us of the four rocks in the hills near where we ate. ("Someone told this to me in a Waz once; I don't know if it is true," he introduces his tale by disclaiming.) They were once four girls escaping from their enemies, whose friends prayed they be saved, and so they were turned into unusually graceful forms of stone.

. . . Mirad's mother is ill, so he is off to Mazar. I find myself inundated with compliments in my classes, now, and generally have to be less strict . . . The season's first cucumbers . . . and the season's plum-like fruit with stone-like shiny seeds in quartets enters our house. I go over to see Zeebee while Baba takes Habibullah to the bazaar, and she tells me Mirad's mother had health problems this past winter. Zeebee insists that the ailment was brought on by being alone in her house with her children gone, and with her grief over the deaths of her daughter's family.

Zeebee speculates. "She is old and wise with nothing to do but worry herself weak." Then Zeebee shares her own worries about Daud's diarrhea . . . and she speaks also of the crazy family across the way whose boys are always pelting the window and wall with stones, and whose women protested when an old grass cutter came into the compound when they were there to cut grass . . .

Mirad returns, medicine having been obtained for his mother. He shares with us some music on the radio, a song called "Ay Taza Gul" by Khyal, and another song specially by Rafi Sahib and a female singer, Zhilla. Later, we hear the first reference to "the war the U.S. lost in East Asia . . . ." on the BBC.

Yesterday afternoon a U.N. film came to my school. Everyone was crushed into the corridor to watch, with the *modir* procuring electricity from the town generator, with a special permit. But today, my students claim that it was only about mules and microbes and it had been too hard to see or understand . . . .

Friday I am to be Paregul's guest for lunch . . .

May 10, 1975

Thursday morning, Dan and I leave for Mazar in the front seat of a short-charged tan model Toyota, which is full of pilgrims of all shapes and sizes. All are intent, in the first few moments, on knowing what relationship Dan is to me, and whether or not we have cars as broken as this one to take us places in the States. One gaunt, black-bearded, prophetic looking man begs for a seat, running after the vehicle until we are almost through the toll gate. However, though we have room in the front seat the driver refuses to take him for 15 *afs*.

The desert spreads out, full of shepherds, flocks of young lambs, a frieze of the last red flowers in the green plains. At Mazar we first visit the bank. Then, as I wait to have my check approved, the chief clerk brings out a technical industries letter, full of such words as "cognizant of," "unskilled" to translate. We are sent over to the Sufi who disperses bills and then out into the bazaar circle, among *kutchi* women selling bracelets, their dark skins tight across withdrawn eyes and blank faces. We stop at the carpet seller's shop, but he is engaged in a serious discussion over some new purchases, so we detour to have photographs taken for future documents. After a brief pause at the old school teacher's shop to pick up candy and butter, where we find him a little cool or distracted, we set off with the volunteers.

Everyone launches in to a brief discussion of why educational innovations here will never have any meaning, nor be implemented, until the teachers can understand what the purpose of their teaching is . . . Likewise, something as basic as a lesson plan becomes a form filled out, with no connection to the actual schedule or pace of instruction, when the teachers have no sense of continuity at all. Also topical, and scalding, is what some deputy administrator from the Ministry had said about the placement of PC volunteers, contradictory to the current practice: "Well, we believe in keeping an American presence outside of Kabul."

I go back then . . . and with my note from Mohammad Mirzad Daud and a few queries from shopkeepers, set out to visit my landlord's house. As I approach it, a string of children escort us to the gate, and Daud's wife peeps out nervously, then comes back to get us.

We are escorted to a room with beautiful rugs and photographs of Ruhsamrah, Daud's daughter, a teacher-student now at the DMA teacher college, thin white curtains in the window (opened to host a hundred flies), a rope bed, the usual cushions on the floor, these covered with beautifully embroidered pillowcases. A handsome blue-eyed man in his late 20s, in matching *tanbon* and *peron*, comes in to sit decorously with us. He identifies himself as a nephew who had been a soldier in Herat, but was recently transferred back to Mazar. Twelve years before, he had had an American teacher in his school. A tray (two or three) of cake, cookies, candy and tea arrives, which we take as the second course after having eaten our own brownies, and our lunch. Soon the daughter, brightly dressed in a clean tailored pantsuit, her hair high on her head in a French roll, arrives with a rich bouquet of flowers.

We talk a little, the nephew leaves to go to a celebration of the Red Crescent Society Day, behind troops of boy scouts and cub scouts in knee-high socks and beanie hats. Then we receive an invitation from another relative. This is a dark man whose intonations and face gestures are all a little exaggerated and whom I remember from several of the family weddings as being . . . accepted in both men and women's chambers alike. He asks us to come to Balkh for the afternoon with him someday. The family itself invites us to stay for the night, but we excuse ourselves and leave, back through modern-dressed Russians and stubby old-fashion bodied Eastern Europeans—who likely thought me a spy—who live in this neighborhood. We go back to find the pictures are still not ready, so return to the cab stand to get a ride back to Tashkurghan.

A young beggar girl moves her hand over my purse, and I rudely turn on her, pitiless, "What are you doing?" I jerk away, firm but sorry to not have more compassion.

The ride is a good one, the other passengers intrigued with this pair of my brother and me, and after that is set down and who I am and what I do, the driver demonstrates his mastery of world affairs with a discussion of Kissinger, whose religion (Jewish) thrills him openly and whose unsuccessful recent trips to the Middle East have permanently removed him from the realm of the immortals, people who do unbelievable things (*"balloi."*) He asks also why English is spoke everywhere, when—unlike Hebrew or Arabic—it had never been given directly to the people by God. Then he asks where the Beetle style car first originated.

During a return visit with volunteers, the Bonds, we hear a good story about Arnie and Kayla Bond's landlord, who studied in the States at some point in Utah, and is now president of the Cement Company in Puli-Khumri. The man lives in great opulence in a plantation on the edge of the city where the Bonds visit sometimes. At the last visit he seated them on his patio in the garden on carpet pillows and gave them whiskey with unclean ice, all grandly executed until a chicken came running out and knocked over the glasses and then cleaned itself on the rugs, and until the "educated man" proceeded to talk about the book he was reading and which he considered an excellent study of American society. He brought out a sex-thriller, the cover displaying naked or thin chemise-clad girls, and a blurb on the back describing a plot involving a drug addict who was now in the wife's bed, etc. So much for the sham, or grace, of Western education.

Ziadeen joins us for dinner and leaves without thanking us, as usual, and we . . . study the image of stars and a bright red phantom blaze on the western hills . . . .

Friday then . . . . Paregul comes to get me at 9:00 a.m. She sits nervously . . . over tea she seems reluctant to even be here—then we all three—Dan, myself, and Paregul—set off via my school and the old *baba* to her house, where we enter the clean carpeted room and the beginning of a comfortable day for a young male (Dan) among young ladies (quite un-Afghan in that respect) begins.

We are immersed in relations and conversations, a sister-in-law quite pregnant, another with her first born, a tiny wet black-headed two-month old. This one intuits that while Afghans live in the past, Americans fly in the sky; and while Afghans don't even all have bicycles yet, Americans go to the moon. She notes that cars that are used in Europe or the U.S. until they're broken or eight years old, are taken to Afghanistan and declared "new." She is quite a caustic, but thoughtful, young women, this new mother.

Her mother and a mustachioed, chunky tall old woman come in to chant and stroke the *chillum* (water pipe), to engage in light talk, and then we are presented with a huge lunch, one I imagine the family has slaved to perfect since dawn. Later, we wait in the garden for a driver, and then are carried off to the springs.

On the hill, as we are splashing in the water, the afternoon moves to darkness. The assembled learn from Dan how to make stones skip on the water, and carefreely pelt some pompous government men usurping their would-be place below. Then we decide to move out too, meet Najiba's family, and the *chadris* pass as ghosts. It turns out that our car has been appropriated by the local commandant and his relations, so now we are stranded outside town. Eventually we start a strange parade down the highway, the hills mute, until a car comes and we're whisked off. Danny practices the Dari words to say to his hostess, "You are like my sisters" in Persian. Then as they give us a big bouquet of flowers we go back down the alley to our house, to find Tom watching out for an old student of mine, Anifa, whose mother had sent strange food and *kimah* earlier, and then promised to come herself after dinner. However, they don't come that day . . . .

Yesterday I sat for my *'bey-car'* hours in the laboratory with Nazifa, the *modir's* wife, and Najiba, all intent on discussing motherhood and mother's day, colds, and visits to people's houses. Then the wraith sad figure of the spunky little girl clerk came in, Mowgul, whose father had died the week before, and left behind Shegul in the 12th class and her mother, the shopkeeper, and one brother who is a *gaudiwan*. During the break the modir tells his wife she should be in class. Later, we see Mowgul briefly, fainting, crying in the 12th class . . . . Will the sisters now be taken out of the school?

Home then and the arrival of Habibullah's 12-inch ascosis worm, ("Momma, a snake came out," he had cried). Then Azarullah arrives.

He is followed by Anifa's family, so I step out with them and the neighbors across the way (buck-teethed, dark-skinned Pushtoons) to go to the gardens. The whole way they grumble, berating the rudeness of Khulm men whom they imagine staring at them, although they sit mostly with their *chadris* "masks" down. The old student Anifa raves about her beautiful rich family by marriage and the huge garden they have in Aybak, and the hard luck she is in, now that her husband has gone off to be a soldier for a year.

They scrape their broad feet inside the building, unaware that it is not yet a museum, start for the main room, and then turn back. The class three brother acts as a petty tyrant dictator over all of them, telling them they can't let up their veils, while Anifa continues to complain about having to be so *"kite"* (restricted). Some vague relative, a snotty class eight boy who is playing hooky from school goes in swimming with a bleached brown group of other boys in the never-changed reflecting pond water, and after some unusual questions about my salary, childlessness, etc., we set off via the hotel garden and another rich relatives' home, for my own house.

With half of them I share tea, as the others wander off, and they pick at the corn cake, and spill tea on my photographs . . . The women move on double eyes through the house and kitchen and question the salary of Mirad, then finally leave among exclamations of how "clean" his work in the kitchen is. Meanwhile the local "nut," the Hajie Biron teacher, has arrived. The women crowd together, awkwardly, back into the now deserted living room to avoid his eyes, and then leave . . .

When Azarullah goes out, half an hour later, we cross over into Mirad's yard to see Mirad's mother and her bevy of shots and medicines (mostly tonics, vitamin C, and some antibiotic). He asks us how to best give the shots in the vein without hurting her; we decide he must continue to give it behind the elbow since that vein is easiest to find . . . .

About 8:30 Amore M'med appears. In hand are my 75 pictures, which he had picked up for me in Mazar . . .

Sunday. We ingest a note from the provincial head of education. He has dictated that all female teachers and students are to dress in the black uniforms or comparable garb, and show no colors. Further, all the male teachers must cut their hair to a specific length.

. . . I am given an exam schedule which will leave me here until the end of the exam period . . . I walk in on a bizarre scene of the three pregnant teachers (the wife of the *modir* and the two first grade teachers, all sitting in the laboratory, intensely bent over papers of salt, eating white chicory passionately.) . . .

May 13, 1975

We again have a failed attempt to go up the mountain. It is scalding hot and I have less energy than anyone else. As we strike out beyond the edge of town, trampling symbolically across several graveyards, the sun's sheen in the face of the desert plateau in front of us makes me dizzy. I walk about an hour and then . . . decide to go back . . . Upon seeing my red face, a *gaudiwan* insists I must take a ride, but I "tashekoor" him and smile, then walk on.

We have dinner at Azarullah's on Sunday, with the old round aunt who motions for me to enter the house as she undertakes her prayers, and Anifa's chattering mother. Eight other guests arrive, invited by the father, and brought by a judge to the neutral party to discuss a quarrel. Consequently, our meal is divided. The male half talks on the other side of the wall, shadows and echoes, and the women move about their tasks without talking. My stomach hangs ready to empty itself, but I manage to eat of the rich feast, slowly, and for once no one is monitoring my portions. With tea Anifa's father enters to enthusiastically describe for us all the techniques of catching everything from *cawk* to deer to tiger in the mountains or on the desert, and to share his own particular favorite times and experiences. He remembers one episode with the famous Yuri and Thaddeus, predecessors and volunteers in this region from years ago, and further immortalized. He speaks of the founding of the original cities of Khulm and Tashkurghan out in the desert going toward the Oxus. Collaborating the almost mythological story we have now been told several times, he explains that the founding occurred when a daughter of the king of Balkh quarreled with her father and was thrown out. Somehow she was able to take some of the father's riches with her and build a huge fortified place out at the site, and then later was reconciled with her father again. But the village's main buildings remained.

In the half lights I slowly grasp the story, ending for them all when the Mongol invaders shattered the town. Yet, because it had been a rich city, people today still go out to look for lost gold and jewels left there from centuries before.

Monday is a hot day and we receive fresh brown bread filled with leeks from Zeebee on top of the evening meal. We sit, watching the first shadows on the mountains around us, wondering about the land beyond, cool now, and Mirad comes over to ask about the gifts he wants to sent to our families in "Am-ri-ka." He sits down with us, then begins to tell stories of the Communist society, where—he had heard—everyone had enough to eat and steady work and housing and clothing, thanks to the order of the government. He recalls the street widening in Mazar and the Afghan government's plans to let Russia build a petrochemical plant there and provide work for thousands. Then, in a realm closer to him, he speaks of the discrepancy between the landed rich and the landless here, of how there are beggars, thieves, and chronically hungry people all because the rich do not give enough of their excess to the poor, and because they have no one to make them do so.

I think about the premises of a government, of a democracy, of a civil society. I believe it is the obligation of those with much as citizens within a society, to assist others; and that it is the job of government to provide protection, employment, basic human needs for its citizens. It seems so simple: citizens pay taxes, needed revenue is raised, and then it is dispersed to bring a measure of care and equality.

There is a custom among his people, Mirad explains, that when the various crops, especially the first grain of *"joa"* (barley) is ripe, that several landless friends go to the field of a wealthy man and offer to cut it for him for their meals and a small percentage of the crop. There is a harvest festival; the men work hard for one or two days. They have all their meals in the field and sleep there until the crop is all harvested. Then they receive the grain they need.

Mirad, the cool night air fresh on his face, looks back up the mountains and speaks of how his people and many others always like to go out to the hills in this weather because now they can sleep outside without any fear of cold.

As he returns to his home, I wonder with whom he has been speaking, or what programming on Afghan radio, has taught him the concept of communism as a society that takes care of its own. Ironically, Tom and I start a—Monopoly game—that carries our grinning shadows into a 10:30 dark, the lantern flickering steadily, our tiny red candles carving out rare light . . .

This morning, already as I leave for school, it feels warm. The teachers in the office grumble about the fleas in their houses, how it begins a bad season for them now, and so will it be, someone ventures, until the barley crop is in. Another announces the *modir's* wife's plans for a luncheon for the mullah, to insure she receives the right blessings said on her pregnancy. Someone else, the class 1 teacher, proudly shares how she had seen my brother Danny in the bazaar and, figuring out who he was, had invited him for tea and talk; and so on. Self-consciously, the *saer-malim* greets me with a strange, toothy smile, in remembrance of the pictures of himself I had given away. And the students seem languid, but are not rowdy . . . full of little kind sentences, such as "No other American will be as good as you."

I toss my head gently and tell them the new teacher will be just fine, if not better.

Kabul: May 2002

The airport: still little more than an open landing strip
in a field lined and riddled by bombed-out military planes,
twisted metal, and wrecked tanks,
the former building a shell without windows, electricity or running water,
floors pitted with rocket hits, barely more than heaps of shattered stones.
Like most buildings around the city,
the walls resemble Swiss cheese from the barrages of bullet holes.

Years before, it had been a classy place, whose marble walls,
tiled floors and restaurant, basic but clean,
drew people even not in transit
to collect here for a meal some nights.

Even this far from the city
lines of homeless children, the street beggars and orphans,
call to arriving cars,
offering single cigarettes or a shoe shine
for the price of a tenth of a piece of bread.

It is hot, dusty, noisy—
old *gaudi* drivers ringing their bells to get a rider,
bicyclists darting across the rutted road and shrieking,
the constantly pressed horns of lumbering trucks
laden with construction equipment,
old taxis so decrepit they seem held together
with yarn and glue and rubber.

And the ubiquitous military trucks, jeeps and Humvees,
soldiers in torrid green camouflaged uniforms
and protective gear
wielding their arms nervously.

scattering the groups as they pass.

XV

FAREWELLS

May 15, 1975

A merciful cooling off . . . with rain like a fresh heave of grace, and cloudy weather welcome for once.

In the afternoon Azarullah brings over Mir Wias, one of Tom's best students, and while Tom and I are delayed in the bazaar trying to find materials for a dress and *peron and tanbon*, Dan has to host them. They thumb religiously through the Sear's catalog, and as they debate the relative merits of machine-made clothing, Dan interrupts with a question across cultures, as to whether or not machines are good. Azarullah emphatically claims that they must be, thinking he must have misunderstood, clearly uneasy with my brother's blatant philosophical and rather dreamy approach to all discussions. Later, when Tom and I return Azarullah erupts into a quick-tongued, detailed description of various people in his acquaintance, never mincing words. We hear how certain boys at school dance like women kneading flour, or the water wheel at the mill, and how the *modir* of my school is tall like some fruitless tree while the *modir's* wife is like a churn for squashing *toot* (mulberries). He shares a story of the escapades of some of the boys at the school in Mazar. Last year, they mischievously fed some kind of emetic weed to the afternoon teachers at school during one free exam lunch period. The teachers were forced to congregate out in the *tashknob* and no one could proctor tests. Subsequently, everyone had their field day for free answers, and standbys in the school year had a good sight (*khuyb sile*).

He tells how another time some boys at this high school stole the meat for the teacher's soup, hoping to make them too hungry to be able to teach or proctor that afternoon. Then we hear—again—a favorite jest again the old science teacher, how the students always tease Hagi-sibe about his lesson on microbes, when they all firmly believe he could find a fair share of them on his own beloved, but ill-kept person.

Later, the young Mir Wias recites some of his poems, and Azarullah tells us the source of one of his: All are in traditional Persian form and tell about unrequited love, and the sad life of the unsuccessful, the always yearning, lover after his beloved. The pieces resonate with a few absurdist, along with classical images, of the heart being skewered like a kabob, of writing with the blood of flower petals, only to have rain wash it all away, and of craving green meadows and a sharing of wine.

This afternoon a local storyteller, a man called Ismail, appears at our house. We recognize him as Azarullah's guest the night we were there, a garrulous, deep-voiced man who had shouted in animated, unending dialogue his impressions of the fruit trees, and of all Tom's students (for he thinks Tom is a teacher at the girls' school) and the sterling good qualities of the town for "sights and stories, guests and entertainment," etc. A tad under the weather, I stay in the bedroom, but his voice booms out in such enthusiastic explanation, it is impossible to miss his every word. One could scarcely accuse me of ease-dropping.

He describes the "chicory" from the hills and how the plant once it has "eaten the rain," is in the best form then for people to eat, as opposed to when it turns to rhubarb, a dry and less favorable product. He asks Tom if he can draw, and claims that if he had himself gone to school he would have become quite good in drawing. He speaks of all his relatives and friends in the bazaar and how Ismael has all the foreigners stay at his house.

He tells us, "If the man had had his way when you and your *xonum* first arrived, you too would have lived in his house, and been near the school, a water supply, and my endless sources of local history and folk tales and general knowledge."

There is a long pause and Danny's flute comes wafting from the "chapel" room, the small storage vault adjacent to the kitchen, where my brother has laid claim and sleeping bag.

Earlier, under the mulberry tree, Mirad, Zeebee and Azarullah devour the rain-sweetened fruit. On one ladder, fresh and childlike in a pause, the man had been drawing a picture of a hunting scene with the gunsmen and animals in the wings awaiting action.

Now we hear his questions and opinions on sleeping outside on the roof on fresh grass and a cotton pad (necessary), and on the benefits of having only a few children as opposed to one in every corner engaged in mischief. Animatedly, he applauds the travels by my brother or others from the States to this city, and how other tourists manage to come. Then he offers to have his good friend arrange and take care of everything for a mountain climbing expedition for one day and a night out of town. On a pet peeve, he outlines then the processes involved in the building of the "cooked" road just the spring before we came, by the Russians, and how much better all had been with the ancient old road through the bazaar made by the people themselves here. Then, smiling broadly, he leads us on, commending how good conversation is among friends, and how well the lives of all people pass when they spend some of it talking with friends. He brags softly about his gardening skills (he uses some hybrid seeds)—And so the afternoon passes, like so many others, and yet unique today with this rich bearer of tales.

May 17, 1975

Verily coming to an end as teachers and residents here, as we are now, each day has no real chance to blur into the other, and yet it does. Saturday, Azarullah and a 10th grade student Sadiq, and my student Shahzadah and her newly-shorn brother sit outside in our yard until 7:00, while Dan broaches his usual questions, about the universe and other states of being, and solar years and light distances, over cookies and tea and a dimming day. This mixed gathering exudes a kind of excitement in the air, and soon the group is glancing at the selected slides from Greece. Out of nowhere, the otherwise profligate tax collector's son worries outloud at his poor English abilities and how this lack of knowledge will limit his career.

Then Mirad's brother, the elder, appears and we hear that their mother continues to worry and wane.

The next night we dine at the principal's house. The air is cool, the sounds enchanting, nestled as it is beside a running stream. Again we enjoy a delicacy of seating and food, with his wife swooning as the night air comes down. Through the lantern-lit bazaar, we thread our way back to our own house, and sleep through the rushing s-s-s-s-s breeze and the rattle of windblown windows.

The morning begins lustily with the caws of crows, the rooster crowing on the porch, and Zeebee and Habibullah gathering mulberries from the ground. Quickly the sky conjures a thunderstorm to accompany us, and firm in my classes and school office, I bask in the school's mellowness these days. *[There are letters from many at home . . . including a college friend now in law school, Joan Bennett, whose writing on an aerogram is sadly undecipherable, adding to her sense of being remote.]* We learn our gentle farmer friend, the PCV Pat Gruner, is being thrown out of the country because he will not shave his beard. He invites us to visit him in his home state of Nebraska any time we can; and another volunteer, Sue, tells us she has brought the Lashkagar-made costume dolls for us.

In the afternoon Paregul and her sister Jamila and the little nurse, and Danny try to tell a fairy tale, and the girls eat, then climb in the mulberry tree, as we hear a brief flute concert. When they leave, a handkerchief flutters behind, like a flirtatious girl's last thought . . .

Today then is the last day for teaching; I stroke a gentleness and resignation among all my students. We exchange pictures and addresses, and prize books are handed out. Some work has come to an end.

But sadly, elsewhere, life and death go on. There is the announcement of how a 17-year old boy, Paregul's cousin (10th class) was shot to death the morning before by a 24-year old camel driver. The camel driver had worked for some man and taken a liking to his 7th grade son, and attempted to lure him off for "bacha bauzi" but was caught in the act by the since murdered youth. So the man had killed the cousin. (The story goes on: every resident here and for much of the country is related to someone else. The "abducted" boy is the nephew of Kamila of Class 12). My students claim these things happen once a year. Some say once a month, and Islamadeen, laughingly, claims it happens every week. But we feel for the fallen "hero."

There is a meeting for all the teachers after school, an event squeezed in unprofessionally and the modir speaks clearly and slowly so that I can follow all the contents. The questions posed are fundamental: Should the exams begin earlier in the day than regular school or later? Should the teacher have authority over discipline and cheating, or should a principal and proctor? Should food be made at school for the teachers? The last sets off debate for about half the meeting as the shy female teachers await delegation of responsibility to cook on the days they have no lessons, since they are all elementary teachers.

Mirad got back, his mother still alive. Everywhere around us are conversations on "enlightenment" and "social responsibility" and the world of the West murdering the East . . .

. . . I see again the sad, battered expressions of certain students today who realize these really are our final days together, that I will be leaving. I see Zeebee's mellow manners with the boys, and yet something of my troubled sister Louise there, too, both of them having lost their first two girls, both of them caught in new and certain exile.

May 21, 1975

The date should be distant, as it always was, a reality we dared not focus on. Impossibly, here we are galloping up to the time again.

This morning we all rise at 5:00 a.m. and I accompany Dan to the highway to find transportation to Kabul. It is cool and breezy at that hour; and as each person, particularly the traffic policeman and the old motor *saro*i-keeper, vow to help him get on something and look a little roguishly askance at the fact that Danny still doesn't know Persian. Morning pulls itself out magically from the high lighted hills, across the deathbed of graves and shrines along one side of the highway, creeping boldly into the base of the valley.

Is he married? What work does he do? Has he been a soldier yet?

The traffic policeman, thin and eagle-beaked and rusty-colored, smiles at him eagerly, then flags down the first bus and he gets him a seat on a Haji Aqub. Thanking the policeman, barely getting a goodbye off to Dan as the bus pulls away, I set off for the town. On route, I pass some of Tom's teachers; they stare, bewildered to see me alone at this hour, then ask if Tom is at the school.

Half an hour earlier, Tom left for the day. All the boy's *lycee* teachers are gathering at the Chesma for a "Teacher's Holiday." Sometime around

8:00 in a now hot morning, Mirad's family scatters under the trees to gather mulberries.

The wheat is higher than any man in Sare-pul, Mirad tells us when he comes back from there, and despite some hail that killed a little fruit with stones half a kilo in size each, it is green, flourishing now, and water is plentiful.

He lowers his voice. "But things are different here in Tashkurghan." He relays details of the recent murder here, claiming that of all the places in Afghanistan from Badakshan to Jalalabad to his own town where he had lived or had knowledge of, Tashkurghan out did them all in the number of—and persistence of—gamblers.

"Further," he reminds us, "no one ever gets together with another person without talking about his gambling exploits or challenging his friend to bet on something. Even *moie-safeds* engage in it enthusiastically."

The teachers at school sometimes unwittingly mimic western entrepreneurs racing against time: they all check their watches (those who own one) each morning to synchronize them, and always one or the other's—Esfandyar or the *saer-malim* leading—will be off a few minutes. The *modir's* wife and Sherafad the 1st grade teacher and Najiba and Nasreen the "lab keeper" and the clerk from last year's class Mowgul, gather in the dank laboratory to nibble unripe fruit during the break or fix their hair, or to giggle inevitably over some aspect of their recent contact with someone. Enthusiastically, they shake hands and greet each other, every morning and afternoon, and they go on and on about good food they have recently eaten, will eat, or are eating, the good fruits of Tashkurghan or the birds in the fields and mountains they'll catch or have caught before, or their salaries. They note again, doggedly observe my ever present pile of books, questioningly, acknowledging that I can carry all these "preparations," but they really can't. Giving me a good-natured tease, they mingle other times with respect at my persistence. Or Islamadeen regales me with the exploits of his cousin in Tuscon AZ, who writes that he misses a lot of fruits and vegetables that don't grow there, or shares how he himself must go back to the Higher Teacher's College in Mazar for two more years, starting next year. Then, asking me how old I am and hearing "just 24," he shakes my expectations by claiming he thought me at least 30.

I record the wise sayings, mostly character judgments, pieced together from Mirad and Azarullah, the student:

There are special nicknames for people, according to their personalities or behaviors:

Ladies call other ladies, *tota chusham* if they are a person with eyes like a parrot, i.e. immodest.

You say a man has a heart made of glass, (he is a coward). He is *sheesha dill.* Hypocrites are called *gurgay atashee*, a wolf of fire, someone from Satan. A compliment is made about someone who is meek and mild. This is a *gurbay miskeen* (a gentle cat). A spiteful man is a *shutar keena*, because camels revenge and hold their grudge for ever, then attack. They *(shutar)* never forgive. If you say someone is as rich as a *Quarun*, it's a reference to *Chawn* (Charon, in Greek mythology) who they think takes the gold coin from the tongues of the dead before taking them across the Styx, and thus has gotten very rich.) Not surprisingly in this society, henpecked men are laughed at, and moneylenders are despised. On the more hospitable side, is the saying, which has been largely epitomized in the respect with which our non-Moslem state has been received from the beginning: *"The Farungees in their religion and we in ours."* meaning, people must be tolerant. Put another way, this goes, *"God is the Palace of Truth and there are many roads leading up to that palace."*

The 11th class questions me about "used clothes" from America. Tajenisa testifies (again) that no other teacher will be able to take my place, Suraya's haughtiness is simmered down with a nod from her friends who tell her to mind her manners and she actually apologizes for asking for one of the books I had given as prizes to the best students. There is quiet awe ruling the 9th class, a few heads down crying, even the 8th class silent, and the 10th class is suddenly my ever-admiring friends, with Parwin speaking solidly to the effect that it was good I fought with them as I did, because with me as their teacher there had never been an idle day. The 12th class lingers, dewy-eyed, devoted, seeking my signature in their "memory book."

The Country Director, Dick Howard and wife Jodie, and a professor from Buffalo arrive for a brief visit. Ziadeen pops in moments too late, feeling defeated, having hoped to secure another Peace Corps teaching job for the summer.

Mirad is off to the bazaar to get a haircut (a shave), in the best Afghan summer fashion, and the *alef-chopper* (grass cutter) is in the garden filling up bags with his goods. The house is quiet except for the buzzing flies. It is a hazy afternoon courting words in bound volumes; tomorrow the 11th class will finish their courtship with my English methods.

> *[We have more visitors, Arnie and Kayla Bond from Puli, professors from Harvard and Montreal, and a Dr. Ash and others studying the Kutchis and nomadic pastoral life, for five years, living among them,and making a film. Dr. Ash bluntly notes his sated experience with less than enlightened PCVs in a training session for Gambia, volunteers who rebelled at his insinuations of needed understanding for cross cultural communications. It is a shame that every volunteer is not a diplomat or a committed participant.]*

Tom shares his stories of his day with the teachers, how childishly free it had been . . .

The teachers had all teased and chased each other, and concentrated mostly on their pranks on the ever vulnerable Hagi-sibe, taking his hat and winter coat (he still wears it now), tying his belt to a tree so he fell down when he tried to stand up, dropping river crabs in the bag of fish he was collecting from the river. They all spent the morning in a grove about two kilometers from the Chesma, playing cards and fishing. In the afternoon they "swam," or at least Tom and one fellow fish dived in the pure, clean water of the spring, at its deepest 12 feet, and Tom called it among the most refreshing water he had ever been in. Here, too, they teased old Hagi-sibe, in his baggy trunks missing a safety pin, by getting him into an inner-tube (absconded with from the hotel manager who was out in it trimming the sides of the marsh plants), and then pulling him out to his genuine terror to the middle of the pool. It is the play of schoolboys, bordering on torture: Afghan men in their forgotten free moments.

Today's exam for the 11th class comes off flawlessly, with three girls carrying straight 10s, and most of the others close behind. I share lunch with the teachers, a greasy broth, bread, potatoes, and some student-donated *awshak*; and there is a lot of teasing to find me a miniature fork and spoon. But it is a good meal and company.

Home then, I find Tom off to proctor exams, and then to paint the traffic sign at the Bande (highway), something his *modir* had volunteered him to do. I sit with Mirad and Zeebee and Habibullah while Daud sleeps in the hammock Dan left, and the sun blazes on. Then Zeebee shares a woeful tale of her period returning after four months and how she has great trouble with this bleeding. Daud wakes up and vomits. I think what in my first aid pack might help either of them, but, as always, frustrating it is to not know how to heal, or how to help them maintain their health and avoid the deadly parasites and microbes.

May 24, 1975

Yesterday was an expedition to organize our household to be shipped to Kabul in tact when Raheem comes down. We found blood and excrement from hundreds of flies on our sheets this morning.

I have no assigned exam, so sit with Mowgul in the office and hear her praise her past, her years as a smart school girl in Samagan, her time in the hospital, her love for Diane a PCV nurse there several years ago, and her knowledge of typing, and cooking and sewing under the breezy shade trees. In the sun the old men nod within their loose cotton sacks, bones boiled dry.

I return to school at 10:30 to find Tajenisa being scolded by the principal in a circle of students in the school yard, for some insult too many she had dropped at one of the women (the wife?) It makes me sad and uncomfortable. I like both of them, two sparks of Afghan womanhood who for all their mutual orneriness deserve some support for their spirits.

I give out pictures to 12th class students and promise to sign their memory books, stand inspecting "chef" Esfandyar's soup (melted roghan) lunch treat, then sit in a moment while the aggressive afternoon teachers tease me mercilessly for wearing a red dress and ribbon.

"They are the clothes of a lover," these stern ladies tell me boldly, then ask for details of my love life with Tom. And the two mullahs listen and laugh inwardly when I scold the women for being so naughty *(shokh)*, then repeat and discuss my meaning among the other assembled teachers. Not to be left out, the *saer malim* tauts Tom's excellent spirit to learn Persian and the times at the boys' school when he had let his mind be known. The *modir*, in fine suit and tie, juggling his papers quietly, smiles at me as I leave, when one of the cheeky women pinches my cheek . . .

Tonight chokes with an abominable heat. Even with our thick-walled house, we are in an oven of stuffiness. Outside the air is vibrant, the moon full.

Earlier Amore M'med and his friend who works for the old Hagi came over briefly, in pursuit of some medicine for this former cook, who is again very weak. He has slept for eight days, and coughs continuously. We give him aspirin and cough medicine, he brightens a moment, blesses us profusely, speaks with pride again of the picture I had given him myself, and prays he can stay alive to pray for our safe return to America. I think he will stay for supper, but he eventually excuses himself, and I fell terrible, as if we are deliberately withholding food from a very sick man. He is too tired to walk to the hospital to see the doctor, he claims. When he goes outside he sinks down for a few minutes as if to gather in breath, and then he goes feebly away, still blessing us. Then the evening moves in and his gaunt, thin figure melts into the soft shadows, the figure of a profound pathos, sorrowful and slightly mad.

Mirad is off early, the meal simple for once, heat pressing in. I go to the bazaar to see the tailor's exploits, find a funny uniform dress for me, and the wrong size of *t and p* for Tom. But we both take on their just insignificance next to the multitudes of hungry, sultry night.

May 27-28

We wove heavily through several traumas in the back days, stemming perhaps from the weather, from the fact that we are almost finished here, from our own inability to accept the end as being that, from the ever-present frustration of doing any work in Afghanistan; and from still being in a state of anticipation for law schools to answer. Sunday's test for the

8th class goes all right. Although none of them shine, I don't need to fail anyone either. Lunch, given by the 12th class, is lavish with *pilau, dolk* (sour milk with vegetables in it), fruit, yogurt, stew and meat. I correct and record grades until 3:30, then come home.

About 5:15 an old *baba* comes from Tom's school (Tom, a casualty of the soup he had to eat at the school the previous day, has been resting at home all day). The *baba* tells us that someone has telephoned us from Kabul and will call back. I go over to the unnatural telephone office with Mirad, half-lame with two boils on his leg. There is an inspector, the bookkeeper and the *saer-malim* there, and we go through the formalities of greeting and waiting to see how the telephone call will transpire. It never does. With instructions for Tom to come at 7:00 the next morning, I leave.

The caller, who turns out to be Qorbin, Mirad's brother, does call the next day, but not before Tom and I had speculated on all sorts of possible callers, and he had gone back himself for the call in the uncommunicable office of the telephone house.

Halfway through dinner Ziadeen appears with a petition for the worst of Tom's students, charging him to pass him. Likewise there are petitions for Rozia in the 10th class (Marzia's good friend), telling me she deserves a five. Then he announces that he will be going to Kabul after his job here, and he leaves, ever unceremoniously.

Yesterday culminated with the finality of my wits.

I get to school a little before eight, thinking I was to be a proctor for the seventh class physic's test. It soon turns out that they are to have an English class but that neither their teacher Fakir Khan nor his test has materialized. I hastily make up one, and with a call to Samagan to make sure I have permission to give the test in Fakir Khan's place the principal and I and two other teachers file into the first grade class. Here the noisy 7th graders sit, as I begin the futile job of writing the test on the postage size blackboard, one question at a time, while the students lamely attempt to understand my English letters, my odd Persian accent, and the unpredictable manner of my strictness. When, after a good hour of trying to make sense of them and they of the board, I think they should be finishing their tests, all chaos breaks lose.

Girls complain and weep and shout and buttress, and I find myself running out of the classroom, mortified and defenseless, to cry before an assembly of my own students on the first porch of the school. One of the teachers shelters me back to the room and everyone sticks in a head to comfort or exhaust their curiosity over my red eyes. I still am shaking, close to most unprofessional tears, as the test drags on in total silence, and the principal sits guard himself. The orals spin out of control, as well, more farce than folly, with the young afternoon teacher translating each name for me as I give out numbers (grades), and by 12:00 something like "an exam" is finished, or at least the gesture of one is concluded.

Every teacher who has a relative in the 7th class fingers the papers, scans with shock the poor showing of her particular favorite, cautions me about the need to pass them, then invites me to share another day's lunch with them. At the long table we all assemble, but my stomach unrighteously growls and distorts itself, upset, so that from the start I know that I am going to insult my fine hosts by not eating properly. Still, I try gallantly, turn yellow, and endure a bark of sarcastic play from Caravan, who asks why I came to see Afghan life and people and now cannot eat the Afghan food. Soon I rise, excuse myself, and race weakly for the *tashknob* at the end of the garden. For the first time I use an Afghan stone . . .

Back in the office, more steady, I ask to be allowed to go home briefly. Without further ado, I pick up the exams, but not until I am out in the schoolyard gates do I realize I am going home to correct the papers because I don't wish to sit through another afternoon of having each teacher put in a favorite word for her relative or allow Caravan to nosily pry to see how I grade, what the grades are, or how much flux I allow in my "numbers."

I know I am not going to compromise.

In fact, I arrive home with bad cramps. Tom is grading his 10th class and their performance is poor. I tell my story to Mirad, and Azarullah appears as we are now laughing. He eventually reads the names of the students off their papers for me and tells me I should pass them all (after it was too late to change numbers), humorously cautioning me about certain girls (Najiba's niece, a relative of his, the sister of the murdered boy—she got a 9). I dart out into the scorching afternoon to take back the test and baffle the principal and get a cold look from Najiba and an amused one from several others. I realize again that they think my seriousness in this work is a bit humorous, i.e. foolish.

Doubtless the trial of conscious isn't over yet. Ziadeen appears in person late in the afternoon, to say goodbye before he heads off to Kabul this morning, to pick up our letter of recommendation for him, and to tell me that the grades for that class were too low, since all the girls had gotten low grades at midterm, too. Fakir Khan, acting as an Afghan teacher often does, had wanted to scare them at that point, but intended to pass them all with unrealistically high grades at final time.

It is not worth contesting. So I blunder into "their" system. So it shall be: the class has learned almost no English. I rather doubt that they are any better in their other subjects, and I pity the poor teacher they will have next year who will try to start Book II with them, when they have never learned the basics of Book I.

But they are only children. The real call comes down to the absurdity of these kids studying 13 subjects at a time, and learning none of them, then being pushed on automatically to begin 13 new subjects all over again the next year, when they have rarely mastered the foundations of any given subject. They're always floundering anew with each year's subsequent level of "book," so who cares what my place should be in any of this . . . . Who am I to jeopardize any one's chances for staying in school? Is that really accepting mediocrity?

The flies in the bedroom buzz obnoxiously. Tom is at the teacher's picnic at the Spring, Amore M'med is back in his house donning aspirins, (he came by at 6:30 this morning, sat and blessed, and left a little after Tom did), and my growing hot restlessness turns each corner of a page of thought into fuel for worrying. I crave a huge bathtub where I might float to my heart's oblivion and just stay cool. And perhaps, with that soaking might come someone to make decisions for me.

We receive a gift for "the cradle" from Amore M'med's wife. They dream of children for us, seasoning my January with December's fruit, my November with July's ripe melons, and the old man promises more will be coming.

Alas, this family, so dear, so poor, so eager to please us—we have rarely been able to reciprocate on a scale they need.

Azarullah appears to go over some questions before his English exam tomorrow. Past and present perfect tenses bewilder him not at all, but when he shows us his notes and I attempt to correct the spelling, order of words, etc, he withdraws them protectively, claiming that exactly as he has it in his notes is the way the teacher wants them to spell the words, since in this form is the way he gave them to the class!

Strange words, and a shock to see his assumption instinctively is to doubt me, the intruder, and go with the teacher's word, even though the teacher has about a second grader's grasp of the language and the intruder is a native English speaker. Or, perhaps this dear boy needs only to protect the knowledge he has already learned from my observations that what he has learned is wrong, and that he must re-learn it. Again. So be it.

> *[As always, our days pass with visitors, this time the McGuffys who were PCVs 10 years before, and who are in the Embassy now. They enter with a troop of boys, and complaints of Kabul . . .]*

In the next yard Mirad's father talks to Habibullah; his low, sonorous voice seems to chant, the boy giggles and crows, someone else carries, spills water, and the day burns on. The baby Daud is sleeping in the hammock which had carried Dan through many an adventures, and is now a way to lift an Afghan baby off the dirt. He has butter on his head and herbs at the back of his throat, which seem to have stopped the vomiting. These remedies come from the old wise woman up the street, but the mother and Habibullah still have worms

Outside, the previous evening before Tom arrives, Mirad asks me about the exams, and how students get graded, what a student has to do to pass, and what becomes of him if he fails.

But then he explains, changing the subject, that he has some work he wants to do, and he needs our help to do it, and that is to find a present to sent to Tom's and my parents. Although I insist that is totally unnecessary he persists in asking again if I will help him find something they might like, since he doesn't know well himself. So now he has given himself another task to do. I wish he could appreciate how his work has helped us, how well his stories have entertained and taught us about his country, how much we have gained by having his family living beside us, and how all he has done already has been enough.

I look out: Bright red sour cherries ripen on the small trees, deep scarlet among the pale green leaves; plums are turning from lime to yellow at the other end of the yard; pomegranates burst with flowers into the shape of plants to come; swallows tap in the caves on the porch, riddling the *burrio* slates with their nests, and the lone crackling magpie is king of the old mulberry tree, master of all he surveys, and exclaiming it. Boys in the alley, in the shade of the late afternoon between the tall walls, run after a ball, throw it to each other, take turns catching another boy, play the invented games of every nation and boyhood, in their pajama-like clothes, capped like scholars, noisy as a mob at football.

May 30, 1975

It is a lazy, scalding day. Mirad's plague of boils has made him bedridden for three days, so we're scouring the kitchen for ourselves. Evenings the house is so hot we sit among a plethora of strange flying and crawling creatures on the porch, groveling most calmly for the breeze.

The ninth class exam went well, almost like a charm; everyone passed of her own volition. They were quiet and gentle and Fakir Khan, back from Kabul and some sort of official ceremony for teachers, sat in the back of the sultry room grading his pile of papers, while I alternated reading words for students who couldn't find them, opening the door, and just huddling the more chatterly students like Camargul and Suriya into isolation.

Thursday. Tom is gone, and sleepy in the heat, I watch Mirad's son digging holes, the grandfather in an upside-down beachcomber's hat telling him to show me the flowers he finds. We hear that Ziadeen has secured the teaching job he sought at PC for the next group. We discuss ways to move the household, via the "Rocket", a truck, all the while anticipating 12 hours in the Salang's adversarial realms. It is hard not to grumble, with the heat, the lack of books, and the uncertainty about Tom entering law school and me finding a job, or of us staying to do PC work another year.

June 1, 1975

. . . Ziadeen, a headache more absent than present as my proctor for the 10th class, interferes handily. He measures a grade for his pal Rowzia

Jahbur, while I big-heartedly help Mowgul, the first-grade teacher, pass the test so she can be accepted to go back to school in Mazar or elsewhere, and really train to be a teacher. In the end, to help, to facilitate, to allow those trying to move forward: that is the best we can manage here. Now she has just finished the 9th grade, and is still missing 10th grade credits.

We are to have lunch, after the governor's arrival, as we save the best English speakers in the class for the last, but he and his supporters never arrive, so we move out to the meal, the greasy cold brew of soup. "Today you've made a new flavor," the *modir's* wife teases Esfandyar. *"Bay mazar wa sord"* (without flavor and cold). Najiba's sister contributes *awshak*, which an old *baba* brings piping hot and delicately dished, about desert time, and it is consumed instantly.

In my rushing, I initially enter a grade incorrectly on the official grade sheets for the provincial offices. They are to be in indelible ink and never tampered with, but the *modir*, without a whimper, allows me to correct it, since the mistake is in favor of his housefriend (Marzari's name was first on the list and she got the "10" intended for Shahzadah, and this would have been the end of the game if I hadn't insisted that I be allowed to erase and correct. Meanwhile the great wealthy Caravan of Samagan approaches me and begins asking me for everything from an incubator to a lesson in English, in his tough-nosed, incomprehensible Farsi way, as everyone in the room seems to be remarking on my now excellent command of their tongue (and perhaps my ability now to handle such a braggart). Or, perhaps, they only joke.

I return home, profoundly lonely and restless, and sit in the yard waiting for Tom. Grandpa comes over with Daud, and catching my lopsided humor (mine is a face which broadcasts its feelings, rarely succeeds in hiding anything), he questions me about child-raising, wondering whether people raise their own children or send them away in my country, asking how old they are before the school takes them, asking me then if I am not sad to not have the *malim* there too so we can both talk and pass the time pleasantly. And, of course, he persists in the inevitable question:

"Were you sad for your years here?"

"No, no, it was a gift," I tell him.

Crazy foreigner and a women to boot I head out to the bazaar to get Tom's shirt from the tailor, imagining if not seeing raised eyebrows and frank laughter among other shoppers and *dhukandars* in the idle afternoon heat.

The plums near the *tashknob* are sweet and golden now; the mulberry tree in its middle age fruit is languid; the sour cherries, beautiful, deep red in color, are pickable. It all dawns, the reality of leaving a place as magnificent as this one has been, of knowing that probably never again in our lives will we have such a beautiful, if simple, home, or such a peace.

This morning we start collecting household goods and the last of the books, like disemboweling a home. When the books are all packed, Mirad collects wooden things and tiny items we are throwing out to take with his family to Sare-pul tomorrow. They will leave, as the days grind us toward our end. Grandpa passes a critical eye on all potential wear, and Zeebee is tense and worried about little Daud who has diarrhea and vomiting again, while Habibullah—with the open imagination and heart of a three-year old—excites himself chasing flies or hammering, or scribbling on paper, or just giggling and running after imaginary things.

A year ago today we were in Kabul, working on another plan, to find a respectable summer job for the remaining weeks before taking a vacation. And the girl from Pinjsher was drowned. As Tom put it, the thought of her is sobering. It makes us wonder what we have done with our extra year of life, or of those we have yet to use. *Inshalla.*

June 2. 1975

[Dan comes back from Kabul and Bamiyan]

Dan arrives from the *bande,* just as we are about to take some popcorn and sodas and cake over to Mirad's house for a small farewell party among adults. Earlier we cooked dinner and sent half over to Mirad, then gathered cherries and plums for his fruit basket. All his household bundled up, he left at 5 this morning on a Waz, chickens collected in the cabinet with the screen door over them, clothes and pillows and a few dishes gathered in cloth bound tightly. I kissed them all good bye and they climbed on the Waz. To the last minute Habibullah was hanging back, as if he understood suddenly that someone was leaving, that something was about to happen that he couldn't quite grasp, but could feel.

But last night on his back porch with the boys asleep, we talked of Danny's trip, of seeing coyotes (the dogs with the yellow eyes) and swimming in the lakes at Bande Amir, and being worried about wolves. He had broken down in the Toyota he got in out of Kabul and had to go back to find a cab, and the cab cost him 150 afs to Bamiyan. On the trip back, he had left at 6:00 a.m., but the truck broke down and he reached Puli around five, and subsequently reached here late. He spoke of the Buddhas, who perhaps were never defaced, but only wore gilded golden masks which have now been lost, and of the Japanese writer-musician whom he had met and shared the night with, who is doing articles on the problems of the world and may come here and interview us. He talked of climbing around the lakes, of their azure beauty, of Benson and Susan Marek's home on the bluffs over the valley, of their life of teahouse sitting and reading, of the other (stony) travelers haunting the place, and of some words of Persian he had learned.

This morning we wake slightly refreshed, after a night sleeping cool under the stars, on the mud patio around the yard, the small branches of the apple trees between us and the heights, and the open constellations of the night. Dawn arrives early, with the excited noises of birds breaking day. Something in an Indian poetry book, the Navajo's magpie song, exactly fits our early wakings now:

> *The magpie! The magpie! Here underneath*
> *In the white of his wings are the footsteps of morning.*
> *It dawns! It dawns!*

With breakfast we eat fresh plums off the trees, and after eight Dan troops off to the school with me, to look in embarrassedly on the examinations in session. The girls pose as shy as he is, but the *modir* takes him on a guided tour to look at each classroom, wanting him to hear what kind of questions there are, wanting some of the better students to address him in English. Even the mullah smiles out of his religious zealotries, as he sits correcting exams, and except for one unfortunate quarrel with Ziadeen over this (this very pen), out of proportion to things real, and a few attempts at pictures, we leave after clumsy farewells.

Students trail us on all sides, making last inquiries about when I must leave.

Then we are out in the hot sun, heading toward home, after my always poor attempts to catch poses in the bazaar, or in the schoolyard, of the land and people before me.

Tom's off to school and Dan has been out to try to take some pictures in the bazaar for us, as he has a special license as the visitor and will not insult anyone, whereas we as residents may somehow be considered rude to now take these pictures, unasked, of our neighbors. The afternoon is cooling down a little. Just then, in walks the eccentric storyteller's son with his pictures of the day he went hunting with Yuri and Thaddeus . . . so we'll see . . . .

June 3, 1975

Last night the Japanese philosopher, anthropologist, journalist, musician Tokio Hasekawa, and his reflective friend, Tokio Mariyama, both men whom Dan had met in Bamiyan, arrived.

Tom and I, both aware these are unusual guest, feel some tension as a result. They are brilliant, Renaissance men, but with their long hair knotted on their heads and their Indian-ashram-type dress, and their songs and chants into the night, Tom especially worries that our neighbors will think badly of us. Further, we can not answer the questions they put to us about the music here, the traditional instruments, for we have had little to do with that kind of culture in our small village . . .

Gahwan, 8th class, comes about 10:30 and she sits in the bedroom while I explain to her about our Japanese visitors. She seems to accept it all as quite natural, that my brother would have friends who have also come to visit, that they are dressed like the holy men of another country. She then greets Dan and gives him a hat, then presents me with a bouquet of flowers and an apology for not having more. She bristles as she tells her version of the unfair grading system of Afghan teachers, people who do not even bother to learn their students' names. I take her picture, along with one of me, and she trails out, leaving behind explanations to Tom and Dan both about the purpose of the *chadris*, and how she only has to wear it on the street so people won't think she is a full adolescent displaying herself against her fellow townspeople's customs. She carries herself with such dignity. Yet she is only 14.

> [We are engaged with dinner, cooking, shopping, creating a vegetarian meal.]

We are interrupted by Tiara's visit at the door, her mother-in-law and aunt, and a fine big-eyed baby girl, fair skinned as her mother, looks out of her layers of chubbiness, at the world. I want to invite them in, but again feel embarrassed for all the men in the yard, so tell them of the visitors and allow then to walk away, without insisting that they come in the yard. But I promise a real visit and not just a passing in the alley, before we leave.

With tea the music begins, a strange alien chanting by the poet, accompanying himself on the rebab, product of a Buddhist mountain people, low and persistent and sorrowful, full of pregnant silences. Our guests take out a Japanese atlas of historical maps, showing various historical movements in the world. Seeing them leads the poet to explain about the monk who traveled this route somewhere to carry Buddhism from India to China, accompanied by a monkey and a pig, and of the adventures he had had and had written about . . . .

In the morning they leave, heading toward Balkh, and from there on the old road to Herat, leaving behind their addresses in Japan, and invitations to the mountains where they live. They also share a description and sampling of Tibetan music (a work crew clearing a tree on a mountain, the dance movements of the flowers) and tell us sadly of the life of the Tibetan refugees now, and the intolerance of India and Nepal alike for these people forced to flee their lands. After showing us a woven band the elder poet-anthropologist, Mr. Hasagawa, got from some refugee, they head up to the *bande*.

June 8, 1975

The mountain, Tak Azar, ("1,000 gunshots" is its meaning), the one we call "the wave," stands firmly as the border of our valley.

Thursday, we entertain Mary and her two sisters and brothers and a dark uncle and cousin from Mazar, a dark haired Semitic family, with Mary herself looking like an old-fashion Warsaw Jewess.

On Friday . . . we take a trip to the springs in a Waz full of burlap bags of hay, and a big round faced mullah *hagi*, and a flushed Turkomen merchant, and a moon-faced, wizened Uzbek, and farmers of a plethora of blended tribes, along with half a dozen crusty barefooted boys and youths. There are no women. Tom answers questions, that day a full set of them, on marriage in America and birth control pills, military service and the population of the U.S. and its main products, of prices for airplane and overseas/overland trips, of the road to Mecca. The boys swim and I watch. There is a tribe of muscular Mazar males present, plus some soldiers from across the road—all enough of an inhibiting influence to keep me dry.

We rode back in a Toyota beside a young Kabuli, whose English soared. He had known Mr. Billy and Mr. Bob who had lived in Baglan last year and who had worked in the Intercontinental Hotel. The man is now manager of Afghan Fertilizer, and is often mistaken for a foreigner.

Mirad, returned from Sare-pul, presents us with hats as gifts for our family in the States. Then he launches into packing with a vengeance, and after working the clothes and between eating bazaar *pilau*, he enlightens us about another bad accident in our Tangi.

A truck with 250 thousand afs worth of rice was coming back from Khanabad one night, and a young man from Sarepul was the owner and a driver. A helper and the truck's owner were accompanying the truck, along with some passengers. Somehow the driver fell asleep, missed his turn, and the front of the truck snaked into a wall (Foolora's estate). The cab was crushed, killing all its occupants, as well as the driver and the helper in the rear. One only person escaped; he was miraculously flung into the *jewie* with only a broken arm. The bodies were taken to the hospital in Samagan and identified, and the families of Sarepul and Aqcha notified via Mazar and Sheberghan. Mirad said the family of the young Sarepul boy had cried without stopping, for all the nights he was in town; the boy was to have married this year, with the savings from his work, and had already begun to build a family home . . . .

. . . Saturday I go to school . . . sit in the hall, and watch the *"rasiem"* (drawing") examination. The students had to copy a most unrealistic duck Muzdah had sketched; and I saw the display of original and non-original embroidery work for *"heyotee"* (sewing). After saying goodbyes and hellos to students, again and again, I finally take a picture of all the teachers. It is then almost noon, and I diligently began writing out my address and trying to joke with the old *babas* and the clerk about going to America with me. Then, at the *modir's* wife's suggestion, and Najiba's paraphrasing. I again begin my clumsy goodbyes, with Ibrahim Sayyed and Fakir Khan speech-making elaborately about all my virtues. Biting my lips, forcing myself to stay strong, I only burst into tears when it comes to shaking the hands of the white-turbaned Persian teacher Abdul Hafez Khan and Islamadeen. They were, somehow, for all my initial muteness, the kindest here, always had been gentle and comforting.

But all my carefully prepared speeches are never said: In full tears I shake the shake each students' hands, bawl out "I can't tell you goodbye," to Paregul and Magfirate, and limp out trying hard to smile and wave under the brightness of the noon sun.

In the afternoon, Tom returns from Mazar with all our money. Dan is ill with the predictable "Kabul Quickstep," and lays sleeping under the mulberry tree, when Shahzadah appears for a three-hour sit. Then we have dinner and a story hour from Mirad. For a moment, we relax, like children tucked in for the night by a loving parent, as he tells us the name origins of the various Afghan cities:

Kabul comes from an erosion of the words "Caw" which is the chaff of the wheat that blows away, and "pul" which is money, because traditionally money never lasts for anyone in Kabul. It's the place where money blows away like dry chaff.

The name Shebergan goes back to the time of a famous old miser-hermit named Shebrer who had a craggy disposition. People after him who were equally close-foreheaded and tight-eyed, and squawked in anger or distrust, took his name. So all of the people of Sheberghan have to walk around with their faces all tight and their eyes half slits because there is a bad, dusty wind blowing there always. Thus, they became known as the people of Sheber, and the place as Sheberghan.

Aqcha is a corruption of "cha," referring to Kallemchas, the small woven rugs and "taq," meaning the best, the wisest, the first quality. The "t" was eventually dropped, to represent the place where the best rugs are made.

Sarepul means, "the most money," referring to all the rich merchants who have traditionally lived here and the families who make and sell rugs and other expensive, high quality things. "Sang gliah", the cool, high, productive village another day beyond Sarepul is named for all the stone it has there, and the odd measurements and standards it has, equal to a quarter of Kabul standards.

Sleep comes . . . a wind storm blinds us and makes us choke for much of the night. Then Sunday dawns, our last in Tashkurghan, consumed in packing, resting, buying. Before us rests the prospect of final visitors, and the slowly evolving trip "home."

June 11, 1975

Before, Sunday afternoon most of the 11th class comes to drink Fanta and give me handkerchiefs, and to see Dan, to surround his feverish form under the mulberry tree, and to tell me goodbye. I kiss them all in leaving; it can not really mean they are not to be before me ever again. On Monday comes Paregul (11th) and Jamila (8th) and Fouzia and Ziagul (8th) to sit until lunchtime, and tease Dan and ask me a few questions (Can we send you food in America?) After the other two groups have left and we can't find lunch, Tom brings *pilau* and bread for the remaining Paregul and Jamila, while I try to say encouraging things about the future to cheer them up. The sun beats mercilessly, always a reminder of the time and place, as I speak of trying to find a scholarship to the States for Paregul. Then they too leave about 2:30.

There is no word from Mirad; but about 4:00, we get a call. I go to the bazaar telephone with the clerk, pass Najiba, Kamila, Foolora, and Shagon on the road; and tell them to please go ahead and I will join them. I shout and misunderstand, on the phone, but finally get Mirad's message.

I have just returned to sit with the girls when Tom arrives. Dan, on his feet again, and up and off to find Fantas, tells him the tale. Tom bends, laden with last minute bazaar purchases (a long turban, a small rug seat cover, a beautiful Kutchi bag, a vest), and after finding yet another bundle in which to put the new purchases, he runs off again to tell his school and make final farewells.

We sit. Another student and her sister and mother come for only a moment (Ziagul again), then leave with tearful farewells, and Zahra and her sister arrive. I write in someone's memory book, quoting Cavafy or Shakespeare; they talk of tests and social affairs, my admirers, but somehow already removed from me, then stand bare-faced on the highest roof of the house, oblivious to how all the town gestures and points (for any watching). I like their defiance.

We all stroll in the garden, and they sample new fruit and nuts and then drink some more of our inextinguishable supply of orange flavored water. After the perfunctory photo, I am saying goodbye to them, too.

Azarullah and the little boy (Anifa's brothers) cluster around us for a few still minutes as we return to our side of the yard. He and Tom, with various students, had spent much of the day on the other side, on Mirad's high porch, perched under the mud arches catering to breezes. There are a few moments of good quiet, when suddenly my *modir*, tall, silent and graceful and Muzdah-jan, his wife, appear. They sit into *shawms* (sunset) and wish us a calm farewell, shake Dan's hand, then all of ours firmly, give us their telephone number in Kabul and depart.

Azarullah, this man-child who has shared so much with us these past two years, takes his leave emotionally, and then the house is silent, Briefly it is only our own. We clean the last crumbs up, drink powdered milk and nibble cucumbers and bread for our evening repose, and then fall asleep.

The day of departure dawns.
Jammed impressions, we can only catch them.

The whole town lines up, heads bowed, nodding as we pass with our buggy of baggage.

It is behind us now; we've left Tashkurghan.

Yesterday. At dawn we are up for the last of of the packing, and Azarullah, the bookkeeper at Tom's school, all assemble for a piece of bread and tea as we wait for Mirad and the hired Toyota. We share a last handful of fruit from the garden, while Amore M'med and his half-mad family file in to collect old boxes, wood, and cans we had left behind. The elder is almost crying for a minute, then calm again, repeating "the *malim mirra*" (the teacher is going), as all of them, ant-like, carry their morsels on their back to their house and return back for more. The principal of the bank ventures in with his two gaunt adolescent sons to tell Mirad that if any money is left owing to us, he will make sure it all clears. But Tom, tired, tense, misunderstands and bluntly informs him we have no debts and anyone who says we do speaks *"drogh"* (lies). The little gray man, taken aback, disappears before all the teachers, students, and passersby into our alley.

Everything is finally loaded and we leave our home, turning on to the old main street to see the eccentric Hagi-sibe pacing in front of us. Tom jumps out of the truck as he comes around blindly to the door, then goes the other way around the truck as Tom comes from there, until they finally find each other, embrace, blow out words. Then the truck is moving again, Tom leaning out the window to tell him a final good bye, while the bewildered wise fool of the town looks puzzled at the rapidity with which it had all seemed to end.

I am, of course, in tears, see the corner *dukhadars*, the road and passing market-bound men and boys, the *chadried* women, the stone walls of the hotel and the clinic, and the old plateau in the distance, all through a screen of incredibility, as I catch in the wind the faint call of my students, "*Ba mona xoda,* Ms. Frances." Then we are entering the gorge, our Tangi, passing the spring, solidly rolling down the last—the only—road to Kabul, Khulm's greenness and rare oasis-waters, left behind. The more typical rough and tumble arid terrain of Afghanistan is now our fate and history.

The bus plows through, as do pedestrians, villagers, the thousands who live among them, the mounds of earth outside Kabul. These latter, I remember, are called *"toda"* or "Khakay Bokhara." People claim the army of Afghanistan had been defeated and had fled to Bokhara in Turkestan centuries ago, but they returned to try to retake Kabul. They had no rations, so they filled their knapsacks with "half sand and earth and the other with grass." Fiercely then, they stormed the capital and captured it. Victors, upon entering Kabul they were ordered to empty out their bags at the gate to commemorate the victory. They did, and the result was the heaps on its edges.

June 12, 1975

No sooner do we arrive in Kabul then we are inundated with the usual gossip and complaining. We swallow a mild annoyance from having seen Rahim's PCV van in the Salang and not having been allowed to "ship" with him. But this is paltry. We find a karachi to bring our stuff to Brenda and

Chris Mahoney, where we will stay a few days, and whose landlord worries we might be moving in.

The contrast could not be more stark. I watch a Kutchi woman walk along the far wall at the International Club while white-clothed children dance on the tennis courts below her, all observable from the top of Gwen and Jack's house in Share-re-naw . . .

> *[Tom is not in any law school,the files are incomplete, so we begin our plans for the trip home and the return . . . We will begin with a few days in Austria.]*

June 20, 1975

We spend our two years of savings, some of the government money, to buy a blazing assortment of gifts for our families, and we carefully agonize over how inappropriate some embroidery piece, a hat, a book of prints a vest, a *kutchi* dress, might be for people with their special interests. We gaze at the well-dressed Shari-nau wealthy, the patched-clothed Hazaras in their secret walled huts, the dark Kutchi women balancing a jar, a baby, a begging *"bakshesh"* hand.

Then, in this noisy city, we have time at last to remember Tashkurghan, to have the new reality dawn on us, that we are soon to become Kabulis, too, with all the noisy, smoke and dust-filled streets, the callous PC machine, the often indifferent fellow volunteers, the double prices of food, the incessant unhealthy air, the long winter. But perhaps we must tell ourselves, perhaps we must at least try to find the cosmopolitan gifts of the city, its music groups, and language lessons, its dancers from China or India, its educated class, its students also eager, hungry to learn.

Year Three
August 1975-July 1976
Kabul, Afghanistan

It had been said of King Aminullah Khan (1919-1929):

> *"King Amanullah is too wise to drench the rather conservative Afghan mind with a sudden and wholesale dose of foreign culture. And above all, he is careful to strain the draught through the muslin-mesh of Afghan customs, carefully adapting each innovation to the peculiar requirements and mentality of his people."*
>
> *—From Sirdar Ikbal Ali Shan, "Afghanistan for the Afghan," Bharana Books and Prints, New Delhi*

Mirad and family

Our house in Tashkurghan, 1975

XVI
ADJUSTING AGAIN

August 15, 1975

In our big-windowed houses then, with our Tashkurghan crafts and cotton mats huddling in the corner, overcome with all the space, we begin to settle into this third year, one during which we are to teach at the university, develop curriculum, and be mentors for the provincial teachers whom we left. Yet we know we have stayed on for reasons shaped far away in the States: the lack of a secured teaching position or other position for me, the failure of Tom's LSAT scores and applications to top law schools to be properly delivered or reviewed in time to allow him to be admitted, our own ambivalence about the future, including of ourselves as a couple, sadly. And, my brothers and one sister in my own first family fester, their conditions unresolved, themselves needy.

Mirad will continue as our cook, although it will be a very different job than he had in Tashkurghan, with our daily flood of Volunteers and other visitors. He has moved into the salon/living room, and so we're really living in two rooms now, with the former study our bedroom and the front bedroom our sitting room.

Outside we have the grape arbors, boasting three kinds of grapes, and beyond our gate, the rumble of cattle and hand-drawn carts shoulder to shoulder in a shattered time with the municipal buses and taxis or private cars. We spend a few mornings weeding the garden and now have the prospects of our own tomatoes, broccoli, and late corn. Oddly we discover the physical completeness which comes from pulling the roots of the weeds from the harsh ground, separating the true plant from the false . . .

The sounds, smells, and lights in our new house magnify: birds in the arbor chirp, wind prowls quietly between the rooms, and bright and airy sun flirts through the tall the windows, pulling our vision up the wide walls, back to the pale bamboo woven floors. Beyond our wall, a neighbor plays his tape and radio a bit too loudly; a flaunted decadence, some new East, pilfers our night's quiet with its lovesick moaning songs. Another night it is English music, British and Beatlesesque, delivered in what must be a foreign tongue to what we assume to be a wealthy Afghan family listening.

In our living room we have hung up a Kutchi bag and a bright woven-embroidered wall hanging from Tashkurghan, constructed a bookshelf with cinder blocks and put down our standard, unfailing flowered *toshaks* and pillows and blue curtains. Our bedroom has a wooden bed, wide and sturdy, the *ghilim* from the Turkomen's bazaar, another wall hanging (green and gold), two crooked Lokaii strips, and a long table-desk for our "work." We are to get some chairs when the PCV nurse leaves from her apartment. The kitchen and bathroom have medieval but quite competent tubs and basins; the former has shelves and tables. Now equipped with a three-burner electric hotplate, we've put our personable and well-used kerosene stove to rest.

Ours seems a most anonymous place on the edge of the city, a blend of modern and traditional, the walled compound indistinguishable from the others along the road. Yet people note where we are: One day on the Share-nau bus as I sit daydreaming and forget to get off at the stop before our house, the conductor calls out: "Malim-sibe, xona-shemma aes" (Teacher, here is your house).

I stumble off, mystified.

August 18

. . . The Bamiyan PC couple and Brenda and Chris Mahoney, just returned from their break, are full of stories of hiking high up into the Foolodi Valley and exchanging their packs with Kutchi women. One woman had run about like an animated doll, as soon as Brenda put it on her shoulders, and then ceremoniously helped Brenda get it back on. Later, the whole group appeared on all sides at the higher altitudes to offer bread and yogurt, and to request, take up the ever present cry everywhere they went, for *"dawa,"* (medicine) because life at 18,000 feet had burned their eyes badly and they were always squinting, red-eyed among the mountain lakes where they pastured their herds.

We hear again of the extreme poverty in Bamiyan, of the people who waste nothing, of the children with tins strapped to their backs following the cows and sheep around to pick up their droppings, to be dried and used as fuel for baking their life's staples, of the problems in the PCVs' house with water. Water has to be carried from a hill beyond their house, which is itself built into the hill. The walls of the channel or the conduit collapsed and neighbors dug to try to find the water source with pick and ax for a week. Finally, the townspeople built a temporary embankment again. They spoke of their landlord who has a shop in the bazaar and ends up giving his produce away because he has so many friends whom he wants to help. They told of their students in rags and ski boots (hand-me-downs, used clothes bazaar finds) and the Afghan tour buses of rich Europeans who sit in the hotel on the hill and rush in their platform shoes and wincing breaths to see the mystical Buddhas, and the entrepreneurial restaurant and hotel keepers from Kabul who come up for the season to cull their profits in this poor valley.

. . . [We do not know our place now: Do we lavish ourselves like expatriates in the international community, or do we try to live simply, and/ or will we just hover around and get bitter about Peace Corps, this minor government organization which inevitably represents bureaucracy and inflexibility to us as its "employees?". . .]

One day, likes birds alighting briefly, Mirad's brother Qorbin, and his *namzad* (wife-to-be), a shy, round-faced little girl who finished the 7th grade in Herat, come to visit. They sit demurely in our house, and while the brother speaks of his job in Paghman and of his house in Kabul and his need soon to find other work, and as Mirad details how he had finally finished the chores necessary to get his work papers, the child-women looks out demurely from behind her *chadris*. She meets my smile, slowly, dares never initiate a word; so when they leave and she slips on her pointed-toed Kabul patent and leather shoes with shiny buckles, and the brother pauses wide-eyed to see Mirad's big empty room, I taste again a little presence of the provinces. It rests with us again.

Last night we lay awake, hearing a loud, almost bellowing solo singer, coming over a loud speaker from a neighbor's house nearby, where a wedding was under way, or perhaps a supernatural wake, at one in the morning . . .

August 29, 1975

On our next break, we visit Bamiyan again. We come back from Bamiyan and Bande-Amir, having done lots of healthy hiking in the sun at 9,000 to 11,000 feet, speculating on beauty as a green valley or an emerald lake stretched beneath us. We had come back As our Mercedes minibus winds and bumps down hill, delivering us back to Kabul around four, we remember.

Impressions of those days, that region: crisp cold apples at dawn from Benson and Susan Marek and Susan's small apple trees tucked in green natural earth planters in their dusty yard along with pink and purple flowers Susan's students planted for her one day when she was sick, and the rows of a garden of snow peas, beans and lettuce, and one winding morning glory plant; their small-doored, low windowed, tiny-roofed hobbit house built into a hill of what must have been a perfect Buddhist stupa; the sound of running water everywhere in the valley.

One afternoon we follow their jewie into the opening of Foolodie Valley, while a brother and sister watche us from across the water as we sit down to rest. In the honeycomb caves, we find old monk's cells, the strange funereal array of human skulls and a bed of mud and wood and the geometric shape of the base of the tomb, eerie and unnatural, as the valley of falling evening stretches out below us. The Hazara women climb the nearby cliffs to their houses and the workers in the fields move into the end of day and a night's needed rest. Buddhists turned Moslem, this heathen practice of stark revealed bones, is not a part of their scene.

We had been here before, but now we understand much better. At the Red City, the old deserted city at the edge of the valley, three layers of buildings and watch towers once housed nobility and its protective armies. Then, after Genghis Khan's grandson was killed there, the Khan vowed to revenge his death by destroying the whole valley—which he did, ending with Share-Golgotha, where the daughter of Suleiman Jalladin betrayed the whole town by sending a note (legend tells) to the fierce Mongol telling him how to cut off the city's water supply. She was herself later murdered for her betrayal by the conqueror. We sit on the top of the city, several brick towers, still intact, with the little Tajik-Hazara guide who listens to the wind and points out all the directions, the Hazigah Pass, the Cuh-e-Baba Mountains, Foolodie, the road to Doshi.

Himself down earlier, goat-footed and racing to bring up another group to the top of the ram-shackled hill, he asks us about our Persian and our life here as well as his own, then walks us later to the teahouse beside the road where we patiently wait for three hours for a vehicle to come and take us back to Bamiyan. It is a 10-mile trek, but we pass the time well as the friendly people question and instruct us. Our young guide sings and plays *dutar*, and an emir of the Shar-Zohak area who has been out supervising the construction of a hotel at the base of the city, tells us how much he likes American teachers. Like glittering pebbles at the bottom of a rushing stream, we glimpse the concerns behind his questions: what about races, religion, children, and produce in America? He queries us as to how we like Afghanistan, and how life in Tashkurghan had been, and whether or not we had swum in the lakes at Bande-Amir. While goat herders doze in the sun and their flocks nibble, two old men (their faces dry and lined, beard and ear hair grown together, crusty-handed) pray under the straw roof of a wall-less structure across the road from the teahouse. A truckload of Kutchi women on a bangled, brightly-painted truck eat under their dusty blankets, their voices a low rumble, complaining and nibbling their dry bread while their men eat at the teahouse. Then we observe the tourists in the bazaar; the bulk of them this time seem to be made up of thin, lightly—garbled French couples, and I reflect how people in groups always seem slightly arrogant.

Making up the Waz to Bandi-Amir the next cold morning, when we float suspended until the first lake comes into view, are the shopkeeper Shafiq who is also the Mareks' landlord, and his brother the mullah at the General Store, and the battery of "malim-sibes." These are all of the shopkeeper-innkeepers at the little tourist town establishment, inhabitants of paltry buildings at the foot of the austere mountains, from which the lakes stretch beyond them.

Here, too, we note the discrepancy between two Afghanistans, where in one rich Kabulis can set up a camping tent complete with lawn chairs and umbrellas and barbecue stand, identical to a family outing in the U.S., while their countrymen cling to the thin sides of the mountain, living in black-sooted caves, and others, the nomadic Kutchi follow their herds living in real tents. The strange clamor from the children, "baksheesh, baksheesh" swells up everywhere around the lake, while the herdsmen and their wives further away from the town shout after us, asking for "dawa," (medicine) pointing out a sore arm or a place on their face, talking of younger brothers or sisters who have such sores, of three days of walking needed to reach the one barebones basic clinic.

We move on, above and around the cliffs, until we are tired and dry and our zinc-oxided faces have turned red. Pausing, we take in the rare beauty of the colors in the lake, the inhuman grandeur and size of the dry hills and plateaus around. Nights we sit in the damp mud room on rope beds under mountains of covers. Another visitor, a youth from Belgium, coughs loudly in front of us (he spent most of his boyhood in Zaire, the former Belgian Congo, where his family three times lost all of their household when they were forced to leave). And out alone on the hill from the *kenerab,* we look out to the frontier-like camp of the town below, the wide starry night, the slightly howling wind, the chatter of the tourists excitedly absorbing every angle of this world until they too crawl off to bed.

And then dusty, cold morning light. We remember: meeting the neighbors, openly friendly women in colorful dresses, their children tiny and silent; walking one day to see the Valley of the Dragon, the rift, a cleavage at the top of the stone structure which looks exactly as if someone had sliced it with a sword (and the Hazarajet legends tell that Hazrat Ali did this act), the minuscule springs representing the perpetual tears of the slain beast, the rock his scales, the color his blood; seeing the Afghan Tour people on horseback and their guide, a young Frenchman; swimming in the icy arms of the lake, sitting on the salty white dry banks of another, and just walking then. Oddly this is a reversal, as we meet the native inhabitants of the area, for the traveler now is the wealthy one and they who have homes and a place to stay are the poor . . . .

Mirad tells us about the *'lublubchas'* (beets), a plant so sweet that people lick their lips when they eat them, and thus the name.

Mirad's friend Asef speaks of the importance of having work papers to establish your legitmacy to work for foreigners, in Kabul. His friend had been working for some Germans one year and the woman came home from the university and ate lunch with her husband as usual. Then the man went off to his job at the zoo, and the woman went upstairs to rest. She took a heart attack and died. But Asef was innocent in it all because he had had his work papers in order that year.

Hearing details of our trip to Bamiyan, Mirad also describes the place beyond Bamiyan where a rock stands. No matter what size you are, if you can squeeze through, you are proven to be without many sins. But, if you get stuck you are a very sinful person. We didn't find the rock.

We toss out as many of the Afghan sayings and expressions as we can, among ourselves, translating from the English, or the Farsi, using a small collection published in Kabul a few years earlier and noting the ones which resonate best. In these stark mountains, mostly devoid of human echoes, all of human nature seems reduced to simple sentences:

> On hypocrisy: Under his arm the Koran, and his eye on the bullock.
>
> On a bad-tempered person: Like a mad dog he snaps at himself. Or, You can not clap with one hand alone.
>
> On courteousness: Be it but an onion, let it be given graciously. In another mood: Though your enemy is a rope, call him a snake.
>
> On resoluteness: Do not take hold of sword grass, but if you do, grasp it tight.
>
> On industry: Whosoever loves, labors.
>
> On the reliable: Doubt destiny's faith as salt does money. Also, God will remain, friends will not.
>
> Parents say, "Our boy is growing." They forget that life is, in reality, shortening.

Others similarly reflect our obtuseness, or our disappointments:

> The ungrateful son is a wart on his father's face. To leave it is a blemish, to cut it is a pain.
>
> Shoes are tested on the feet, a man on trial.
>
> When a knife is over a man's head, he remembers God.
>
> A frog mounted on a clod and said that he had seen Kashmir.
>
> Even if a mouse were as big as a bullock, it would always be the slave of a cat.
>
> To say, "Bismullah" brings blessings, but not in wicked pursuits.
>
> Though the clouds be black, yet white drops fall from them.
>
> Finally, love of wealth in old age is scorned: "Oh thou Greybeard, thou eateth earth."

About the idyllic trip to the Bande-Amir plateau and the village of Bamiyan: the people who live half the year in their mud straw huts with their cattle in snowbound cold and work almost ecstatically in the fertile summer months to raise wheat and alfalfa, feed for themselves and their cattle, and who have irrigated their high valleys so that the sound of running water is everywhere, who eat the grass itself, so little do they ask to keep themselves alive—these people have water to drink—according to a lab analysis made on Benson and Susan's water source, a "spring" behind their house—that is 80% fecally-contaminated.

In Bamiyan the boys are all short of sight, from vitamin deficiences and the harsh sun and weather and dust. Classes are conducted in the sun because it is too cold in the buildings, so there are always distractions and the sound of floating voices from some other windowless, wall-less "class," and the whir and descend of dust as a car or truck passes on the town's main street. The dust billows and stretches all the way to the back of the school yard, and there is no chalk or paper anywhere . . .

And the Mareks' kind landlord, Shafiq, has a many-tentacled family, several sets in from west of Bamiyan now, come to spend the winter there. So Shafiq, although the landlord and shopkeeper, must sleep at the volunteers' house (where all their fare of food is humorously strange to him, but where the warm stove makes all other strangeness inconsequential). He loves the heat and the room all to his own. When the B's come down for vacation after finals in a month, they must take all their things with them, as his relatives will move in to the house and surrounding shelters while they are away, so precious is shelter.

There is intense cold at 8,000 feet, the *jewis* all frozen in early morning, and it is the last of the harvest: people sleep in their fields to collect potatoes and grains, their only food stock for the coming seasons' austerity. And young boys with barely a cotton shirt on walk on hardened dry skinny legs out to collect water and grain.

Back in Kabul our yard is looking bare now; some creature knocked down about half of the corn stalks and most of the large grapes are gone. Yellow plum tomatoes seem prolific; the more standard, staked red bushes aren't readily producing. Broccoli is up and soon to be eatable, and the small green seedless grapes are sweet.

. . . The week out of Kabul convinced us again that Afghan people are uniquely warm, generous, and courteous. Everywhere we went people had only to hear we spoke Dari, and they enthusiastically took us under wing to talk, to pass stories, to become friends.

Will we have to haunt the old bazaars in Kabul and keep those elements alive around us, so we don't get discouraged by the big city solitude?

August 31, 1975

It is Pushtoonistan Independence Day, but it is a day not officially recognized and therefore we're not supposed to celebrate it, because the U.S. Embassy doesn't—with good reason, perhaps. But that doesn't make the U.S. any more loved by the Afghan government, for whom the issue of Pushtoonistan Independence is a major one. The areas immediately across the Durand Line, another British absurdity, where their Pushtoon brothers dwell, they claim as they own, and insist should be an independent Pushtoon country. It is a only the other provinces beyond these that they would delegate to Pakistan.

A Kutchi wedding takes place on the street beside the AID compound. Children are made up like round-eyed ghouls with heavy make-up, women in silver jeweled bracelets and lockets and in bright purple and scarlet dresses, toss and swirl their hair, as drummers and tambourines play a procession down that most unculturated street. Perhaps the group has come from a camp beyond the ivory-walled American complex.

September 2, 1976

. . . In the morning I go to the bank to take out money to pay our visible debts, and mail somethings at the Big Post Office. I wander with a stiff determined gait in the largely all-male crowds of boxer-short and loud *ghilim* sellers, past carnival boards, a burst-the-balloon booth, around instant refreshment stands in hideous garish colors, and the million used clothes and banged pots and old book bazaars, all melting into notations on a perpetual village fair.

Then Ziadeen appears at Peace Corps and comes over to our house. Our old teacher, speaking quickly, in clear English now, unloads on us all the gossip and news of the people we mutually know: Our old *modir* is teaching at Avicenna High School now and his wife, who had lost another child, is teaching at a school 30 kilometers out of the city, a morning bus ride away. Most of the Jalalabad teachers have returned to Jalalabad now and he himself is to be sent back to Tashkurghan for a little while, though his wife, eight months pregnant, will stay and his cousin, who is soon to be acting *modir-e-mareft* of Samangan, will get him an easier job, a transfer to the school in Aybak. He has been teaching Pushtu to one American couple, and a German couple, but while the latter had worked hard and learned a lot, the former had indicated that they didn't consider Pushtu important enough to pursue, although they were doggedly intent on going to Logman. PC wanted them in Samangan. He said no single volunteer would go to Tashkurghan, as per our recommendation.

Then he promises to take up the letters for my students, borrows some money he insists he will pay back in a week, and launches into an explanation of how the very religious people of Khulm had made up bad stories about his living in Mazari's house. He announces that Mazari is now engaged to a rich man who already has a wife and five children in Kunduz, and how she will be "sold" for 80,000 afghanis. Meanwhile, her cousin, and Paregul and Solyra, had all failed and Shahzadah's father is about to be transferred to another province, so that this year's 11th class is almost non-existent.

. . . I laugh. We spend an absurd morning trying to get our introductions to the University, and can only be critical, and a tad ironic now, of the way Jawid handles it. He fails to make a call and so when we get to the *powhantoon* (university) we find that both of the people to whom we are to be introduced are absorbed or engaged in meetings. He does not intend to interrupt or wait until they are over, so we return home, the status of our work there still unresolved. But my impression is that I should just go and introduce myself the first day of school, this Saturday.

September 4, 1975

Ziadeen arrives angry, but now is free of sad looks, for he has just learned that he will be transferred to Jalalabad Province and then to some tiny village up near Nuristan at the Pushtoonistan border. Shockingly, her explains that this is where four teachers were killed in the post-Jeshen uprising by the network of religious mullah party adherents triggered and supported by Pakistani agents. In fact, they are the same group who killed commandants and officials and soldiers in Gulbahar, Kandahar, near Gardez, and "a few other places besides this *kenorab*." He is simply one of the 1,200 Jalalabad teachers sent out to do teaching in the provinces for two years and now transferred back to Jalalabad, which still does not have enough jobs for them . . .

We remind him that the transfer could change tomorrow. Everything does. But we say nothing about the relative who was to find him an easy job.

And my old *modir* visited the PC office, and spoke of visiting the Faculty of Adabiyaat (Arts and Letters) at Kabul University. Not seeing us, he did not share where he lived, but spoke of some problems his wife was having, and then left . . .

September 5

Mirad tells us that superstitious people speak of tonight as Borat, the night before the start of Ramadan, when the spirits of the dead come out of their graves. Hungry ghosts abound, it would seem.

September 7, 1975

Sitting at the university in a sterile room of three desks, I have yet to be formally "introduced," though the importance of that daily diminishes, and the classes have yet to begin, with the official calendar saying there is registration this week and the start of classes on Saturday. At the same time, with the dismissal of the faculty's assistant dean, the individual who was primarily in charge of scheduling, there appears to be little chance that "unscheduled" classes can begin as (un)scheduled.

I wonder why he was dismissed. Is it his proximity to the Americans, who started this program?

Yesterday marked the beginning of Ramadan. Mirad tiredly returned from Sare-Pul where he left two sons healthy and his wife and parents solidly stocked with wheat and fuel for the winter . . . His brother Qorbin secured a job with a U.N. family (Egyptian husband and Swiss wife) in Share-nau and they would have hired Qorbin's wife, too, but he opposed her becoming anyone's *"nana"* at any price. In his pin-striped suit and fashionably long hair, Qorbin could pass for a rising businessmen . . . with male comradeship and smooth talk . . . and by contrast Mirad maintains a shy, countryman's air which makes him more enduring.

When Mirad arrived the morning of Ramadan, he told us he had begun his fast, and had heard the gun sound at 3 a.m. to announce the beginning. And although not totally sure this was the official start until morning, he now felt it was definitely Ramazan. Yet he had seen Afghans on the road coming over eating or smoking, defiling their religion or ignorant. (But, he tells us, a true Moslem must always be prepared to begin his fast, because if he fails just one day to preform the fast he negates all the good of fasting the other 29 days). This is severe . . .

Today I meet some of my university colleagues (Rick Dwyer and Dick Pettey, the latter here until December), and a few Afghan students or instructors popped in their heads for a moment's talk. The American PCVS seem to pride themselves on keeping their distance from everyone here, except a few students from very wealthy families who are so well implanted in Afghan political and historical life that they are invulnerable to coups or official changes.

One such had his story told by this fellow named Dick, who claims the student is about to be married to a girl now off visiting in the States.

The wedding is slightly rushed because his father, main adviser to Daud, is currently involved in the decisions and acts which keep him occupied full time—in effect stemming from some Western oil company interests in Afghan fields. There has been an ultimatum from the company to the effect that they would develop nothing here as long as Afghanistan was as Soviet-looking as it appeared now. So Daud is supposed to gradually ease out his "Russia-soft" cabinet members, in the greater interest of Afghan development. Meanwhile, the rich student's brother-in-law, chief of police or likely the controller of political insurgents, is nightly in the dungeon room at the base of one ministry (Ministry of Foreign Affairs) working with old style Soviet and universal horror techniques to torment his prisoners (members of the religiously-extreme Mullah Party) and force them to reveal all the aspects of the religiously radical party. This latter is judged as synonymous with the Pakistan-supported series of assassinations.

Will we get answers to these questions?

Since there is no university bus, I wait for the city bus, but one after the other overflows with little school children, so each pauses and goes on. I speak to a teacher from the Faculty of Letters who teaches English, Linguistics, and Anthropology. She asks accordingly what I do (the conversation is a perfect repeat of the one I had had with the janitor in the Engineering building, who had started out with a question as to where the two PCVs, the yellow and red-headed husband and wife—the T's—had gone to).

[I sight Tom up the hill, so jump off the bus and join him.]

A Kabul city bus between the hours of noon and 6 o'clock is like a frozen Noah's ark, overcrowded with a sampling of each genre of people here, but heaviest with the black-dressed white-scarfed school girls and the little clinging school boys in their baggy western pants and too-worn shirts. I dangle from a strap or a bar, standing most of the way, fighting for a place on the bus, the second one, once it finally comes. Around me hover the women, whose numbers are only slightly less than the men, but they are compelled to sit in one-quarter of the area, among the overrun of frantic school girls.

September 9, 1975

. . . Yesterday marked the official entrance into the academic world here. I attended a faculty meeting, met the Dean and some of the more talkative staff, and gained more faith in my contemporaries, or at least one of them. This is a volunteer who came here last December, who had spent two years as an English teacher in a small central Afghan village, and whom we had met before, an extendee from Brenda and Chris Mahoney's cycle. He had lived simply, read the classics, shared the distinction of being a foreigner in a village with some Italian and French nurses and priests at the local clinic, eight hours away from the nearest volunteer (whom he could only reach by going to stand on a half-road and catching a truck or something going that way) since there were no buses.

The faculty meeting itself turns on a discussion of students about to be failed or dropped from the faculty for low averages, a professor being rehired who had previously quit to take a position which never materialized for a government industrial bank, and a plan for faculty leaves. The interplay of personalities is impressive here, with the rigid Parliamentarian sort who sits on the edge of his seat waiting for a mistake to cite as out of order; the even-toned, small, quiet chairman (the Dean that day); an energetic, strong-minded professor who challenges every approved motion introduced by the thin American professors of engineering in their cotton, short-sleeved colored shirts and gray faces and thinning hair, and who looked active but bored. All in all the Afghan professors exhibit meticulous and fluent English and obvious competence and intelligence (which makes me all the more appalled at any unprofessional-ism among my PCV colleagues).

Street scenes: one of the hand-pedaled wheel chairs for Kabul's crippled, loaded down with the poor man's three children, moves steadily beside traffic downtown; the dry, mucous-like deposit of the Kabul River where a few brightly scarfed women sit swatting their laundry and thin boys in shorts splash in upstream; several hundred city workers, drafted soldiers, move stones to make a temporary dam across one end of the river, shuffle in their gray worn uniforms and dark-burned faces, and shaven heads in the small space like prisoners of time; an old man sends his two huge lopping camels galloping across the street between insanely stuffed buses, trucks, diverting cars and taxis; the Kutchi sisters, wandering in tears behind their four sheep, come from the road behind the palatial AID compound (where I had seen the Kutchi wedding the night before.)

September 12, 1975

. . . I love my talk with my fellow professor, Ms Azur, who speaks proudly of her husband's trip for a month to Germany last spring for a conference. He has now been promoted to a higher office in the Ministry of Mines. A number of students from that half semester I taught a summer ago come back to greet me, congenial and a little mischievous, one of a pair of juniors especially so. One of T's students from the same time sits down and in perfect English lays out his plans for the future: he has gone into architecture along with most of the other good English speakers in his class. They intend to go through all of the government low-pay jobs, but maintain a lucrative private practice on the side. "And, of course," he interjects: "Civil engineering has a lot of humanitarian value to it, with all the poverty and such in Afghanistan, but these kinds of projects are not being implemented yet, so I must begin where work exists."

He had tried to get accepted as an AFS student and go study in the States all through high school, but every year those eligible had been one class ahead of him. Then, by the time he graduated from high school there weren't any more students going, period. By government decree, no Afghan student could participate.

We harvest some of the garden corn this morning, a totally freakish crop like something out of an art supply store—a twisted cross of Indian corn—purple, black and large-toothed, irrationally placed gems of lavender and gray and yellow. Mirad suggests that we preserve the seeds and take the cobs to an official during some holiday (after an old custom often done with a particularly large pad of cotton), and collect a slight "baksheesh" for the oddity. But we just eat it . . .

Mirad stood before us, aghast at the news that his friend Ghafar's PCV had spent 20,000 afs. on dishes and stuffed woolen pillows, and 1,000 afs. for flowers. Meanwhile, news came from Tom who had pedaled off to the USIS compound to watch "Godspell", that we could subscribe to an eight-part music series, offered here, with the first performance scheduled at the Goethe Institute on October 1.

The nights and mornings are unquestionably chilly now; we have a sudden sense of being high in mountain air. By day, the sky is blue. The sights and sounds in the morning: the call of a *"konah-forish"*, a figure out of "Aladdin and the Magic Lamp," the old man who goes about each neighborhood intent on buying odds and ends from each compound, which he will in turn sell to some jumble of bazaars "down town." A small boy with a thin donkey carrying a huge burlap bag full of giant tomatoes comes to ring the doorbell at the sumptuously large yard next door and a young servant girl in scarf, *unchadris*-ed, comes out to bargain for the family's purchases in a blending of ancient barter and modern convenience.

. . . One of my projects underway here is to make up lots of pamphlets of supplementary reading for the provincial schools, and to work on organizing the PC library. I want also to keep up my writing [the genuine "hobby" Tom credits me with having, while he has none].

September 14, 1975

. . . It is enlightening to get some glimpses of the volunteers' life in Kandahar, these volunteers who came and taught as we did, but who were settled in the heart of the Pushtoon world. They have come to admire the kind of pride and clannishness of their Pushtoon neighbors, the very qualities we so often would criticize as outsiders. Further, they are entrenched in a fairly comfortable lifestyle with German friends also living in their town, and enjoy their teaching jobs, their schools, the fruits from their gardens, the bazaar always running-over with tropical fruit, banana, coconuts, grapefruits, all winter long. They admire the old, old *chadris-ed* women who perch outside the hat shops in Kandahar to sell their handmade specialties; and have even come to understand the Pushtoon's version of a Pushtunistanstan, a land which would stretch to the Indus and most certainly include Peshawar . . . .

Today in my first semblance of classes, I amble in bright-eyed to start the first hour with a Freshmen section. But attendance starts with one, grows to two, three, then seven by the end of the period, a quiet, gentlemanly group, at whom I smile too much, as I collect names and background, and disperse a parcel about my own background, and then dismiss. With a colleague, Paul Oldsman, I then venture to meet the section of Technical Vocational Engineering students. There are 10 enrolled and today five are present, including two from Badakshan. We meet in a small, untidy classroom behind an architect's drafting studio. My examples for them come slowly, and I struggle with the tiny blackboard, my crumbling chalk, their timeliness and silent, tireless watch, as I press on and on with questions from their inimical grammar book. It makes me quite blind and mad by an hour and a half, by which time most of their alloted period for the day has been used up. With a load of books to weigh me down. I beat a hasty retreat home to shuffle over a hundred options for the two classes, ways to fill up fourteen lecture hours.

Like a clear omen of obtainable success, I smile to myself; I have a legitimate seat on both illusive, bundle-bursting buses between the university and home, as a dark-eyed, timid girl of four clings to my knee, looking frantically back and forth between my grinning face and her *chadrised* mother.

. . . . In his best *tanbon* and *peron* and on Tom's bike, Mirad rides off to be a dinner guest, after he has finished his chores here. Earlier he had exclaimed over the plants from the Mahoneys, the country boy who loves beauty, collecting all that is green as beautiful in his eyes. Again, as he has on silent nights last year back in Tashkurghan, he retells memories of his army days in Badakshan. The thoughts are set off by my questioning him about a language called Sharsaglree. He explains that the language is spoken in a village of the same name, high in the mountains, a place so cold the people wear heavy felt clothes and woolens most of the year round, and ride on yaks *(gahwarees)*. His first year he was in a small town south of Faizabad, his second year way up at the Russian border and Oxus River, a place all the soldiers in his company had to walk for ten days to reach. He, however, got to fly in because he was carrying the official papers from Kabul. But, he tells us, Badakshan, is even further up in the mountains, and there had been a famous donkey-eared king who had once ruled there.

"To keep his secret, the donkey-ears, the king would have each barber killed, one after the other," Mirad relays in Dari.

September 17, 1975

I meet for real the regular Freshman section today and discern a fair number read well and do so with good comprehension. They sit, the men sixteen strong, one woman, silent and polite, as I chatter about the elements of the course.

. . . For dinner we have the Leighs (we of the Ivy League graduate corps—Jeb went to Yale, just as our Bamiyan master Benson went to Harvard, and I am the spawn of Columbia and Tom of Princeton), and Mikita . . . They share a picture of the gossip of Kabul, pass on the sorts of stories of broken or dangerous relationships that friends sit around and tell each other at tranquil afternoon teas, I guess, anywhere in the world.

One involves a couple who had been forced to marry against their wishes and who live in a house over the river in northern Kabul. Nightly the husband and wife would scream and tear each other up and knock each other down, until the girl's family began to make threats to the effect that something had better change quickly. A flood of sorts descended on their house and, the husband claimed, swept his wife into the river and drowned her. The local officials searched the river and found another woman's body. The wife's was never found. The husband was never tried, never punished in any way.

Another story involves the popular Afghan singer-poet (was it Ahmad Zahir?) who was made to marry a girl whom everyone knew to be a tramp. She was pregnant before the marriage, or pregnant by someone else afterwards, and was found killed about the time of the Paghman flood after Jeshen. The man was arrested in his home in Paghman, at the time of the arrest surrounded by three unmarried girls, and given seven years in prison for each woman found his his presence.

Yet another tale, this told by the Grants of Lagman, involved their former landlord's son and one of Patricia's married students. The couple, against all rules, chose to meet, and selected the Grants' garden as the site for a rendez-vous. When, out for a stroll, Jacob, came upon them in the midst of some heavy lovemaking, he was stumped and they fled. There was nothing to do but for the Grants to move out. Their cook, scornful of the affair, claimed that the women's husband had known about it all along, but being a kid (not a man, who—Akbar the cook claimed—would have seen the girl punished by death), he just let it go on.

One more Romeo and Juliet episode gone sour comes from the Grants in Lagman. They had offered their garden as a site for some photographs for a student, but the student had arranged a tryst with an admiring girl, one of Patricia's students, all under the guise of having himself photographed with her. After the photo shoot, the couple continued to meet, people heard, and one day the boy came running to ask Jacob to hide the gun he was carrying because "they" were after him. Soon after that, the boy was evicted from the town but, Mikita claims, he has since made himself much in evidence in Kabul for she has seen him several times.

Mikita, with her wry humor, reports on her high school's preparation for International Women's Day festivities. One side detail for the event has been student essays, prepared on the assigned subject and uniformly copied, which share the common phrase that in the past "the life of women here was all bad." When having some of her teachers and their boyfriends over for tea once, she was overwhelmed by the obnoxiousness of one particular Kabuli male who put on his girlfriend's make-up and shirt and begged cab fare to his Rabia Balkhi rehearsal. Later, the saner teacher dropped this man and saw him get married off (but the romance of an affair had long blinded her). Then the man appeared as the singer of the "Pink Tulips" band which was practicing at her school for the International Women's Day event, and she could scarcely believe it.

September 19, 1975

I have now had a series of my classes. All the students are there now, and Wednesday and Thursday they began to take on faces for me, to have real distinguishably qualities. A lot of them act rather solicitous with me, coming up to ask questions, to outline and query a particular point I have stuttered over in class. One is always conscious of being listened to, of not having every point absorbed at face value, but at least of having someone's attention. I'm shocked at how quiet they are. I stumble to a stop and the pause seems unearthly long. Okay, I must be more inventive in the class and find ways to keep them interested.

[With friends and friends of friends we have tea and dinner and] . . . eventually we are all drawn into the talk of Ahad, a medical student, and Tom, about the Moslem's idea of non-believers: The thought goes that all of us after Mohamed who have not enlarged our knowledge of God beyond the three books, are to go to hell, even as our ancient ancestors who lived before Mohamed are still eligible for heaven if they were faithful to their prophet in their time. We discuss half in jest, half seriously, the overtones of this statements. Finally Ahad defended (or rejected it?) all by telling us that Ahad himself couldn't understand why a God would exist who could decide whether people went to hell or to heaven, because that would make him a selfish God, and why should man honor someone with such petty interests . . . . Is it not the classic question?

The medical student spoke of how difficult it is for any student to get a passport to leave the country for the West, that each passport costs 2 ½ *lag* (250,000 *afs*), and before the stage in which you are actually asking for a passport, you have to *baksheesh* a lot of intermediaries. Of course, even after gelding their palms, they may not even go on to the next step for you,and deliver what you need.

Jeb Leigh had been in the Ministry that handles these things that very morning and witnessed one Afghan's solution to intolerable bureaucracy: a large *khan* came strutting in and demanded to see the principal of the bureau, and when a clerk behind the counter looked at his passport and told him it was no longer good for travel, he shook the house rafters with his stream of invectives, sending the clerks huddling in a corner. Finally one of the clerks called the *modir*, who promised to come right in, as the others tried to calm down the blustery man.

Somewhere in the conversation, the call for evening prayer unfolds, marking *iqfal*,the end of the fast, and the two Afghans leave us.

September 22, 1975

> *[Discussions are rich in this city, but they are among the expatriates and a few edge-hanging educated Afghans, and travelers. So we chat about literary and political issues, music and history, physics and reality, and about my youngest brother . . .*

with one of Danny's former Reed friends on route to India, an Englishman named Peter Child and his significant other, Sally]

We go to see a young Indian dancer of Kathak dancing, age 12, who has the suppleness and wild beauty of her progeny, something of the frenzied ascetic in her purity, as well as the soul of sensuous age and dignity, the skilled professional in her perfect dance. Much struck me as strange: the place of her chanting in between dance sets, the hand motions, the delicate silver bells on her ankles, each obviously a stylized interpretative gesture revealing some part of the story or an emotion . . . Also what came out was the difference between an eastern and a western audience, how much talking and movement is allowed in the former, how the audience comes to behave naturally, unrestrained while a performance goes on, following the way of the bamboo, bending naturally with the currents, and how they see the dead silence and stiff formalness with which we westerners attend a performance as tasteless. The first half we saw was guileless, interesting, if strange; the second half warped with PA popular songs and tinny music, seemed to undermine the traditional, but likely it also represents blending of styles and time endemic to Indian culture, syntheses. Syncretism.

Sept. 25, 1975

[Others have visited Tashkurghan and speak of its familiarities and charm). After their trip, the Leighs report back to us that all the children say "misses" for women. One day when they were wandering near the girl's school, indirectly on route to the boys', they ran into a line of little black-dressed, black-bagged girls just out of school, who froze at the sight of them. Asked where they were going, they then repeated *"moktab"* (school) four times in unison, before the Leighs scurried over the rickety bridge and out of their gentle sight, and the girls moved on. Another day John wandered to the Bagh-e-Jemoriat and came upon a young workman huddling behind a wall walloping a melon, breaking Ramazan fast—In one second the culprit tried to persuade Jeb to join him, in order to lessen his own crime, by "hosting and welcoming a stranger." Another scene that impressed them was the coming of night at the hotel and how the old Baba put out his little table and carefully set up a glass of water and some nan, and then went to find himself a melon from his garden, before

seating himself ceremoniously, eagerly ready for the *azad* (call to prayer) to sound . . .

We read a letter from Brenda and Chris Mahoney [our replacements]. They are sharing a house with a widow and her son who help with water and wash on the first floor. Brenda says my students vow to always love me and they shower her with a thousand questions a day about me. Her husband has inherited both 10B classes, one notorious 10-B of last year having failed in total, plus one eleventh and one twelfth class . . . So that dogged struggle goes on.

Yesterday morning my old *modir* from Tashkurghan came to visit: Mr. Shukor ceremoniously leads me to room 116 from my own office, where I shake his hand and Rashidullah goes through all the formalities of asking about my family and Tom and my job. Awkwardly, because he is always so quiet and I generally am too in such situations, he finally reminisces with Shukor about old friends and faculty at Adabiyaat (Arts and Letters), from which they both graduated, and shares with us the not surprising troubles Muzdah had with her job, and the illogical course of the government when it comes to providing jobs for Afghan teachers. Then, as I rise to go to off and give a quiz to a freshman class, he stands, too, and presents me with an envelop with an invitation to dinner at his house for tomorrow night . . . He bows, saying he will meet T and me at the PC office a little before the time and take us to his house . . .

Last night we were the guest of the Leighs' friend, Ahad, in a house on the hill in Jemominah, the "real city," behind the university, with pungent open latrines emptying into the dirt roads and steep winding paths going straight up the hills (there are three hills, with slight indentations below them).

A moon-filled night, the chewed crescent hovers between the dark outlines of the hills where a thousand brightly lit houses vouch for the patterns of its inhabitants. An old woman from Wardak (his home town) had stood on his roof halfway up the mountain one night that week and told him that the sky had fallen down into the land and when a light was turned on in a dark courtyard, she exclaimed that "they must not put their burning basket near her head because it would be too much warmth."

His medical student Zmaria from Herat is present. He's a fourth year, one of the surviving 28 from his original medical class of almost 200, in the year when 28 fellow students from Lycee Sultan in Herat were accepted into the university, more than half to the Faculty of Medicine, around 11 to Engineering, the others to Arts and Letters. Seated in Ahad's room, we introduce ourselves to three of his brothers and one 8-month old niece as the evening unwinds. The youngest brother serves us: rice and stew and yogurt, melon and grapes and tea.

Ahad describes the "adult" high school he goes to. Peace Corps had hired him to work for them when he was just a bright 15-year old, had him as a language teacher for five years, one year of which had been in Colorado in Estes Park. So he missed graduating high school and now he goes every night to make up courses. In six months he should finish the 12th class, and then must begin again his battle to get out of the army. A tour with Yasir last year lost him his PC job . . . After that he worked as a translator for the SUNY team in a demographic survey, and for a while (an unpleasant one), he worked as a clerk who managed the inventory at the USAID commissary. Apparently the ever popular, omnipresent Mr. Shukor of my faculty taught there a while, also, but was ridiculed and fired because he never prepared his classes, or tried to get his students' respect. This is our host's take on it, but I question his harshness on my colleague, pretending not to hear this latter slander. Surely, like they say of the Irish, Afghans "are a fair people who never speak well of each other."

The student Zmaria flushes excitedly as he recalls an Afghan heart specialist who now works at Johns Hopkins and makes 12 thousand dollars a a month, having defected from a conference he was sent to in India and then gone on to the States. Its the same area of specialty Zmaria hopes to pursue. Like medical students everywhere, he sighs and reiterates the tremendous work involved in being a medical student, the tons of materials they must absorb. When I ask him if there are many girls in his class, since I know to become a doctor is a huge ambition for the best female students, he pauses, looking around.

"Actually, girls do not do very well because of their weaker stamina. And, of course, they can not easily adopt the kind of male openness about anatomy that is needed. In fact, our traditions make studying in the same room with men virtually unacceptable. But, some make it, will succeed, and yes, they are very much needed."

. . . We take a star-dazzled stroll down the hill, out into the night, to the road again, the lip of the university, to hear Ahad speak of how the compound people regard the moon as a holy place where the angel who will announce the end of the world lives. (He'll play on his "flute," as Ahad describes it, and the earth will get flat). This is why few Afghans can understand about the "moon shots." Then, a clever mime, he gives a little solo skit showing the differences in vocabulary and gesture of Afghans from Herat to Pinjsheer, to Tashkurghan. (About seven or more years ago, he had worked during a cholera inoculation when there was an epidemic in the north and the town of Tashkurghan was closed off, quarantined).

. . . Again, the regimen, the rituals of my class, a mountain of work to appease them: worksheets and quizzes and study guides to type, and writing assignments to check. I return a batch of papers and am amazed to see the student's shy kind of shame at any numbers under 90%. These are all captains of their high school classes, the "creme de la crème." Yet some seem slow and do not respond to my questions, my direct prodding. They act so much younger than I originally thought of them as being, and are in fact almost contemporaries. In any case they'll keep me busy, and for once, learning English, the language of all textbooks and research in this faculty, makes sense.

On the bus coming home (crushed and thriving) I have a short talk with a sophomore in the Engineering faculty who has known our previous colleague, Mr. T. (the red-headed southern) and admires his good teaching. "It is so important for a teacher to have good methods," she shares. When she asks if I have seen any other cities in Afghanistan, and I tell her, she responds slowly, not really grasping how I could have lived in Tashkurghan for two years, and gone to and fro to Samagan, Aybak, and Mazar. Settling in, she compliments me on my Persian, praises Herat's historical sites, and exits the bus.

Sept. 21. 1975

Last night: a warmly received, comfortable evening at my old *modir's* house, with Rashidi (Balkhi) and Muzdah (they share it with her sister, mother of three). Also present are the sister's silent, intensely drawn husband, one slightly taunting son, a quiet sixth class sister, and Zudrah, who is still unemployed, still unaccepted at the university, at large since her graduation from high school over a year ago. As she did before, she still mopes about the horrible time she spent in Tashkurghan our first spring there, when she was visiting her sister, and was forced to sit dully around the house. By contrast, here she goes to movies and the park and walks about at will . . . She is a little too sophisticated for my tastes, without her sister's sense of humor, but I would not judge her, for what options does she have?

And the brother is a science graduate of the university and currently teaches at Habibia H.S. for 1400 afs a month. He had had Mark Havel as his teacher way back when, and admired his excellent Persian and ability to know Afghans on all levels. Clearly a thoughtful man, one who enjoys "the big questions," he speaks mostly with Tom, and sometimes with my old *modir*, about religion and science and their need for and possibility of a marriage. He takes the lead in bringing up the characteristics of Darwinism, and how the sociological improvement analogy could be applied to Christianity versus Islam (slavery, feudalism, bourgeoisism, socialism.) Either to him is an improvement on the former; Tom concludes that it is more important for a religion to teach people how to live in this world and this life and not in some future one, that in theory none of the simplest principles of Christianity—brotherhood, tolerance, care for the poor, peace—have ever been applied to actual life, that there is a huge discrepancy between acts and ideas in all the world's religions.

The highlight of the evening, inevitably, is our presenting the photographs I had taken from Tashkurghan. Muzdah enumerates the names of all the teachers, and speaks delicately about how she and her husband look. I hear of the death of the infant son of Sherifa, whose picture I had taken, who was sick one day and then gone, of the marriage of one of the 12th class teachers, of the transfer of various teachers to Mazar, and of the possibility of Najiba (the only female graduate of the 14th class around) becoming a *maimon* or someday a *modira* there . . . .

Oct. 1, 1975

. . . I am still in the first stage of organizing some regular 60 to 74 English stories to be distributed to the provincial schools . . . in between absorbing *[comments on the US Embassy, Joyce's genius as discussed by Anthony Burgess, and the prickly truisms and caveats of the German writer Boll].*

Oct. 3, 1975

With the approaching festivities, all the students in their well-cut suits begin gathering after class to greet each other, a visions of their holidays to start in the air today (although officially Eid is not until Sunday—today is Friday). Anticipation gives a mischievous merriness to them as a group,

I scour the *Travels of Marco Polo* for some descriptions of sites in Afghanistan. Southern Russia and Iran we recognize. It is clear that—rave reviews—the quality of the produce is fairly unchanged since the 13th century.

> *[I am also reading of sexual practices and prejudices in different cultures, and seeing the heart-wrenching consistency in offering women as benefits for guests, etc., and the connection between violence against women and violence against nature, as beautifully discussed by Patricia Griffith. Also, I am reading Neruda, and Edith Simon: The Golden Hind]*

Oct. 5, 1975

This midnight Eid begins. I've noted the fast less this year than when in Tashkurghan.

Mirad has traveled to Pinjsheer with his friend. Of all strange things, we entertain a visit from two German women, who present themselves as Jehovah Witnesses, a mother and a daughter. Do they not know that proselytizing is strictly forbidden in this Moslem land?

I run across a poem (thought) from Joel Dagan's *Dust:*

> *'It would be dishonest to pretend that /I went because I wanted to turn the desert into a garden or to realize dreams that were/thousands of years old./ I went because it was different/ because I had nothing else to do, because it was a road/ that might*

have an end.? I knew I would not stay forever;/I never thought of tying my future to this newness /I knew I would take the road back one day,/but perhaps carrying with me a particle/of the night's silence/of the day's honesty."

[Reading, reading, reading these months, these years: 30s Protest writings, as well as talking to Howard about his PhD work in psychology, attending a concert in the British Embassy ballroom, thinking of getting pregnant and how too orchestrated our lives have become, working to order the PC library, and taking in stories and meals with families of expatriates who have both children and unique past histories to share.]

. . . Mirad returned on Friday from his trip with Ghaffar to the mountains with tales of the fatted calf . . . He is full of praise for the beauty of the town, Tanger, larger in area than Tashkurghan he claims, but with fewer shops. He brings us a rich variety of pomegranates, full of juice, red and vibrant as they are sweet, all homegrown in the mountain valley.

. . . Our return to the full-time job at the university is well-founded and yet it is, also, cut into by the full-time job of organizing the library and writing the stories up in "graded English" to use in provincial schools. I would hate to be idle here.

Why Good People Still Try to Work in Afghanistan 2010

It is for the two dozen small girls who sit with their heads bowed in the dark, damp classrooms, listening like small doe caught in a headlight, their wondering eyes tense, having trekked into class and determined to study and learn, even though the previous evening, a shrouded figure delivered another night letter to the school, threatening them with death or maiming and their teachers with beheading if they continued to attend this school.

It is for the young Joya who walks to school every day past the very spot where her sister was murdered four years ago when she tried to escape from a *bad*, a way of mending a vendetta, a forced marriage between families in which a child is made to pay for the crime of her brother or father by marrying the family enemy and becoming the family's slave. Joya persuaded her parents to let her attend school and try to learn how to make her community and future better, to help her country as a doctor one day, to prevent that kind of injustice from ever harming another girl, another sister, another son.

It is for the young and re-entered teachers who struggle to show them how important their school is, what possibilities await them to help Afghanistan once they have gotten an education. It is for these classrooms where children sit and where their parents have sent them with worried eyes, never knowing if the children can come again, tomorrow, whether this school building will be standing. And yet, here they are, teacher and student, eager to learn as much as they can, fueled by their desire to study and to teach despite the barriers, eager to nurture the life and soul of Afghanistan itself.

It is because of those stories and people that crossed time and oceans, to follow on the courageous travels and initiatives of Suraya Sadeed from her initial humanitarian assistance to a forgotten land to her groundbreaking work with peace education and state-of-the art community-based girls' schools, narrated with energy and humility in her book, *Forbidden Lessons in a Kabul Guesthouse: The True Story of a Woman Who Risked Everything to Bring Hope to Afghanistan.* It is to honor the initiatives of Sima Wali in decades of work with refugee women, and on behalf of human rights. It is in celebration also of the challenges faced by Ann Jones in *Kabul in Winter* as she volunteered to teach Kabul women and advocate for their injust incarceration in a climate of foreign military intrusion and international for-profit investment that hindered more than helping. It is for the gripping and redeeming stories of shattered social means and abusive marriages, of friendship and love, which introduced this troubled land to book readers and moviegoers in the States and around the world in Khalid Hossain's *The Kite Runner* and *A Thousand Splendid Suns.* Perhaps courage lives in fiery indictments and rare acquiescing reports by RAWA, the *Guardian,* AfghanistanOnline, Rashid Ahmed (*Taliban*), Steven Coll (*Ghost Wars*), and dozens of others who have written with passion and truth about this country over the past decades.

It is to add to the story that gets told, that is always the same: The culpability and ignorance of the U.S. who "meddled so long and so recklessly in Afghanistan"(Jones 57); the creation of the Taliban; the funding of psychotic killer Hekmatyr and religiously extreme former *mujahadeen*; the neglect of common Afghans; the propping up of a failed client government; the expanding of NGOs, private development and drug lord, which bring almost nothing to the vast majority of the Afghan peoples; the fanaticism spilled across borders and fed by foreign states. It has all been said, ignored, or known but not said, or not said and not known, for decades.

It is for the individuals trying just to survive at the geopolitical fault line of a volatile ending twentieth, beginning twenty-first century. It is about reversing the patterns: nations more committed to their own agenda and interest in stark black and white (Soviet and America, West and Islam, Communist states and democracies), and more committed to using military interventions and arming of clients than to investing in stabilizing, long-term development and the facilitation of livelihoods, to better the lives of children and families around the world.

It is for the line of cornflower-burqaed women clutching infants and toddlers waiting in a clean and accessible health clinic, and the engaged, employed, eager staff of returned Afghan nurses and doctors; and the programs which provide health screening, maternal and prenatal care, inoculations, and free medicine. It is for this scene multiplied thousands of times in Barkai-Barki, Kabul, Peshawar, Rostaq, or Faizabad, affirming, supporting, enabling life, in belated but powerful reaction to the 50 to 100,000 citizens killed or debilitated under the 1978-1979 Khalq government when the US—by admission of Stanfield Turner, then CIA director—used "other people's lives for the geopolitical interests of the US", the 2 million Afghans killed by the USSR and its clients by 1992, the 600,000 maimed, the 6 million forced into exile as refugees, the 2 million IDPs and the "perhaps one and a half million driven insane by ceaseless war."

It is for the soldiers killed and maimed and damaged for life, Americans as well as those of other nationalities.

It is to try, to believe, in, righting a wrong.

XVII

KABUL LURES, KABUL LIFE

Oct. 14, 1975.

[Tonight we went to the USAID staff house with Cheryl Paul and some of her Fulbright friends . . . to hear Margaret Mills (who had visited us in Tashkurghan) talk about "Storytelling in Herat.". . . She begins by defining storytelling, explaining that it is really a lowly profession because the person is recognized as a trader in *drogh* ("lies"), but that almost every family has someone who can tell the old stories. With the advent of radio and the passing of the need to break the cotton by hand, the frequency of storytelling has declined. People let the stories pass in and out of oral tradition, over generations; many details, whole stories get forgotten. A woman tells stories usually about women, a man about men, and the stories are usually about magic or about romance and heroes (military, religious, thieves).

She launches then into reading from her translation of a celebrated storyteller, one of her favorite stories about Khasta Khamarah, or the Snake Man and the Human Brick.

All stories start out about a virgin, a prince, or a thorn picker, and this one begins with the adventures of a poor thorn-picker who finds a rich storehouse of wheat under a stone while he is picking thorns one day. He takes it all home to his family who are excited at the new wealth and go back to the hole the next day to clean it thoroughly. There he meets a snake, who asks him what he has done with the grain.

The man explains he had found it and taken it home to his wife and three daughters.

"Very well, then," said the snake. "Then give me one of your daughters as a bride or I'll eat you."

The old man goes home, crestfallen, and asks his first two daughters. In no uncertain terms they refuse him, saying they are young and he is old, and rather than make them take a snake for a husband he should let the snake eat him. But the third daughter says she will do it, feeling it must be God's will for her.

The old man tells the snake, who gives him directions as to how the child must be dressed and cleaned and set on a white camel to wander the next day. And this is all done, but a hoard of snakes also come into the house with the new clothes and a white she-camel; and the girl goes off.

Well, it turns out that the snake is really a beautiful man under his skin and is really a *peri* (a divine who can assume human form), so handsome that "his sister would even fall in love with him just seeing him from the back." And the snake man, Khasta Khamorah gives the girl everything she needs and they live in a beautiful house under the ground, complete with the most elegant of clothes and rugs and a magic ring. The girl and her husband love each other very much. But the husband, it is understood, must change back and forth from his snake to his man state, and vice versa.

One day the sisters come to visit and incite the girl to burn the snake skin. Despite the husband's warning and a night "when he slapped his wife so hard her head spun around to the back" and then feeling bad "he slapped her again so her head came back to the front," they go ahead with their plans and burn the skin. (I wonder about this sanctioned spouse abuse, on both sides.)

Then the *peri* explains that his wife will not be able to find him again, until she wears out seven pairs of iron shoes and seven sets of iron clothes and even then will fail because his relatives are all *devs* who eat human flesh.

So the riches of the house underground disappear along with the husband, but the girl gets the iron things and begins walking, walking for days and months and years until she has almost worn out the last pair, only to find herself near the husband's house.

Follows the intrigues and adventures she has among the *dev*s who are determined to eat her: she must sweep the house of straw, wash a black cloth white and a white one black, and her master—by magic—dopes each of her adversaries. Then she is sent to get scissors, mirror and comb from the aunt's house and Khasta Khamorah tells her how to escape with her life there by calling a river of pus, yellow oil, a pool of blood, good mulberry syrupy, and a crooked tree, a straight tree; by giving a dog some bones and a camel some straw, by escaping from the *dev*-aunt when she gets back to sharpen her teeth (she had one pair of feet and found another). All of these things (pool, river, dog, tree) refuse to stop her because she had flattered them by calling them nice names, while the old woman had insulted them by calling them what they were and mistreating them.

So the final trial comes. The snake man is to marry his cousin; the night of the wedding the brother-in-law ties candles to the girl and makes her walk in front of them to the wedding chamber, but Khasta Khamorah gets the mother to let the "servant girl" stay in the bedroom that night and when he sees how they've burned his human wife, he boils the new cousin-wife in oil and hides her under her *chadris* and turns into a *dev*. Then he takes needles and straw and a cup of water and escapes with his human wife.

In the morning the aunt and mother, hungry to eat the "servant girl," wait until noon for the "couple" to get up, then find the charred cousin. Outraged, they set off to find the fugitives. They're stopped a little by the needles which stick in their feet and the straw which burns in their eyes, but almost catch up with them. At that point, the snake man changes his cup of water into a huge ocean between himself and the pursuers. When the mother asks her son how they got across the water, he tells her they must take heavy rocks under their arms and jump in.

So the old *devs* do so and drown, and the snake man and his wife go back to their human kingdom, where they are happy in their home under ground.

"And they live on that side of the *jewie* and we live here," Margaret finishes.

All the stories are about impossible love one way or another, and the goal is to marry someone outside your family, tribe, or realm.

On the university bus yesterday, I receive a formal introduction to Ms Gholami, who is often on the bus when I am. A blond-haired women who teaches in Tom's faculty, she explains gaily all about her years in

Beirut at American University, and of her teaching now at USIS in the afternoon.

"It is unfortunate, is it not, the sick social system in a Moslem country which prevents boys and girls from meeting each other?" she queries, as she goes on to describe the friendliness and sincerity of her three American roommates, of her other Moslem friends there and especially the Afghans with whom she could be "Naughty." Finally she invites me to her house, along the bus route, vowing we should get to know each other.

I eagerly agree; I hope we can become friends.

October 16, 1975

. . . . [Days pass reading *A Canticle for Leibowitz*, a Richard Hughes novel, and Gunter Grass's *A Tin Drum*, noting the new urban look and taste of Mirad, missing a visit from my old *modir*, meeting and sharing writing ideas with Arthur and Yvonne Alpert, the wife of the assistant country director, another brilliant and well-traveled couple).

It is raining tonight, a rehearsal for winter snow: clouds dark and dusty shroud the city most of the day. I look out eerily at dusk across the Peace Corps garden to the distant hills, the higher mountains, hear the filtering sigh of the call to prayer, see the wind massage the dry leaves on the tree: our fall of sorts.

Oct. 18

. . . We had a visit yesterday from the medical student Zmaria and his friend, Ahmed Khan, who spoke again, warily, of the various problems of being Afghans in an imprisoning country. The medical student, thin and serious, has been collecting false x-rays and prescriptions for himself. These he will present at the end of his studies at Kabul University, to the Ministry of Public Health, to explain his need to leave the country and receive special treatment abroad. Once out, he will stay out, of course and begin studying for his specialty. There is no other way, as medical students are not granted passports generally, and the few scholarships that come in each year are given nepotistically to the less than deserving relatives of various commandants and ministers.

Once when he was in class 11, this medical student from Herat was selected to be an AFS student (he had told a version of this earlier); on the dawn of departure he was told he couldn't go and someone else went in his place. That was in 1968. Meanwhile Khan is involved in trying to get out of the army so that he can finish his high school and then be eligible for only one year of service, or get into university, and then teach and thus get out of it entirely. He was on route to bribe someone with 6,000 *afs* to get a "deferment." The other option is for him to go into the army and then simply run away after a few days, then go back and finish his schooling, after first heftily bribing the commandant in Wardak, his home, to not bother his parents.

Oct. 21, 1975

In yesterday's classes at the university, I field a sudden enthusiasm and passion from the freshmen, who have finally realized that they will in fact have a test on Tuesday and have just had their last chance to prepare. It, not surprisingly, is a dribbling poor performance, by prof and class both perhaps. Meanwhile, we rip through a chapter with the TV (technical vocational) freshmen: the patterns taught—strict grammar—seem of minor value . . .

There is always something on the ride home on the public bus. I get on at the university, barely clinging to the open door, little boys and girls under my feet, and then up on the main road I humbly back down so some students, like pelting stones, can fall off at their stops. In their enthusiasm and pushing, I lose my balance, fall backwards on the street, tear my shirt and stand up embarrassed, trying to push it all away with a smile.

But the little girl who had also fallen behind me shouts at me angrily, "Mister, go away."

Stung, I reply that she herself should get lost. "Why are you being rude?" I question.

` The whole bus watches me crawl back on, the girls gather giggling around the bus driver, who gives me a strange look. and two women squeeze together to open a seat for me this time.

Humiliated, the outsider, scarred, I want to be away, to shout at someone, to disappear into thin air, but instead I just look down at the floor of the bus, hard-faced. To them my embarrassment must seem something trivial and foreign, my whole person remote. Perhaps they all assume I do not speak Persian, despite my frustrated comments to the child in perfect Dari, but an explanation, some words of comfort from them, would have been worth a lot.

Or, what? I miss the conversations, the always "on" of Tashkurghan . . .

> *[Rashidi Omaid is to type my manuscript. Our Country Director, Howard, is back from the provinces and according to his comments does not think volunteers are very interested in having teaching resources brought to them. This is a new job he is trying to define for T.]*

Today, along with our lunch, in wander two frosty Bamiyan lads. We welcome the soldier from the Red City and his cousin, the first quite bold and not shy about taking food or tea and fruit, the second, ruddy cheeked with chapped skin and winter blown hair, eats lightly(though we are only having soup), and barely speaks . . .

I watch our neighbor, a stout well-dressed Indian man from the "apartment" house beyond our next door's compound who has a military jeep honk for him every morning. His sons, in British school boy's uniform, shorts and knee socks, swing briefcases and thermos jugs to take off to their school, then lessons, after him each day . . .

Oct. 22, 1975.

Tom will assume the position of Volunteer Regional Representative beginning in January. He will have a truck and driver and spend about two weeks every month in the provinces spreading TEFL resources and running errands.

As always, I have my own little adventure, starting with the Freshman test which four out of the 24 manage to fail, ending at the university with my attendance at the faculty meeting, where Dean Sayed is both kind and good-humored. As a representative of the English Department, which now had full status within the faculty, I can vote on their various parliamentary debates. The crux of the meeting: approving the minutes from two weeks before, and then a wild debate on whether or not to give credit to some students. It was, the professors attested, the make-up test grade for five students who had since taken another make-up exam, almost two years after the original, and received a 29. Should their integrity be questioned, should the mark given by the professor in absentia be accepted or should one accepted by the committee (they had spent 15 hours inspecting the exams)? The recommendation follows, taken as official from that advisory committee, and the word (in the form of an authorized letter) of the first make-up test given by a professor is accepted.

While trying to find a watch for T's birthday near the Spinzar Hotel, I am told by a shopkeeper there from Kunduz that a "Miss Nancy" had had all the boys in town in love with her when she worked in Kunduz five years before.

At Agha-gul's meeting, we follow a discussion of how eventually all the PCVs will be replaced by Afghans. That sounds correct to me. My sense is also that we should have colleagues who can assist, and thereby we could spend more time with the Afghan professionals than with each other . . . .

Events aplenty. A Miss March is in country, a friend of my sister Evelyn's California legislator Bill Carpenter . . . . There's a simple birthday party for Tom with Mirad and Qorbin, and presents.

Oct. 26-27

[Visitors, a bad movie, meals, the Bamiyan couple]

Classes are lengthy. They begin early (8:00) and end late (4:00) but twice a week there is a gap from 10:00—2:00. Usually, I pass my break by seeking a spot in the sun in the chilly offices and watching the shape of mountains around the bowl of Kabul . . . writing curriculum guides and revisiting stories for provincial school lessons.

. . . On United Nations Day, half a holiday, we went to Paghman to catch a bit of the fall colors, reds from the turned apricot trees, among yellow and orange and lime which could have dotted a Vermont woods, all in the soft high air of that garden resort town above Kabul. We walked from end to end of the town, finding ourselves once in the now private gardens of Daud, another time in a a teahouse between bearded men and agile boys drinking tea and eating our packed lunch of crisp fall apples, eggs and brownies, and nibbling on fresh baked bread. The best of the day: the afternoon hours spent in the old king's beautiful formal gardens with marble pools and fountains and terraces, well-tended, with a spacious view of Kabul to the east and the white heads of the snowy Pinjsheer Mountains to the North. Here, too, we found the king's old house, now used by ministers up for the weekend; it is full of wooden Swiss balconies and round sun rooms with geranium window boxes and carved wooden ceilings and a flavor of elegant continental provincialism.

Walking up the road to the gardens from town, collecting a few perfectly turned leaves, and munching apples, we hear details of a new birth, all natural, in Susan Marek's family . . . Her sister-in-law in the States has a daughter.

I take in another tale from Tom, of a strange girl student at the college who tried to commit suicide at least once after being *namzad* to a boy she didn't want to marry. This girl is the sister of Fareiba, someone from our training staff. He speaks also of a colleague, a Volunteer who rarely comes to class, and whose nonchalance affects all student attendance.

In my own faculty, we remain in a cold, cold office, with no prospects for a good heater, so one can literally sit and turn blue in the habitual damp shade. even though we keep on our coats, hats, and gloves to work . . . The classrooms are better.

October 28, 1975

> *[I recall again the pivotal idea of Ivan Illich, listen in on the fascinating life and views of my California visitor, Mrs. Ruth March, and go off shopping for a "new" coat in the used clothes bazaar.]*

. . . Today Mirad brings wood for another volunteer, Randy Jenner, and finds himself challenged to a dual by Randy's "little cook," who took it all as an insult to his territorial rights. The "duel," with sticks of freshly bought wood, is abandoned, following Mirad's pretended apology and his explanation that it had all been done only to help the other cook, that people should not resent getting help . . .

We have the usual run of days at school, but clearly there is more than a modicum of educating underway. These students want to succeed. Because I am having trouble keeping a voice lots of the time, the return of a stubborn laryngitis which had gripped me here several seasons, I give quizzes which show how far above head my past teaching had been.

We are pleased to receive a letter from Hagie, the old science teacher in Tashkurghan, who says, "the school goes well."

We laugh indulgently, knowing what he really means is something encapsulated in a Dari proverb:

"He wet a hundred heads, but has not shaved one," referring to a barber who only preps but never delivers. Or perhaps "It is because of an uncle, that there are grapes on the vines," targeting the reality of how only those with a supportive family or other connections actually have a chance at "success."

We are off to the fields to see *buz kashi*: It is a blaze of colors; we are separated with the rich Afghans and the foreigners. The teams race, hold onto horses by magic, the soft feet flying on the dry grass. Binoculars are welcomed and passed around by every child in our radius. Samagan and Bamiyan both lose their matches, the sun glares, the heavy slaughtered calf is tipsy, prostrate. The crowd turns: at intermission the finale, a thousand people scatter on the field. Leaving the grounds, I experience my first ever crude shuffle with Afghan "stags" in a pack. I strike out to hit a "someone" who represents them all, then withdraw hastily and just leave . . .

"Adam bashane." (Be humans.)

Still, there are magic moments. As I am standing before the lumbering bus, a girl of ice with the clear porcelain face of a delicate eastern princess, in frayed shawl and dancer's limp dress, waits beside me. She turns, stares, asks incredulously where I am going. As I board a bus a day later with Ruth, my visitor, an old women shoulders us abruptly, but when she sees me with the older woman, her face explodes into smiles of generosity. She asks if we are related, then points out her grandchildren to us proudly. When we are about to alight, she asks, solicitous, if we have gotten off at the right place.

And night falls over marketplace and bazaar and teahouse, that stolen scene of life still somehow timeless even in bustling Kabul: the guards at the austere Russian-built ministry gates like soldiers in a dark fairy tale, they are so stiff, so superimposed; the dolled-up, high-skirted, wealthy Afghan women. Airplanes on route to tomorrow. Night's daily end.

[I am reading Malcolm Lowry's post-death novel, Dark as the Grave within which My Friend is Laid—] and think about the way a piece written years before never quite gets completed by the writer. Out of the dirth of his creativity he can only re-write it, reducing a whole experience to one small detail. For example: "on one occasion a dead lemon in an ashtray had taken on the aspect of a cowled old women shivering, sitting in the cold rainy snow." Or, "Mexican babies, aware of man's tragic end, do not cry."

Or, on sunset, on the night of an eclipse:

"They heard the pure voice of a Mexican singing somewhere on a balcony, as if rejoicing that the world had relinquished its shadow and the moon was with them again."

"I wrote a book about running into the past."

"It was certainly not a street, no vehicle could possibly climb it, huge boulders, very steep and shinny, adobe thatched huts, cats, dogs, chickens, lizards, children. Mexico was a sestina of these words, if it came to that . . ."

"No darkness had the same quality of hopelessness as the darkness in Mexico."

A door closes, but can not shut out the past.

Nov. 6, 1975

> *[We are house-sitting for the Howards while they travel north, and their kids are in school. It offers a kindly regression—. warm cinnamon buns for breakfast, childhood games, a TV . . . .*

On the bus with Ms Gholami and her wit, I praise her teaching and her good experience with it. She is respected by others, yet in her reiteration tells it with such warm fun, I can't think her vain. A mysterious pair board the bus—a brother and sister from Bulgaria, who are studying Persian and art at the university.

We have lunch at Dr. Sahar's house. He is the linguist and language supervisor for Peace Corps/Afghanistan. His house has a large ranch-like decorum, stucco walls with just a little too bright old fashioned curtains. The whole PC staff seems present—Agha-gul and wife, Jawid and wife, and Yasir, Dr. Sahar and his little kids and bustling young wife (we learn later that she finished high school last year, and wants to continue to study, but that for now Dr. Sahar makes her stay home to care for the kids), and Dr. Stern and his wife . . . We consume a huge lunch, as well as stories of other countries and services, and then thumb through Iranian magazines full of articles on poetry, fashion, and engineering . . .]

Agha-gul's little wife, one week married, is as tiny and delicate as a singing bird. In a slim dress and high-heel shoes she moves like a dancer, sits in her modesty, a pretty child . . .

And the weather, rumor goes, has put snow on the mountains. From Hushamenah, Sahar's neighborhood, the flat valley leads into the awesome mountains on all sides. There's a sense of unlimited space, eternity, and as this afternoon brought on an ominous change of temperature, we expected to see the storm roll out of the mountains like a great bass opera star ready to perform on the valley stage.

And on Chicken Street, we buy a flute, wooden, lightly carved with trellises of grapevines.

Nov. 9, 1975

Situated in the icy bowels of this English office at the end of the sun (give it until 2:00 and it will warm gloriously), my pen is almost too cold to flow, my hands dry and tingling as if submerged in cold water . . .

My bus friend, Ms Gholami, fills me with good humor every morning now. She gets quite animated talking about her teaching and praise and a book on abnormal behavior, socialization versus anti-socialization. She is a bright, cheerful sort able to laugh at the incongruities of men always having seats and women having to stand (she refers to "buses," but we both know the image can easily be extended to all aspects of their lives) . . . delightfully normal and curious and alive.

We recall the oven houses we had heard of in Bamiyan, how fires were built under the hollowed-out ground, like that of a bread oven, and the people inside kept pretty warm. Howard then describes the Korean homes, the ground tile canals in the floor of houses fed on coal, and how in the thin, tight houses of Korea, whole families succumb every night to the coal dust fumes, an odorless killer of those who seek its warmth, as the carbon monoxide escapes through leaks from the tiles that snare maze-like through the house.

Back again in the enslaving originator of my ghostly clinging cold, students colder than I am come to ask questions. Snow has dusted the mountains around Paghman, telephone lines are down from a storm in Taloquan, and though we haven't gotten any of the white ice yet, the wintry blasts are pre-imminent: clothes set out to dry in the optimism of yesterday morning are frozen solid by moonlight, we discover when we retrieve some pants and a shirt by night. Yet at home we have fires, somewhere warm to go.

Tom quizzes me as to what he should do with certain of his female students. One is quite bright but is always absent (she married last spring and lives in Share-nau), and an arrogant, prissy sort to boot. He doesn't want to fail a second semester Senior, and yet she scarcely asks for anything better. Another girl, mentioned before, has the queer habit of coming into the classroom when Tom is alone and closing the door. At that point he absently excuses himself and goes out to round up his class. Yet another young woman, daughter of a former ambassador to Japan, reads and writes English fluently, almost as well as a native, so he uses her like an assistant teacher and she makes his teaching a pleasure. But there is yet another girl who seems to be quite enamored of the other PCV and who spends time with him at his house (Mirad's friend, the volunteer's cook, Ghafar reports) . . . Should he interfere? Of course, this can not end well. I remember the parable: "If a blind man is walking around a well, and you do nothing, you are sinning."

> *[Some of the single volunteers leaving do socialize with Afghan women, under the name of being tutors hired by their fathers, and likely they will not get their visas renewed because of their social lives and PC's recommendations against them.]*

In my own classroom the betrothed, or the cousin unbetrothed, of Shahzadah of old, has started to come to class infrequently. We were reading a text yesterday, our first time to do so when he was present, I guess. When I call on him to read, he falters, then fails miserably after a few lines. The other students tell me he just has a problem with stuttering, so I stop him and let someone else continue reading . . . So perhaps he is okay after all.

In another world: we hear radio reports on the march into the Spanish Sahara, by Morocco and Mauritania. Again there are people marching across land someone else claims is theirs. Is it all a taunting, for war, more war in a whole arch of the Middle East and Northern Africa? Another beginning?

> *[I read Joyce Carol Oates's Wonderland and do not like it, but by contrast found Kazinsky's book intriguing; and another, The War Anthology, mandatory. Gauguin's diaries are scintillating, this man in good humor a delightfully boisterous rogue, his descriptions of other painters memorable.]*

From Gauguin:

"One remembers one's childhood: does one remember the future? Memory of the before . . . memory perhaps of the after? I do not know precisely. But when we say, 'It will be fair tomorrow,' are we not remembering the past, the experience that makes us think as we do?"

"If you are aspiring to sleep with a dancer, do not permit yourself to hope for a single moment that she will swoon in your arms. That never happens; the dancer swoons on the stage."

Nov. 12, 1975

> *[I got the typed manuscript back from Rashidi—]*

At Rashidi's house, seated on the sun porch, she is primed perfectly, her face in beautiful colored lines, her finely spun hair shaped to fashion, her trim posture trim. She tells me of her whole family who live here, and how she intends to go to India and study English and get some credits and courses in secretarial work and be, in this way, independent. A graduate of the French school, she only learned English after high school with some courses at USIS and Peace Corps . . . Although she invites me to lunch, I must refuse, so she bring out a huge bowl of almonds which she says her father, a merchant, sells . . . . Meanwhile, her small nephew carries the heavy typewriter we had lent her to a taxi . . .

Oddly, my only traumas of late are around trying to keep warm. But now there are finally electric heaters for our office, except that the electrical system can not support them. So first thing yesterday the whole line went out, or at least the ones to which our office is connected, plummeting us again into eternal chill. And this is a school of engineers.

. . . On the university bus, I relish the chance to talk to a few more Afghan women, a little island of acquaintances in the otherwise arctic world it seems. There's the girl with the degree in guidance from Indiana U., named Hosie who looks very Hispanic and who was mistaken for a Mexican with her coloring and her name. She spent two years in the States and visited in Colorado, Texas and Boston, with friends or relatives. (Her brother was at MIT those years, and so she has seen movies, and TV and lived in an apartment and generally enjoyed her American experience, the travel and freedom in particular, as well as the acquaintance of a few Iranians to help her keep up her home front.) How strange must be her life back here where she has a job—on paper—but no legitimate work, it seems, since neither university nor ministry will acknowledge the need for a guidance department at the university level. Maybe it will change, for her sake.

Another women is teaching biology at the Faculty of Medicine and—charmingly, innocently—asks me all the school girls questions, about my family and husband. She explains how she came to learn English from courses her brothers showed her. She radiates with pleasure, thinking of her work in the university, and she insists that she has always been able to live in Kabul, free, and that only a natural shyness keeps her from speaking out more.

> *[I read* Freedom or Death, *about Crete in the 1870's; and some Russian fairy tales:* A Mountain of Gems: Fairy tales of the Soviet Lands; *along with some Bertrand Russell). Ford refuses to bail out NYC and says it can go bankrupt. Meanwhile we struggle with our isolation from the "real, poor, struggling Afghanistan," bewail how we now are just "more foreigners"*

living off of but away from real people's daily battle to survive as "we are professional teachers, engaged in a business this year."]

Nov. 13, 1975

Mirad seems sometimes back in our circle, and socializes more with us, now that Mike and his cook have moved to the other side of town. He has some time to just be at home with us in the cold fortress. After supper now, as in the old days, he often sits with us and tells us his impression of things. One day, his attention caught by a pamphlet on transportation, he asks about a strange spindle-wheeled cycle—a tricycle—and then about the age of cars and airplanes. He is delighted with the notion of a balloon as big as a room with a chamber below for passengers, the zeppelin.

The conversation turned to loan sharks he had known one night. He tells us one of whom is the infamous Ghulam, and how the daughter of the highest mullah in the country had wanted to marry, but her fiancee did not have the amount of money required to buy her himself,. Subsequently, he took loans from a lot of people. Now the amount of money he has to pay as the interest alone is around 60,000 *afs* a month, exorbitant. Shaking his head, Mirad wonders at this, how it is surely a clear indication of things being amiss in the world of Islamic non-interest loaning, and how for a holy man it is a complete violation—by banker and usury both.

It comes to me suddenly, a flashback of the epiphany Howard experienced as he sat in the back of a Bamiyan classroom, in the village which at 8,000 feet has been having winter for two months already. He was sitting next to a student in a room without glass in the windows or heat and watched the poor boy try to concentrate on an English lesson, although the child had no textbook or notebook or solid socks and shoes . . . .

Nov. 26, 1975

[Notes on intense lovemaking]

I am sitting in the window of the PC library as the late day's sun, winter setting, moves in through the glass, and the clouds form over the mountains. A guard props a bike against a tree in the yard before me and polishes it, and our Indian and his family squabble over some homework problems at a card table on their patio porch across the nearby street . . .

The students have me give two lessons outside, claiming that under the sun was a better place for learning than in the shadows of the huge, cold rooms. I don't disagree with them the first day, although it is uncomfortable standing up in the direct sunlight in my my multi-layered garb (for I had been able to arm myself against the expected cold rooms), and with them all in sleepy poses at my feet. A rim of other students form, ease-dropping at my back. Then, the second day a dust storm and a continuous chilling breeze wagers for their attention and pretty much wins.

[I am a tad discouraged. The stories I had written for the high school curriculum have been relegated to less than inspired fellow volunteers. I also regret being on the fringe of the university community . . . And Mirad, disappointingly, who is doing less work for us and likely for his family, has asked for money for winter clothes. Of course we provide it, for he has long since become a close friend, as much as a cook, but we feel counterfeit.

Last night we attended a German troubadour performance. It was remarkable, but is it now bread and circuses for us?

We get news from Tashkurghan that Bashir of Rowkia's cousin-uncle fame and Mary of the 11th class (old Mirzad Daud's granddaughter-niece) had been married the week before, the social event of the season, and that Najiba, with support from Ziadeen (this man does have political pull, and did end up back in Tashkurghan and not the deadly village edging Pushtoonistan and the mountains), is to become *modira!* How rapid has been her rise, and how exciting for the school. The town had snow the first week in November and also in mid-October, with the expectation of more *"barf"* on the way.

How I miss the town where I spent so many days wasting time being unhappy, initially. Now I grieve in retrospect because the days, that experience, is irretrievably gone, and more than the days, the people.

[I read a book about a Kikuyu Kenyan, another about a 5-year old child, Hungry for Me *by S.I. Wilson. We are*

suddenly, unexpectedly, having issues with Mirad, who is really not needed by us anymore in this city of so many options, for food and shared meals, and with Tom away half the month . . .]

The drafting teacher at the Engineering Faculty, a short slightly stout fellow in old tortoise-shell thick-lensed glasses, always has a welcome word for me. On Sunday he asks about my views on the weather and on my students, smiles a bit mischievously, an old western-trained Afghan lush, to tell me he had had a girlfriend who came to visit him when he was an Engineering student himself and "had been drawing his drafting lessons carefully." On the bus this day, a young doctor, of the handsome Afghan stock, speaks softly, decorously to the young female biology teacher from the Medical Faculty, and I sense a pure sort of harmony and naturalness between man and woman. as I've rarely, if ever, seen before in Afghanistan.

. . . Winter and the sharpness in the air: the hurrying figures of old men looking for the sun, and the workers bound up in faded coats like swaddled children. An old team of cobblers in a small kiosk shelter against one street, their tools and piles of shoes around them, polished and bound, and the head cobbler himself wears rags knotted around his legs and feet.

Tonight there is to be a full eclipse of the moon, and already at sunset guns sound from the fort. Mirad explains that a wise man had announced it on the radio already the night before ("How wise he must be to have known even before it came." Mirad insists); and that during the night the robbers and holy people must say special prayers, while the people who don't understand it all must affirm their belief in Allah.

Nov. 21, 1975

. . . . A brilliant and wise and world-traveled French girl named Catherine, who my brother Dan had met at the Belgian commune where he had worked before he traveled across continents to see us, appears and she fills us with lively and thoughtful conversations, about the spectrum of young and old who have migrated to life on the commune in the Belgian countryside; the harrowing expectations and rigidities of the

French education system; the amazing array of languages in the world and how they had each evolved, in "families" and uniquely alone, such as Basque; the traditional life still evident in most of Iran; the richly empirical and ancient flavor of Herat; and the enviable and special Afghan pervasive hospitality, etc.

Yet Tom bristles, especially intense and cross and quarrelsome. Perhaps his job frustrates him.

And how well Afghanistan disguises its poverty: how the sheer smallness of the population from the large infant mortality rate keeps the masses from increasing into hungry hordes. Yet is this the best way and who are we to tamper . . .

Darwin, etymologies. What is human and what inspires and respects the sacredness of all life?

November 23, 1975

[We are discussing the Hopi language as presented in Benjamin Whorl's *Language, Thought and Reality.* A visiting Chilean medical student, tells us about wars and how poor boys are made to fight rich men's conflicts all over the world; we hear more on the inflexibility of the French school system; about an ecologist in Paris and the arms sales by the French; along with details of the French student demonstration of 1968 and Catherine's socialist grandfather*. The Chilean describes a trip across the U.S. and how, despite a series of car breakdowns, he and his colleagues successfully completed their transcontinental journey. This leads into the subject of racism—against Arabs and North Africans by the French, against the Turks by the Germans, against the indigenous Indians in Brazil and elsewhere as highways are built and mining introduced on their lands, and by too many in the U.S. against Blacks and Chicanos . . .]

Speaking of streets and demonstrations, we talk of Afghanistan's government, of the anti-monarchist movement about five years before the coup when the striking students at the university had just been shot, no questions asked, for participating, and also in some of the high schools, how students had been beaten if they showed their political views.

. . . The Chilean had liked Afghanistan the most of all the places he had traveled, for the people's unspoiled way of life, touched by the modern world only superficially, is beautiful to him. Yet he knows that underneath it are all the realities, death and frustration, and a narrow world view . . . .

November 25, 1975

. . . Well, the potpourri of Afghan government will allow a new training program to come after all, but no more people can go out to provincial sites, we are told. In fact, PC is effectively being taken out of secondary education, or so that is the "official word." Today.

Nov. 27, 1975: Thanksgiving

Students are restless, off to study after getting back an exam. These canny kids wonder why we have class on an American holiday. We hear of a film at USIS, venture out for the long wait, among dismissive Americans. Eagerly we talk with Mikita, a PCV, who speaks of her Japanese-American grandmother's burial, and of mystics in California . . .

Back in the brittle air, smoke in our words, the lighted city on the hills around us . . . we look out at midnight and walk halfway home until a crowd of us flags a taxi. He drives, thinking us all mad, the stereotypical *haragees* able to party all night. We get home and quickly fall asleep.

It should have been a good walk: the sort of undefined placement in that Kabul mountain night, the rest of the town asleep, a lone policeman at an intersection, the soldiers at the prison shouting their alarms, and the shadows of other soldiers, government cheap labor in the barracks around the prison, seen through the high windows . . . . but I mourn being wasteful in such leisure with co-patriots, the playing at still being high school kids . . . . We did not come here to live among a "little America."

[We are all invited to Thanksgiving dinner at the Alpert's house. Arthur was a conscientious objector in W.W. II, and interviewed POW in Korea after that war and its torturers. Yvonne is from Belize. They are 50 and 35 respectfully, and have an infant son and a 6-year old daughter. All the PCVs and staff attend, and I enjoy perusing the contents of their house, each item a story reflecting their time in Africa and Afghanistan, in Central America, in Korea, in the U.S., for they are not just regular Americans but world spirits.]

I read with interest Yvonne's article, in parts very nicely done, as she sketches the world around her during one day. Hers is unique in its point of view: she speaks as a Third World woman who finds herself in a highly superficial role in a Fourth World country as the" mem-sahib" among the poor. Frustrated, she struggles to touch the new world and herself as well . . . . The house is full of mementos of those other worlds: the expansive, expressive African art, masks and gourds (calabashes) from the Yorubas or Igos, and the painted cloth with the impish jumbled figures, angular and somewhat universal in their confused humor turned to fear; the sacred Turkish Sufist spoon, the woven rugs, the painted lacquer boxes . . . Guitar music, first from somewhere in Central American, then from the Hungarians and the Romas, wafts among us. Yvonne explains slightly about the Central American Caribs, the Black descendants of the original slaves brought from Africa, and who still have the dances and the black magic, the yam and crushed grain dishes of their African ancestors, Thus, when she went to Nigeria she realized that she was quite at home there, that all these things had also been on the street she grew up on as a girl, in her own Belize.

[I am scolded for my "rejection" of Tom, over wanting freedom, over having to patch up instead of stick to my stance when we quarrel, for my sense of being callous, of being self-indulgent and again missing the good.] J.F Power's image of darkness. Flannery O'Connor's everything, Whorf's book on language.

We ponder how Mirad, by his own confession, has become too fond of his radio and bicycle—and we wonder if we have blurred our role with him such that he considers himself part of our family, and yet . . . . we are the "mem-sahibs," still, as his paying bosses. There is never a right way for us, when it comes to hiring folks to help.]

Ms Gholami laughs uproariously on the bus, after I tall her of a mis-thought trip to the local movies across town. She says she goes to Hindi movies sometimes and sits through their long stories and goes home with a headache, mad at herself for having wasted her time. But she claims the worst thing about the Indian movies is their lack of realism, how people are supposed to be in love, but never kiss (banned by the state), and how through impossible circumstances, years of separation, people stay true to each other. Ever the gentle philosopher, Ms Gholami contends that love really has to be fed regularly or it dies. She recalls that an American movie by Charles Bronson was a lot more realistic to her as it portrayed how a beautiful doctor's wife eventually turned her interest elsewhere when her husband was always away at work, was no longer feeding their relationship. All such comments seem quite astonishing from this modern but rather Emily Dickensonesque Afghan woman, for whom the prospects of marriage with some brilliant loving man, as each year passes, grow more farfetched . . . .

One student, the courteous Bashir, returns, having asked after his father and gotten his distinguishing beard shaven and his hair cut.

> *[At the theater of the International Club, we watched the Russian movie of the "Sleeping Beauty" ballet by a Leningrad company (the Bolshoi?). Another concert was at the Lycee Istequell, the French School, a palatial establishment by all standards, by a young male pianist, a prodigy at Chopin, Debussy, Beethoven, We sit among largely French, German and American audiences at each. Finally, there was a film of adapted from* Anna Karenina. *I finished Durrell's writing on Corfu and Mary McCarthy's memoirs].*

Mirad tells us about the dogfights on the edge of Kabul; the beasts are carefully primed and trained to attack. One giant mastiff requires three people and ropes to hold him before he has his quick battle. These fights are a sharp barbarity, but a small one compared to the things people do to each other as nations.

I keep finding myself standing before my Freshmen classes attempting to explain to them, how quirky is the tangle of the "world powers" these days, how fragile is the peace that holds the opposing countries back from warfare, how insane is the very notion of having nuclear battles, which would eliminate a continent in a matter of seconds, as all life perished or sickened in radioactive poisoned days . . . .

November 30, 1975

Ushering November out with a sunless day, a god of sand, wetted and cold, hovers low over the city, turning the mountains into ghostly forms. School enacts itself as usual. The weathermen have promised snow, but though we can see our breath outside and a splattering of rain has fallen, as yet there is nothing white . . .

> *[The ever evasive foggy fellow Daniel Curt, a PCV, is to leave immediately . . . .]*

My student, Faruddin Wafi, with due *salaams* in the middle of a reading about Marco Polo's visits to Badakshan, presents me with a few small ruby pieces (or are they just amethyst?) and a square of lapis lazuli as an after thought. I refuse the gifts, of course, but he insists. If I keep either we face a regular dilemma, for no gift is a free gift.

XVIII
SCOUTING OUT A FUTURE

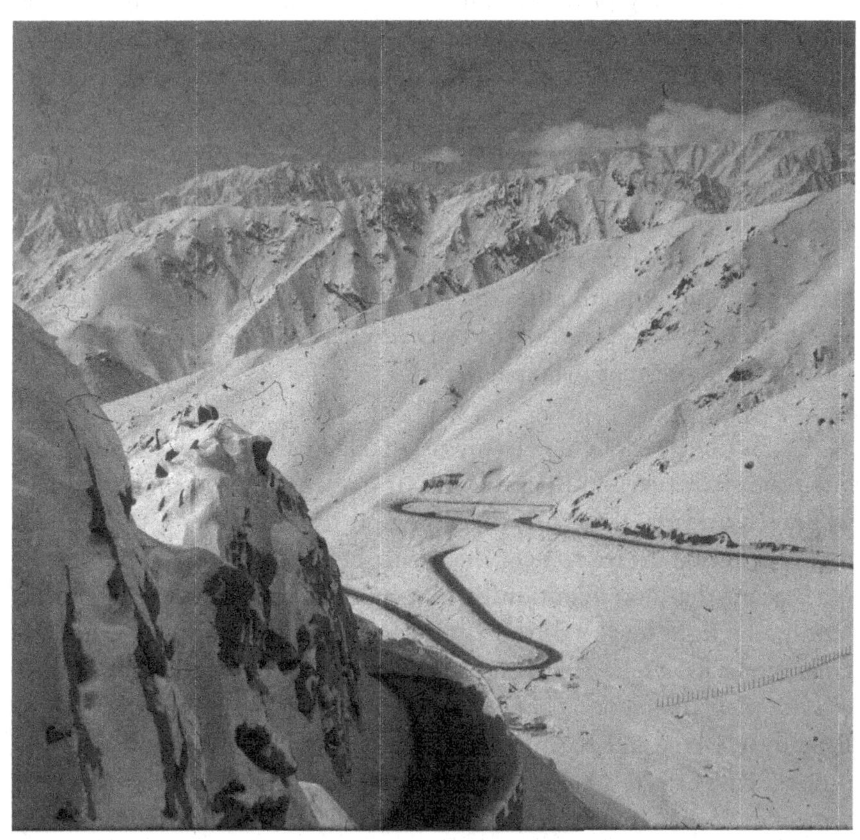

Road to the Salang Pass

Dec. 2-5, 1975

[Tom worries about the LSAT, and again we open our house to visitors—James and Lena Auchincloss from Herat, Benson and Susan Marek (with Benson suffering bad conjunctivitis); and we hear a recital by volunteers and others. We're joined by Brenda and Chris Mahoney, and their old language teacher Koshan, and then we make a wedding cake for Qorbin, Mirad's brother.]

We imagine: The 18 hour trip from Herat, music in the rear, a fussy baby, a half blind driver after Ghazni who insists on creeping for his hour's worth to Kabul when snow flurries develop. We see the desert expansive, ungraspable space and time caught in the ambiguity of dark—a frightening prospect, unnamed dimensions around that belittle you. You stamp in your insignificance. You could react by hating it all, daring it to try to touch you. But it touches you, is unavoidable.

How Westernized is the dress of these students; the modish shoes and pants and hairstyles. They are disproportionately the wealthy of the country, so that those of a few rungs down economically stand out in their shabbiness. Tom's students especially exude style, and one poor man's son among them, although at the very top of the class, wears his one drab suit and shoes and posture every day. He may not be hired by slick-looking foreigners who pay well.

. . . With the Mahoneys in town, we talked about Tashkurghan, this one-time challenge and the pride of our lives. I quiz and the Mahoneys volunteer, and the details of their life and teaching there come out in total: the initial dream state of the town's beauty, the sudden changes of the season, the total adoption by and immersion with their neighbor's family, the tight loyalty of the 12th class to me and consequently their failure to be too excited by Brenda, the new-found awakening in the other classes, their interactions and small squabbles, the pending wedding of Esfandyar, Mary and Bashir's nuptials, the change in them all after the unions, Pat's trip to Qaddar with the teachers, carefully covered up in someone's *chapan*, the exit of the old *talwador* at the boys' school and my little *keteb* clerk at the girls', Najiba's performance as *modira-sibe.* (She has not yet taken the test, the *saer-malim* grumpily watches it all, and—quite unprofessionally—she has her knitting too much in evidence), and so on.

[Tom's exam did not come . . . .]

. . . Chris appears with a huge package from home, full of such loving things as two giant maple leaves, a sand dollar from the Oregon coast, fruit-flavored candy canes, dried apricot pull, socks, undies and a pink gown, guitar and recording books, a long card full of down home pictures, and a Sierra Club calendar . . . and we eat pancakes for lunch.

Afterwards we make a mad dash to the university to find the dormitory where two Tashkurghan girls receive us in moments, like lost family. Outside by the gate, we are beckoned in, after Brenda tells them she bares messages for two Freshmen girls from their "watan" (home). In fact, the girls' neighbors had sent word and goodies. We walk through a complex of drab rooms without seats, a configuration set up to discourage any social life. Finding there is in fact no place for receiving guests in the "girls' dorm", we end up squeezing into in the tiny dorm room the girls share.

One, Mahadi, the other Malekah, are both in Arts and Letters, and as possibly the first home-grown girls from Tashkurghan to go to the university, they accept their status with mixed love and hate: Homesick, cold, anxious to find themselves in the middle of all the Kabuli students and sophisticates, the girls waver in strange moments. We want to take them with us to Tashkurghan for their break, and then bring them back in a few days, but they have four days of exams beginning in a few days, and therefore cannot possibly take the time to go home. Still, there were some spilled beans, as Brenda tells them about a robbery at Mahadi's sister's house and how she had had to go live with her mother again—(the neighbor had sworn that the girl was already told, had acknowledged it back in the village via a letter, but that turned out not to be the case, so Mahadi was shocked, as was Brenda). Afterwards, all the provincial girls in the dorm, anxious to have a visitor, come over to speak with us. We note a few carefully entered and exited male visitors coming to visit certain girls. Meanwhile, a half-witted but loving *nana* whose job it is to supervise the gate and the girls' food, just stares out, allegedly watching everything. There is an accepting easiness to it all, so different from the stiff encounters I've grown accustomed to elsewhere.

Afterwards, we drive down a street on an old clunky bus to find Asef's house, the one he now tends. Greeting us, he runs out to buy baklava and make tea and the conversation roars in the freshness of the Mahoney's admiration for him, as they tell of their life up in Khulm. Inevitably the subject of Thaddeus comes up and Asef wants to know why Thaddeus hadn't married Noushin while she was studying in the States. Of course, none of us know the answer for this legend of a volunteer from years before. And then he sees us off . . .

Benson's neighbor from Bamiyan, Shafiq, nervous into tears, comes to our house, anxious over Benson's eyes. He scolds us all around for not having come earlier and impresses on us Benson's need for visitors when he was ill . . . .

Subsequently, we return home to chatter in detail now over students, by name, to find that people always tell Brenda that "Frances did it this way, so why don't you?" until she must surely have come to hate me. She explains how she perceives the students I had known, the changes in them.

Somewhere in the conversation, we get a description of a gift for Ziadeen who does teach at the school and also gives them language lessons. It seems that Rozia, who failed the 10th class, had worked all term on a sweater for Ziadeen, only to have him reject it as too small so she had to pull it all out and start over. And there is the woman next to the house where they live, an ageless creature of 42 who takes care of their washing and cleaning, and can always come up with a *pilau* if they have a lot of guests. When they first came and left their dishes by the *jewie* to be washed, little girls from next door came over to do them. Initially, this woman hid her face from Chris for three weeks, and then showed it. After that she began to confine in him, more than she ever had in Brenda, about her life and its challenges.

We laugh as they share how the woman passes on her impressions of how often they have sex (based on the flow of water down the *tashknob* pipe every morning) and how she had gotten crazy, ashamed over losing their good smelling "Wicks" (Vicks) in the *jewie* one day, although the thing lost was actually a kind of Indian incense. Another time she tried on some of Brenda's dangling earrings and manged to "forget" and walk out the door with them, but it was all done with such love and good sport it seems.

Their approach to this life is enviable; they seem immersed in the village and neighborhood, not some odd pair of foreigners sequestered far away from the village's daily life. Tom and I, with his New England reserve, and my shyness and acquiescence to his preferences, had missed much, sadly.

Then there's Ziagul (last year's ninth class) and her merchant-mullah-baba-father who had them all for dinner and then apologetically near the end asked permission for one question.

The question came: "I have heard there is a broom in America which eats dust (demonstrating the sound of "whoof") and that although it is made of gold, most households have one."

Chris quickly agreed to his first proposition and vetoed the second one, setting straight an image of a plastic and aluminum, and not gold, vacuum cleaner.

And then there are the conversations that her neighbors have about interesting personal details . . . They ask Brenda pointedly for all the specifics on married life, and without the least hesitation or inhibitions, my dear and creative friend provides the facts.

December 7, 1975

Behind us is the proper wedding of Mirad's brother, our first in Kabul: The bride's family, we learn, is all of Iranian roots, Turkomens from around Tabriz, with the high cheek bones and round heads of their tribe, along with a gentle, friendly manner. As guests, foreigners, we are treated like royalty.

So we venture up the hill of Jema-minat, alight with the coiled electricity of the poor Kabul neighborhood, into a yard replete with scrubbed clean dignity, to be separated in the dusk, Tom to the men's world, me with the women. The room I enter shimmers, dressed up like the bride herself in a hue of soft lights, a cheery stove in the middle, and around them in their covered scarfs and robe-like full clothes, in ages descending like the rungs of a ladder, sit the women and the girls, from the family of Sheringul who have appeared there. Hossain's child wife, who already has three children, who once danced during the evening with her sad gracefulness, sits suckling her two babies, and shakes her head mutely at everything I say, even when I question.

She has a son of six now, who walks cockily around the room though only a midget, and flaunts his sister's handkerchief like a matador, and tells me that he goes to school now and has learned his *alef-beys.* (I wonder, watching his chameleon quickness, an impatience that could grow into wrath if his father who gave him his looks and provides for the family, also gave him some of that unstable pose, the hashish dreams, the craving for belly-dancing women.) There is also a young daughter of the bride's family. This latter includes the man at the Engineering faculty who runs the labs, and another husband-father who works for the museum and spends a lot of his time outside of Kabul at various digs, and had been to India and projects a trip to London; and an old father who once worked for the government in some capacity and has since been called back out of retirement to supervise a project. This is a distinguished group.

The young sister dances while a neighbor girl, the landlord's much more pushy family, crowds around with questions and stares. A mother is also there, who conducts the ceremonies, later, when its time for the bride to come in. The groom is decked out and the bride looks pale, moving in a sombre gait, held up by the oldest daughter, Leilah, of the family whose mother, along with the bride's sister, goes out of her way to ask after my state of mind, to feed me the quick story of her sister, to cautiously collect a detail or two from me. The Iranian mother takes me to her heart, with her god-spelling charms telling me my welcome and giving me a grin of shrewish old lady's teeth, whitened like fossilized bones.

There are diversions: the drum playing for the men in the courtyard, then the silence of eating a well-spread meal; the always deferring to me, the foreigner, the professor-*estawd* who came with her foreignness to grace their room this night. I keep waiting to ask the fragile mother Sheringul if she is happy, but the answer is evident from one look at her heavy head, the helpless children clutching for her love, and then the contrast with those moments as a coy maiden in her dance, her changing clothes three times like pealing skin trying to peal off layers of a youth that was taken from her prematurely like a pulled tooth.

There is a different spirit in the daughters of the house—the tiny, gentle cow-eyed wife to be who wears her green and then her white bridal gowns like ornaments to seasons, spring and winter, youth and age, and her new wristwatch, and the wand of plastic paper flowers, like a veneer all over the 10th grade student's fright. She was officially a woman, then, and all the weeks and years before would make up a rule in her mind somewhere about what kind of days she gives to future children And her sisters hug me and tells stories and jokes.

And then there is another radiant child-woman, big with eminent child, in her pink gown and bright red stole and dark hair and eyes and pale sheen: some statue to maternity in ageless desert gardens like a poem to youth turned womanly but preserving nature. There is much talk about fruitfulness and barrenness and the need to have a husband like a line out of a song: giver and taker of seed, the caller of the years.

Of course, there are some riddles about tribes, and the impact of buying brides like selling candies. The Iranian Turkoman speaks up boldly for the cause of "free love," of natural gifts rather than purchased ones, and asks me if my *"mohdum"* (people), like her own, don't believe that way. There is, of course, the usual conversation about babies and not having them, and ways to prevent pregnancy, or induce fertility. The women mention other foreigners they have met, travelers who do not know any persons in Afghanistan, strangers, but who give these Iranian-Turkomen women a strange angle of thought: how narrow their own lives remain since they never travel.

Then, in comes a street family, poor Hazara folks . . . .

Tom takes pictures: the rainbow cake is served, the gathering of tribes like a parade of belief in the future. Then the celebration ends, and we are winding down the hill again to find a taxi in the cool night, and think of Afghan specialties:

There is a day and another and then at the university we are all sent out to parade "spontaneously" in the streets for Padogovny, the Russian President, and though the students protest, the babas are sent out to run them into the streets. I work in the steely quiet halls for a few hours, and then set off to walk home, first via a jumbled bus, and then on my own feet.

December 10, 1975

Early this morning we rise with the chill predawn and like pack rats or beasts of burden, sleepy as the light on the snow crest mountains, set off for the Suleiman Bus, a beehive of activity, with everyone bundled and eagerly collecting seats.

We are going back to the village then, to Tashkurghan, for a short visit . . . and the familiar landscape passes us: the streams of shabbily wrapped and bundled farmers and sons and their untidy heavy loads, their arms in the ceremonial long *chapan* sleeves, the snow like dust outlining the rills of the rising and falling mountains, the backbones of the country narrow and thin rites of mountains; the hay pulled up inside and over houses like thatch, the russet fields of dry cotton plants, the beseechingly naked fruit trees, the land that was florid and green like song last spring but turned to muteness.

And then the city: Tashkurghan, the hills, the bordering mountains, the feeling and curve and design of the land, a picture for a policeman, the *gaudiwan's* tale of how we came to be here, the mud lanes and dome houses. We reach Chris and Brenda's yard, and meet their neighbors, friendly pilau-bearing, one jaundiced woman. There is a flood of recollections, entering and exiting before: I see it and need to cry, and feel drowning in this other feeling, a desire to cast off and yet stay still, to find a new source of love awake in me. I remain as mute as the seasonal terrain.

Among a whole melee of passersby—who can say which we will remember, which forget? I think of Thomas Wolfe's sentiment crystallized, that you can never "go home" again. You can wake a morning and watch the sun come up over the mountains, the rays sliding across the velvet and harsh shattered textures, like a memory to the old rag pickers clothes which turned to gold and silk when the wand of a kind magician moved over them. Morning in this valley is ageless, and the birds, huge arrogant magpies, saunter across the grass, flirt and swoop down from tree to tree like prehistoric sailors, and the trail of smoke, thin, wispy as blown powder, comes from the ovens of every family, where the daughters and the mothers make their meals.

On the Thursday after we arrive, we find a gray day and the alleys have filled up with mud and the sphere for splashing extends into a world without borders where everything is wet. We tread the way through a thin drizzle, going first in the morning after tea and pomegranates like shining sweet rubies, to hail the *gaudiwans* and neighbors, the shopkeepers and students, sexless children in bright garb. We enter Shahzadah's house and sit around their stove to meet her brother's new wife, to be invited twice by her mother and father to see the sisters, all in that house where we first were, now turned to a kind of a barnyard, the same mud dried . . . turned to mush: Shahzadah protest a little too much, her eyes on Brenda, whom she adores, and her memory short; she had been sick with a cold for a while, received the story of Makadi and Makaha with a sardonic grin, and wouldn't listen to any conversation about her cousin, potential *namzad*, Mr. Wali.

In the days to follow, I see her again, gather from her eyes a kind of hardened scorn, feel hurt by the way she comments on the differences between Brenda and me, (how quickly her Persian has grown, how rich her stories are, how beautiful her coloring is, over and over.). But in her own place I try to understand the girl, always the outsider, the rich tax collector's daughter from more advanced ways, who would cut her own classmate, this town, out of the snide childish sophistication exclaiming her brightness.

On then, after some shopping, to Paregul's house. Paregul of the letters, who receives me with hugs and shaking knees like a long lost friend, Paregul of the now 12th class, always closest to my heart. We go inside and sit around the *sandali*, the coal table covered with heavy blankets, the heart of a family where it gathers to have meals, tea, talks. There is just a little silence, as the other women of the family come out to greet us, her brother's wife and child, his mother, then her sister who is studying typing at a special school in Mazar.

We remain only an hour or so, warm in the household, then I excuse myself to go "home," to warm up a little lunch, and then when the men return from their morning, we all set out again, this time to visit Rozia and Hamida and Camar. The first house of course was that at the end of the *culcha*—the tall two-story room of Hamida's family where we are seated and greeted by her brother, Abdul Salaam, who is about to graduate from the university. In all directions, the world in sight, stand mountains and gardens. Her two smaller brothers come in, fresh and grinning as garden sprites, and sit down too. Hamida herself is in the bazaar, so we meet her older sister, with her round, classic Uzbek face, pure-complexed and smiling, full of a sad, winsome beauty, herself a recluse of sorts.

We were to learn her story the next night at a dinner at their house, how the mother had fallen ill after the last son was born and so this sister had had to stay at home and do the work, and raise the others—how she taught Hamida, did all her letters and homework for her until she was in the fourth grade and started studying Pushtu, when suddenly Hamida began to understand herself.

The older girl sits quietly, fetches us a wondrous tray of tea and candies, and her college-graduating brother (he had been a teacher here for several years, a graduate of the Higher Teachers' College in Mazar and Kabul), speaks of his love of the land and all its sorrows. He recalls the cluttered noisy dorm rooms in Kabul, the poor quality of the instruction there, the poverty, unemployment, and chronic hunger of the people—and how he has a friend in Pittsburgh who had gone to study there, had loved it, and had found the streets all but paved with gold. Although interrupting gently, politely, we try to tell him that all is far from rosy in the States, but he persists in saying at least it is modern and its people happy.

That all remains to be seen.

When Hamida comes, we kiss her after their fashion and there are tears in her sister's eyes, out of joy, out of all the passed opportunities, out of the mistakes life gives our children, out of remembrance of how by the hand of her father, and her mother's illness, she had lost out of a whole way of life.

We come home then, with an invitation for dinner for the next night, and stop to invite Camargul. At the Mahoney's house I grow sad, cry like my weak self, feel far from Tom, and then put the feelings, all feelings, far away.

Friday then dawns exuberant, a sky clear as beauty itself, and I follow Brenda, first to visit her neighbor (the night before we had made cakes and then in the afternoon of Friday were to receive compliments of students), the family of the girl at the university. I have met one sister, whose house had been robbed of everything, and who now is also suffering from hepatitis, her young face, though mother of three, lined with weariness. They also bring out candies and tea, and we gather under a *sandalie* and talk, then after farewells pass to the bazaar, then home again in time to set the table, exchange impressions of Zahne-Miahshaw, when the first group of students, Gahwar and her sister, troop in. Next come Shahzadah, Rozia, and Camargul, later Ruhnai and sisters and Zaiman, Magfirat and Fazilat, and a parade of students I only half know, from classes I never taught.

They hear me calling one the wrong name, to my tired heart so desperate to be loved to immortality, I guess, seem always to compare me to Brenda—and the reality of their lives seems all too clear, how they could know and reflect on neither a past nor a future, how the only reality apparent to them was the reality of the immediate, the now apparent.

But I am tired and overly sensitive, so to my skewered ears even beautiful and brilliant Magfirat gives me a gentle blow when she informs me that once my hair had been as light as Brenda's, but it had gotten dark. There is a little laughter. As a group they do not mix that well, each group by class keeps to themselves and shares their own stories. For long minutes I watch through the window; Brenda's worker sits there too, and I detect tears in her eyes, as she gazes at us all, in her old shabby tarnished pantaloons She carries the sad smile of someone's swan song. (I think again of Sheringul, dancing at that wedding), the poor among the rich, a disease never to be corrected.

After they leave Nacira and Fanzia, the little sister, come, squat beside us in their easy manner, veils up to show nifty jump suits, their little sister also there. They, too, talk, then vanish, and we have only a few minutes, it seems, before it is time to go to Hamida's for dinner.

Was it that night the fight began? Was it another?

Around six we troop down the muddy lane to the house and sit again in the *bawlabad*-spread room with the brothers and fathers (and a brief Hamida). Spread out before us were some 50 dishes, for each of us servings from six or seven different things. Conversation ensues among all the rich eating: the food spread out aesthetically, beautiful in color and texture, the light catching at a piece of china, a child's eye.

Later we talk about women (made to work too hard), students (fortunate to be able to atted classes but a little spoiled and wasteful of the gift), and *chadris* and reputations (Hamida wants to go without chadris but her brother won't allow it here). Following the simple script of being *mamons,* next we go down below to drink tea with the mother and quiet sister. One tiny brother adopts Brenda as his own; they tell us how as a child he had drunk the milk of many mothers and so is not afraid of people, but takes to everyone very naturally. And around the *sandalie*, the older sister's story emerges, as the mother watches us all with love and a calm, buried sadness. Hopping up and down, grinning, the brothers exude energy in this otherwise solemn setting.

At our leaving there are gifts of apples; the oldest brother walks us home, sits awhile, pleased to be in Brenda and Chris's house. After twenty minutes, taking the hand of another brother, this one also kept out of school, silent like the older sister, and the gregarious child who accepted everyone, he nods, gives thanks, and leads them out.

I balance on a small stoop outside a long time watching the sky shift, trying to think what is in my mind to turn so much light into darkness, why I am so full of comparisons, so jealous or hurt by the realities around me, why I can't just accept how things are. Fiercely, I see Tom as a kind of villain, always clipping my wings, and as night deepens, cloud covered, I sit in the yard and think of my capacity for love, and if I even have any, of people I liked in high school, of Joe and Steve, of Washington U. Tom Spirer, of Nova Scotia Francoise, of people who had touched me callously when I was first in college, of my longings after all sorts of Tom's Princeton classmates and current colleagues . . . to whomever. Who knows how there is in me such a black selfishness that numbs me to anyone who doesn't try to make me happy, who is not able to always be telling me as much, who mirrors back to me a sense of my worth that I do not internalize myself.

How weird and selfish to be so needy, especially here.

Yet, I feel also a desperate need to give even more than I want or need returned, to have a person or persons in whom to share all this love and care and attention that defines best who I was, am, or want to be.

Had T. somehow not accepted that from the start? Had I never whole-heartedly given it to him?

The mountains are gone, one light burns in the house, Tom is snoring softly under the covers, a wind blows, and still I sit trying to find something. Then, too tired and cold, I just go off to sleep.

Saturday then, we have the lunch at Camargul's, one of Brenda's special students, surrounded by a bevy of the loud-speaking women in bright clothes and coiffured hair, undaunted as they ask us about sex, love, men, making very little effort to include us or make over us, yet in their own right kind and generous. Chris sits alone in the women's hall with us, while a uniform of men pass through, and after we say thanks a dozen times and eat our fill, we give in to a plan to go out to the Hajie Biron where a *buz kashi* game is to be underway.

It is a howling windy, lonely day out there somehow. All the women in *chadris* on the hill stare at us; the students whom I greet seem remote and even gentle Nerulhoda tells me she is sorry I am forgetting some of my once excellent Persian (as I had written them I had, although it is also that I am not speaking much with anyone on this trip, I think), and suddenly I feel the whole world has collapsed, that no part of any of those students or this town can be mine anymore. A comment from Shahzadah follows, her usual snippy observation about some word, some dress; and I have to leave that crowd, to trudge down the hill to the men's world, to let the horse's dust fly in my face a little, to stare away from the silk cloaks, the turbaned crowd, and let the hills, mountains, and bowl of desert, the steppe lands, textures from sand and stone, drying cotton fields, colored dirt houses, the round roofs and square cut walls, the curved rows of post-season plants—the huddled blowzy figures on the hill.

We find Tom and Chris, and again I am weeping. Needing an exit, we take our leave from the hill and then set out for the road.

Unexpectedly, we meet Syfora's sister and sister-in-law, and after being tightly packed into a car, with her husband and with Islamadeen and his brothers and Ziagul and Tajenisa—we stop at the latter's house to have tea and exchange stories. I rally, lifted by the beautiful, kind faces of that family—a cousin from the telecommunications school who speaks with an "okay" for "yes" in delicate scrambled English, the enthusiastic praises shared of the strange brother who is a soldier now in Badakshan (later it turned out to be near Baglan), the good-natured Chris's "oo's" and "ah's" which the girls emit upon seeing mellow Chris, the girls own classic Persian beauty taken in.

On down the road we wander then, with an invitation to return to the house and share breakfast at 7:00 a.m. the next morning.

Thursday. (Back to Kabul, Dec.16. 1975.

I have yet to finish Saturday's happenings, which consisted of walking in the gathering dark back to town, shaking hands and telling stories to old students and teachers of Tom, old *mafatishes*, old friends, until we got to Azarullah's house, where we were seated again under a *sandalee.*

Something was awry: our dear Azarullah seemed sullen, rubbing his eyes a lot, still a little wizened, looking way too old for only a boy. The electricity wasn't to come on for a long time so we sat in his lanterned room as father, than distant cousin, little and big brother came in to tell their stories. There was gossip about all the thieves in town, and the teacher at Tom's old school who had been apprehended several times for his behavior. There had been one famous robbing of sheep in which the teacher had supposedly carried a whole herd over a high wall using ropes, and was finally found when the police followed footprints to his yard and found the sheep there. Or, was he actually caught in the act that time? Anyway, he, the others, got off almost immediately (The husband of Majhan, Brenda's neighbor whose whole life possessions were carried off, would sit in the Mahoney's house the night before we left and tell us her full impression of the *"rahwat xord"*—dishonesty—prevalent in Afghan law).

Azarullah's father talked about the unfairness of the system, and of the narrow chances for a university education for his son. The cousins removed spoke of Mazar and a soldier's school, of their friends at the Faculty of Engineering, their pretty boy smugness seeming to send Azarullah under the table. There followed dinner and conversation, a half hour with the women, mother and sister and neighbors in the darker, dank room, a radio cassette playing, the smallest son petted. Then we were tumbled out into the night, lanterns swinging as our host took us to Mahoney's house.

All across town and up the alley, our bundled figures, shadows projected big against the wall. It was comfortable, to find in the house a resonance, our host and hostess pleasantly resolved in each other, so that watching them I felt old and unloved, and yet acted even more distant from Tom.

Sunday then, a predawn dressing, a *gaudi* ride and wind in our faces, we trekked out to the big manor house of Ekramboy, and with the sisters scurrying, we heard of the mother's bad eye weeping, the son peacock-like stalking, the late teachers gathering. There was a slaughter in the uncle's yard next door, and the day emerged into gray. We sat around a brazier of coals, a blanket over us, and were served candied carrots and quince marmalade, a family specialty of soup made from the Qorbani, consisting of sacrificed lamb, his melted fat and marrow, and *sambazaks* (meat sugared patties-pastries); and large loaves of round, wet bread, and bowls of *kimah* (skimmed cream and curds). Afterwards we talked about my students in Kabul, my one girl student in the Freshman Engineering class and a few others in more advanced years, the economy and how much English now governed our days, so we had little need, sad to say, to use more than basic Persian some days. But fluency rebounded here as we chatted about babies, the Noor clinic, the price of bread, the dormitories for girls at the university; and how I must come back again, and how Brenda must always also visit them.

Soon it was off to walk briskly home, as their greetings and hugs rang in our ears still, the day decidedly mellow and soggy and brisk with unwarmed earth around us. We were almost to the Mahoneys' when we ran into their landlord, who protested at our never visiting him, who insisted we must come tonight. We refused of sorts—a tad amazed that someone who had not invited us in our two years there, like Ziadeen and this man Nadem Khan, should now be so fawning and protective when we were only in town for four days.

Back at their house, we found dear old Amore M'med, who kissed my hands and made signs and blessings like a father to a daughter, praised us, spoke of nothing, then asked Tom for *baksheesh,* which angered Chris, and then was off to do an errand for us, to purchase *tel* (gasoline) with his Turkomen friend Habibullah.

On then, all of us gathered at 11:30 to go to Shahzadah's for a huge lunch and further conversation, a bit more intellectual than others, on revolutions and Russian history, presidential elections and the attitudes of the rich to the poor. The tax collector spoke matter-of-factly of how he had walked to *buz kashi* the previous afternoon in order to show everyone there that he had no false pride and was quite willing to do as poor people did. We spoke of the trials of students at Kabul University with their bad living arrangements, and the geographical origins of the father's family and his wife's (Jalalabad and Kabul), and there were jokes about Chris's quietness. (He was supposed to be so full of food his vocal cords didn't work anymore that afternoon). And so on, while the little room, once our whole house, shabby and dark with an over productive *bookerie* stove, sent us all into a drugged heat. The neighbor's girls were there along with us, Azra and another friend. They spoke little but readily about how Mahadi, the girl at the university, had always been smart but just lost points because she did not always get along with her teachers and that was why it was perfectly right that she got into the university despite their *nombre sardan.*

We were off home again, Tom and Chris before us like different worlds, Tom in the Gatsbyesque western Florsheim shoes and turtle neck sweater and coat and overcoat like an old man in injured dignity, and jaunty pace; Chris in a ski jacket and bluejeans and boy's galoshes, old lumber man's wool cap, East and West. Tom disappeared, presumably to bid Azarullah good-bye. (It turned out that he went to *buz kashi*) and then to his old student's, and I joined Brenda to go home to rest. But of course we were interrupted within a quarter hour by some unknown students, neighbors of unknown quantities, who had to have a tea tray set in front of them, a conversation directed, some meeting arranged, which we did with joy, if also with bit of weariness.

It was almost dark as we trekked off to Paregul's house, and on route met Tom and white-turbaned, robed Rasuddin, the ghoulish mullah, who in a turn of face greeted us kindly. We moved into Paregul's house, dark as a cave, ten faces of unknown women nursing babies, all made up, sitting in a ring of candle like kerosene light around a *sandalee*. For a long time we rested silent against the pillows, with Paregul away busy preparing the meal, and conversation moved at cross currents. I caught myself close to dozing, absently taking in the sun and shadows, the play of light across shaky faces, the turns of noses, the function of maternity, the old Beebe's manlike form, the sisters-in-law from Kabul and Mazar, the ogre-like neighbor and her daughter, *namzad* at 12. And so, the sense of it.

Then it was dinner and a feast even better than all the others: chicken and three kinds of fruit, *kafta, kebab, pilau* and meat, pudding and *nan*, spinach—and we ate heartily despite our over-stuffed stomachs. Afterwards the little cousins danced, eyes flashing, the old mother-grandmother a solid, quiet dignified form smiling and tending one or the other of the many infants between their nursings from their mothers. We were just about to take in tea and let the conversation rise like a natural wave after the long day's work, when Chris and the landlord came in, and we clumsily extracted ourselves from an awkward mistake. I had told them to come too early, at 7:30 in fact.

The landlord, Tom's old *saer malim,* fumed, the alley stretched like a mushmeal of mud in places, but we trooped on, only a little peeved, back to the house, and collapsed. But it wasn't over. Enter the neighbor, the tow-haired Azarullah, the mother, a jaundiced Mazan, the husband, the old father, another Zeagul and Aziza and the sisters. The men (Chris and Tom) hid in the bedroom and we went through yet another display of hospitality, all the time chatting about the inevitability of thieves—this family having but recently been the target of some—and the physical route over land and sea to America, the two in no way connected. Ostensibly the women came to give me some things to bring to Mahadis and to rehearse me carefully in the proper news to tell her, minus my tale of thieves and sickness. And so on with reality, and immediacy.

I listened, shook my head, understood their concern, and promised to do what they wished.

Time, then, and could we sleep? I saw images: the mountains in all their seasons, the passing faces of certain students. But there was more: floor after floor full of food set before us; a tear in the old housekeeper's eye; the skitteringly happy but timid face of the adopted Turkomen boy; the sweet way our friend Chris looked out while strumming his guitar and singing, and his brotherly kindness, instinctive, when he put his hands on my face in the kitchen to calm me when Tom exploded one day; and Brenda's always easy way of conversation, in contrast to my own clumsy reticence.

Until it was another early day, full of breakfast and casualness. We made a not so well timed and awkward goodbye to the house and its sirens and silences, then moved off to school. In each class I faced the suddenly shy watching faces of my students to whom I gave candy, and the already elsewhere pre-occupied faces of the teachers, of Najiba's kind warm enthusiasm, of my own stronger sense of it all this time.

Then we were seated in a *gaudi*, again leaving town to meet Tom at his school. Squeezed into a Toyota, we bumped along to the crossroads of Puli, the turn off to Kunduz, where we took a taxi into town, bargained for a *gaudi* to the *saroy*, then found another Toyota at take us all the way to Kabul, and a another taxi—9 hours later—to our door. In our chilly house, we found a letter of thanks on the table from and Lena and James, who had stayed there, and two chocolate bars, for which we knew they had paid dearly on Chicken Street.

. . . We checked in at PC, had a light dinner at the restaurant of dim lights and haunted folklorists, and vowed to start all over tomorrow . . . .

The country had been splendid in places, moonlight on the starving mountains, the patterns and textures of winter deserts, the always burdened workers in each field or valley—We knew the road well, weren't especially sensitive to any newness, and in a moment losing my groundings. I could have been a child again being driven to my grandparent's old far in eastern Texas, or identified as my own driver in the old Rambler going up to Maryland or in the trip to California with Dan and Mother I had taken the summer I graduated college.

Our driver was young, without even a full beard yet. People were quiet except in that first Toyota to Puli—when Tom had to go through the answers to all the questions we had answered for two years here, about salary, wives, work, family, distances, funerals, airplanes, marriages, wars, soldiers,—and so on, as if all the world needed only to know these few details, and the rest, like windblown dross, today was dispensable.

Dec. 18, 1975

I am back to the realities of teaching; in short I'll be giving my exams the very end of this month instead of January 8-10th . . . The Dean wants his pre-engineering course to start as soon as possible. As its Department head, I'm to be here the full month . . .

[I'm enjoying Yoshida Kehno: *Essays in Idleness,* even as I struggle with my desire for T and his odd rejection and a reversal. I note my own discontent with being here and not advancing in writing or career prospects, with finding T's moods obsessive and his style slow and non-liberating, with blaming my being "an adolescent at heart" . . . still expecting some deus ex machina to enter and "to give me the privilege of thinking myself brilliant, beautiful, witty, and successfully employed." Another book, fuel for thought, Aye Kwee Armah: *The Beautiful Ones are Not yet Born.*

We continue to shuffle dates for the Indian trip we wish to plan for semester break, ourselves typical of our colleagues here, who live for the next travel opportunity.

Dec. 22, 1975

A play of sorts gathers at the University about the dates of exams and pre-engineering course. A meeting with Dean Sayed yesterday yielded nothing except a vague expectation on his part that we should all be around for any work he decides on. In truth this is fair: he has a right to demand hours and days from us, as we supposedly are committed to doing work on behave of the university and faculty, not just entertaining ourselves. Still, it would be easier to have firm dates, around which to work, in terms of preparedness for the coursework here, and for any vacation days of which we might take advantage.

Today the landlord's small daughter comes knocking at the door . . . to ask if rent had been paid for this month and if so, when. Tom and I had brought it over last Tuesday and given it in a person to the exclusive *sibe-xona.* But, afterwards we had misgivings as to whether or not it had gone to the correct house, so this was a slight jolt. Shyly, she listens, then nods, her long lashes demurely down, her small animated form slightly bobbing from side to side. As quickly as she has arrived, she leaves, only to knock on the door again five minutes later.

"Do you need any milk or butter?" she asks softly. "Please excuse me if it has been trouble for you for me to come inside again." Perhaps her new job, spurred by natural curiosity, is just to discreetly check inside the house, and see how we are keeping it, or to peek at some of the other foreigners who frequently visit here . . . .

It snows, but by noon most of it has melted, leaving only the illusion of a jeweled shawl on the mountains above us, the sky clear and blue for the first time in several days. Inside, our classrooms radiate chilliness and hard stones. Teeth shaking, the students whisper their anxiousness to be done with the semester and winter both.

I continue to present the students with more sheets of exercises and readings each week than other teachers had in a month . . . . I only hope they help them.

But apart from my silly self-indulgence . . . the truth is, this is a world—Afghanistan, its provinces, its cities, but most other non-Western countries—where people's lives are little better than those of teams of insects or hoards of animals. The poor people who make up well over half of the world population live each day in a struggle against death by hunger or disease or exposure, their hours consumed in trying to make a living, their children dying every year. Theirs is a realm where few can read or write, they are a people who know nothing before death of that whole soothing fantasy or faithful world of words which sometimes help to alleviate reality, individuals who will spend all their days in one place, like the Egyptian faluddens beside the polluted stream on the edge of the desert or the Mexicans in the shanty towns on the edge of the modern capital whose fathers and brothers are unemployed, where children are skinny and undernourished, whose selves go through the daily ritual, with little dignity left . . . .

. . . I don't know, couldn't even speculate on what's the correct way for the world. All my believes on some sense of Reason up there falter and yet I am forced to believe there are powers totally beyond us, beyond all humanity, which will act out their senses of things, the eternal cycles no matter what man-child we come up with to try to alter it. Twain's sense of a game, Dante's sense of scaled hells and heavens, Buddha's sense of no-resistance, of nirvana, all point to the same realization that in the end a kind of enlightened stoicism is the very most we can hope for.

But still, all those wretched lives go on, nothing helps them, nothing alleviates their pain, nothing inspires them in their hopeless quiet dignity and those who could change it are so rotten in the heart with their queer ideas and ready luxuries and comforts, they are the real walking, waking dead.

Greed, greed, greed.

Yet out of this, the words of Tolstoy and others, that possessing and giving love is the most important quality of living

Dec.26, 1975

> [Christmas, presents exchanged, Mirad's memories of the foreigners in Jalalabad renting a *gaudi* and going around the town singing Christmas carols three years ago. We go to midnight mass.]

It is a grand old pedaling ride out to the Italian Embassy in the deep night, along the car-less, lighted avenue past the high, white-walled, sprawling compounds of the city's leaders, native and otherwise, and we arrive early at the church in time to pick out a seat on the edge and watch the jolly big-hearted Italian priest, fluent in at least five languages, greet each new arrival. He blesses each, while the musicians practice on flute, organ, guitar and recorder in the background and the Christmas tree in the choir sends out a wave of changing light.

The mass itself, international in flavor, pulls in the ambassador or *charge d'affair* of the U.S., France, Germany, Italy and Spain to read the nativity gospel in each native tongue, and the congregation or the choir and musicians join in a Christmas carol in the same language after each reading, in a classic Celebration of Carols and Word. We grin at the flurrying, good-natured motions of a stage director with which the little Italian priest handles each grouping of internationals. When he invites the Spanish representative to read the Spanish section, the man gestures dramatically that he will need to borrow glasses to do so, and magically a pair appears. We sit behind three English daughters with their porcelain pale faces and blond hair, the children dressed in purple and green and blue velvet dresses and don hats, to receive the Christian mass in their sleepy wonder. We are nurtured by the familiar elements of the mass, float with the flute solos, ancient music recital, and guitar accompaniment; smile with the ivory-faced, gray-habited nuns and stoically over-plump or wizened Italians in one flank; and listen intently, to the two English priests—Brothers Martin and Malcolm—officiating over their communion service in sombre brogues. Everywhere there are candles, and candles, and candles: mesmerizing, shimmering, giving warmth.

We bike home again in the early Christmas hours, the whole city magical and fully ours, the silence beautiful, past the shadowy figures of cold, uniformed soldiers scattered before the official buildings, catching the inside lights of an occasional taxi at some intersection. Home again we fall quickly into bed . . .

At five, already dawn, we wake to the sound of sushing water. We race to turn off the water pump, and discover a deluge lays around us. We clean up, sleep an hour more, rise to the day.

Outside, it has begun to snow. By 9:30 the city hosts a veritable white Christmas. After teas and bread and a cold walk around the city turned to snow-cleaning labors, we bask in a private shared sense of Christmas, a beloved secret between us, while the rest of the world shakes and skates and moves to maintain its regular survival . . .

[Later, guests in the rituals of the holiday, we join a party at the Country Director's house, a space full of a rainbow and atlas of nationalities, and children . . . . The sense of shared community revives, and spirits rise, promising a better tolerance and acceptance of all things to do with people and Tom and myself . . . . In retrospect, among the food and desserts, the drinks and enthusiastic faces then, some images emerge: catching sad-eyed flirtatious R. Dwyer give a passing fancy to a girl who receives one look and turns away; musing on the old music teacher Rahmgul with his massive pitted Pushtu nose and great gentle eyes and laughter playing the *rebab* and singing and preparing a drum, and searching a scale along with James Gareth before the brick fire-place with its design of a Incan sun across the screen; our PC staff, Rona and Parwin and Sadja, dressed up, fresh as Parisian models, in their late 20's and husband-less; and the snow transpired so quickly this early Christmas mornings like an afterthought by nature to set the scene right.

Exams this week . . . . At the moment there's a grand confusion in our disheveled ranks at the Faculty, all arising from the fact that no one is or was to give exams early. The Dean doesn't have the power nor desire to re-arrange the mess, so we must. Mr. Wali, head of scheduling, etc. and the committee feel that another final should be given all students on the day of their regular scheduled exams, and thus they'll be abiding by the rules. However, that change creates a bind: Paul's sections have already finished their tests, and half of Rick Dwyer's and mine have exams announced and planned for tomorrow. Students, staff, none is about to spring up and like the idea when there is so little logic or convenience in it.

A plan arrives: Tom and I think we should announce that all students must be present for another exam, although, in fact, they need not be, and then on the official day, exams can be given to other sections and any of our sections which have already taken one will just need to sit in on the test one hour and then leave. Will it work?

Of course the whole thing went sour due to the comments of Rick Dwyer early last week; he penned Paul and me letters suggesting that the Dean allow us to give our exams early, so that we would be finished in time to take a week's break and still be back in time to begin the Pre-Engineering course, slated in his myth-swallowing eyes at that time to be beginning in early, early January. But, in fact, this was only Rick D's take on it. Thus, the confusion.

I get late Christmas cards from two students, one signed, "your faithful students." How dour and at once childish I must often appear to these classes, the way I'm always given to hearing their point of view on anything, their democratic decision as to whether or not to have class, my accepting late work with small penalty, and so on. I believe I do a decent job of teaching them, but perhaps less of being a mentor or professional acquaintance. Obviously the latter can rarely be comfortably possible for a foreign woman in a faculty of almost total males. In reflection, I continue to miss all of my students from Tashkurghan; yet I know I was always a little distant from them also.

I seem fated to have lousy luck with preparing final examinations on ditto machines.

I troop off to USIS early and tell the "ditto man" that I want some things run off, have gotten permission from someone in charge earlier. I watch him run off my exams, package them in a paper and hand them to me, then arrive back at PC and find about half of his pages, especially the whole set for the last test for the Freshmen section, has bled so badly, from too much fluid, that they are totally unreadable. Calmly I find some forms and retype then, but then I'm wary that I may have used the wrong stencils . . .

[We are making plans for the Indian trip, dealing with delayed visas, Further, we welcome back Bruce Letts, the coordinator for all TEFL teachers. I've been reading Kate Millet and pondering how men could have eternally been so controlling . . . . and if women will simply become "worst men" as they "achieve" in a more even playing field. These are European and American women, but our sisters in this land and in most of the world, have no such option . . .]

Interminable gray skies linger with the promise of cold, but only a little comes, In a clearing we see the mountains again, a patch of the virgin cold, and the cycle goes on; we feel the cold especially since the clouds and sun are heavy, the latter invisible before the former.

January 1, 1976

The new year comes in as wet and soggy as used tissue: a gray inversion over the city between the mountains and a cold wet drizzle that could never quite make it as snow.

Yesterday our exams finally finished. After posting my grades at the university, I take a bus to the Indian Embassy, where I am rudely introduced to a whole new style of bureaucracy: I.E., no one ever gets their passports at 11:00 and we should have known better than to have come at this hour expecting them to have our passports. So after a mild public rebuke, I return home, type some of Tom's law school applications, and return at 1:00 to stand in a crowded line. Of course, upon reaching the end, a young bureaucrat waffles and intones: the visa will not be ready until two more days . . .

On the bus coming home from the University today, in the middle of the big intersection near the Traffic Police and the zoo, I encounter a funeral. A congregation of men, single file carrying a covered bed, move solemnly into their neighborhood, and out to find a graveyard on the hill somewhere above the city. They shuffle, slowly, with their stiff, lifeless burden, between the cat-like darting taxis and the smoky lumbering buses, the fruit vendors on the sidewalk, and the pacing soldiers on the wall above the prison across Damazang.

At the Indian Consulate, a Jordanian boy borrows my pen to fill out a passport form. Later his partner comes in, but he gestures him away; they are determined to turn in their passports regardless of the hour or the day. A clerk at the post office refuses to cancel my aerogram with its 2 af stamp properly despite his supervisor's scolding; and a weary, cross-eyed dizzy American traveler sidles down beside me on the seat at the Indian Consul and begins to tell me of his travels—Europe, Turkey, Iran, Afghanistan, next India . . . .

Mirad initiates a bit of a detective task . . . He has to go with his brother and Ghaffar to some village in the eastern mountains tomorrow to take care of some kind of money exchange or loan and Ghaffar is on permanent guard duty at the training center and thus can't ask for leave, although he needs to go along. So we are tasked with finding

Azerly, the Administrative Secretary in charge of staff and such things, and through Howard locate his brother at the flower shop on Chicken Street . . . Meanwhile Mirad's oldest brother, the famous shopkeeper from Sare-pul, comes to our house. He is a large, heavy-set man and Mirad's thin, chistled features are almost lost in his ruddy full face. After hearing previously of the family split, how this brother has almost nothing to do with Mirad and his father, it is intriguing to see him and wonder if the two mysteries, the one with money and the other with his appearance, are related . . . .

> *[We took our trip to India, were away for ten days and returned on January 18, but Tom came down ill with malaria-like symptoms. We sought the PC doctor, as his fever reached 103 F. and he shook with chills. Is it dengue fever, not malaria?]*

January 19, 1976

At the university, the Dean is now less certain that the Pre-Engineering class can go forward, because he must bring in 50 extra students, based on the results of the Concorde, and then let the first semester separate out "knows and not-knows." It seems odd, in reflection, as I previously thought the intention was to help students with weak backgrounds to catch up with the others. All of which could mean I do not teach again until school officially opens in the middle of March. I will meet with him to determine how to use our teachers and resources to further his plans.

I return home via the regular bus, the fact that men sit while women stand squashed and unbalanced, bothering me today . . . then stop in at the post office and the PC office.

Qorbin came visiting, having just left his job at the Sudan-Swede's house because—he tells us—he no longer has a bicycle to get him to and from work and can not rely on the public buses at 8:00 a.m. In any case, the PC doctor has thought about hiring him, but Qorbin is a little worried about being able to handle a job at that huge house and also wonders about not having a bike. One wonders why certain foreigners here can't hire more than one person to handle all their work . . .

Kabul is in sad shape this winter; there has been only one day of snow and it hasn't even been that cold. There's a big change in climate worldwide, strange weather patterns, as illogical as can be, in best Joycean tradition, "as unpredictable as a child's bottom." Our small collection of hand-me-down plants are hardly prospering, the big sprawling ferns wilted . . .

January 19

> [Tom is better. Between trips to a local lab, I pick up a package at the Post Office with all the bureaucracy involved, only to discover it is for the Hatfield's old cook, Zaman, and is an expensive Timex, some photos and junk jewelry. One of the PC office folks then helps in extracting it from customs. And we leave it for someone to pick up at the center and deliver to Zaman.

It is supper, then, and from his bundle of blankets besides the blazing *bookerie* fire, Tom moves sluggishly to drink some more of his medicinal salt and sugar water; for the first time he eats a portion of rice. Transfigured with the flood of carbohydrates, afterwards he sings lyrics from a Brendan Behan play.

At 7:15 I pedal out to a lecture on Ai Khanoum, by a French archaeologist. Ai Khonoum was a Greek city built west of Kunduz at the junction of the Oxus and a smaller river, which a French team has been excavating for eight years. His slides and talk are fascinating as we watch the classical city of palaces and temples and courtyards emerge from the debris. It was built, or at least at its best, at the time of Alexander in the 3rd century BC and the archaeologists have found plaster castes of many famous Greek statues made in the style of Alexander's court sculpture, as well as Corinthian columns (also Ionic and Doric), bathrooms with perfect drainage and fireplaces and small tubs, and a well-preserved mosaic in one bathroom floor complete with nautical emblems of crabs, dolphins, and dragons. This latter is as good as any of the ancient ruins we'd found in Crete perhaps, evoking the same sense of well-cultivated life in bygone millenniums. In addition, the city, which existed there briefly before the Turks and others overran it, included:a gymnasium and theater, and the layout shows it was atleast 1 1/2 by 3 kilometers in size,

On the way home I pedal madly, making it back to the house through the cold, then suddenly realize my watch has slipped off. Retreating on my heels, I circle back to USIS, now locked and with no one there except one little soldier. He responds with surprise and sympathy to my tearful entreaties, but is unable to open the door, so I cry my way home. A block away from the house I meet Tom, shockingly not only up on his feet but out on a bike; he had found the watch in the yard, and pedaled after me to let me know. We both settle back into the house, cold and tired and blessed, grateful for a chance to sleep, after a little reading. Mirad must have thought us entirely mad, first me pedaling around in the dark, then Tom who had been on his death bed all night and day suddenly racing out into the cold after me, and then our silence (except as I sneak into the kitchen to steal the last piece of yogurt pie for Tom who was much recovered and had a healthy appetite for the moment.)

Up at dawn today, I futilely set off for the university, where I grasp only too quickly that there is yet no specific assigned work for me.

[I am intrigued by Drabble's book, *Waterfall,* on how marriage makes women ghosts, how it provides a way to evade your gifts in inactivity. Is that to be my path? I found a poem "The Cow" by Mary Gordon, my old Barnard College classmate, in the *American Review,* along with an interview with the mystical composer, Karlhunz Stockhauen]

January 20, 1976

This morning I idle for hours at the university, without any students . . . Mr. Shukor comes in and shuffles quietly at his desk in the office. He is such an odd fellow. When here, I never see him reading or writing or anything, but rather it appears that he is just passing time, drifting. In fact, he always has questions about things we are teaching, even if he raises a point three weeks after the rest of us have taught that section.

Today he told me how his son wants to enter the Faculty of Medicine and so as he told us two summers ago, he has borrowed books from there so the 14-year old can spend his vacation reading them.

I see a notice posted for a meeting of the faculty, and thinking it the usual faculty meeting which we have on Thursday, I set off at 1:00 and brazenly enter the conference room, ready to be greeted. Immediately, I find myself in a full room of professors and administers, all male, in the midst of a seminar on the future and present needs in Afghanistan for engineering and agricultural programs. The assembled trade details on development, dropping the English words like "urbanization" or "industrial plants," in between the Persian rhetoric. I listen carefully, participants nod, but after 30 minutes I realize I am not actually supposed to be there, so I turn and usher myself out, a tad flustered.

The days then are mostly wide open, to be used for our own work, for reading, for planning. Tom appears to be all well again. The weather is springlike, damp with just a chill of winter, the mountains cradling. Next month had better bring real winter weather or the crops and water supply will suffer.

Recalling the scene in the faculty meeting earlier, I remember hearing of a murder in this Faculty the year we had first come to Afghanistan. Kabul University, like most centers of higher education, has had its radicals of all persuasions since its start in 1940, and has also been the smelt from which generations of national leaders come. Likewise, the Faculty of Engineering, admittance to which requires, along with the School of Medicine, the highest national exam grades, has always had its quota of the brilliant, its projectors of the future.

Ahmad Shah Massoud (later to be the martyred, leader of the Northern Alliance)was an engineering student in the early '70's, at which time he was a member of the student wing of the Jamiat-i—Islami party, led by (future President) Burhanuddin Rabbani. Rabanni had studied Law and Theology at Kabul University and and been a professor there himself. Other members in this Jamiat student group had been Gulbuddin Hekmatyar (future warlord and head of Hezb-i-Islami), as well as the head of Jamiat's student wing, although he had been in prison for his role in the murder of a student from a rival Communist group, the event about which I had heard rumors in 1976. Not surprisingly, the ideological disputes between Hekmatyar's radical faction and Rabbani's moderates soon caused a split in the university-led movement, all of which foreshadowed the first phase of the civil war.

Engineering education, as it was practiced during the time I was there, had grown out of the Faculty of Science at Kabul University in 1956, then become part of a joint Faculty for Engineering and Agriculture in 1958.

By 1963, a modern, independent Faculty had been established, one which used the curriculum, teaching materials, and teaching staff typical of any American university, and over the next decades the Faculty received major assistance from the University of Wyoming (1950's-1963), followed by a consortium of eleven U.S. institutions (Georgia Institute of Technology, Purdue University, Rice University,University of Cincinnati, Carnegie Mellon University, North Carolina State University, Stevens Institute of Technology, Illinois Institute of Technology, University of Notre Dame, Washington University, and Indiana University) through 1974. As part of the aid, Afghan professors trained at a wide spectrum of U.S. universities. Through USAID, from 1974 to 1978 (at which time following the communist coup, they withdrew from the country), major help for the Faculty of Engineering came from the University of Nebraska

The Faculty consisted of six departments: Civil Engineering, Electrical Engineering, Mechanical Engineering, Architecture, Vocational Technical Education, and Agricultural Engineering (administered jointly with the Faculty of Agriculture). Likewise, traditional U.S-style courses, a five-year program spread over nine semesters and with a six month practical training required, led to B.S. degrees in civil, electrical, mechanical and architectural engineering. In 1974, to address the need to train qualified lecturers and instructors in electrical, civil and mechanical engineering for technical colleges and schools in the country, the department of Vocational Technical Education was transferred from the Faculty of Science to the Faculty of Engineering.

In the initial five semesters, students mastered mathematics, physics, chemistry and introductory subjects for civil, electrical and mechanical engineering; while in the remaining four semesters they concentrated on specialist subjects in civil, electrical and mechanical engineering. The departments of architectural and vocational technical education followed appropriate, but separate curricula.

At government urging, as various industrial and commercial sectors were progressing rapidly in Afghanistan, the number of students admitted to the Faculty of Engineering had more than tripled from 300 to 1000 by 1977.

Afghanistan 2002

In the immediate months following the fall of the Taliban, analysts estimated that that post-conflict Afghanistan would need around one thousand dollars per head, or for a population of 25 million about 20 million dollars, plus an additional 500 million to clear landmines. When a country has lost everything, it does not take a lot of speculation or research to realize where reconstruction must go. The country needed a strong and honest and creative government who would put as its first priority finding the means to repatriate and resettle its scattered citizens, employ its people, and provide the means for them to resume agricultural production. They needed to rebuild irrigation canals and provide seeds for crops to again move citizens toward self-sufficiency in food and possibly resume export of traditional goods such as dry fruits, nuts, textiles, carpets, and gems. The people needed basic housing, clinics, hospitals, and schools, especially for girls. The government needed to build sources of electricity, water, and a network for communication (telephones and broadcasting). Afghanistan desperately needed to re-develop, rebuild, retrain, and maintain, a police force, courts, public administration, national government buildings, a central bank and treasury, and courts.

It was a country with a life expectancy of 41 years. Here one in 60 women died in child birth, with 15,000 dead in 2000 from pregnancy-related causes. Annually, 3,000 died from unexploded land mines. Some 77 per cent of the population lacked access to safe water and 88 per cent had inadequate sanitation. An estimated 3. 8 million had been dependent on food aid (2000-2001) and 123 million were affected by the three-year drought. And the only "stability" in the Afghan economy came from a dependence on opium, with 95 % of households in some provinces raising and selling opium.

Across the country in the optimistic early days of 2002, with the very powerful exception of major pockets of resistance from warlords and pro-Taliban forces, in the south and along the Pakistan border, Afghans celebrated the fall of the Taliban, the security promised by the alliance's presence, and the onset of involvement and aid by the international community. But among people neglected, exploited, manipulated, and punished for more than a generation, trust and confidence in any new regime shouted its fragility. Much work, many desperate voices, beckoned to be tended to.

XIX

COUNTDOWN IN EVERYTHING

January 22, 1976

Tom is sick again . . . At the university I am immersed in a plan to teach a special course for the German Technical Vocational section. All negotiations were arranged in Persian, so the instruction should be something like it was for me when I taught in Tashkurgan's Lycee Mahasty and often had to use more Persian than English, in order to explain concepts beyond the students' vocabulary.

We gather for a memorable faculty meeting—the real one—The names of the 53 students up for graduation are introduced, and three of them are censored for disciplinary reasons. This gesture brings out tales of horror from various professors who have each had incidents with these three in particular, students infamous for a kind of swearing, pressuring smugness it sounds like, students who have never let up insulting certain professors. One of the victimized professors stands to make his statement and explains that he has particularly been harassed and that now it has reached the point where he has no recourse but to carry a pistol around with him.

The Dean appears noticeably ruffled. He gives a speech about how while the students in the faculty may have incidents of disobedience, the only means the professions have of disciplining them is academically and that once they are dropped from the faculty, for whatever reason, the police and the courts, could take over. Then some students who were borderline cases for passing were brought up (third year students) and their cases half-discussed. Their grades, one by one, were painstakingly publicized on the blackboard. Then the administrative portion of the meeting ensued, and at high noon, we adjourned, with most items having been referred to specific committees to be further resolved.

I bus home to lunch and a drowsy Tom. We prepare for a panel for other PCVs, at which we are to present about our experiences.

One volunteer observes of Herat and Kandahar: empty drugged faces of world-wearied but not wise travelers in Herat hotels, the Persian classical landscape and the excellent architecture of the Jama Masjet.

I hear of a boy who lived in Tashkurghan for 18 years. After falling on his head and allegedly "dying "once at age four, he came across as mildly retarded, a gentle soul who just wanted to pray in the mosque each day. He also liked to splash in water and on several occasions almost drown. In fact, the story went, he had "died" a second time, but when he returned to consciousness, was again alive, he was no longer crazy. His father, a *rue-safed* (white-haired man) had meanwhile been forced to go into the army after many years of deferring it. After the last accident, the boy had been locked in a room and with his father, his only family member, gone, he was simply forgotten and eventually died. The townspeople then sent for the father, but following Moslem law, which requires an individual to be buried within 24 hours of his death, they had gone ahead and buried the boy. His father's bus arrived an hour too late for the burial.

Other Volunteers speak of the student from Arizona, a Tashkurghanee, with a degree now in hydrology who came back to his family after five years at the University of Arizona. The college graduate grew sick, felt broken and lost in their primitiveness, dreaded being home, where he spent hours with his family being asked questions like: Is America under the earth and do they have sun and water there? It is the classic case of the man from a medieval society whose dream is fulfilled to learn about modernity, who adapts better, faster to that lifestyle, and then cannot return to his roots . . .

Surely there is a job for this educated man in the capital? How can he get to study abroad anyway, if he does not have connections and money? Or, is this belated punishment for a connection with the old king and his family, which had allowed him to leave and get the education, but which now blackballs him from professional work in this country?

Jan. 25, 1976

> *[Tom now has an office at PC set up. Meanwhile, Howard's son Troy is deathly ill with an infection. All staff resumes have been posted, and I keep looking at jobs on the UVA mailings. Or anywhere . . .] . . .*

I brave the clouds and rain-turning-to-snow to go by public bus to the University, to be a presence. Two students, one the top in my Freshmen class, the other his friend, come in to the ofice to ask me about studying and working in the States. I monitor their reality a moment, but have to send the friend away discouraged, telling him it is pretty impossible to get into an American school unless his command of English is superior. Another soon-to-be Freshman knocks and enters timidly, to ask me if he could be in the Saturday class, and an old student comes in to plead his brother's case, a student special from Badakshan: "Can't he just sit and listen to your teaching?" Again, they are wrangling to have admission to this special class to begin on Saturday. A Mr. Sarouish from Arts and Letters (formerly of Engineering) drops in to ask about the pre-engineering program and to explain that if he doesn't get confirmation soon that this job is definite, he'll have to find other employment for the interim. It is the same for all of us, but the Dean is in and out these days, or at special meetings, so I can't question him directly. Instead I write him an earnest note, and put it decorously on his desk.

Students continue to cluster in the halls of the Faculty. Is it just a warm, dry place for them to be, or do they have some work there? After the chill of the previous semester, I am surprised any part of the building seems warm. Likewise I see other teachers sitting in their office on alternate days and likely discussing problems peculiar to their courses. But who knows?

The trip back home on public bus though wet is neither too slow nor crowded at noon. Perhaps most daily travelers just stay in because of the bad weather. More likely now that Kabul schools are closed the normal brood of pushy, squirmy, undaunted school children is simply not there to ply their trade and take up the exuberant and not always polite space that children inevitably do.

We have a scare in the night as one bedroom reeks of burning straw or wood. Mirad and Tom check on the roof but find nothing except two pipes spouting smoke, (there should have been just one). There is nothing on the roof but mud, but we are left with a sense that something between the walls was on fire . . .

January 26, 1976

Feeling strangely mute in a world all white and cold as death, I set out to the university. I am the only women on the bus in the streets at 7:30 a.m., it seems, and have a seat alone directly behind the driver, a good place to watch the mist and sleet snow building up outside the windows. The day before too I had gone out in that snowy quietness, to be a foreign female, in the males' everyday morning: I didn't feel I was in Afghanistan, but rather in the midst of much more, the gathering in of universal separateness.

Then coming home on the same bus in the first seat again, I watch a well-known head come out of the cluttered reflections on the glass partition between the driver and the first seat. It is my old *modir* from Tashkurghan and suddenly, choked by that mad shyness I am forever struck with, I do not rise to greet him. In fact, I jump up and off the bus without ever acknowledging him.

All the way home, walking familiar blocks, I try to rationalize my inexcusable action, that it was a fulfillment of that state that Brenda and Chris Mahoney had described when everything is at its best, and how that is the time to just walk away, so that your memory, which always out lasts the reality, is at that golden time and not of something else. Is that a reason to not speak to a kind principal with whom I had worked for over a year? But it is not him, or anything really about him. It is me and my shyness and my sense that I did not do as well as I should have and that fills me with shame and a desire to turn my back on that assessment. In anything. It is that I walk away from . . . .

Yet so has it been with Tashkurghan and every one about it, and long before Tashkurghan with people, with moments I have loved. I idolize individuals from a far and then let them drop away—It's as if, mortals that we are, we are afraid of clutching things we love too much to us and so we let time and distance carry them away. At first I was always thinking of my students in Tashkurghan, and how I must send things and let them not forget me; but since our trip there over Eid, and its fractured, sad and full episodes, I feel that they have been removed from me once and for all, and that is as they should be, that they and I both must remember how it was for us those two years when we knew each other, saw each other almost daily, rather than to try now to create new memories. So, is that what we have done?

Mirad shares his theories as to why we have mold growing all over our walls. He thinks it is not just from the *oudon* or the *bookerie* always giving out moisture, an idea T. had suggested, but also from the pipes which lie along one side of the house and which also continuously pour out water and keep the interior exterior walls *"nam"* (damp). He spoke to a *gilcar* (mason) friend of his who says that when the spring comes and we open the windows and take out the *bookerie,* we can just whitewash the patches and the surfaces will all be clean again.

Mirad came back from his trip of secrets into the mountains; we never heard if the money was procured or not. Meanwhile he has news and greetings from his family. Poor Habibullah, it seems, has some kind of nodule, a tubular perhaps, God spare, in the back of his throat. And will it get no care?

I offer for his son to be brought to Kabul for an examination, and he thanks us and says he will see how that could be, but that for now the child must stay with his mother in Sare-pul.

Jan. 27, 1976

[I just finished The Passionate State of Mind, *by Eric Hoffer]*

. . . I do not go to the university this morning, and then had regrets for not going out there to meet with students and review possible new classes or materials. Tomorrow . . . .

Mirad's sister came this morning, perhaps just another relative. In any case, she sat in his warm, bright room until he returned from helping Qorbin cook for the new PCV cycle's party Thursday night.

Today is one of those bristly clear blue days when the mountains are elegant in their white mantles and the whole world seems wryly perfect in its balance of light and shadows, and yet the human folks, myself in particular, grow restless from it all—the calm, the repetition—and barely look on the grandeur

It is a cold, brisk night—

> *[Reading Apollinaire in French and English . . ."You are only masks upon masked faces." He dazzles with gorgeous imagery on love, and mortality, time, cities of France . . . .]*

January 28, 1976

At the *powantoon* (university) . . . today I obtain a room for the special, though still unofficial, class which is to begin on Saturday. Subsequently, there is the chance to finally start assessing and shaping the curriculum and sorting over the areas we will need to focus on in the class. Still, there's that element of uncertainty. Meanwhile, the students all morning long open the door to my office, stick their heads in, and say, "Cas-e n'as?" (No one's here?) To which I pipe up, "Bali, malim'aes." (Yes, the teacher is here.).

[We see Chris and Brenda, who are now talking of terminating early but admit they prefer to keep the free ticket home and avoid the shipping expenses. Are these dear folks serious? And what has made them so disillusioned so quickly?]

Mirad and Qorbin are supposed to make 250 *awshak* (Afghan dumplings full of meat and vegretables) for the party tomorrow. Mirad is also talking about what it is like living in Jema-minat, the waterless, steep hills in the middle of Kabul, and how everyone must pay to have their water brought there, and how a friend of his may give him a house to live there one day . . .

So will he be among the "ethnic minority," a target one day, too?

January 30, 1976

> *[I ventured forth and almost bought a rug through Arnie and Kayla's Turkomen bargainer, but it fell through. We*

> *attended the welcome party for the new cycle; and discuss with Yvonne Alpert and others about* Fear of Flying, *the title of which Jong stole from Germaine Greer's book. Yvonne's sense is that these points are those of one who has some growing to do, that sex is not just about aiming for spark and stars which never come, that if we have no initiation into that life, we make instead a cult of it, as we do of the young in general at the price of the old. For it is the sages whose examples and presence we exclude in modern life . . . . We touched on how our hired cooks and nanas become our surrogate families here, because they know us best and therefore feel free to teach us and interact . . . .*
>
> *I wandered home to don pajamas, only to find more visitors at the door . . . Sleeping that night I had a Freudian dream about ships and trains, lost purses and secret compartments . . . And dear Tom is still sick]*

We sleep then, backside to stomach, always something in this country, because there is such a process of settling into our cold bed, warming the blankets until we are comfortable, falling asleep. I wake up with a stomach ache and a full bladder at least once during the night, and trudge out to the cold toilet.

Snow has been falling softly all day long, each particle and flake too small and fine to last. There is a cold heaviness in the rest of the air. A glowing Afghan girl passes me on the sidewalk and, village-open, like a Tashkurghani, asks after my health.

"Khub aes'tan?" (you re well?) I perk up and ask her back. But she is already down the road.

February 1, 1976

. . . There is yet the indefinite pre-engineering syllabus, and the confusion as to whether to begin or not to begin. And in any case, I am greeted with the disturbing news that in the interim, for the next month or two, I will have no more than 10 hours assigned for teaching, with most of it—probably half of it—going to observing student teachers. As department chair this cycle, that should be fine, but I know I will be much happier if I am endlessly busy, not idle and made to feel unneeded and unused.

Today when I talk to Agha-gul he insists there will be other jobs I can do for two months, that summer leave and replacement would be discussed when there is a meeting, but that the Dean is not pleased with the last way "things" (alas, my dear but arrogant co-patriots, again) were resolved . . . So there is also the rather snooty attitude of Dean Sayed and Mr. Wali, based of their past and completely valid reasons for being peeved. But, some of us who have only wanted to work and tried to do so professionally and competently, now suffer from the bad reputation of our predecessors.

And the present class, of widely varying abilities, I've been teaching 2 ½ hours a morning . . . and tutoring and extending one-on-one help whenever they come in to seek it. I could expand the office hours to an informal tutoring session, if the Dean gives approval.

Yesterday a Mr. Hameed who has studied for years at Georgia Tech and knows the Volunteers, Bridget and Eli Masterson well, plops down gently in our office to chat with me, to inquire about my living arrangements, to gossip about past PCVs. Specifically, he explains about the legendary Thaddeus, who used to lecture in Persian to his thermodynamic classes here, using Omar Khayyam the mathematician-poet to explain the unity of all things, to demonstrate how the laws of thermodynamics describe life more than some dead theory, to dramatize how philosophy, and confirmations of life, are in everything, and how the best scientists discover the connections with the arts.

Bravo! That was a man and sentiment after my own heart.

Yet no one is free in this country, during this Daud-era when there is tight censorship of writing and imprisonment of poets, I am told by small voices behind thick doors among the most trusted company. To hide their anti-government sentiments, writers use a poetry of symbolism, the images of night which represent what is lost, of enclosed gardens for ideas and freedoms which no longer flourish, of stars which seem mute, like muffled or divested voices, all to oppose tyranny and social aggression.

Names float, silently, the old and the young, some published or recited abroad, others dead or soon to be, yet others still waiting to be born:

Ashqan(1894-1979), Huydar Wujad(1939-), Razeq Rawin (1946-), Shuja Khurasan (1963-), Layla Sarahar Roshan (1960-2005), Kazim Kasimi (1967-), Ghafur Liwal (1973-), Qahar As (1958-1994), Abdul Hadi Hadi (1969-), Abdul Samay Hamid (1969-), Partaw Nadir (1953-).

Another teacher from the vocational training program, just returned from Wisconsin last fall, greets me with the announcement that he is thoroughly shocked to hear that I have survived for two and a half years in his country, since "it is not a good place to be." He compares the States, his two years there, to being in paradise, and praises the angelic goodness of the Wisconsin people in Menomee, a few hours outside Milwaukee. He points out his mud house on the hill behind the bazaar, and asks me to contemplate the lives of the people who live on the hills, who walk up and down every day collecting water, whatever bare essentials they can afford or they need. He claims that he would also have liked the opportunity to have traveled and lived in another society like a Vista volunteer or a PCV, but that was never an option. A felt hunter's hat turned New York Jew's banker derby awry on his head, his first assignment from a class on "Curriculum Planning" in his brief case, he saunters off, cheerful.

There is something of the sense of passing days like Boll passes through his descriptions of the nuns, the priests, the recurring ladies and men in his novel *Group Portrait with Lady.*

Working in his office today, collecting pictures for a lending library of visual aids, Tom has to endure Agha-gul's advise on how to mount and write stories and pictures and how they must be carefully selected so as not to insult sensitivities—We both swallow: My goodness: we have been doing this for two plus years, and perhaps need rather to have that acknowledged than to be told as if we knew nothing, did nothing. I have a special frustration that the stories I'd done last summer, and which were to be disseminated to the schools, have literally disappeared . . . [I hope they have found good homes and are not just being used as trash.]

February 3, 1976

So life and work go on, in teaching the class each day, assimilating and stapling the Provincial Stories . . . for I have resurrected another batch, which is ready for a journey out.

We have other visitors. Today it is the Randalls, a couple from Kajikai, a bandit-infested dam site in the south where they teach the engineering crew for the electrification projects. Earnestly, they share their stories. To their chagrin, the other Americans there are afraid to eat anything from the bazaar, certain they will become ill. Nor do these other expatriates wish to appreciate or explore anything about Afghan-Pushtoon culture. They receive no orientation or guidance it appears, are just offered an exorbitant salary and transportation and housing and sent here. For example, a fellow recently landed in the middle of the night in Kandahar before a bandoleered soldier. He was four days out of his San Francisco law firm, where a fellow had walked in one day and said, "We need you in Afghanistan."

Granted, their site is a kind of wild west setting. At Kajikai there is a tiny bazaar, but all night long the trucks roll through it, smugglers from the borders, carrying opium from the Helmand fields (a small embarrassment to Uncle Sam that his irrigation project should go to bringing water to thriving opium fields). A Swiss doctor friend of theirs there went down to the south once. This is where a swampy excess of land separates Iran and Afghanistan, and where the smugglers cross by pushing rafts across the marshy land, to transport opium to the west. They turn around and come back with goods (so that goods from Iran, materials, pots, etc. are cheaper on their tiny bazaar than in Kabul). This doctor had simply planned to do some duck hunting. But, at dawn he saw a large form, the loaded raft with a man pushing it, coming toward him, and he fired and then disappeared in terror as it occurred to him what must have happened. He was seconds from being abducted, murdered or just "disappeared," miles from anything and in the company—the no man's land—of any international smuggling ring. He fled in his NGO van.

The main entertainment in the villages around the dam is a round of rock throwing. Once Bill Randall and an American "bigwig" were in the middle of a crowd and decided to leave—But before they could get out, some kids threw rocks at the Americans, which promptly hit the nearest kid in the head. As the shopkeepers who know the PCV couple well saw what was happening, they summoned the police, who in turn terrorized the kids. News spread and soon everyone knew of the incident, and the locals were apologetic for weeks afterwards. The Randalls describe how they also have jackals in the area, thin creatures who come down from the mountains and sit in their yard, pinging on their garbage lids. Further, their amicable gardener, and scavenger neighbors, clean out that same garbage pail free of inquiry, as well as helping themselves to non-thrown away things (mops, brooms), if left out.

Bill apparently works the electric plant along with his students on days when they're working and he can't teach them. The couple have also taught elementary school to some American kids, and cooked up a storm—to pass the days—for recreation down there.

They speak specifically of the wild individualism of the area. There was one attempt by the Afghan government to make the people pay taxes. To make their point, the government had soldiers brought in and then lined up unresponsive locals, in front of cannons, and shot them, but the people didn't budge. Another time the mullahs told the people they could float on their scarfs in the water. So a lot of protesters just jumped into the water and the soldiers were ordered to shoot them. Another time the original village was totally destroyed in a battle between government officials and townsmen. Unbending, the townsmen simply moved further up the river and made a new town.

The story of Lashkagar and the Helmand River Valley, of the Kajikai Dam and the Helmand Dam, was already a common source of gossip and disenchantment among most Volunteers by the time our cycle had arrived in Kabul in 1973, especially so as an example of the kind of culturally-insensitive, expensive, US-based labor, and equipment "development work" we were led to believe our own efforts would be a vast contrast from, and improvement on. In our minds, USAID, which had taken over the project in 1961 after the incomplete (but, for them, highly lucrative) efforts of the mega Morris-Knudsen engineering firm (builders of the Hoover Dam and the San Francisco Bay Bridge), and the discarded plans of the U.S. Bureau of Land Reclamation, was tantamount to the worst in imperialistic venturers. In fact, we sometimes undeservedly sanctimonious PCVs equate that boondoggle with the ongoing and impervious UN "Experts" who float through the country on well-gilded magic carpets, drinking fine whiskeys and living like the Raj. None of the models put forward by any development group, or bank, we have long since surmised, has either the ambition nor the means to really touch the people, to really help Afghans themselves find ways to move their lives out of the 13th century and establish a better and more just quality of life, respectful of their traditions, but not swallowed by them.

We had heard of the flourishing opium crops springing up everywhere in the successfully irrigated fields fed by the Helmand dams, and the thriving business in illegal drug trading through Iran and up to Europe and beyond; of the "Little America" of Lashkagar where American engineers prospering from their hardship pay in this alien country still barely held on to the remnants of the model city once planned for the region. These included a never completed full network of irrigation ditches to allow the production of food crops; a skirted 1951 plan to build four villages with 120 single-story multi-family dwellings in long rows with one apartment per newly resettled Afghan family and a half-acre garden, and access to another 10 acres outside each village; and a 2,000-acre experimental farm which never got seeded, Specifically, there has been decades of exhausting funds, first the 100 million from foreign exchange and gold accrued by the royal family from the sale of karakul during WWII, then the loans from the U.S to the tune of $55,000 "to finish the project," as well as a cycle of paperwork and endless expanding of the plan and then the shrinking of it. We knew how the U.S. had earmarked 75 per cent of its aid to Afghanistan to the Helmand project between 1960 and 1970, yet by the time we arrived in country in June 1973, and officially in 1974, the project had stopped cold.

February 7, 1976

In a downtown carpet shop, hosted by a Turkoman merchant, we pass a lovely afternoon discussing carpets, weighing the virtues of native versus the German dyes, all in a kind of conspiratorial whisper, while the man's youngest daughter, eight or nine and all dressed up in a brocaded long dress and Turkomen's women's cap, sits catching my eyes and smiling.

[Days race, a jumble. Inner and outer charades, and colleague talks. Tom's medical diagnosis remains incomplete, although he is told he has some kind of "flexamania" strain. We inhale, seek out, expire other volunteers and their tales. I complete the next round of the reading stories for the provinces and Tom is ready to go south for his first trip, once he secures some help from Asia Foundation and other pending resources.]

Restless, my desire resists, wants to be done with "this" and get on with my life. I do not like so much leisure, nor so much isolation for the writing . . . I pass hours on a good day contemplating how Tom as a lawyer will right the wrongs, environmentally, socially. In come letters from friends and the wordly Californian, Ruth March, and U.S. and world news that rankles: the decision of an unelected appointee of an unelected President, the Secretary of Transportation, to allow the Concorde to land in Dulles and its certain environmental impact; the obscene antics of the South Boston residents against the Blacks in the busing battle forcing the whole school district to be put under Federal control. Racism? Poverty? When will either cease?

A bleak as dry leaves day: rain, then snow, fall awhile, but there is nothing strong enough to make the ground lay still, nothing to mute the harshness.

Feb. 11, 1976

Tom left Sunday morning, the simplified English stories in hand, a heavy snow falling on the streets, undauntedly, as he set off with the truck full of volunteers' support resources . . . Mirad has been serving incredible vegetarian meals for our guests, the Bamiyan Mareks, who are back in Kabul, ill again. Benson, weak with a staph infected leg, along with an amoebic dysenteric Susan, are staying with me] . . .

[I continue looking for jobs in the States for next Fall, determining how to quickly get state teaching certification, once Tom's law applications are completed.

There was an earthquake in Guatemala, 5,000 dead;

The Mareks describe their time in Ceylon and Dharamsala, of seeing Tibetans with faces like maps of their journeys, like Curtis' portraits of American Indians, with the hollow deep-lined faces of great chiefs, and the tranquil eyes.

Soon it is evening. The decision is final: The Mareks will have to terminate early and return to the States, because of their bad health in poor Bamiyan, because of a year of almost unmitigated bad health.

Tonight a rain falls on Kabul, that ageless placeless sound, then the mildest protestation of sky against earth.

On route to the university I watch a young boy pulling a cow away from a pile of thrown-out cauliflower stalks, and beside me on the public bus going the other way stares out a blue-eyed Afghan matron. At one stop an impish Yankee entrepreneur boy tries to sell plastic ducks and a snake to the women's compartment. This morning, after a meeting with Agha-gul, to organize the new trainees at the Faculty of Engineering, I wander with Susan through both used clothes bazaars with no luck; we carry away only mud and confusion, and find nothing we want. Meanwhile Benson is having blood taken, chest x-rays examined, eye examination completed, and a gold crown fitted. Later, his infection dressed, I hear his lunchless tummy growling.

Mirad has been in several nights now, perhaps because of the weather, perhaps for another reason. How he must miss his family, so far away, yet he works without complaining, is there when we need him, takes our praise gratefully, quietly. Yet the city life makes him different, too.

February 16, 1976

It is the eve of another departure. Tom will leave tomorrow for the North and not get back for five days. He returned Thursday night, reported . . . a good reception from Volunteers and Afghan teachers.

He describes one adventure in Kandahar when he went by motor rickshaw to the staff house for dinner and was stopped by army barricades at 10:00 while he was going back to town. He just missed having to go to the city police with the driver and a soldier, because foreigners and drivers are both forbidden to be outside the city after 8:00 p.m. As they neared the city, a second soldier stopped them and looked for the license on the vehicle, was told to go look in the back, and when he did the driver simply stormed away. A few kilometers further on, the little overworked scooter broke down so Tom and companions ended up walking into the city, apparently without further incident.

He is entering a whole new realm of employment, staff meeting and secrets and juggling of administrative news and details, writing letters and reading memos. So he's always between talks and a typewriter, animated and furiously engaged, late for dinner and suited all day long . . . [Several pending volunteers have been asked to leave for insulting and irresponsible behaviors. T. is also balancing his time and duties with those of Rahim, so as not to usurp his job. It is a delicate business.]

The Pre-Engineering program is struggling to begin. Finally, we gave placement tests yesterday and Paul and I struggled all day to get the exam graded.

Today we begin making up the selections and I meet with the six who are to teach in the program (new PCVs). Having looked at their portfolios earlier, Tom emphasizes that they each have decent educational backgrounds. They all seem serious enough . . . Tomorrow then, we'll complete the positioning of sections, and match teachers with class sizes and numbers, post everything and hopefully begin first lessons.

> *[There are always complaints from serious volunteers about non-serious ones . . . Someone's visit to and praise of beautiful Tashkurghan makes its way back to us. T's last application, this to Antioch in D.C., was sent out.]*

Meanwhile a beautiful white snow falls, the second time this week, and the world turns mellow and pure. But already, on the university bus, Ms Gholami laments how ugly the snow will look this noon as compared to yesterday morning when it lay fresh and clean in great boughs and clusters.

"It reminds me of how everything man touches get dirtied," she says shyly, uncharacteristically sad.

> *[In Lessing's* The Golden Notebook, *I am bothered by the obsession with women who only feel complete when in bed with men, etc., It seems dated, a neon banner for the new sexual liberation . . .]*

Quote for the day: "Only the stupid and children seek cause and effect in the same story."

Feb. 17, 1976

A bright day, the mountains majestic, Tom is off at 8 with all his gear in tow.

I go all day, first the class and discussion with the new teachers, then lunch and a trip to pick up photographs, then the abominably long wait on stencils. Dinner seems only an hour after breakfast, and after the slightest break to read [etc.], I race out to make more stencils and then frantically run them off at the PC office. Back to a chilly house, every bone tired with a sense of aloneness, I nod contentedly, pleased that the day has been so full.

How stark and beautiful is this world, as we stand outside the Faculty building waiting for our bus, our secular discussion raging small against the background of sheet, snow-covered mountains and a procession of men carrying a dead man on an old bamboo bed, who pass solemnly by. This image makes a part of every day, and some marvel and stare. I feel the small majesty of human life and death within the drama of the mountains and sky. The cycles move simply—snow and thawing—beside human life, poignant and amazing.

We bring home the rug we looked at before, a Mauri Sarwah, well made but expensive. Tomorrow I shall march down to the man and buy it, after picking up a bit more cash at the bank. We'll then have a $400 art piece on our floor, although—not knowing the future—we may not always have walls and a roof.

With 35 strong in the classroom, with a blackboard that likes to totter over, I set a pace today I can barely keep up with, and keep having to check my own "cue cards." The new teachers talk intensely of all the newest techniques in TEFL-ing, using rods and charts and golden rulers, spouting bibliographies of source materials, and voicing an uncompromising commitment to things like "silent way," etc. I know these educational terms but find most of what they purport to do intuitive to me now. Still, by their standards, my techniques may appear archaic already. I, too, can learn . . . . I am thrilled to have serious new teachers in the Faculty now.

A cat crawls into the *bookerie* outlet in the wall at the PC and meows quite loudly until she is rescued and driven outdoors, where she sets up a new howl. Howard, on his way home, stops back in the library to tell me they have saved me from the lion . . . .

Feb. 19, 1976

Yesterday, the latest cold spell (snow every other day, a howling wind) set my hands to freezing. I start the day by meeting a new volunteer and going by cab (the trees like car paws on the soft snowy streets) with her to the university. After explaining all the basics, I dash off to my class, where my teaching is observed mildly by the three new comers (now we have nine teaches besides Paul, Mr. Shukor and me). Then, back in our cavernous office, I tutor an over-achieving fellow from my section who generously asks me to help him translate the introduction in his math book. Meanwhile, the office resounds with one duet of teachers-to-be, analyzing the situation.

[Off to the bank, lunch, then off to buy "the" rug. I confront some initial resistance at the bank, because the book is not signed by both Tom and me, but the clerk disperses the money in the end.]

Then, in an act of daring, I take a cab to the *chaman* with my 22,000 afs in an envelop and other (500 and 250) in a packet under my bundled coat. I march in and introduce myself, and the *dukhandar* shows me the receipt in his book, which Tom had earlier written up and signed. Then I hardily present my opinion on how much my husband and I have decided to pay.

Just as nimbly, he emphatically claims that the amount agreed on by Tom and him had been 22,500, and that this already represents a deduction of 500 from 23,000 afs.

Within seconds it becomes clear that he has simply made up his mind and that nothing I might say will change it. So he drinks tea, gives me some, and we sit, neither moving.

Never good at bargaining, or hiding my feelings (and he has figured me out well ahead of this), I grow visibly quite nervous. I try a script: "But sir, I only came to do what my husband told me. I have only brought 22,000 and just came from the bank. This is all I have on me." Eyes down, I go through the elaborate process of counting the money a few times. Then, sighing, I plead the case of justice and how he had told our friend another, lower price. "So, why do you tell us more?"

Finally, almost in tears . . . I offer a time to bring the rug back since we absolutely can not pay more than 22,000, and he just says, *"par wanez,"* (it doesn't matter). So the farce has to come to an end. I empty out my pockets (save one), and show him 300 more *afs*. He gives me back 50, and we shake.

It stands, a golden compromise, honor on both sides preserved. I sign the receipt saying the transaction was done, and then leave, energized to walk all the way back home, to build a fire, to correct papers, and to read *War and Peace* as I gaze at the beautifully wrought patterns of this new rug . . . .

I fall asleep, realizing my discontent of the moment stems from simple boredom with teaching English grammar . . . mixed with the reality that I do not share the others' interest in techniques . . .

Outside, Kabul glows with the snowy beauty. Today is the first of Hoot, tomorrow my 27th birthday . . . Tom should be spending the day in either Sheberghan or Mazar, a lucky, esteemed traveler . . .

Feb. 22, 1976

So a celebration of my birthday passes, a day joyous in its air, the city its most beautiful, the mountains resplendent with the light. In the morning the day's name is given, as I discover new PCV Alsie also has a birthday; so we gossip about the coincidence, pleased with our respective twin, and then I set off to class to the coldest lecture hall in the building and address myself energetically to the students, who watch my animated pacing with envy as they sit freezing in their seats, clutching pen and pencil with red fingers. Then class finishes, several points of grammar put to rest, I go back to the office. Empowered after an interview with Dean Sayed, who is as always smiling and a tad indefinite, Paul and I are sent over to the Economics department. After a respectful pause, a young man leads us and a line of *babas* to pick out four excellent classrooms. It all takes less than 30 minutes.

Back in time to catch the bus, we ponder the reasons this class assigning had taken so long, then melt into the sense of physical graciousness surrounding us, the figures of the mountains in their pure white outlines, standing out like dream images, against the valleys of

Kabul. On the bus I talk to Hooshie who, after three yeas in India, is rather bored with the" things" of Kabul, and its lack thereof . . .

. . . We see a telegram from Benson's doctor parents, who seek confirmation that he is able to travel . . . Pleased to help as much as possible, we also hosted Shafiq, the Marek's Bamiyan landlord, who has braved the cold blizzard of the Shibar Pass to come down and tell dear Benson and Susan good-bye. (He went to the dentist, lunch, the bazaar, a quiet and saintly and unpretentious small Bamiyanite.) Then the Mareks and I troop over to the Howards, where I am gifted with chocolate cake, cards, and a tin of cocoa. It is both my lovely birthday and their poignant farewell, a time for taking leave from two fine Volunteers and good people.

As we sit eating carrots with our dinner, Howard recalls well a story from Susan Marek about how the children in Bamiyan can't see, suffer from vitamin A deficiencies, among others, because they never get any vegetables. The story is validated by Shafiq's acknowledgement that there are only potatoes up there now.

Back home, I humbly receive a little silver-coated pewter vase from Mirad.

February 23, 1976

Tom arrives . . . with the news that 18 boys and four girls, my former students at Lycee Mahasty—Zahra, Kamila, Homira, and another—have been accepted to the university.

> *[Today we are off to the airport to see off Benson and Susan Marek.]*

. . . How mystical and sad I feel, exuberant and tearful, standing on the Kabul airport observation deck, chilled and anticipatory, while that great lumbering gray bird performs its slow ablutions and then is suddenly speeding, rising, soaring up toward the dozing snowy mountains, the clouds and sky, soaring into another realm, graceful as birds in formation.

How strangely short a life is, to find friends, touch and be touched in a foreign land, and then how quickly again they move out of our lives.

Tonight they'll be in Tehran, tomorrow Zurich, that same evening or the next day in Davos, *Magic Mountain* in hand. Their lives forever resonate now with memories of other magic mountains.

A change in pace and sentiment, off to the university to untangle some confusion over rooms, and then again to teach. I deliver slowly, they pick up and act bored . . . then after racing home, I type stencils and run them off on contraband paper.

At sunset on the hill where the fort stands behind our house, someone plays a lonely flute.

. . . Tom returns with stories of his adventures, the blizzard in the Salang, the rigid change to blue blinding skies, his exit from a sure-to-be endless formal meeting in Tashkurghan by pulling up his collar and pulling down his cap and slipping through the receiving line with "salaams," as he moved rapidly out; of meals and the threadbare carpets in the Mazar Hotel, of the cement bazaar in Sheberghan, of the eerie sight of the snow piled around the blossoming almond trees everywhere, this year's crop killed by the uneven cold.

February 29, 1976

Days go.

> *[Return of various PCVs, a trip to Jalalabad for Tom and Howard, a performance by the Tokyo String Quartet and by the Charlie Byrd Trio; conversations on literature and contemporary society; 860 American dead in a week of influenza in the Atlantic and Middle and New England areas*
>
> *Work and teaching and enjoying a bit the solitude, but finding the teaching boring with the required grammar drills . . . reading Mark Twain's biography, putting down my lack of uniqueness and laziness . . .]*

March 5, 1976

> *[Guests, frustration with Tom's job and his helping with decisions on volunteer placement, and arguing for more money*

for provincial school with USAID folk and others, and both of us tired of scaling endless mountains of the impossible]

A volunteer's sister was raped in Morocco; Nixon was invited to Iran after his China trip.

March 10, 1976

[A mimest, Darium Adam, performed . . . I learned how to run the movie projector and showed films to the classes at the Faculty I am getting to know Troy O'Dell and other new volunteers, as Tom is off to the south. I have dinner in Amanullah's old palace, plush and delicately built, a well-preserved and larger version of the one in Tashkurghan. There is dancing, flirting, and an Afghan coordinator of the English program at Agriculture and his shy wife, who tells me at the end that she likes me. Then, more news: the Howards announce they are leaving in a month to go back to Washington, D.C., where he will take a job in the national offices.]

March 17, 1976

Tom is off to Jalalabad for a conference . . . and I am babysitting for the Howards . . . The classes are finished, although briefly a few were left uncovered, as the new volunteers were pulled out of Engineering to begin their house search, and their replacements remained a little shaky in their boots. I meet with the coordinator of Academics, Mr. Wali, who concludes that more teachers are needed. At the same time, he dispatches a memo to PC staff about the time being right to encourage the bringing in of Afghan teachers to be trained to run the department alone.

I agree wholeheartedly and tell him so.

This, again, should be our goal: to be entirely replaced by Afghan professors. Yet, I suspect there is something political behind this sudden sense of using host country professionals instead of Americans. Will there in fact be Russian staff? Might we soon hear of all the American-trained Afghan faculty being booted and the entire school realigned with a pro-Soviet sentiment?

Friday a wet, rainy day and I stay at the PC office to type and cut out visual aids . . . From my perch inside, watching and unseen myself, through the round windowed office, I view the passing world. Mirad, earlier off to the mosque this Joma, (Friday) hears the words read about the Prophet's birth and death day. He tells me that the Prophet, like Essa, (Jesus) also rose into Heaven

> *[The evening rebounds as I join other volunteers, in talk, and games of Scrabble, until it is lentil dusk, and Alsie and I head off to a restaurant to sup on Quik Snack portions, at a table of awkward silence . . .*

The next day I give a test to my students . . . and feel blue.

Mirad tells me about the carnival grounds up in Jema-minat, with the wooden horses and a carousel, and many shopkeepers with special holiday sweets and fried foods. He offers to take me to see it all if I want. At school Mr. Shukor mentions how he took his sons there, but how he didn't know whether to take them on to a parade showing the agricultural program display planned for NaRoz, all part of a elaborate political propaganda ploy.

> *[I listen, smarting slightly, pulled into a long and delving talk with this Alsie, a fellow Pisces, who "is not always wise in her choice of lovers but never long without one . . ." Others in the PC office begin teasing all the bachelors, visualizing their predictably wild lives . . . We take in a movie with Chaplin from USIS, then Bruce Letts and Troy O'Dell bunk down for the night at our house because their own is leaking. Staff and volunteers share NaRoz gifts, as we pass more time at the Howards . . . take in more long talks and biographies.]*

We talk a little about girls (Afghans) and women going crazy from being cooped up in compounds or forced into repressive marriages, and in the midst of our American chatter, we stop to ask Haleem's opinion occasionally. We pose the whole philosophical question: whether or not we (the west) do well to introduce so many options to these people, that although their right to food and health, and to living children, seems undeniable, do we not upset some more subtle balance, their natural kindness, whatever, their closeness to the cycles? Who can know?

> *[And the Volunteers who have come to know and admire her intelligence and modesty, comment on Rashidi, educated in all the arts and philosophies of a French minister of culture, and protected, a niece of the royal family . . .]*

March 21, 1976

NaRoz day, the new year wakes us about 8:00. Our Country Director, Dick Howard, stands gaunt at the door, his face pale, his eyes tense and expectant. Inside, he quickly shares his news: there has been an earthquake in Tashkurghan. There is no reliable source of news, but Afghans have heard the report on the radio. The first tremors struck at 4:00 a.m. Friday. Allegedly 500 houses have been destroyed, snd hundreds of people killed and injured. Officials, Red Crescent Society staff, along with soldiers from Balkh, Mazar and Samangan, have all been dispatched there to help the homeless and injured.

We taxi over to the Saroy-Shamulli where some taxis and Toyota drivers claim that there had been an avalanche (*coorse aftidan*) the day before at 1:00 p.m., but that all the Toyotas had gotten through and the road was open again although Tangi-Tashkurghan had been closed for a while after the mountain fell down. From there we gather at the Howards for breakfast and a morning of debating how best to get someone up to the village to check things out. After calling the Embassy and various Americans on duty, Howard discovers that these groups refuse to participate at all, feel nothing could be too serious, are apparently happy to go off to their shiny and less testing engagements after calling a few Afghan officials at offices where no one answers. Further, the Ambassador's plane is grounded with one engine gone, so the possibility of flying up is ruled out.

Then begins a search for the PC drivers, along with Agha-gul or some other Afghan PC staff official; it is decided that Tom and the Doctor and a PCV driver should go on ahead to appraise the situation and call as soon as they have any information. Perhaps by then Agha-gul and another driver could be found and sent off.

We gathered blankets, food and water and at about 11:30 Tom and the Doctor and a driver set off. The rest of us stay on at the Howards for lunch . . .

When I return home, the doctor's wife comes over to commiserate, visibly upset that her husband has been involved in this. Her concern matches my own worries for the injustice of the damage done to the village and its people, my fears for Tom's safety, and my worry about Chris and Brenda, who are stuck in the middle of this all. Off flies, like a self-driven motor, the usual PC events—meals, talk, news of a theft at one house. The day before we had heard that Tom was accepted to NYU and U.Penn law schools.

School is to begin again tomorrow.

March 26, 1976.

> *[This batch of letters confirms: My brother John is back in the mental institute; Kathy is gone.*
>
> *There are acceptance letters for Tom also to Notre Dame, Boston College, and George Washington. This round, with all materials apparently secured, he has been admitted to every school to which he applied.]*

Tom calls on Monday to say they would be home the next day, and that the Mahoneys are all right.

So, the next day he arrives full of news as the staff party for Dr. Saher is taking place. Road weary, he has to tell the story a hundred time:

He establishes that the entire town was not destroyed but that 100 people or so had died, crushed under houses and walls, and that over all damage was extensive. The Tangi Tashkurghan, the gorge, collapsed, as did the Jahan Bagh Palace, the Government Hotel, and the White Mosque. The Teem, and other parts of the ancient covered bazaar, stand severely damaged, if not completely flattened. The Mahoneys were anxious and hesitant to stay on, but they did not want to just leave. Yet. Many of Tom's old students had been sent to work and watch in the Tangi, where the fallen rock had already destroyed most of the road and was continuing to destroy more. Traffic was backed up, with 50 buses from Mazar stuck. Meanwhile, there were rising vapors, dust, and smoke, the air fetid. The wall around our old house had tumbled down.

One image stands out for him as he recalls details: that of two old men buying a cow to sacrifice with prayers at the mouth of the Tangi, seeking justice from Allah. Their entreaty was answered the next day when worse debris came amid after-shocks—volcano-like shuttering and more cracks and shattered roofs and walls.

Just then, Chris Mahoney found a communication station somewhere, and called down to ask if someone couldn't evacuate them, or at least keep an ear set for news of more problems in Tashkurghan . . .

Thursday passes as our faculty staff waits for schedules . . . I remember the conversation with the student Kaum today who wants me to help him go to the U.S. and find work who will come and talk to me again about it. Sadly, I can give him no promises or even any leads.

Standing a few minutes on the roof, looking out to the mountains, and the mud houses of Kale-Pushte and Kale-Fatkhan on the edges of Share-Nau, I watch the figures moving along roads, the motion, the stooped forms suggesting time captured in spaces between distances and night, seasons and a pause . . .

On Sunday Tom is supposed to leave again for Kunduz and the north with his teaching aids and supplies; Wednesday we will see the Howards off, their tenure here complete, with a party . . .

And it is still winter at night, although in the sun the days are warm.

March 27, 1976

[I waver, swerve, feel confused in mind and intention . . .]

I go out early to school, intending to get schedules all in order and act officially in getting a class in order as well. A discovery comes: There is a faculty Dept. of English mailbox full of our schedules! Hastily the staff rushes out to meet their students and I successfully collect and teach one of my current two classes.

I leave at noon to have lunch with my colleague in the department, Troy O'Dell, via the Hazara neighborhood at the foot of the university. At a small kebab shop he discovers a Kamard hat, and so we enter the *dhukan*, where the workers there cluster around him gleefully, all recognizing him as "the teacher from Kamard."

At the stubby table in the back of the shop, with the Afghan clientèle in the front ignoring us, the oily *chashbbish kebabs* and bread and tea before us, calendar tops of a fake blond women staring down from the walls, he tells me about the Tibetan Mahayana Buddhist monks' meditation. It is directed toward assimilating all of the body rhythms, the positive and creative forces, toward controlling and totally understanding the moment of death, so that in the next reincarnation they will have good karma behind them, and move out of the cycles of human suffering entirely. He had spent one month in a Tibetan monastery outside of Kathmandu, getting taught and disciplined by a lama Tbuten Twarpat, a monk and teacher, who spoke on meditation.

Troy's eyes widen, he smiles quietly, as he shares how Tbuten Twarpat led the students himself, and how, as a living saint in such harmony with all the emotions and rhythms of the world, he and the other monks could actually read minds.

The mediation instruction demanded a hard, rigorous exercising of the mind—and for Troy, it was like being reborn.

Continuing, he speaks of basic doctrines, how the Buddhists believe in the high dignity of human beings, how for a being to be born as a human being, in a perfect human form, is as rare as for a sea turtle swimming the wide ocean to come up above the surface once in a hundred years in the exact same spot where a round marker might be floating at the moment he raises his head. And he goes on further, describing the eight meditations, what people should spend time doing each day—meditations on the perfect human birth, on ways to assume all other people's burdens and sorrows, and so on. His first time at the monastery, he took a vow, to never hurt any living thing. Then, going back a second time, last winter, despite a lot of temptations to keep him from going there, how he had had to fight with himself to again acquire acquiescence, and how he made a vow with the monk this time to keep the pure principal of sorts—no intoxicants or bad sex or lying or stealing or excess of things. So he brought out how the meditation he does is really a kind of ethical code for living, how Mahayana divided from Hinayana in its service code, its egalitarian spirit and its sharing, and its belief that all people can create their own Nirvanas . . .

We take a taxi to Share-nau to hear Arthur Alpert's lecture on Development . . . and later in the day, with Mirad's hospitality in hand, at our house I entertain other visitors, among them two of Tom's students from Tashkurghan. They had come in the rain to see us yesterday, but found no one home. They stare out of sad faces, unpeeling like desperate fruit, tales of how they had come down last Friday only to hear of the earthquake, and how now they were worrying about their families. At the same time, since school was not officially open, despite their having been told otherwise, they had had to spend a week (until this Thursday) alternating between a cold, foodless hotel and the small house of a distant relative of one of the boys. They feel mistreated, but have now settled in at the Polytechnic dormitories, an hour's walk from the campus. As it is wont to do, conversation than turns to the bad events in other parts of the country. They share news of floods all over the south of Afghanistan, and detail a strange case of four men in a car who had been swept into the river.

"And they sat inside, up to their heads in water, until someone pulled them out . . ."

There is a strange problem with the Mahoneys, who will be on their way here tomorrow from Tashkurghan. In a grand miscommunication, they had thought to be evacuated, and are furious that they were not. And yet, that's exactly what Tom and the doctor had gone up to do, we all thought . . . Perhaps they had just wanted to give it another day, had wanted Tom and the driver and doctor to wait there until they decided and then help them leave. Let's hope this can be resolved and that they can return to their work in the village schools.

What of the great burdens of work to be done in Engineering this term . . . ?

Oddly I am seeking a teacher, clearly out of recognition of the need in myself to strengthen something there before it all breaks, to avoid (my family's) hysteria, perpetual fear, and a barb of intimidating self-consciousness. Perhaps I have always thought for Tom to give me that extra strength, but he seemingly can not, doesn't have enough of it himself most times. My own emotions remain too close to the surface, can turn to anger and then to tears. So I look elsewhere . . .

And for reconciling Catholic guilts: "Catholicism is really an insult to the intellect, the way its presented." Teilard de Chardin.

April 1, 1976

Tom has been gone since last Sunday . . . my emotions remain flighty. There had been the incredible load of work at Engineering and the realization that the Howards really and truly are leaving, and then my confused little girl crush on this new found colleague and wannabe intellectual and mystic, could draw me further away from Tom . . .

I indulged again in talking at the PC office about grad programs (Would I study Chinese, comparative lit?), and then drift off with some volunteers to have dinner with another pair in Cote-Parwin. We chatter, share stories of our families, but I mostly focus my listening on Troy, then we all walk together down the hill to go back to my part of town.

Monday is a full day of work. Chris and Brenda Mahoney are at the house, recuperating and thinking of their future. I attend an excellent lecture by Bruce Letts, share dinner once more with a horde of PCVs, and later follow them to the sweet shop, where I confide in Brenda about the mounting missteps with my dear Tom . . .

Wednesday, I work in the office after my class, leave around noon, then later go out to the University again in the afternoon to see Mahadi and her roommates and Malekah. They are wearily returned, had come down with Mahadi's father from Tashkurghan, sit red-eyed and weary after the quake-induced sleepless nights. They describe a destroyed estate, and the particular damage to Zahra and Homira and Zahra's father. In from a class of English, they tell us their schedules, assess their work. Mostly I listen as each person tells his/her version of the earthquake, and of the fate of different relations and relationships. The recounting surrounds us until about 5:30, at which point we leave them and walk down to the main road . . .

It is the hour to go out to the farewell party at the Intercontinental for the Howards, an event for the "whole community." We travel with "Johnny the Doorman, "in a taxi driven by a student at Arts and Letters who reads his secreted book (*Tales of Wisdom and Folly*) at each stop. Halfway there, his license plate clanks off onto the pavement, and he halts the car, jumps out, and attaches it again . . .

Then it is Thursday, and Troy announces before class that thieves had come to his house the night before while he was at dinner and Bruce Letts was at the Intercontinental, and had taken his tape player and tapes and cut open Bruce's suitcase. Even as he came into the house, he had known the thieves were still there. After class, as we board the university bus, he elaborates, sharing the details of how he'd come into the house, thought the thief was in the bathroom, and waited, rigid, listening. Finally, he opened the door and went outside, where he found the doors to the compound and the woodshed wide open. Only then did he realize that the culprit had only just fled . . . It is frightening.

We chat about seeing my students from Tashkurghan, about the huge difference between village and Kabul girls, about how resilient the fathers had been in their old turbans and *p and t*, baggy jackets, bags over shoulder, telling their stories and still concluding that "*Xoda Mehrabahm aes*" (God is kind) . . .

[There is time for a nap back at my house, and then to dress up for another reception for the Howards. This latter takes place a few houses over from our own, a large walled area rented by some British diplomats. I wear my long Scottish sweater, greet the Howards and others formally, then return home, where my doppelganger Brenda and I chat about the madness of sudden emotions . . . .]

Kabul, Afghanistan
December 2002-July 2007

Has anyone ever produced a mirror out of mud and straw?
Yet clean away the mud and straw,
And a mirror might be revealed.
—Rumi," Love is a Stranger"

"A liar has no memory."

—Dari proverb

In Samuel Becket's play, *Waiting for Godot*, two closely intertwined friends chat back and forth about their incessant wait for the arrival of "Godot," their conversation an elegantly stark repertoire of clichés and repeated phrases. Each night as they move languidly to sleep, they observe that they will try again the next day. Early in the play, the line comes, "We are at the wrong place."

The boom or bust mentality of re-development in Kabul by 2007 seemed to be flourishing as the city buzzed with the pounding and hammering of new construction cranes and machinery.

The nascent buildings rose above clouds of dust, as traffic gnarled with Humvees, SUVs, 4-wheel drive vehicles, and Mercedes shared newly paved and often rutted ancient camel trails with public busses, pick-up trucks, man-pulled wooden carts, diesel-sputtering convoy trucks, bicycles, livestock, and pedestrians.

The native and refugee population of over two million, and the staffs and directors of some 1000 international NGOs, contractors, UN experts and NATO's multinational International Security Assistance Forces (ISAF) rushed to make a living, make a meeting, make a sale, and perhaps make life stable.

Guns and *burqas,* ubiquitous beggars and smoky *kebab* stands, a hundred thousand miniature whirling generators, and steel shipping containers functioning as bullet-proof shelters, offices, and rooms appeared everywhere among the traditional open air shops, rug sellers and colorful produce stands.

Children—often the sole bread winners for their families—hawked post cards, phone cards, cigarettes, shopping bags or washed cars along the sidewalks and in the streets; and craftsmen bargained to perform every job from shoe repair to barbering to bicycle re-tiring.

Meanwhile, the accouterments of a ravished infrastructure—wells, clean water and sanitation, garbage disposal, steady electricity, and telephones lines—remained spotty or nonexistent.

Mistakes happen, and big mistakes happen largely.

The blush of alleged initial success in Afghanistan turned suddenly dark and constricted. To be facile, one can talk of the lost energy that went into hunting down bin Laden in the first stage of the U.S. occupation in 2001-2002. Or, fault the resources poured into invading and then trying to secure Iraq, and the subsequent failure to sent sufficient troops to secure Afghanistan. But there are many stories here.

The manner in which "development" had proceeded in the past reflects three huge problems—poor planning and coordination by those who have made Afghanistan their arena, a lack of real expertise, and a resulting failure to employ or engage Afghans in this work. Fist and glove with this fundamental formula for failure has been the corrupt government itself.

The excess of disconnected and overpaid "experts," expatriates and Afghans has compromised Afghanistan's future. Millions has been invested, thousands have been employed to make changes, but these expenditures have disproportionately boosted the donors and investors. less significantly the Afghan people and their needs.

Kabul, the once mandatory stopover for WT's of the 60's and 70's, ("world travelers", a name given to young international backpackers living on pennies a day in their worldly journeys in more innocent times), had changed beyond recognition by late 2007. Once Chicken Street was synonymous with cheap hashish alongside alleged recycled chain mail armor from the time of Genghis Khan, a land at the crossroads of empire builders and empire destroyers from Alexandra to Gorbachev.

By 2007, its surrounding area not only hosted a luxury enclosed mall and a five-star hotel, the Serena, but also offices for FEDEX, sleek cell phone billboards and sales outlets, traffic lights, and a multi-lane highway. The brightly painted trucks which ply the thinly-laid pavement brought in imported foreign goods—fresh shrimp, toiletries, fashionable European shoes, and every manner of electronics, as well as firewood or melons.

"Development," then, proceeds in a truncated and ineffective way. Kabul's touted development is happening primarily in just one area, the product of several large corporations, or private companies

There are new buildings in Share-nau and Kabul City Center, a huge mosque under construction at the bottom of the hill of the Deh Afghanon neighborhood, another multi-story commercial building being constructed across the street from the Majed-e-Haji Yaqub. Prices at restaurants geared for expatriates and foreigners are high and there is even a golf course facility on the edge of the city.

There is a major contrast between the few blocks developed by malls or high rise hotels, versus the real world of the people who have nothing. The unevenness of new construction in Kabul and elsewhere continues to create small, atypical pockets of wealth, surrounded by ancient and untouchable poverty. Much of the city is still in shambles.

Beyond the new mini-mansions and the modern buildings, there are still the *jewies* (open sewers) and the hill-clinging mud houses, and the ruins of 23 years of war. Behind the booming modern constructions and broad highways, tiny, makeshift shops vie for occasional power from patchy electrical grids, and unemployment, and dirty water dominate the average resident's life. The roads out of Kabul are still narrow, even as thousands of cars drag through the city streets along with rickshaws, motor cycles, donkeys, horse carts, and humans, and tiny children weaving in and out of traffic to sell things. And the bulk of rebuilding still takes place in Kabul.

Outside the cities, in its villages and fields, Afghanistan remains a country still suggestive of the Middle Ages in terms of quality of life.

Stupidly, even at this point, the need for consistent investment in all aspects of Afghanistan's recovery and development continues to be profoundly ignored. The country is desperate for intelligent and productive investment in roads, agriculture, irrigation, mine removal, schools, safe water, electricity, health clinics and basic social services. Hunger and homelessness and unemployment must be addressed. There has been little real or long-term "nation-building", and more and more of the population, both those in their villages and those returned refugees, is neither engaged nor employed.

Basic shelter is at a premium for the Afghan villagers, refugees and IDP's who have swollen Kabul's population over the past 20 years, even as the nouveau riche take over and rebuild mini-palaces and walled villas in Sherpur and Shari-nau. In the process they bulldoze and evict the homes of squatters, many of whom live in the shells of former government offices. In Kabul, as in many of the small cities of Afghanistan, rents are high, well beyond the reach of the average Afghan.

More and more the typical Afghan realizes from how much he is deliberately being excluded, not just the opulent Serena Kabul Hotel or Hyatt Regency, or the dazzling glass-covered malls at Roshan Plaza and Kabul City Centre, but also the accouterments of Western luxury and progress whose images shout at them from every corner—Toyota Land Rovers, Coca-cola, cell phone outlets and sleek, foreign banks and offices.

Outside Kabul, in the parts of Afghanistan which need them, most roads continue to be little more than rocks and gravel, or old macadam littered with broken potholes. The U.S. invested $25 million to make one from Kabul to the U.S. base in Kandahar, but already most had developed problems. Likewise, the logical objective of a circle road beyond Kandahar to Herat should be to reach Iran. But, apparently, the military incentive for the US to construct that road is minimal, since Iran can always be reached by long-range missiles from Afghanistan. Even so, a circle road is unwinding.

The road from Kabul to Puli-Khumri is now completed, with new smooth asphalt stretching 130 miles northwest of Kabul. At the Seroy-Shomali on the edge of the city, vehicles bargain to take passengers north or east to Baglan, Taleqan, Kunduz, and Faizabad, or to Samagan, Tashkurghan, or Mazar-i-Sharif, as they always have.

Along the route, inverted tank treads have been embedded in the asphalt to act as "speed bumps," and locals have dug ditches to force passing traffic to go slower and to make purchases from the roadside stands. These stands sell a rich variety of fruit, like fresh strawberries in season, or vegetables, bottled water, soft drinks, as well as random "antique" items ranging from old *rebabs* (a stringed instrument) to rugs. Here, too, services are offered for everything from car repairs, car washes, flat tire plugging, to while-you-wait shoe shines. Old-style single pump gas stations still function, but many new, standard American gas stations line the way, either finished or under-construction.

As of late 2007, the road continued from Puli-Khumri to Mazar, over the Salang Pass as a two lane road, with one lane of traffic in each direction, no middle line, no tolls and no services. While travelers report the buses or minivans being stopped at road blocks to check for narcotics smuggling, at no point does anyone have to show a driver's permit to negotiate this serpentine road over a 12,000 feet high pass. But of course that kind of cavalier attitude toward drivers is hardly limited to Afghan drivers. It is rather pervasive over most of the world

In fact, looking at the road situation in Afghanistan, without roads it is virtually impossible for a farmer or merchant to transport regular produce to market, and every other aspect of life and substance dependent on transport and communication and accessibility is hampered. At the same time, wood which provides fuel for both cooking and heating is sought everywhere and anywhere outside of Kabul. Subsequently, mountain side and valley trees not destroyed by 23 years of bombing are now rapidly bring eliminated in much of the country, leaving behind naked, barren land, susceptible to mudslides and erosion.

And, again and again, there is the impact of opium. The opium economy still rules, a reality embedded in the poverty of the farmers.

In the newly expanded small cities of Puli-Khumri, Mazar, Samangan and Kunduz, growth has exploded without comparable planning, so congestion, pollution, and lawlessness go hand in hand with the thousands of cars, carts and trucks crowding the roads, and any and every attempt at commerce and the real infrastructures of modern entrepreneurism.

Around the mosque in Mazar women sell clothes and earn from $1 to $1.40 per item of commission, while other women spread out their embroidery on the sidewalk to sell. But, nearby, hundreds of men collect and wait each day to be selected for daily labor, while others linger around construction sites, where the demand for labor comes no where near to matching the pool of workers desperate to work and support their families.

The mood in Mazar, always an ethnic blend and once a relatively quiet city famous for its Blue Mosque and peace doves, is equally ruthless. The simplicity and apparent tolerance once synonymous with its people has largely disappeared, another fatality of war. There is little that is innocent there anymore.

In Kunduz, a commercial market thrives, with sidewalk shops and areas on the road set aside for business, an extended downtown with much new construction, and a population three or four times the size it was thirty years ago. New restaurants prosper beside the energetic bargaining at *dhukans* selling fruits, vegetables, clothing, electronics and bread. The main high school, Lycee Shwer Khan operates in four shifts—morning, afternoon, evening and late evening to try to meet some of the needs of the expanded population.

Similarly, all of Samagan Province has more than doubled its population in 30 years and roads leading into Samagan are crowded, lined with new businesses, hotels, stores, and shops, all side-by-side with old and new government buildings, as new returnees crowd the available facilities in the main city of Aybak. In an area which had housed four high school and seven middle school in 1975, there are now 17 high schools and 158 middle schools.

Rebuilding projects by the U.S., E.U., G8 countries, U.N., Japan, China, India, Pakistan, and Iran are evident, particularly in the central, northern and western parts of the country. But even as the cities and large towns take on the trappings of more modern settings, the countryside remains rural, a place where people struggle to both survive and maintain their traditional ways of life. In most cases, these people are not eager to enter the 21st century.

Meanwhile, the monthly income for the average Afghan household remains about $6 while child labor continues to be rampant. Yet, self-sufficiency, subsistence agriculture and the clan at the village level have always been the basis of Afghanistan's economy. To enable the bulk of Afghans to return to their fields and grow food and sell, it is essential to support the population.

How can any country expect to function when so many are marginalized, when so many have lost hope, when such a majority of the population—as viewed by their own eyes, as pushed by fundamentalists groups, as presented on ubiquitous television and radio reports—questions where their country is going and the pace with which it is going there?

Obviously these for-profit groups and corporations who do the vast majority of investment in projects, structure-building, and business development, choose to focus on the bottom line and their ability to generate income. Driven by their own agenda, they exist to make money, not to serve or necessarily change the lives of the Afghan masses—the villagers, the children, the most vulnerable and the largest group.

At their peak, there were close to 1,000 NGOs and international donor groups in the country. Further, these groups effectively take over and run many of the functions which the Afghan government itself should have been running. The government lacks the money, while the NGOs and international organizations have billions. What development that was completed was done at a higher price, and with much less local Afghan involvement or employment, than it would have been, if the money were simply used by Afghans themselves to do the work.

Further, Afghanistan, of course, suffers desperately from a shortage of skilled labor, compelling most firms to bring in their own (like the 30,000 laborers from Pakistan brought in in 2007 alone). But usually the U.S., European and Afghan expatriates employed in projects leave out the Afghans themselves.

In late 2005, the previous Afghan Minister of Planning, Ramazan Bashardost, had asked for an accounting of aid money use by the NGOs. The response to his request was swift and irrevocable.

He was not just removed, but his entire office was eliminated. He had insisted that multinational and international organizations needed to be accountable, and not just the ministries. Further, Bashardot had asked that the U.N. and NGOs provide publicly accessible records to show to what extent the billions allocated for reconstruction was actually going for overhead and profit, versus the amount used for actual projects. He had also recommended that some 1935 registered NGOs leave Afghanistan, even as he exonerated the work of 420 others.

In fact, few people contest the extent to which much of the money intended to go to help the Afghan people was lost between waste, inefficient or non-existent accounting, the payment of *"bakshish"* (bribes), the demands for security, and inflated expenses for a Westerner to secure housing and living expenses.

The government has made the Ministry of Economics the umbrella for all the NGOs doing work in Afghanistan, yet it fuels the arrogance of the large organizations and the private corporations, and only requires the small NGOs to file paper work on accountability.

And the U.S. government did not fund non-government organizations (NGOs). Instead, the Bush administration made all of its grants to for-profit organizations, to promote corporations.

As has been documented over and over, other national experts, in this case American "experts, "receive handsome salaries and a "healthy package." Their special compensation for being in a "hardship post," includes vacation time and settlement expenses, all this despite the fact that in many such cases, the "experts" never get out of their offices. Thus, again, the Afghan government and its clients, for all its "experts," project an ignorance and indifference to the "real" Afghanistan, the 80 per cent of the people still living in villages and in poverty.

At this time the corruption in the government is also horrific. Many consultants hired by the government, and Karzai's advisers, are returned Afghans from Europe or the U.S. who never really knew their own country nor had respect for the average Afghan or traditional Afghan culture. They draw salaries of $40,000 a month from the World Bank and other donors, live lavishly with Land Rovers and villas, and in large part are drawn from the most elite pre-1979 Afghan families.

This scourge of greedy government officials is propped up by a culture of elitism and corruption, and on the next tier of workers by a tradition of bribery and graft. At the least, the dishonesty of this second tier of workers could be addressed by training all government employees, insuring they have appropriate credentials, and providing them a salary which would allow them to live and support a family. The courts are another area of weakness, since they lack skilled judiciary and still have a built-in corruption of bribery. At the same time, they remain inaccessible to the common citizen seeking justice on lost land claims or anything else.

The greatest challenge to "democracy" and stability in Afghanistan is the dominance of the former warlords within the government. This include such notables as Mujaddidi, General Dostum, Fahim, Qununi, Sayeat, Rabanni, among others. At the same time, the fundamentalists in government continue to clash with those who are Western-educated, and together with the warlords are able to block needed changes by voting against the ideas and persons of a small core of educated and progressive Cabinet members.

The U.S. yields an unhealthy amount of power behind the Afghan government. They could remove Karzai, and call on someone else to better represent their agenda. But, such actions, as instituted on such a scale in Iraq, are only part of a failed policy, a divide and rule mentality, which eventually brings everyone down. Bribing, paying off people to support you, may gain you time, but it always fails because you have not gained loyalty or really developed leadership or a population capable of change. You have not been given commitment. You have manipulated and been manipulated and that builds neither permanent loyalty nor agents of change. That does not grow leaders, nor lead to honest, capable governments.

Badly the U.S. has failed at implementing its originally-stated plan of cleaning the country of Taliban forces or helping Afghans reclaim their own lives. So you add to this explosion in "development" and "expertise" only a small part of which means a better life for the average Afghan, a powerless government made up disproportionately of corrupt, recycled ministers and staff, the growing stature of the Taliban, and the ingredients for a problematic stew are blatant. But there is more.

There is an occupying foreign military force, often perceived as arrogant and misused. There is an odd and dangerous mixing of humanitarian work with military work in the use of the PRTs for projects.

And, there is a lack of security or any means to guarantee it. So many of the U.S. forces are just kids who come, terrified and pumped up, who lack the maturity or resources to tolerate the stress of guerrilla battle in current Afghanistan. Too many plunge into all the drugs around and act like potheads.

The soldiers are disproportionately recruited from our poorest neighborhoods and states, and often are only minimally educated. Coming from an "out-and-out' part of society, many may also be the victim of tough backgrounds, and poor family values. Further, as part of the recruitment effort, they are built up to believe that they will do "good," when they are in Afghanistan, that they'll be helping a backward country, and most of the time that does not happen.

But, in fact, the reality is something totally different. These young men and women can not mingle with the local people at all now; they are in their own prisons.

The country whose rugged terrain and fiercely independent tribesmen displaced occupying army after army (the British three times in three wars) now hosted three U.S. bases, and 20,000 troops from NATO and 20,000 from the U.S. (as of October 2006, 12,000 of these U.S. troops served under NATO command). The largest U.S. air base being at the reclaimed Soviet base of Bagram on the Shomali Plain about 30 miles north of Kabul.

In 2007, this base was a world of U.S. Rangers, Chinooks, Blackhawks, Apaches, MRES (Meals Ready to Eat), Cheesy Nachos, Pop-Tarts, peanut butter, Hot Tamales chilies, T-Rats and A-Rats, M-16s,

SARs, covered Bibles, graphic obscenity and tents in a line called Viper City.

The bases were surrounded by enterprising Afghans who have set up stalls to sell everything from wool *pakul* hats, carpets, and boxes and bags of foreign goods pilfered from the bases' dump or unknown sources—to fruit drinks, canned meats, old military belts, smuggled vodka, and home-grown hashish.

Local Afghans even recycle the scrap metal from the practice ranges, so they can sell them for food.

Few breathing and thinking people have not realized the complexity of the U.S. relationship with Pakistan, and the extent to which the Afghan-Pakistani border has generated problems with everything from insurgents to smugglers, on top of decades of bitterness between Pakistan and Afghanistan.

The extent to which Pakistan has interfered with Afghanistan in the course of the past 23 years is hardly a secret. It served as the base of the *mujahadeen* groups and conduit of weapons for the most radical factions, the deliberate training grounds via *madrassa* for a generation of the Taliban, the principal supporter of the Taliban while in power, and it is now an on-going lifeline for insurgents and multi-national extremists and Taliban organized and hidden on their frontiers. Yet Pakistan rests secure with more than half a century of pro-Pakistan policy by the U.S. From the beginning the US kowtowed to Pakistani interests instead of allying with those who opposed the extreme *mujahadeens,* warlords, and Taliban. Now regional rivalries continue to play out. India also has an eye on development projects in Afghanistan and is also keenly aware of the dangers needing to be counterbalanced in the uncontrollable nature of Pushtoonistan

NATO straddles a challenging position. On one hand, the ISAF forces have to fight this insurgency, and on the other hand they find an indifference and even treachery among some local people. Finally, they are confronted with the fallout of a very weak national government, from which they had initially expected a lot, but from which they will get nothing.

The Provincial Reconstruction Teams (PRTs) was the famous "winning hearts and minds" program of Secretary of Defense Rumsfield, but it not only has not won hearts but it has lost minds, and in terms of compromising the lives of the staffs of NGOs, mingling of NGOs with PRTs jeopardizes the NGOs. This entire program is worrisome. It is a disaster to mingle humanitarian work with military work, because it undermines the work, does not give us protection, and as a result hurts everyone.

Afghans are incredibly accepting people in some ways. The poorest and least enfranchised there like their common brothers and sisters in poor countries around our globe are long-suffering in the truest sense of the word. But, no one should underestimate the fragility of their trust, nor the length of their pained memories. Even the NATO forces headed by the British represent another thumb in the eye of the people of Afghanistan, for whom the history of the Afghan-British wars is still not that distant. They have not forgotten the need to route the enemies, and would-be "occupiers," especially in the south. Nor should any ever forget or underestimate the recent painful history of the Soviet occupiers, and how much it shapes an Afghan's view of "occupation."

Right now Americans and our troops are trespassers, seen as simple invaders by most Afghans, foreigners who violate cultural values and traditions. In total disregard for basic rights to privacy, the troops break into people's compounds and houses on raids in search of insurgents. Too often, they radiate an arrogant attitude and disdain for the people. And, as they play the life and death game of hide and seek, in their Humvees with the full gear and the night vision goggles, under layers and layers of security, they look more like aliens than fellow human beings.

Like the "developers," the would-be government "experts," and the international NGOs, the troops must also work with the elders of each community, to respect their positions, and involve them in any decisions. They must develop trust among the people whose future they are supposedly there to defend, one person, one village, one action at a time.

Nothing can be imposed on people if it is not their will to change.

(Comments were adapted from interviews with an Afghan-American humanitarian aid director, 2006-2007, and other sources. As with much of the historical record on events in Afghanistan, I have drawn from hundreds of readings and discussions over the past decades.)

XX

TEACHING AND OTHER DIVERSIONS

April 7, 1976

I pass another week as an overly-dedicated teacher, learning to balance my emotions, and my intellectual questioning, with my responsibilities. Tom returns home late Friday night when, after a sleepy afternoon at the Howards, the Mahoneys and Brenda's visiting brother have already gone to bed. He comes in sad and tired, with tales of the aftershocks, the "rumblings" of Tashkurghan, the wild poppy tulip fields and patches of the desert road between Kunduz and Tashkurghan, the gift bread from Azarullah's family, the ordeal of getting through the Salang where a stalled arms carrier had blocked traffic for hours . . . .

On Saturday all of the department emerged out at Engineering. We were part of a meeting on Development at USAID, a tête-à-tête group of PCVs.

[It is dawn and the day of the Howard's departure. How strange it is to have outlasted two country directors. I walk to the university down a winding neighborhood to Xushal High . . . Then we have lunch at Troy's. It is magical. His tiny, earth-moist rooms are perched along the rocks, the floors covered with *guleems,* donated or gifted, and an ugly selection of *towshaks,* also cheaply bought. We nurse two tea cups and an old rusty pot, along with some dry bread, as the landlord's handy man totes bricks to lean against the window above our heads. His bluff seems the ideal sitting place for a mystic with a unique world view on two sides—north and west and east Kabul and the Hindu Kush; and then the immediate peopled hills beside a graveyard, where I follow the moving blocks of school children, the silent, bowed women, the clouds and air.

Mostly we sit in silence . . . floating a word or two about the ineffable and his always rather trivial practice of debating with himself (or me or whoever is there, he insists) as to what he should do about a house or cook, the heights or the plains. So in his veritable Hans Castorp complex, with its juggling of the concept of self-consciousness and of Nirvana, he mostly looks out and feels overwhelmed by the view, that world picture.

Then I scramble down in a minute to the university, to my attentive class, after which I enjoy an hour or so to sit in the office and watch the hills from that level now.

[I am reading Kafka's letters to Melina . . . I bus home to talk with Tom, to share my feelings, and his concerns, as he hesitates, suddenly thinking law school a bad idea after all . . . I struggle to make the discussion light, to try to believe and say that it need not be a lifetime sentence, that he can yet reconsider, but he grows more serious . . .]

I pause at the image of trees seen growing over the tops of high private compound walls, out of those unknown roots. I muse how I can not touch one man except with my eyes and can do nothing but touch another with child's hands; and recall the daze in which I ride the city buses, collecting faces in the back of my mind, my thoughts weaving and wavy like palm leaves on a beach, sensing it all, but never quite understanding how these disparate emotions and directions fit together.

Departures, that becomes a recurring motif.

Yarrow stalks from sacred graveyards.

April 10, 1976

> [More Kabul meetings, one with U.N. people, another with Mary McMahon (a painter and equestrian), on and on and on again discussions now with Tom: my seeking some breathing room, some needed independence. I know I am afraid I can't support him this first semester in law school, as I have yet to procure the promise of a job. And, I know how strong and silly is my search, for a kindred spirit . . .]

This afternoon we almost weep together, grow warm and close in our sadness as thunder and lightning and rain reign outside in a dark, tumultuous world. He tells me how he doesn't have any real friend except me, that he loves and needs me. I try to respond, sense the truth in what he says, plummet sadder still because I can not give him this simple thing that he—so proud a man—asks for.

Why?

All my confidants are rooting for a reconciliation. There is a letter from Mother about John's improvement, and news that there had been 41 tornadoes in the States one weekend.

I grind out my role in the university . . . where I am seen as super responsible . . . . Thinking how to again write, and how to make my work in this country have meaning, I seek and accept . . . Yvonne Alpert's offered advise. I realize how she too has juggled much, reconciled much, and that there is no easy answer for any of us who would love and write and travel and serve . . . And then one day begin a family.

April 15, 1976

All week it has been sunny; today it turns chilly and as dark gray as winter, except that the air whispers the laughing lightness of spring and the noises beckon birds in the trees about to bloom

[I dangle, swim, drown in many catharses—Between classes and home, I balance long talks at his house with Troy about suffering and the Buddhist view of life and relationships, about logic and our families.

Then Tom again strikes out at me, hurt, and we enter a densely packed discussion, desperate to sort out how we were not being reconciled sexually. He uses the image of making love to the ocean—feeling empty and suicidal afterwards. And I, I vow I am more aware and feeling then ever before—at least socially—and then ponder what we need to do to reconcile both . . . my space and his, my needs and his . . . It is sad and then healing.]

Our dear student friend from Tashkurghan, Azarullah, comes to the house, full of his trials of adjustment to dormitory-university life. I wash clothes, old ones which still fit, and the day elapses, no longer limping. We rest in a quiet resolve.

Meanwhile, we have little bags of water hanging from all the grape vines in our yard, which Mirad put there to catch the moisture from the arbor, because some old *baux-wan* who was in chopping up the ground told him that this water would make his hair stay in longer if he used it. And there is the special letter from the mullah in Jalalabad, who Mirad had asked for advice about his son Habibullah's growth on his neck, his sickness, which of course he couldn't read, but which he sent off to Sare-Pul that very day.

And there are the men and the *jewies* in the street; the city is re-doing all the ditches, widening the roads with concrete slabs and putting up a row of unstable-looking slab curbs, along with rock walls in the ditches. Several hundred men in dusty faded brown uniforms work as a manual labor regiment, each digging or wielding rocks or observing, or passing weight, all along the streets that form a "T," in front of us, and they make strange comments at us, "the foreigners," as we come though, as they work at their projects with its built-in obsolescence.

And there are the blooming apricot trees, wafting fragile pink blossoms.

> *[Bits of the I-Ching, Gabriel Marcel, Confucius. So we come full round in our talks, and thoughts of the itinerary—how in a few months a route will take us from Delhi to Kathmandu to Rangoon to Bangladesh to the Malaysian coast . . . Or, instead it could take us to Europe by way of Delhi and a stop in Ireland for me, as Tom re-enters the States and I join him a week later . . . . Which will it be?]*

April 18, 1976 Easter

At 6 a.m. I venture out to the elegantly tended grounds of the British Embassy. A half-mad man, claiming we are going his way, also jumps into the cab. Then, flinging open the door, he exits quickly at an intersection, without so much as a nod in any direction. The driver comments: "Not all people have all their brains."

At the Embassy, we stand on the fresh green grass and sing old Protestant hymns, while the sun rises over the mountains, dazzling and huge. The arching old trees around the lawn bend in the motion of near-leafing, and a splattering of fruit trees already in bloom add an element of delicate simplicity, while tiny purple and yellow flowers sprouting outside the flower beds seem like holy drops on an earthen rug. The music, one lone trumpeter behind me counting the peals, soars pure and beautiful, drawing me back to all those years as a teenager watching choruses of tympanists and trombones and processions, anticipating Easter eggs, participating in the choir myself at our liberal, suburban St. Louis Methodist church.

I tumble, Alice-in-Wonderland-struck in a moment with that old image of the receding mirror windows into your past, chiming at you, echoing, with a wealth of memories down a long hall. I feel sad at the pause in time, the sheer beauty of singing hopeful songs about immortality in a setting as grave and majestic as this Kabul bowl, and I think of my family and all their traumas never to be touched or healed. And the unknown and well-known tragedies here.

I return home to find Tom slowly getting his things together for a week in the provinces . . . I pen him a note full of encouragement, and leave it in his box at PC, along with my three purple flowers from the Embassy grounds at dawn, and then set off for school on the public bus. There I meet a fifth year architect student who talks excitedly about his work prospects, and how she enjoys this profession. She grins, impressed that I am both married and the holder of a Masters degree, then queries me as to why I and my husband had both gone into the humanities, instead of the sciences.

. . . Back in our office, Paul Oldsman . . . wrathful at the incompetence and laziness of our pathetic co-workers, etc., explodes. I remind him that this, too, will pass. My own class moves with confidence and ease; the second class is even easier because all the Sophomores plead that they yet lack their books, so the lesson should not go on. I surprise them with a small quiz and they dissolve, penitent. Home for lunch, I then venture out to the full wrath of the day, now glorious but hot, to buy a few Easter candies and flower seeds to put anonymously in my co-workers' boxes, to give 10 afs to the shoeshine boy when only five is called for, to just miss buying endless bouquets of wet red poppies from begging children. I must go off to the Embassy to find out about reissuing my passport, and to have passport pictures taken . . .

[We have visits with other PCVs, and I catch a sense of Bruce Letts' goodness. He is soon off to be with his wife in law school.]

It's as mellow, as lonely as childhoods of summer when you pause in the warm fresh air at dusk with a timidity, when you want to be brave and take in the season, aware that the sun has turned, but that you are unable to, because you are somehow too small in it all.

On the bus to the university yesterday (I went back in the afternoon to deliver a letter and money to Magadess, and then set about correcting awful Sophomore essays), when coming home from Share-nau, I watched a tiny little woman with a gold-knobbed cane sit down beside me. Something about her sitting there, made me happy, made me feel there was magic in the air. I need the small relationships with other people I can get mornings, evenings riding on the public bus. It is a small connection, an eye on their world, but at least I am immersed in it in those moments.

And the flute seller boy who wanders the streets passes by with his shrill song. Night has come.

April 19, 1976

[I am doing a study of Bonhoeffer.]

Tom should be in Grishk tonight.

On Tuesday the passport procedures begin at the Embassy . . .

There is a little more light and humor in the office now, my fears swallowed and a kind of false joy carrying me away. I have found my place, ceased to demand.

Rona, a PC secretary tells me in her proud beauty, her stony countenance, how her grandfather came from Tashkurghan, had land in the Tangi, and how she had never been there. Her father, now deceased, had first gone there when he was 30 or 40.

[Again, our chatter, our making of the expatriate's community, our seeking comfort in what is familiar. We talk about childhoods and travels, fathers and other things with PCVs.]

Mirad's pictures were ready today. We look at them with him. The colors are none too good, but we see much: all his family in Sare-pul, little boys crying, his oldest son refusing to grow, the over-powering light, some beautiful Uzbek pieces, the elements of patriarch, children, women, old men.

> *[I am measured for a dress; and I am fearful after a set of rejections from school districts to which I had applied. A big dinner pends.]*

April 22, 1976

> *[I collect quotes from Virginia Woolfe, and from George Sands in* Three Guineas*]*

I jump up, totally awake this morning (past my first waking at 5:30) to find it is 8:30. Our landlord enters to tell me that he has put the water pump back on, but that the gate to our neighbor's had been left open all night.

On Wednesday night Mirad's little son Habibullah, his father and the father of his sister's dead husband, come down from Sare-pul. I greet the child who looks small and dizzy in the big house, lend out *toshaks* and such. Then, after giving Mirad the next day off, so he can take Habibullah to see some "woman on the hill in Jemal-minat" and to a doctor, and so that he can accompany the distant, toothless relative to get a pair of teeth, I . . . pedal out to hear a classical guitar concert by William Matthews.

Before we leave the performance, I met Hooshi from the University, with her friend and former classmate, a woman in thick glasses, who is introduced as one of the only women judges in Afghanistan. It is a warm night and the doors to the outside of the auditorium gap open: a damp, cool breeze passes through, giving something of the milieu of a sidewalk cafe. So the performer comes, tall, pale, awkward, with his simple guitar, his heavy beard which gives to his covered lips a goofy smile, his small, deep-set myopic eyes which he turns to watch his strings as he plays them, his perfectly bald egg-shaped pate (as if whisked from the infirmary to perform . . .). But he plays beautifully. Listening in the summer night to "Lochamae Pavan," a Renaissance piece, one thinks of long-skirted, small-bosomed women holding lutes in gardens of nightingales and gallants, sad as season's end or season's beginnings. And meanwhile two moths flutter in, circle about the lights, dodge his head. We listen silently to a Mexican work, Manuel Ponce, done for Segovia, which consists of some twenty variations on the theme "Folia de Espina" and a Fugue, most of which Matthews plays. Parts of it twinkle, sheer magic, as his hands come up with the peal of bells and than a crescendo like waterfalls.

During intermission, Hooshi and her friend leave (they had been talking through the performance; it had not interested them.) I talk with a woman who had been visiting with other PCVs our first Christmas in Mazar, whom I remembered as small, southern and infinitely feminine and submissive, who is engaged to an Afghan musician now, and who will go to the States and marry she hopes. Now she is just "playing house," has lived with him for a while, even had an abortion of his child illegally . . . I am flabbergasted. In short she has had a rather strange time. I begin to ask her about clear future plans, but just then her fiancée returns, and instead we talk of the earthquake in Tashkurghan . . .

. . . My favorite (piece) of the evening is "Recuerdos de la Alhambra" by Tariega, which literally transports one to the southern Spanish kingdom, to scents of jasmine and perfumed fountains, to noble arched doorways and glistening ocean cliff bottoms . . . .

And I do so miss Tom . . . . [Have I squelched the yearning, found the comradely peace on the other front, once I realized this was not my salvation? It is only a friendship with someone who has a cross of saintliness, humor and aloof vanity. And who is also gay, and thus brotherly. I vow a new beginning with Tom.

I acquire a new passport, and a new dress, do my university work, stay in the office until 5, then have a long talk with Paula Frank at the Dunns house, and absorb her sense that there is no eligible partners for her here, even as we share thoughts on the States.]

She maintains that people have gone mad, that our contemporaries back in the States are flooding into professional schools in the hope of avoiding a financial debacle, the apocalypse, that people with jobs are lording over those without them, that everyone has a sinister glare about their faces, an achievement-oriented glint, that everyone has turned conservative . . .

Everyone?

Later as we sit in the window, the stormy sunset past, cool night hovering, low lights in the room, we hear the pure tones of a flute. It is Ann Dunn practicing in her house, across the green yard and shrubs and pigeon-houses trees, the sound coming like an opening on night . . .

Back at our house the windows are open again, as are those in all the neighbor houses, so we hear their too loud radios, the cheap Afghan-Indian pop music, the too dramatic soap operas. How hard we must listen to catch the birds, alone in their frantic songs only early in the morning . . .

[Anais Nin's *Seducton of the Minotaur . . . a strange piece.]*

April 30, 1976

Finally it is another week, today a full blown blue day, after all those strange half-turned, stormy ones. Friday, we attend a party at the Jenkins' home . . .

Habibullah, who has joined his father in Kabul, needs our help. So we begin the week's work of shuttling him to doctors. It takes only one test to find that he has TB, that this is the source of his nodules, of his swollen glands and stomach.

Mirad takes him to the children's hospital, where he waits among long rows of silent people, children in all manner of pain and illness, waiting to be seen by a doctor who doesn't have time or medicine to spare to heal them. Then, Mirad visits the general TB hospital where they give Habibullah a test and medicine. At the Noor Clinic, he is thrilled, tears in his eyes as he recalls. He describes the gentleness, the clean set-up there, the intelligent and caring staff. They give him medicine for Habibullah's eye, so that the child's bright black eyes are wide open again in a matter of days. Later Mirad approaches us shyly, to ask what he should feed the boy, how an old man had told him that for 40 days the child should have nothing but tea and bread.

I think Tom's opinions prevail; he tells Mirad what to do about all the medicines, explains how important it is that Habibullah stay here and go regularly for his medicine, explains how necessary it is that the child eat good and varied food and grow strong.

By contrast, I put down my own adventure going out to the Noor Clinic to have an appointment with the Scottish doctor, and how no one knew who I was or what I was doing there:

A sprightly be-glassed woman with the peppy stride of a former gym teacher tells me, "All can be worked out," and finally locates the doctor to see me. The able man has just completed a delicate operation; forty-five minutes later he finally gives me a prescription for tetramycin cream to be used for 40 days morning and night to alleviate the symptoms I had of glaucoma (mildly convincingly so) and tells me to get off the pill and Aralen, and to make my own test that way to see if the problem recedes.

I have a raucous voyage by bus back to Damazang, back to the university because I think to have left my key (and where I find Bruce Letts, looking for a disappeared Rick Dwyer, who follows me back into the office to ask about correcting the Freshmen test.) Then I hurry back to Share-nau and over to PC . . .

. . . My students are fearful of low grades on last week's test; these are the sleepy Juniors, who it turns out can't ever hear a word I say in those barn-like classrooms . . . Or so some warn me.

Wavering, I seem about resolved to leave as early as possible, to do what Tom recommends . . . seeing how senseless it is to stay around here and organize curriculum . . . Yet I am sorely tempted to stay on a little longer and earn some more months of my salary.

I find myself in an exegesis on the concept of precocity and apotheosizing.

So my Tom returns from his provincial trip, with golden shoes which turn up at the toes and beautiful colored hats from Herat. Only days later does he share that . . . the volunteers there (except Lena Auchincloss) had been totally non-cooperative . . . as he observed classes and offered the storybooks.

One night we go off to the concert at the Italian Embassy, a mammoth modern building, a cross between a hotel and a museum, with its sad-eyed dark Madonnas, a candelabra and open arches and wooden stairs, so much more visible than we remembered from the Christmas mass. The potpourri of people, this international audience, inhale the 15th century music, recorders and flutes, harpsichord and guitar and mandolins. The concert radiates the magical, is a pleasure to attend, and in that strange décor one could catch all the strains of a song, reduced to a clear haunting melody of a flute, of a dance.

> *[I read Selksy:* The Devaluation of People; *even as Tom struggles with more shigella . . . }*

Again, the greening of the earth dazzles us. I have not seen a spring so precious in a long season.

May 1

> [As a group we are planning a poetry reading. Individually, we take in news/shared stories of siblings who are crazy or on drugs and parents divorced or otherwise broken, poems by Sandburg. From, "Little Girl, Be Careful What You Say," and "For You" ("The peace of great door be for you/wait at the knobs . . . ."]

May 4, 1976

> *[I've been reading about Native American Indian wheels, contemplating moonlight, talking to Brenda Mahoney's visiting younger brother and the Milwaukee-bred fellow teacher at Engineering.]*

Strange conversations continue, with Brenda's brother from Oregon who at 20 shows, a kind of naïve cynicism about America and at the same time a real wisdom, too. He came to Kabul to eat banana splits without bananas in the western establishments, to have beer at the Staff House, to take in a cultural and sociological tour, to read all the latest *Time* magazines and interpret them for us, letting us know what is the real spirit of the times back in the U.S. He explains how he has friends (female) who are into trucking appreciation, how everyone is using trucker radio broadcasting now, and has short wave radios which monitor the police band (so that they can know whether to speed up or slow down at some given stretch of highway, so in effect they are always trying to imitate the irresponsible kind of trafficking of those burly marathon makers of the great America.) A new set of values evolves, none of them very inspiring.

I take in a dissertation on moonlight (preened of course by the lunar ludic one, who can watch it all from his rock-hanging house above the city) and how the waning moon fills us with certain excess energy, how in short we can or cannot attune ourselves to that intense atmosphere. I reiterate, speak about my vivid memories as a child of waking up with my head in the window and intense moonlight falling on me, and how terrified I would be thinking that it would make me go crazy if I unknowingly slept with that strange, strong light on me for a long time. I can't verbalize it all those rich tapestry-like details, the aspects of moments when I was intensely aware of the moon, felt conscious of it, and for those facts no one could contradict me, delve into me, or in any way extract those minute particulars. Troy has of course done a lot of moon-watching from his place in Kamard.

May 6, 1976:

> *[As always, confusion, this time as to when I will terminate, as I have classes until late in June and feel I should stay until the end so that someone reliable will be here to get all the grades in, to coordinate complaints, to function as a regular and paper signer between the various realms (official and office) . . .].* After all, I am Chairman.

May 7, 1976 (Joma)

Once upon a time on a stormy night quite given to the cool spring clouds and invading modernity, some of us gathered in a cool Kabul garden to read poems by candlelight. There was Dylan Thomas, Yeats, Marvell, Eliot, Richard Hughes, William Stafford, e.e. Cummings,

John Keats, Seferis and an unnamed Biafran poet . . . two poetasters themselves . . . Thoreau and Chinese classics and Japanese haiku, Kenneth Rexworth and Tom Clark, and several unnamed on love, loneliness, time passing, memory, the night mists, fragile beauty—all were there, as well—and peopling the voices were Tom, me, Brenda, Alsie, Chad, the Kellys, Randall, and a moody friend of his . . .

Earlier, at dawn, Ben Hedges (Brenda's brother) rose and set off to take a bus to Herat. In the early dawn I sat through tea with him. At work the long lingering: I had to make up a test on the spur of the moment for the Afghan Tour entourage. Tired, I returned at 4:00 by cab, only to find that everyone was peeved because proctors had yet to be set up for the exams the next afternoon . . . A small party for Mirad, stylish cake and our picture album as a gift, and yellow and purple flowers from his brother, Qorbin.

We visited the Kabul Museum on Tuesday afternoon, two and three-quarters years almost since we first saw it . . . for a study of those fragments in my mind, the details of the stories introduced to me a thousand times and which I have yet to absorb—There is still a certain other-worldliness in going through the rooms of gathered artifacts, the union of ages (Greek, Chinese, Indian in the land around Kabul, the Buddhist monasteries, the Persian-Arabic pottery, the prehistoric doodled-on rock from around Balkh, all the symbols and monuments to current ages and past, man and deeds, over and through it all a kind of tired anticipation of how it all might have been had one generation (radically non-innocent) replaced another. And then the strange, unrelated gods of Nuristan, like firm animistic carved wooden African totems.

Then it was down to Demazang on a bus and walking to the University . . . standing in direct sunlight of late afternoon, and reading our colleague's questions stated in a letter . . . staying to 5:40 with Rick Dwyer, bewailing how complacent and uncreative most of America appeared these days, how people, youth in particular, have stopped asking questions, but just complacently accept things as if there were no options except those with which they were born. I.E., they follow their parents. And, we weigh in, how they are again caught up in appearances, looking good with a car, clothes, girl, job, what have you. How sick the whole thing is, how little is given to culling lives which are not hollow stalks, how there's no tension per se (no wars?), and so complacency is the fill of the day.

Dinner comes, after a wearying walk through returning school children loud in their scorn, and their teasing, of us.

And other afternoons. Yesterday grading the test for the Afghan Tour and reading a report with the Dean. Waiting, Dave Dunn and Tom and I talked of WT's who had been in jail here and returned to jail, of wealthy Afghan student families who are prisoners of government disfavor or the government itself, of ways of shipping things home, of boy scouts . . . of the TASK ball Dave and Kay Dunn were to attend, of rumors that Bill Calhoun had had an affair with some embassy underling and was now ostracized by the community . . .

May 8, 1976

[Some silly Paris revue performance, partially attended . . . myself dressed in a jacket, blue skirt and stockings . . .] I go to a meeting third hour to hear the Dean and others extemporize on how each department must make up a curriculum committee and once that has been settled, each of the participants must reiterate the ideas of the others, to insure everyone's input had been secured. I delicately break up the meeting by moving forward to my class, to cue the Dean to the fact that we have scheduled classes to go to . . .

Tuesday un-tender, the day darkens this 11th cycle of the month, the sun gone and only evening light left, although it's only 3:15. Tom traveled off to the North yesterday before noon, and I journeyed on to long class hours and a party of expatriates—a Dutch UN expert who was collecting children's street games as a hobby, and Rashidi Omaid from the PC office.

. . . We bought a second rug, the Mauri from the village north of Herat which is famous for the exquisite work of its weavers, eased in our transaction by the fact that Tom's father sent us 1,000 dollars from our bank savings account back in the U.S . . .

In the hall yesterday, the betrothed of Gulzada and the brother of an upper class student in Lycee Mahasty (Suraya) stopped me to ask if I was the woman who had taught in Tashkurghan, and if so had I known Gulzada? He continued then, "What kind of 'mind and morals' did she have?" It was a strange throw back to that other time, that world of the village, so soon to become something else.

A strange, albeit timid, woman talked to me at the dinner first, a Bryn Mawr educator whose husband is here writing a book, and who has lived all over the world. She has a Princeton-easterner polish, a certain overbearingness to her, and I sensed her need to abandon me for richer fields after an interminable length . . .

Night's upon us too soon. But the scent of acacias, the graceful white hanging flowers from all the trees, adds a note, a scent of blessed times . . . .

[The PC doctor is in Nepal, and Tom was asked to be acting country director while everyone was at a meeting! Amazing. Still, I am wondering why there are no jobs from the school applications I have sent out . . . .] . . . Perhaps friendlessness is a vocation after all . . .

Wednesday I conducted a meeting of sorts to catch the department's opinion, then dashed home for lunch, rushed back on the public bus to school, then went on to the Used Clothes Bazaar . . . .

At home . . . all night the sound of the wind blowing, the trees rustling, doors and shutters banging, like a peopled field, frightening and sudden.

Thursday May 13, 1976

I climb up on the roof, via a crotchety ladder, my spiral of sorts to some remunerative eye-spot, and see in a moment the moon—round, wafer-thin but circling full and luminous, consuming the gray sky, itself inimical, unquestioned in its regal place, around it the stars, small and tremulous. Back again, the air redolent with spring greenery filled with a languidness. I want to watch the tones of night, evoke long dead, never procured conversations with those who people our past, still extant (since memories, however untruthful, are always implacable), but I come inside and instead read poems from an old issue of *Shenandoah* and then whizz through a selection of e.e. cummings (for a moment there, I conjured up my high school friend and mentor, Terry Lazar, austere and overly intellectual, studying a poem in Miss Henry's French class 10 years ago.)

[Excerpts from e.e. cummings, comments from Bruner's Essays for the Left Hand.]

May 16, 1976

Yesterday I saw the Howard's old compound guard, now shepherding on Damazong. He walked by, with a flash of his relatives' sheep, hot and sad, gentle and old.

Last night I heard a magic concert . . . a musician/magician on strings named Jack Glatzer, master of pure beauty and drama and humor and charm, in selections from a Beethoven Sonata, a Bach Partito, Paganini,

. . . Tom has returned with tales of the north, floods in the Salang, land slides and closed roads, and a new reconciliation. He describes the trauma of showing films in Tashkurghan, success at the boys' school, but blind mob action at the leaderless girl's school, of him also—this same recognition has saddened me back in December—feeling a certain distance from the Mahoneys. and their possession of the town.

The overload of work from the Dean's office waits for me, plus the regular class load, as I focus on a batch of inquiries and applications to send out and then wait for responses. I dread, but must, get recommendations, endorsements, and so on.

May 21, 1976

I rise at 5:30 to birdsong, Tom's warm pleasant form curling beside me like an extension of a mellow scattered song outside, and my mind writhes with memories. I'll try to collect last week in a line of words, a paragraph indented with its own sense of itself, pleased but brazen.

There was first the element of the sun, strong and indomitable now from mid-morning to mid-afternoon, so that one easily turns red with no exertion at all. There's the full-blown lush green of the grape arbors shading, shadowing all our comings and goings by the compound gate, by the porch beyond the sun porch and our bedroom window; and all over the city, there is the coming of the roses, soft and fragrant and of every hue.

There were the hard grammar lessons to teach the self-persevering classes to balance, the long conferences (set up as one-on-one, one student and me) for three days, to discuss most often non-existent research, to repeat in every mouthing 27 times that the form of things like footnotes and bibliography was important. In the Freshmen classes there was the restless advent of their spring and maleness, and among the Sophomores there was the fear of too many unknown facts beginning to crescendo on their heads . . . .

[All this is lightened, distanced, with lunches, dinners with colleagues.]

Tom arrived Saturday night; we have a new lilt in our bones, all things seemingly reconcilable, if we will but pursue them with patience and radical (Yeatsian) innocence.

For months there have been regular, if excessive, meetings with the Dean, a stream of notes and memos for him. Suddenly, there are no more invitations, no more meetings, and I lose myself in a sullen anger until I realize that in fact I had likely avoided a meeting I should have attended. He had allowed me to do it without rebuke immediately, but none of my avoidance has gone unnoticed.

One noon I catch a lunch with Tom at Kabul Hotel, with its old, decaying colonial flare (although Afghanistan was never a colony), the white-coated attentive waiters, the businessman's special, and a table with vases of flowers before long mirrored walls . . .

[Tom purchased a handwoven Harris Tweed and a pattern of plaid blue and brown, both to be made up in debonair jackets . . . . We entertain other friends and hear their tales, one Chad who had been mentored by Richard Hugo . . . another with a grandmother who used to take the kids out of school to have their palms read by gypsies because she thought schooling before age 12 was way too constrictive and influential . . .]

And Wednesday had been the poetry reading, under the grape arbor, candlelight on a low table . . . the air kind, our voices curious and loving or light and querying, the night well-posed in memories and reflections, and a presence by half-light of something noble and remote, of our immediates all turned to backward looking pauses . . .

Yesterday, after a full morning, all the classes in a row, I was to meet Tom at a softball game at noon . . . Off we went in a semi-exploding cab, activated by a boy who did not even know where the main streets of Kabul were, who seemed half-consumed by the dark black fumes of his discombobulated motor, inhaling the sour wind . . . . [We chat, ferociously, about another volunteer who likes to lure people already taken in order to show her power . . . arrive to find there is no game and no news, and detour instead to the Afghan Department Store]. We are soon squashed into the noon rush bus where T. holds some man's flowers and the duplicating paper, and I am eye-balled and sweating out the door. Suddenly we pass by two bus-loads of Russian children, the girls in bright ribboned hair and clean white smocks and pinafores, the boys all in red scarves and tight short pants and old-fashioned cotton shirts—

Upon arrival at the store, Tom shares a story: Sneezing one day, inattentive for a split instant, he almost got hit by a car, and another time while he simply stood in place by the road, a bus almost backed into him.

We go up then to the top of the regular thriving restaurant, choose tables, then go to wash up after the heat. Coming back. I find Tom and Kirk . . . The meal begins slowly, even as we eye the Russian contingency in the adjacent table, the other diners, well-pressed and animated, the scenery about us . . . Later, we indulge in a treat, ice cream at Tretonnes.

Mellowed, at home, I type some tests, bathe in a dream of bubbles and hot water, eat dinner and talk to Tom about an article he has read advocating bi-sexuality by an old professor at Princeton. We bring in the study of history, of society, ending rather grimly with my recapitulations of Brenda's brother's observations on the present mediocrity of American youth . . . Against our will, we are again swept off to a party next door, whose loud music plucks at us, and we hear stories from Chad and his days in Montana . . . .

Morning brings the cycle full round. Against our will, again, we wake to our neighbors jarring Hindi movie music at 7 a.m., the too loud radio standing out like a naked man in the usual clothing of the heavy rumble of trucks and buses on the outdoor pavements, and an unidentified carping bird . . . .

May 23, 1976

. . . . Mother's letters come, four strong, like little religious epistles tidied away with velveteen ribbons in an old parson's attic chest: Her religiosity is only slight tamer than her faith. She reprimands me for my worry, telling me of the good treatment my brothers John and David are getting at the hands of concerned doctors, then shares an odd little description of how they called on her to say a prayer at the end of the Sunday School and she did eloquently, I guess, and everyone was moved.

I'm fearful of going home to see them: the age heavy in my father in his real estate unreality job, like the scattered ashes on the butt of his cigar habit of years; mother's hair grown out gray now, her dresses a bit old-fashioned and sack-like, her glasses thick over those child soft brown eyes, her form a skeleton body of that of her child-bearing years, the warm, full mother of my childhood. The house with the holes dug in the yard for the never-to-be-finished greenhouse, David's spiritual project, the old musty mattresses, the empty bedrooms, my locked college trunk like a stalwart of a preserved temple in the temperamental cascade of the varied heat-heavy rooms. Yet I want to see them, hug them, know them all.

. . . Yesterday we all gave a test to our Freshmen . . . then graded our papers, sharing a soft camaraderie . . .

The shape of Tom's form against me in the night, the impulse to huddle against the known before the unknown, carries us on.

At the university, between classes, our colleague, Troy, tells me his notion of how he had to water down anything he wrote home, to fill it with pleasantries because none would understand subtleties. Somehow from there we go on to discussing writing and this friend tries to say it is all empty emotions, non-glorious, that only the Buddhists found worthy writing—and maybe Blake or Whitman in the West, persons who describe their epiphanies for others to absorb. As I speake of "worthy" writers, (my Dostoevsky, Faulkner, Welty, McCullers, Marquez, thousands), it turns out that Troy, like my Tom, had never read many of them.

I try to speak of dialectics, the need for conflicts, for something better to be borne out, of a sort of evolution—we move on to a definition of wisdom, the absolute that all is changing, the notion that suffering is self-induced, and so on. He tells me that his intense satisfaction with art, music,and poetry has all been pre-empted by his meditation experience. In effect, none of it could measure up to the cathartic, brilliant illumination of that experience.

Somehow we are back again defining "love," as something non-particularized, and I am saying it had to be first particularized before it opens and adheres to the godhead, because once at that point it wouldn't seek itself in lesser particulars, one-individualized forms.

And it is 1:30 and he has a Farsi lesson; neither of us has had lunch, and my own class is to begin at 2:00. Philosophy settled, behind us a rain storm blurs the mountains and wind's scouring grit and dust floods the sky; he speaks of how intellectual purity has a place in the world, how his uncle had written a great treatise unintelligible to the common world first, and now has written a more approachable book which would lead to help for a lot of people whose sexual preferences now ostracize them from society. As I express not such sincere skepticism in the possibility of man, the world evolving to a better state, we hit again on some definition of absolute, how temporal we are as creatures, how our mistakes in judgment come from our inability to transcend this artificial cycle, our failure to be able to accept the more than cyclical way.

. . . I arrive home in a rain burst, in a shared cab with two students who didn't pay this time. There is news of Tom's three ordered suits . . . and a letter from Tom's father about a burglary in the house next door. Tom's mother had watched the entire thing, thinking all the time the burglars were just one of the boyfriends of this neighbor's strange daughter!

And in the morning we wake to find Mirad has picked twenty little roses and placed them in a bowl on the sun porch table, and their perfume redolent, the room swims in the sweet pinkness. In the world beyond, roses are everywhere, spring waning, summer burning in like some unasked for wrath, yet the flowers are rich, will be sturdy in their delicate perfectness through it all, symbols before the mountains of a certain tamed but indefatigable energy.

Tomorrow we're to give more tests, this time to Sophomores, and in the effervescence of a tardy reprieve, we can close down our school day for a bit and go off to an adventure.

Tom is planning now a trip to Jam in the first week in July, a trip to carry us to the mountain's long dry womb, to pluck secrets and barrenness like prickly cactus stems and press it into leaves of a book of recollections we'll give a title to in older age, and heighten with experience.

What is the source, what the moment, a moth beating its wings every night against the glass, thinking to want in, but not knowing what inside is.

May 28, 1976

We come then in two days of unraveling traveling along roads dedicated to dessication and emptiness, beneath the sky like a blinding strip of some indelicate painter, come to the end of the road, deserts and mountains within and without behind us, to sit in a room in a large garden of apple trees, roses, pomegranate bushes, and wild zinnias and sip tea that comes all the way from China. We left in the cool morning of Wednesday in the truck that bounces on its torpid springs like some grasshopper of elastic steel. Boiled eggs and a kilo of ginger snaps, Troy, Kirk, Brenda, Sher Khan, Tom and I, a collection of women's poetry and Woolfe's *A Room of My Own.* (There had been on Tuesday the chocolate frosted cake for Anne, the reading of Gwendolyn Brook's *Seven at the Golden Shovel*, the losing softball game with PCVs, the conversation started but never finished the day before on truth turned now to laughter, a joke about everything in pants, a reference to the criticisms by Renison that women poets have no sense of humor.

Off then to Kandahar, a pause to dip ginger snaps in the oily tin of peanut butter at a town made of mud shelters, a thin stream of water, a child alone in the hot road, squeezed on either side by thin poplar trees and the cast shade. In Kandahar, we join the volunteers, have a meeting with a woman teacher, then do a walk in the bazaar to find the correct prizes for wannabe gifts. It is a journey into the land of men, me shouldered by Troy and Kirk, Brenda in her bold buxom teeshirt and etched out waist, well behind us, into the town and past the monument, the central circle encased by the storefronts of kebab shops and future memorabilia, down sidewalks thick with commerce—the guns and plastic jars, shoes and old rugs, parallels of food and embroidery. Toward dark, time cooler now, the people enlivened by the stale winds reprisal, we pause at a nan shop, with bread hanging up shared like commas, take in the aviaries of strange interbred pigeons, the whipped cream apparel of the dark-faced turbans on men with hard legs.

What images are we chasing—a tale of the Buddhist *saddhus*, the people doomed to kill, spectral figures with long emaciated arms and legs and bulbous bellies; another of the water djinn, the fourth traveler in any trio, and the shrine to him at the edge of Kabul, where one can wander into the hills to find a natural spring, the holy place where rock hitting stone, gave his magic birth: the word ziaggarets, connoting the crooked hats of middle earthmen, balanced on a dry hill and raised to heaven.

In Kandahar a trip to the staff house, peopled by the surly contemptuous Afghans who look upon the ill-bred drunken American construction workers there, as on swine, it would seem, and the Americans, set down in this land when in their own they would be strangers to me, fat and falsely ruddy-faced, ghoulish in their exaggerations, ill-kept, unkempt.

The lights go out upon our arrival: when they come back on we consume grand cheeseburgers and play ping-pong or pool. I am animated.

At 10:30 we all go home, play our roles in trying to seduce sleep. Set down to Ophelia I giggle, a spectral Mr. O'Dell in a sheet becomes Julius Caesar. Brenda lays quiet in her corner, Kirk rises looking for water and fingers all the wares on the table above me. I try first to sleep in the windowsill, thinking to get the breeze, but Indian neighbors on an adjoining porch set up the legendary havoc, heads rocking, radio blearing, lights bobbing on and off. As I finally struggle to fall asleep a stench as of the inside of garbage cans bursts in redolent, so I move down to the floor beside Tom, and wonder for several hours and a brief sleep, what the other figures in the room are thinking, whether or not they are awake and wondering too. I want to sleep touching someone. (This image will be forced on the world the next day in the truck when I sit in the front with Troy and fall asleep moving in the bobbing world against his brotherly shoulder and wake to more consciousness, his motion, his form beside me. Subtly I crane to tell him I am sorry if I'd leaned on his shoulder like a drunken New Yorker, and he rather rationally replies it does not matter, since he has been asleep a while too). So I keep kicking out my feet to touch Tom's, warm figure in half-rest, and want to move about and watch, dart out to the "john," in true Ophelia form my robes blowing, and eventually between three and five sleep, at peace a minute.

We are out on the road again, the long morning at a languishing river in Grishk where we sit in a tea house, then drive through the shaded village streets to find the volunteer in Patrick and Shelley West's old house, a jewel of shade under a big mulberry tree. We squat then, eat some fruit collected in best shaken limb tradition, and soon are again in the truck driving on, and on and on, to eat lunch somewhere, fly-full, and watch rivers and narrow green valleys, but mostly the dry land and mountains around a rare curve between dips in the road, the patches of violet, flowers new sprung from the cracked earth, the dry wooden structures which make up the eternity, the timeless vignette of the southern life.

We pass a nomad's caravan which sits itself on the stolid plains like the impersonal figures in a Dantesques canto, the children little men at ten in their dry crusty faces, the women in rich dusty garb clustering beside a spring at one stretch of road lined with trees.

I tell a story of driving to California, of two sisters, and hear of a trip across Milwaukee in an old battered car held together by spirit and beer. Sometime I read Woolfe, discuss a quote by Boswell's Johnson, paraphrase a final paragraph.

New York-like, Herat rises above us, the mushrooming from the sentinel trees lining the road, an infinity of sameness. Dinner, a trip around the hallow-glazed mosque, a chat with an Australian sheep expert, candlelight and restless sleep. A ringing.

Sunday, May 30th

We arrived back yesterday at 7:00 p.m., having started the day in a semi-dilapidated state:

The alarm fails to go off, my internal clock haywire, and so after a night of being eaten alive by flies and mosquitoes and small crawling things which go bump in the night, I have to be awakened by the driver. I hear, as if a pair of rough hands jerking me from a dark, soft womb, the driver Sher Khan calling to James Auchincloss, our PCV host here.

"It is 25 after 4 and we'd better hurry, *malim-sibes*."

So I grab my things (Tom has more trips to take here), and with fellow volunteer Rob Linnekin dart off to the truck to be deposited before the full Qaderi bus, looming huge with its lights and mountains of bundles and baggage in the turning dawn. We crawl aboard, and as this May 30th day defines itself in heat and light, I write, read a little, meditate on the past days. I doze, oblivious to the scenery, stomach clutched and physically sick, too hot and dry and tired most of the time to let it touch me, but in moments something passes over my weak parameters and comes into focus—the variety of lined, wizened oriental or Caucasian or semitic faces and garb which surround us, the garbled voices of the brash Pushtoon speakers, a child with all the features of an American or European stock, a scarved Arab who approaches us with perfect English, the thin rivers between the miles and multitudes of burnt out land, the mountains' mirages, the constant-changing light.

I have left Tom, a tad too casually, as I have seemed to treat him during the whole trip, all too consciously. We've had no physical contact in three days, and even less mental sharing. Nursing the distance, the apartness, it is as if I choose a kind of step-childish mischief, act out my roles before his censoring with a kind of pre-destined quality, indulge with curiosity to see how far I can rock my boundaries. Yet I hate myself for hurt I might bring to Tom, but lack the control, the desire to reckon with the mishaps. He has projected an irascibleness the whole trip, obviously uncomfortable in his role of business man—for we were tagging along on his official trip to the Volunteers. While we were holidaymakers, he was all purpose, and he did not want us to forget the division of roles. And I, who genuinely want to flip wings and be light and a little silly, lovely and a little wild, chafe at his reproaches when Troy or others and I play word games together, discuss readings, tell anecdotes, all in a kind of high pitched good humor, a mocking that excludes everyone else. He has a right to not be ignored, and in all the years I have known him rarely has been. For his is a strong and vibrant personality.

But perhaps I also have a right to be myself, to not be taken for granted, to soar and laugh and socialize and—even—flirt. So tomorrow when he returns, how will we deal with each other, this man who has known my body, my soul for eight years now? Or, so we believe.

But, if I slow down, I can go back and set down the little pieces, the little details of the trip that make me happy, but that also sadden, the dichotomies. The night after dinner in Herat, the first night there, when Tom went off to hold his meeting, the Australian sheepherder specialist from the World Bank and Brenda and Troy and I sat in the vanished light—there were only candles—talking, mostly listening to the man Ian's description of his work here. He detailed its nature, the process of buying sheep and building up herds and recognizing the patterns. When I went out to get my stuff from the car, the speech turned to the subject of solitude, and as I returned I heard Troy claim he liked it that way, being alone, that he hadn't slept the night before because of all the people in the room

"Ah, yes," Ian remarked. "But, you can't live alone too long without crossing over and being forever forced to maintain your solitary style because you then no longer can know how to live with anyone else."

Perhaps more was said, but the meeting ended, everyone left. I washed and went to bed. Returning, Tom watched me, cool, questioning.

Earlier I was sitting in the window of PCV Rob Linnekin's dusty, dirty house watching Troy play guitar, as he focused on the cook's shy, beautiful four-year old daughter. The child sat at my feet, watching, and I felt dizzy from the heat, the fear.

Friday morning I got up to write, to reflect, the life-long habit that keeps me vaguely stable, I suppose. Then around 9 we all piled into the truck and set off for the sites of Herat, and a long morning of seeing Jumi's tomb and its shade trees and tied strings of promises; the old tomb and court of Sadi; tombstones and legends and mosque archways; a carved black marble coffin elaborately and mutely beautiful; the minarets, stone curling; stove pipe factory stakes on the horizon; and the shrine on the hill where a mullah blesses you and you must roll for salvation. Only Tom participated. Lunch was Pushtu kebabs in an upper room full of smoke in the town, a shaft of light from the smoky vent falling on Pat, the Nepalese PCV we'd met, and the illusions to Christ and the Last Supper extended as we partook heathen-like of the carnivore's host.

In the afternoon I surrendered to a brief nodding sleep, and then went over with Brenda and Rob, just returned from a trip to a nearby village by bike—to play at reading a dictionary, while Tom met with other Herat volunteers. Afterwards, we assembled for an ice cream-making session. For a few minutes Troy and I sat looking at Rob's pictures, American relatives, suburban middle class elements, and we laughed good-humoredly at American values versus our international ones, seeking a reckoning, commenting on faces in the group pictures, the redness of the people. Meanwhile, dear Brenda, always puzzled as to why the awesome Troy never talked to her, watched, a tad scornfully, as we well deserved.

Then with the shared ice cream, came ease-dropping and timid laughter, a mischievous duo and some guitar tuning, and a scanning of *Playboy* jokes, Troy, looking away, comments that the Hefner empire and its products are exclusively for impotent 80-year old men's vicarious thrills.

After ice cream we indulged in more useless talk: jokes about the Australian's accents, reflections on the Nepalese music by Pat (its an incantation, each raga a creation of the goddess), and Kirk's titillation, laughter from what he read in *Playboy*, and my own Tom grinning and austere in turn. Then a separation, for it was a workday for half of us: Lena and James Auchincloss set off to their house with Tom, while I joined Kirk and Brenda, Ian and Chris to visit the bazaar, for what had become a cool afternoon. We went to sit in a poshly upper class teahouse with its selection of English brews, called The Samovar. A line of us watching, the walls heavy with hangings, the musicians playing expertly but without much spirit, the couple across from us a beautiful ebony girl and a sullen boy, supping on yogurt . . . Troy spoke of decorating a New York apartment with these crafts, then decided he would too soon find them gauche. We ordered yogurt and later mint tea, and shared a skewer of Brenda's kebabs. Troy talked of an otherwise perfect cousin from Rochester who died of a weak heart at sixteen, and of her sister who had five beautiful children and just kept having children, and how—good Catholic—she wanted it that way, and how almost all of his family and relatives were "teacher sorts."

The Herat glass catches me, dusty blue at my back. Troy had carried a piece home for his sister, the previous year, but it had broken the week she got it when a knickknack shelf fell down in her house. I followed with a description of how my mother had sent me a jar of Noxema and I'd shattered it after its 14-month journey the first day I opened it. He spoke of the Bonds in Puli-Khumri and how they came to be his friends, then told how he was found with typhoid fever and brought slowly back to life among the Macdonalds . . .

[Finally, we went back to the Auchincloss's house, and from there each to his own destination.]

Then came the wearying 18-hour trip on the bus yesterday morning . . . leading to sleep like salvation last night. Back at work, I re-establish a routine.

Pam visited in the afternoon, like the angel Gabriel, wise and beautiful, balanced, rendering harmony and thought. She had come to ask the questions, and I gushed out my guilty secret, this silly schoolgirl infatuation with a brotherly PCV, the famous Troy O'Dell, to which she responded, eager to straighten me out like an aged, gentle weaver, untangling the first work of an apprentice at the loom. She spoke of her changed concept of time—how it goes anyway, of her desire to leave here and start nursing school and then go into a practitioner position four years hence in California. As to my own problem, she assessed this crush, this obsession with another in the waning days of our Afghan life, this cooling toward my own faithful husband, to be caused by my love of drama, and that Tom and I both suffered from this energy. She listened to my description . . . then gave me her own version, and concluded that the object of my interest was in fact immature, egotistical, and shallow, and that all the good that I seemed overwhelmed by there is in large part of my own creation. She noted how smug dear Troy was for someone who has supposedly had so many intense experiences.

Then she spoke of her own recognition of a need to be alone and in solitude, but also loved, and of her leaving Fung after five years, and seeing him marry an old friend. Sadly, she acknowledged that being here in Kabul generated a kind of artifice, a lifelessness, a permanent distance from the genuine, as one after another we gave in to being an expat in an unloved community, of having to battle constantly with Afghan and American bureaucracy. And, she acknowledged, she hates TEFLing.

So she left glowing, and I sat down to continue the conversation, in my head directing it now to Troy, so that I can be purged and stable by the time Tom arrives tomorrow.

I ask him (insane women face peering at the mirror, changing poses and eyes), if he hadn't always just considered me, if he considered me at all, as a kind of wild child fighting my own practical maturity—the reference to the Eloise brat-genius of the TV play/book. And—in my head—I ask him how someone who had had such rich experiences could be so oddly, at least in the face he presents to the world, untouched by them, as if it were all a pose, for a picture, a story he'll take later. I go on, explaining, how it is as if it were all to show off himself—for example the way he speaks of his meditation, his house on the hill, the Florentine lady, the minaret over Paghman, as if he were most enchanted by his involvement in it, and not really touched, moved, changed by what he saw. I thought of the time he told me how his mother couldn't recognize that his adopted cousin loved her more than anything else; nudge him to recognize why he couldn't apply all that to himself and other people. I remind him of his infinitely rational facade and how, after all, it has some thing ossified and counterfeited, too static about it.

I remind him (in this mirror to face practice dialogue) how my being "smitten" with him has been excessively time-consuming, how there has been so much more I could have done these last months but instead I have been putting all my energy into this (the university, lightening his tasks, seeking his ideas and company, allowing . . . his centrality there); until it has all resolved itself into a dew, much ado bout nothing perhaps. Then, in my ghostly, purging querying, I ask him about his friends here, Marty, Kitty and Rick Dwyer, Arnie and Kayla Bond, wondering how he could seek them out, literally waste his time with them if he was really so sincere in his devotions to higher things, since they were all rather nice but narrow young adults, with parts of them far from thoughtful or introspective.

On it goes: I ask him to justify his way of blocking out people, making some important to him one day and some another, the general fickleness in his timing (Pam said he was a child for whom all the world was just a toy to play with, since he doesn't know what he wants; Rob, skimming the surface, had told me that he didn't really regard me blindly, that he must be aware of my attraction to him). So, I stop the talk there, measuring an occasion to say it all, reflective. But not yet purged.

Brenda's brother leaves tomorrow. I'll go to the airport with him at 6:00 and recall my own and others' exits by air, past and future. And meanwhile, I go over again Pam's crystallization of many facts, a reference to how she's always read books about atrocities in which people lost their humanity, and how she had learned that it doesn't take a crash in the Andes to teach a person he is a cannibal, or a concentration camp tormentor, that daily things work to de-humanize us and that our only recourse is our own determination, our recognition of the fact that only we are responsible for our destiny, our creations.

Oh, Tom. How will we ever grown together again?

"If you do not have the heart of a lion, do not travel in the way of love."

-Dari proverb

(June 3rd came and went in here somewhere.)

Strangely spent days. I'm in the PC office waiting for Tom to come out of a meeting which started at 1:30. Yesterday his return and the falling out of grace because Brenda's principal had complained of her absences for too many days. Just generally, Agha-gul was annoyed at the prospects of Tom having taken on volunteers for the trip to Herat when none was legitimately excused from work. Of course, it was not Tom's choice to do so. Troy hasn't come back yet and his absence is also calculated it seemed. Of course the fact that PCV staff chief Wahili has just taken a week's trip to Herat with all his relatives doesn't daunt anyone, but for a volunteer. . . . yech. How sick I have grown of people; now they seem fit only to disappoint us.

Then we hear Mirad's saga of how his cousin, Ghulam who had run away from the Army for twelve years, was now being sought. Consequently, as a kind of collateral, Mirad's father and uncle were put in jail in Sare-pul until he is found, and brought up there. So Mirad has had to turn him in to the police in Kabul and in retaliation Ghulam now claims that they (Qorbin and Mirad) owe him a lot of money and that'll he'll run away to Pakistan if they don't pay him. Meanwhile, despite the "turn-in," the old fathers are being kept in jail.

Then, as if we are all opiated in some love-hungry air, Kirk shares with me a strange confidence, how he loves Fareda, an Afghan PC teacher, and has for a long time, but always discretely of course. It seems that only that afternoon she has agreed to marry him and go with him to the States. But, in truth, now he has no way to get her out, since the government, the family . . . have tight bounds, restriction, ways of imprisoning its people. And we hear of other American-Afghan romances and how they have had the potential for better luck—Gulnar can met Paul in Iran, Sajia can wait for Rick from America . . . and so it goes. How oddly unsolvable it would seem, and so we talk on until 10, thinking of solutions, laying out on route all the superficials of PC, its frustrating element, its inability to control and inspire its own.

Research papers and Junior tests are coming out of my head: I sit working until 4 today almost nonstop from 10:00, grading and grading. So is it any wonder that it is a dry brain in a dry season?

A few soft details: the cherubic baby with button eyes on the bus in front of me yesterday, who stared until his eyes were stars at some unfocused fascinating thing, while her sister smiled at me shyly, posed to receive the ticket for the one *af* ride.

And yesterday at the airport where I had gone to accompany Ben Hedges, the faces, the styles of those departing, the hard calloused French tourists, who never looked back, the young son with all his female relatives in tears around me and waving, the wild American contingency—wide cowboy hats and clinging children and southern drawls. And the inspiration, the sad pause as a plane landed, another took off, so that watching I had to cry to remark somehow in a non-verbal way on this realm so close to us and so fragile: that heavy bird coming out of the mountains, going into it, and we people standing below, watching it all like a movie or a visual prayer.

June 4, 1976

Today my brother Dan begins his 21st year around the sun . . . Alas, the strange parallels of youth and age. We gather and take the realm into ourselves again, and also continue a conversation three days long with the late inhabitants of a provincial site, Puli-Khumri, and their realm of reflections. One principal at the girl's school on a trip to Beirut in the name of some sort of international conference, got a diagnosis for Valium for her nerves, and now—an Afghan pharmacist loves her—she takes her medicine, and claims to have "eaten William." In a house which could certainly rival a creation out of Jane Eyre's Gothic English Moors, she lives with her insane mother and sad little sister, the father having been thrown out years ago. There is some discontent: one time the mother made a chicken for the neighbors next door and fed it to them, without ever cleaning out the old bird.

There are also stories of the irresolvable ingratitude of Kabulis (PCVs who fail to grasp the need for a love and tolerance in this country, who are content to ape American values and then complain about the hard price of living.)

Taciturnity

[Dinner parties, dinners out, concerts by Arnie Bond and Troy, guests at our house all the time and spending time out with them, reunions, and closed shops on Friday, pizza at Salims', which equal, more distancing from Tom . . . .

One joy: riding home on the bike at 10:00 p.m., I find the whole city, the tired, walled neighborhoods full of mystery, and going by three figures in the dark, I imagine one of them a kind of mythic mold, all the time himself unknowing . . . .

June 10, 1976

Good speeches by the Juniors at the university . . . They do make profound progress. This program works.

[Guests come and go, and work goes on well. I reach a resolution with Tom: he feels that we can not coexist, that we diminish each other. I suffocate and rebel under his sadness and anger and sense of pending violence; I feel that he can not provide for me what I am seeking . . . . On and on, and I seem still stubbornly in pursuit of some time with the silly Troy, despite all I know and all I realistically want. There are conversations and movies and missed contemplation . . . . I have given in entirely to the expatriate's life, perhaps, not one that makes me proud, one that keeps me too my idle.]

June 11, 1976

. . . The chameleon on our window stands static, stoical, misunderstood, the silent watcher on the metal screen to all our goings and comings. And the moon grows full.

It is a rare pleasure, to sit and collect other people's stories, the histories and anecdotes of their lives . . . .

Tom shares again his experience at a Kabul wedding (he came home at 2:30 a.m., reeking of cigarettes and sweat). It was a cold, noisy affair, stilted and boring, with food eaten upstairs in a room where everyone had to stand. The dancing by the men and women was entertaining to a small extent, and a famous mime called Johnny Walker performed sexual mimes and acrobats to stimulate them all. Speaking of weddings, I recall Troy's tale of one in Kamard where a drama was performed: an old man and a young boy dressed up and stalked other attendees. Likewise, I think of Arnie and Kayla Bonds' experience at a wedding where a man without instruments—in mime—played each in time for hours, putting in his version of their sound as he piped, played flute, *rebab, tabla,* etc. I visualize again the three cronies-hags at the first Tashkurghan wedding we had attended, and their washboard tunes and old dry bodies, performing. Tom speaks of seeing Jhat women perform in Herat one time, at a party at the Australian's house, and how they were provocative in their movements, collecting money for their special turns, and propositioning as they left. In fact, one aggressively invited a foreigner to come to her house and see her other instruments.

[At the bazaar, we purchase cloth for the Kandahar embroidered shirt faces, and gather stares, Still . . . Unless we are personally known, we are forever the odd *haragees,* objects of disdain and penetrating inspection.]

Kerry and I discuss our combination of anxiety and eagerness, as we approach time to return to the States, and to be out of this female-repressive society

> *[And so it continues, as well it might our entire lives: musing on the relationship, how to repair, how to rationalize it all as aggravated by my being in Kabul. which is such an artificial world for an outsider, so that it made me invest more in Troy or others than was normal, since I did not want to be alone. Or, perhaps, after the confinement I just need to be more independent. But I never wanted, in doing so, to lose or hurt Tom . . . .*

June 18, 1976

> [We attend a good-bye party by Tom Jefferson at the U.S. Embassy, and take in an evening concert at the British Embassy in full splendor]

Work dominates. We have Dave Dunn's departure from the department and Fred Cozzen's advent, and a new tension in the office, beyond the usual confusion of classes and ambitions, myself physically and mentally drained, by the whole prospect of the waste of time and energy I've put into running that place and relating to its people (American people, not the students). And now it is all finished.

[As quickly as my self-imposed infatuation started, it ends. Now, I am just distant strangers with Troy. I temper a quarrel with Tom Lords and wife, whose puppy we've kept for 10 days,] I recognize I am just a too punctilious women who has occasional disjointed flights of fancy, neither a friend nor an enemy, as he loves to apportion out the world in his pseudo-Buddhist teleology. I can only look back at this whole one-sided relationship or parley with him as a rather perverse and ill-timed use of my last semester here: the fact is that I was always giving so much thought, creative and otherwise to how to relate to him, and in the process sadly ignored Tom, put him at a possibly irreparable distance, and did almost nothing, nothing, of the other work I had established for myself, the completion of "the mss," the additional writing, the parsing of a plan for the future. What moved me to try to put so much faith, so many confidences into hum, who really is stuck sadly upon himself, and seems a complete opportunist, grabbing a person's attention only in so far as that attention can further his cause, his getting insurance forms filled out, or mailed, or a recommendation form furthered or typing practice utilized, or a free meal donated, or an ego boost in a listened-to-conversation, or—But I can't criticize him because he never pretended to be other than he was, whereas I should be cajoled and scolded for projecting my own mind. So be it then. Finit.

And Tom's new suits arrive. They stylize him from ambassadorial to sporty professor to wealthy consumer, and the craftsmanship is first-rate, as are the fabrics and colors . . . .

June 25, 1976

We just realize this is the third anniversary of our departure for Afghanistan and that our wedding anniversary (number four) passed us by last Friday, unremarked. Will it be that way every year?—[And Kayla and Arnie Bond, Dave and Kay Dunn, Bethany Carroll, are all off . . . People have moved on, departed now, and it is the end of our stay, too.]

At the Faculty, I oversee the administration of final exams, with the Dean immobilized with broken legs (and I will visit him tomorrow)

[I attend a birthday celebration for friend Troy, who'd spent his 23rd in a Greek prison, his 24th near death with paratyphoid, his 25th in Kamard unhailed, and his 26th, this one.

[Visitors are in from the provinces and are always less vitriolic then those in Kabul . . .]

. . . Yesterday we participated in a conference (enclave or conclave) at Paghman to discuss the future and present of PC. On the beautiful estates of the Aimaq family, we sat restless, conversation was bogged down within particulars, repetitious particulars. Then, for dinner that night, we heard Margaret Mills and her stories . . . .

The story: The beginning is something about a king who had seven wives. The *peri*-queen, one of them, took the eyes out of the others, and the wives were forced to all live in a cave, but none of them had children until Khajii Khez (the fourth presence whenever three people are together, the third when two are there), gave them instructions on how to get pregnant. They all do at the same time and one gives birth to a son who is a great strong boy and grows up to be the hero of the story. This latter throws rocks a lot to bring food for his mother and the other wives, until one day he kills the king's herald hawk and the king calls for him (not aware that this is his son) and puts him to work And meanwhile the *peri*-queen, who has figured out his identity, dislikes him intensely, of course, and sets up a series of trials he must go through so that she can get rid of him.

The first is to go get *"sheer-e-shear, in pashee shear, pashe te sheer"* (lion's milk on a lion's skin, on a lion's back.) Khajii-Khez helps him, tells him the secret way to get there (to the kingdom at the back of the world), and actually gives him a magic walking staff to carry him there. Of course the garden of the lions is owned by a beautiful girl, whom the boy must court. He is told to go to her veranda on Friday when she is combing her hair and when the woman calls three times, "I'm burning" because he pulls her hair, then "Everything will be all right. All is done" he is to take action.

He goes, she calls fire, then turns around and falls in love with him. Smitten, she tells him secrets, such as how to kill the white *devi* who loves her and is a danger to the boy (on the second trial). The trip to get the lion goes fine, the task to kill the threatening *devi* is aided by the girl, who will eventually marry the boy. The white *devi* himself tells how he can be killed—by going to a certain field where a bull roams and making him stand still and cutting him open and taking out a cage of birds and killing a sparrow wherein rises the soul of the white (and while the white *devi* is telling this story, the bewitched boy, tuned into a needle in the girl's lapel, listens.)

Some place in here, there is a hunt, an old man who kidnaps the beautiful girl in his flying pot, who all the time is stirring the pot himself. And there is a hunt to find them and many magic birds of Khajii Khez help chase them. But, only one helps the boy and finds them and then the bird becomes the boy and latter a sparrow and another bird which is killed because they are the souls of the *peri*-queen and her mother (who has all the wives' eyes). Finally, all is returned to order, and so it ends . . .

. . . At the end of the evening, attendees move by alkaline lanterns down the mountain . . . the hills around us vibrate with the twinkling lights, as we try to imagine the views before electricity came to Jamal Mina. Silently, the hills and the parables resound. This is a world defined by the wall and the door . . .

And in the afternoon at Paghman, when the meeting is raging in its vapidness, I wander away and stand on a terrace and look down to see old Baba Pieda in prayer, his silhouette among the late afternoon shadows, also mounting words, but his silver head somehow in a better time. a better meaning to his methodical prayers (and the inevitable sense of humility, of those who must touch the ground.)

Today, I go shopping, for Kandahari shirts, dress fronts, and Russian peasant dress materials, and a silk wall hanging for the Uncle Al collection . . . Coyly in the morning while I am working in the Peace Corps library, all our books returned, as well as those of others, old Baba Haji comes in with flowers behind his back and tells me how sad he is that we were leaving,.

"Please take these flowers and when you go back to the States and your family, you should remember how one day the old baba brought you flowers and told you how there were no other people like you and Tom." He goes on to describe his two daughters, how one is at the university now, how they are good and smart like me, and how he hoped they did as well as I did.

Tears well at remembering such a beautiful gesture.

We are then to try to leave at the end of the week. How strange it will be . . .

> *[Letters from the Mareks. It appears his Harvard researcher doctor/mother has gone senile, after being hit by a bus while crossing the road . . .]*

The yard is redolent, verdant virgin green with forming grapes, nubile and youthful, the arbors heavy with the fruit. And hollyhock bushes in five or more hues bristle proud-headed in their regalia. Evening here lifts us, so fresh and green, and the people stroll beyond our walls, their adventures emerging . . .

June 30, 1976

My last hour, my last class, passed today. The last grade calculated, the last time sitting at my desk in the office, the finish of this community, of that lifestyle. Some students, an envoy, come to thank me. I was touched, numb, distant, not able to properly muster all their names or faces, conscious suddenly of having nothing more to say to all their polite enthusiasm. The day before I'd told my Freshmen good-bye, and now have done the same for my Sophomores.

One afternoon . . . I trooped across the hazy late afternoon campus to the hospital to visit the Dean in his double cast, joyful and jesting enough on his back, nodding at us politely from the iron hospital bed and telling us how he is reading lots of English magazines. Sharing a ward with him lays an old man whose friends and visitors are all turbaned and baggy-panted. In the doorway I pause to look at wilted flowers, think back on the conversation on the way over . . . .

All afternoon and morning Tom and I had looked at prayer rugs and lapis, and finally gotten something, letting go of our money all too easily, forgetting to dream in the context of the articles, matter-of-factly measuring the dimensions. The corridors of the hospital echo with memories of the remnants of paste jars from elementary schools, antiseptic . . . The university cafeteria, a shoddy structure with draped burlap ceilings like heavy gossamer in some raised rathskeller or catacomb, calls us for tea . . .

> [Tom and I and departure, like a third between us, are reconciled. We listen to the plans of other PCVs. We decide that Language is a kind of means of dividing up realities . . . .]

July 2, 1976

> [Farewells, talks, deserts: we are to leave.]

. . . Then it was Wednesday. All morning we are at the bank buying traveler's checks, the strange phenomenon of a national bank with Afghan currency supply depleted and people having to fight for their right to get money, the sign "Cashier Closed" a solid wall of defiance. Still some fought on: a Turkish UN expert, and a Swede, both got what they wanted. A dizzily well-dressed American business women (Easter chic) got hers, a student with an engineering student got his.

Then, I bus over to the university for my really last day, meeting the Sophomores and giving explanations for Charley—my replacement—as a few hurried words . . . In the morning I take over the grades and slide them under the office door, and tack up a note, then run into Yousef, the old science emir from Samagan, energetic and petite and polite, Jerry Kissinger's old counterpart. Outside, looking up to the house on the hill, to the early morning motions of the city, the rivers and the mountains unfolding, time is again long and silent. But, a hurried morning follows, in contrast, as we move all our possessions out, or into Mirad's room, as he will take them.

In the evening we have a dinner at Mirad's, at the compound in Kalow-Fatellah, along with his old uncle, round faced and kind, Qorbin with a wall of calendar pictures and women, the sly-tongued Hossain and his wife, a son of an old man, another uncle or in-law from Sare-pul whose father we had gone to Mazar with once, but who is now dead. After a rich meal, meat and cherry sauce and *kabuli* and *burani* and potato *korma*, and fruit in the rich hues of harvest, purple grapes, ruby plums, yellow apricots, tea and cookies, we all sit and talk: Of the tram line being built in Kabul and the funny things with Afghan currency and dollars at the bank, of the relative value of other currencies. Qorbin's wife's mother and Mirad's mother, great Turkomen-Hazara, Mongol-carved faces, sit like sleepy owls, nodding at it all, until it is 10:30 and—all visibly tired—we thanks our hosts and take our departure.

Today then, we rest in our house which is no longer our house, with most all our stuff gone to Mirad (including a few mistakes, such as my pink nightgown). In this house he has dimmed with curtains on every window, we feel a spartan emptiness with mounted wooden candle holders without candles, and stiff *charpor* chairs and only setting for four for food stuff. I had woken at five, full of the thoughts of the last days, and a deep longing . . .

[Some volunteer, hearing of our future plan, warns me: it will be hell ahead for you both with him in law school and you trying to support you both . . .]

The itinerary: we will fly out of Kabul with Ariana on Tuesday to Amritsar with a connection to Calcutta, and then use a duet of days there to secure a visa for Burma. Then we'll fly to Rangoon, from which base we will go outside the city to explore some corners of this secret land for a week, before we go on to Bangkok. From there, we have a commitment to go to LA via Asia (Taiwan, Hong Kong, Japan). It costs more money to fly to Calcutta but hopefully we can make all the connections and save a few more days to make the trip worth the extra $100 per ticket.

Shots then in the afternoon. I am immersed in the weird sensations of fainting dead away, come to again to find the new nurse looking at me, who has gone through a whole lifetime before consciousness, struggling to place myself back in this world.

Together, Tom and I try some word puzzles, but I crave an engaging book.

July 7, 1976

[Calcutta, India]

We sit beneath the whirling draft of an old ceiling fan while another shoots back our own moisture at us from the air, in an old British mansion turned hotel called the Fairlawn in Calcutta.

The frayed hot motions of getting here are now behind us, as we sit in this moment of damp sultry suspension (our verisimilitudes of comfort dangling back in a cool grape arbor in Kabul).

It was a strange departure, jelled as it was first on Monday, then the day spent in diminishing our list of things to do before we could actually leave—the clearing out of our last particles and articles of self from the house, starting about 6:30 with the piles of *toshaks* and give-away clothes, bundling what we intended to take with us, making a joke of Tom's suitcase which is an extra 15 kilo of three year-old used clothes bazaar shoes, and diarrhea medications, and the last of the books we had failed to ship among our 190 kilos.

In the PC office at 8:30 we finished our list of things to be signed, milking poor Bhasin for our financial clearance and getting rewarded with the announcement that, "No, I can't be all that glad to be finished with you, since after all others will come in your place!" A chat with Kit A. and Scot M., who are still trying to solidify their plans for cross-culture for the new training cycle, but who are continually diverted by their female colleague's nonchalance, her retreat to the bath or bed conveniently at all the times they call for confirmation.

Finally we set off to check money, find that we must first count it all, at which point Tom goes back to PC to see if he can have his language test, after which Tom and I stop at the money bazaar to convert all of our *afs* to dollars and then some. Taxi-deposited at the mouth of the *saroy* of moneychangers, a veritable warehouse for mercenaries, we enact our business with "Khalil and Brothers" in the office full of speculators clutching briefcases of script. We make our last sortie to the used clothes bazaar behind the post office and offer a careful hour of searching and bargaining, then walk away with the price of a finely-cut light sports coat. We catch a cab then to PC where we explain that we can't actually go to lunch yet after all . . . Mirad is awaited; he is to come to the house and take away the last of the things . . .

[After all we stop at the Italian restaurant for lunch, talk of Jung and images and normal life . . .] return to the PC office to get an incident-less inoculation against cholera . . . to post letters to Shukor and Baba and Mrs. Azur . . . to find we can not get a language test because Agha-gul and Jawid are out of time. Tom reminds me of the need to make certain purchases on the bazaar—[PC staff contributes, gallantly; the PC truck is to move us from house to one-night lodgings to the airport.]. Then, it's off to the German department store—Hamizadah—for socks.

I speak with Tom K. who will be at Engineering, filling him in dutifully on the curriculum and needs, and take a letter from him to be delivered to a priest in Bangkok who had married him and his wife several years before and was to help them adopt a Thai child . . . . [Then, it is all good byes, thoughts on leaving. And on staying too long . . .]

Tom is called to a meeting, interrupted and ended only by the somber arrival of Azarullah and a friend from Tashkurghan, who sit like tearless, voiceless statues of frozen thoughtful sorrow for about an hour, speechless, and then leave. Sitting with them the sadness surrounded me, confirming as it must inevitably that this was a final meeting, a final farewell, that this boy who had been so much more than an Afghan friend was now on his own, as were we, that PC was more than just an organization we now left—that both these people and this country—were about to be extracted from our lives.

[Ironically, in the last hours in the country, we were introduced to one final gossip trail: Someone insists on telling us about all the gay single volunteers here . . . .]

. . . Yesterday morning, then, we got up and had . . . breakfast, then set off to PC to shake hands in a round of good byes with everyone from Bashir and Nalang and Hagi to the gardener and Rahim . . . With Sher-Khan at the wheel, we set off to the airport . . . where we stood ghastly quiet after we checked in. Agha-gul came around, with a lot of salutations, and there were the perfunctory greetings from him for other Afghan officials. He pointed out the Minister of Culture to us, a gynecologist, short and stiff looking. Soon enough we realized we must take our final leaves and move into the waiting room. Hugs again . . . handshakes . . . and at Agha-gul's turn we get an unexpected Afghan trio of kisses on the cheek. A salute and then we were off, clear and quick through customs. A loquacious heavy Canadian, just behind us and waiting for the same flight, came to talk off our ears with her itinerary of travels and moralizing notion of what PC must be all about (we gritted our teeth and walked away at the phrase "converting the non-whites"). But we were finally relieved by the announcement to board, looked back and found that our friends hadn't stayed to wave after all, sat down on the last patch of Kabul soil—and took off, born upward.

The pilot gave us a complete tour of the valley as we soared above its jagged and whittled off peaks, before we moved away. When the plane took off the impact of the years in this land, ended now, finally fully, overwhelmed us. Through tears, a flood of memories we watched the familiar sites below us—Jamal Mina, the university, Bazhe Bala, and the old King's tomb, our own Share-nau house to one corner, the sad harsh land so vulnerable below us, reduced now to a level of dry, direful mirthless simpleness and sorrow. They have so little, for so many centuries, generations, have subsisted hugging the drops of seasonal water that creates the few patches of green, that allows the hard mud houses to adhere to the ground. We dreamed, somber, across Jalalabad, all of Pakistan.

Then, as we came down in Amritsar, Ariana Airlines earned its ludicrous name for itself by skimming a crack a few seconds off the ground, the huge jet veered sharply to one side almost to the left, straightened briefly, then like a tipsy cap tipped sharply to the right, again. As we all sighed, it smoothed, leveled. Indignant but grateful now, we saw the great plane put down on gripping pavement . . . In India.

So there is now, the rest of our lives, as we look back and realize the smallness of our discomforts and the hugeness of our youth, as I recognize with each passing month how a kind of tension under-girded my life with a husband in Afghanistan, from day one, coming as I did from an all-women's college in the late 60's, early 70's, being married only a year before we set off, finding myself backseat to many discussions. And, realizing how both of us had been somewhat untested with others, myself having dated through college and my year of graduate school, but my partner having never known any other girlfriend, or that social ease.

I was 24 when we arrived, Tom turned 24 that fall. We were young, and while adamant about not being "typical Americans," we sought out the familiar when the unfamiliar became too much, enjoyed the camaraderie of our fellow PCVs, relished the streams of visitors from all over the world who appeared on our doorsteps, summoned from their wanderings or a bazaar passing, to meet us, the fellow haragees, the American malims, especially during the two years in Tashkurghan, less special, less integrated during the final term in Kabul's international milieu.

I knew from the beginning I was escaping as well the sadly disturbed family I had grown up with, in many ways, the brothers who suffered manic depression—solid a moment with a new start in life, then off the deep end again,—a sister likewise ill and unstable, her problems complicated by the horde of children she bore, an elderly father old enough to be a grandfather, a mother who took it all onto herself to resolve . . . a younger brother who had more wits and talents than any of us and yet who seemed to be wandering the globe (he caught up with us), not getting on with his college education, etc. etc.

And perhaps Tom was also distancing himself from his family. Or, perhaps this husband had embarked on this most atypical experience because he wanted to please me and my adventurous, unbridled self. Will I ever know?

We are changed. Forever. And Afghanistan . . . .

> *The true lover never seeks union.*
> *His companion is separation and his friend imagination.*
> *"Layla and Majnun" by Firzuli*

Kabul Revisited: January 14-20, 2008
Violence Returns

Never, never and never again shall it be that this beautiful land will again experience the oppression of one by another.
—Nelson Mandela

Kabul had become a city where foreigners valued their regular or occasional perk in the gym or coffee shop of the Serena Hotel, this high end luxury establishment, like an out-of body experience in the normal grit and hassle of navigating Kabul Streets, and when the hotel was bombed any who reflected would haver realized that its marble-walled corridors, and fancy European layout and furnishings acted like a poke in the eye to average Afghans, and particularly the Islamic fundamentalist insurgents always hovering ready to strike by then. This was an attack on what everyone who resented the foreign community and their "development projects" considered most opulent. To these insurgents, in a city of over 2 million whose government and crowds of international experts and entrepreneurs could not even provide water to its residents, a "serene" and elegant haunt that smacked of money and western values such as this hotel, screamed to be targeted and made an example of.

Three months before in Baglan, on a bright, breezy November day, hundreds of children had gathered at the gate of the new sugar factory. They came to sing and present flowers to Parliamentarians arriving for the factory's dedication. Suddenly a suicide attacker detonated a bomb, and in the carnage that resulted, 65 young boys and girls from the neighboring school lay like bloody and broken vessels among the dead, and another 115 suffered injuries.

This was the winter when, in parts of Afghanistan, bowing under one of the worst winters in 30 years, temperatures plummeted to 25 degrees in January and February, and both the homeless in Kabul and those in isolated pockets in the provinces needed desperate basic humanitarian assistance to survive. Like a scythe, the harsh weather sliced through the most vulnerable—children, the elderly, the internally displaced—as the icy winds howled out of Tajikistan. The dark clouds pushed across the milky gray sky and dropped heavy snow, froze rivers, and blocked roads. Frigid temperatures and ice killed livestock and closed down villagers' access to food supplies, fuel and transportation in areas where shortages had been growing for months. In the cities like Kabul and Herat, they shut-down always vulnerable electricity grids.

International teams slipped and shivered over ice-blocked roads to reach some of the camps for the newly-returned refugees. In the snowy field, faces and bundled forms materialized from shabby tents and bare adobe huts which spread across the area. Hand over fist, they lined up to receive shoes, warm clothes, blankets, coal and other winter supplies. Here were the far-flung residue of all parts of what had been an Afghan nation, a huge group of women and the elderly, Tajiks and Hazaras, who had fled the drought in Badakshan; families of ethnic Pashtuns from Pakistan; Kutchi nomads who had no fodder for their livestock and no defense for themselves against the ruthless cold. Here, as in places like Charai Qombar outside Kabul, and throughout the country, thousands continued to flee regional tensions, as well as stricter policies by Iran and Pakistan which had closed down border refugee camps and detained and deported Afghan laborers.

In the areas of highest risk, poor security, impenetrable blocked roads and rough terrain, thwarted efforts by the World Food Organization, the Afghan Red Crescent and other Afghan and foreign organizations, NATO-led Provincial Reconstruction Teams, and local residents to bring assistance. To even clearly assess the extend of these cold and hungry villagers was impossible. Further, with up to an 80% increase in recent months in the price of staples such as wheat flour, in the face of decreased exports by Iran and Pakistan, widespread hunger again haunted many Afghans. Yet, as a local relief group explained, just 70 cents was enough to help a vulnerable family through a day, while $56 could support a family through three winter months.

All across the country in January and February, as people bundled up in donated blankets and coats and huddled around smoky stoves in their mud-walled houses or in temporary shelters outside cities, the death toll rose. According to the Afghan National Disasters Management Authority and UNOHA, there were over 500 reported weather-related deaths by the end of January, and daily tens of thousands of victims of exposure, hunger and lack of medical supplies waited for relief in the hardest hit areas—the northern, western and central western provinces of Herat, Badghis, Ghor and Farah. Trapped in the bitter cold, thousands of families in Masklakh, Shardai, and Minaret IDP camps (internally displaced person camps) and settlements around Herat subsisted on daily rations and distributions of blankets, mats, heaters, and personal hygiene items. Thousands of others in camps in Helmand and Kandahar, where the fear of terrorist attacks prevented deliveries from U.N. agencies and other NGOs, faced little chance of relief.

In the newest parts of reconstructed Kabul, traffic congestion reigned, cars and every manner of human, animal and cart inched past shiny new buildings edging the roadslip of central Kabul, past the crossing of Asmaye and Salang Wat Road near the striped rectangular Ministry of Education building, where a huge billboard advertised the latest Hindi movie from its perch above the curving Plaza Hotel and its rows of shops. The tall, all-glass face of the Marshal Business Center, one of Kabul's modern enclosed malls looked out like a mirror or a mirage, its smooth surface throwing back the scattered towers and roofs of the rising center city, the incongruous City Tower sitting in midtown like some misplaced airport tower; the octagonal former guardhouse of Shahrara Tower, with its floors of closed archways and decorative rims; and the distant smudge of the old government building at Pul-i-Baghe-Omumi with its attached high rise wing, one of the highest buildings in Kabul.

From most of the city one could look out to an expanse of mud and mortar, of rubble and high rises, of stiff and shining glass and steel offices and stores and lopsided leaning adobe and bamboo shacks and shops. Beyond the center of Kabul lay the U.S. Embassy, a fortified compound whose protective fences, barricades and checkpoints spread across the area of Wazir Akbar Khan. Would it be long before all of the liveliness of Kabul, its very heart had to be choked in barrack-style armaments? Would a mini-Belfast, or small Beirut or a Baghdad Green Zone evolve here, with Wazir Akbar Khan and the neighboring areas which now housed most government ministries, the offices of the UN, most embassies, and the old palace be closed off in some kind of protected zone?

Meanwhile, the stories of Taliban strongholds in the Pakistani territories, and bulletins about horrific suicide bombings and roadside explosions on both sides of the border, continued to dominate the headlines. Again, it became apparent, that the even greater strength of the insurgents lies in the ability—once again—of their Islamic clerics and armed soldiers to swiflty enforce the only order in town, negotiate property disputes, recruit young and disillusioned youth to be their ground forces, and in essence run a shadow government. To gain such a foundation in the country, systematically, the Taliban have gone through four stages, since 2002. Most went underground, fled to Pakistan, or simply, pragmatically, changed alliances. As their leaders began to return to the south and also make inroads in the north starting in 2005, they moved easily into the power vacuum and struggles, and inflamed resentment of corrupt local officials and of the "Christian invaders" among largely illiterate and poor peasants. By the end of 2007, they were in a position again to actively recruit—not just unemployed, angry local Afghan youth—but also an over-layer of groups from nearby provinces, the south, and overseas.

Also, with the rising number of civilian deaths in Afghanistan, with an estimated 698 civilians dead between January and the end of June in 2008, for example, (UN data), the Taliban had had more than enough fuel to challenge attentive Afghans to vilify the U.S and NATO forces and hold them responsible. If there was ever any doubt, the Afghans have for the most part, since the initial desperate and confused welcoming in 2001-2002, hated the idea of foreign forces operating on their soil. Low numbers of NATO troops on the ground, in impassable and unforgiving terrain that had flung off invaders for thousands of year, continued to make airstrikes the main strategy of defense.

And the mistakes multiplied. As the security situation in Afghanistan and Iraq daily deteriorated, and more and more Afghans struggled to survive, one had to wonder how many schools, teachers, doctors, books, roads, houses, and jobs might have been created and sustained in these fragile lands by the $1.6 trillion the U.S is estimated to have spent between 2002 and 2008 to sustain the Iraq and Afghan wars (Congress' Joint Economic Committee, October 2007). This translates into a cost of $20,900 for a family of four. How many thousands of Afghan families might that have sustained?

As Edward Giradet explained in his 2011 book, looking at the situation a few years later *(Killing the Cranes,* 2009), the United States spends approximately $100 million dollars a day for recovery efforts in Afghanistan, but shows few results. By mid 2011, 2500 U.S., British, French, German, Italian, Canadian, and other nationals were dead, 18,000 Afghan soldiers had lost their lives, and 40,000 soldiers were wounded from IEDs. One remembers over and over the British-Afghan Wars. In January 1842, for example, 4500 British soldiers and 1200 camp followers were killed in Jagdelak between Jalalabad and Kabul, trapped in an exit route in which the Kabul River meandered on one side, and high steep cliffs closed off escape and provided enemy fire, on the other.

Giradet goes on to explain, how by 2001, when the U.S. invaded, the drug traffic industry equaled $3 billion annually. However, by 2010, it was making $194 billion annually, a sum which equals the G.N.P. of Iran and Finland. Finally, illegal trade in falcons and birds of prey by wealthy Arab princes and hunters represented another lucrative business.

In June 2008, barely on anyone's radar, a first-ever comprehensive Afghan national development plan had been developed and presented. Priced at $50 billion, it detailed the necessary steps and strategy to rebuild the nation, and was presented at a donors' conference in Paris. Mahmoud Saikal, a senior adviser on the Afghan government's new strategy claimed the plan could "pull Afghanistan out of poverty by 2020 and "provide a road map for everything from electricity to railways to social justice." In fact, international donors led by the United States pledged more than $21 billion "to help the country develop infrastructure and institutions and combat drugs, poverty and violence." (*Washington Post.* June 13, 2008; Page A11). These pledges came in addition to the $25 billion that had been pledged by international donors to Afghanistan since 2002. Only $15 billion of those earlier pledges, however, had been delivered because of ongoing issues of mismanagement, incompetence and highly visible corruption among some Afghan government players and their partners, and a deteriorating security situation.

The scenario, more common daily, evolves:

Sirens go off and a convoy of Humvees, the young soldiers staring out from the rear in their padded uniforms and goggles like creatures in some lost lagoon horror show, passes by. It is a possible bombing, a block away. But the only sound is the sirens piercing the hot, muggy air like something sour and sharp. Traffic shirts, swerves around, the soldiers, moves to the edge of the maelstrom of mule-pulled carts, bicycles, yellow cabs, swerving pedestrians, and thundering overloaded and smoking trucks.

Each driver honks, as much as brakes, as he moves, inch by inch, forward.

Glossary of People and Organizations

While names have been changed and places and actions have been sifted though the fine net of memories and years, the actions and people in this book are all real.

July 1973:

T (Tom): my husband
Peace Corps/Afghanistan—Kabul
Tim Macdonald, TEFL Coordinator
Dr. Jenkins, first PC doctor
Yasir Maiwand, Peace Corps staff
Chad and Wanda N., PCVs in Gardez
Jahandar, the N's cook
Jake, PCV in Gardez
Spogmia, teacher at Wanda's school in Gardez
Gulmamadudi, Pushtoon teacher in Gardez
Mr. Van Hollen, Dutch UN specialist Gardez DMA teacher's college
PCV from Kabul collecting samples of turtles, moths, and lizards for the
Stephen and Ava Mansard, PCVs and training language partners
Smithsonian, in Gardez area.
Wasim, Dari language teacher
Dr. Sahar, PC Director of Cultural Orientation and Language
Daud, uncle of King Nadir Shah, new President following coup in July 1973
Fareiba, TEFL staff
James Gainer, PC Director
Ambassador Newton, U.S Ambassador to Afghanistan

Hussain Ali, PC coordinator of transport ion and logistics
Mark Havel, Afghan expert, previous PCV in Afghanistan
Leila Doorani, Farsi teacher
Maury Heligman, Khanabad PC teacher
Gulnar, a PC staff language teacher
Sajadi, PC staff driver
Devon, PC volunteer, Baglan
Norwegian Norm, a doctor working for the UN
Nourshin, PC staff language teacher
Fariad, PC staff provincial coordinator
Fariad's Swiss wife
Modir-e-mareft (Samangan)
Commandant in Khulm
Under-governor in Khulm
Russian brother-in-law of Under-Governor
Baba at Khulm Hotel
Modir at Boy's Schoolboys
First Modir at Lycee Mahasty: Faroodullah
Saer-malim: Fakir Abdul
M'med Ali Jan, Pushtu teacher at Lycee
Pierre and Michell Michaud, anthropologists
Landlord, Iotallah
Armoe M'med, initial cook in Tashkurghan and long-time supplicant
Jerry and Sara Kissinger, PCVs in Samagan
Tanettas, PCVs in Kabul who had served in the Phillipines
Syfora, student in 9th class
Tajenisa, student in 10th class
Zahra, student in 11th class
Trent and Candy Hatfield, PCVs in Mazar-i-Sharif
Janice Brown and Prissy Halliday, PCVs in Mazar-i-Sharif
Sayed Shah, temporary cook in Tashkurghan (he lasts a week)
Ghulam Azer, PC cook in Kabul
Shahzadah, town tax collector's daughter
Azarullah, Tom's student who visits faithfully
Shogul, Gulsom, Soliha, Zahras, Falora: 11th class students
Zeagul, student in class 8
Ruhna, student in 9th class
Tiara, first bride, 12th class

Modir Rashidi/ Rashidullah (Balkhi)
Modir's wife, Muzdah
Modir's sister-in-law Zudrah
Jamila, a teacher
Hamia, a teacher
Rozia, 9th class
Maury M., PC Volunteer, nurse
Bethany Carrol, PCV
Denise Blake, PCV in Kapisa who drowned in June 1975
Lena and James Auchincloss, PCVs in Herat
Mike P., PCV in Bamiyan
Ghazni-jan, PC coordinator for southern provinces
Mrs. Azur, professor at Kabul U. Faculty of Engineering
Mr. Shukor, English teacher in Faculty of Engineering at Kabul U.
Billy Young, Barb Shelton, PCVs in Kabul
Hossain, cook for Jason McCabe
Jason McCabe, PCV

September 1974

Aman, cook in Tashkurghan who did not watch house during summer 1974
Zeagul and Tajenisa, students in 11th grade (2nd year)
Najiba, new teacher at Lycee
Foolaria, student in 12th class, whose father dies
Mogul, 12th class (graduated 1973)
Fazuna bride at wedding, September 1974)
Wahidullah, Mary: PCV staff dismissed by Howard
Fazuddah (also Fouzia) student in 12th class, married 1974
Mirad, cook to the end
Zeebee, his wife,
Mohammed Ali, his infant son
Habibullah, his 2-year old son
Najibullah, his 10-year old brother
Ziadeen, Farsi teacher from Kabul at Lycee Mahasti, who tutors us
Parwin, teacher at Lycee
Sherafad,student in grade 8

Jawid, Afghan PC Co-Director
Ruhara, class 9, married and in Russia
Rhusamarah, Mirzad Daud's daughter
Morad M'med Daud, new landlord
Marguerite and Rob Rawls, PCVs terminated in Aybak Province after domestic quarrel
Teddy Roberts, PCV, banker and later diplomat
Alyson Kennedy, PCV in Mazar
Hossain (cook for Alyson)

Pendarullah, rich man in Khulm, married to one of old landlord's (Haji-sibe) daughters
Bashir, son of Pendarullah, one of T's best students
Others of Haji-sibe's family: Assadullah plus five others, by two wives
Pat Gruner, PCV in Lashkargar, in agriculture
Patrick and Shelly West, PCVs in Grishk
Teacher from Hajie Boran (a communist)
Arthur and Yvonne Alpert, PC staff (assistant director, and his writer wife)
Rashid Parwani, PC staff
Patricia and Jacob Grant, PCVs in Kandahar
Anifa, student in class 8
Brenda and Chris Mahoney, PCVs, replace us in Tashkurghan in Sept. 1975
Mr. Rahbudeen, teacher at Lycee
Fakir Khan, teacher, Lycee
Gwen and Jack, PCV's (briefly)
Paregul, Sohliha, Zahara, Shegul, Gulsom, Monira, Katzah, Kamila, Foolaria, Rabia, Mumlekat, Suraya: 12th graders now
Esfandyar, 1st grade teacher at Lycee
Esfandyar's sister, Sahera
Sabera, Syfora's sister-in-law
Hossain, Mirad's cousin, his wife Shirengul, and kids Mina and Zmaria, fired by Alice in Mazar initially
Paregul, excellent student, with Magfirat, Class 12 (1975)
Arnie and Kayla Bond, PCVs in Puli-Khumri
The Lyttons, PCVs in Jalalabad (1971-73), for whom Mirad had worked
Babur, PC staff language teacher
Bruce Letts, new TEFL coordinator, former PCV in Kunduz.

Ahlia, 8th grader, married 1975
Nacia, student in class 10
Qorbin, Mirad's brother-in-law
Abdul Salam, friend of Azarullah and brother of my student, Hamida, captain class 8
Jaglagar, teacher at boy's school and watch repairman, with reputation for domestic abuse
Lawalahan, another disfavored teacher at the boy's schoolboys
Leilah, student in 8th class
Mayor of Khulm
Mayor of Hazrat Sultan
Sherafad, 1st-2nd grade teacher at Lycee
Suraya, student in 9th, whose father died
Kamshad, new Lycee teacher, Communist
Nafiz, sister of Paregul
Fazilat, student in class 11
Ibrahim Sayyid, best teacher at Lycee Mahasti
Daud's family (the landlord) including Mary in class 9
Hagi-sibe (s) eccentric teacher at boy's school (not the former landlord)
Lulah, Seeman, Suraya, Shazan Leelah, Zeagul, students in 9th class
Eqromboy, richest man in town, Tajenisa and Zeagul's father, l
Hushi, little sister of Tanenisa and Zeagul
Nasreen, another sister of Tajenisa and Zeagul, in class 7
Kabirmullah, teacher at boy's schoolboys
Islamadeen Khan, teacher at Lycee
"Rahnee Dahwanee," the communist teacher
Margaret Mills, Harvard PhD candidate, storycollector
Mirzad
Mir Wais, one of best students at boy's school, friend of Azarullah
Sadiq, 10th grader at boy's schoolboys
Kamila, student in class 12
Jamila, Paregul's little sister
Mowgul, the clerk (female)
Islamadeen, teacher, Lycee
Abdul Hafez Khan, Persian teacher, Lycee
Jawid, PC staff, Kabul
Jeb and Caitlin Leigh, PCVs Kabul
Shorts, of Kandahar (PCVs)

Bus lines: Gulhana, Hagi Pushtoon, Hagi Aqub

Year 3 (Sept. 1975)

Rick Dwyer, PCV, teacher at Faculty of Engineering
Dick Pettey, PCV, teacher at Engineering
Troy O'Dell, PCV from Karnard, third year taught at Engineering
Dave and Kay Dunn, PCVs in Kabul
Dean Sayed, Dean of Faculty of Engineering, Kabul U.
Mikita, PCV in Kabul
Ahad, Afghan student, friend of the Leighs
Zmaria, medical student
Cheryl Paul, PCV in Kabul (future diplomat)
Rashidi Omaid, PCV secretary
Agha-gul, PC staff
Ms Gholami, Kabul U teacher, friend on faculty bus
Daniel Curt, PCV (made to leave)
Mahadi and Malekah, students fom Tashkurghan accepted to Kabul University
Thaddeus (old PCV) involved with a Noushin (not the same teacher)
Benson and Susan Marek, PCV's in Bamiyan
Shafiqal, landlord and friend of Mareks
Camagul, Nacira, Fanzia,Nerulhoda: students from Lycee Mahasty
Gahwar, Zaiman, Magfirat, Fazilat, Rozia, Zahne-Miahshaq, Shahzadah—students who visited from Lycee
Randalls, PCVs in Kajikai
Paul Oldsman, PCV, Kabul U.
Fred Cozzens, PCV, Kabul U
Ben Hedges, brother of PCV Brenda Mahoney.
Randy Jenner, PCV, Kabul
Magadess, Student at Engineering
Baba Pieda, janitor at PC office
Rob Linnekin, PCV, Kabul
James Gareth, PCV, Kabul
Alsie Scott, PCV, Engineering
Kit Adelson and Scot Masyers, PCV trainers
Pam Johnson, PCV, Kabul
Gayle Pindar, PCV, Kabul

Paula Frank, PCV, Kabul
Tom Lord, PCV, Kabul
Chad Talbott, PCV, Kabul
Kirk Chan, PCV, Kabul

List of Named Places (in order of appearance)

Gardez: village on road to Kandahar south of Kabul, solidly Pushtoon area

(UN compound
DMA school
compound rented by O's

Kabul locations:

Shari-nau, Kabul
Ashraf Hotel, Kabul
Bost Hotel, Kabul
Jema-mi-nat, Kabul
Puli Sukta, Kabul
Kabul University
Intercontinental Hotel,
Babur Gardens,
Salim's (pizza)
AID compound
USIS Library
Kabul Zoo
Paghman, old royal summer home outside Kabul
Kabul Museum
Hindi movie theater
Kalow Shadalm and North Garage: lots where busses and vans left for routes north and east from Kabul

Baglan, small town on road to Salang

Puli-Khumri, small town on road to Salang
Kunduz, major town in north
Khanabad, town in north
Spinzar Club, Kunduz
WHO farm, Kunduz

Parwan Province, capital is Charikar and includes Salang Pass
Samagan-major city of north

Mazar-i-Sharif, major city of north
Balkh, old village outside Mazar
Haji Peodah shrine Balkh, archeological site
Jemoriat Gardens, Tashkurghan, gardens under constuction

Takht-e-Rostam, Samangan, archeological site
Begram, village on road to Puli-Khumri (later US base)
Shibar Pass, mountain pass on road to Bamiyan from Kabul
Shari-Golgatha, ruined city outside Bamiyan
Shari-zahar, ruined city from siege by Genghis Khan, outside Bamiyan
Bamiyan, site of Buddhas and Hazara population

Kajikai Dam, construction project on Helmand River
Hadjie Boran—village and site of graveyard outside Khulm
Jalalabad, major town on road to Khyber Pass
Charka Gardens, Jalalabad
Hedda, Buddhist-Greek ruins
Lagman, village outside Jalalabad
Charbaugh, village north of Lagman, with old Nuristani houses
Kuh-e-Safed, White Mountains
Rostana Jethur Camel Hiri, archaeological site
Shawa, village famous for lacquer furniture and containers

Glossary of Selected Dari Words

adomee barfee: snowman
afghanis: unit of money
askar-e xoda: soldier of God
aton: national dance

awshak: dumpling-dish made with leeks and yogurt sauce
auspos khadan: kitchen, cooking area
awmak: stupid

baba: old man
badal: injustice
balloi: overhead loft, above
ba mona xoda: good-bye (go with God)
bande: traffic circle outside town
batcha awal: first boy in class, head of class
batcha buzee: male taking a young boy as a lover or pet
bilbour: nightengale
bookerie: potbelly stove for heating room
cawk: bird used for fighting
chablank, chapan: long robe with ceremonial sleeves
chadris: full-covering for women with mesh screen over eyes, pleated; burqah
chapoti: rope bed
chaprose: janitor
chawki: bitter curd
chimchuk: sparrow
chinar: oak tree

choie-xona: tea house
coorse aftidan: avalanch
cucha:alley
dek: sad, lonely
doz makinum: to steal
djinn: imaginary spirit
diwan: collection of poems
dhukan, dhukandar: shop, shopkeeper
esta whot kadaen: to nap
dagtar: girl
gaep-e-ajeb: gossip,
gao: cow
gaudi: horse-pulled carriage
gilcar: mason
gilim: woven wall hanging or floor cover
gorg: wolf
gou-gush: weeds
gulloo dart: sore throat
gustee-hukh: pork
hakim—sibe: sub-governor
haragee: foreigner.
Hazara: one of ethnic groups of Afghanistan, with Mongolian features, mainly living in central mountains

honum: wife

jewie: open sewer ditch
joa: barley
jung makadan: to fight
karachi: wagon for moving or carrying things, often pulled by a man
kenerab: outhouse
ketab choie:
ketchalow: potato. "Mister Keetchalow," derogatory name for Europeans
korma: stew
kosmak: sour cream
kouteb; clerk
Kutchi: wandering herders who follow sheep herds into mountains and across into Pakistan seasonally.

loya jirga: traditional meeting of all ethnic groups
mafeesh: inspector
malim: teacher
malim-e-sports: sports teacher
mamon xona: guest room
modir: director, principal
modir-e-mulliyat: bank director
modir
moie-safyed: old man, "white-hair."
morc: chicken
morcha aspekee: horse ants
namsad: to be engaged
nan: bread
nangi pakhtana: honor
nashaib—faraz: ups and downs
naquel kadaen: to cheat
naswar: snuff
owdon: water container for washing hands
pay shawnee torsh: closed forehead, someone who is private
peron tanbon: long shirt and baggy pantsm traditional Afghan male garb
pilau: rice dish
powantoon: university
putch: empty (as in a head)
Pushtoon: major ethnic group of Afghanistan, crossing into Pakistan, speakers of Pushtu

reshwot: bribe
roghan: grease, cooking oil

saer malim: head teacher, assistant principal
sandalie: heating mechanism for room made of low table with fire or coals under it and a blanket over it, under which people sit around the table
sharee-xorlie: engagement party
shawlo: blanket worn over coat
shawn: sunset
shi'ite: second major group of Moslems, a minority in Afghanistan, predomonantly Hazaras

shokh: naughty
suras: books of the Qoran

tabreek: congratulations
takiak: review by rote
taklef: trouble
taxiwan: cab driver

yawd amad kadaen: to remember
zambaris: bees
zardaloo: apricot

Some Sources

In recollecting these journals, I have found sustenance and new facts in the following, to the authors and writings of which I am most grateful:

Ludwig W. Adamec, ed. *"Mazar-i-Sharif and North-Central Afghanistan" in Historical and Political Gazetteer of Afghanistan Vol. 4*.(Akademische Druck Kahay U. Verlaggsanstratt, Graz-Austria 1979).

"Afghanistan" <http://reference.allrefer.com/country-guide/afghanistan>

Bahawodin Baha: "Improving Technical, Vocational and Engineering Education in Afghanistan," University of Brighton, UK, MY 2006.

Rajiv Chandrasekaran, *Little America: The War Within the War for Afghanistan.* (New York: Vintage Press, 2012)

CNN, "Saturday Morning News," October 20, 2001 <transcripts.cnn.com/TRANSCRIPTS/0110/20/smn.29.html>

Jason Elliot, An Unexpected Light: Travels in Afghanistan, (London; Picador, 2001), p. 28.

Edward Giradet, Killing the Cranes, (White River, VT: Chelsea Green, 2009):

Douglas Hostetter, "Report to the Moslem Peace Fellowship on the joint Help the Afghan Children delegation to Afghanistan." 2002

Institute for War and Peace Reporting, "Afghan Recovery Report: Lebanese Conflict Reverberates in Afghanistan," September 7, 2006 <http://www.iw

Arley Loewon and Josette Michael, editors, *Image of Afghanistan: Exploring Afghan Culture through Art and Literature. (Karachi, Oxford Press, 2010).*

Ahmed Rashid, *Taliban: Militant Islam, Oil and Fundamentalism in Central Asia* (New Haven; Yale U. Press, 2000

Olivier Roy, *Afghanistan: From Holy War to Civil War* (Princeton: Princeton U. Press, 1995)

Barnett R. Rubin, *The Fragmentation of Afghanistan: State Formation and Collapse in the International System* (New Haven: Yale U. Press, 1992).

Mir Hakmatullah Sadar, *Lemar-Aftaab.* January-February 2001, "Afghanistan's Internal Refugees: 'Trapped at the Margins,' http://www.afghanmagazine.com/2001/articles/internalrefugees.html

Shah Sirdar Ikbal Ali, *Afghanistan of the Afghans,* (Quetta: Shah Sirdar Ikbal Ali, 1978).

The White House, Office of the Press Secretary, "Event Backgrounder: The President Meets with Iraq and Afghanistan Non-Governmental Organizations," Washington, DC, March 21, 2006.

Acknowledgements

Much of what is presented here comes from the author's journals kept as a Peace Corps volunteer from July 1973-July 1976.

Thanks go:

- To the hospitality and faith of the thousands of Afghan families who shared bread and tea, laugher and tears, stories and hope.
- To the numerous cited and un-cited writers, reporters and writers who have brought to the world's sometimes closed eyes an honest and in-depth picture of the struggles of the Afghan people over 30 years
- To the Peace Corps who gave a generation of young Americans the opportunity to live among and come to understand the decent and hard-working and gracious Afghan people in a a breathtakingly beautiful and enchanted world before the 26 years of fighting; and to its returned Volunteers who continue to "bring the story home," to advocate on behalf of the poor, the disenfranchised, the sick, and those in need of the liberation of education.
- to Suraya Sadeed who has published her own story in the beautiful, *Secrets Told in a Kabul Teahouse,* and from whom I had to privilege of learning about her work and the situations in Afghanistan during her humanitarian and educational work there over the past 20 years; the staff of Help the Afghan Children, in the US and Afghanistan for their devotion to touching and changing the lives of Afghans in this shattered land; and to HTAC's Board. partners and donors who support important work, not the least of which has been the expansion

of girls' education on a level and in a place hitherto unknown, and the initiation of Peace and Mediation studies as part of the Afghan Ministry of Education curriculum for every school in the country.

About the Author

Frances Garrett Connell currently teaches for the University of Maryland University College. Since her years as a Peace Corps Volunteer in Afghanistan, she has raised three amazing and world-wise sons, navigated 30 years of marriage to Washington attorney Tom Connell, and worked as a community volunteer in school, church and social service programs. She taught in secondary and adult education programs and at five colleges and universities; directed ESL, refugee resettlement, hunger education, and US repatriation programs; and wrote a dissertation on "Literacy and its Indigenous Forms in a Traditional Afghan Village" for her doctorate at Columbia. Author or editor of eleven other books, several of them as part of her A Reminiscence Sing oral and family history endeavors (and including compilations of work by two brothers—John and David—mentioned in this journal and a Tibetan sister-in-law, wife of brother Danny who had visited in 1975), she has published poetry and essays in 27 magazines. Most recently, she moved from a spacious, woodsy home in Silver Spring, MD to a tiny studio in Washington Heights (NYC) with a glimpse of the Hudson, and became the grandmother to Gabriel Dylan Hu Connell (b. Oct. 8, 2012).